Cripping the Archive

DISABILITY HISTORIES

Series editors: Stefanie Hunt-Kennedy, Kim E. Nielsen, and Michael Rembis

Disability Histories seeks scholarship that explores the lived experiences of individuals and groups from a broad range of societies, cultures, time periods, and geographic locations, who either identified as disabled or were considered by the dominant culture to be disabled.

We conceive of disability and disabled experiences broadly and seek to include scholarship that spans a range of embodiments, including the emerging field of mad studies. We are especially interested in scholarship that not only employs innovative approaches to using disability—in constant interaction with systems of race, class, gender, and sexuality—as an analytical tool to deepen our understanding of larger power relations, ideologies, and institutions, but also engages in meaningful dialogue with other subdisciplines within history, such as legal and political histories, social histories, histories of technology, science, and medicine, histories of the body and sexuality, and histories of the development of capitalism and imperialism. We welcome submissions from a variety of geopolitical locations, especially those that situate disability history outside European and North American contexts, including regions or nations that would become identified as the "global South." We are interested in scholarship that moves beyond traditional disability frameworks and offers methodologies and approaches to disability history that are rooted in decolonial, transnational, and transimperial perspectives.

For a list of books in the series, please see our website at www.press.uillinois.edu.

Cripping the Archive

Disability, History, and Power

Edited by
JENIFER L. BARCLAY AND
STEFANIE HUNT-KENNEDY

Foreword by Jaipreet Virdi

UNIVERSITY OF
ILLINOIS PRESS
Urbana, Chicago, and Springfield

Manufactured in the United States of America
1 2 3 4 5 C P 5 4 3 2 1
∞ This book is printed on acid-free paper.

Cataloging data available from the Library of Congress

ISBN 9780252046698 (hardcover)
ISBN 9780252088797 (paperback)
ISBN 9780252048036 (ebook)

This book is dedicated to disabled people around the world — past, present, and becoming — whose experiences and knowledge have been silenced and erased.

Contents

Foreword

History cannot be written without the archive. Yet the archive itself is a process embedded with biases and power negotiation between the custodians, researchers, donors, and public. Wedged between the physical storage space of collections and layers of metadata for cataloging and digitizing, the archive is a site of power. By assembling which histories are worth preserving, the archive is fraught with inequities, too often replicating colonizing forces leveled against minoritized, colonized, or vulnerable people whose records tend to be neglected or lost. Fragments and erasures abound within the archive, shaping what kinds of histories are written or unwritten.

However loud the silences, disability echoes within and beyond the archive. Biases in collection, inaccessible institutions, and outdated language in the metadata collectively shape how disability appears in the archive and how historians approach disability as an analytical category for assessing archival evidence. In disability studies, language is crucial for contextualizing issues and experiences of disability. If metadata does not capture accurate perceptions of disability—if it captures any at all—then the archive cannot accurately reflect the presence of disability. A search for "prosthetic" or "prosthetic leg" in a museum collection can yield no results, but "leg" brings up results for artificial legs alongside table legs, signifying that personal prosthetics can hold no intimate meanings for users and are but mere inanimate objects that prop up bodies. If we center the perspectives of disabled archivists, researchers, and other custodians of knowledge, how can the archive be reshaped or recreated to offer more than fleeting glimpses into disability histories?

Emerging out of a period in which immense accessibility options were made available for work and social participation, while archive restrictions and closures simultaneously challenged researchers' productivity, *Cripping the Archive: Disability, History, and Power* is both a memento and a blueprint for a crip futurity. The volume explores how the structural power of ableism informs the organizing, politics, and spaces of the archive, presenting different tangents for unearthing disability from the archive across global contexts. Some offer solutions. Others remind us there is still work to do. As the editors emphasize, the archive process is not value-neutral, but is rife with complexities about what encompasses a physical or digital archive, the ethics of collection management, and the paradoxical presence of disabled people and disability as both "hypervisible and invisible" within historical records. Disability is always present in human societies, and even through fragments it has a presence in the archive, especially when layered through documents of colonization, enslavement, capitalism, and other power inequities of class, gender, and race—alongside joy, magic, and other elements of human experience.

Archives are attempts to immortalize a shared historical past, but as we witness all too often, they are fragile, fleeting spaces of preservation. The 1973 fire at the United States' National Personnel Records Center destroyed approximately sixteen to eighteen million military personnel files, including evidence of disability and disablement critical for understanding layers of war service from World War I through 1963. War, too, destroys the archive and impoverishes history. The Librarians and Archivists with Palestine (LAP), a network of librarians, archivists, and information workers, has maintained a list of damages caused by Israel's ongoing genocide of the Palestinian people. The destruction wrought on cultural heritage sites, the bombing of the Central Archives of Gaza City and the Rafah Museum, and the displacement, injury, or death of archivists, librarians, and other custodians all have demolished irreplaceable historical materials. These forms of destruction are literally and figuratively silences of power that create and curate the worlds people inhabit, but they also, perhaps more importantly, affirm why disability justice is essential for memory-keeping.

Jaipreet Virdi
November 10, 2024
Written on a plane over the Gulf of Mexico

Acknowledgments

From its initial inception to its final stage of production, this collection has operated on crip time, bending the clock to meet our bodyminds and not vice versa. We enacted crip time as a practice and not just an abstract concept, both for ourselves and our contributors. It has been an absolute privilege to work with such a fantastic group of authors and an honor to learn from their scholarship and collective wisdom. We hope they are as proud of this collection as we are. Throughout the time it took to complete this project, we received invaluable support from our home institutions. We appreciate the support of our departments—the University at Buffalo's (UB) Department of History and the University of New Brunswick's (UNB) Department of Historical Studies. We are especially thankful for the financial contributions of our institutions—UB Humanities Institute/Office of the Vice President for Research and Economic Development Faculty Publication Fund and UNB's Harrison McCain Grant in Aid of Scholarly Book Publishing Award.

As with any creative project, many people contributed behind the scenes in various ways. It was important to us to make this volume affordable and accessible. Whereas the funding from UB and UNB allowed us to offset the purchase cost of this volume, Jay Dolmage met with us early on and shared his expertise in accessibility and open-access publications. We were also fortunate to have thoughtful reviewers who gave generously of their time to read and provide insightful feedback on such a large collection. We would like to thank the University of Illinois Press for its support and enthusiasm from the very beginning. We are especially grateful to series editors Kim E. Nielsen and Mike Rembis, and acquisitions editor Alison Syring, who immediately recognized the significance and necessity of the volume, championed it, and provided us critical encouragement and intellectual support. Finally, we are incredibly grateful to the disability communities that make our work possible.

Cripping the Archive

Introduction

JENIFER L. BARCLAY AND
STEFANIE HUNT-KENNEDY

In history, power begins at the source.
—Michel-Rolph Trouillot

In 2017, *Oxford Essential Quotations* included disability historian Douglas Baynton's well-known refrain: "Disability is everywhere in history once you begin looking for it, but conspicuously absent in the histories we write."[1] While this acknowledgment of such a quotable quotation signals a growing public awareness of disability history, it still leaves many significant questions unanswered. Why is disability enveloped in this paradox? What forces and factors create this dynamic? How is disability everywhere and nowhere, present and absent, obvious and overlooked in both the historical record and historians' interpretations of the past?

Cripping the Archive: Disability, History, and Power is a collection of interdisciplinary scholarship that responds to these questions by considering not only how but why physical, sensory, and psychological disabilities are underrepresented, erased, or distorted in the written and material historical record. Building on the recent work of a small coterie of scholars who put the issue of disability on the map in the field of critical archival studies, the collection's contributors probe the machinations of archival power by uncovering disability in contested archives, challenging the boundaries of how we define "the archive," exploring the creation of inclusive archives accountable to and centered on disabled people and disability justice, and disrupting ableist power structures and dynamics within the archive.[2] By exploring the ways in which ableness informs the politics of the archive as a physical space, a discriminatory record, and a collection of silences, *Cripping the Archive* allows for an intersectional and interdisciplinary approach that bridges disability studies, history, and archival studies.

The idea for this collection emerged from a conversation between the editors about our own experiences with finding disability in the archives of slavery. Having both recently finished our first books on the historical relationship between disability, slavery, and race, we were discussing the difficulties of foregrounding the lives of disabled enslaved people in an archive marked by the dispossession of enslaved people. As slavery scholars have noted, the archive of slavery reflects the power, inequality, and racism that undergirded Atlantic slavery, and we are indebted to their poignant understandings of archives as not only sites of knowledge but as sites of injustice.

In our first books, we attempted to (in the words of slavery scholar Marisa Fuentes), "narrate the fleeting glimpses of enslaved subjects in the archives."[3] And yet, we quickly discovered that centering disability in histories of slavery generates more challenges in archival excavation and takes the question of the archive in new directions. Disability added another layer of complexity, erasure, and discrimination to the archival experience. We encountered challenges in Caribbean and U.S. archives that reflect the pervasiveness of ableism and its influence on the archive as a place that protects, preserves, legitimizes, and sanctifies certain documents, while it negates and destroys others.[4]

There are examples of archives that are mindful of disability and accessibility, but this is far from regular practice and disability often remains problematic.[5] The archives we visited offered no resources that facilitated locating disability, and many sources were not digitized, preventing the use of in-text searches and screen readers. Most archivists were not versed in disability history and, therefore, were unprepared to give us direction. Our search words for various materials—from the sources themselves to related resources such as archival catalogues, finding aids, container lists, and collection descriptions—were things like "lame," "crippled," "mad," "insane," and "invalid," a lexicon shaped by a long history of pathologization, biomedical and cultural oppression, and power. These challenges are also refracted through larger socioeconomic inequities within countries and between them. For instance, although Caribbean archives are some of the best in the Americas, they lack the institutional support, funding, and international recognition that is often granted to their northern counterparts. Archives in the global South, broadly, are less likely to receive funding and support for technological innovations such as digitization, which securely preserves the historical record and makes it more accessible to scholars, disabled or not. Materially, the lack of funding prevents archivists and institutions from ensuring that there are technologies in place to find disability in the archive or make brick and mortar archives physically accessible. Ideologically, ableism justifies the denial of allocating already scarce financial resources to the nuanced work of recognizing, calling attention to, and validating disability in the archive and its finding aids. Through trial and error, we both discovered that to find disability in slavery's archive meant to look for sources steeped in colonial violence that told many different and sometimes competing stories of disability. At the same time, we each "discovered" disability hidden in plain sight in primary sources like the well-known autobiographies of Frederick Douglass and Mary Prince.

As our excitement grew over our shared experiences with researching disability, we knew there was something to be said about how power and ableism frames disability in the historical record. We connected these ideas to a myriad of theories that shaped our own intellectual trajectories over the years—from the significance of "unmarked markers," the influence and ubiquity of the "normate," and the obliviousness of privilege to the profound but often overlooked role that disability plays in intersectionality and how ableism shapes the production of knowledge and the very content and form of the historical narratives we construct.[6] We knew, by the end of that conversation, that we wanted to crip the archive by demonstrating what a critical disability approach teaches us about history and power.

Feeling energized by our shared struggles and insights, we put out a call for contributors to an edited collection on disability and the archive. To our delight, contributors responded from diverse personal and intellectual positions with a range of understandings of this issue. The authors in this book come from different professional ranks, geopolitical locations, temporalities, and proximities to various disability identities. In the summer of 2021, we organized a "Meet and Greet" with the contributing authors to introduce ourselves and our scholarly interests. It became abundantly clear that, collectively, we recognized not all was well with the relationship between disability and the archive. Through that first meeting and in each draft of their work since, the contributors to this collection challenged and expanded our understanding of the contested space that disability occupies in the archive between visibility and invisibility. With their reflexive scholarship and compelling approaches to cripping the archive, they pushed our questions further and nuanced our understanding of how power works in the archival process.

Terminology and Methodology

The chapters assembled in this collection embrace and reflect the many valences of the term "crip" vis-à-vis the archive, which we understand as formal and informal spaces—material and virtual—that gather sources from and about the past. Crip signifies a process of reclamation and pride, wresting an ableist term from those who champion a fantasy of "being normal" and investing it with a more nuanced, accurate set of meanings based on the complexities of disabled people's lives. Crip also encompasses an identity and sense of community based on shared experiences of disability and ableism. To crip the archive in this sense means to center disabled people, find creative methodologies to reclaim their histories, and confront the limiting nature of how their experiences appear in primary sources, if they appear at all.

But as disability studies—and specifically crip theory—teaches us, "crip" is also a verb, an analytic, a framework that moves beyond identity-based approaches to disability and, instead, challenges us to reckon with disability as a set of ideas that change over time and structure larger systems of privilege and oppression alongside race, gender, class, sexuality, and other salient social categories. Indeed, "disability" is a nebulous and often contested term that largely depends on who is defining it, according to what metrics, and why.[7] These variables emerged and changed dramatically in different historical moments; when considered cross-culturally, entirely different understandings of the body, mind, bodymind, and even disability itself become clear.[8] There are also nuances of disability experiences—whether a condition is acquired or congenital, permanent or temporary, episodic or chronic, singular or plural. "Cripping," then, is the process of critically interrogating "how private or privatized versus public cultures of ability or disability are conceived, materialized, spatialized, and populated," particularly in repetitive ways that maintain the hegemony of what Robert McRuer calls "compulsory ablebodiedness."[9]

Archives play a pivotal, but often unacknowledged, role in producing and sustaining social and cultural norms about the body from the kinds of sources they house and their content to how these materials are made available and to whom. The archive is most often thought of as a brick and mortar building, usually with a governmental or institutional affiliation, that stores documents from the past. As historians, we are trained to think of the archive as a place that contains traceable sources, however tangible or ephemeral they may be, and one that serves as a meaningful interface among scholars as they discuss and debate various interpretations of the past. Perceived as "traditional," archives typically house materials defined as "legitimate" or "authoritative" by archival specialists, which often undermines or discounts disabled people and their experiences as sources of knowledge.[10] Cripping the archive necessitates a revaluing of what we consider to be legitimate historical sources and who can produce them. This more nuanced perspective invites people, in and outside academia, to engage with a more expansive definition of the archive and what constitutes a valid primary source, one that creates "a different center."[11] This process allows us to focus on the production of disability knowledge, which requires us to question what counts as an archive and embrace the friction that this question evokes as a productive force. While this opens up exciting possibilities, it also risks abstracting the archive to the extent that it "can, at the extreme, conjure an image so corrupted, so impenetrable, and so totalizing as to leave no room for encountering the actual past except through contemporary memories of it."[12] Striking a balance between these extremes allows us to encounter traditional archives anew, while also embracing the possibilities of unconventional archives, all of which has the potential to expand and enrich our understandings of disabled pasts.

In the past decade, archival institutions have increasingly moved to digitize documents, making historians less dependent on the physical archival building. The digital uptake has also seen the creation of many digital archives that are not associated with a governing body. Historians themselves have created online archives, many of which are open-access. Even so, the archival process—the act of deciding what gets archived and what does not—is not a value-neutral process. The increasing digitization of archival sources across the globe has important implications for scholars everywhere, but particularly for those of us who face obstacles in accessing brick and mortar archives. Digital archives allow disabled and chronically ill scholars to access primary sources from the comfort of their homes and without the financial and environmental costs of overseas travel. However, digital archives are not in and of themselves accessible. Digital accessibility is not only an ethical responsibility, but it is also legally required by the Americans with Disabilities Act (ADA). Under Title II of the ADA, companies cannot discriminate against disabled people "in the full and equal enjoyment of . . . public accommodations."[13]

When Congress passed the ADA in 1990, the internet was not a part of our daily lives in the way it is now. However, the Web Content Accessibility Guidelines (WCAG), a worldwide organization with the goal of providing a shared standard in web accessibility, has set a precedent for individuals, companies, and governments.[14] As some of the contributors in this volume argue, the creators of digital archives must remain attentive to accessibility by choosing content management systems that support accessibility, speech-to-text software, alt-text descriptions, screen readers, and providing open-access content, among other best practices. The shift to accessible, digital archives reminds us that, even with these developments, not all archives are created equal.

In addition to using a critical disability lens to analyze the types and modes of archiving and content within various repositories, how we interpret archival evidence is also key to cripping the archive. At the basis of every historical narrative is a question about positioning, and this is also an ethical question. Whose history are you telling? And from whose perspective? The representation of disabled people in the historical record often reflects the medical, social, colonial, and legal systems that created the record, resulting in evidence of fragmented personhoods, stories of "overcoming" or pity, sensationalized and exploitative representations, and complete erasures and silences. Even in historical scholarship, disabled individuals remain underexplored in spite of the expansion of disability history. Disability historians carefully quilt together remnants of these past lives to move disabled people from the peripheries of history to the center. *Cripping the Archive* questions the historical record's framing of disability across time and space, reflects on the disabled scholar's experience in the archive, and creates counter-archives by expanding our definition of an archive beyond brick and mortar.

We see this collection as an example of engaged scholarship inspired by disability justice and the critical work of scholars and activists.[15] Disability justice is both theory and praxis—a form of movement building that embraces the power of disability while simultaneously identifying and resisting the role that ableism plays in determining the distribution of power in society with disproportionately negative effects for multiply marginalized people. A disability justice approach begins from a place of intersectionality, recognizing that disability is not a single-issue identity. In other words, disabled people live with intersecting identities that span gender, race, class, sexuality, nationality, and other significant social categories. These intersecting identities create complex forms of oppression that are not reducible to one aspect of lived experience.

In many ways, disability justice is a response to disability rights, which amplified the voices of white disabled people with mobility impairments, often at the expense of disabled people of color, disabled queer and gender-nonconforming folks, and individuals with other types of disabilities and impairments.[16] Disability justice is inherently intersectional, moves beyond the singular practice of using legal means to procure individual rights, and confronts the overlapping histories of racism and ableism. As disability activist Patty Berne explains it:

> The histories of white supremacy and ableism are inextricably entwined, both forged in the crucible of colonial conquest and capitalist domination. We cannot comprehend ableism without grasping its interrelations with heteropatriarchy, white supremacy, colonialism and capitalism, each system cocreating an ideal bodymind built upon the exclusion and elimination of a subjugated "other" from whom profits and status are extracted.[17]

The suppression, erasure, and negation of disabled people's histories is a form of cultural oppression parallel to—and, indeed, an intrinsic part of—the same processes of colonial violence that attempted to silence and rewrite the histories of colonized people across the globe. And the kinds of histories we write are dictated as much by personal interests and hegemonic politics as they are by the contours and content of the archives themselves.

Both Jenifer and Stefanie were drawn to these more complex stories of disability and personhood in large part because of our personal identities and proximities to disability. We both grew up in rural towns, in working-poor families, with disabled siblings in culturally disabled homes, and we have both moved in and out of various disability identities. Our proximities to and experiences of disability along with our experiential knowledge of the vicissitudes and precarity of poverty have shaped and expanded our capacities to understand other people's struggles, even when they are not our own. As white women from working-poor backgrounds with complicated relationships to disability identity, we acknowledge the contradictions of privilege and disempowerment that inform our views and experiences of the world.

Our lived experiences influenced the fields of history that we gravitated to and how we position ourselves in relation to our work. As scholars of Atlantic slavery—Stefanie a historian of the Caribbean and Jenifer of the United States—we understand that writing history is, whether or not you are conscious of it, a decision about one's relationship to power. Scholars are continuously confronted with the choice to engage in a process of historical production that either reinforces existing power relations or, instead, uncovers and challenges them. We are committed to the latter.

This collection is also a call for scholars across disciplines to reject ableism in their encounters with the archive and to acknowledge how ableism operates and intersects with other forms of oppression. Historians have embraced the familiar triad of gender, class, and race, but all too often view disability as unique, abnormal, exceptional and, therefore, beyond the scope of comparison and analysis. According to this logic, disabled lives are unexplainable and, thus, attempts to study disabled people and to use disability as an analytic are futile. The irony of this perspective is that disability is the only universal human condition. Disability does not discriminate; each of us, regardless of age, sex, gender, nationality, race, or economic status, will likely become disabled in our lifetime either through accident, disease, or natural processes such as aging. Confronting the ableism that is inherent in the archive and centering the lives of disabled people offers alternative ways of understanding the past that challenges and displaces dominant narratives that have achieved widespread acceptance and circulation, which has implications for contemporary issues, too. Ableism in the present requires ableism of the past. To paraphrase historian William Loren Katz, "If you believe people have no history worth mentioning, it's easy to believe they have no humanity worth defending."[18]

Chapter Contributions

What does it look like for *Cripping the Archive* to use a critical disability approach to study the archive? The collection begins with chapters that examine the ways that disability has been hidden and erased in the historical record and how scholars can challenge these silences to unearth disability from the archive. Part I, Uncovering, takes readers on a tour of various historical records to demonstrate the multiple ways that disability is silenced and the different methodological approaches researchers take to confront these silences and reveal disability histories. We chose to open the book with this section because we wanted readers to understand what we mean when we say that disability is silenced and erased in the archives and in historical scholarship. What does that look like, and how do scholars confront silence in the archive?

There is no one way to locate disability in the archive. Indeed, the chapters in Part I highlight various methodological and theoretical approaches to uncover disability. Emily Cock, for instance, illustrates the challenges and merits of open-access digital archives. Through an examination of *Trove*, a digital archive of primary sources on Australian history, Cock illustrates that access to historical documents has served to challenge the white-settler national narrative of Australia and recenter immigrants and, in particular, disabled runaway convicts, as significant historical actors in Australian history. But, as Cock explains, digital archives are still not neutral resources; obstacles to accessibility continue to restrict access to these so-called open-access websites.

Other chapters in this section explore traditional and nontraditional archives and challenge us to think anew about the way ableism shapes what documents are considered archivable in the first place. Radu Dinu's chapter explores the dearth of disability history in Romanian historiography in the context of high Stalinism and its state socialist legacy. Since the mid-twentieth century, the Ministry of Internal Affairs has controlled the archives, which has had serious implications for disability history because governmental bodies responsible for welfare and health policies (with which disability is inextricably intertwined) often withheld their files from the National Archives. Thus, Dinu shows how this silencing of disability at the archiving stage can perpetuate silencing at the retrieval and writing stages of historical production.[19] KJ Cerankowski uncovers disability in the archive of Jemima Wilkinson and the Public Universal Friend via the intersections between disability, illness, and queerness. Through an examination of the archives of the Friend and archives about the Friend, Cerankowski considers the afterlife of illness and the ways in which illness, rather than merely passing, can leave a permanent mark on the embodied experience, which can then shape subjectivity. Together, the chapters in this section illustrate how the silences surrounding disability can also reveal truths—truths about societal ableism in the past and present and how it shapes lived experiences, archival processes, and the histories we write.

Other times it is not the absence of disability in the archive that produces silence but rather scholars' reluctance or unwillingness to engage with disability in the archive. This is the case in the chapters by Nina Vollenbröker and Isabelle Lawrence. Through an exploration of the archive of the highly influential modernist German architect Adolf Loos (1870–1933), Vollenbröker's chapter uncovers Loos's hearing impairment as critical to the spatial and sensory dimensions of written and built projects. Vollenbröker places Loos in the broader history of the standardization of bodies and pathologization of difference at the turn of the century. Lawrence's chapter confronts the ways that museums have perpetuated and reinforced problematic representations of disability. Her chapter asks what is at stake in such representations and what is the responsibility of museums, as spaces of public knowledge production, in shaping public perceptions of disability and disabled people. Drawing on a series of workshops that took place in 2021, Lawrence illustrates how involving individuals with lived experience of disability in the decision-making process can serve not only museums but the public in gaining deeper awareness of the social, cultural, and political issues of revealing the so-called hidden histories of disability.

Part II of the collection, Obscuring, captures the myriad ways that formal archives intentionally and unintentionally obscure the everyday histories of disabled people, the role of the state in this process, and the significance of context for understanding how and why this happens. The chapters by Audra Jennings and Sarah Handley-Cousins highlight how even the most well-intentioned state actions work against scholars' ability to access disabled people's personal histories. Jennings considers how thousands of archival records pertain to the U.S. states' efforts to contain or mitigate disability in the first half of the twentieth century, yet details about disabled people's everyday lives remain elusive. Barriers to accessing this information result from context-specific language related to the state's varying perceptions of disability, a flood of documentation across various agencies, and records about disabled people produced by nondisabled people, all of which reside in disconnected federal and state archives. Handley-Cousins's chapter similarly explores the role of the state in obscuring disabled people's historical record by considering the impact of laws that restrict access to archival materials dealing with sensitive patient files, specifically those related to mental health such as New York's Mental Hygiene Law. In mapping the tangle of state laws and often contradictory ways they are operationalized even within a single state, Handley-Cousins illuminates the tension between patient confidentiality and disability scholars' use of medical records as sometimes the only avenue to access the inner worlds of disabled people in the past. In attempting to protect the privacy and dignity of patients, these laws inadvertently obscure their lived experiences and primarily target those with psychological (as opposed to physical or sensory) disabilities.

The chapters by Maria Cristina Galmarini and Francine Almash and Jan Valle further illuminate these themes and the importance of contextualizing disability to understand the power of formal archives to erase and obscure. Galmarini analyzes how Cold War politics veiled and even destroyed early records of the international blind movement, specifically the World Council for the Welfare of the Blind, in both Eastern and Western archives. In the West, because the World Council included socialist states and celebrated a particular kind of state-centered disability activism, the end of the Cold War rendered the organization obsolete and out of tune with Western liberal ideas of equality and civil rights. As a result, few efforts were made to preserve its records. The archives of former socialist nations, on the other hand, obscure the lived realities of blind people with persistent narratives of achievement, triumphalism, and overcoming that record only the stories of "supercrips" and the "able disabled." Almash and Valle similarly emphasize historical context—in this case, the politics surrounding race and disability in public education in the 1960s and '70s—to examine the archival erasure of New York City's "600 schools" that served as sites of removal and segregation for Black and Puerto Rican students labeled "socially maladjusted" or "emotionally disturbed" in the 1960s. By the 1970s, these schools morphed into District 75—a segregated district for students with disabilities—the only district of its kind in the country then and now. Despite their importance to the fight for community control and the historic 1968 Teachers' Strike, these schools and their impact on current special education remain little more than a footnote in history. As the authors demonstrate, they are often erased in formal archival records and require researchers to utilize a range of creative methodological approaches to piece together their histories and the histories of students of color with disabilities who attended them.

The chapters of Part III, Decolonizing, challenge readers to recognize and counter Western biomedical framings of disability that implicitly and explicitly shape the content and structure of most formal archives in the global North and erase or pathologize the disability experiences and situated knowledge of Indigenous people throughout the global South. In their chapter, Heather Vrana considers the limitations of Guatemalan and, more broadly, Central American archives of disability resulting from the historical logics of the state, the church, and biomedicine that either erase disability outright or frame it only as an issue related to health or charity. Instead, they turn to the Pasillo de Milagros, or Hall of Miracles, in the tourist town of Antigua where disabled people from Guatemala, El Salvador, Mexico, Nicaragua, the United States, and other places leave offerings—like prosthetics and orthotics—for Saint Hermano Pedro de San José Betancur in gratitude for answering their prayers. This space, Vrana explains, bears witness to Latin American crip worldmaking and serves as a unique community-based archive from which disability scholars can develop more nuanced understandings of care, cure, and faith.

The section's other two chapters both deal with Native people, and those connected to them through settler colonial projects like boarding schools, in North America. In their chapter, Jess Wilcox Cowing examines the disabling nature of Indigenous boarding schools through the narratives of two white women, Minnie Braithwaite Jenkins and Estelle Aubrey Brown. They argue that low-level white women employed by the Bureau of Indian Affairs to enforce ableist-racist assimilation policies ironically experienced disabling effects themselves, which captures the legacy of disability produced and exacerbated by state violence and carcerality. Sarah Whitt, Traci Brynne Voyles, and Susan Burch's chapter more specifically defines settler ableism, a tool of settler colonial ideology rooted in Western biomedical understandings of the body that colonizers used to justify the institutionalization of Native people in the nineteenth and twentieth centuries. With careful intentionality, the chapter models egalitarian and ethical scholarly practices through its framing as a dialogue and use of citational practices that showcase the work of Indigenous scholars and others who employ a critical disability perspective. Rigorously analyzing how formal archives reinforce and legitimize settler ableism (and, in turn, settler colonialism) through its selective content and structure, the authors also model alternative methods to navigate archival limitations such as working from a different, Indigenous-focused archival center and re-storying narratives of archival silences. As Sarah Whitt so poignantly puts it, "The archive, as it proves time and time again, is inadequate to the task of remembering—but has never stopped us from trying to resist its investment in forgetting."[20]

The chapters comprising Part IV, De-Centering, displace the pervasive hegemony of ableism in the archive and challenge readers to reckon with archives and archival practices that, despite their flaws and limitations, center on disabled people. The two chapters that bookend this section—"Deafness and Silences in the Archives" and "Privileged, Oppressed, and Liberated"—examine how deaf archives decenter simplistic, inaccurate representations of deaf people, even as they grapple with the overrepresentation of white, male, upper- and middle-class experiences that these collections reproduce. In their chapter, Octavian E. Robinson et al. reflect on the history of deaf representation (or lack thereof) in archives curated by hearing scholars and consider the emergence of deaf-focused archives at Gallaudet University and the Rochester Institute of Technology in the United States or Døvehistorisk Selskab and Doof Verleden Vlaanderen in Denmark and Flanders in Europe. While the authors provide a layered critique of audist and ableist practices in traditional archives, they also make the powerful point that "deaf-centered archives replicate the power relations and silences found in archives more generally" by privileging some deaf experiences and ignoring others.[21] In their chapter, the Holcombs demonstrate what a deaf-centered archive looks like by constructing a multigenerational family history that draws on their privately held personal collection, while also reflecting on the problems and limitations of their materials.

Similar to the ways that Deaf scholars call attention to forms of linguistic chauvinism that value spoken and written English over ASL, Part IV's other chapters also focus on the need to decenter ableist practices in the content of archives and in the ways that scholars produce and interpret archival materials. In their chapter, Osnat Katz and Samuel Goldstone-Brady argue that while oral histories have been a powerful tool for reclaiming and recording previously hidden histories of disabled people, this methodology inherently privileges those who communicate verbally. With its focus on orality and a particular kind of linear narration, oral history excludes and constrains some groups of disabled and neurodivergent people both as participants and as researchers. Liana Cole likewise calls on readers to reckon with the ableism that shapes how we value and interpret archival material. Cole examines Vanda Vieira-Schmidt, an artist in a German inpatient psychiatric facility, whose creative expressions are not considered art but rather evidence of her insanity. Cole centers Vieira-Schmidt and other Mad artists as worthy of being archived not in a manner that pathologizes them and their work but rather documents their creative output as evidence of their artistry and politically active pursuits.

In the final section of *Cripping the Archive*, various authors explore the experience of accessing and creating archives of disability in ways aligned with disability scholars' and activists' long-standing practice of drawing on their own experiential knowledge to inform their work and prioritizing accountability to disability communities, especially those that are multiply marginalized.[22] In the opening chapter, Gracen Mikus Brilmyer discusses the affective experience of disabled researchers when confronted with primary sources about disabled people from the past. Through interviews with disabled scholars, artists, activists, and community members in the United States and Canada, Brilmyer explores the impact of archival research on disabled individuals and how they imagine themselves in history. Others in this section discuss the experience of creating archives. Nicki Pombier, for instance, discusses the experience of creating an archive from the neglected documents of the Pennhurst State School and Hospital (1908–86) in Pennsylvania with a team of community archivists, former Pennhurst residents, self-advocates with Intellectual and Developmental Disabilities, support staff, family members, and multidisciplinary artists. Employing innovative methodologies, Pombier explains that the project "engages with but does not enact archival practices."[23]

Pombier is joined by other scholars in this section who show what it looks like to not *retrieve* from the archive but *create* an archive. The chapter written by Shuko Tamao and Aaron Rubinstein discuss the many barriers to creating accessible archives and best practices for creating access from the perspective of both the historian and the archivist. With a focus on the Robert S. Cox Special Collections and University Archives Research Center (SCUA) at the University of Massachusetts, Amherst, their chapter considers what the archival experience would be like were archives to use "nothing about us without us" as an operational principle. They envision that a user- and disability-centered approach to archives would create "a more expansive interpretation of the human condition by revealing the contested nature of health, human rights, autonomy, and independence."[24] In a similar vein, coauthors Sona Kazemi, Hemachandran Karah, Efrat Gold, and Mary Jean Hande discuss the creation of a digital *living* archive designed to maximize accessibility across ages and bodyminds. An extension of Kazemi's Instagram account and informed by the principles of disability justice, the chapter discusses the process of creating an interactive digital archive and multilingual dictionary of disability and care. Significantly, this project aims to connect diverse communities of disabled and mad people in the global South and other places in the world that have been largely ignored by disability scholars and theorists of the global North. These scholars illustrate what happens when we center disabled people in the creation of archives, where disabled people are not simply invited to sit at the table, but rather are active participants in setting the table.

Cripping the Archive makes three significant interventions in the fields of disability history, disability studies, and archival studies. First, it challenges the "compulsory able-bodiedness"/able-mindedness inherent in the historical record by locating disability in the archive. In recent years, scholars have paid increasing attention to the archives as sites of knowledge *and* sites of power and inequality. Their work has brought renewed visibility to the fact that not all pasts are deemed worthy of being documented, archived, retrieved, and written about. And yet, disability remains absent from many of these discussions, ignoring the lessons that disabled people's lives teach us about the past. Several chapters in this collection uncover disability stories from the historical record. By centering disabled people as historical actors, not passive recipients of medical care or heroes who "overcame their circumstances," our collection demonstrates that retrieving and producing their histories is necessary to counteract the hegemony of ableism.

Second, *Cripping the Archive* dwells on uncomfortable junctures in the historical record, where disabled people are paradoxically hypervisible and invisible in the archive. Although disabled people appear in the archive in a variety of familiar sources—from curiosity cabinets to medical records—their voices are often marginalized, silenced, or distorted. Authors in the collection read against the grain of the archive, simultaneously piecing together archival fragments to reconstruct the lifeworlds of disabled people and calling attention to the ways they were obscured to begin with. They read against the politics of historiography, which often restricts scholars from understanding the "complex personhood" of disabled people, to use Avery Gordon's words.[25] For instance, historical sources overwhelmingly detail disabled peoples' oppression and marginalization, but as the authors in this collection reveal, disabled people also experienced joy in the midst of oppressive conditions. Like disability itself, "disability joy" is historically constructed and must be understood in specific historical situations. In other words, the survival strategies and various ways that disabled people thrived under violent conditions may not constitute joy by contemporary understandings, but constituted important moments in the lives of disabled people in the past. Authors in this volume demonstrate various ways to hear the silences around disability joy, see the undocumented moments, and recognize unrecorded feelings to uncover disabled people's full human experiences.

Lastly, this collection aims to bring attention to the ableist nature of the historical record and the archive experience, and the ways in which this ableism informs the scholarship we produce. What are the challenges disabled researchers face when conducting archival research? In what ways do the methodological demands of the historical discipline reflect the pervasiveness of ableism, and how might a critical disability perspective challenge these expectations? How do disabled scholars experience disability in the archives—what are the emotions and traumas relived in these encounters? By showcasing a variety of interdisciplinary and theoretical approaches, the collection offers new methodologies to explore archival imbalances, uncover systems of power, and deconstruct their influences on the historical records that inform our work. Haitian scholar Michel-Rolph Trouillot wrote that "history is the fruit of power," and it is for this reason that we must study its production. *Cripping the Archive* seeks to reveal how power produces an abyss of silence and absence about disability since, in the words of Trouillot, "the ultimate mark of power may be its invisibility; [but] the ultimate challenge [is] the exposition of its roots."[26]

Notes

Epigraph: Michel-Rolph Trouillot, *Silencing the Past: Power and the Production of History* (Boston: Beacon Press, 1995), 29.

1. Susan Ratcliffe, ed., *Oxford Essential Quotations*, fifth edition (Oxford: Oxford University Press, 2017).

2. Laurie Block, "'An Invented Archive': The Disability History Museum," *RBM: A Journal of Rare Books, Manuscripts, and Cultural Heritage* 8, no. 2 (2007): 141–54; Sara White, "Crippling the Archives: Negotiating Notions of Disability in Appraisal and Arrangement and Description," *The American Archivist* 75, no. 1 (Spring/Summer 2012): 109–24; Rachel Corbman, "Remediating Disability Activism in the Lesbian Feminist Archive," *Journal of Media and Cultural Studies* 32, Iss. 1 (2018): 18–28; Bill Kirkpatrick, "Disability, Cultural Accessibility, and the Radio Archive," *New Review of Film and Television Studies* 16, no. 4 (2018): 473–80; Natalie Spagnuolo, "Mobilising Historical Knowledge: Locating the Disability Archive," in Katie Ellis et al., eds., *Interdisciplinary Approaches to Disability: Looking Towards the Future* (London: Routledge, 2018): 153–63; and Susan Antebi, *Embodied Archive: Disability in Post-Revolutionary Mexican Cultural Production* (Ann Arbor: University of Michigan Press, 2021). The single- and coauthored works of Gracen Brilmyer are also deeply relevant, such as Brilmyer, "Archival Assemblages: Applying Disability Studies' Political/Relational Model to Archival Description," *Archival Science* 18, no. 2 (2018): 95–118; Jessica Tai et al., "Summoning the Ghosts: Records as Agents in Community Archives," *Journal of Contemporary Archival Studies* 6, Iss. 1, Article 18 (2019); Brilmyer, "Toward Sickness: Developing a Critical Disability Archival Methodology," *Journal of Feminist Scholarship* 17, Iss. 17 (2020): 26–45; Brilmyer, "Toward a Crip Provenance: Centering Disability in Archives Through Its Absence," *Journal of Contemporary Archival Studies* 9, Iss. 1, Article 3 (2022); and Brilmyer, "'I'm Also Prepared to Not Find Me. It's Great When I Do, But It Doesn't Hurt If I Don't': Crip Time and Anticipatory Erasure for Disabled Archival Users," *Archival Science* 22, Iss. 2 (2022): 167–88.

3. Marisa Fuentes, *Dispossessed Lives: Enslaved Women, Violence, and the Archive* (University of Pennsylvania Press, 2016), 1.

4. Randall C. Jimerson, "Embracing the Power of Archives," *The American Archivist*, vol. 69, no. 1 (Spring-Summer 2006), 20.

5. Some libraries contain extensive disability holdings, such as UC Berkeley's Disability Rights and Independent Living Movement Project and the University of Toledo's Regional Disability History Archive. Others, like Yale University's Cushing/Whitney Medical Library, contain single collections such as the Robert Bogdan Disability Collection. In other cases, libraries and organizations are taking steps to make disability-related materials more apparent to researchers by compiling aids such as the Oklahoma Historical Society's "Researching Disability in Oklahoma, 1890–1960: A Collections Guide" that extends across state agencies, private entities, and state archives and libraries, or the Society of American Archivists' web-based resource "Documenting Disability in the Historical Record" (https://www2.archivists.org/groups/accessibility-and-disability-section/documenting-disability-in-the-historical-record), to name just a few.

6. Ruth Frankenberg, "Introduction: Local Whitenesses, Localizing Whiteness," in Ruth Frankenberg, ed., *Displacing Whiteness* (Durham, NC: Duke University Press, 1997): 1–33; Rosemarie Garland Thompson, *Extraordinary Bodies: Figuring Physical Disability in American Culture and Literature* (New York: Columbia University Press, 1997); Peggy McIntosh, "White Privilege: Unpacking the Invisible Knapsack," in *Peace and Freedom Magazine* (July/August, 1989): 10–12; Kimberlé Crenshaw, "Demarginalizing the Intersection of Race and Sex: A Black Feminist Critique of Antidiscrimination Doctrine, Feminist Theory and Antiracist Policies," *University of Chicago Legal Forum*, no. 1 (1989): 139–67; Patricia Hill Collins, *Black Feminist Thought: Knowledge, Consciousness, and the Politics of Empowerment* (Boston: Unwin Hyman, 1990); Christopher Bell, *Blackness and Disability: Critical Examinations and Cultural Interventions* (East Lansing: Michigan State University Press, 2012); Hayden White, *The Content of the Form* (Baltimore: The Johns Hopkins University Press, 1987).

7. Licia Carlson and Matthew C. Murray, eds. *Defining the Boundaries of Disability: Critical Perspectives* (London: Routledge, 2021).

8. Raewyn Cornell, "Southern Bodies and Disability: Re-Thinking Concepts," *Third World Quarterly* 32 (8) (2011): 1369–81; Shaun Grech, "Decolonising Eurocentric Disability Studies: Why Colonialism Matters in the Disability and Global South Debate," *Social Identities* 21, no. 1 (2015): 6–21; Esme Cleall, *Colonising Disability: Impairment and Otherness Across Britain and Its Empire, c. 1800–1914* (Cambridge University Press, 2022); Madhwi, "'Able,' 'Disabled' and 'Invalid' Labourers: Disability and Indenture in Mauritius and Natal, c. 1840–1910," *Global Histories of Disability, 1700–2015: Power, Place and People*, ed. Esme Cleall (Routledge, 2023): 40–56; Nirmala Erevelles, *Disability and Difference in Global Contexts: Enabling a Transformative Body Politic* (Basingstoke, UK: Palgrave Macmillan, 2011); Helen Meekosha, "Decolonising Disability: Thinking and Acting Globally," *Disability & Society* 26 (2011): 667–82; Jenifer Barclay, "Differently Abled: Africanisms, Disability, and Power in the Age of Transatlantic Slavery," in J. F. Byrnes and J. L. Muller, eds., *Bioarchaeology of Impairment and Disability: Theoretical, Ethnohistorical, and Methodological Perspectives* (2017): 77–94; Barclay, *The Mark of Slavery: Disability, Race, and Gender in Antebellum America* (Urbana: University of Illinois Press, 2021); Stefanie Hunt-Kennedy, *Between Fitness and Death: Disability and Slavery in the Caribbean* (Urbana: University of Illinois Press, 2020).

9. Robert McRuer, *Crip Theory: Cultural Signs of Queerness and Disability* (New York: New York University Press, 2006), 72.

10. Penny Richards and Susan Burch, "Documents, Ethics, and the Disability Historian," *Oxford Handbook of Disability History*, eds. Michael Rembis, Catherine Kudlick, and Kim E. Nielsen (Oxford: Oxford University Press, 2018): 161–74.

11. Carol Padden and Tom Humphries, *Deaf in America: Voices from a Culture* (Cambridge: Harvard University Press, 1988), 41.

12. Emily A. Owens, *Consent in the Presence of Force: Sexual Violence and Black Women's Survival in Antebellum New Orleans* (Chapel Hill: University of North Carolina Press, 2023), 6.

13. Sec. 12182. Prohibition of discrimination by public accommodations, Americans with Disabilities Act of 1990, As Amended. https://www.ada.gov/law-and-regs/ada/#subchapter-ii-public-services-title-ii/.

14. Web Content Accessibility Guidelines, https://www.w3.org/TR/WCAG21/.

15. Leah Lakshmi Piepzna-Samarasinha, Mia Mingus, Stacey Milbern, Leroy Moore, Eli Clare, Sebastian Margaret, Patty Berne, and others, for instance, show us what disability justice in action looks like.

16. Sins Invalid, "What Is Disability Justice?," https://www.sinsinvalid.org/news-1/2020/6/16/what-is-disability-justice. Also published in *Sins Invalid, Skin, Tooth, and Bone: The Basis of Movement Is Our People, A Disability Justice Primer*, second edition, 2016.

17. https://www.sinsinvalid.org/blog/disability-justice-a-working-draft-by-patty-berne/.

18. Katz's exact quote, "For if you believe that a man has no history worth mentioning, it's easy to assume that he has no humanity worth defending" appears in "Let's Set Black History Straight: An Interview with William Loren Katz," *The Reader's Digest* (July 1969), 2.

19. Trouillot, *Silencing the Past*, 26.

20. Sarah Whitt, Traci Brynne Voyles, and Susan Burch, "Settler Ableism: Indigeneity, Unsettling the Archive, and Accountability in History," 206.

21. Octavian E. Robinson, Meredith Peruzzi, James McCarthy, William T. Ennis III, Brian H. Greenwald, and Joseph Murray, "Deafness and Silences in the Archives," 251.

22. Alice Wong's acclaimed work, for instance, captures the importance of community-oriented and community-led projects and signals the tremendous need to critically examine disabled people's lack of representation in conventional archives beyond clinical descriptions written by and for medical professionals. See Wong, ed., *Disability Visibility: First-Person Stories from the Twenty-First Century* (New York: Vintage Books, 2020); Wong, "My ICU Summer," Disability Visibility Blog (August 2022), https://disabilityvisibilityproject.com/2022/08/07/my-icu-summer-a-photo-essay/; and Wong, *Year of the Tiger: An Activist's Life* (New York: Knopf Doubleday Publishing Group, 2022). Similarly, "community elders" like 2022 Ford Foundation Disability Futures Fellow Corbett O'Toole are living archives of the history of disability and disability activism. O'Toole's public engagement, art, and autobiographical writings both document and testify to the marginalization, misrepresentation, and oversimplification of disabled people's intersectional experiences in formal archives. See especially her classic work *Fading Scars: My Queer Disability History* (Fort Worth, TX: Autonomous Press, 2015). Other scholarship, like that of Jaipreet Virdi, makes clear how lived experiences of disability shape the kinds of questions that scholars ask of particular disability archives. See *Hearing Happiness: Deafness Cures in History* (Chicago: University of Chicago Press, 2020).

23. Nicki Pombier, "File/Life: Remediating the Pennhurst Archive with Community Archivists," 392.

24. Shuko Tamao and Aaron Rubinstein, "Accessibility Widely Defined: Making the University of Massachusetts Special Collections and University Archives' Disability Collections Available to Everyone," 386.

25. *Ghostly Matters: Haunting and the Sociological Imagination* (Minneapolis: University of Minnesota Press, 1997, rpt. 2008), 4–5.

26. Trouillot, *Silencing the Past*, xix.

PART I

Uncovering

CHAPTER 1

The Missing Romanian Chapter in Disability History

RADU HARALD DINU

The ideal which we imagine in history is unquestionably ablebodied.
—Katherine Ott

Introduction

New historical research has enriched our understanding of disability in Eastern Europe and contributed to decentering Western narratives during the last decades. However, the limited number of studies revolve around Soviet and Central European experiences, while the history of disability in Romania is still in its infancy.[1] How can we explain this lack of interest in Romanian historiography? This chapter proposes to shed light on the missing Romanian chapter in disability history. The first section provides an overview of existing research and of available archival and digitized resources, which have been widely omitted from established historical narratives. The second and third sections interrogate country-specific factors, such as institutional hindrances, ableism, the general lack of interest in disability among academic historians and the (in)visibility of disability within Romanian politics of memory. Reflecting upon the Museum of the Blind in Bucharest, the only museum that displays objects and artifacts related to the experiences of disabled people in Romania, the last section addresses the challenges of exhibiting and conveying disability history in a Romanian context.

The chapter is based on previous research and five expert interviews that were conducted in 2021. The semi-structured interviews revolved around the question of why disability has virtually been absent from Romanian historiography, archives, and museums, a trend also observed in historiographies of other languages, including English. As the respondents are experts in their respective fields (history, archival studies, and museology), the interviews also tackled the issue of why established institutions of memory and cultural heritage have failed to integrate disabled perspectives into their collections. To guarantee the respondents' anonymity, pseudonyms have been used throughout the study.

Previous Research and Available Sources

It would be an exaggeration to claim that the history of disability in Romania has not been studied at all hitherto. A few Romanian scholars have investigated various aspects of disability from a historical perspective, but these studies remained on the margins of mainstream historical research, are typically descriptive, and simply served the purpose of documenting organizational or educational aspects.[2] While the following outline should not be seen as exhaustive, it illustrates the need to infuse Romanian historiography with critical approaches to disability.

Available historical bibliographies attest to the fact that disability has been widely omitted from mainstream historiography and history of medicine before 1989.[3] While the history of medicine evolved into an established subdiscipline after the Second World War, influential works remained committed to Whiggish narratives of medical progress and disregarded the topic of disability.[4] The only noteworthy study published in 1968 was a multi-authored volume on the history of special education in Romania, focusing on the history of blind and deaf education during the nineteenth and twentieth centuries. The contributions to this volume were exclusively written by special educators, a fact that tellingly illustrates the gap between traditional historiography and the few historically interested scholars of disability.[5] Attempts to write histories of disability were also made by the Association of the Deaf and the Association of the Blind, which were the only state-sanctioned interest organizations for people with disabilities in socialist Romania. Both members and able-bodied specialists regularly published articles on the history of the blind and the deaf in the associations' official magazines, *New Life* (*Viața nouă*) and *Our Life* (*Viața noastră*). This absence mirrors prevailing discourses during state socialism that focused on normalizing society and rendering disability invisible. As Kolářová and Winkler put it succinctly, state socialist regimes in Eastern Europe exhibited a "deep trouble with difference," highlighting the "chasm between the (proclaimed) desire for and promises of justice and equality and the rigid notions of normalcy, and ablebodiness or ablemindedness."[6]

After 1989, this general picture did not change substantively. A few authors outside the traditional field of academic history have documented the history of various institutions and schools for the deaf, as well as the history of special education. However, these works tend to be descriptive and lack critical perspectives or insights from the fields of disability or deaf studies.[7]

Hence, few works have been written by academic historians, and these are usually scattered across various disciplines or have only a limited reach outside

Romania due to language barriers. Ligia Livadă-Cadeschi was the first historian to investigate philanthropical institutions and the history of the "poor and unfortunate," which historically included the disabled, in the Romanian principalities of Wallachia and Moldavia. While her work does not address disability explicitly, it sheds light on marginalized groups of society that are still absent from mainstream historiography.[8] In a similar fashion, scholars in both Romania and the United States have investigated Nicolae Ceaușescu's pronatalist policy that resulted in, among other outcomes, a large number of institutionalized disabled children.[9] The inhuman living conditions of these children, who were placed in state-run asylums and termed "irrecuperable" during Ceaușescu's reign, were revealed to an international public in 1990. While their fate dominated the political and academic discourse on disability during the postcommunist years, other groups of disabled people remained rather invisible.

A number of recent historical studies raise hopes that this lacuna will be addressed more broadly in the future.[10] The establishment of a working group dedicated to studying the history of disabilities in Eastern Europe, spearheaded by Maria Bucur and Maria Galmarini, marks a significant milestone in bringing the history of disability in Romania and in other Eastern European countries into the spotlight.[11] One of the key initiatives that emerged from this endeavor is an upcoming edited volume and special issues in the journals *Slavic Review* and *Transilvania*. These and other forthcoming studies on disability in Romanian history inspire hope that they will elevate the field's visibility within mainstream historiography.[12]

Attitudes and Mentalities

When Nicolae Ceaușescu's communist regime collapsed like a house of cards in December 1989, postcommunist elites inherited a malfunctioning welfare system that had exerted a devastating impact on the lives of the disabled. Romanian state funds for health care and social services dramatically decreased from around 1.4 percent of the total state budget in the 1970s to 0.3 percent in 1989.[13] Additionally, the catchphrase "socialist humanism" had for many years contradicted the harsh reality experienced by disabled people. After 1989, the rule of institutionalizing disabled persons was perpetuated, leading to the fact that a large number of disabled people still live in residential institutions.[14] Ever since the state socialist period, many of these facilities are situated in rural areas where access to employment is scarce. Additionally, ableist and infantilizing attitudes toward persons with intellectual disabilities prevail in contemporary Romania.[15]

The neglect of disability in Romanian historiography can partly be traced back to these political and social upheavals during the second half of the twentieth century. It would be wrong, however, to ascribe historians' general disinterestedness exclusively to the state socialist legacy or to the years of transition.

Gabriela, one of the respondents who works as a university professor in history, identifies various historical trajectories that led to a general disinterest in social questions within the Romanian public discourse. "Traditionally, Romanian elites never developed a significant sensibility towards social problems," she emphasizes. Far from being a national stereotype, the widespread indifference toward marginalized groups has historical roots that can be traced back to the eighteenth and nineteenth centuries. First, the Romanian Orthodox Church did not encourage charitable organizations comparable to Catholic charities for the poor. Similar to other autocephalous Orthodox churches in Eastern Europe, the Romanian Orthodox Church historically "remained close to the political power center, instead of committing itself to underprivileged groups of society," as Gabriela emphasizes. While there are counterexamples, such as the Eastern Orthodox monk Paisius Velichkovsky (1722–94), who welcomed the poor and sick to the monastery of Neamț hospital during the eighteenth century, "this was an exception," as Gabriela states. "The care for the 'deserving poor' was never essential to the Orthodox social teaching." She highlights that the widespread indifference to social questions is also mirrored by the fact that volunteering is poorly developed in Romania. Second, political reforms that were implemented during Romania's nation-building process in the nineteenth and twentieth centuries remained a top-down project, carried out by political elites who disregarded the needs of the peasant population or disadvantaged groups. A third explanatory factor is what Gabriela calls "the appetite of a broad electorate for rightwing policies" that is interconnected with the aforementioned elitist political culture. In contemporary Romania there is a widespread opinion that sweepingly incriminates recipients of social benefits: welfare beneficiaries, including the disabled, "are frequently denounced as moochers of public funds and as impostors," Gabriela states. This "rightwing rhetoric that incriminates public spending" is being embraced by a large majority "who still refuses to debate the causes of social problems." Caius, one of the respondents who works as a university professor in history, draws similar conclusions and points to the manifold continuities between the inveterate national communism[16] of the Ceaușescu era and political currents during the postcommunist period:

> While the United States has its own history of WASP constituencies, one could say that Romania has been marked by a White—Romanian—Orthodox electorate after 1989, which favored nationalism over minority rights. This is why there is a widespread reluctancy towards historical research on minorities, disability included. [These people] claim that studying marginalized groups would denigrate Romania's reputation.

This reluctancy is also mirrored by historians whose views were formed during the national communist years. Even after the Revolution, "these historians dominated key positions at universities and archives and reproduced national communist mentalities far into the 2000s," Caius claims. Part of this mindset was a monumental type of history writing, to borrow Nietzsche's concept, and according to Caius many historians regarded disability as "embarrassing and troublesome" for the self-image of the country.

Another reason why poverty and disability were neglected by historians is that these subjects are generally not regarded as "sensational" topics, as Gabriela states. The fate of Ceaușescu's orphans stirred some debates during the 1990s because they offended public sensibilities. Other groups of institutionalized and disabled persons, by contrast, caused less attention because they were not perceived as "spectacular" enough. Ada, one of the respondents who is head of a historical archive, confirms this picture. "In Romanian public discourse, disability is still widely perceived as a misfortune . . . or at least as a private matter." This also clarifies why the dysfunctional social care system in Romania largely remains off-topic until distressing incidents of mistreatment toward disabled individuals come to light. In a poignant echo of past mistreatment of children in orphanages that once shocked the world, Romania found itself embroiled in a new scandal in July 2023, this time centered around care homes for elderly disabled individuals. Private care home operators prioritized profits over the well-being of vulnerable residents, leading to a wave of severe abuses, neglect, and tragically, even deaths. Direct links between high-profile politicians and those responsible for the mistreatment raised serious international concerns anew about the malfunctioning social care system in Romania.[17]

Historical Archives and the (In)visibility of Disability

Archives do not merely represent a disinterested collection of historical records but rather serve as sites of political power. They can assist or impede transitional justice, and they can empower or exclude groups. As Verne Harris, former archivist of the Nelson Mandela Papers, once emphasized, archives' "indelible imprint of power either marginalizes or excludes (in terms of both 'content' and 'access') the weak, the poor and the outcast—society's aliens."[18] Michel-Rolph Trouillot similarly contended that silencing is "already inscribed in the sources, regardless of what else they reveal."[19] This logic applies no less to the Romanian context since political control of the National Archives spilled into the postcommunist period. Historical archives still select their documents and privilege certain perspectives while ignoring others. Those who have historically held the power to amplify their voices are the most visible to historians, with their voices echoed and their stories preserved.

Since 1951, when Romania was marked by high Stalinism, the state archives have been operated by the Ministry of Internal Affairs.[20] Even after 1989, this organizational structure remained unaltered, and the Faculty of Archival

Science, where several generations of archivists and custodians have been trained, was never transformed into a civil higher education institution, but rather was put under the auspices of the Police Academy (hence under the Ministry of Internal Affairs).[21] Only during the past years has the change of generations brought with it new impulses among archivists and historians, but due to the prevailing state control, many institutional hindrances remain. According to the National Archives Act from 1996, governmental institutions are required to transfer their files to the National Archives.[22] However, governmental bodies that historically have been in charge of welfare and health policies including disability issues withhold their files.[23] This picture is in accordance with Ada's experience as head of an archival institution:

> In Romania there has never been a tradition of accurately collecting and archiving official documents. State officials never cultivated professional ethics that respect administrative law and regard documents as a valuable public good . . . . This shortfall eventually translates into an issue of democratic accountability as documenting and archiving official decisions and actions determines whether state authorities can legitimate their position towards citizens.

In order for archives to ensure their autonomy and accessibility, factors such as stable funding, training, and experience of archivists, as well as legal protections against outside interference, must be in place. Instead, political pressure on archives has entrenched undemocratic practices after 1989. Apart from the fact that government bodies such as the Ministry of Health[24] have overlooked their basic public administration duties and neglected the preservation of their archives, historians are given virtually no access to several ministerial archives.[25] One of the few exceptions is Doboș and Jinga's research project on Ceaușescu's pronatalist policies, which received permission to access these files.[26] This attests to what the historian Adrian Cioflâncă has called a widespread "secret-mania."[27] In May 2022, following a series of measures by the Ministry of Internal Affairs, both central and local branches of the National Archives have been compelled to further restrict access to their collections by introducing a new requirement to verify selected files for the presence of "classified" information, resulting in additional delays and obstacles for historical research.[28]

The other side of the coin, according to Caius and Ada, is that Romanian archives have consistently struggled with logistical problems and lack of space and resources. As a result, archivists are not able to secure good working conditions since their hands are tied by political decisions. In reflecting on this nexus between memory politics and institutionalized barriers, Caius underlines that in order to get access and preserve important archival material, historians need to raise consciousness at the EU level. This is because decision makers in Romania themselves invoke EU legislation, such as the General

Data Protection Regulation (GDPR), in order to hamper access to historical documents. When it comes to disability and communism, which are still considered to be peculiarly sensitive issues, attempts to conceal important documentation will most probably continue to plague historians in the future.

Besides these external pressures, another factor explains why research on marginalized groups has been limited to a handful of historians in Romania. Documents from the early modern period are handwritten and use the Romanian Cyrillic alphabet, so to read them one must undergo time-consuming paleographical training. One example is the so-called registers of the "guilds of the poor" (*breasla calicilor*).[29] Many historians today do not have the necessary paleographical skills and are decreasingly interested in dedicating themselves to these documents.

The (in)visibility of disability in Romanian archives can also be explained in terms of supply and demand, according to Ada: "The questions we ask determine how archival records 'talk back' to us. If we start to pose new questions, historical sources that had been invisible up to now will be uncovered." In this context, Ada draws a parallel between the lack of attention given to women's history before the 1970s, and the fact that traditional history writing in Romania today renders disabled people insignificant.

Despite the fact that disabled experiences are missing from mainstream Romanian historiography, archives and libraries in fact hold a plethora of documents that have the potential to unsilence voices of disabled people. My own research at the National Archives in Bucharest is based on a collection that documents the Central Union of Craft Cooperatives (UCECOM), which maintained a wide network of sheltered workshops and became the biggest employer for disabled people during the state socialist period. These materials, however, have scarcely been consulted by other historians up until now. Similarly, the collection of the "National Office of War Invalids, Orphans and War Widows" (*IOVR*), founded in 1920, or the "Public administration of hospitals" (*Eforia Spitalelor*), have only received attention from historians outside Romania.[30] In addition to these archival sources, libraries are increasingly digitizing their historical periodicals collections. The University library in Cluj has made the main journal of the Romanian Association of the Deaf, published between 1932 and 1949, accessible to the public.[31] Although not digitized, other periodicals published by the Association of the Blind and the Association of the Deaf are available at the library of the Romanian Academy and other university libraries.[32]

Even if historians begin to utilize these collections, our picture will inevitably remain fragmentary if the history of disability is told from an exclusively institutional, top-down perspective. As archival records are mainly based on official documents, marginalized groups only become visible once they interact with state authorities, and this relationship has been habitually conflict ridden. For the most part, contacts between disabled people and authorities remained limited to those between doctors and patients and between people entitled to receive state-funded pensions and their caseworkers. Ever since the interwar period, the social insurance system in Romania has been, however, "rudimental and generally restricted to few beneficiaries, such as war widows, veterans and orphans," as Ada points out. In illustrating historical AIDS research, Virginia Berridge has termed this phenomenon "archives on the run" or "ad hoc archives." Archives are "picked up, sometimes literally, where they present themselves . . . . 'Ad hoc' archival provenance necessarily brings a particular bias to the subsequent historical account."[33] Against this backdrop, writing disability history in Romania inevitably entails a reliance on personal accounts and oral histories, which have been published to a limited extent in recent years.[34] Additionally, published ego documents—such as memoirs, diaries, and fiction—can serve as noteworthy examples.[35] Nicolae Ionescu's autobiography from 2005 offers a compelling history of the blind community, while Max Blecher's autobiographical accounts vividly depict the lives of individuals grappling with chronic illness and disabilities in interwar sanatoria.[36] Nonetheless, it remains imperative for historians to delve deeper and unearth additional valuable sources.

Lastly, historical archives also raise questions of accessibility. Melina, one of the respondents and the only archivist at her workplace who is physically disabled, depicts her own employer in surprisingly positive terms. After a serious accident that left her physically disabled, she was relocated to a unit for academic publishing and documentation, which she describes as a substantial career advancement. As to the physical accessibility of her institution, "the fact that the archives dispose of a wheelchair ramp, facilitates the access to my workplace." However, accessibility concerns not only the removal of physical barriers but also the provision of assistive technologies such as website accessibility: "A manuscript I was working with was in such bad shape that it was hardly possible to decipher the letters. For people with a visual impairment, these types of documents, which are additionally decomposing quickly, would be completely inaccessible." This is why Melina stresses the necessity of digitizing records more quickly to secure their accessibility for a diverse range of communities in the future.

Conveying the History of the Visually Impaired and the Blind

History museums have traditionally neglected bodily differences, and most of them still do not include objects that attest to the history of disability. In omitting these objects from their collections, museums "not only reify the idealized human form" but also present "a historically inaccurate view of the past," as Richard Sandell has asserted.[37] Yet, museums have the potential to play a more central role in reframing visitors' historical knowledge.[38] With regard to the representation of disability, Katherine Ott has contended that museums are crucial for performing "the important heritage work of historical validation," remembering the lives of disabled people through the material and visual culture they have left behind. In selecting and exhibiting artifacts and objects otherwise lost, museums can accomplish an "archaeology of the disappeared and hidden."[39]

The Museum of the Blind in Bucharest is a typical example of this type of archeology. Although located in a central urban district, colloquially known as "Bright Home," or *Vatra Luminoasă*, the museum is only visited by a few people, and its permanent exhibition continues to be unknown by a majority of city dwellers. As Ciprian, one of the respondents who is in charge of the museum, asserts, "few people know about our exhibition. Those who happen to visit the museum are in fact here to visit our school or association." The peripheral status and location of the Museum of the Blind within Bucharest's urban landscape are an evident reflection of the systematic invisibility of disability in historical narratives. As discussed in the first section of this chapter, scholarly efforts to examine the history of the deaf and blind have been limited and have barely influenced mainstream historiography, museology, or heritage preservation. The origins of *Vatra Luminoasă*, aka the "Quarter of the Blind," are intrinsically connected to Carmen Sylva (aka Elisabeth of Wied), the first queen of Romania. As a typical representative of philanthropic endeavors at the fin de siècle, she corresponded with Helen Keller and helped to fund the first institution for the blind in the Romanian capital, the "Bright Home Settlement" (*Așezământul Vatra Luminoasă*), which consisted of a primary school, an asylum, and sheltered workshops.[40] The museum was set up during the early 1960s as a part of the Bright Home special school for blind and visually impaired students and consists of a single large hall.[41] Among the museum's exhibits are Braille typewriters and a printing press from 1869. The museum also owns unique manuals from the nineteenth century, printed in the Moon and Klein type—embossed symbols derived from the Latin script as alternatives to Braille developed by William Moon (1818–94) and Johann Wilhelm Klein (1765–1848). Among the more outstanding objects are a musical notation on cords similar to the string alphabet (see Figure 1.1), and exhibits from various international meetings and conferences of the association's sister organizations in the Eastern Bloc during the Cold War.[42]

Additionally, the museum functions as a modest archive and library where fragmentary issues of historical periodicals, books, and newspapers in both Braille and standard print are preserved.[43] One of the exhibits is early editions of the association's own periodical *Our Life* in Braille, printed on plastic pages during the postwar years due to widespread paper shortages. As compared to other historical museums in Bucharest that are publicly funded, the Museum

Figure 1.1. Musical notation on cords, one of the exhibits at the Museum of the Blind in Bucharest.

of the Blind is restricted by extremely limited resources and its dependency on voluntary engagement. Against this background, it is hardly surprising that the design of the exhibition is rather traditional, with exhibits enclosed and protected behind large showcases. Visitors are left with the impression that the museum has remained unchanged since the 1960s.

As places of public memory, museums are not only regarded as crucial for the formation of citizenship and national identities but also subjected to market forces as they need to compete with tourism industries.[44] Museums in Bucharest are also exposed to various economic interests. In this respect, the Museum of the Blind is not part of the local cultural heritage market: "On a free weekend," Ciprian emphasizes, "no one would say: 'Let's go to the Museum of the Blind today!' Those who are interested in history rather visit the Military Museum or the National History Museum in the city center as our exhibition is off the main tourist tracks." When answering the question as to how the museum plays a role in shaping the identity of the blind in Bucharest, Ciprian paints a rather sober picture:

> A majority of members of the blind community live in the vicinity, and many people maintain contacts with our school and association. Therefore, our museum ought to play a much more central role . . . . However, the museum does not have enough resources to become a nodal point for the

blind community. There is a deep spirit of solidarity and community among the blind in our neighborhood . . . but what we need are funds, more exhibits and personnel who can develop and modernize our museum.

Conveying the history of the visually impaired and blind is not only a concern of the museum but rather a task that falls to history teachers at the adjoining senior high school for the visually impaired and blind.[45] However, the national curriculum for history does not leave space for teachers to integrate alternative perspectives, as Ciprian suggests: "We do not teach disability history at all on a regular basis. Sometimes we find time slots and can guide our students through the museum, but history teaching in our school exclusively consists of narratives of national or international history." This picture is in accordance with an educational project financed by the corporate-funded Orange Foundation, a charity that seeks to improve access to education, health care, and culture for people with sensory impairments, particularly visually impaired or deaf children.[46] While the educational platform employs both auditive and tactile learning strategies, aiming to promote "history through sound and touch," teaching materials mainly draw on traditional narratives from an able-bodied perspective.[47]

Ciprian and his colleagues have discussed the option of weaving blind history into their own history lessons: "The history of blind massage therapy, for example," an established profession among the blind, "would be highly relevant for our students, but unfortunately, our hands are tied by the national curriculum." Since final high school examinations are very demanding, "we cannot jeopardize our students' grades," Ciprian explains. The only remaining possibility is to teach blind history outside regular lessons: "As we meet our students on a daily basis, they sometimes pose questions about blind history and we do our best to convey the history of our community during our spare time."

Finally, Ciprian attests to the fact that there is no exchange whatsoever between academic historians and the blind community. "There are only a few established historians who have investigated the history of the blind or other disabled groups, and the few historians who have contacted us did so by accident, mostly because they were interested in the biography of our former queen." Although Ciprian reveals that university programs in history are popular among blind students who have graduated from the senior high school, "contacts with the academic world remain scarce." Established historians in Romania generally "do not have any knowledge of disability history," Ciprian acknowledges.

Museums and Archives as Empowering Institutions

Through an engagement with the history of disability, museums can become a powerful force for challenging and reshaping contemporary discussions about normativity and ablebodiedness. In this sense, museums can truly become what Mark Lilla once defined as democratic and empowering institutions. However, to achieve a genuine sense of a "shared cultural experience" among citizens, museums need to rethink their practices and behaviors.[48] Creating an inclusive experience is a challenging and complex task for many actors in contemporary Romania. This issue also applies to archival practices, spaces, and materials that still need to rise to the challenge of enabling a more diverse community to interrogate their specific pasts. The purpose of this chapter has been to discuss these challenges and to tackle the ways in which Romanian historiography, archives, and museums can confront increasing demands for reconfiguring their representational practices. Historians, archivists, and museologists need to reframe their narratives and materials if they are to uncover histories of disability. Time will show if these emancipatory impulses, discussed by historians of disability for many years now, will inspire the Romanian historical imagination to "crip" the archives and to represent disabled people in more equitable ways.

Notes

Epigraph: Katherine Ott, "Disability and the Practice of Public History: An Introduction," *The Public Historian* 27, no. 2 (2005): 11–24.

1. Radu Harald Dinu and Magdalena Zdrodowska, "Disability in State Socialist Eastern Europe," in *The Palgrave Encyclopedia of Disability*, edited by G. Bennett and E. Goodall (London: Palgrave Macmillan, 2025), https://doi.org/10.1007/978-3-031-40858-8_237-1.

2. For example, the recent study by Ruşeț: Răducu Ruşeț, *Momente din istoria dizabilității. Repere cronologice și aspecte sociale* (Cluj: Editura Presa Universitară Clujeană, 2022).

3. Ioachim Crăciun, ed., *Bibliografia istorică a României*. 6 vols. (Bucharest: Editura academiei române, 1970–1989); Mihai Popa, *Bibliografia medico-istorică 1914–1945: Transilvania* (Cluj: Institutul de Medicină şi Farmacie, 1965); Vlad Popovici, "Bibliografiile Româneşti als istoriei medicinei," *Clujul Medical* 83, no. 4 (2010): 712–15.

4. Valeriu L. Bologa, *Istoria medicinei româneşti* (Bucharest: Editura Medicală, 1972); Nicolae Vătămanu and Gheorghe Brătescu, *O istorie a medicinii* (Bucharest: Albatros, 1975).

5. Gheorghe Anastasiu et al., eds., *Contribuții la istoria învațământului special din România: Culegere de studii* (Bucharest: Editura Didactică şi Pedagogică, 1968).

6. Kateřina Kolářová and Martina Winkler, eds. *Re/imaginations of Disability in State Socialism: Visions, Promises, Frustrations* (Frankfurt am Main: Campus Verlag, 2021), 21.

7. Roxana Bejan and Ruxandra Foloştină, *Istoria dezvoltării educației speciale* (Bucharest: Editura Universitară, 2017); Gheorghe Moldovan, *Literatura Surdologică În România Interbelică* (Timişoara: Editura Politehnică, 2015); Gheorghe Moldovan,

Istoria Învățământului Bănățean Pentru Surdomuți (Timişoara: Eurostampa, 2010); Gheorghe Moldovan, *Începuturile Învățământului Special În Timişoara* (Timişoara: Politehnică, 2007).

8. Ligia Livadă-Cadeschi, *De la milă la filantropie: Instituții de asistare a săracilor din Țara Românească și Moldova în secolul al XVIII-lea* (Bucharest: Editura Cuvântul Vieții, 2020); Ligia Livadă-Cadeschi, *Meseria cerşutului în pământul aceştii patrii: Fragmente de istorie socială românească. 1800–1900* (Bucharest: Editura Universității, 2013); Ligia Livadă-Cadeschi, *Sărăcie şi asistență socială în spațiul românesc—sec. XVIII–XX, masă rotundă, iunie 1998* (Bucharest: Cris Cad., 2002).

9. Leyla Safta-Zecheria, "Away towards the Asylum. Abandonment, Confinement and Subsistence in Psychiatric (De-)institutionalization in Romania" (PhD diss., Central European University, 2018); Cristina Doboş and Mia Jinga, *Politica pronatalistă a regimului Ceauşescu* (Bucharest: Polirom, 2010); Lynn A. Morrison, "Ceausescu's Legacy: Family Struggles and Institutionalization of Children in Romania," *Journal of Family History* 29, no. 2 (2004): 168–82, https://doi.org/10.1177/0363199004264899; Gail Kligman, *The Politics of Duplicity: Controlling Reproduction in Ceausescu's Romania* (Berkeley: University of California Press, 1998).

10. Recent contributions include Radu Harald Dinu and Staffan Bengtsson, eds., *Disability and Labour in the Twentieth Century: Historical and Comparative Perspectives* (London: Routledge, 2023); Radu Harald Dinu, "Medical Discourses on Dis/ability in State Socialist Romania: A Critical Genealogy," in *Dis/ability in Media, Law and History: Intersectional, Embodied and Socially Constructed?*, edited by Micky Lee, Frank Rudy Cooper, and Patricia Reeve (London: Routledge, 2022), 76–89; Maria Bucur, *The Nation's Gratitude: War and Citizenship in Interwar Romania* (New York: Routledge, 2022); Maria Bucur, "Natalia Milița Geormăneanu: Microistoria unei 'nesupuse' ca demers în studiile de gen," *Transilvania* 11–12 (2020): 9–17; Marius Rotar, "Between Marginalisation and Integration: Practising Deaf Sports in Interwar Romania," *Sport in Society* (2020), https://doi.org/10.1080/17430437.2020.1820990; Harieta Mareci-Sabol, "'Ridicând din poverile vieții.' Institutul pentru orbi (şi surdo-muți) din Cernăuți (1908–1918)," *Analele Bucovinei* 27, no. 2 (2020): 427–52.

11. Association for Slavic, East European, and Eurasian Studies (ASEEES), "Working Group on Disability Studies," accessed June 25, 2024, https://www.aseees.org/about/affiliate/interest-groups.

12. Forthcoming studies include Maria Bucur, "Five Faces of Disability in Interwar Romania" (manuscript in progress) and a special issue of the academic journal *Transilvania* in Romanian edited by Maria Bucur, Leyla Safta-Zecheria, and Radu Harald Dinu.

13. Bogdan Murgescu, *România şi Europa: Acumularea decalajelor economice (1500–2010)* (Iaşi: Polirom, 2010), 338.

14. Leyla Safta-Zecheria, "Challenges Posed by COVID-19 to the Health of People with Disabilities Living in Residential Care Facilities in Romania," *Disability & Society* 35, no. 5 (2020): 837–43, https://doi.org/10.1080/09687599.2020.1754766.

15. Leyla Safta-Zecheria, "Biopolitics, Care and the Transformations of a Large Institution for Children with Disabilities in Romania from 1956 to 2015," *Journal of Contemporary Central and Eastern Europe* 31, no. 1 (2023): 45–66, https://doi.org/10.1080/25739638.2023.2182504.

16. Lucian Boia, *History and Myth in Romanian Consciousness* (Budapest: Central European University Press, 2001); Katherine Verdery, *National Ideology under Socialism: Identity and Cultural Politics in Ceaușescu's Romania* (Berkeley: University of California Press, 1991).

17. Cristian Ștefănescu, "Romania: Authorities investigate abuse at care homes," *Deutsche Welle*, accessed June 25, 2024, https://www.dw.com/en/romania-authorities-investigate-abuse-at-care-homes/a-66209699/.

18. Verne Harris, "Archons, Aliens and Angels: Power and Politics in the Archive," in *The Future of Archives and Recordkeeping: A Reader*, ed. Jennie Hill (London: Facet, 2011), 107–26.

19. Michel-Rolph Trouillot, *Silencing the Past: Power and the Production of History* (Boston: Beacon Press, 2015), 27.

20. Cristian Vasile, "Comisia Prezidențială pentru Analiza Dictaturii Comuniste și accesul la arhivele comunismului românesc," in *Fără termen de prescripție: aspecte ale investigării crimelor comunismului în Europa*, eds. Sergiu Musteață and Igor Cașu (Chișinău: Editura Cartier, 2011), 201–15.

21. Ministerul Afacerilor Interne, "Ordinul nr. 14/2017 pentru aprobarea Regulamentului de organizare şi funcționare a Academiei de Poliție 'Alexandru Ioan Cuza,'" *Monitorul Oficial* no. 121 (February 14, 2017). The Faculty was suspended in May 2021: Guvernul României, "Modificarea şi completarea Hotărârii Guvernului nr. 294/2007," *Monitorul Oficial* no. 504 (May 14, 2021).

22. Parliament of Romania, "Legea nr. 16, 2 April 1996," *Monitorul Oficial* no. 293 (April 22, 2014).

23. Elena Dragomir, "The end of archive research on communist and post-communist Romania?," H-Romania. August 6, 2022. Accessed June 25, 2024, https://networks.h-net.org/node/7941/discussions/10356425/end-archive-research-communist-and-post-communist-romania.

24. The official denominations of the Ministry of Labor and the Ministry of Health changed over time: Mihaela Lambru, "Asistența socială în România. Două secole de evoluție instituțională," in *Sărăcie şi asistență socială în spațiul românesc*, ed. Ligia Livadă-Cadeschi (Bucharest: Colegiul Noua Europa, 1998).

25. Cătălin Botoșineanu, "O himeră și un abuz legislativ. Documentele clasificate în cadrul Fondului Arhivistic Național," *Archiva Moldaviae* 13 (2021): 239–54; Cristian Vasile, "Un proiect de lege și multe restricții" and "Câteva considerații pe marginea proiectului de lege privind Arhivele naționale, L636/2018" (unpublished manuscripts, January 23, 2019), typescript.

26. Doboş and Jinga, *Politica pronatalistă*. This comprehensive study is the outcome of a research project conducted by the Institute for the Investigation of Communist Crimes and the Memory of the Romanian Exile (IICCMER), initiated in mid-2007. Due to its state-funded status, IICCMER had enhanced authority to

request access to the archives, facilitating the research process more effectively than other independent researchers.

27. Cosmin Năvădaru, "Adrian Cioflâncă (istoric) despre lupta pentru arhivele comuniste," Hotnews, accessed June 25, 2024, https://life.hotnews.ro/stiri-prin_oras-10550079-adrian-cioflanca-istoric-despre-lupta-pentru-arhivele-comuniste-erau-ascunse-fonduri-intregi-erau-scoase-file-din-dosar-era-lupta-primul-razboi-mondial-metru-metru.htm.

28. Iulia Popovici, "Secretele lor sînt secretele noastre. Cum au ajuns să fie clasificate regimul Antonescu și istoria României comuniste," December 2, 2022, https://www.observatorcultural.ro/articol/secretele-lor-sint-secretele-noastre, accessed on June 25, 2024; Dorin Dobrincu, "Noua direcție a adevărului: distrugerea memoriei istorice românești," May 29, 2022. Accessed on June 25, 2024, https://www.contributors.ro/noua-directie-a-adevarului-distrugerea-memoriei-istorice-romanesti/.

29. Livadă-Cadeschi, "De la milă la filantropie."

30. Bucur, *The Nation's Gratitude.*

31. *Răsăritul nostru: Organ pedagogic cultural și social al surdo-muților din România* (published between 1932 and 1949).

32. *The Gazette of the Deaf-Mutes* (*Gazeta surdo-muților*), *Our Life* and *Voice of Silence* (*Viața noastră* and *Vocea Tăcerii*, after 1989) were the official organs of the Deaf community. The Association of the Blind published *New Life* (*Viața Nouă*), a successor of the interwar *Braille Magazine* (*Revista Braille*), which had been established in 1925 and was discontinued in 1933. Roman Danilă, "Din istoiricul scrierii Braille în limba română," in *Contribuții la istoria învațământului special din România: Culegere de studii*, eds. Gheorghe Anastasiu et al. (Bucharest: Editura Didactică și Pedagogică, 1968), 70–83.

33. Virginia Berridge, "Researching Contemporary History: AIDS," *History Workshop* 38 (1994): 228–34.

34. Anemari Monica Negru, *Viața pe front în scrieri personale* (Târgoviște: Cetatea de Scaun, 2019). Georgie Popescu, *Frânturi din viața unui medic* (Iași: Editura Olm, 2012); Radu Cărpinișianu, *Suferințe și speranțe: Destine dintr-un cămin spital de invalizi mari mutilați* (Alba Iulia: Fronde, 1997).

35. For example, Dimitriu-Leorda's novel about deafness in interwar Romania: Vasile Dimitriu-Leorda, *Înfrângerea destinului. Romanul unui surdo-mut* (Bucharest: Unknown, 1938).

36. Nicolae Ionescu, *Azilul de orbi Regina Elisabeta. Vatra Luminoasă* (Bucharest: Pandora, 2005); Max Blecher, *The Illuminated Burrow* (Prague: Twisted Spoon Press, 2022); Max Blecher, *Adventures in Immediate Irreality* (New York: New Directions Publishing, 2015).

37. Richard Sandell, *Museums, Prejudice and the Reframing of Difference* (London: Routledge, 2007), 147.

38. Catherine Kudlick and Edward M. Luby, "Access as Activism: Bringing the Museum to the People," in *Museum Activism*, eds. Robert Janes and Richard Sandell (London: Routledge, 2019), 58–68.

39. Katherine Ott, "Collective Bodies: What Museums Do for Disability Studies," in *Re-Presenting Disability: Activism and Agency in the Museum*, eds. Richard

Sandell, Jocelyn Dodd, and Rosemarie Garland-Thomson (Hoboken: Routledge, 2013), 270–71.

40. Helen Keller, *Helen Keller's Journal, 1936–1937: With a Foreword by Augustus Muir* (Great Britain: Michael Joseph Ltd., 1938), 175; Robert Monske, *Vatra Luminoasă. Regina Elisaveta* (Bucharest: Inst. de Arte Grafice Carol Göbl, 1908); Friedel-Wulf Kupfer, "Carmen Sylvas Wirken zur Verbesserung der Lage der Blinden in Rumänien," *Zeitschrift für das Sehgeschädigten-Bildungswesen* 106 (1986), 214–18.

41. Constantin Marinescu, "Das Blindenmuseum in Bukarest," *Die Gegenwart* 24 (1970), 114–16.

42. For a study of the blind community during state socialism in Romania, see Radu Harald Dinu, "Becoming a Productive Citizen: Labour and the Blind Community in Socialist Romania," in *Disability and Labour in the Twentieth Century: Historical and Comparative Perspectives*, eds. Radu Harald Dinu and Staffan Bengtsson (London: Routledge, 2023).

43. Canal 33, "Muzeul Braille—unicat în Europa—aflat în sectorul 2," filmed June 3, 2020, video, 42:01, https://youtube/7G16TKnVCdU.

44. Pille Pruulmann-Vengerfeldt and Pille Runnel, "The Museum as an Arena for Cultural Citizenship: Exploring Modes of Engagement for Audience Empowerment," in *The Routledge Handbook of Museums, Media and Communication*, eds. Kirsten Drotner et al. (London: Routledge, 2018), 143–58; Dallen J. Timothy, *Cultural Heritage and Tourism: An Introduction* (Bristol: Channel View Publications, 2020).

45. Officially "Queen Elisabeth" special senior high school. Direcția Generală pentru Administrarea Patrimoniului Imobiliar Sector 2, "Despre noi," accessed on June 25, 2024, https://invatamantsector2.ro/school/liceul-tehnologic-special-regina-elisabeta/.

46. Fundația Orange, "Despre noi," accessed June 25, 2024, www.fundatiaorange.ro/.

47. Fundația Orange, "Nevăzătorii din România învață Istoria prin Sunet și Atingere," accessed June 25, 2024, https://www.fundatiaorange.ro/comunicate-de-presa/nevazatorii-din-romania-invata-istoria-prin-sunet-si-atingere/.

48. Mark Lilla, "The Museum in the City," *Journal of Aesthetic Education* 19, no. 2 (1985): 79–91.

CHAPTER 2

Deafening Architectural Modernism

Reconsidering the Archive of Adolf Loos

NINA VOLLENBRÖKER

"Ask an architect about their work, and you may learn more about the style, form, materials, structure, and cost of a building than the bodies or minds meant to inhabit it," disability theorist Aimi Hamraie writes. "Examine any doorway, window, toilet, chair, or desk in that building, however, and you will find the outline of the body meant to use it."[1] The built environment is deeply connected with people, as Hamraie eloquently points out, and yet the variety of human bodies—bodies in wheelchairs, bodies of disabled veterans, deaf bodies—rarely bears upon architectural discourse. This tendency to elide the body also concerns architects: just as a building constantly communicates with those who *inhabit* it, it also traces the bodies of those who *imagined* it—and their diversity has similarly been ignored. Staying with Hamraie's critical gaze on architecture's difficult relationship with disability, this chapter considers the body and the work of the highly influential modernist architect Adolf Loos.

Adolf Loos might be seen as an architectural all-rounder—one of those few practitioners whose acclaimed designs and built projects were matched by his output as a thinker and writer. During his tumultuous forty-year career, Loos lectured internationally and published dozens of essays, focusing mostly on architecture, but also touching on other topics ranging from furniture, utilitarian objects, and clothes to food, music, and haircuts. The most significant of his writings is "Ornament and Crime," a manifesto for modernism printed in the interdisciplinary journal *L'Esprit Nouveau* with a foreword by the celebrated architect Le Corbusier. In his short opening text, Le Corbusier unmistakably claimed his Austrian contemporary for the modernist movement when he announced: "Loos is one of the predecessors of the new spirit."[2] Loos was, as Le Corbusier affirms, one of the very first but also one of the most significant

Figure 2.1. Adolf Loos cupping his left ear with his hand. Photograph by Emil Theis, Dessau, c. 1930. 22.5 × 16.7 cm. Wienbibliothek im Rathaus, ZPH-1443.

modernist architects.[3] He created numerous revolutionary interiors and buildings, among them social spaces like the Café Museum (1899), the American Bar (1908), and the highly contentious Haus am Michaelerplatz (1911), as well as many residential projects, most memorably the Haus Steiner (1910), which immediately became a pilgrimage site for architects and was reproduced in virtually all literature of the modern movement, and the Villa Moller (1928) in Vienna, Austria (see Figure 2.4), and the Villa Müller (1930) in Prague, Czech Republic (see Figure 2.11).[4] Reflecting on these canonical works, architectural theorist Beatriz Colomina concludes: "Adolf Loos is the only architect of his generation whose thinking is still influential today."[5]

Loos was born in 1870 in Brünn, now Brno, in the Czech Republic. The son of a stone mason, he came from a background of construction and brought a distinct understanding of and appreciation for materials to his architectural journey. He studied in Dresden, Germany, worked in the eastern United States for three years (between 1893 and 1896), spent time in England, and then settled in Vienna where, on and off, he ran the Adolf-Loos-Bauschule and an architecture office.[6] At the time, Vienna was a lively center of creativity and critical rethinking, and this suited Loos, an eccentric, controversial, and often outright difficult person by any standards.[7] The architect established himself as a central figure in Vienna's cultural and intellectual life, where he was regarded as "an equivalent of Ludwig Wittgenstein in philosophy, Sigmund Freud in psychoanalysis, or

Arnold Schoenberg in music."[8] He counted vanguards such as Peter Altenberg, Oskar Kokoschka, and Karl Kraus among his closest friends, and, between 1902 and 1932, no less than four women called themselves "Mrs. Loos," with his final wife, Claire, being the daughter of a client and thirty-five years his junior.[9] Yet while Loos enjoyed rubbing shoulders with the capital's creative and wealthy elite, his dissonant architectural stance often sparked chilling incomprehension, and his unorthodox ways pushed away friends and supporters alike. Loos famously denounced the popular Secessionist artists, worked in radical opposition to mainstream architectural taste, and published highly controversial essays. He was notoriously unreliable, regularly got into confrontations with building authorities, and frequently delivered building projects late as well as considerably above budget. In 1928, Loos was convicted of sexual misconduct; in 1933 he died penniless of syphilis-related ailments.

The Loos Archive is held across two prestigious institutions in Vienna—the Graphische Sammlung Albertina and the Wienbibliothek im Rathaus—and has been part of UNESCO's prestigious Memory of the World register since 2018.[10] However, it remains "a collection of fragments" at heart: Loos destroyed many of his office documents in 1922, and any surviving records—including architectural drawings and models, written communication, photographs, and travel documents—continue to be gathered from Loos's companions, friends, and partners in Austria, the Czech Republic, and France.[11] While the Archive has served as a foundation for much influential scholarship considering Loos and his work from a multitude of nuanced angles, its absences and silences are palpable.[12] What is more, they remain mirrored by the relating voids and omissions in the Archive's readings. "[T]he research into Loos is organized by *gaps* in the archive," as Beatriz Colomina puts it. "All of the writing is in, on, and around the gaps."[13] One such neglected aspect—a glaring *gap*—is the fact that Adolf Loos was profoundly deaf by the time he produced his most influential works.[14]

Adolf Loos's overlooked deafness is not the only hearing impairment that has escaped architectural scrutiny. Architect Hansel Bauman confirms that deaf spatial authorship remains barely recognized within spatial discourse at large and, given that "the unique sensory and spatial dimensions . . . of deaf experience hold intrinsic architectural implications," points out the resulting significant loss to scholarship.[15] In the case of Loos, however, the context in which he both lived and worked make this scholarly shortfall particularly unfortunate. Loos's life essentially traced the rise "of statistical averages, standardized forms, and other narrowly defined ideals" and the connected, highly problematic processes of regulating bodies, pathologizing difference, and suppressing linguistic diversity in particular.[16] In addition to these currents, architectural debate was, at the height of Loos's career, beginning to circle around normative understandings of human bodies: as functioning, fit, and able; as a source of mathematical dimensions and standard proportions rather than a source of individual experience, knowledge, and needs; as representational, uniform, and ultimately interchangeable.[17] Understandings of "people as fleshy, corporeal matter," as Rob Imrie puts it, and as being in a mutually constitutive relationship with architecture, were largely absent from discussion.[18]

Addressing this gap in the Archive and scholarship relating to Loos, "Deafening Architectural Modernism" tugs at records relating to the architect's audiological condition amid the rich, interconnected layers of the Albertina and the Wienbiliothek's collections. This chapter does not intend to establish definitive insights or to rewrite Loos as a person or as an architect. Instead, it aims to foreground his deafness for the first time, to offer it as a critical modality to consider moments in the architect's written and built projects, and to point to new ways of thinking about space. The chapter is divided into two sections, each firmly guided by a set of archival items and arguing that key elements of Loos's visionary architecture were rooted in his deaf sensory experiences and abilities.[19] The first section mostly considers the architect's earlier years. It approaches Loos's life and work from a sensory science perspective and places an architectural focus on walls, investigating the perimeters of Loos's spaces through notions of vision and touch and asking how they came to be radically reduced in form but rich in their materiality. The second section considers the architect's later life, approaching it from a sociocultural angle. It places a focus on interior space, investigating how Loos's interconnected rooms and distinct circulation routes frame unexpected communications and experiences. The entire chapter is guided by archival material and draws upon architectural historians and Deaf studies scholars, as well as on critical disability, cognitive science, linguistic, and feminist perspectives.[20]

"The Walls of a House Belong to the Architect": Perimeters of Stillness and Concord

On first sight, the Adolf Loos Archive foregrounds sound rather than silence.[21] Loos's pocket calendar for the year 1926 suggests he took regular dance lessons, his polemic writings repeatedly draw on musical imagery, and his architectural plans return, again and again, to musical instruments and to spaces for the performance of concerts.[22] The architect was a self-confessed Richard Wagner fan and regularly attended Vienna's many concerts. His close friend, Arnold Schönberg, was one of the twentieth century's most influential composers, and Loos's archive underscores that, while Austrian society struggled to grasp Schönberg's sparse, atonal music, the architect was always a firm supporter. "Centuries may have to pass," Loos once noted, "before people wonder what it was that made Arnold Schönberg's contemporaries get themselves into such a state."[23] Once Loos reportedly bought up all tickets for a Schönberg concert that was threatened with last-minute cancellation due to insufficient sales. At the end of another performance, while the scandalized audience remained disdainfully silent, Loos jumped to his feet and applauded vigorously. "It's easy for you to clap for this music," he was told to a backdrop of sneers from fellow spectators in the room, "you are *deaf*!"[24]

Loos inherited his deafness from his father. A hearing loss is recorded in his 1896 military documents; by 1905 Loos did not easily follow conversations around a table.[25] A few years after that, he no longer heard individual voices and stopped taking questions at the end of his public talks.[26] Loos still spoke internationally and with great passion and energy—in fact, his architectural lectures were reviewed as "explosions of light" in the press—but by 1914 he prepared for subsequent discussion by distributing sheets of paper among his audiences so that their thoughts and comments could be communicated in writing.[27]

Around this time, Loos was given a business card by Jacques Fränkel, a childhood friend of Schönberg's (see Figures 2.2 and 2.3). In the Wienbiliothek, this small, yellowed piece of paper survives next to well over a hundred similar cards embossed with the names of Loos's many clients, acquaintances, and friends. On its back, Fränkel's business card bears the handwritten words: "Hearing exercises with Professor Urbantschitsch."[28] Victor Urbantschitsch was an Ear, Nose, and Throat doctor at a Viennese institution for the deaf and had supposedly developed a set of ortho-phonetic and ortho-acoustic exercises to improve residual hearing in deaf patients. This therapy was being recommended to Loos, and while it's not clear whether Loos visited the professor, the reference accentuates a complex moment in time: the moment when Loos continued to surround himself with concerts and speaking commitments, the moment when he was losing access to most day-to-day sounds, and the moment when he, importantly, wrote, delivered, revised, and eventually published his most significant text, "Ornament and Crime."[29]

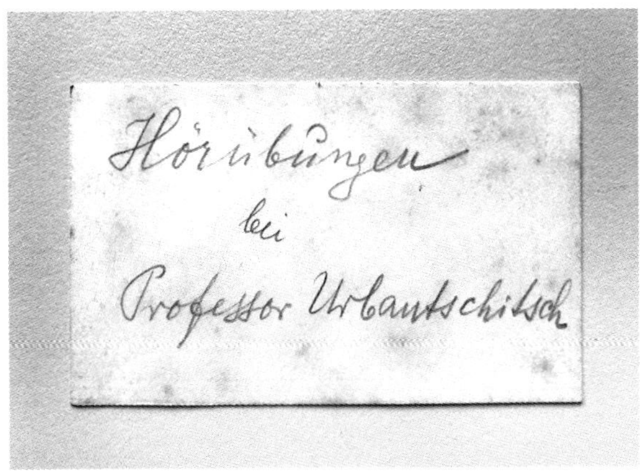

Figure 2.2. Back of a business card bearing the note "Hearing exercises with Professor Urbantschitsch." Photograph by author, 2021. Wienbibliothek im Rathaus, HS, NL Adolf Loos, ZPH 1442, 3.4.15.

Figure 2.3. A selection of business cards from the Adolf Loos Archive at Wienbibliothek im Rathaus. Photograph by author, 2021. Wienbibliothek im Rathaus, HS, NL Adolf Loos.

It is hard to overstate the influence of "Ornament and Crime." Architectural historian Christopher Long contends that "[n]o other architectural tract written over the past century has had either the trenchant impact or the long afterlife of Adolf Loos's little essay."[30] In this text, Loos argues that everyday objects derive beauty from their usefulness and should not be further embellished by ornamentation.[31] He casts decoration as inauthentic and outdated, proposes that cultural evolution was gradually causing ornamentation to disappear, and judges the creation of new forms of decoration as regressive and unmodern.[32] "Ornament and Crime" was, no doubt, partly a response to its time. Loos vehemently disagreed with Vienna's prevailing architectural taste—the profuse ornamentation of nineteenth-century historicism and the subsequent Jugendstil movement—and overtly criticized his Austrian and European contemporaries who employed applied decoration in their buildings.[33] In parallel, he welcomed the first voices calling for buildings and objects to be divested of superfluous ornament, including those of sociologist Georg Simmel and architect Hermann Muthesius, who were arguing for the removal of art from utilitarian objects, especially from items mass-produced in factories.[34]

But while his surroundings may have fueled Loos's offensive on ornament, his revolutionary stance on architecture should not be separated from his deafness. Feminist theorist Donna Haraway has firmly established that the perception of any situation is always a matter of an embodied, located subject. Coining the term "situated knowledge," she explains that understandings are never neutral but rather shaped, on the one hand, by the many intersecting aspects and dimensions of society and, on the other, by the individual reality of corporeal experience.[35] Haraway further extends situated *knowledge* to include a similarly located form of creative practice—situated *imagination*—which produces from this experiencing body.[36] Deaf studies scholars have built on Haraway's work. Concepts such as "Deaf Gain," "deaf critical insight," and "positive difference" have shown *deaf knowledge* as a distinct form of situated awareness rooted in deaf individuals' social experiences, bodily experiences, and, as architect Hansel Bauman has argued, distinct spatial experiences.[37] "Deaf people inhabit a rich sensory world in which lies the seed of a profound approach to experiencing our built environment," Bauman explains. He asserts that deafness does not merely adjust the way a person *understands* space but also influences the way they *create* space. Deaf individuals, he proposes, operate from a special position when it comes to "shaping the foundational aspects of architecture."[38]

His deafness, then, might be seen as having afforded Loos a particular understanding of, and a particular creative approach to, space. Bauman goes on to suggest that *vision* and *touch* are central to deaf relationships with the built environment, so the following paragraphs will pay attention to these two senses when considering Loos's archive and his architecture.

Research into deaf sensory abilities proposes that the spatial distribution of visual attention is different in deaf people compared to their hearing peers. Hearing individuals typically give less consideration to what happens in peripheral locations of their field of vision than deaf individuals. This specific area of the visual field benefits most strongly from auditory–visual convergence, meaning a hearing person relies on the joining of two senses—seeing and hearing—to discern what happens in the margins of their visual awareness. Deaf individuals, on the other hand, use visual attention only. They do not rely on the same merging of these two senses but instead develop enhanced visual cognition to monitor their peripheral visual field.[39] This superior cognition and acuity at the perimeter manifests itself in everyday spatial experience. Brain and cognitive science research suggests that the "greater attentional resources in the periphery . . . predict that *peripheral* distractors will be more distracting" for deaf individuals.[40] Related research rooted in spatio-scientific approaches goes one step further, proposing that deaf people have less "tolerance for *visual clutter* and discontinuity" in particular.[41]

An attention to visual orderliness and continuity, an aversion to clutter, and a distinct treatment of those architectural components that define the *periphery of vision and space* are undoubtedly at the core of Adolf Loos's work.[42] A particular treatment of boundaries—of architectural perimeters—can be discerned in the way he uses walls.[43] The walls that enclose Loos's revolutionary houses are regular, geometric surfaces defined by straight lines and an overwhelming lack of color. The facades of these buildings, including Villa Winternitz, Haus Schnabel, Villa Müller, Haus Brummel, and Villa Moller, do not distract with any excess information: the walls' expansive surfaces are white, clean, and sober; the window openings, which appear to have been punched out of them, are small and reveal little about the spaces they enclose; the lack of decoration gives no clues about the social or economic status of a house's inhabitants.[44]

The external facades hence wrap the building within a clutter-free perimeter, and this continues through to the interior. Here, Loos continues his language of highly controlled, undecorated architectural perimeters, but the walls lose the monochrome severity of their exterior to a different palette of materials, including wood, stone, painted plaster, and even the draped folds of lightweight cloth. In Loos's own Bösendorferstraße apartment, a screen of white fabric wrapped itself around an entire room, smoothly veiling any doors, windows, wardrobes, and other elements of storage.[45] The fabric fulfilled a central architectural aim that Loos explicitly addressed in his writings: it essentially removed the messiness of domestic life from the perimeter of the space.[46] Other efforts to calm the visual margins can be found across most of Loos's buildings. His designs for high-level windows and plain wall paneling, for example, are intended to fold the gaze inward, away from a room's edges and into the center of the space.[47] Further, Loos occasionally allows the straight trajectory of an internal wall to meander, its calculated detour carving an intimate recessed area—a "Nischerl" in Viennese—from the larger space of a room.[48] Intended as seating nooks, these intimate areas further hone the experience of spatial tidiness at the architectural perimeter: the walls on three sides envelope the person using the seat, banning peripheral distraction by excluding the larger room's outer edges, and guiding the eye to the interior's center—Loos created spaces that do not distract at the margins.

One of his recessed alcoves can be found at Villa Moller, a house located in northwest Vienna and completed for Anny and Hans Moller in 1928 (see Figures 2.4 and 2.5). Here, the main living area takes over the first of the building's four stories, and the seating nook is carved from the volumetric space at the center of the house. Occupying this intimate area, a person's view is cleanly directed down into the high-ceilinged living room and, through a door, flows further into the music room, which in turn opens up into the dining space and the garden (see Figure 2.6). This suite of interiors has been reviewed as geometrically harmonic and organized according to a rational system, but

Figure 2.4. Villa Moller, Vienna. Main facade. Photograph by Martin Gerlach jun., 1927–28. Albertina, Wien, ALA2445.

while Loos is routinely credited for stringently obeying the laws of simple geometry, there has been scholarly discontent with his use of not-so-simple finishes. Loos's selection of materials—painted plaster, Okoume plywood paneling, travertine columns, matte ebony parquet—have led architectural historian Kenneth Frampton to conclude that the space is "permeated by one subtle disjunction after another." Frampton detects "discords" between Loos's stark purist forms on one hand and his rich palette of colors and materials on the other.[49] Other architectural historians notice the same friction sensed by Frampton. Joseph Rykwert found it "curious" that the "archenemy of all ornament" should employ such a rich material palette so freely in his built work, and others detect architectural "paradoxes" or perceive Loos as "spoiling" his rationally conceived space with the "choice of materials he used."[50]

These perceived spatial "dissonances"—to use Frampton's term—might, however, be understood as the exact opposite: a remarkable concord.[51] "Perception of the outside world," brain and cognitive science research shows, "results from integration of information simultaneously derived via multiple senses."[52] Deaf individuals may not, as previously outlined, benefit from the auditory–visual convergence that assists a hearing person with gaining a thorough appreciation of their spatial perimeters. However, the body can also pair

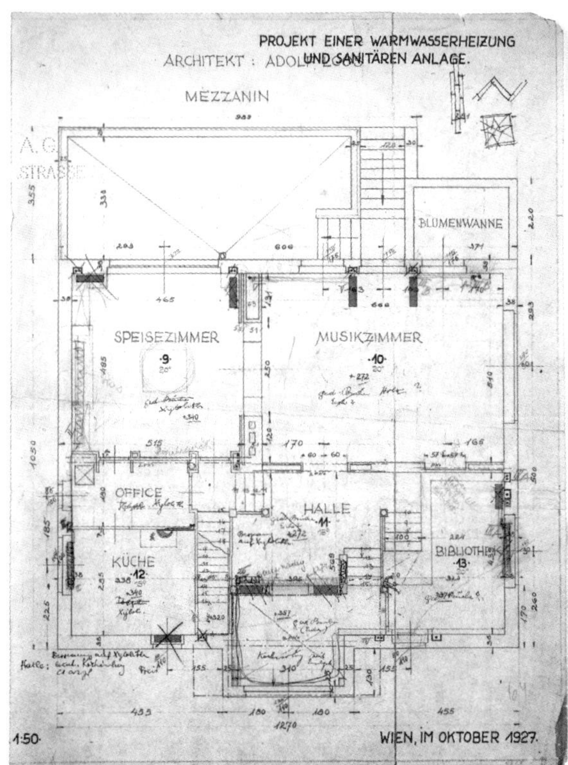

Figure 2.5. Villa Moller, Vienna. Plan of the main floor showing the seating recess and openings between rooms. Dyeline copy with annotations in ink. 1927. Albertina, Wien, ALA905.

Figure 2.6. Villa Moller, Vienna. View from the music room into the adjacent dining room. Photograph by Martin Gerlach jun., 1927–28. Albertina, Wien, ALA2453.

other senses, especially if they have commonalities. In his architecture, Loos might be seen as turning to such an alternative merging of senses: he brings together not sight and *sound* but sight and *touch*—a sense known to operate with "increased . . . attention and acuity" in deaf individuals.[53]

Loos actively reflected on this visuo-tactile convergence in his writings. "[W]hat I want is for people to *feel* the material in my rooms," he noted in an essay. "I want them to know about the closed space, to feel the material, the wood, to perceive with *their sense of vision and their sense of touch*, sensually."[54] Loos here preempts an understanding of spatial perception that has only just begun receiving scholarly attention: the fact that, as anthropologist Tim Ingold puts it, vision can "switch from its optical to its haptic modality." This haptic vision, Ingold explains, allows us to tune into architecture's texture, complexion, and affective expression.[55] In keeping with his desire to *feel* his spaces through vision and touch, Loos does create rich, haptic surfaces. A building's inhabitants frequently come into contact with some of these surfaces: a moving body will brush against walls and columns, and will habitually touch floors, handrails, door handles, and pieces of furniture. But Loos's strong haptic qualities noticeably and deliberately extend to surfaces that are out of reach—such as ceilings and high walls—and their materiality, grain, and texture are explored by vision rather than touch. Upon entering a space, it is possible to *feel* the cool evenness of a Cipolin marble or the tangly friction of fur, to *see* the smoothness of a coffered mahogany ceiling or the muffled acoustics produced by a curtain wrapping around the entire room. Loos's very tactile, rich materials, as architectural historian Nathaniel Coleman puts it, "communicate directly to the body"—even at a distance.[56] The tactile can be seen, the building can be touched through vision. Loos himself referred to this ongoing, continuous exchange between material and body as a "peripheral physical sense of touch"[57]—being deaf, he defined his architectural perimeters by haptics, not by sound as is typical, and the material palette that underpinned this visuo-tactile approach has come to be "the touchstone of his astylistic style."[58]

"I Master the Language of Others": On Conversations in Space

The Wienbibliothek has thoughtfully categorized all artifacts held in the Loos Archive into individual sections.[59] The sections bear titles such as "Envelopes addressed to Adolf Loos," "Photographs," "Business cards," "Bills," "Newspapers and magazines" and, importantly, "Conversations."[60] The latter comprises a total of twenty-eight items that vary greatly in their appearance (see Figure 2.7). There is an old order book filled with scribbles. There is a folded pocket map of Florence with the handwritten sentence: "Striding forward is easier than staying behind."[61] There are small notepads and loose pieces of paper filled with words

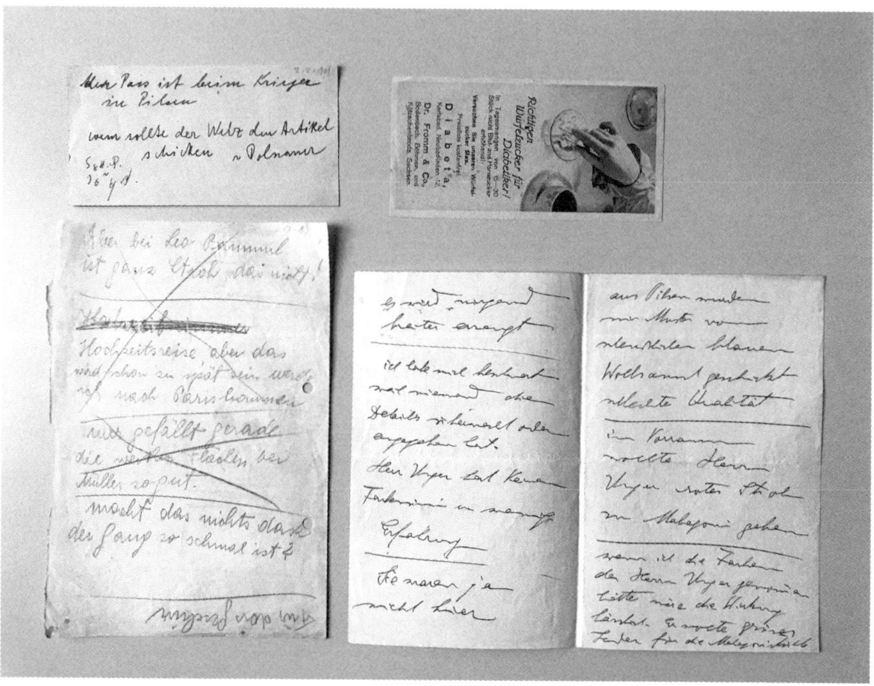

Figure 2.7. A selection of "conversation papers." Photograph by author, 2021. Wienbibliothek im Rathaus, HS, NL Adolf Loos.

and quick sketches. Some have been repurposed from thin, shiny advertisements. Others are lined sheets of writing paper, folded and faded or torn around the edges. Business cards and envelopes also bear quick notes. Most messages are recorded in pencil and address everyday concerns. "Dolphili, my love!," one message from Loos's wife Claire reads, "I want to shout out into the world that you are the greatest human being alive!"[62] Another set of sentences is written by the composer Anton Webern, a friend of Loos's and pupil of Arnold Schönberg. The two men appear to have discussed music, Webern offering a frank and thoughtful analysis of his own work in writing: "My music is lyric, that's why it is so short. It is poems." A second line, also in Webern's hand, promises: "I will return with Schönberg."[63] Schönberg was living in Berlin at the time.

Within the Archive's "Conversations" section, these diverse items have been filed as "Speech papers." They date from a time when Loos was actively referring to himself as deaf, both in personal letters and in newspaper notices he published, and his inner circle relied on pen and paper to communicate with him in written rather than spoken language.[64] Complementing the Wienbibliothek's "Speech papers" are a set of photographs kept at the Graphische Sammlung Albertina. The images show Loos, sitting at an outside table, engaged in a conversation with a woman (see Figures 2.8 to 2.10). Always keenly aware of his looks, the architect wears a suit, white shirt, and tie; his hair is neatly combed back. In

Figures 2.8–2.10. Adolf Loos in conversation in Pilsen. Photographs by Willy Kraus, 1930. Albertina, Wien, ALA 2106, 2107, 2093.

two photographs he smiles and speaks, his hands gesticulating, then moving energetically across his upper body. The woman listens, looking at Loos. The third photograph is different. Loos is still. Now wearing glasses and a focused expression, he leans in toward the woman. Lying on the table is a small writing pad on which she is recording her handwritten contribution to the discussion.[65] The images were taken in Pilsen, Czech Republic, in 1930. They capture a spatial communication, involving glances, movement, and repositionings in space, through gestures and within translations—crucial themes that are also at the center of a house a hundred miles away: Loos's Villa Müller.

Villa Müller sits on a hillside overlooking Prague and was built for Milada and František Müller. Its design—like its architect—is not one to conform or to take heed of advice: between January and December 1929, the house was refused planning permission no less than *ten* times (in fact, although building works commenced in the spring of 1929, permission was not granted until June of that year). Villa Müller is the most developed example of Loos's revolutionary notion of Raumplan, a complex arrangement that does away with segregated rooms, instead allowing interior space to flow between all areas and across varying levels of a building. Speaking just after the completion of the house, Loos explained: "My architecture is not conceived in plans, but in spaces. I do not design floor plans, facades, sections. I design spaces. For me, there is no ground floor, first floor etc. Storeys merge and *spaces relate to each other* . . . . [I]t is just this spatial *interaction* . . . that thus far I have best been able to realise in Dr Müller's house."[66] At the center of Villa Müller, Loos emphasizes, are spatial interaction and interrelation—a form of architectural communication. Importantly, the house was finished in 1930—the same year Loos himself was photographed in conversation with the young woman.

Considering Villa Müller in parallel with the photos of its architect taken at the very moment of the building's completion, the Raumplan takes on additional meaning. The Pilsen photographs show Loos engaged in what is, above all else, an *embodied* and *visual* communicative act: his gestures, facial expressions, and movements, the processes of writing, and the lip pattern reading together form a language that is inseparable from his physical person.[67] Literary historian Rebecca Sanchez links richly layered, physical, and relational interaction—like the one depicted in the photographs—to her concept of "language-in-body." She proposes that communicating bodies might be seen as *inscribed with words*, or as literally being composed of words, and reflects on how this particular communicative state positions people within their physical surroundings. "[I]f '*human bodies are words*' and the words 'are in you,'" she concludes, then "considerations of language become part of everyone's daily existence."[68] To put it differently, if we understand the body as *language in space*, then space necessarily becomes molded, pierced, and shaped *by* as well as *for* this language.

Building on Sanchez's concept, it might be argued that language located in the body demands, and creates, a different kind of architecture. Hansel Bauman notes that "deaf houses"—buildings that "emerge out of the ways deaf people inhabit and construct their spaces"—demonstrate clear common attributes: the absence of secluded rooms, the creation of openings between spaces, and the presence of vistas that oscillate between different points in a house to allow for communication.[69] Loos's Raumplan, at its core, can be seen as providing this: space that dismantles traditional frameworks, fractures small-scale enclosure, and creates visual connections. "Through the staircase," as architectural historian Julius Posener sums up the internal articulation of space at Villa Müller, "a person sitting in the dining room becomes aware of . . . the lady's room and the library; through its wide opening to the central hall, the dining room almost becomes an annex of the hall. That's the Loosian Raumplan."[70] Here, and in other houses, Loos's Raumplan locates the body's presence at the interstices between walls and vistas, orchestrating opportunities for communication operating in a visual modality—between rooms, across levels, along complex circulation routes through a large opening in the wall, a semi-veiled window, or even a fish tank integrated into a balustrade (see Figure 2.11).[71]

The open spaces of Loos's Raumplan allow for communication—through glances, gestures, utterances—between the people experiencing them. The intricate interconnection of rooms permits space to flow, actively weaving a storyline of glimpses, sightlines, and connectedness through the Villa Müller.

While the overall Raumplan was undoubtedly at the center of Loos's design, he also gave each individual room in the house precise attention, especially when it came to their specific lighting schemes.[72] From the outside, Villa Müller's windows have been critiqued as "randomly placed" and as appearing "smaller than they actually are," but they are neither oddly located nor oddly dimensioned.[73] Instead, the windows correlate to the rooms behind them:

Figure 2.11. Living room of the Villa Müller with a view of the opening to the raised dining area. Photograph by Martin Gerlach jun., 1928–30. Albertina, Wien, ALA2490.

spaces with more human interaction, such as the living room, generally have larger windows and more natural daylight; spaces with less interaction, such as the library—a "reservoir of quietness" that is "set apart from the household traffic"[74]—have smaller windows. A rooflight, furthermore, brings brightness to the central stairwell. Openings cut into interior walls borrow a soft glow of daylight from adjacent rooms. In many houses, windows are located above eye level or filled with opaque panes of glass, making them a mere source of light rather than frames to the outside world (Loos thought that "[a] cultivated man does not look out of the window; his window . . . is there only to let the light in, not to let the gaze pass through.").[75] Electric light fittings are positioned and integrated into the buildings' fabric with exceptional care, and Loos also used mirrors, analogous to lamps, to spread light across rooms.

"Adolf Loos was a master of space . . . but he should also be recognized for his manipulations of light" is how architectural historian Elise Wasser King sums up this attention to illumination, concluding that "Loos' lighting was . . . more than purely functional. Like his exquisite materials selection, his lighting added interest, warmth and beauty to otherwise austere spaces."[76] Villa Müller's atmospheric interiors, bathed in varying levels of luminosity and radiance, has led scholars to understand it as a space of suspenseful atmosphere, of theatricality, and of performance. Beatriz Colomina argues that the building's "inhabitants become both actors in and spectators of" a dramaturgical event, occupying either an illuminated stage or a gazing across the interconnecting rooms framing the recital.[77] For Colomina, Villa Müller is a "viewing mechanism" whose distinct spatial qualities—the "Raumplan" layout, the windows, the electric lighting—allow one occupant to detect another, "just as an actor entering the stage is immediately seen by a spectator in a theater box," and to observe their actions.[78]

In addition to seeing the movements of one body in space, two people might also see each other's gestures, facial expressions, and lip movements. An extended interpretation might, therefore, understand Villa Müller's carefully lit, open spaces as fostering a more balanced relationship between all its occupants, placing an emphasis on two-way communication (rather than one-way observation)—spoken, signed, or otherwise—as an act of embodied interaction that is so perfectly supported by Loos's most accomplished building.[79]

Conclusion

"What do we look for in an archive?" cultural theorist Ariella Azoulay asks, offering a poignant response: "That which we have deposited there."[80] She draws on Michel Foucault's understandings of the archive as establishing a monopoly over systems of knowledge and on Jacques Derrida's figure of the "archon," the guardian of the archive who controls its boundaries, deciding which documents and artifacts are preserved (or not), how they are classified (or not), and who has access to them (or not).[81] Azoulay goes on to highlight the many silences, avoidances, and erasures at the center of most archives. She argues that incomplete archival histories construct incomplete physical presents, thus perpetuating privileged social categories while sidelining those who are less visible, less documented, and therefore ultimately less valued. These archival distortions, silences, and even complete erasures, in other words, affect historically marginalized groups — including deaf and disabled communities.[82]

What is more, where archival material does exist, this frequently remains unconsidered. Historian and theorist Lennard J. Davis points out that "successful disabled people . . . have their disability erased by their success."[83] This has certainly happened in the case of Adolf Loos, whose work is lauded as "occup[ying] a truly exceptional place in the history of architecture" but whose deafness has been overlooked during nearly a century of architectural and academic attention.[84] However, in the Adolf Loos Archive—at the Graphische Sammlung Albertina and Wienbibliothek im Rathaus—the architect's deafness can be traced. It is there, present in a handwritten recommendation for therapy, in official portraits and casual snapshots, in the many tattered notebooks employed as communication devices, and in the photographic record of Loos using gestures in conversation. It is palpable in his writings, his drawings, his spaces. Still, the fact that Loos was profoundly deaf when he produced his most acclaimed works of architecture has been given virtually no scholarly attention. If mentioned, it receives an oblique, diluted glance, often with a negative spin. Douglas C. Baynton writes that "deafness is usually conceived by hearing people as merely a lack, an emptiness where hearing and sound ought to be" and Loos's deafness is habitually dressed down as an unfortunate, near-irrelevant infliction, an inopportune deficiency in an otherwise truly gifted—if complex—architect.[85]

This chapter, building on the work of those scholars who have looked at deafness, disability, and architecture—Jos Boys, Elizabeth Guffey, David Gissen, Aimi Hamraie, Sara Hendren, Barbara Penner, Bess Williamson—has aimed to pull at the photos, "Speech papers," and other under-considered items in the Vienna archives in order to disturb the narrative of Adolf Loos, his writings, and his spaces. "Loos sought to redefine architecture for modernity," Coleman writes, mirroring the many architectural histories that firmly establish Loos as a cofounder of architectural modernism.[86] The architect is thus intimately linked to a movement that championed standardized living practices, mass-produced furniture, and universal building types—aims based on normative understandings of *obedient, interchangeable* human bodies.

We have seen that Loos did not have an *obedient, interchangeable* body—nobody does.[88] Loos's archive, between its many gaps and loose ends, traces his deafness, and his deafness shaped his spatial experience and authorship.

Loos's differently sensing body interconnects with his passionate offensive on ornamentation and with the clean architectural perimeters he constructed—his outrage-inspiring facades without clutter, monochrome and nondistracting. This difference can also be seen as a driver for the sense of haptic vision flowing through his buildings. People without hearing, President of the National Association of the Deaf George Veditz insists, "are first, last and all the time *the* people of the eye," and Loos's materials communicate their texture, sound, and sensuous warmth directly to their spectator's sense of vision.[89] Finally, Loos's Raumplan, with its intricately interconnected spaces and careful lighting, can also be linked to the architect's deafness and use of embodied communication.

The Adolf Loos Archive, then, when considered through the lens of the architect's deafness, suggests that it was his particular body that allowed Loos to generate his acclaimed, provocative spaces and that laid the foundations for so much of the architectural thinking, writing, and practice that came after him.

Acknowledgments: I would like to thank the Architectural Research Fund (the Bartlett School of Architecture, UCL) as well as the Royal Institute of British Architects Research Fund for supporting this chapter. Gerhard Murauer at the Wienbibliothek im Rathaus was exceptionally helpful. I am also grateful to my colleagues at the Bartlett School of Architecture, especially Jos Boys, Megha Chand Inglis, and Stelios Giamarelos, who read earlier versions of this chapter, to Barbara Penner, and to Jonathan Hill, who always supported me and whom I will never stop missing.

To my youngest son, Lukas, thank you for opening my eyes to deafness.

Notes

1. Aimi Hamraie, *Building Access: Universal Design and the Politics of Disability* (Minneapolis: University of Minnesota Press, 2017), 19. For other key works focusing on architecture and disability, see Jos Boys, *Doing Disability Differently: An Alternative Handbook on Architecture, Dis/ability and Designing for Everyday Life* (London: Routledge, 2014); Jos Boys, *Disability, Space, Architecture* (London: Routledge, 2014); David Gissen, *The Architecture of Disability: Buildings, Cities, and Landscapes Beyond Access* (University of Minnesota Press, 2023); Elizabeth Guffey, *Designing Disability: Symbols, Space, and Society* (London: Bloomsbury Academic, 2018); Sara Hendren, *What Can a Body Do? How We Meet the Built World* (Penguin Publishing Group, 2020); Bess Williamson, *Accessible America: A History of Disability and Design* (New York: New York University Press, 2019).

2. Le Corbusier, "Foreword to Ornement et Crime," in *Corbusier, L'Esprit Nouveau* 2 (November 1920), 159.

3. See Murray Fraser, Alicja Gzowska, and Nataša Koselj, "Eastern Europe, 1900–1970," in Fraser, ed., *Sir Banister Fletcher's Global History of Architecture*, vol. 2, 958.

4. Panayotis Tournikiotis, *Adolf Loos* (New York: Princeton Architectural Press, 1994), 75–78.

5. Beatriz Colomina, "Sex, Lies and Decoration: Adolf Loos and Gustav Klimt," in *Potlatch*, Issue 3 (Adolf Loos: Our Contemporary Unser Zeitgenosse Nosso Contemporâneo), Fall 2012, 1.

6. Loos's architecture school had students between 1912 and 1923. Loos worked mostly from Vienna but regularly took projects on the road with him and, between 1924 and 1928, lived mostly in France.

7. Local thinkers, writers, musicians, architects, and artists included Sigmund Freud and Ludwig Wittgenstein, Peter Altenberg, Hugo von Hofmannsthal and Karl Kraus, Gustav Mahler and Arnold Schönberg, Gustav Klimt, Oskar Kokoschka and Otto Wagner, many of whom were Loos's close friends.

8. Fraser, Gzowska, and Koselj, "Eastern Europe," 958.

9. Loos married Lina Loos in 1902, Elsie Altmann Loos in 1919, and Claire Beck Loos in 1926. Bettie Bruce, who was in a ten-year relationship with Loos until 1914, referred to herself as "Mrs. Loos" although the two were never officially married.

10. The Loos Archive was added to UNESCO's "Memory of Austria" chapter in 2018. In six archival boxes and one folio box, the Wienbibliothek im Rathaus (WBR) holds the written archive ("Schriftlicher Nachlass")—2,322 items including handwritten and typed essays (addressing, besides architectural matters, clothing, art, table manners, music, and exhibitions), letters, and official documents. The Graphische Sammlung Albertina (Albertina) holds Loos's sketches and drawings as well as photographs of Loos and his built work. Outside the official Loos Archive, the court documents relating to his sexual misconduct trial are kept at the Archiv der Stadt Wien (Metropolitan Archive).

11. Beatriz Colomina, "Archive," in Beatriz Colomina, *Privacy and Publicity: Modern Architecture as Mass Media* (Cambridge: MIT Press, 1996), 1. While researchers must be aware of a certain personal choice for silence, given Loos's destruction of much of his papers, it is important to highlight that the archives created over the past decades have been crucial to nuanced understandings of the architect and the person, especially in relation to Loos's sexual misconduct charges.

12. Much recent writing focuses on the architect's residential designs with a recurring emphasis on theatricality, power relations, and sexuality. Beatriz Colomina memorably interprets the interior of Loos's villas as dispersed stages where the gendered roles of domesticity are acted out and observed, somewhat voyeuristically, from a series of "theater boxes." Farès el-Dahdah and Stephen Atkinson touch on notions of sexuality, race, and architectural subversiveness in their consideration of Loos's house design for Josephine Baker. Philip Ursprung highlights Loos's considerations of labor relations in architecture, while Frederic J. Schwartz and Christopher Long have both scrutinised Loos's 1928 court case and its implications for his architectural practice and theory. Beatriz Colomina, "The Split Wall: Domestic Voyeurism," in Colomina, *Sexuality and Space* (New York: Princeton Architectural Press, 1992); Farès el-Dahdah and Stephen Atkinson, "The Josephine Baker House: For Loos's Pleasure," *Assemblage* no. 26 (April 1995), 72–87; Philip Ursprung, "Working with 'Ornament and Crime,'" in *Potlatch*, Issue 3, Fall 2012, 71–75; Frederic J. Schwartz, "Architecture and Crime: Adolf Loos and the Culture of the 'Case,'"

The Art Bulletin 94, no. 3 (September 2012), 437–57; Christopher Long, *Adolf Loos on Trial* (Prague: Kant, 2017). On Loos's court case, see also Andreas Bruner, "Gruppenbild mit Kindern," in Markus Kristan, Sylvia Mattl-Wurm, and Gerhard Murauer, eds., *Adolf Loos; Schriften, Briefe, Dokumente aus der Wienbibliothek im Rathaus* (Wien, Metroverlag, 2018), 283–93.

13. Colomina, "Archive," 3, 1. Emphasis added.

14. I use the term "deaf" to refer to Adolf Loos's audiological spectrum of deafness as a physical state. It is this audiological condition that should become a critical modality when considering Loos's architecture. Loos was born with at least partial hearing but became profoundly deaf in later life. He was not a sign language user and, while repeatedly referring to himself as "deaf," might not be seen as having adopted a Deaf cultural identity although, as Rebecca Sanchez points out, "the distinction between deafness as a physical state and deafness as cultural identity is not always (or ever) a clear one." Rebecca Sanchez, *Deafening Modernism: Embodied Language and Visual Poetics in American Literature* (New York: New York University Press, 2015), 153.

15. Hansel Bauman, "DeafSpace: An Architecture toward a More Livable and Sustainable World," in H-Dirksen L. Bauman and Joseph J. Murray, eds., *Deaf Gain: Raising the Stakes for Human Diversity* (University of Minnesota Press, 2014), 379. While Loos's deafness is briefly mentioned in some scholarly texts, it is never at the center of considerations of his work. One investigation that interprets Loos's architecture as a site of bodily (rather than spoken) communication is Ines Weizman, "Tuning into the Void: The Aurality of Adolf Loos's Architecture," in "Did You Read Me?," *Harvard Design Magazine* (2014), 8–16.

16. Elizabeth Guffey and Bess Williamson, "Rethinking Design through Disability, Rethinking Disability through Design," in Elizabeth Guffey and Bess Williamson, eds., *Making Disability Modern: Design Histories* (London: Bloomsbury Visual Arts, 2020), 3. The greater arc of the process of standardizing bodies, charted by Lennard J. Davis, largely parallels Loos's lifetime. Davis traces the field of statistics, from nineteenth-century logging and categorizing of bodily measurements, to Alexander Graham Bell's eugenicist speech on deafness, and into the early twentieth century with its normative attitudes and the fierce cultural encoding of corporeal difference. Lennard J. Davis, *Enforcing Normalcy: Disability, Deafness and the Body* (London: Verso, 1995), 32. See also David Serlin, "Disabling the Flâneur," *Journal of Visual Culture*, 5 (2006), 193–208; Rosemarie Garland Thomson, *Extraordinary Bodies: Figuring Physical Disability in American Culture and Literature* (New York: Columbia University Press, 1997), 6. The process of increased norming and regulation of the body developed a particular focus on hearing and speaking: in a drive for "communicative norms," language diversity was targeted, accents were silenced, and nonverbal, embodied communication was branded primitivist, even nonhuman.

17. See, for example, Ernst Neufert's 1936 reference book for standardized spatial requirements in building projects; Le Corbusier's aim to establish his stylized six-foot "Modulor" as a basis for all architectural measurement and proportion; modernist discussions about "machines for living in," and the Bauhaus school's aspirations for good design in every home. See also Rob Imrie, "Architects' Conceptions of

the Human Body," in *Environment and Planning D: Society and Space* 21, no. 1 (2003), 47–65; and Natalia Pérez Liebergesell, PeterWillem Vermeersch, and Ann Heylighen, "Designing from a Disabled Body: The Case of Architect Marta Bordas Eddy," in *Multimodal Technologies and Interaction* 2, no. 1 (2018), 4.

18. Imrie, "Architects' Conceptions of the Human Body," 51 and 63.

19. This study draws primarily on Loos's built and surviving domestic spaces. Since his deafness was progressive, particular emphasis is placed on Loos's later work.

20. Kenneth Frampton, "Adolf Loos: The Architect as Master Builder," in Roberto Schezen, ed., *Adolf Loos: Architecture 1903–1932* (New York: Monacelli Press, 2009); Tournikiotis, *Adolf Loos*; Burkhardt Rukschcio and Roland Schachel, *Adolf Loos; Leben und Werk*, (Residenz Verlag Salzburg und Wien, 1982); Paddy Ladd, *Understanding Deaf Culture: In Search of Deafhood* (Clevedon: Multilingual Matters Ltd, 2003); Davis, *Enforcing Normalcy*; Bauman and Murray, eds., *Deaf Gain*; Annelies Kusters, Maartje De Meulder, and Dai O'Brien, *Innovations in Deaf Studies: The Role of Deaf Scholars* (Oxford: Oxford University Press, 2017); Donna Haraway, "Situated Knowledges: The Science Question in Feminism and the Privilege of Partial Perspective," in *Feminist Studies* 14, no. 3 (Autumn 1988), 585–86; Daphne Bavelier, Matthew W. G. Dye, and Peter C. Hauser, "Do Deaf Individuals See Better?," in *TRENDS in Cognitive Sciences* 10, no. 11, 512–18; Boys, *Doing Disability Differently*; Boys, *Disability, Space, Architecture*; Guffey, *Designing Disability*; Hamraie, *Building Access*; Hendren, *What Can a Body Do?*; Barbara Penner, "The Flexible Heart of the Home," *Places*, May 2018, placesjournal.org; Williamson, *Accessible America.*

21. Adolf Loos, "Die Abschaffung der Möbel," in Franz Glück, ed., *Adolf Loos—Sämtliche Schriften* (Herold, Wien, München 1962), 390.

22. Calendar for 1926; WBR, HS, NL Adolf Loos, ZPH 1442, 2.2.25. Musical imagery features in "Glass and China," "Beethoven's Sick Ears," and "Poor Little Rich Man." Drawings of music rooms and instruments: Haus Hans and Anny Moller (ALA A13, 0133, and 932); Villa Dr. Ing. Frantisek and Milada Müller (ALA59); Apartment with Piano Room (ALA557v); Wohnung Dr. Weissenstein, Kaminzimmer, Grundriss (ALA477r); Wohnung mit Klavierzimmer, Grundriss (ALA557r); Atriumhaus, Grundriss (ALA662). Chair and sheet music storage are considered on dedicated drawings (ALA A13, 919, and 930 respectively). A cello or violin has been montaged into the display case on a photograph of the Villa Moller music room by Martin Gerlach (1927–28), ALA2453.

23. Adolf Loos, "Arnold Schönberg and His Contemporaries," in Adolph Loos, *Ornament and Crime: Thoughts on Design and Materials* (Milton Keynes: Penguin Random House, 2019), 244.

24. Rukschcio and Schachel, *Adolf Loos*, 182. Emphasis added.

25. Compare Rukschcio and Schachel, *Adolf Loos*, 35; Kristan et al., eds., *Adolf Loos*, 106.

26. Rukschcio and Schachel, *Adolf Loos*, 35, 102, and 192.

27. Robert Scheu noted "Was er redet sind Explosionen des Lichts . . . " in *Die Fackel* Nr. 283/284 Wien 26.06.1909. For his international lectures, see Cecile

Poulot, "Adolf Loos und seine Netzwerke in Paris um 1926," in Kristan et al., eds., *Adolf Loos*, 271.

28. WBR, HS, NL Adolf Loos, ZPH 1442, 3.4.15. A total of 120 business cards can be found in Archival Box 4 at the Wienbibliothek im Rathaus. For cards with annotations, see items WBR, HS, NL Adolf Loos, ZPH 1442, 3.4.1–3.4.66. All translations from German by the author.

29. Adolf Loos, "Ornament and Crime," in Loos, *Ornament and Crime*. The history of the essay is complex: Loos first presented a version of it as part of a Berlin lecture entitled "Kritik der angewandten Kunst" in 1909. He wrote "Ornament and Crime" in early 1910 and gave a related talk in Vienna that year. The first publication, in French, appeared in 1913. See Christopher Long, "Ornament Is Not Exactly a Crime: On the Long and Curious Afterlife of Adolf Loos's Famed Essay," in *Potlatch*, Issue 3, Fall 2021, 31–48.

30. Long, "Ornament Is Not Exactly a Crime," 31.

31. The text has a series of inexcusable flaws and has been rightly criticized for its deeply troubling racist and colonialist tone. Loos problematically links ornaments to the tattoos of Indigenous people of New Guinea and the tattoos, in turn, to criminality. He also references other non-European nations in a condescending tone.

32. The text refers not just to architecture but also considers language, food, and objects of daily use, assessing applied ornamentation to be economically wasteful, culturally backwards, and physically oppressive in all of them and arguing for forms that relate to their own making and cultural history. Loos, "Ornament and Crime."

33. Taking aim at two well-thought-of architects, Joseph Maria Olbrich and Henry van de Velde, he proclaimed: "The modern ornament has . . . no past and no future. It is greeted with delight by uncultivated people to whom the greatness of our age is a book with seven seals, and repudiated shortly afterwards." Loos, "Ornament and Crime," 196.

34. Georg Simmel, "Das Problem des Stiles," *Dekorative Kunst* 11, no. 7 (April 1908), 307–16. Hermann Muthesius, "Wirtschaftsformen im Kunstgewerbe," lecture at Volkswirtschaftliche Gesellschaft Berlin, January 1908.

35. Haraway, "Situated Knowledges."

36. Haraway, "Situated Knowledges," 585–86. See also Marcel Stoetzler and Nira Yuval-Davis, "Standpoint Theory, Situated Knowledge and the Situated Imagination," in *Feminist Theory* 3, no. 3 (2002), 315–33.

37. For Paddy Ladd's concept of positive difference, see *Understanding Deaf Culture*. For deaf critical insight, see Davis, *Enforcing Normalcy*, 100–25. For "deaf gain," see Bauman and Murray's "Deaf Gain," in Bauman and Murray, eds., *Deaf Gain*. For deaf knowledge as situated knowledge, see Michele Friedner, "Doing Deaf Studies in the Global South," in Kusters et al., *Innovations in Deaf Studies*, 130.

38. Bauman, "DeafSpace," 375. See also Hansel Bauman et al., *DeafSpace Design Guidelines*, unpublished working draft, Gallaudet University, 2010, 10–13, accessible at https://infoguides.rit.edu/deafspace/principles, which contextualizes DeafSpace as a contemporary project founded by deaf spatial practitioners to research the

"architectural implications of deaf ways of being" and subsequently conceive spaces with and for deaf sensibilities.

39. Bavelier et al., "Do Deaf Individuals See Better?" For investigations into how sensory modalities interact, see also Lei Yuan et al., "Seeing Is Not Enough for Sustained Visual Attention," in *Proceedings of the Annual Meeting of the Cognitive Science Society* 39 (2017), 1412–17.

40. Bavelier et al., "Do Deaf Individuals See Better?," 514. This study focuses on visuo-spatial communicators, but the importance of being deaf rather than a sign language user is added in Matthew Dye, "Seeing the World through Deaf Eyes," in Bauman and Murray, eds., *Deaf Gain,* 203–4.

41. Bavelier et al., "Do Deaf Individuals See Better?," 514. Antti Raike, Suvi Pylvänen, and Päivi Rainò, "Co-Design from Divergent Thinking," in Bauman and Murray, eds., *Deaf Gain*, 402–20. Emphasis added.

42. For an understanding of what constitutes visual clutter, see Ruth Rosenholtz, Yuanzhen Li, and Lisa Nakano, "Measuring Visual Clutter," in *Journal of Vision* 7, no. 2 (2007), 17 and 1–22.

43. While Loos's houses are site-specific rather than interchangeable, architectural theorist Panayotis Tournikiotis has highlighted similarities between buildings that, he argues, "allows a consideration of the projects as successive manifestations of a single rational approach." Tournikiotis, *Adolf Loos*, 59.

44. Tournikiotis, *Adolf Loos*, 59 and Frampton, "Adolf Loos," 15.

45. Martin Gerlach jun, "Wohnung Adolf Loos, Wien I., Bösendorferstraße (früher Giselastraße) 3/5. Stock, Schlafzimmer" (ALA3130). Loos's use of fabric to cover messy details is also visible in Martin Gerlach jun, Wohnung Paul Khuner, Wien IV., Möllwaldplatz 4, "Blick vom Herrenzimmer ins Wohnzimmer" (ALA2307).

46. "What must the truly modern architect do?," Loos ponders in one of his texts. "He must build houses in which every item of furniture that cannot be moved must be concealed inside the walls." Loos, "Die Abschaffung der Möbel," 390.

47. See also Beatriz Colomina, "Intimacy and Spectacle: The Interiors of Adolf Loos," in *AA Files* no. 20 (Autumn 1990), 5.

48. "Nischerl" might be translated as "small niche." These built-in alcove seating areas are noteworthy in Loos's architecture since, unlike some other architects, Loos did not typically furnish his buildings. A "Nischerl" can be found in drawings in the Loos Archive in the Albertina: Wohnung Hirsch, Esszimmerecke (ALA680r), Villa Dr. med. Josef Fleischner (ALA150), Villa Dr. Ing. Frantisek and Milada Müller (ALA59), and Haus Hans and Anny Moller (ALA905). The Nischerl in Loos's own apartment is visible in a photograph in the Albertina: Martin Gerlach jun, Wohnung Adolf Loos, Wien I., Bösendorferstraße (früher Giselastraße) 3/5. Stock, Kaminnische, schräge Innenansicht (ALA3128).

49. Frampton, "Adolf Loos," 16–17. The internal detailing is, indeed, sensuous and intense. While Loos often sourced materials locally, manipulated them minimally, and installed them to be durable in the face of fashion cycle changes (thus aligning himself with the drive for ornament-free architecture and production he preached in his writings), he did use a variety of textures and materials. See Nathaniel Coleman, "Loos (1870–1933): Not the Material But What Is Done

with It," in Nathaniel Coleman, *Materials and Meaning in Architecture: Essays on the Bodily Experience of Buildings* (London: Bloomsbury Visual Arts, 2020), 37–60.

50. Joseph Rykwert, "Adolf Loos: The New Vision," in *Studio International* 186, no. 957 (July–August 1973), 18. Quoted in William Tozer, *A Theory of Making: Architecture and Art in the Practice of Adolf Loos*, unpublished PhD thesis, University College London, 2011, 24. Coleman, "Loos (1870–1933)," 37. Dragana Vasilski, "In Search of the Roots of Minimalism in Architecture: Formal Silence of Adolf Loos," in *Arhitektura i urbanizam* 31 (2011), 17.

51. Frampton, "Adolf Loos," 16–17.

52. Nadia Bolognini et al., "Tactile Temporal Processing in the Auditory Cortex," in *Journal of Cognitive Neuroscience* 22, no. 6 (June 2010), 1201.

53. Donna Jo Napoli, "A Magic Touch," in Bauman and Murray, eds., *Deaf Gain*, 225.

54. Adolf Loos, "On Thrift" (1924), in Loos, *Ornament and Crime*, 257–58. Emphasis added. Beatriz Colomina writes: "Loos privileges the bodily experience of space over its mental construction: the architect first senses the space, then he visualises it." Colomina, "Intimacy and Spectacle," 11.

55. Tim Ingold, "Surface Visions," in *Theory, Culture & Society* 34, no. 7–8 (2017), 99–108.

56. Coleman, "Loos (1870–1933)," 45.

57. Loos, "On Thrift," 258. Emphasis added. Loos also links "sensing" and "seeing" of material qualities in his essay "The Principle of Cladding," in Adolf Loos, *Spoken into the Void: Collected Essays, 1897–1900* (Cambridge: MIT Press, 1982), 66.

58. Frampton, "Adolf Loos," 17.

59. Loos's lifelong friend, the playwright, essayist, and poet Karl Kraus, wrote: "I master the language of others. Mine does what it wants with me." Frampton, "Adolf Loos," 14.

60. See the Loos Archive's register, "Teilnachlass Adolf Loos, Wienbibliothek im Rathaus, Handschriftensammlung, ZPH 1442." Titles refer to the following sections: envelopes addressed to Adolf Loos, section 3.5; photographs, section 10; business cards, section 3.4; bills, section 2.6; newspapers and magazines, section 13.1; conversations, section 2.2. See also Markus Kristan, Sylvia Mattl-Wurm, and Gerhard Murauer, "Vorwort," in Kristan et al., eds., *Adolf Loos*, 11.

61. WBR, HS, NL Adolf Loos, ZPH 1442, 2.2.28.

62. WBR, HS, NL Adolf Loos, ZPH 1442, 2.2.6. Translation by the author.

63. WBR, HS, NL Adolf Loos, ZPH 1442, 2.9.23, and 2.9.24. Translation by the author.

64. For details about Loos referring to himself as deaf, see Rukschcio and Schachel, *Adolf Loos*, 344–45, 347, and 349. Unlike his contemporary the deaf American architect Olof Hanson, Loos did not express a particular interest in learning about or actively creating architecture for deaf people.

65. The process of communicating via written notes is also described by Loos's wife Claire Beck Loos in Claire Beck Loos, *Adolf Loos: A Private Portrait* (Los Angeles: DoppelHouse Press, 2011), 90.

66. Loos speaking at a lecture in Pilsen, 1930. Transcript from the Vienna Centre of Architecture, https://www.azw.at/en/event/adolf-loos-nachleben/, accessed October 3, 2022. Emphasis added.

67. While Loos did not use sign language, his wife Claire confirms he did read lip patterns. Beck Loos, *Adolf Loos*, 65. Loos might thus be seen as engaging in "total communication," which Peter Jackson defines as the combined use of "speech, writing, sign . . . and reading." Peter Jackson, *Britain's Deaf Heritage* (Kippielaw: Pentland Press, 1990), 343.

68. Sanchez, *Deafening Modernism*, 26. Emphasis in original.

69. "These practical acts of customization are commonly recognized traditions within Deaf culture," Bauman further explains, "[They] . . . are exemplified by the notorious phrase 'this is a deaf house.'" Bauman, "DeafSpace," 378–79.

70. Julius Posener, "Julius Posener Vorlesungen II," in *archplus* 53 (1980). Aachen: ARCH+ Verlag, 38. Translated from German by the author.

71. See Haus Rufer (1922), arguably the first to fully use the interior spatial notion of Raumplan, Haus Tzara (1926), and Villa Moller. Joseph Rosa in Schezen, ed., *Adolf Loos*, 92.

72. Architectural historian August Sarnitz notes that Loos's "architecture is defined by the quality of space, light, proportion and colour." See Tozer, *A Theory of Making*, 35.

73. Rukschcio and Schachel, *Adolf Loos*, 611. Translated from German by author. The review of Villa Müller's facade is by Robert Scheu.

74. Ludwig Münz and Gustav Künstler, *Der Architekt Adolf Loos: Darstellung seines Schaffens nach Werkgruppen/Chronologisches Werkverzeichnis* (Vienna: A. Schroll 1964), 149.

75. Le Corbusier, *Urbanisme* (Paris, 1925), 174.

76. Elise Wasser King, "Harnessing Light: Illuminating Lighting in Adolf Loos' Early Commercial Designs," *Journal of Design History* 25, no. 2 (2012), 152.

77. Colomina, "Interior," in Colomina, *Privacy and Publicity*, 244.

78. Colomina, "Interior," in Colomina, *Privacy and Publicity*, 250, 238.

79. Villa Müller is frequently seen as Loos's "most complete building." See Fraser, Gzowska, and Koselj, "Eastern Europe," 958.

80. Ariella Azoulay, "Archive," in *Political Concepts, A Critical Lexicon* 21, Issue 1 (July 2017), www.politicalconcepts.org/issue1/archive, The New School for Social Research, 2017, accessed February 22, 2022.

81. Jacques Derrida, *Archive Fever: A Freudian Impression* (Chicago: University of Chicago Press, 1996). See also Michel Foucault's understandings of the archive as establishing a monopoly over systems of knowledge in his *Archaeology of Knowledge* (London: Routledge, 2002).

82. See Gracen M. Brilmyer, "Toward a Crip Provenance: Centering Disability in Archives through Its Absence," *Journal of Contemporary Archival Studies*, vol. 9, article 3 (2022). Other marginalized communities are also affected by this. See Saidiya Hartman, "Venus in Two Acts," *Small Axe: A Journal of Criticism* 12, no. 2 (2008): 1–14; Ann Laura Stoler, "Colonial Archives and the Arts of Governance," *Archival Science* 2, no. 1–2 (2002): 87–109.

83. Davis, *Enforcing Normalcy*, 9.

84. Hilde Heynen, *Architecture and Modernity: A Critique* (Cambridge, MA and London: MIT, c. 1999), 75.

85. Loos's deafness is sometimes linked to other characteristics perceived as negative. Joseph Imorde portrays Loos as borderline psychotic and links this mental state directly to his "suffering from a hearing impairment." Joseph Imorde, "Adolf Loos: Der Raumplan und das Private," in *Kritische Berichte* 34, no. 2 (2006), 41 (translated from German by the author). Paul Davies links Loos's deafness with his lifelong sexual promiscuity, incorrectly claiming that Loos became "deaf from syphilis contracted from a youthful visit to a brothel." Paul Davies, *Architectural History Retold* (New York: Routledge, 2015). Ines Weizman puts a direct focus on Loos's "deteriorating" hearing and its gradual "decline," and endeavors to establish how the "setback" he experienced caused his buildings to become "prosthetic devices—extensions, perhaps, of his trusted hearing trumpet." Weizman, "Tuning into the Void," 10–11.

86. See, for example, Le Corbusier's attempt to establish his "Modulor" as a basis for measurement and proportion, Ernst Neubert's related reference book for standardized spatial requirements in building projects, modernist discussions about "machines for living in," and the Bauhaus school's aspirations for good design in every home. Le Corbusier, *The Modulor* (Basel; Berlin; Boston: Birkhäuser, 2015); Ernst Neubert, *Architects' Data*, fourth edition (Oxford: Wiley-Blackwell, 2012); Le Corbusier, *Towards a New Architecture* (translated from the French by Frederick Etchells) (London: Architectural Press, 1970); and Walter Gropius, ed., *Neue Arbeiten der Bauhauswerkstätten* (Munich: Albert Langen, 1925).

87. Quoted in Rob Imrie, "To Body, Disability and the Radiant Environment," in Boys, *Disability, Space, Architecture*, 27. The material realities resulting from this approach clearly constructed the difference that had been denied in the first place, devaluing and excluding those bodies whose legs, arms, and eyes were not as assumed by Le Corbusier and his contemporaries.

88. Bodies, Davis argues, are "deformed, defeated, amputated, obese, female, perverse, crippled, maimed, blinded." *Enforcing Normalcy*, 72.

89. Quoted in Douglas C. Baynton, *Forbidden Signs: American Culture and the Campaign against Sign Language* (Chicago: University of Chicago Press, 1996), 10. Emphasis in original.

CHAPTER 3

"Brain of Woman, at 30, Half an Idiot"

Recovering Disability Histories from the "Footnotes" of the British Museum Collection

ISABELLE LAWRENCE

Introduction

If disability has been "buried in the footnotes" or the "unglamourous backwaters" of history in museums, how should it be recovered?[1] Since the 1990s, museum professionals and academics have increasingly asked this question, problematizing the absence or misrepresentation of disability in museum displays and heritage spaces. This critique has prompted a multitude of projects intended to reveal what can be considered hidden histories in museum collections, provoking discussion about how disability could be reframed and the role museums could or should play in shaping perceptions of disability and disabled people.[2] Significantly, academic and professional scholarship has become increasingly mindful of the ways in which museums shape the production of knowledge through processes of selection and omission, to the point that key scholars have argued that museums actively contribute to the negotiation of social, cultural, and political values.[3] This has resulted in academics and museum professionals critiquing ways museums perpetuate or reinforce problematic disability representation. However, these discussions also illuminated the potential to encourage audiences to think more critically about the imagery and ideas they are exposed to within and outside of museums. Creating an environment in which museums could, theoretically, actively seek to counter negative attitudes and assumptions creates opportunities for objects to be given new meaning and to be mobilized in efforts to reimagine disability.

What could or should this mean for how museums approach engaging audiences with their collections? Drawing on a series of consultative workshops and meetings that took place in 2021, this chapter considers the impact that involving people with lived experience of disability in decision making could have on how museums understand their own role in the production of knowledge surrounding disability. It examines both the significance and risks envisaged for a single object in the British Museum collection: a photographic print allegedly representing the "brain of woman, at 30, half an idiot." This object provoked significant questions surrounding how to contextualize and communicate difficult histories in a way that mitigates against the potential ramifications of displaying objects with the potential to dehumanize the people represented. This object, after all, relates to human remains, however directly or indirectly, and also to medicalized practices now deemed highly unethical.[4] Raising the question of how we, as researchers, museum professionals, and visitors, can avoid becoming complicit in the injustices we study, this chapter considers the need to develop deeper awareness of the social, cultural, and political issues at stake when we reveal these hidden histories.

A Positive Impact? Museums and Disability Representation

It is important to acknowledge that this photograph was discussed in several workshops that took place between January and November 2021 as part of a collaborative collections research project entitled *Hidden, Revealed*.[5] Organized and facilitated as part of a PhD project in museum studies, the design of this research was therefore heavily influenced by discourses within this interdisciplinary field. This includes discourses that surround the representation of disability and draw on ideas originally developed by disabled activists and disability studies scholars. By extension, moreover, these discourses also include those that emphasize the importance of representation more generally, and the need for museums to be accountable for their social, cultural, and political impact, increasingly advocating that museums should attempt to impact positively on society.

For over two decades, academics and professionals have pointed to the lack of disability representation in museums, creating the perception that it has been "buried in the footnotes," problematizing historical and continued deprioritization of disability and its history.[6] In response, museum scholars and professionals have examined the ways in which these institutions replicate or reinforce pervasive and problematic archetypes of disability. Many liken these institutions to the cultural locations in which disabled peoples' lives have been devalued.[7] Importantly, this problematization of disability representation emerged in the wake of discussions surrounding the impact that museum practice has on the production of knowledge, through selection and omission when collecting, cataloguing, and interpreting objects.[8] Prompting academics and professionals to question the neutrality or objectivity of museums, these organizations have increasingly been seen as embedded in "the contemporary political and social world within which they exist," shaped by, and shaping, the world around them.[9]

This has raised the question of museums becoming socially purposeful, progressive, "activist," and "useful."[10] While these concepts differ, they each emphasize the museum's potential to have a positive impact on society. Critically, each concept presents this potential impact in terms of encouraging critical awareness or introspection, adopting practices "based on contemporary values and a commitment to social equality," or creating "circumstances" in which individuals and groups can self-empower.[11] Attention has therefore shifted to focus on the effect that museum practices have on the wider world, which has inevitably led to new questions surrounding the ethical responsibilities of museums.[12] This new understanding stresses moralities and the relationship between museum representation and human rights. With an emphasis on the willingness of museums to be accountable or radically transparent and to share authority, professionals are required to be reflexive, considering the implications of the narratives they construct and the way in which they are constructed.[13] In practice, several museums and heritage organizations have subsequently engaged with subjects previously omitted from traditional historical narratives, including their own historical links to the British Empire and the production of knowledge more generally. Many have achieved this by staging interventions ranging from explicit reinterpretation of objects in museum displays to the development of staff training designed to encourage institution-wide introspection and self-critique.[14] Although many of these changes have met with resistance, they have nonetheless involved actively engaging with contemporary activism. Ethical museum practice is thereby reconceptualized in terms of museum engagement with issues relevant to the ever-changing sociocultural and political landscapes in which they operate.

It is within this context that academics and professionals have sought to challenge the problematic representation of disability in museum and heritage spaces. This has often involved employing specific models of disability as a means of developing new critical frameworks or lenses through which to interpret museum collections, while also asking who is involved in the construction of these critical frameworks.[15] Repurposing emancipatory research principles, the involvement of people with lived experience in any decisions made about the representation of disability has become an ethical priority.[16] While the power dynamics involved in any kind of participation can be far from straightforward, creating some form of trading zone in which lived experience is respected as valuable expertise has been established as an objective to aspire toward.[17] Whether in the guise of consultation, collaboration, inclusive curating, or curatorial fellowships, emphasis is placed on inviting disabled people to exert different levels of control over the production of knowledge within museums.[18]

Hidden, Revealed: A Collaborative Collections Research Project

Hidden, Revealed was designed in response to this discourse, with the intention of improving understanding of how collaborative methodologies, inspired by emancipatory research principles, could shape new, ethically grounded forms of disability representation in the British Museum. This project drew heavily on the expertise of a consultation group of twelve participants, made up of a combination of artists, activists, academics, and British Museum employees. Building on a combination of lived experience of disability, experiences of researching and engaging audiences with disability history, and also knowledge of the British Museum collection, this consultation group selected the themes that would be explored in later workshops and fifteen objects that I would research further. Additionally, individual participants made decisions surrounding which of the three themed workshops focused on object selection to attend, and, in the final workshop, which objects and related ethical issues they wanted to discuss further.[19]

Sampling the collection in this way made it possible to identify and engage deeply with ethical dilemmas that the museum would need to navigate to avoid undermining the overall mission of improving disability representation. Throughout this process, key themes and ideas continued to emerge, establishing a loose but ambitious mission for the project. For example, participants wanted to contribute to histories that centered the experiences of individuals with impairments. At the same time, they wanted to contextualize these narratives within the shifting meanings attached to disability and individual impairments across time and culture. For example, they wanted to account for the impact of forces like intersectionality, empire, colonization, and changes to medical knowledge on individual experiences. Underlying this interest, moreover, was a desire to challenge preconceived ideas surrounding disability in our shared past and present, including stereotypes connecting disability with ideas of victimhood, dependency, poverty, fraudulence, and personal tragedy. Effectively aiming to expose the social and cultural construction of disability, participants emphasized the need for future museum interpretation to encourage audiences to reimagine the place of disabled people in the past and present, thereby working toward a better future.

These priorities fundamentally shaped how participants interpreted the photograph of the human brain in the group's second workshop, which explored the theme of "Disability, Medicine, Empire and Control," and its final meeting, in which participants examined digitized images of the photograph and the historical context in which this object was created and considered the ethical ramifications of display. Some participants interpreted the photograph as part of a history in which disability was weaponized in the construction of racial hierarchies and in which bodies categorized as subnormal were collected and displayed without the consent of the individual. Initially, this object inspired debate among participants surrounding what is meant by the "weaponization" of disability. In the final workshop, however, the discussion centered on the risks of displaying dehumanized remains. These discussions shaped the ways in which participants interpreted the object's complex and troubling significance and mapped out the risks of encouraging audiences to engage with such a difficult object. After a brief introduction to this object, the remainder of this chapter considers how participants interpreted this object's significance, and the ethical challenges it might represent.

"Brain of Woman, at 30, Half an Idiot"

Found in the British Museum collection in 2017, this photographic print appears to represent a human brain, which is interpreted simply as the "Brain of Woman, at 30, Half an Idiot. 35 oz" in a handwritten inscription. We are given very little information about the woman whose remains are represented in this way, when this photograph was originally produced, or how it was disseminated. However, we do know that it was found by museum professionals and a former PhD student in the pictorial store in early 2017 among other previously undocumented material relating to the craniologist Joseph Barnard Davis (1801–81). In the museum's online collections database, for example, the museum explains that it was found among material acquired for the museum at multiple auctions in 1883, following Davis's death in 1881.[20] Critically, this information locates this photograph within the anthropological interests of a man determined to measure and categorize the intellectual capacity of different racial groups.

Davis's collection consists of over four hundred objects. It ranges from objects representing the material culture of communities across the world, to photographs, portraiture, and sculpture depicting individuals from different racial backgrounds, particularly people from areas that were then occupied by the British Empire. This broader collection reflects the anthropological interests pursued by Davis during his lifetime, interests that involved interpreting the bodies of people deemed racially different to support his polygenist belief in the separate origins of each of the human "races." Arguably, the photograph of the brain of "half an idiot" represents a direct link between Davis's anthropological collecting interests and his work as a craniologist. Davis was a prolific collector of skeletal remains, amassing a large collection of "race crania," with which he sought to demonstrate the utility of "racial craniometry as an analytical tool to classify the world's 'races.'"[21] Classifying the weight of the brain as a "race-character," a fixed quality that could not be changed through education, culture, or environment, Davis sought to demonstrate the "essential and ineffaceable" differences between different racial groups.[22]

This was, moreover, part of a wider anthropological discourse deeply informed by ideas of intelligence, and what was called idiocy, imbecility, and, later, feeblemindedness. Like other medical practitioners at the time, Davis was an active member of multiple anthropological societies across the world and served as editor of the *Anthropological Review or the Journal of the London Anthropological Society* for an unknown number of years between 1870 and his death in 1881. Within these societies, anthropological interest in the material culture of different community groups combined with a fixation on categorizing the intellectual capacity of the people of the racial groups within these communities. This discourse subsequently informed whether these cultures were deemed civilized, barbaric, or savage, and therefore whether they were capable of self-governance, often shaping colonial policy.[23] This discourse was heavily informed by studies about individuals categorized as idiots, imbeciles, and, later, the feebleminded, including those who lived and died in hospitals or asylums and whose remains were later dissected.[24]

This collecting history prompts speculation surrounding the place that this photograph held within both Davis's research and wider anthropological discourse. The photograph's caption categorizes the woman as "half an idiot," a designation that points to the later emergence of the terms "feebleminded" or, in the United States, "moron." By the time of Davis's death 1881, evolutionary theory increasingly discredited his arguments surrounding racial origins. Nonetheless, medical practitioners, anthropologists, and policy makers simply reconceptualized preexisting ideas about race and intellectual capacity in ways that seemingly aligned with emergent evolutionary theory. With the advance of eugenics in the late nineteenth and early twentieth centuries, "the poor, the uneducated, criminals, recent immigrants, blacks, and the feebleminded" were collectively framed as "evolutionary laggards" or "eugenic misfits."[25] Significantly, eugenics established feeblemindedness as threatening racial degeneration.[26] Encompassing individuals whose perceived defects were believed to be more difficult to detect than those of idiots and imbeciles, so-called feebleminded men and women acquired an insidious significance in early-twentieth-century society. This was partly due to perceived difficulties of monitoring and restricting the ability of such persons to marry and procreate, which was perceived to risk lowering the intellectual capacity, morality, and fitness of the population more generally.[27] Arguably, the "Brain of Woman, at 30, Half an Idiot" foreshadowed the "clinical photographs" of the twentieth century that concretized feeblemindedness as a "physical, objective condition with clear visible causes" in medical and popular imaginations, enabling audiences to "perceive and understand the threat of feeblemindedness."[28] This problematic photograph therefore reflects the early production of a pseudoscientific discourse that later enabled those with expertise in this discourse to cement their own positions of power by categorizing bodies and minds within a hierarchical framework.

The Significance of the Photograph: Critiquing the Weaponization of "Feeblemindedness"

Within the context of *Hidden, Revealed,* this object was bestowed with a peculiar significance that was rooted specifically in its potential to engage audiences in discussions surrounding how disability has historically been weaponized. Participants identified this weaponization of disability as a priority in the first meeting, with several expressing particular interest in pursuing objects that demonstrate the role ideas of disability had in the development of scientific racism and colonial policy. Critically, several participants advocated in favor of engaging audiences with the photograph and what it might demonstrate about how ideas of intellectual capacity have historically been utilized to empower or disempower different groups of people. One participant, who has chosen to remain anonymous in this chapter, felt strongly that the object, and its relationship with Davis's wider collection, would highlight how anthropology, craniology, and phrenology were "fed by objects and images from across the Empire."[29] They further argued that this particular object and collection presented an opportunity to engage with the ways that medical practitioners, anthropologists, and colonial officials constructed ideas of what constituted fitness that, in turn, shaped ideas of racial difference in the popular imagination, colonial policy, and experiences of Empire and colonial occupation. As they explained,

> the uniting theme is essentially that fitness, physical and psychological and intellectual, could only ever be ascribed to Europeans. And this is the undergirding intellectual principle of imperialism, of colonisation.[30]

Effectively, this photograph was understood to offer an opportunity to interpret the role of both the photograph and the wider collection in the production of pseudoscientific knowledge pertaining to race and its sociocultural impact. Other participants developed this point further, alluding to literature that perpetuated academic racism throughout the twentieth century.[31] Interestingly, an exhibition guidebook published by the British Museum (Natural History) in 1965 entitled *The Races of Man* was specifically mentioned.[32] By referencing literature that promoted the fiction of a "really scientific appreciation of racial and individual variation" more than eighty years after Davis's death, it was clearly felt the photograph could be mobilized to critique wider histories of knowledge production and academic racism.[33] Referencing museum literature, moreover, raised the possibility of recognizing the role of UK museums in these discourses, including the British Museum and museums that it was closely associated with.[34]

Importantly, participants also emphasized the need to examine the attitudes underlying this weaponization of disability. Participants stressed the need to use this photograph as a tool to encourage reflexive and critical thinking surrounding why so-called feeblemindedness could be weaponized in this way in the first place, but also in terms of how this might compare with attitudes in the present day. Early discussions surrounding this object involved negotiating the definition of "weaponization," with different participants interpreting this concept in varying ways. Most of the participants initially defined it in terms of the deliberate creation of physical impairment as a form of corporal punishment, or in terms of using the threat of impairment to discourage specific behaviors or practices. Nonetheless, each definition seemed to emphasize the political utility of framing disability either as something that can materially disempower individuals and communities or as something to be feared, transforming it into a political or military tool. For some, this was an idea that could potentially be critiqued or unpacked when interpreting the photograph and Davis's collection more generally. They discussed, for example, ableist language used in online political discourse, and considered what these historical and contemporary examples might teach us about "how we still think that disability is a condition to be ashamed of."[35]

Participants developed this idea further in the final workshop, arguing that the museum also needs to mitigate against the potential for audiences to simplistically historicize these practices without consideration of their relevance to the present. Stressing the need to encourage visitors to consider how historical discourses "inform modern ableism," for example, another participant warned that it would be too easy for visitors to assume that these practices "happened in the past" and "that doesn't happen anymore."[36] While this point was not expanded upon at the time, it is clear that there are parallels that could be drawn with incidents in the UK's relatively recent past, each of which have compounded distrust of medical and educational authorities among marginalized communities. Notable examples include the placement of illegal "Do Not Resuscitate" orders in the medical files of patients with learning disabilities during the coronavirus pandemic, which raised concerns surrounding the devaluation of disabled lives in medical settings.[37] Specific to Black British communities, moreover, a particularly pertinent parallel is presented in resurfaced scandals surrounding the disproportionate number of children of African Caribbean heritage who, having recently emigrated to the UK, were categorized as "educationally subnormal" between the 1960s and the 1980s.[38] Provided that the photograph is interpreted in a way that counteracts oversimplistic historicization, the object therefore acquires a wide-ranging significance. Effectively, participants advocated in favor of developing critical interpretive frameworks around Davis's collection that could encourage audiences to confront ableism, and its relationship to racism, in the present.

"Freakification" and Dehumanized Remains: Perpetuating the Legacy of Collecting and Displaying Disabled Bodies

However, participants were concerned by another issue at stake. Repeatedly, they drew attention to the fact that the photograph depicts the disembodied remains of a human being who likely had no control over how her remains were treated and represented after her death. Admittedly, there is some uncertainty over whether the photograph directly represents a human brain, rather than a cast, sculpture, or even a model based on the cumulative findings of anatomical dissections of multiple individuals. While these are possibilities with the potential to complicate the way in which we interpret it as a representation of human remains, this object was nonetheless taken at face value for the purposes of the project. Participants chose to take for granted that the brain once belonged to a specific individual: a thirty-year-old woman who, at some stage of her life or in death, was categorized as "half an idiot." This woman is unidentifiable without further research into the photograph's provenance. Yet, in the latter half of the nineteenth century, when she likely died, the extent to which individuals understood how medical practitioners and scientists would treat their remains after death, and whether they would have consented to this, is questionable. As Johanna Parker puts it, as a medical practitioner, Davis "would have understood the role of consent, but like many of his contemporaries he viewed the law as an anachronistic impediment to achieving scientific progress."[39]

Participants viewed this issue as an important part of this object's significance and emphasized the need to engage audiences with questions surrounding consent. Situating this woman within a much longer history, in which bodies have been appropriated, pathologized, and displayed because of their difference, participants became concerned with the question of how to draw attention to and counteract the impact of this medicalization. For Jeannette, a project curator at the British Museum at the time of the workshop, this photograph was created to "prove certain things about either people with disabilities or from different ethnic backgrounds" and to distance the viewer from the woman.[40] In particular, participants emphasized the dehumanizing impact of "anatomization" or "atomization" of disabled bodies—reducing disability to a single, disembodied organ dissociated from the person to whom it formerly belonged. As highlighted by Jeannette, "it's very easy to be removed from a brain, because it doesn't have a face . . . so it can be just seen as an object."[41] The brain depicted is simply categorized as that "of [a] woman, at 30, half an idiot. 35 oz." This clinical description distances the viewer from the woman represented under the guise of medicalized objectivity. This language focuses attention on the measurable, including the weight of the brain, and the interpretation of those measurements to denote a subnormal level of intelligence. This lens encourages the viewer to look at the brain as an object of scientific and anthropological interest, not to think more deeply about the person it formerly belonged to. Echoing concerns surrounding the objectifying implications of other museum practices surrounding human remains in museum spaces, such as those expressed by Angela Stienne in relation to the act of physically or virtually unwrapping mummified remains, this anatomization or atomization had a discomfiting effect on several participants, who compared the photograph with other encounters with human remains in museums and collections.[42] As Participant 1 explained, "as an epileptic, that brain makes me feel really uncomfortable. I mean really, really uncomfortable . . . because epilepsy is often represented in medical museums, often in these atomized ways."[43] Clearly, the dehumanizing processes involved in the production and consumption of this photograph need to be tackled in any interpretation of its history, but this also raises the question of the impact of such dehumanizing representation on audiences in the present. One of the key issues to emerge through these discussions therefore concerned whether it is possible to counteract this effect by reducing the distance between the viewer and the viewed, re-humanizing the woman in the photograph. Jeannette, for example, emphasized the need to "return back to the people who were abused in that way," turning attention away from the perpetrators of this abuse to focus on the individuals anatomized in this way.[44] Effectively, it was felt that the museum should seek to remove or shrink this distance between the viewer and the person represented by challenging the artificial, impersonal, and clinical layers of interpretation that helped to create it. Although it is not possible to explore in detail, this was a sentiment shared by other participants with regard to other objects relating to human remains, who felt the importance of reminding audiences that the human remains on display once belonged to people with their own beliefs, relationships, and aspirations in life, regardless of whether such experiences and their significance is known to us. This approach would, moreover, be compatible with the British Museum's human remains policy, which emphasizes the need to avoid voyeuristic display practices and treat the remains of individuals with "care, respect and dignity."[45]

Despite conversations about how to display this photograph in a more ethical fashion, several participants expressed strong reservations about displaying such material at all. The uncertain provenance of the photograph, for example, proved a source of concern, particularly given that this woman might represent a community historically dehumanized and exploited within colonial and medical power structures. Fearing that the museum could, through display, perpetuate this legacy, these participants also cast doubt over how far the museum can anticipate and mediate audience responses. Critically, much of this concern surrounded spaces in which collections engagement is relatively unfacilitated. With regard to both this photograph and other objects relating to human remains, participants feared that such spaces could inadvertently encourage a form of voyeurism, regardless of the intended messaging or best efforts of the museum. Comparisons were drawn, for example, to "human zoos" in which visitors were encouraged to "gawp" at the "odd people" on display.[46] Drawing on past experiences of encountering human remains of disabled people in museum displays, participants were also quick to point to the risk of reinforcing the problematic narratives or archetypes, regardless of the intention behind such displays:

> [A]s much as I think they're trying to talk about human diversity, what really ends up happening is the freakification of disability.[47]
>
> [T]he risk of reinforcing those narratives, even if you're trying to challenge them, is real.[48]

With the problem of "gawp[ing]" visitors, any future displays of such material are arguably positioned as part of the legacy of this practice of collecting and displaying disabled bodies, risking behaviors that could continue the "freakification" of the disabled bodies on display, however unintentional.[49] This raises an important consideration. Museum audiences are not simply passive recipients of information but are involved in the production of knowledge, negotiating the messages they take home. After all, audience research used to demonstrate the positive impact of museum interpretation on visitor perceptions of disability also demonstrates that visitors nonetheless interpret such content through the prism of their own preexisting attitudes and experiences, sometimes in ways that are "at odds with the aims of the project."[50] If the photograph were to be displayed, is there therefore a risk that audiences would take it at face value without reflecting on the challenging histories involved in its creation, collection, and display?

Mobilizing the Photograph of the Human Brain?

Is this a risk worth taking? Throughout these discussions, participants clearly demonstrated the potential significance of this object in providing opportunities to critique assumptions surrounding both disability and race. At face value, mobilizing the photograph of the human brain and encouraging audiences to critique the way in which ideas of idiocy were weaponized could therefore enable the museum to work toward a more ethical future in which stereotypes are dismantled. Participants emphasized that these discussions about race, consent, and the anatomization of disability need to be had, and that the museum would be a "powerful space" in which to do so.[51] However, legitimate concerns raised in these sessions remind us that museums do not operate in a social or cultural vacuum. Instead, they need to contend with the same legacy of reductive interpretations of disabled bodies that we intend to critique.

On a practical level, this raises the question of how ethical futures can be reached in responsible ways. Participants suggested a range of possible solutions. These included the creation of highly mediated spaces in which facilitators who are both "historically literate" and "conscious of the racial politics and imperial pasts" could guide discussions.[52] However, at a more theoretical level, these concerns also raise unsettling and potentially unresolvable questions about the risk of becoming complicit in the historical injustices we study, whether we engage with these objects or hide them away. In her discussion of sideshow photography, Jane Nicholas asked, "For the historical researcher sifting through such material, where is the line between modest witness and curious gawker?"[53] Pondering whether researchers can be "vulnerable to history," Nicholas highlights the potential for historians to become embedded in the power relationships involved in the creation and use of such photography. She describes the tension between the urge to protect the people represented from "the voyeuristic gazes of historical researchers" by repressing the evidence and the desire to research and tell their stories.[54] In so doing, she questions her own role in perpetuating their status as sideshow attractions or freaks, or, alternatively, of silencing or hiding this aspect of the past. Building on the work of Antoon de Baets, she asks how researchers can balance their responsibility to recover marginalized histories, with their duty to preserve the dignity of the dead.[55]

A level of reflexivity is thereby demanded of anyone seeking to mobilize this photograph. Encouraging us to consider how to best serve the dignity of the woman whose body is depicted in this dehumanizing way, this mobilization raises interesting questions. By displaying or engaging audiences with the photograph, even in the context of dedicated or facilitated discussions, how far would the museum perpetuate the status of this woman as an object of study if not as a medical specimen? How far would museum visitors become complicit? In fact, by focusing attention on the photograph in the workshops, how far have I implicated myself, my participants, and my readers in this process?

While these are not questions that can easily be answered or resolved, the reflexivity that this could inspire is arguably desirable for an institution with a collection and history as controversial as that of the British Museum. After all, if the progressive museum is "undergirded and invigorated by deep engagement with key ethical issues of the day," the uncertainty generated through these discussions is arguably a good starting point, prompting deeper engagement with the issues at stake in the representation of such difficult histories and their legacies in the contemporary world.[56]

In fact, taken further, such uncertainty could also feed into broader debates surrounding the display and care of human remains in museums more generally. These debates are often characterized by increased scrutiny on the extent to which research and display interventions involving such remains perpetuate harmful stereotypes, objectify the deceased, are invasive or, alternatively, are in what's considered the public benefit.[57] With critics conceptualizing and rationalizing this dehumanizing and invasive potential in conflicting ways, the moral value and perceived public benefit attached to such collections can fluctuate drastically, ultimately leading to questions surrounding whether such material should be repatriated. These debates are largely beyond the scope of this chapter because questions surrounding repatriation were not the primary concern of the *Hidden, Revealed* research project, which instead focused on the question of representation and display. However, if the uncertainty surrounding whether displaying the photograph of the brain of "half an idiot" would be in the public benefit is applied more broadly across museum collections containing actual human remains, it could potentially raise further questions surrounding the morality of acquiring and retaining such remains in the first place.

Arguably, the uncertainty inspired by the photograph therefore hints at the in-depth insight that working collaboratively with people with lived experience of disability could generate, not only in research that interrogates the ethics disability representation, but also in projects exploring broader subjects, including the ethical treatment of human remains. While early discussions revealed the very real potential to uncover and critique stories that had been hidden, buried, or overlooked, deeper engagement also revealed the sociocultural quagmire that must be navigated to realize this potential in ways that cause as little damage as possible. Raising new research questions in need of investigation, this could eventually lead to ethically grounded engagement that fully considers the social, political, and cultural impact that such engagement might have.

Collaboration and the Potential for Deep Engagement with the Complex World of Disability Representation

The title of this book is *Cripping the Archive*, prompting us to consider what it would mean to "crip" practices throughout the archival, museum, and heritage sector. For Alison Kafer, to "claim crip critically" is to deconstruct binaries surrounding the categorization of disabled and nondisabled, to "jolt people out of their everyday understandings of bodies and minds," and to work toward "crip futures" that "imagine disability differently."[58] Drawing on the work of Robert McRuer, for example, Kafer argues in favor of "critical attempts to trace the ways in which compulsory able-bodiedness/able-mindedness and compulsory heterosexuality intertwine in the service of normativity" that, in turn, is "used to justify discrimination against people whose bodies, minds, desires, and practices differ from the unmarked norm."[59] Effectively, Kafer imagines crip futures in which disability is critiqued not solely as a distinct concept or category but as being informed by the same standards of normativity that inform concepts of race, gender, sexuality, and class. To crip the archive or museum would therefore be to find a way to work toward these crip futures.

This chapter has demonstrated the value of collaboration as a means of ensuring that museums and other heritage organizations work toward these futures in ways that are actually useful or progressive. The discussions that took place during *Hidden, Revealed* arguably uncovered immense potential for the British Museum to do so through critical engagement with its collection. Revealing opportunities to encourage audiences to critique assumptions underlying the concepts of idiocy, feeblemindedness, and race, the potential for the museum to challenge or jolt future audiences "out of their everyday understandings of bodies and minds" is tantalizing. Involving people with lived experience of disability, as well as historical and political literacy, provided opportunities to develop understanding of the object's significance. However, this chapter demonstrates that the value of collaborative methodologies also lies in their ability to enable deeper engagement with issues that cannot easily be resolved, even if this involves problematizing the potential or significance initially identified. Unearthing the very real risks of putting disabled bodies on display, the uncertainty generated could encourage the reflexivity required to fully understand and mitigate against them, ultimately encouraging museum staff and audiences alike to identify, deconstruct, and challenge the subtle but dehumanizing messages about disability that the photograph, and other such objects, might project.

In this respect, the cripping of museum spaces therefore necessitates careful but unflinching engagement with uncomfortable subject matter underpinned by collaborative and reflexive discussion of such ethical questions. As these workshops were organized as part of doctoral research, the scope and impact of *Hidden, Revealed* was inevitably limited, with little scope for participants to take up active research roles. Additionally, the participants who opted to discuss this photograph were predominantly from an academic background. This raises questions surrounding how it would have been interpreted by participants from a wider range of backgrounds, particularly those with lived experience of learning disability. Actively involving a wider range of such participants in future projects surrounding such material would be essential to taking this research further. Interestingly, the British Museum is increasingly experimenting with collaborative methodologies in which participants are more heavily involved in decision making, research, and interpretive processes.[60] Within this context, perhaps the potential for the museum to engage more deeply with these challenging subjects might increase. Perhaps then it will become possible to recover buried histories in ways that help to achieve ethical crip futures.

Notes

1. A. Delin, "Buried in the Footnotes: The Absence of Disabled People in the Collective Imagery of Our Past." In *Museums, Society, Inequality*, ed. R. Sandell (London, New York: Routledge, 2002); C. J. Kudlick, "Disability History: Why We Need Another 'Other.'" *American History Review* 108:3 (2003), p. 765.

2. J. Dodd et al., *Rethinking Disability Representation in Museums and Galleries* (Leicester: Research Centre for Museums and Galleries, University of Leicester, 2008); J. Dodd et al., "Disability Reframed: Challenging Visitor Perceptions in the Museum." In *Re-presenting Disability: Activism and Agency in the Museum*, eds. R. Sandell, J. Dodd, and R. Garland-Thompson (London: Routledge, 2010).

3. See E. Hooper-Greenhill, *Museums and the Shaping of Knowledge* (London: Routledge, 1992); S. Pearce, *Museums, Objects and Collections: A Cultural Study* (Leicester and London: Leicester University Press, 1992); R. Sandell, *Museums, Moralities and Human Rights* (London: Routledge, Taylor and Francis Group, 2017).

4. There was some uncertainty over how directly this photograph represents human remains, specifically whether it directly represents a human brain instead of a cast or model designed to represent a specific "type." However, this object was taken at face value for the purposes of this project, and, as will be discussed, the participants expressed concerns over the prospect of displaying such material. In turn, this raises the question of whether it is appropriate to reproduce this photograph in this book, and I have therefore decided to not include it out of respect for these concerns.

5. This project was organized and facilitated as part of my doctoral research, which is funded by the United Kingdom's (UK) Arts and Humanities Research Council (AHRC). It was facilitated as part of a collaborative doctoral partnership with the University of Leicester and the British Museum. The British Museum provided additional funding to facilitate the workshops, and several British Museum employees volunteered their time to support me as I facilitated these workshops.

6. Delin, "Buried in the Footnotes"; J. Dodd et al., *Buried in the Footnotes: The Representation of Disabled People in Museum and Gallery Collections* (Leicester: Research Centre for Museums and Galleries, 2004); see also J. Majewski and L. Bunch, "The Expanding Definition of Diversity: Accessibility and Disability Culture Issues in Museum Exhibitions," *Curator* 41:3 (1998).

7. R. Sandell, "Disability: Museums and Our Understanding of Difference." In *The Contemporary Museum: Shaping the Global Now*, ed. S. Knell (London: Routledge, 2019), p. 178; S. L. Snyder and D. T. Mitchell, *Cultural Locations of Disability* (Chicago and London: University of Chicago Press, 2006).

8. Hooper-Greenhill, *Museums and the Shaping of Knowledge*; Pearce, *Museums, Objects and Collections.*

9. Sandell, *Museums, Moralities and Human Rights*, p. 142; R. R. Janes and R. Sandell, "Posterity Has Arrived: The Necessary Emergence of Museum Activism." In *Museum Activism*, eds. R. R. Janes and R. Sandell (London and New York: Routledge, 2019); S. Knell, "Introduction: The Museum in the Global Contemporary." In *The Contemporary Museum*, ed. Knell.

10. See J. Marstine, "The Contingent Nature of Museum Ethics." In *Routledge Companion to Museum Ethics*, ed. J. Marstine (London: Routledge, 2012); B. Lynch,

"Introduction: Neither Helpful nor Unhelpful—A Clear Way Forward for the Useful Museum." In *Museums and Social Change: Challenging the Unhelpful Museum*, eds. A. Chynoweth et al. (Abingdon: Routledge, 2021).

11. R. Sandell, "Museums and the Combatting of Social Inequality: Roles, Responsibility, Resistance." In *Museums, Society, Inequality*, ed. R. Sandell (London, New York: Routledge, 2002), p. 21; Lynch, "Introduction: Neither Helpful nor Unhelpful"; R. Sandell, "On Ethics, Activism and Human Rights." In *Routledge Companion to Museum Ethics*, ed. Marstine.

12. This shift has caused some controversy. It has, for example, been framed as "destructive" by conservative commentators and politicians, who perceive a threat to the free and "objective" scholarly pursuit and communication of knowledge, and present debates surrounding repatriation and the so-called culture wars in terms of censorship or being canceled. It is not the purpose of this chapter to engage with this debate. However, on repatriation, see, for example, T. Jenkins, *Keeping Their Marbles: How the Treasures of the Past Ended Up in Museums—And Why They Should Stay There* (Oxford: Oxford University Press, 2016) ProQuest Ebook, p. 322; regarding the culture wars, see S. Heffer, "A Meghan Markle-Style Cult of Truth Bending Bullies Is Hijacking Museums," *Telegraph*, April 4, 2021. https://www.telegraph.co.uk/news/2021/04/04/meghan-markle-style-cult-truth-bending-bullies-hijacking-museums/; O. Dowden, "We Won't Allow Britain's History to Be Cancelled," *Telegraph*, May 15, 2021. https://www.telegraph.co.uk/news/2021/05/15/wont-allow-britains-history-cancelled/.

13. Marstine, "The Contingent Nature of Museum Ethics," pp. 14–17.

14. For examples, see R. Atkinson, "Exploring New Stories: Shifting Perspectives, Leeds Art Gallery," *Museums Journal*, October 13, 2022. Accessed October 15, 2022, https://www.museumsassociation.org/museums-journal/reviews/2022/10/exploring-new-stories-shifting-perspectives-leeds-art-gallery/#; S. Burn and T. Cisneros, "The Social Justice Curriculum at Wellcome Collection," *Stacks, Wellcome Collection*, February 15, 2022. https://stacks.wellcomecollection.org/the-social-justice-curriculum-at-wellcome-collection-cceeaf76bd72#:~:text=The%20Social%20Justice%20Curriculum%20is,stakeholders%20and%20our%20Advisory%20Group.

15. See Dodd et al., *Rethinking Disability Representation in Museums and Galleries*; J. Dodd, C. Jones, and R. Sandell, "Trading Zones: Collaborative Ventures in Disability History." In *The Oxford Handbook of Public History*, eds. J. B. Gardner and P. Hamilton (New York: Oxford University Press, 2017); S. White, "Crippling the Archives: Negotiating Notions of Disability in Appraisal and Arrangement and Description," *American Archivist* 75, no. 1 (2012); C. Barnes and G. Mercer, "Breaking the Mould? An Introduction to Doing Disability Research." In *Doing Disability Research*, eds. C. Barnes and G. Mercer (Leeds: The Disability Press, 1997); C. Barnes, "'Emancipatory Disability Research': Project or Process," *Journal of Research in Special Educational Needs* 2:1 (2004). Accessed May 26, 2020, https://onlinelibrary-wiley-com.ezproxy3.1ib.le.ac.uk/doi/full/10.1111/j.1471-3802.2002.00157.x; H. Hollins, "Reciprocity, Accountability, Empowerment: Emancipatory Principles and Practices in the Museums." In *Re-presenting Disability*, eds. Sandell, Dodd, and Garland-Thompson.

16. See R. Sandell in interview with K. McSweeney and J. Kavanagh, "A Reflection on Participation." In *Museum Participation: New Directions for Audience Collaboration*, eds. K. McSweeney and J. Kavanagh (Edinburgh and Boston: Museum Etc, 2016), p. 589.

17. Dodd, Jones, and Sandell, "Trading Zones." In *The Oxford Handbook of Public History*, eds. Gardner and Hamilton.

18. J. French, "Auto Agents: Inclusive Curatorship and Its Political Potential." In *Museum Activism*, eds. Janes and Sandell; J. French, *Inclusive Curating in Contemporary Art: A Practical Guide* (Leeds: ARC Humanities Press, 2020); see also Hollins, "Reciprocity, Accountability, Empowerment."

19. Please note that due to the limited scope of this doctoral project participants chose from a finite range of objects suggested by me. My decisions surrounding which objects to suggest for discussion (and further discussion in the final workshop) were based on my own interpretation of the guidance that participants generated in earlier workshops.

20. British Museum, "Object: Brain of Woman, at 30, Half an Idiot." Object Record. British Museum website: Collections Online. Accessed March 15, 2022, https://www.britishmuseum.org/collection/object/E_2017-2005-1/.

21. J. Parker, "Navigating the Nineteenth Century Collecting Network: The Case of Joseph Barnard Davis." In *The Routledge Companion to Indigenous Repatriation: Return, Reconcile, Renew*, eds. C. Fforde, C. T. McKeown, and H. Keeler (London: Routledge, 2020), p. 501; British Museum, "Object: Brain of woman, at 30, Half an Idiot."

22. J. B. Davis, "On the Weight of the Brain in the Negro," *Anthropological Review and the Journal of the Anthropological Society of London* 7, 25 (1869), p. 191; J. B. Davis, *Thesaurus Craniorum: Catalogue of the Skulls of the Various Races of Man, in the Collection of Joseph Barnard Davis* (London: printed for the subscribers, 1867), p. 40.

23. S. Jarrett, *Those They Called Idiots: The Idea of the Disabled Mind from 1700 to the Present Day* (London: Reaktion Books, 2020), p. 186.

24. See Jarrett, *Those They Called Idiots*, p. 208.

25. H. A. Washington, *Medical Apartheid: The Dark History of Medical Experimentation on Black Americans from Colonial Times to the Present* (New York: Anchor Books, 2006), pp. 190–92.

26. J. W. Trent, *Inventing the Feeble Mind: A History of Mental Retardation in the United States* (Berkeley and Los Angeles: University of California Press, 1994), p. 141; M. K. Simpson, "Idiocy and the Conceptual Economy of Madness." In *Intellectual Disability: A Conceptual History, 1200–1900*, eds. P. McDonagh, C. F. Goodey, and T. Stanton (Manchester: Manchester University Press, 2018), pp. 200–204.

27. P. McDonagh, *Idiocy: A Cultural History* (Liverpool: Liverpool University Press, 2008), pp. 274–80; P. McDonagh, "Learning Difficulties: The Transformation of 'Idiocy' in the Nineteenth Century." In *A Cultural History of Disability in the Long Nineteenth Century*, eds. J. L. Huff and M. Stoddard Holmes (London and New York: Bloomsbury Academic, 2020); P. McDonagh, "Visiting Earlswood: The Asylum Travelogue and the Shaping of Idiocy." In *Intellectual Disability*, eds. McDonagh, Goodey, and Stanton, p. 251; O. Barden, "Learning Difficulties: A

Cultural History of Learning Difficulties in the Modern Age." In *A Cultural History of Disability in the Modern Age*, eds. D. T. Mitchell and S. L. Snyder (London and New York: Bloomsbury Academic, 2020).

28. M. Elks, "Clinical Photographs: 'Feeblemindedness' in Eugenics Texts." In *Picturing Disability: Beggar, Freak, Citizen and Other Photographic Rhetoric*, eds. R. Bogdan, M. Elks, and J. Knoll (Syracuse: Syracuse University Press, 2012) ProQuest Ebook, p. 82; E. Chaloupka, "Imagining Cognitive Disability: Recursive Reading and Viewing Processes in Henry H. Goddard's *The Kallikak Family: A Study in the Heredity of Feeblemindedness*," *CEA Critic* 77, 3 (2015), p. 273; see also A. Maxwell, *Picture Imperfect: Photography and Eugenics, 1870–1940* (Eastbourne: Sussex Academic Press, 2008).

29. Participant 1 in *Consultation Group Meeting 2*, facilitated by author with support of Jess Starns. February 19, 2021. Online Meeting: Zoom.

30. Participant 1 in *Consultation Group Meeting 2*, facilitated by author with support of Jess Starns. February 19, 2021. Online Meeting: Zoom.

31. Penny in *Consultation Group Meeting 5*, facilitated by author with support of Jess Starns, Kayte McSweeney, and William Westwood. November 2, 2021.

32. Penny in *Consultation Group Meeting 5*, facilitated by author with support of Jess Starns, Kayte McSweeney, and William Westwood. November 2, 2021; S. Cole, *Races of Man* (London: Trustees of the British Museum (Natural History), 1965).

33. Cole, *Races of Man*, p. 10.

34. The British Museum (Natural History) (which became the Natural History Museum in South Kensington in 1992) was originally established in 1881 as an offshoot of the British Museum to store and display the museum's natural history collections. The British Museum (Natural History) was legally separated from the British Museum by act of Parliament in 1963.

35. Participant 1 in *Consultation Group Meeting 2*, facilitated by author with support of Jess Starns. February 19, 2021. Online Meeting: Zoom.

36. David in *Consultation Group Meeting 5*, facilitated by author with support of Jess Starns, Kayte McSweeney, and William Westwood. November 2, 2021.

37. J. Bass, "Learning Disabilities Should Never Be a Reason for a Do Not Resuscitate Order," *Health Service Journal*, April 25, 2020, https://www.hsj.co.uk/mental-health/learning-disabilities-should-never-be-a-reason-for-a-do-not-resuscitate-order/7027489.article; J. Tapper, "Fury at 'Do Not Resuscitate' Notices Given to Covid Patients with Learning Disabilities," *Guardian*, February 13, 2021, https://www.theguardian.com/world/2021/feb/13/new-do-not-resuscitate-orders-imposed-on-covid-19-patients-with-learning-difficulties.

38. See W. B. Coard, *How the West Indian Child Is Made Educationally Sub-Normal in the British School System*, fifth edition (Kingston, Jamaica: McDermott Publishing, 2021); *Subnormal: A British Scandal*, directed by L. Shannon (London: Rogan Productions, Lammas Park, Turbine Studios), aired May 20, 2021, BBC One. Accessed August 25, 2022, https://www.bbc.co.uk/programmes/m000w81h/.

39. Parker, "Navigating the Nineteenth Century Collecting Network," p. 511.

40. Jeannette in *Consultation Group Meeting 5*, facilitated by author with support of Jess Starns, Kayte McSweeney, and William Westwood. November 2, 2021.

41. Jeannette in *Consultation Group Meeting 5*, facilitated by author with support of Jess Starns, Kayte McSweeney, and William Westwood. November 2, 2021.

42. A. Stienne, *Mummified: The Stories behind Egyptian Mummies in Museums* (Manchester: Manchester University Press, 2022), pp. 192–97.

43. Participant 1 in *Consultation Group Meeting 5*, facilitated by author with support of Jess Starns, Kayte McSweeney, and William Westwood. November 2, 2021.

44. Jeannette in *Consultation Group Meeting 5*, facilitated by author with support of Jess Starns, Kayte McSweeney, and William Westwood. November 2, 2021.

45. A. Fletcher, "In Respect of the Dead: Human Remains in the British Museum," *British Museum* (blog), June 12, 2014, https://blog.britishmuseum.org/in-respect-of-the-dead-human-remains-in-the-british-museum/; Trustees of the British Museum. *British Museum Policy: Human Remains in the Collection*. London: British Museum, 2013. Available at https://www.britishmuseum.org/sites/default/files/2019–10/Human_Remains_policy_061218.pdf, last accessed March 15, 2022. See also D. Antoine, "Curating Human Remains in Museum Collections: Broader Considerations and British Museum Perspective." In *Regarding the Dead: Human Remains in the British Museum*, eds. A. Fletcher, D. Antoine, and J. D. Hill (London: The British Museum, 2014).

46. Penny in *Consultation Group Meeting 3*, facilitated by author with support of Jess Starns. May 13, 2021. Online Meeting: Zoom.

47. Participant 1 in *Consultation Group Meeting 5*, facilitated by author with support of Jess Starns, Kayte McSweeney, and William Westwood. November 2, 2021.

48. David in *Consultation Group Meeting 5*, facilitated by author with support of Jess Starns, Kayte McSweeney, and William Westwood. November 2, 2021.

49. Penny in *Consultation Group Meeting 5*, facilitated by author with support of Jess Starns, Kayte McSweeney, and William Westwood. November 2, 2021; Participant 1 in *Consultation Group Meeting 5*, facilitated by author with support of Jess Starns, Kayte McSweeney, and William Westwood. November 2, 2021.

50. Dodd et al., "Disability Reframed," p. 107.

51. David in *Consultation Group Meeting 5*, facilitated by author with support of Jess Starns, Kayte McSweeney, and William Westwood. November 2, 2021; Participant 1 in *Consultation Group Meeting 5*, facilitated by author with support of Jess Starns, Kayte McSweeney, and William Westwood. November 2, 2021.

52. Jeannette in *Consultation Group Meeting 5*, facilitated by author with support of Jess Starns, Kayte McSweeney, and William Westwood. November 2, 2021; Participant 1 in *Consultation Group Meeting 5*, facilitated by author with support of Jess Starns, Kayte McSweeney, and William Westwood. November 2, 2021.

53. J. Nicholas, "A Debt to the Dead? Ethics, Photography, History, and the Study of Freakery," *Histoire sociale/Social History* 47, no. 93 (2014), p. 143.

54. Nicholas, "A Debt to the Dead?," p. 151.

55. A. de Baets, *Responsible History* (New York and Oxford: Berghahn Books, 2009).

56. Marstine, "The Contingent Nature of Museum Ethics," p. 5.

57. N. MacGregor in J. H. Taylor and D. Antoine, with M. Vandenbeusch, *Ancient Lives, New Discoveries: Eight Mummies, Eight Stories* (London: British

Museum Press, 2014), p. 7; Antoine, "Curating Human Remains in Museum Collections," pp. 6, 7; Stienne, *Mummified*, pp. 192–97.

58. A. Kafer, *Feminist, Queer, Crip* (Indiana: Indiana University Press, 2013), pp. 13, 15, and 45.

59. R. McRuer, "Compulsory Able-Bodiedness and Queer/Disabled Existence." In *Disability Studies: Enabling the Humanities*, eds. S. L. Snyder, B. J. Brueggemann, and R. Garland-Thompson (New York: Modern Language Association of America, 2002); Kafer, *Feminist, Queer, Crip*, p. 17.

60. L. Cruikshanks and S. Hunter Dodsworth, "Partnerships and Plurality: Evolving Practices at the British Museum." In *Museum Participation*, eds. McSweeney and Kavanagh.

Hidden, Revealed Consultation Group Meetings Referenced

Consultation Group Meeting 2, facilitated by author with support of Jess Starns. February 19, 2021. Online Meeting: Zoom.

Consultation Group Meeting 3, facilitated by author with support of Jess Starns. May 13, 2021. Online Meeting: Zoom.

Consultation Group Meeting 5, facilitated by author with support of Jess Starns, Kayte McSweeney, and William Westwood. November 2, 2021. Online Meeting: Zoom.

CHAPTER 4

Cripping the Convict Archive

EMILY COCK

This chapter engages with disability and the digitized archive through the open access *Trove* platform of the National Library of Australia. *Trove* offers tremendous resources for diverse kinds of Australian and transnational history since the printing of the first newspaper in 1803, many of which include the critical contributions of disabled people. Here, the focus is on disabled people transported by the British government as prisoners, or "convicts." This chapter crips the *Trove* archive in three ways. First, it draws on disability critiques of digital history and the digital humanities to evaluate the accessibility of this resource as an important international archive, juxtaposing it with the subscription website *Ancestry*, where the State Archives of New South Wales (SANSW) has placed digital versions of some of its microfilmed convict records. Second, the chapter introduces an unused set of digitized sources for disability history: descriptive advertisements for runaway convicts in the New South Wales (NSW) penal settlements, published in the weekly *Gazettes*. These sources offer rich opportunities to capture individual agency and experience and illuminate the diversity of the convict population. Finally, the chapter offers a model event for bringing this digital archive to public audiences and creating new archives through them.

Between 1787 and 1868, Britain sent over 160,000 prisoners to the Australian colonies, starting with NSW in the land of the Eora Nation (now Sydney) then Van Diemen's Land (Tasmania). Relocating this population relieved the crowded prisons, secured the colonization of Australian territory following the invasion, and perpetuated the ongoing displacement of the Indigenous people. Historians have demonstrated that the Australian case operated within global systems of forced migration and colonialism, elevating the significance of the case study.[1] The Australian runaway notices parallel advertisements for people fleeing slavery and indentured service in the Anglo-Atlantic world, which have been the subjects of excellent scholarship and digitization projects.[2] This includes work utilizing the advertisements' physical descriptions to trace disability in enslaved populations.[3] My identification of advertisements for disabled Black runaways in NSW, including formerly enslaved people, extends this scholarship. Inmate descriptions from British prisons are also online, capturing changes in individuals' bodies prior to transportation, and variations in perspective and language around bodily and mental difference.[4] The potential benefits of analyzing these digitized archives comparatively and in tandem to understand global discourses and experiences of disability are immense. The consideration of disability and forced migration intersects with the regulation of free migration studied by Esme Cleall and Jennifer S. Kain, where an ever-increasing policing of disabled people's migration was characteristic of the British imperial project and a constant source of tension between the colonies and metropole.[5] Colonists utilized ablest and racialized tropes to distinguish themselves from the Indigenous population, and formed local branches of worldwide philanthropic movements to manage aging and disabled free and emancipist settlers.[6] Though there were many points in the convict system at which a disabled prisoner might escape transportation (e.g., ship surgeons could refuse to embark them, or they might successfully petition for a pardon while still in Britain), the colonial authorities could not refuse them once they landed. Thus, unlike the free immigrant Cleall and Kain discuss, the convict population is one in which it is possible to find innumerable disabled arrivals alongside those who acquired impairments in the colonies.

Most NSW prisoners were not locked up in secure facilities. Rather, authorities assigned them to work for free white settlers. These private assignees formed the majority of those who absconded and appeared in subsequent advertisements. Others escaped from general or mental hospitals, road gangs, or the Female Factory (a semi-secure women's prison). The advertisements vividly illustrate the diversity of people transported through the penal system: men, women, children, people of color from across the world, and people with bodily and mental impairments. These descriptions were created in an onboard muster before prisoners were allowed to disembark in the colony—creating an "indent"—and amended and expanded through further surveillance and documentation.[7] The indents included sentence and crime details, family links in the colonies, literacy levels, and other details. By the 1830s, they were printed and distributed to different administrative bases. The advertisements draw out the details most useful for spotting the prisoner in NSW: the person's age, ship, occupation, place of origin (hence accent), and a detailed physical description. Read alongside the indents, they also allow us to document changes in prisoners' bodies and circumstances during their sentences.

The thorough documentation of convicts has made this a uniquely well-archived population in comparison to their free poor neighbors back home—the archives were thus added to the UNESCO International Memory of the World Register in 2007. Scholars are accessing the *Gazettes* on *Trove* to research diverse topics of transnational nineteenth-century public sphere and press history.[8] The examination of convict tattoos, including through the runaway advertisements, is a thriving subfield.[9] It is possible to compare multiple runaway notices for individuals alongside the other archives of their penal experience, such as new arrest registers and tickets of leave that are hosted on *Ancestry* and linked through digital humanities projects like the *Digital Panopticon*.[10] The digital platforms have increased public and professional historians' ability to not only identify trends across the convict population, but also to flesh out the stories of individuals within the nineteenth-century "paper panopticon."[11] For example, Michaela Ann Cameron has used digitized newspapers and trial records and further resources to reconstruct the life of convict and "diminutive cripple" John Donne, known in nineteenth-century Parramatta as the self-styled "Lord Donne."[12] Crowdsourced digital history projects like *Convict Records* (inaugurated through the State Library of Queensland in 2011) allow people to bring information about individual prisoners into the public domain. Much of their research is through *Ancestry* and, in turn, *Ancestry* includes the *Convict Records* profiles in its search results.[13] The organization and preservation of the massive physical Australian archive has only been a priority since the 1950s, since previous generations were ambivalent at best about the impact of the "convict stain" on national and family histories. Neglect and destruction have left unnecessary gaps, and for many years historians were not allowed to name individuals, lest it disturb living descendants.[14] In the nineteenth century at least, there remained the belief that criminality itself could be an inherited disability, and influential early historiography emphasized physical and mental weaknesses among the population.[15] Lucy Frost describes how the arrival of microfilm copies suddenly "made it impossible for gentlemen in Hobart [Tasmania] to control the academic writing of history" by restricting access to and use of their physical documents, reminding us that the use of technology to increase access to archives is nothing new.[16] But mass digitization, offering unprecedented levels of global access, searchability, and linkage for both academics and the public, raises new ethical questions. Having a convict in the family might have shifted, as Frost says, "from secret shame to source of pride" for many, but what if research shows that the ancestor was a violent Bill Sykes rather than a cheeky Artful Dodger?[17] Or they were a victim of violence or constraint in one of the colony's lunatic asylums? Changes in archival access mean that publicly illuminating individual stories is now far more possible, but—as many of the chapters in this book discuss—they create new imperatives to balance subjects' privacy with historical understanding and the interests and emotions of public stakeholders.

Disability in Convict Australia

Historians have investigated the health and physical strength of people selected for transportation in a number of ways. Convict indents with physical descriptions have been read for evidence of health and impairment in comparison to other British populations, generally linking transportees' poor health and short stature to their lower class and urban origins.[18] The extent to which convicts were accepted or rejected based on factors including health and disability has been a hot topic of debate. Andrew Piper goes so far as to argue that "Britain deliberately and systematically used the transportation system to convey invalid convicts from its shores to the Australian colonies."[19] On the other hand, Deborah Oxley, Richard Ward, and Lucy Williams have argued that youth, good health, and physical capacity were desired criteria for transportees, but that there is no evidence for any systematic use of them in sentencing.[20] Older felons might be imprisoned rather than transported, but this was not universal.[21] Men who might have been eligible for a reprieve conditional on assignment to the army or navy, but were impaired, might instead be sent to Australia. An explicit example is Thomas Poore (transported 1796) who possessed a "lame hand [rendering him] unfit for the navy."[22] In her pathbreaking examination of disabled male convicts transported to NSW, Beverley Earnshaw found that in the 1826–29 arrivals, 5.1 percent of men were described in their indent as having a physical or mental impairment, which decreased to 3.9 percent in 1836–38.[23] She hypothesized that many were veterans of the Napoleonic Wars, finding several examples of men attributing impairments to war injuries.[24] The advertisements contribute to a more nuanced picture of impairment in the penal colonies, showing both a wide range of impairments carried over by the transportees, and a further range acquired within Australia. Even if health was desirable, impairments such as deafness, immovable or missing limbs, impaired vision, and more were no barriers to transportation.

Health care onboard ships and within the colonies played important roles in managing and creating disability within the convict and wider populations. Mortality and morbidity rates varied significantly between ships, and have been investigated by many historians.[25] The historiography of convict medicine has highlighted the detrimental impact of communicable diseases, malnutrition, and accidents over the long journey.[26] From 1798, convict and free emigrants to Australia enjoyed reasonable health care en route due to increased regulation of surgeons on board.[27] Using linked archives, scholars tracing the life courses of the transported population are further illuminating the role of transportation in shaping experiences and incidents of debility and disability in the colonies, and their place in transnational disability history.[28] These stories are part of a long history of disability within criminal justice systems.

Convicts received access to medical care and, in some cases, improved living conditions compared to the cramped poverty spaces that many of them had left in Britain. Some studies suggest that this led to better health outcomes for themselves and their descendants. For example, children in the Australian colonies grew taller than their British contemporaries.[29] They were supported by the colonial medical service, and in 1816 a new Sydney General Hospital was built at the command of Governor Macquarie.[30] The General Hospital, Hyde Park Barracks, and lunatic asylums at Castle Hill, Tarban Creek, and Liverpool served as temporary or long-term homes and care spaces. There were also "invalid gangs" for convicts only capable of light duties. Earnshaw argues that assignment to an invalid gang was extremely restricted, and required a warrant from a magistrate.[31] Musters from Port Arthur, Van Diemen's Land, show these crews assigned tasks such as working in vegetable gardens.[32] Nevertheless, numerous men in the advertisements had run away from an invalid gang, suggesting either a greater level of fitness than Earnshaw suggests, or a tactic of pretence to disability to be assigned to that crew. Women could be sent to the General Hospital or to the Female Factory. Elizabeth Gilligan (b. 1808) arrived in Australia in 1831 with a broken right leg that caused her to "halt" and was first sent to the hospital.[33] She still carried this injury when she ran away from her mistress, Harriet Howell, in May 1833.[34] She apparently returned, because she ran away again on the second of June.[35] Gilligan escaped yet again in August, still with the effects of her injury: "right leg been broken and halts."[36] Her limp was thus no impediment to either assignment or escape.

Access and the Convict Archive

Scholars have already produced remarkable quantitative and qualitative research into convict Australia by working across digitized archives. These include not only *Trove* and *Ancestry* or *Find My Past* but diverse genealogy and local history sites that are so often the places in which the nonfamous of history are first noticed. The accessibility of these archives and research methods, however, requires ongoing assessment and improvement.

As other chapters in this book demonstrate, physical archive access can carry particular considerations and difficulties for disabled academics. Elsewhere, in an illuminating article, Ryan Lee Cartwright writes of the additional time and money that he must spend for wheelchair-accessible accommodation and transport before even entering the archive, and the additional negotiations he requires within it.[37] The two physical archives most relevant to the NSW convict materials employed here—SANSW and the UK National Archives in Kew, London—both use their digital platforms to provide detailed accessibility information for visitors. This includes, as of 2021, a "Virtual Tour" on the SANSW website.[38] Understanding and facilitating the diverse experiences and needs of researchers are key to ensuring that archives can serve the widest possible audiences now and in the future.

Although digitization remediates some access issues of the physical archive, scholars of accessibility and the digital archive are demonstrating that it does not automatically result in equal access for all. Andrew Prescott and Lorna Hughes note Cokie Anderson and David Maxwell's opinion that "the number one reason for digitizing materials is to improve accessibility" but argue that this has focused on addressing *geographic* distance, rather than wider accessibility.[39] Convict paperwork is indeed a good example of significant distance between intertwined archives. Lara Putnam observes that the digitization of archives has significantly increased the potential for transnational studies by reducing the need for expensive and time-consuming trips to individual archives around the world.[40] Teaching resources improve, both in class and as students are able to integrate more primary sources into independent research projects. Digital humanities practitioners are continually seeking to improve accessibility for their processes and outputs, but there is still a long way to go.[41] As Elizabeth Ellcessor pointedly remarks, "merely making material available is insufficient to promote genuine access."[42] The resources utilized in this chapter are further subject to the standard criticisms of sampling, economic access, searchability, etc., of all digitized sources and digital platforms utilized for historical research.[43] While I originally stumbled on the advertisements through a now-forgotten *Trove* keyword search, systematically working through and correcting each issue has been necessary to build a complete dataset. The historical profession also privileges physical archival work as the "real" research, although it is debatable how long the perceived authority derived from this—which Carolyn Steedman discussed over two decades ago—will persist as digitization booms.[44] This is especially the case when even travel to the archive results in being directed to a microfilm reader or computer if the items are available in these formats.

Subscription platforms like *Ancestry* are now key gatekeepers of the digital archive.[45] As Putnam notes, the production of and access to digital archives are contingent on personal or institutional technology and funding.[46] I accessed the library edition of *Ancestry.co.uk* through the Cardiff council library and, in 2021, was able to do this from home due to temporary COVID-19 allowances. On January 1, 2022, however, access reverted to in-library use only. Additionally, budget crises make me skeptical about the institution's continued subscription. Like a physical archive, in-library-only access disadvantages vulnerable people—particularly disabled people—who are shielding, cannot travel, are less able to visit during opening hours, or negotiate other issues that make this difficult. Unlike most archives, libraries are also bustling community spaces with coffee shops, the Citizens Advice Bureau, and diverse activities for children and adults, all of which increase potential distractions and distressing sensory stimuli.

Because *Ancestry* is designed for genealogical research, search functionality privileges names and locations. Even though full scans of convict indents including physical descriptions are included, the descriptions have not been tagged or transcribed, meaning that they are neither searchable nor legible through a screen reader. In this, they parallel the online indexing of the physical Colonial Secretary's archive by Joan Reese, Linda Bowman, and Aileen Trinder, which also prioritizes convict names.[47] Finding disabled individuals requires knowing who you are looking for, rather than searching for historically appropriate key terms as can happen in other digital archives. Katherine Roscoe also notes that genealogy research facilitated by sites like *Ancestry* privileges historical individuals who have reproduced.[48] Any person whose impairment was significant enough to impede their marriage prospects (and given that male prisoners outnumbered women by about five to one, the men's odds were already poor) or whose children did not survive or reproduce would therefore fall by the wayside.

Trove was established in 2009 to integrate resources from digitized archives across Australian collections of books, manuscripts, music, images, newspapers, and more. While new materials are continually being added, including audio and visual sources to better capture Indigenous perspectives, the colonizers dominate the early nineteenth-century resources. In this, *Trove*—like *Ancestry*—typifies broader concerns about the dominance of global North and especially English-language sources in digital archives.[49] It has its own budgetary concerns thanks to unstable government funding, which in 2022–23 saw users united in a desperate campaign to #SaveTrove. Though funding is promised until 2027, it seems likely to be a recurring negotiation.

Trove follows Australian government accessibility expectations, informed by the National Disability Strategies (2010–20; 2021–31) and Web Content Accessibility Guidelines (2008).[50] It uses Optical Character Recognition (OCR) to generate searchable text from scanned print materials. An enthusiastic body of approximately sixty-four thousand "VolunTroves" are then guided in correcting errors, adding annotations and keywords, uploading images, and other activities to enhance the metadata and research collection.[51] Like the ability to zoom into page scans, clean, full-text OCR is another assistive technology that allows all users to more easily navigate the data and website. This is true whether searching for key terms linked to disability in this period, or tracing the fates of known disabled individuals. But as Eric Harvey points out, OCR text that is clean, accurate, and coded correctly is a sine qua non of operability for people using tools like screen readers to access a website.[52] I tested *Trove* with the open-source NonVisual Desktop Access (NVDA) screen reader, developed by blind Australian software engineers Michael Curran and

James Teh. NVDA highlighted the lack of image descriptions for pictures on the home page, and the necessity of the OCR for making the scanned newspapers useable: otherwise, hovering over the page resulted in the very unhelpful description of "image." Correcting the OCR text within *Trove*, facilitated by *Trove*'s openness for this community editing, thus becomes a necessary step for researchers wishing to not only use the archives themselves, but to facilitate their use by others. Within resourced research programs, this should create opportunities (or requirements) to use research budgets and timelines to accommodate this activity.

Relying on audience contributions to fix the existing OCR provides opportunities for community engagement in archive accessibility. But it also carries risks. It relies on all users acting in good faith to accurately transcribe records without adding, amending, or omitting text, and to encounter terminology and content that may be upsetting or run counter to the user's beliefs. This leaves both the user and contentious histories vulnerable, which might include Indigenous, LGBTQIA+, and disability histories and VolunTroves. These platforms create an encounter with potentially difficult history that combines the private reading of the professional historian with the wider engagement of visitors to a museum or heritage site. In *Trove*, this is directly managed for materials identified as including Indigenous Australians.[53] The *Trove* home page opens with a pop-up of "Cultural Advice" for Aboriginal and Torres Strait Islander users stating that "Trove contains images, voices or names of deceased persons." A "Find out more" button adds that some terminology and viewpoints "may not be considered appropriate today." It gives the option to "Show cultural advice," which activates "cultural advice notices before viewing materials on *Trove* that may be considered culturally sensitive [to Indigenous users]," although this only works for materials *tagged* as such.[54] Enabling this advice (effectively "trigger warnings") for sensitive materials throughout the archive would require identifying and coding all relevant holdings, prioritizing materials, and revising classifications and terminology, all of which would demand immense resources. But it would also improve searchability and forewarning for all researchers, enabling new forms of accessibility.

Disability History in the Convict Archive

Advertisements for runaway convicts in early nineteenth-century NSW are an evocative example of the disability history resources freely available on *Trove*. In our 1831–41 sample, there are over thirty thousand advertisements, but there are far fewer individuals involved, as many advertisements pertain to repeat offenders, reclamation notices, or long absences. These advertisements feature vivid descriptions of the prisoners, followed by lists of those apprehended since the last edition, allowing historians to trace their movements. The average advertisement format was as follows: name (usually "surname forename"), ship, prisoner number, age, place of origin, occupation, physical description (including height, "complexion," hair, eyes, scars, injuries, tattoos), who/where they ran from, and if they had run before. The runaways' physical descriptions were usually based on the pre-embarkation indents. The NSW indents are available digitally on *Ancestry*, but there is no OCR for the descriptions.[55] Conversely, the *Digital Panopticon*'s indent data for Van Diemen's Land is searchable by description, but the information has not always been included in full. The advertisements therefore significantly improve searchability of detailed convict descriptions. Moreover, the convicts' descriptions have often been augmented by their acquaintances in the colony (especially the person to whom they had been assigned), and significant changes in appearance noted. They therefore offer a richer and more responsive view of the convicts' characteristics over a period of time.

The advertisements were printed in the weekly *Sydney Gazette and New South Wales Advertiser* (1803–32) then *New South Wales (NSW) Government Gazette* (1832–1900) under the authority of the Principal Superintendent of Convicts' Office. The *Gazette* was the first newspaper printed in Australia, and despite problems of paper and ink supply, provided a reasonably regular venue for official news.[56] In early years the *Gazette* was one double-sided page, which may partly explain the brief lists of only names for absconded prisoners. Another likelihood is that in the first decade of the nineteenth century the Sydney population was small enough that people could not escape for long. There are stages of increasing information, such as where they had run from (1814) and their occupations (1816).

Permanent impairments appear throughout the records, contributing to the debate on the role of health and capacity in guiding sentencing decisions. Shoemaker John Fitzgerald, age thirty-nine, ran away in 1831.[57] Identified as deaf and dumb, Fitzgerald had been transported on the *Earl St Vincent* in 1818 for stealing property. At his trial, "evidence [was] communicated to him by an interpreter."[58] He enjoys a greater presence than most in disability histories of both Britain and Australia, thanks in part to the searchable *Old Bailey Online* that makes his trial stand out.[59] Charles Duche, an 1816 runaway (elsewhere Dyche; *Baring*, 1815), who was a sawyer-turned-publican, was "either from infirmity or imposition . . . employed a considerable time in the Invalid Gang."[60] Although some people with significant illnesses or impairments were unable to run away and, therefore, do not appear in these advertisements, Duche is just one of many for whom long-term infirmity was no impediment to their break for freedom.

The Sydney advertisements offer further material for scholars investigating the transportation of disabled people from across the British sphere of influence, who included formerly enslaved Africans and Americans of African descent, free people from Africa itself, Māori from New Zealand, Hawaiians, Americans, Canadians, and South Asians, as well as people from across England, Scotland, Wales, and Ireland. Roscoe argues that the details of Asian, Black, and Indigenous individuals at the Cockatoo Island prison "are recorded less fully and with less accuracy than white inmates" in the records: "bodies of people of colour were erased, with 'race' acting as their primary descriptor."[61] There are certainly some sparse descriptions in the newspapers: Henry Dunn (*Hadlow*, 1818) is recorded as "40, Seaman, [from] America, 5 feet 9, black eyes, black hair, black comp[lexion]," despite it being his fourth time running and that he had only recently been returned to the Hyde Park Barracks.[62] He was able to conceal some details as he was moved between different assignments: while only identified as from America in 1830, in 1825 and 1833 advertisements he was identified as specifically from Philadelphia.[63] It is therefore likely that some nonwhite prisoners' disabilities are lost in these records, if their racial appearance was considered sufficient for them to be recognized.

However, my sample of advertisements so far indicates a richer archive in the indents and advertisements, as additional detail is often included. This was perhaps because more description was necessary for identifying people out in wider society than in confined holding sites. In 1816 a group of five absconders from the *Lady Elliot* included two men listed by name only, "Peter Franks, a man of colour" and "one Sysew, a goodlooking Lascar, about 24 years of age, and nearly 6 feet high."[64] This tall and "goodlooking" young man would have been one of many South or East Asian sailors passing through the colony on British ships. Black men from the across the African diaspora abound, and many receive a level of detail on par with other entries.[65] The repeat runaway Robert Abbott from Demerara (Guyana) was twenty-five, "[occupation] cooper, 5 feet 8¼, black comp[lexion], black and woolly hair, black eyes, scar on right cheek bone, scar on outer corner of left eye."[66] These details copy his indent listing, with the notable deletion of one descriptor: "a slave."[67] Black Cuban servant Isaac Brown (*Champion*, 1827; convicted of fraud in Middlesex) was missing the "last joint of right thumb" and had a "scar corner of left eye."[68] His certificate of freedom reveals that by 1835 he had lost "one front upper tooth" and acquired "three scars on left temple [one of which might be the scar here], scar on left shoulder."[69] The shoulder scar may well reflect his life in the colony: in 1829 he was sentenced to fifty lashes for running away from the road gang.[70] At twenty-three, Jamaican William Evins already had "black woolly and grey hair" when he ran from Henry Incledon Pilcher in 1836, along with "black eyes, nose broad and flat, lips thick, scar centre of forehead, another on left eyebrow, scar outside left eye, scar on right cheek bone, [tattooed] RSWA inside lower left arm."[71] The ship Evins was on, the *Strathfieldsay*, carried twelve Black men from Jamaica and another from "Africa," which might have encouraged the particularly detailed indent descriptions that this notice copies.[72] But after January 11, 1837, when he ran again, his tattoo was even *corrected* in advertisements to "RSWE."[73] "James Gough" was singled out with capitals for his name and an additional note in 1824: "32, [from] Isle of Wight, 5 ft. 5¼, black eyes, black and woolly hair, black comp., [escaped from] Hyde Park Barracks, Desperate Character, upper lip shot away, and otherwise disfigured by gunshot and other wounds about the neck and body: lately escaped from Macquarie Harbour, Van Diemen's Land."[74] This was actually John Goff (*Marquis of Wellington*, 1815), who would go on to lead convict revolts and a mass escape from Norfolk Island in 1826, for which he was executed the next year.[75] Thus, a racialized description was no barrier for including disability or disfigurement information in these advertisements.

While there may have been sufficient Black men in the colony for detailed descriptions to become necessary, smaller population descriptions also reveal disabled individuals. A woman named Priscilla—who is a very rare example of a woman of color in these advertisements—merited additional details that provide evidence of her medical history: "44, Jamaica, housemaid, 4 feet 11 inches, black comp., black and woolley hair, black eyes, lost a front upper tooth right side, *mark of cupping on each temple.*"[76] Even a Black Muslim man from "Bussorah Arabia" (Basra, modern-day Iraq) received a significant level of detail: nineteen-year-old groom Mahomed Sidy Maccors was "5 feet 5 inches, [with] black comp., black and woolly hair, black eyes, scar on forehead resembling a horseshoe, several small scars below both temples, lips thick, mole right cheek, front teeth decaying, nose broad and flat, scar left shin."[77] His name in the ship indent is Sidy Baynenoria Mahomet, and he was convicted of mutiny in Mauritius.[78] He arrived on the *Symmetry* with fellow mutineers, including a twenty-five-year-old footman from Calcutta named "Hurroo," who had his racialized description supplemented by details of "R[eads] & W[rites] own language," "two scars over right eyebrow, another under same, right ear pierced, large scar inside of left arm, blue mark inside lower part of same."[79] Combining these archives therefore offers excellent opportunities for finding detailed descriptions of this diverse population.

It may be that individuals with significant, visible physical differences were not afforded the same level of individualistic description of tattoos, etc., as their peers. James Shelly (aka Skelly; *James Pattison*, 1830) was given a sparse description when he absconded in June 1832: "22, Herdsman, Westmeath, 5 feet 9, grey eyes, brown hair, dark ruddy comp. wants left arm."[80] Shelly remained at large until August, and must have been moved to the invalid gang after his capture, since he ran from this team in July 1833.[81] Cheshire horse driver William Broster (*Dunvegan Castle*, 1830), missing his right arm, received the same limited descriptors in June 1833.[82] However, in August 1832, John Knight (*Waterloo*, 1829) absconded from a road gang for the second time and though he lacked a right arm was nevertheless given a very full description: "26, Labourer, Lewis, 5 feet 11½, blue eyes, brown hair, ruddy comp, wants right arm, [tattoos of a] woman, J. K. M. H., and a variety of letters on left arm."[83]

The advertisements include invisible disabilities such as speech impediments that may not have been noted at the arrival muster. Mary Ann Read was a shoebinder, needlewoman, and housemaid from Kent, who had absconded three times already when she ran away from Bathurst innkeeper William Nathaniel Kable in September 1836.[84] Read had arrived on the *Roslin Castle* in 1830 and was immediately sent to Bathurst for assignment: first to Alexander Watt, then to John Liscombe.[85] Read's advertisements show use of both the indents register and additional details, probably provided by her first supervisor. Along with her hair and eye color, place of birth, and occupations, the advertisement takes the descriptions of her tattoos from the indent: a child on the right arm, and "9 July 1808 James Fuller" on the left. But it adds that she speaks with a lisp.[86] This probably wasn't noticed in the visual inspection for the indent, but became apparent as she worked in Watt's house. Liscombe omitted this level of detail from his advertisement, perhaps to save money, or as a decision of the printer to save space in a busy week: either way, the lisp was interpreted as a less important identifying detail for the average person to notice. John Hall (*Marquis of Huntly*, 1830) absconded from a road gang in 1836 and is described in his advertisement and indent as "wanting speech."[87] In an 1834 gaol entry record it is described as an "impairment in speech," which was the term used when Hall ran away from William Lawson in February 1834.[88] The level of impairment is therefore ambiguous, and may be linked to the brevity of the interactions used to generate the gaol description: the registrant may have been hesitant to describe Hall as having a total lack of speech in case he was just being reticent, whereas the witnesses on the road gang would have felt safe with such an assertation after spending more time with him.

Impaired mental health and intellectual disabilities are also in evidence. Irish laborer Michael Mostfame (*Sir Godfrey Webster*, 1826) was described in advertisements as "an Idiot" and "Idiotic."[89] His *very* frequent absconding may reflect psychological distress he experienced within the convict system. Mostfame had been transported for vagrancy, which may or may not have been linked to an intellectual disability and inability to find work in his native Louth. His indent entry is blank beyond his name, "vagrant," and Louth, with a note "Muster not completed on account of the mans [*sic*] Deafness."[90] It is interesting that even his visible characteristics like hair and eye color were not recorded, but the note is more telling for the role of the prisoners's testimony in constructing these documents, and the potential for verbal and aural impairments to disrupt this. It is also indicative of a lack of interpreters available, which may have made his six-month voyage a particularly lonely one. Mostfame's frequent escapes ironically give us a good picture of his whereabouts, including that he was initially retained at the Hyde Park Barracks rather than sent to an assignment.[91] While at large in 1828, he was arrested on suspicion of murdering a stockman and stealing his clothes; though acquitted, the reports show he already had a public reputation for lunacy.[92] He was sent to the Liverpool Barracks (ran away June and December 1829), and must have been assigned to a road gang late that year in order to run from it in February 1830 and again in 1831.[93] Perhaps on account of these escapes, Mostfame was sent to the hulk for removal to Port Macquarie, where a specific settlement for "invalid" prisoners had been established. The Inspector of Hospitals and an assistant surgeon directed that he be removed from the hulk to greater "confinement and security" in Hyde Park Barracks, and thence to a lunatic asylum, "owing to his insane and violent conduct." These letters—not digitized—show that he was assessed in comparison to two other "lunatic" men and was the only one not considered stable enough to be sent to Port Macquarie.[94] Mostfame's 1833 certificate of freedom gives additional details and shows some change over his time in the colony: where in departing Ireland and in the 1831 escape he was described as having a pale complexion, by now it was "ruddy & pockpitted," suggesting exposure to the sun and the survival of a bout of smallpox. He had also "Lost nearly all the front teeth in upper jaw. Very deaf. Large scar ball of left thumb. *Lunatic*."[95] But he had also progressed from his 1831 position as a "labourer" to possessing the occupation of "weaver," suggesting economic capacity as he entered emancipist life, and perhaps reflecting activities undertaken within the asylum.

As with Mostfame's journey, one of the richest uses of the advertisements and linked records is for tracing changes in health and acquired impairments and their impacts over individuals' careers. Londoner John Deane's (*Countess of Harcourt*, 1828) indent describes a "cast in right eye" and "scars on neck & right cheek," which are included in the advertisement.[96] But the advertisement describes "large scars on both cheeks and under both jaws," showing it was not just an administrative copier but the testimony of someone who had seen Deane for themselves.[97] This may have been the result of accident, but could also be from a disease like scrofula. We cannot know for certain if the scars had grown or just been more fully described, but Deane was running from the invalid gang, which suggests that he had been suffering from significant ill health or injury. An 1831 escapee from the lunatic asylum was Peter Cosgrove (*Fame*, 1817), who is described as a "Soldier and Labourer" and an "Idiot."[98] He ran away from the asylum again in November 1832, with the same occupational and mental descriptors.[99] Cosgrove was from Longford, Ireland, but was convicted on the Isle of Wight in 1816 and transported for life. He was not sent to the asylum immediately: the convict muster for 1825 shows him privately assigned to Reverend Samuel Marsden, in whose employment he had been since 1822 after first working in a road gang.[100] He also received a ticket of leave in 1829 (as a "labourer"), which was revoked in 1831 "in consequence of his being insane and having neglected his masters."[101] The ticket itself did not mention lunacy, nor does his 1840 conditional pardon, where records like Mostfame's would lead us to expect them.[102] It also only lists him as a soldier. Cosgrove and Deane are therefore examples of how the advertisements can capture details and fluctuations in health that are otherwise hidden in the digitized convict archive. Moreover, Cosgrove shows the importance of the physical archive in completing his story, especially after emancipation: in 1846 he was arrested for stealing apples, but the prosecutor and magistrates took pity on him as "acting under the duress of other parties," "paralytic in one side, idiotic to a certain extent, and quite unable to earn his living, he has subsisted here for some years upon charity." It was therefore arranged for him to be admitted into the care of the Benevolent Society.[103]

Finally, work assignments revealed by the advertisements can hint at how disabled prisoners could, to some extent, be supported by well-chosen tasks. John Hennessy was nineteen and convicted of theft when he arrived on the *Mangles* in 1824. His 1832 advertisement describes him as a "Cripple," and as working for the Reverend Thomas Hassell as an "Usher."[104] Was this only a temporary impairment? Was it how he ended up with employment that wasn't physically strenuous? A similar concession to impaired physical strength appears with Michael Hart (*Fergusson*, 1829). Hart's indent describes him as a weaver, but his runaway notice in September 1832 notes that he is "paralytic [on the] left side."[105] This could be why he was assigned to the Escort to Roads rather than his former occupation. Hart escaped again in January 1836, still "paralytic on left side," but now from the more secure No. 2 Stockade.[106] Drawing the advertisements into discussion with the better-known records—indents, tickets of leave, etc.—offers excellent opportunities for nuanced life-course examinations of disability in the convict population.

Bringing Digital Archives of Convict Disability to Public Audiences

Within Australia (where I grew up) and in Britain (where I now work) there is an image of the convicts as white, British, able-bodied, generally male, young adults. In the song "I Am Australian" (1987), made famous by The Seekers and learned ever since by Australian primary school children, the speaker "came upon the prison ship / Bowed down by iron chains," but then holds the strength to have "*fought* the land, [and] *endured* the lash."[107] Novels from Marcus Clarke's *For the Term of His Natural Life* (1874) to Bryce Courtenay's *The Potato Factory* (1995) comprise a long literary tradition depicting the impacts of hard labor and injury on the bodies of the convicts. This injuring labor is part of the penal creation myth: "A convict, then a free man / I became Australian."[108] It is much less common for individuals to *start* transportation stories with impairments or disabilities. Such stereotypes of physical fitness and endurance of both men and women hold key roles in the settler colonial mindset.[109]

Public history can perpetuate or challenge these ideas and the invisibility of disability in the colonial past. In 2019, researchers from Face Lab (University of Liverpool), University of Tasmania, and National Trust Tasmania showed "average" convict portraits at the Hobart Penitentiary Chapel. This exhibition emulated nineteenth-century photographic techniques to amalgamate late-nineteenth to early-twentieth-century photographic records of Van Demonian prisoners, raising important issues of physiognomy, identity, and compassion. As project leader Hamish Maxwell-Stewart commented, this process created "a face that's got amazing symmetry . . . all of the blemishes tend to disappear, and what you get is the things we find appealing" and images of "lots of sexy offenders . . . these people look really good!" The averaged faces deliberately echoed nineteenth-century practices of anthropometric criminal studies, and were accompanied by textual exploration of some individual life stories to remind visitors that there is a "human story to every court encounter."[110] But the visual component did not only necessitate a loss of the individuals within the composite, and a flattening of the range of people who comprised this population: it also traded on contemporary biases that associate aesthetic beauty and absence of disfigurement with good morality, which face equality advocates are constantly challenging.[111] The indents and newspaper advertisements offer an excellent alternative resource for introducing public audiences to the *diversity* of the convict population in a literally warts-and-all fashion. I have started to do this in a public engagement activity, and by using creative response methods we can generate new imaginative archives reflecting contemporary interpretations of the documents.

In 2019 I received a small event grant for the UK Being Human "Festival of the Humanities."[112] The premise of my event was simple: it would create imaginative visual portraits for historical people who did not have them, and introduce event patrons to the unexpectedly diverse mixture of people transported to the Australian colonies. The main event took place on one November evening in Cardiff, but I also took it to the Festival launch at the Foundling Museum, London. I commissioned a Cardiff artist, Rosemary Baker, to create five A5 pen and ink portraits of convicts who had vivid descriptions in the advertisements (Figure 4.1). Each of these were accompanied by short biographies I produced using the advertisement details, further research into the individual, and contextual information about the type of convict they represented (e.g., children). I transcribed a large number of further advertisements to go into a "lucky dip" bag, and at the event people could draw out a convict to "meet" them. After we had a brief discussion to help them understand the details in the listing, the patron would then draw the convict. After this, they had the choice to find out what crime their convict had been transported for. Most people did choose to learn this, although it is difficult to know whether this was a morbid curiosity about their subject's criminal past or a simpler desire to get to know them better in any available way. We built up a table of portraits over the night, and gave visitors a different perspective on the Australian penal colonies. The art materials were kept simple and cost-effective—colored pencils, basic clipboard easels, etc.—and were then donated to a local children's group. After the event, the portraits were gathered into an online archive on my blog (participants had been told this in advance).[113] After COVID-19 interrupted subsequent sessions, I was finally able to repeat the activity in a number of South Wales public libraries in the summer of 2022, where the pencil portraits are now part of the exhibition component. I look forward to building this archive further and moving the images into a more sustainable and accessible online platform.

As a public disability history event, accessibility was key. The event was free, and was held off campus to encourage wider community attendance

Figure 4.1. Portrait of Mary Hely by Rosemary Baker. Hely was transported for theft in 1831, and described as follows when she ran away: "23, Housemaid, Limerick, 5 feet 0½, hazel eyes, brown hair, fair pock-pitted and little freckled comp. upper lip hairy, two scars on back of left hand, scar on lower left arm, finger nails small, scar on centre upper lip, from Mr. John Morris, Sydney" (February 13, 1833, 63).

than the standard "town and gown" crowd and to create a relaxed atmosphere. The planned location was a local café called Aubergine, which is a community-engaged enterprise specifically run by autistic managers to "empower other autistic people through accessible environments and innovative working practices."[114] The event budget thus included money for consultation with them over event accessibility. Unfortunately, the café was forced to relocate unexpectedly, and we eventually agreed they would not reopen in time for the event. Finding a new family-friendly, affordable, and wheelchair accessible evening venue at late notice was difficult, and one venue was politely but explicitly told that their bid was unsuccessful because of a lack of wheelchair access. All key information—for example, the biographies, the event posters, a description of event format—were reiterated by text and translated into Welsh to meet Welsh Language Standards requirements. Further considerations of noise levels, free movement in the space, and the invitation to get in contact about any specific requirements as part of registration followed Cardiff University guidance on inclusive and accessible event planning.

Despite the lucky dip format of the evening, there were a number of factors that curated this group of portraits. First, I selected advertisements that had a good level of detail that could be depicted visually. This meant the loss of invisible disabilities from the record. I would revise this in the future: discussions highlighted the interpretation and historical understanding required for depicting even objectively visible impairments (such as a patron who was unsure how to depict a club foot, or those unfamiliar with smallpox scarring), and the role of the visual in the creation and use of these sources in context. As such, the portraits are themselves new archives of public disability history interpretation, and an alternative research method.[115] Second, I targeted more of the unexpected demographics, which meant that groups such as Black men, people with highly visible impairments, or even women, were statistically overrepresented. I was concerned that the visitors might be inclined to draw their convicts in "mug shot" style, so I explicitly asked Baker to draw more naturalistic portraits. In the end, no one depicted their individuals in this way (although there were a couple who, as one attendee put it, are "a bit Jean Valjean/Hugh Jackman"), and I wonder whether my stressing that the convicts were living in the community rather than within a prison inflected this.

The events were small but encouraging. The local library sessions were even smaller, but this proved beneficial to patrons who remained wary of large gatherings due to COVID-19 or other factors. It facilitated relaxed and informal engagement, and brought forth many fruitfully challenging questions and observations about the archival materials and my research.

One of the convicts selected on the first night happened to be James Shelly (Figure 4.2). The beautiful imaginative portrait created by Jo Rigby—who is herself a disabled artist—was based on the advertisement printed after Shelly

Figure 4.2. Portrait of James Shelly, created by Jo Rigby at the *Facing History* event. Shelly was described as "22, Herdsman, Westmeath, 5 feet 9, grey eyes, brown hair, dark ruddy comp. wants left arm" (June 13, 1832, 136).

ran away from an invalid gang in July 1833. In Rigby's portrait, Shelly appears as a young man with skin reddened by the sun, stubble-chinned and wearing his brown hair a little long, as might be expected for a man without access to a barber. He is thin, though the advertisements don't mention build. His right arm is crossed over his chest, gently highlighting the empty shirtsleeve that hangs on his left side. This compassionate crowdsourced portrait brings life to the curt descriptions provided in his indent and advertisements, and hints at the potential for engaging the public imagination with disability history and the archive.

Conclusion

The descriptions provided in advertisements for runaway convicts fundamentally challenge myths of the Australian settler colonial nation as white, British, male, young, and free of impairment or disfigurement. As forced immigrants, the convict population offers evidence of the interconnections of disability with nineteenth-century transnational penal systems that intersect but also diverge from the management of disabled free immigrants. Linking individuals through digital projects and resources like the *Digital Panopticon* and *Ancestry* has immeasurably increased the capacity of family, public, and academic historians to trace their life courses. It is also more possible to capture incidents of injury and illness and to identify long-term impediments that reveal the intersections of disability through the British justice system: within the British Isles, across their colonial and trading regions, and in the offshore penal colonies. The digitized records of *Trove* are an excellent accompaniment, and in the case of the runaway advertisements show particular moments of agency that are missed in the administrative documents that have been more frequently utilized to reconstruct the lives of transported Australian settlers. Mapping individuals' stories can show how their impairments changed and affected (or did not affect) their positions in the colony.

Access problems with *Trove* and *Ancestry* are illustrative of widespread concerns about inclusion and access for digital archives and digital humanities projects. They demonstrate clearly that there is significant work to be done in facilitating inclusive access for all researchers, whether on the basis of disability, language, economic or geographic restriction, or other factors. Explicit planning and budgeting are required for digitization projects to embed accessibility in their design and functionality, and to address any tensions in inclusion and access for crowdsourced material like OCR. As public-facing resources, they raise similar requirements for accessibility as public engagement events, but on a significantly larger scale. Utilizing these resources for public engagement events provides a space for mediated access to them and can highlight and prioritize disability for public history through attentive event design and framing. Ironically, these descriptions of runaway convicts show that disability history in the Australian colonial context is inescapable.

Notes

My first thanks go to Cardiff University students Anna Rixson, Caitlin Duggan, and Amina Marshall, who worked with me to process the advertisements from *Trove* as part of the Cardiff Undergraduate Research Opportunities Programme. Their enthusiastic engagement with the material was invaluable. I am very grateful to Jo Rigby and Rosemary Baker for allowing inclusion of their portraits, and to the editors and reviewers for their feedback on this chapter. My further thanks go to the Being Human Festival and Harriet Hopkins and the Awen Libraries team for supporting the portrait events.

1. Clare Anderson, *Convicts: A Global History* (Cambridge University Press, 2022); Emma Christopher, Cassandra Pybus, and Marcus Rediker (eds.), *Many Middle Passages: Forced Migration and the Making of the Modern World* (Berkeley, London: University of California Press, 2007).

2. Simon P. Newman et al., *Runaway Slaves in Britain: Bondage, Freedom and Race in the Eighteenth Century*, https://www.runaways.gla.ac.uk/; Bristol Archives, *Index of Early Black Presence in Bristol, 16th to 19th Century*, https://archives.bristol.gov.uk/indexes/earlyblackpresence; *Freedom on the Move* (North America), https://freedomonthemove.org/; *The Geography of Slavery in Virginia*, http://www2.vcdh.virginia.edu/gos/; John Hope Franklin and Loren Schweininger, *Runaway Slaves: Rebels on the Plantation* (New York: Oxford University Press, 2000).

3. Gwenda Morgan and Peter Rushton, "Visible Bodies: Power, Subordination and Identity in the Eighteenth-Century Atlantic World," *Journal of Social History* 39.1 (2005): 39–64; Stefanie Hunt-Kennedy, *Between Fitness and Death: Disability and Slavery in the Caribbean* (Urbana: University of Illinois Press, 2020), and "'Had His Nose Cropt for Being Formerly Runaway': Disability and the Bodies of Fugitive Slaves in the British Caribbean," *Slavery & Abolition: A Journal of Slave and Post-Slave Studies* 41:2 (2020): 212–33.

4. Numerous archival series from The National Archives (UK) and New South Wales State Archives are spread across *Ancestry*, *FamilySearch*, and *Find My Past*, and are part of my continuing research.

5. Esme Cleall, *Colonising Disability: Impairment and Otherness Across Britain and Its Empire, c. 1800–1914* (Cambridge: Cambridge University Press, 2022); Jennifer S. Kain, *Insanity and Immigration Control in New Zealand and Australia, 1860–1930* (Cham: Springer, 2019).

6. John Gilroy, Jo Ragen, and Helen Meekosha, "Decolonizing the Dynamics of Media Power and Media Representation Between 1830 and 1930," in *The Routledge Companion to Disability and Media*, edited by Katie Ellis et al. (Abingdon: Routledge, 2019), 36; Karen Soldatic, "Disability's Circularity: Presence, Absence and Erasure in Australian Settler Colonial Biopolitical Population Regimes," *Studies in Social Justice* 14.2 (2020): 306–20; Brendan Gleeson, "Domestic Space and Disability in Nineteenth-Century Melbourne, Australia," *Journal of Historical Geography* 27.2 (2001): 223–40; Tanya Evans, *Fractured Families: Life on the Margins in Colonial New South Wales* (Sydney: UNSW Press, 2015).

7. Deborah Oxley documents the indent process in *Convict Maids: The Forced Migration of Women to Australia* (Cambridge: Cambridge University Press, 1996), chapter 1.

8. M. H. Beals, "The Role of the *Sydney Gazette* in the Creation of Australia in the Scottish Public Sphere," in John Hinks and Catherine Feely (eds.), *Historical Networks in the Book Trade* (Routledge, 2016): 148–70.

9. David Kent, "Decorative Bodies: The Significance of Convicts' Tattoos," *Journal of Australian Studies* 21:53 (1997): 78–88; Simon Barnard, *Convict Tattoos: Marked Men and Women of Australia* (Melbourne: Text, 2016).

10. Barry Godfrey et al., *The Digital Panopticon: Tracing London Convicts in Britain and Australia, 1780–1925*, www.digitalpanopticon.org.

11. See, e.g., Rebecca Kippen and Janet McCalman, "A Test of Character: A Case Study of Male Convicts Transported to Van Diemen's Land, 1826–38," in *Lives in Transition: Longitudinal Analysis from Historical Sources*, edited by P. Baskerville and K. Inwood (Montreal: McGill-Queen's University Press, 2015), 19.

12. Michaela Ann Cameron, "My Lord Dunn: A Tragicomedy," *St. John's Online* (2016), https://stjohnsonline.org/bio/john-dunn/ (accessed November 1, 2021).

13. "About," *Convict Records*, https://convictrecords.com.au/.

14. Lucy Frost, "The Politics of Writing Convict Lives: Academic Research, State Archives and Family History," *Life Writing* 8:1 (2011): 19–33.

15. Oxley, *Convict Maids*, 106–9.

16. Frost, "The Politics of Writing Convict Lives," 25.

17. Frost, "The Politics of Writing Convict Lives," 32.

18. Brian Gandevia, "Some Physical Characteristics Including Pock Marks, Tattoos and Disabilities of Convict Boys Transported to Australia from Britain c. 1840," *Australian Paediatric Journal* 12 (1976): 6–13; "A Comparison of the Heights of Boys Transported to Australia from England, Scotland and Ireland c. 1840 with Later British and American Developments," *Australian Paediatric Journal* 13 (1977): 91–97.

19. Andrew Piper, "'Mind-Forg'd Manacles": The Mechanics of Control Inside Late-Nineteenth Century Tasmanian Charitable Institutions," *Journal of Social History* 43.4 (2010): 1046.

20. Oxley, *Convict Maids*, 60, 112–13; Richard Ward and Lucy Williams, "Initial Views from the 'Digital Panopticon': Reconstructing Penal Outcomes in the 1790s," *Law and History Review* 34.4 (2016): 893–928.

21. Ward and Williams, "Initial Views from the 'Digital Panopticon,'" *passim.*

22. *The Digital Panopticon*, Thomas Poore b. 1766, Life Archive ID obpt17921031-53-defend506. https://www.digitalpanopticon.org/life?id=obpt17921031-53-defend506. Version 1.2.1, consulted February 7, 2022.

23. Beverly Earnshaw, "The Lame, the Blind, the Mad, the Malingerers: Sick and Disabled Convicts within the Colonial Community," *Journal of the Royal Australian Historical Society* 81.1 (1995): 26.

24. Earnshaw, "The Lame, the Blind, the Mad, the Malingerers," 26–27.

25. For example, Hamish Maxwell-Stewart and Rebecca Kippen, "Sickness and Death on Convict Voyages to Australia," in *Lives in Transition: Longitudinal Analysis from Historical Sources*, edited by P. Baskerville and K. Inwood (Montreal: McGill-Queen's University Press, 2015), 43–70.

26. Katherine Foxhall, *Health, Medicine, and the Sea: Australian Voyages c. 1815–1860* (Manchester: Manchester University Press, 2012).

27. Gary L. Sturgess, Sara Rahman, and George Argyrous, "Convict Transportation to New South Wales, 1787–1849: Mortality Rates Reconsidered," *Australian Economic History Review* 58.1 (2018): 62–86.

28. Janet McCalman and Rebecca Kippen, "The Life-Course Demography of Convict Transportation to Van Diemen's Land," *The History of the Family* 25.3 (2020): 432–54; Emma D. Watkins, *Life Courses of Young Convicts Transported to Van Diemen's Land* (London: Bloomsbury, 2020).

29. Barry Godfrey, Kris Inwood, and Hamish Maxwell-Stewart, "Exploring the Life Course and Intergenerational Impact of Convict Transportation," in *Intergenerational Continuity of Criminal and Antisocial Behaviour*, edited by Veroni Eichelsheim and Steve van de Weijer (New York: Routledge, 2018), 64.

30. Fiona Starr, "The 'Sidney Slaughter House': Convict Experience of Medical Care at the General 'Rum' Hospital, Sydney, 1816–1848," *Health and History* 19.2 (2017): 75, 85.

31. Earnshaw, "The Lame, the Blind, the Mad, the Malingerers," 31.

32. Hamish Maxwell-Stewart, "The Rise and Fall of John Longworth: Work and Punishment in Early Port Arthur," *Tasmanian Historical Studies* 6.2 (1999): 104.

33. SANSW, *Annotated Printed Indents, 1788–1842*, 339–31, *Hooghley* (3), 1831.

34. *New South Wales (NSW) Government Gazette* (1832–1900), May 15, 1833, 181. Unless noted, all subsequent newspaper citations are from the lists of runaway convicts in the *Gazette* and accessed online through *Trove*.

35. June 3, 1833, 211.

36. August 14, 1833, 311.

37. Ryan Lee Cartwright, "Out of Sorts: A Queer Crip in the Archive," *Feminist Review* 125.1 (2020): 62–69.

38. *NSW State Archives and Records*, "Visit Us," https://www.records.nsw.gov.au/archives/plan-your-visit (accessed August 15, 2022). Also "Information for Disabled Visitors," *The National Archives*, https://www.nationalarchives.gov.uk/about/visit-us/information-for-disabled-visitors/ (accessed June 3, 2024).

39. Cokie Anderson and David Maxwell, *Starting a Digitization Center* (Oxford: Chandos, 2004), 5, cited in Andrew Prescott and Lorna Hughes, "Why Do We Digitize? The Case for Slow Digitization," *Archive Journal*, September 2018, https://www.archivejournal.net/essays/why-do-we-digitize-the-case-for-slow-digitization/.

40. Lara Putnam, "The Transnational and the Text-Searchable: Digitized Sources and the Shadows They Cast," *American Historical Review* 121.2 (2016): 377–402.

41. George H. Williams, "Disability, Universal Design, and the Digital Humanities," in *Debates in the Digital Humanities*, edited by Matthew K. Gold (University of Minnesota Press, 2012), https://dhdebates.gc.cuny.edu/projects/debates-in-the-digital-humanities.

42. Elizabeth Ellcessor, "A Glitch in the Tower: Academia, Disability, and Digital Humanities," in *The Routledge Companion to Media Studies and Digital Humanities*, edited by Jentery Sayers (Routledge, 2018), 108.

43. Ian Milligan, "Lost in the Infinite Archive: The Promise and Pitfalls of Web Archives," *International Journal of Humanities and Arts Computing* 10.1 (2016): 78–94; Charles Upchurch, "Full-Text Databases and Historical Research: Cautionary Results from a Ten-Year Study," *Journal of Social History* 46.1 (2012): 89–105.

44. Carolyn Steedman, *Dust* (Manchester: Manchester University Press, 2001); for further reflection on affective qualities and privileging of the material over the digital, see Emily Robinson, "Touching the Void: Affective History and the Impossible," *Rethinking History* 14:4 (2010): 503–20.

45. Jerome De Groot, "Ancestry.com and the Evolving Nature of Historical Information Companies," *The Public Historian* 42.1 (2020): 8–28.

46. Putnam, "The Transnational and the Text-Searchable," 359.

47. "Colonial Secretary Letters Received," *MHNSW*, https://mhnsw.au/indexes/colonial-secretary/colonial-secretary-letters-received-1826–1896/ (accessed June 3, 2024).

48. Katherine Roscoe, "Is Digital Crime History Too White? Representation in Australian Archives," *History Workshop*, August 26, 2019, www.historyworkshop.org .uk/is-digitalcrime-history-too-white-representation-in-australian-archives/ (accessed February 28, 2022).

49. Gerben Zaagsma, "Digital History and the Politics of Digitization," *Digital Scholarship in the Humanities* 38 (2023): 830–51.

50. "Website Accessibility," *Trove*, National Library of Australia, https://Trove .nla.gov.au/website-accessibility, accessed February 7, 2022.

51. "Become a VolunTrove," *Trove*, https://Trove.nla.gov.au/help/become -volunTrove, accessed February 7, 2022.

52. Eric Harvey, "Beyond Compliance: Thinking Accessibly about the Digital Humanities," Stanford University, January 25, 2022, https://youtu.be/z5Y010Gn9wc.

53. On archives and Indigenous Australian history, see Jane Lydon, "Photography and Critical Heritage: Australian Aboriginal Photographic Archives and the Stolen Generations," *The Public Historian* 41.1 (2019): 18–33.

54. "Cultural Advice," *Trove Australia*, accessed February 14, 2022.

55. They have tagged name, age, trial date and place, estimated birth year, vessel, and arrival port and date.

56. Rachel Franks, "Before Alternative Voices: *The Sydney Gazette and New South Wales Advertiser*," *M/C Journal* 20.1 (2017): https://doi.org/10.5204/mcj.1204.

57. September 15, 22, and 29, 1831. There is no "found" notice.

58. Trial of John Fitzgerald, September 9, 1818, *Old Bailey Online*, t18180909–1.

59. Christopher Stone and Bencie Woll, "Dumb O Jemmy and Others: Deaf People, Interpreters, and the London Courts in the Eighteenth and Nineteenth Centuries," *Sign Language Studies* 8.3 (2008): 226–40; *Deaf in New South Wales: A Community History*, "John Fitzgerald," http://deafinnsw.com/john-fitzgerald (accessed November 2, 2021).

60. September 14, 1816, 2.

61. Roscoe, "Is Digital Crime History Too White?"

62. December 28, 1830, 4. Dunn was convicted of robbery in Bristol in April 1818. The advertisement is repeated into January and February 1831, and again in January 1833.

63. August 25, 1825, 4.

64. *The Hobart Town Gazette and Southern Reporter*, June 29, 1816, 1. Franks must have been caught quickly, because he is soon listed again as having broken out of jail.

65. Cassandra Pybus, *Black Founders: The Unknown Story of Australia's First Black Settlers* (Sydney: UNSW Press, 2006).

66. May 28, 1834, 321.

67. SANSW, *Annotated Printed Indents*, 32–2472, *Hercules* (4), 1832.

68. August 14, 1833, 311.

69. SANSW, *Butts of Certificates of Freedom*, no. 35/46.

70. SANSW, *Gaol Description and Entrance Books, 1818–1930*, 4/6430, roll 851.

71. October 19, 1836, 816.

72. SANSW, *Annotated Printed Indents*, 36–1401, *Strathfieldsay*, 1836.

73. January 11, 1837, 36.

74. December 16, 1824, 1. Emphasis in original.

75. Ian Duffield, "The Life and Death of 'Black' John Goff: Aspects of the Black Convict Contribution to Resistance Patterns during the Transportation Era in Eastern Australia," *Australian Journal of Politics and History* 33.1 (1987): 30–44.

76. September 20, 1850, 1457, emphasis added. She was a Baptist, and tried in Jamaica for stealing tea: SANSW, *Annotated Printed Indents*, 548–36, *Elizabeth* (5th), 1836.

77. March 20, 1839, 341. He ran again in October and was quickly caught: October 16, 1839, 1169; October 23, 1839, 1192.

78. SANSW, *Annotated Printed Indents*, 38–890, *Symmetry*, 1838.

79. SANSW, *Annotated Printed Indents*, 38–888, *Symmetry*, 1838.

80. June 13, 1832, 136.

81. July 17, 1833, 266.

82. June 12, 1833, 219. He arrived with "one arm only": SANSW, *Bound Manuscript Indents*, 30/413, *Dunvegan Castle*, 1830. There is no more detail in his 1843 Certificate of Freedom: no. 43/1389.

83. August 22, 1832, 250.

84. September 14, 1836, 717.

85. Trial of Ellen Smith, Mary Ann Read, and Charles Newman, October 29, 1829, *Old Bailey Online*, t18291029–103.

86. October 7, 1835, 708.

87. January 13 (p. 13) and February 24 (p. 175), 1836; SANSW, *Bound Indents*, 30/1672, *Marquis of Huntly*, 1830.

88. February 26, 1834, 100; SANSW, *Gaol Description and Entrance Books*, 2/2016, roll 759.

89. February 18, 1830, 4; February 3, 1831, 4. He is listed as found on February 22.

90. SANSW, *Bound Indents*, 26–89, *Sir Godfrey Webster*, 1826.

91. Hyde Park Barracks (at large for a few weeks in both cases): September 30, 1826, 4; April 9, 1827, 4. Moved to Emu Plains July 4, 1827, 1; then October 29, 1827, which says it is his fourth escape. Back to Hyde Park Barracks after capture, and runs again (January 7, 1828, 4), which is the period of the murder suspicion.

92. "A Coroner's Inquest," *Sydney Gazette and New South Wales Advertiser* (1803–1832), January 23, 1828, 2.

93. Liverpool Barracks: June 9, 1829, 3; December 15, 1829, 3. Road gang: February 9, 1830, 4; March 23, 1830. Different road gang: February 3, 1831, 4.

94. SANSW, 4/2102, letter 31/4183. The other men are Peter Morgan (*Malabar*, 1819) and Joseph Richardson (*Royal George*, 1828).

95. SANSW, *Butts of Certificates of Freedom*, no. 33/53. Emphasis in original.

96. SANSW, *Bound Manuscript Indents*, 43–1373, *Countess of Harcourt*, 1828.

97. November 15, 1832, 2.

98. November 17, 1831, 4.

99. November 7, 1832, 396.

100. TNA *New South Wales and Tasmania, Australian Convict Musters, 1806–1849*, HO 10/19; SANSW 4/7014, p. 107, reel 6022.

101. SANSW, 4/2114, letter 31/6464.

102. SANSW, *Convict Registers of Conditional and Absolute Pardons*, no. 41/90.

103. SANSW, 4/2738.6, letter 46/1092.

104. June 13, 1832, 136. Hassell (d. 1868) was an Australian-born, Welsh-trained Church of England clergyman in charge of the extensive "Cowpasture" parish. Hilde Shaw, "The Parish of Narellan," *Illawarra Historical Society Bulletin* (February 1971): 3–7, at 3.

105. September 5, 1832, 278.

106. January 27, 1836, 79.

107. Bruce Woodley and Dobe Newton, "I Am Australian." *I Am Australian* (1987). Emphasis added.

108. Woodley and Newton, "I Am Australian."

109. Soldatic, "Disability's Circularity," and "Postcolonial Reproductions: Disability, Indigeneity and the Formation of the White Masculine Settler State of Australia," *Social Identities* 21:1 (2015): 53–68.

110. Hamish Maxwell-Stewart, in Helen Shield et al., "Average Face of 19th Century Convicts Created from Records." *Your Afternoon*, ABC Radio, July 23, 2019, https://www.abc.net.au/radio/hobart/programs/your-afternoon/facelab/11339618.

111. Changing Faces, "About Face Equality," https://www.changingfaces.org.uk/campaigns/face-equality (accessed August 12, 2018).

112. Coordinated and funded by the School of Advanced Study, University of London, in partnership with the Arts and Humanities Research Council and the British Academy.

113. Emily Cock, "Creating Portraits and Facing History," *Facing the Past*, https://dremilycock.wordpress.com/2019/11/19/creating-portraits-and-facing-history/ (accessed March 2, 2022).

114. *Aubergine Café*, "About," https://www.auberginecafe.co.uk/ (accessed March 2, 2022).

115. Dawn Mannay, *Visual, Narrative and Creative Research Methods: Application, Reflection and Ethics* (Abingdon: Routledge, 2016).

CHAPTER 5

The Feverish Saint

A Queer Crip Encounter with the Public Universal Friend

KJ CERANKOWSKI

"The illness is gone." So states historian Paul Moyer in the opening segment of a National Public Radio (NPR) *Throughline* episode devoted to the life and story of the Public Universal Friend. There is really nothing that remarkable about Moyer's statement. Often, the tale of the Public Universal Friend begins with a declaration of an ending—the fever cools, the sickness retreats, Jemima Wilkinson dies and in her body is born the genderless spirit of the Public Universal Friend, the All-Friend, the Comforter, or most simply, the Friend. The Friend then goes on to become a remarkable religious leader most notably known for a kind of genderqueerness. And henceforth, the illness is gone. As unremarkable a statement as this may seem at first glance, it is exactly the plot point I return to time and again in this story. What if the illness isn't absolutely gone, but leaves a lasting impact on the life and embodiment of the Friend; what if illness is integral to the very existence of the Friend? By cripping the archives of Jemima Wilkinson and the Public Universal Friend, I suggest that their stories require bringing illness and sickness to bear on gender, sexuality, and religious zealotry.

Susan Wendell suggests "any adequate feminist understanding of disability must encompass chronic illnesses," and so too must any queer understanding of disability.[1] Following J. Logan Smilges, I also "lean into disability's capaciousness" as a "broad term that encompasses a wide variety of embodyminded difference," including, as pertinent to this study, illness or chronic illness that inevitably shapes and reshapes the bodymind.[2] Thus when I imagine cripping the archive of the Friend, I do so at the specific intersections of illness as an embodied and often disabling experience and queerness as an embodied and political formation.[3] As Wendell notes, there are of course distinctions that can be made between disability and illness—not all disabled people are sick.

But it is also true that illness can be experienced as debilitating—many sick people experience themselves as disabled, whether temporarily or permanently. Accordingly, disability ought to also include and accommodate illness.[4]

Just as I avoid "laying open" the body of the Friend to tell some story of trans history that relies on knowledge of the sexed body, I also avoid making any case for the Friend as disabled, or even chronically ill.[5] As I caution about exporting contemporary gender categories to make sense of trans history, I similarly refuse to export diagnostic categories of illness or disability onto the past. Rather, I argue that the Friend's very being bears an indelible relationship to the experience of illness and that the Friend continued to have a complex relationship to illness, to a sense of health, and to being in time for the duration of the Friend's existence. To recuperate the inextricable links between illness and gender in the story of the Friend is to bring a crip attentiveness to the archive, to refuse to let illness simply pass and to instead recognize the way illness leaves a mark, returns, and shapes a life. Here, I revisit the archives of the Friend (letters, journal entries, ledgers) alongside the archive created about the Friend (historical and pop cultural feminist and queer retellings) to argue that we cannot understand the Friend's gender without accounting for illness—the illness was never simply gone.

Ungendering the Friend

First, a little more context. Jemima Wilkinson was born into a Quaker family in Cumberland, Rhode Island in 1752. Various accounts describe her as a religious but somewhat rebellious girl, who even into her twenties had not yet married, which was uncommon for young women in that time period. Then in 1776, just a month or so before her twenty-fourth birthday, Jemima was suddenly struck by a fever that burned through her body and left her bedridden for days. Just when her family had given up hope and braced themselves for what they thought would be her demise, Jemima leapt from her bed, seemingly fully recovered. But the person they rushed to embrace claimed to no longer be Jemima Wilkinson. Instead, the figure announced that Jemima had in fact died and the spirit of a genderless holy prophet had been sent into her body, heretofore to be referred to as the Public Universal Friend. The Friend then went on to gather a devout following, eventually settling the land of the Seneca Nation in what is now the Finger Lakes region of upstate New York. This Society of Friends then founded a new town there called Jerusalem, where the body of the Friend eventually died in 1819.

I cannot here tell any more comprehensive an account of the Friend's life and ministry than has already been done by numerous historians, biographers, and fans alike.[6] Instead, I am much more interested in how and why the story of the Friend resurfaces, and especially what people want from that story, or, what *I* want from the story. Over twenty years ago, Susan Juster asked, remarking on the Friend's conventional and otherwise forgettable theology, why the Friend should have been so fascinating not only to contemporary Americans in the late eighteenth century but also to us today. Juster answers her own query with the suggestion that interest in the Friend likely has everything to do with the Friend's figure as "the cross-dressed actress or imposter."[7] No doubt, different factions of people show keen interest in uncovering historical examples of crossdressing or in cracking the stories of early religious fanaticism and "false prophets."[8] In fact, the story of the Friend has gone through various cycles of resurgence and public interest. It has been retold by historians delving into the odder religious histories of colonial America, particularly through the Second Great Awakening (the Friend, after all, developed quite a following of believers and practitioners). It has been embraced by feminists as a tale of cunning and patriarchal refusal—a woman who wishes to remain unwed and instead devote her time to learning and preaching the gospel cleverly reinvents herself as a genderless saintly figure. And, most recently, in a new era of gender politics, the Friend's story has been taken up anew by people looking to recover some sort of early queer, transgender, or nonbinary history in the Friend's strange (re)birth.

I am reluctant to assign any gender to the Friend, as gender categories are historical, contextual, and ever shifting. As Joan Scott concisely puts it, "questions about gender are never completely answered." And the Friend's story is indeed a story that refuses complete answers and raises many more questions. Further, to draw on Jamie A. Lee, the archival body is "always in motion" as archives are shaped by and reshape the desires of the researcher. I want to make room for those whose longing has brought them to embrace the Friend as a revolutionary woman who refused the gender norms of her time as well as for those whose longing brings them to the Friend as a nonbinary or genderqueer forebear. But I also want to carve out space for crip archival longings, to build a complicated case for understanding the Friend at the nexus of gender, illness, and religiosity. Even as I respect the complexity of how and why different groups may uphold the Friend as either a feminist hero or as a trancestor, I am concerned that even feminist, queer, and trans versions of the story tend to erase or gloss over the role of illness in the very making of the Friend.

I confess that I myself had been unfamiliar with Jemima Wilkinson and the Public Universal Friend until just a few years ago when one of my friends sent me an Instagram post that detailed the life of this "nonbinary, celibate saint" in colonial America. This story, it seemed, sat perfectly at the intersection of my interests in trans life and asexuality. I snapped a screenshot with the goal of looking into it all a little more deeply. At some point, I typed "Jemima Wilkinson" and "Public Universal Friend" into a search bar, bookmarked some information, committed the name and story to memory, and most probably deleted the screenshot because I have since been unable to recover the initial post that drew me to the Friend (a testament, perhaps, to my own failures as an archivist).

But in my recent search to recover that post, I found an explosion of stories of the Friend in popular media across late 2019 and early 2020, a whole new archive, if you will. While one podcast seemed predominantly focused on reclaiming the Friend as a powerful woman in history (*What's Her Name* podcast), all the other current iterations I came across gestured toward a tale of long-existing nonbinary life in America's past. Some of these recent stories include a *Washington Post* piece from January 5, 2020 titled "A Genderless Prophet Drew Hundreds of Followers Long before the Age of Nonbinary Pronouns"; a feature story on the queer website *Autostraddle* published April 7, 2020, "The Public Universal Friend: A Deep Dive on a Story of Nonbinary Identity, Quakerism and Near-Death Experiences," which includes an embedded video of a YouTube vlog from December 19, 2019 titled "Non-Binary and Religious: The Public Universal Friend"; an episode of the podcast *Cool People Who Did Cool Stuff*, "The Public Universal Friend: A Nonbinary Icon in Revolutionary-Era America" from June 2022; and the NPR *Throughline* episode that this chapter began with. *Throughline*'s tagline describes it as a show "where we go back in time to understand the present." In these instances, going back in time to the story of the Friend activates an attempt to understand nonbinary gender and the singular "they" pronoun.

In addition to popular media, the story of the Friend has recently made its way out of academic literature and historiography into the literary nonfiction market. T Fleischmann's book *Time Is the Thing a Body Moves Through*—a meandering memoir-adjacent lyric essay exploring queer experience and possibility in the absence of being some thing, or being any gender or sexuality—features several pages on the Friend. Fleischmann's narrative of the Friend borrows liberally from two main sources (Moyer and Wisbey) and is plopped right in between stories of online dating, group sex, and trans party scenes. Fleischmann laments trying to tell a disinterested young attendee of a "trans-centric queer party" about the Friend, only to be met with either boredom or offense. It would seem, in Fleischmann's story of the story, no one really cares. But I suspect it was this moment in Fleischmann's 2019 book that turned many in the trans and nonbinary communities on to this story. In fact, when I tell a trans friend of mine that I am thinking of writing something on the Friend, my friend says, "Oh! That's the person T Fleischmann wrote about."

There are multiple readings that might help make sense of why exactly Fleischmann includes the Friend's story in their book, but one core speculation is that the Friend's story reflects Fleischmann's embrace of an absence of identity, a refusal to *be* a certain *thing* that describes a way of being gendered.

What is notable for my interests is not necessarily *why* Fleischmann tells the story, but *how*. Fleischmann chooses to use they/them pronouns for the Friend, even as they acknowledge Scott Larson's essay in an endnote as the first piece they read that "understood" the Friend's gender. The very notion of properly understanding the Friend's gender belies Fleischmann's own proposition that gender ought not be a thing to be and to therefore be understood about a body, laid open.[9]

Larson importantly complicates the narrative by describing the Friend as "a figure at once performing gender ambiguity and divinity beyond gender."[10] As such, writing about the Friend presents one with difficulties of the "grammar of gender" because the Friend, as a genderless being, defies gendered pronouns. While "they" has been taken up as a "gender neutral" pronoun that might be employed when discussing someone whose gender may not be known, it has also been adopted as the most common pronoun used to indicate nonbinary gender expression or identity. Although one may interpret nonbinary as a movement away from gender altogether, our very ability to conceive of nonbinary today presupposes a gender binary. But as Greta Lafleur asserts, the very concept of a gender binary is not contemporaneous to early modern figures like the Friend, as the gender binary is an invention of the late nineteenth and early twentieth centuries. Instead, LaFleur suggests we "sit with the terms that these figures developed for themselves."[11]

And this is where I enter a distinction between agender or genderlessness (without a gender) and nonbinary (gender that is not of the binary man/woman, male/female). The Friend, by way of disavowing the human, arguably also disavows gender categories.[12] Thus, the nonbinary gendering of the Friend, as illustrated in many contemporary iterations of the story of the Friend, is arguably a transhistorical displacement of modern gender categories and grammars that don't quite fit. Accordingly, it seems a better practice to simply avoid pronouns for the Friend altogether (as Larson does and as I do here). It is worth noting that in the historical record the Friend is sometimes referred to as "he" by followers as well as some outside observers, referred to as "she" mostly by nonfollowers and detractors, and most often with no pronouns and simply referred to as "the Friend." Karen-Edis Barzman has also documented instances in which the Friend is referred to as "her him" in some of the Society's papers, which highlights the limitation of a singular pronoun and may well be an early usage of the later practice of writing "she/he" or "s/he" as a more inclusive gesture.[13] And while the usage of the singular "they" pronoun has gone in and out of favor in the English language, there does not, to my knowledge, appear to be any use of the singular "they" to refer to the Friend among the Friend's contemporaries.[14]

All this is not to belabor the question of gender and "correct" pronouns. Rather, the question of the Friend's gender and pronouns deliberately brings us back to the matter of illness. As Larson writes, "To call the Friend 'Jemima

Wilkinson' and 'she' was to deny the story of the Friend's death and miraculous resurrection." Larson continues, "The Friend was genderless, but only by virtue of being a resurrected spirit," as genderlessness was imagined to be a transcended state, the characteristic of a celestial being whose essence is beyond human sexual dimorphism.[15] As such, referring to the Friend as a woman masquerading as a man is not simply a failure to recognize some sort of proto-trans historical possibility, but it is to deny Jemima's transformation from a woman named Jemima into a genderless spiritual being called the Friend. In another direction, by claiming the Friend as nonbinary, one risks suggesting that nonbinary-identified people have somehow transcended the human form and are divine prophets, which is adamantly not what I wish to imply here. To the contrary, I am suggesting that claiming the Friend as nonbinary actually fixes the Friend back into human gender categories. More than any kind of transition of gender, this is a transition of being. To deny this spiritual transfiguration in the Friend's story is to essentially deny the impact of illness and a kind of death that resulted from it.

And so we return to our origin story: the Friend was born in illness. But this is not a mere plot point to move on from. The illness is not gone; the illness is inextricably tied to the Friend's ongoingness as a genderless being. And even more literally, illness does not remain absent from the Friend's life as the Friend goes on to work as a healer of the ill and ailing, but also later succumbs to death after several years of increasing debilitation due to chronic edema. What I therefore offer here is a crip approach to the story that centers illness as inseparably linked to the (a)gendered and religious threads that have to date received the most due attention. The ongoingness of the body the Friend inhabits is an enduring relation with illness, corporeality, and persistence through time. The story must return again and again to illness rather than begin with its end.

Fever Archive

When I first set off in pursuit of the Friend, I imagined myself chasing a kind of "archive fever," as I was quite literally searching for the story of a fever in the archive. But what I was embarking on was far from the feverish search for Truth of Jacques Derrida's *mal d'archive*. I am all too aware of the archive's shortcomings, gaps, and erasures, not to mention the impossibility of any single Truth. Rather, I approach the archive through an embrace of affective experience, the bodily repertoire, archival ambience, and fabulation.[16] The archive fever I had in mind is something more akin to Carolyn Steedman's attention to the archive's materialities, the circularity of dust, how we become infected in and by the archive. Infected, in the sense that the archive can literally make us sick as we inhale old parchment and binding molecules, sloughed skin, and whatever other airborne vectors ride the dust across our lips and into our circulatory systems. But also in a more quantum sense, that even if consuming the archive's material into our organism does not actually make us physically ill, we might still, as Steedman quoting Roland Barthes puts it, "eat history."[17] In so doing, we theoretically take history's ills into our own bodies and let them shape us. I want this intimacy with the Friend, a way to know the ghostly spirit who captivates me, inducing a feverish desire, a fervor.

But as I began making plans to travel to Ithaca in the fall of 2020 to leaf through and breathe in the papers of Jemima Wilkinson, the threat of a new fever interrupted my plans. The onset and ongoingness of the COVID-19 pandemic closed the archive. Before the collections eventually reopened, the archivists and librarians provided me instead with digitized copies of Wilkinson's papers. Left to scroll hundreds of pages of randomized PDF files of letters, purchase deeds, almanac pages, court documents, payment and loan books, death logs, and dream journals on a computer screen, the materiality and its dust elude me. I squint my eyes against the screen, zooming in and in and in, straining to read the script. My head aches, dull and heavy, my neck muscles tighten and tense. The work flares my chronic pain points and tests the limits of my body; one way of cripping the archive is simply *being crip in the archive*—working at the limits of our own bodies to recover the glossed and buried stories of disability and illness.

As I painstakingly read through the files, I am searching for any variable by which a relationship to illness persists in the Society of Friends and particularly for the Friend. Mostly, I find notes of assurance of good health, of remaining yet in time (the Friend and followers tended to refer to death as "leaving time" or being "snatched out of time" and so, to go on living was to remain in time). I find fragments, bits and pieces to a larger puzzle that has no answer key. A letter from the Friend to a James Parker notes that a follower, Sarah (presumably Sarah Richards, who was a close confidante of the Friend and kept a book that is also collected with Wilkinson's papers), was sent "to thee at the time of thy severe sickness viewing it to be a time of great distress and trouble of oppression." Sarah Richards describes a trip to Seneca Lake where she and her party "met the Friend once more in time finding all in comfortable health." The Friend, writing to Sarah Richards: "I am yet in time through the long suffering and tender mercies of the Lord on High." And to another follower, Hannah Wall: "I am yet in time and remain to be the same friend." Among these small notes of either providing care for ill members of the fellowship or of simply reassuring one's state of good health, I find one curiosity in a note from the Friend in a letter to one C Marshall, written in 1795, twenty-four years before the death of the Friend's body: "I am yet in time through the goodness of a long suffering god and enjoy tolerable ~~good~~ state of health." I am struck that the friend wrote "good" and then crossed it out, asserting instead a "tolerable state of health." The Friend continues, "Life is uncertain and death is certain for in such an hour as ye think not death may come." I cannot help but wonder what ailed the Friend at the time this letter was written, or if the Friend was drawing on Jemima's memory of the fatal fever, of the health of that body being forever more tolerable if not good, as long as the Friend remained in the body in time.

There is also, of course, the oft-cited "A Memorandum of the Introduction of that Fatal Fever," which is a third-person account by the Friend of the fever that befell Jemima Wilkinson. The Friend describes how the "Columbus Fever" (since called typhus) spread through Rhode Island from a war ship, bringing death upon Jemima. As she "appear'd to meet the shock of Death," she encountered two archangels calling "Room, Room, Room, in the many Mansions of eternal Glory for Thee."[18] The suggestion then is that Jemima followed the archangels to eternal glory and the spirit of the Friend "took full possession of the body it now animates." I take the time to name what is ostensibly Jemima's vision, albeit described by and through the Friend, of the angels crying out "Room, Room, Room" because it parallels some of the later recorded dreams of the Friend: "The Friend dreamed that a man came to the Friend's house and said tidings tidings tidings" and "The Friend dreamed that a man came with a flag and said victory victory victory." The Friend seems to dream in these ternions, which may raise doubt for some readers as to whether it was Jemima all along who dreamed all of it or simply the Friend's mode of telling all dreams (both the Friend's own and Jemima's) through these triad declarations. I am not particularly worried about whether or not Jemima's spirit actually left her body and the Friend's took over. Rather, I care that the residues of illness variably persist and this story of illness, death, and reanimation is the one that gives way to the Friend's genderlessness.

In other words, had Jemima not become ill, it is unclear if the Friend would have ever come to exist. Susan Juster writes on millenarian prophets in *Doomsayers*, noting that although "cases of miraculous recovery from severe distress are rare," indeed, "a period of physical debility (whether natural or self-induced) was a good way to prepare the mind to receive a divine summons to serve." Juster connects this notion of miracle recovery and divination specifically to the Friend's resurrection (as well as to another prophet, the Friend's contemporary David Austin, who developed "prophetic powers" after nearly dying from scarlet fever).[19] Just as I cautioned against the fallacious logical leap that trans or nonbinary people are somehow more spiritually transcendent, I also want to caution against the idea that sick or disabled people are somehow more enlightened or closer to some sense of godliness. It is worth noting, however, that trans, sick, and disabled people often bear a familiar relationship to the notion of bodily transcendence, experienced as a dissociation of sorts, to cope with varying pains—emotional, psychic, and physical—that often accompany the experience of being trans, queer, or crip in the world. But more to the point, just as I have argued that the Friend's gender (or lack thereof) cannot be separated from the narrative of illness, so too must we understand that the experience of illness (and its ties to gender) cannot be separated from the spiritual and religious context of the time in which the Friend was living.

Further, the embodied experience of illness and spirituality become almost impossible to disambiguate. Writing more specifically about the prevalence of consumption as an archetypal disease among eighteenth- and nineteenth-century evangelicals, Juster describes how the "consumptive" state actually "worked much like the spirit itself—'agitating,' 'seizing,' and 'invading' the body at its weakest points." This is not to metaphorize illness through the spiritual, but to instead bring a crip attentiveness to the embodied experiences of illness and spiritual ecstasy that often appear similar in a physical seizing of the body. The resemblance between bodily suffering through severe illness and spiritual ecstasy is so strong that Juster remarks that "it is difficult to know where physical discomfort leaves off and spiritual enlightenment begins." Although Jemima Wilkinson suffered from typhus rather than tuberculosis, I might extrapolate some of Juster's observances for my purposes of making sense of the "feverish saint" here. When the body is pushed close to death, as Jemima's body was, it may very well be difficult to retreat from the spiritual epiphany that arises from the so-called near-death experience. "The point is," Juster writes, "that for many saints, grace *felt* like illness; they were often hard pressed to distinguish between the two."[20] Whether or not the body that lived beyond the fever housed the spirit of Jemima or the Friend, illness, faith, and gender became inseparable.

To be clear, I am not arguing that queerness is a result of illness, that queer people are "sick" in some way, or that those who believe they have achieved some sort of spiritual transmogrification are "sick." But the pressures of cure, healing, and fixing the body into legible categories of gender, sexuality, and wellness often silence and erase a queer embrace of the formative impacts of illness. What I ask us to do here is sit with the possibility that some of us may be co-constituted as queer through our experiences of illness, disability, and debility. I argue that a crip attention to bodily entanglements of gender, spirit, and health cannot leave illness behind. Instead, illness can change a body (or a soul) and is an often unforgettable part of the dense webs and patterns of our making. Restaking claims to the life impact of illness and to refuse its erasure as something that simply passes is not to pathologize or seek cure, but to recognize the impact and centrality of sickness and wellness to how we become possible in the world.[21]

What I hope to have offered here is a new way to consider the afterlife of fever, to shift our understanding of illness from something that either merely passes or remains chronic and thus disabling to an embodied experience that can shape subjectivity. I have experienced intense bouts of feverish illness at the onset of infection, but after the fever passes, those experiences leave marks on my psyche and sense of self, including the shape of my gender. I am not always sick, and I mostly move through the world appearing able-bodied on a regular basis. But I do sometimes have flares of pain and fatigue that remind me that the illness never really left. It returns not just in the experience of unease and bodily disease in a flare, but in the way I understand who I am in the world, my limits and my capacities. The story of the Friend has helped me follow my own crip recovery of the impact of illness, which even in my agnosticism becomes inseparable from religiosity, a sense of a spiritual self, and gender. A queer crip encounter with the Friend's archives uncovers the way the fever withdraws but leaves a mark. To claim that the illness is indeed not gone is not to wallow in sickness; rather, it is to refuse erasure by naming the ways bodyminds are constituted in and through illness or disability, whether temporary, recurrent, or enduring. Such a recognition makes possible new ways of being and becoming in configurations that joyfully resist cure's imperative to eliminate illness and achieve normative constructions of wellness, gender, and sexuality. And that is, in all senses of the word, an ecstatic way to live.

Notes

1. Susan Wendell, "Unhealthy Disabled: Treating Chronic Illnesses as Disabilities," *Hypatia* 16, no. 4 (Autumn 2001): 17.

2. J. Logan Smilges, *Queer Silence: On Disability and Rhetorical Absence* (Minneapolis: University of Minnesota Press, 2022), 6. Smilges even further explores the provocation that disability might actually be the "bedrock of queer," 22.

3. Regarding the overlap of disability and queer politics, I take direction from Robert McRuer's formulation of crip theory as co-constituted by queer and disability politics in *Crip Theory: Cultural Signs of Queerness and Disability* (New York: New York University Press, 2006).

4. Susan Wendell, *The Rejected Body: Feminist Philosophical Reflections on Disability* (New York: Routledge, 1996).

5. Scott Larson suggests that trans histories must refuse "overexamining" or "laying open" gender variant subjects in order to prove some embodiment of what we now understand to be transgender. Instead, Larson calls for "critical trans-attendance," a method that "shifts the scene of inquiry to attend to alternate frameworks and articulations of power that surround the subject of examination." "Laid Open: Examining Genders in Early America," in *Trans Historical: Gender Plurality Before the Modern*, edited by Greta LaFleur, Masha Raskolnikov, and Anna Kłosowska (Ithaca: Cornell University Press, 2021), 352. Accordingly, I am interested in employing a critical queer crip trans attendance to the retellings of the stories of the Friend to attend to more complex ways that gender and illness coextensively take shape.

6. See in particular the work of Michael Bronski, *A Queer History of the United States* (Boston: Beacon Press, 2011); T Fleischmann, *Time Is the Thing a Body Moves*

Through (Minneapolis: Coffee House Press, 2019); Susan Juster, *Doomsayers: Anglo-American Prophecy in the Age of Revolution* (Philadelphia: University of Pennsylvania Press, 2003); "'Neither Male nor Female': Jemima Wilkinson and the Politics of Gender in Post-Revolutionary America," in *Possible Pasts: Becoming Colonial in Early America*, edited by Robert Blair St. George (Ithaca: Cornell University Press, 2000), 357–79; "To Slay the Beast: Visionary Women in the Early Republic," in *A Mighty Baptism: Race, Gender, and the Creation of American Protestantism*, edited by Susan Juster and Lisa MacFarlane (Ithaca: Cornell University Press, 1996), 19–37; Scott Larson, "'Indescribable Being': Theological Performances of Genderlessness in the Society of the Publick Universal Friend, 1776–1819," *Early American Studies* 12, no. 3 (Fall 2014): 576–600; "Laid Open," in *Trans Historical*; Paul Moyer, *The Public Universal Friend: Jemima Wilkinson and Religious Enthusiasm in Revolutionary America* (Ithaca: Cornell University Press, 2015); and Herbert Wisbey Jr., *Pioneer Prophetess: Jemima Wilkinson, the Publick Universal Friend* (Ithaca: Cornell University Press, 1964). While some scholars tend to draw on David Hudson's *Memoir of Jemima Wilkinson*, as Adam Morris notes, Hudson's account is intended to disparage the Friend, with whom he was engaged in a land dispute. Hudson, *Memoir of Jemima Wilkinson: A Preacheress of the Eighteenth Century: Containing an Authentic Narrative of Her Life and Character and of the Rise, Progress and Conclusion of Her Ministry* (Bath, NY: R. L. Underhill, 1844); Morris, *American Messiahs: False Prophets of a Damned Nation* (New York: Liveright Publishing Company, 2019).

7. Juster, "'Neither Male nor Female,'" in *Possible Pasts*, 357–58.

8. It is in the context of the "false prophet" that Adam Morris, in *American Messiahs*, paints Jemima Wilkinson as a cultish Messiah figure, even going so far as to liken the Friend's tactics with those of Jim Jones.

9. I refer here again to Larson, "Laid Open." Additionally, it is important to note, but beyond the scope of this chapter to unpack further: Fleischmann also cites Larson, "'Indescribable Being,'" on understanding the Friend as a settler. In fact, across many accounts, we find a complicated narrative of the Friend's Quaker-inspired principles that included antislavery ideals and peaceful and equitable relations among Indigenous populations as the United States formed as a nation and expanded its own settler colonial reach westward—a westward expansion the Friend also participated in through the purchase of land and the formation of a settler community on Seneca Lake. Coextensively, the formation of the nation-state further sedimented gender categories, which puts the Friend at odds with settler movements in that regard, even as the Society of Friends purchased and deeded stolen land.

10. Juster, "To Slay the Beast," in *A Mighty Baptism*, 28. Larson, "'Indescribable Being,'" 581.

11. Greta LaFleur, "Epilogue: Against Consensus," in *Trans Historical: Gender Plurality Before the Modern*, edited by Greta LaFleur, Masha Raskolnikov, and Anna Kłosowska (Ithaca: Cornell University Press, 2021), 368.

12. Kit Heyam writes, "[T]he Friend was not a person, but a spirit; hence it's more accurate to speak about them as genderless than as non-binary." Heyam, *Before We Were Trans: A New History of Gender* (New York: Seal Press, 2022), 218.

13. Karen-Edis Barzman, "The Subject of 'Woman' and the Discipline of Early Modern Studies: Jemima Wilkinson and the Publick Universal Friend," in *Culture and Change: Attending to Early Modern Women*, edited by Margaret Mikesell and Adele Seef (Newark: University of Delaware Press, 2003), 348.

14. Dennis Baron, in *What's Your Pronoun? Beyond He and She*, finds a peppered use of the singular "they" in the English language along with a long history of contention around its grammatical correctness, showing that recent debates over the grammar of the singular "they" are just rehearsals of debates dating back to the early nineteenth century. While Baron presents some examples of the use of singular "they" from the late eighteenth century, the majority of his examples come later, postdating the Friend's lifetime. It seems, thus, that the use of singular "they" was still rather uncommon among the Friend's contemporaries. Baron, *What's Your Pronoun? Beyond He and She* (New York: Liveright Publishing Corporation, 2020).

15. Larson, "'Indescribable Being,'" 595–97. It bears significance to note also that the Friend's divine claim not only made possible an ungendered way of being, but also enabled settler possibilities. Larson asserts, "[T]he claim to actually be divine played a role in the Friend's participation in westward expansion, even as the Friend did so in ways that actively sought peaceful relations and violated traditional gender boundaries," 600.

16. Here I refer to Diana Taylor's shape of the repertoire and embodied memory in relation to the archive, E. Cram's understanding of archival ambience as central to sensory memory and meaning-making, and Tavia Nyong'o's and Saidiya Hartman's various uptakes of fabulation as a performative approach to the archive that takes seriously how speculative fabulation can serve as a way for minority subjects to dream otherwise. Taylor, *The Archive and the Repertoire: Performing Cultural Memory in the Americas* (Durham, NC: Duke University Press, 2003); Cram, "Archival Ambience and Sensory Memory: Generating Queer Intimacies in the Settler Colonial Archive," *Communication and Critical/Cultural Studies* 13, no. 2 (2016): 109–29; Nyong'o, *Afro-Fabulations: The Queer Drama of Black Life* (New York: New York University Press, 2018); Hartman, "Venus in Two Acts," *Small Axe* 12, no. 2 (2008): 1–14, *Wayward Lives, Beautiful Experiments: Intimate Histories of Social Upheaval* (New York: W. W. Norton and Company, 2019).

17. Carolyn Steedman, *Dust: The Archive and Cultural History* (New Brunswick: Rutgers University Press, 2002), 27.

18. Jemima Wilkinson Papers 1772–1849. #357. Also transcribed in Mrs. Walter A. Henricks and Arnold J. Potter, "The Universal Friend: Jemima Wilkinson," *New York History* 23, no. 2 (April 1942): 159.

19. Juster, *Doomsayers*, 65–66.

20. Juster, *Doomsayers*, 107–8.

21. Here, I call up Eli Clare's ambivalent relationship to cure, as something that can both ease pain and discomfort, but also erases, homogenizes, and reinforces the concept of the normal, normate, normative human body to be maintained and restored as such, in *Brilliant Imperfection: Grappling with Cure* (Durham, NC: Duke University Press, 2017).

PART II

Obscuring

CHAPTER 6

Disability, the Modern State, and the Archive in the United States

AUDRA JENNINGS

In September 1938, Laura Curley wrote to President Franklin D. Roosevelt on behalf of the teachers and administrators of Jefferson School in Oakland, California who worked with the school's disabled children. She sought assistance on three matters: the school's plans to develop a summer camp for its students, information on the Warm Springs Foundation, and a request for an autographed photograph of President Roosevelt.[1] The letter, like the individual points in a pointillist painting, offers a glimpse of a singular point in a much larger and more complex picture of experiences of disability in the 1930s United States. With its tantalizing clues about the educational experiences of the physically disabled children who attended the urban school, the letter points to the potential of federal government records to elucidate the lived experience of disabled people across the United States. Concern about disability and the fitness of citizens, immigrants, workers, mothers, children, and veterans, among others, informed and motivated significant state growth in the United States in the early twentieth century.[2] During this period of rapid change, state-level policy varied significantly and federal attention to disability shifted considerably across the first half of the twentieth century. Programs meant to understand and address disability, which American society and the state increasingly viewed as problematic, developed, grew, moved between agencies, and disappeared altogether as war, work, medicine, and epidemics changed the incidence and circumstances of disability. This chapter makes the case that the U.S. state's fragmented, shifting understanding of and approach to disability in the first half of the twentieth century both created and obscured rich records of the lived experience of disability. This chapter seeks to make sense of this phenomenon and move toward a methodology for navigating archives constructed in a period when ideas about and languages of disability were shifting rapidly and for locating disabled people's voices in a period when state interest in disability often grew out of impulses to contain, control, and limit disability and disabled people—impulses rooted in racialized, gendered, and class-based ideas about disability.

This chapter examines how the individual points, like those contained in Laura Curley's letter, might be used to develop a more nuanced picture of disabled people's lives. Historical circumstances frame what remains obscured—sometimes the documents themselves and much about the individual lives recorded therein. The chapter addresses the historical circumstances that shaped the archive of disability—its absences, challenges, and the particular kinds of documents produced and collected by the U.S. federal government in the first half of the twentieth century. From there, the chapter looks at three categories of these documents: documents associated with federal efforts to understand disability, documents connected with appeals for assistance—a category that reflected both the dearth of services and a continually changing landscape of aid across this period, and documents related to federal efforts to address disability. Finally, this chapter offers advice on how to navigate the particular set of challenges presented by these sources and archives as well as the challenges that extend to other times and places.

Laura Curley's 1938 letter to President Roosevelt is a single letter in a large collection of documents, which are part of a particularly large archive—the Franklin D. Roosevelt Library archives more than seventeen million pages of documents—in a massive system of archives—the U.S. National Archives contain more than thirteen billion pages of textual records. Yet, Curley's letter offers an instructive example as to how the tiny point or points contained in an individual document might illuminate elements of the lives and experiences of disabled Americans.[3] Framing her requests, Curley explained that the Jefferson School, part of the Oakland public school system, educated sixty physically disabled children in an annex on the school's grounds, circumstances that pointed to the segregation of disabled students whether by design or as a consequence of the inaccessibility of the school. Each day, the school's disabled pupils traveled to and from school by taxi, a detail that suggested the continued inaccessibility of public transportation and city streets. Her description of the facilities highlighted the annex's rest area with twenty-six beds, monitored by a matron at all times. With further study, this detail might help to make sense of medical responses to particular disabilities and the types of concerns that prevented access to public schools for many disabled children in this period. The matron's constant supervision of the space also raises the specter of fears that necessitated this presence. Were school administrators or parents worried about the frailty or morality of the disabled children? Did the concerns begin with what might happen to the children or with what they might do? Curley noted that polio had been "the greatest single cause of their difficulties." The request for a photograph of President Roosevelt revealed one particularly vibrant point of the image the letter allows one to construct. Curley wrote that the school displayed a photograph of the president but that it was "so thumbed by the youngsters" that the school hoped to replace the damaged photograph and frame the new one so that the "little finger prints could be washed off the glass." This oft-touched photograph of President Roosevelt raises interesting questions about how teachers, administrators, and various adults in the disabled students' lives presented Roosevelt and his disability to them. How might students have shaped or reframed those narratives? The numerous "little finger prints" suggest that the children paused at Roosevelt's portrait and felt compelled to touch the image. What might that oft-repeated pausing and touching suggest about what the physically disabled students saw in Roosevelt's portrait?[4]

Even Curley's questions point to clues about particular elements of lived experience of disability at the time of her writing. Her request for materials about the Warm Springs Foundation points to the complexities of polio care in the late 1930s. Roosevelt had founded the Warm Springs Foundation to transform the Georgia resort into what would become the nation's leading polio rehabilitation center in the mid-1920s. In 1935 the foundation announced that it would begin to use some of the money it raised in communities across the country to support treatment, and in the same year that Curley penned her letter, Roosevelt launched the National Foundation for Infantile Paralysis to seek a cure for polio and to provide treatment to individuals with polio.[5] Curley's request for more information about the Warm Springs Foundation may well have reflected the limited options individuals seeking rehabilitation faced—the dearth of rehabilitation facilities, the small number of beds in those facilities, and how the length and cost of treatment limited access to polio care, particularly before the National Foundation for Infantile Paralysis expanded access. The request may also have reflected the reputation of the Warm Springs facility, the need for funds for local rehabilitation efforts, or some combination of all of these factors.[6]

Curley shared that the staff had been discussing, "sort of in the stars," she confessed, the development of a summer camp that would serve the school's physically disabled children and perhaps even disabled children in San Francisco. She asked President Roosevelt if government land in the Sierras could be used for the camp and if the Civilian Conservation Corps (CCC) might assist by preparing the area for physically disabled campers. She also asked if the president knew of other similar camps that might help them to think about what might be necessary to develop such a program. Curley's questions about the availability of the CCC to help realize the Jefferson School staff's dream of a camp for physically disabled children suggests that perhaps she knew to some degree that a range of New Deal alphabet agencies were building or expanding hospitals, rehabilitation centers, schools, and other facilities for disabled people across the country.[7]

Standing alone Laura Curley's letter to President Roosevelt perhaps obscures as much as it reveals, but the document exists in a collection that contains boxes and boxes of documents that highlight absences, expose other points, and begin, when pieced together, to reveal the contours of histories that have been obscured. Curley's letter reflects, to some degree, two of the three categories of documents explored in this chapter. As an appeal for assistance, Curley sought information from the president, in part because the constantly shifting terrain of federal disability policy left it unclear which agency to contact and in part because of President Roosevelt's unique position as the founder of two prominent national disability-focused nonprofit organizations, though similar appeals would be directed at President Harry S. Truman throughout his presidency. The letter also gestures toward some of the major New Deal initiatives focused on disability. To be certain, the letter, and the existence of numerous letters written by disabled people, their families, and myriad officials representing a range of institutions and organizations, local, and state governments, all reflected a particular moment in U.S. history. Profound social and economic shifts, a changing and growing population, economic collapse, war, and waves of reform produced significant state growth in the United States in the early twentieth century. In the midst of that growth, disability and ability, alongside race and gender, continued to shape what historian and legal scholar Barbara Young Welke calls the "borders of belonging," or categories of privilege and exclusion embedded in American law.[8] These borders shaped the state's explosive growth throughout this period. Policy makers and reformers drew on disability to articulate ideas about worthiness for aid, fitness for citizenship and work, and the cost of war, industrialization, and urbanization. This attention to disability reflected two important realities. First, disability served, as historian Douglas C. Baynton has described it, "to justify inequality for disabled people themselves" as well as for other marginalized people groups. He argues that "the *concept* of disability has been used to justify discrimination against other groups by attributing disability to them."[9] Second, many of the significant social and economic changes of the late nineteenth and early twentieth centuries created living and working conditions that increased the prevalence of disability. "Unsafe and poisonous conditions, unguarded machinery, unregulated conditions," historians Gerald Markowitz and David Rosner argue, fashioned an economy in which "disease and disability were endemic in the American workplace" and in which industrial work in the early-twentieth-century United States "was often equated with the risks of warfare."[10] The rapid growth of cities, in particular growth in overcrowded and under-resourced tenement communities, shaped conditions rife with epidemic and chronic disease, both of which could cause disability. Even as improved sanitation helped to control the spread of some diseases, it also created the particular circumstances that made polio more likely to cause permanent physical disability. The First and Second World Wars shaped the number of disabled Americans and Americans' perceptions of disability.[11] Changing ideas about work and the workplace also contributed to growing concerns about disability and stigmatization of disabled people.[12]

This particular moment—marked by state growth, increasing concerns about disability, and growing numbers of disabled people—shaped the types of documents in the archive and how and where they appear. Growing numbers and concerns led the federal government to investigate disability and seek to understand the extent and character of the "problem" disability presented. These investigations often captured the experiences, and sometimes the voices, of disabled Americans. The profound and rapid changes of the period and shifting understandings of disability produced uneven and changing policy, with responsibilities often spread across numerous agencies, creating difficulties for disabled people and their families at the time and for scholars now as we seek to use scattered records to reconstruct facets of disabled people's lives and experiences. The circumstances of state interest, with its shifting sites and changing terms and aims, often obscures disability in U.S. federal archives. For example, Congress tasked the Children's Bureau with managing programs that addressed childhood disability. Yet, the Children's Bureau shared responsibility for disability prevention with the U.S. Public Health Service and worked with the Office of Education when it came to training disabled youth for work. During the New Deal, the Works Progress Administration assisted with and absorbed many aspects of the bureau's work related to childhood disability. Similarly, the Veterans Bureau administered veteran, but not civilian, rehabilitation until the program expired between the wars. The inadequacy of American health, welfare, and disability policies and the confusing and shifting structures that shaped existing programs gave rise to rich documentation of the lived experience of disability. The maze of local, state, and federal laws that constituted the American welfare state often prompted average citizens to petition the president, senators, or congressmen when they or their family members experienced disability. They aired their frustrations, sought aid, aimed to gain access to or learn about existing services, and hoped to influence policy. Finally, records of the various federal programs that sought to address disability also contain critical evidence of the lived experience of disability.

During the first half of the twentieth century, the federal government collected varied data about the incidence and prevalence of disability, the causes of disability, the institutions meant to serve disabled individuals, aid paid to disabled people, and pensions paid to disabled veterans, among other data points. In Bureau of Labor Statistics publications, the *Statistical Abstract of the United States*, U.S. Public Health Service records, and many other agencies' publications and records, researchers can locate these data and extrapolate from them the rough outline of Americans' experiences of disability. Beyond these statistical analyses, federal officials also sought a deeper, more nuanced understanding of experiences of and community responses to disability.

Representative Augustine Kelley (D-PA) led a two-year congressional investigation on disability. He argued that Congress faced "an astonishing lack of knowledge" on the problems that shaped unemployment among disabled Americans. Kelley asserted that Congress needed to study disability to gather the information necessary "to deal with the problem."[13] In 1944, the U.S. House of Representatives established the Subcommittee to Investigate Aid to the Physically Handicapped, a subcommittee of the Committee on Labor. The resolution called for "thorough studies and investigation of the extent and character of aid now given by the Federal, State, and local governments and private agencies to the physically handicapped." It directed the committee to study employment opportunities and "any necessary remedial legislation."[14] The investigation, conducted between August 1944 and June 1946, encompassed twenty-five hearings that considered a range of disability-related issues. It explored specific disabilities and disability broadly defined in specific cities, including New York City, Pittsburgh, Detroit, and Philadelphia. The hearings considered disability in the context of accidents, monopolies and advertising, maternal and child health, rural conditions, and drug addiction, among other topics. The subcommittee also held hearings on legislation advocated by the American Federation of the Physically Handicapped (AFPH). Over the course of two years, the subcommittee collected thousands of pages of testimony from disabled people, activists, labor leaders, employers, physicians, social workers, and government officials, piecing together a significant record of the difficulties disabled people confronted when seeking education, work, and health care as well as local, state, and federal responses.[15]

During World War II and the postwar era, disability activists, union leaders, professionals in medicine and rehabilitation, and bureaucrats fought to expand and define federal disability policy. They argued about the nature of the "problem" that disability presented and what would constitute an appropriate federal response. This struggle frequently played out in hearings before congressional committees, such as the hearings held during the House's two-year investigation; consequently, committee records contain carefully presented articulations of the positions of activists, a range of professionals, and federal officials. The Subcommittee to Investigate Aid to the Physically Handicapped itself represented the AFPH's first victory in Congress. AFPH President Paul Strachan told members that the committee offered disabled people an opportunity to "tell our own story," "from the depths of our personal experience with our afflictions and with the difficulties we have encountered in meeting the problems of economic life, and participating, if we could, on equal footing with the nonhandicapped."[16]

More than just a site of conflict between activists and bureaucrats and a record of the thoughts and ideas of employers and experts on disability, congressional hearings considering questions of disability policy also include letters from average citizens with disabilities, who as encouraged by Strachan sought to share their "own story." For example, upon hearing that the House was investigating artificial limbs, F. A. Tingley wrote to the subcommittee, complaining, "I am 58 years old and have been around the block at least, and I have never in all my life seen any industry or business where there was so much abuse as there is in the artificial limb business." He had worn "a below-the-knee" prosthetic leg for almost thirty years, and in that time, purchased eleven prostheses. He explained that he had been forced to travel to a "strange city" to purchase his limb. Once he arrived after a long train ride, he had difficulty finding the limb factory. He waited for days for service, having trouble finding a place to eat and sleep. Finally, a company official told him his leg would be shipped to him. When the leg arrived, well over a month later, he found that he could not "possibly wear it for 5 minutes." In the end, Tingley had no recourse to get his money back or a better-fitting limb.[17] These letters chronicle experiences with discrimination in education and employment, they describe living and working conditions of disabled Americans from across the nation, and they recount the difficulties many disabled Americans experienced when they sought aid, health care, and assistive devices. Significantly, these letters capture disabled Americans' attempts to educate policy makers with the wisdom of experience.

In September 1949, Mildred Scott, secretary of the AFPH, spoke to an organization of professional women about disability and the need for better disability policy. She told her audience about her own experiences, both as a disabled child and later as a disabled adult seeking employment. Scott asked the women to consider whether they knew where and how to receive services and how they would budget for services if a child or other family member became ill or developed a disability.[18] While Scott's audience of professional women might have had more resources than the average American, many Americans, regardless of access to resources, would have been forced to answer Scott's question in the negative. The reality that many Americans would not know how to access services or be able to pay for them helped to produce extensive records. These records capture everyday Americans' experiences when disabled or caring for a disabled loved one, seeking health care when options were often limited, searching for educational or work opportunities, and navigating the tangle of local, state, and federal laws that shaped community, state, and federal responses to disability. (One would need a ladder to photograph an organizational chart of federal bureaucracies that managed some element of federal disability policy in the post–World War II era.) Limited options, a lack of services, and confusion about the services that existed often prompted average citizens to write directly to the president when they, or their family members, experienced disability. Citizens with disabilities also wrote to congressmen and senators, expressing their disappointment, seeking assistance, and hoping to change policy. These two types of federal sources—direct correspondence with the president or members of Congress—represent a fertile field from which historians can develop a more complete picture of the myriad experiences of disability in the United States in this period.

Such communication appears in the federal archive in many places, depending on the recipient's response (for example, letters asking about particular federal programs were often referred to that program for a response, but in the case of presidential communication, at least, records about the original letter and response to it remain in that president's official file). Because of the volume and geographical reach of the letters, postcards, and telegrams received by Presidents Franklin D. Roosevelt and Harry S. Truman, and because some record remains of a wide range of communications, even if White House staffers forwarded the communication to someone else for response, this particular space in the federal archive documents a diverse range of experiences of disability.

Both the Roosevelt and Truman administrations maintained official files for correspondence from or about "physically handicapped" individuals or organizations of or benefiting them. In both cases, these official files are archived in the Roosevelt and Truman presidential libraries. Both presidents also kept personal files related to disability. Many disabled people and their family members wrote to President Roosevelt seeking aid or assistance in finding aid. For example, in September 1940, Katharine Grant Sterne, of Poughkeepsie, New York, appealed to the president after eight years of being unable to vote because of her disability. In this case, Roosevelt used his connections to have arrangements made for Sterne to begin voting.[19] Disabled Americans also wrote to Roosevelt about their experiences, expressed opinions about federal disability policy, shared photographs of their wheelchairs, and, like one writer, Lydia Dierks, expressed a sense of kinship because of their shared experiences of disability. In 1938, Dierks, of St. Paul, Minnesota, wrote, "Those of us, however, who are handicapped, particularly the polio victims, among whom I belong, feel rather close to and proud of our President."[20]

While the sense of connection that Dierks articulated prompted and framed many letters to President Franklin D. Roosevelt, Americans also sent countless letters to President Harry S. Truman about their experiences with disability. Because these letters might seem more unexpected, and because scholars have not examined these letters as fully as those received by Roosevelt from disabled Americans, this discussion focuses on a few examples from the Truman papers. These letters dealt with education, health care, and employment—all central elements in Truman's postwar vision of advancing economic security through policy—and are particularly revealing of the letter writers' everyday experiences of disability. The Truman administration referred most of the letters discussed below to the Federal Security Agency, which later became the Department of Health, Education, and Welfare, for action and/or reply.

Letters from parents of disabled children were particularly common among letters about education and health care. For example, in 1948, Mrs. Vurl

Thomas from Oklahoma appealed to President Truman for help in finding a school that would accept her nine-year-old, "mute" son. She explained that at least one school had promised to admit him, but after more than a year's wait, her son was still not enrolled in school.[21] The dearth of educational opportunities available to disabled children motivated numerous other parents to write to President Truman. Mrs. E. C. Rowland from Illinois penned a letter to the president in 1948, arguing that it was not enough that some sort of educational opportunities existed for disabled children in a state. She wrote that she had been forced to fight to get her daughter, who had paralysis and hearing loss, into school. The only school that would accept her, however, was far away from their home. That distance and the need to fight to gain access to even a faraway school were unacceptable conditions to Rowland.[22]

Both of these letters, and others like them, demonstrate that what was compulsory for some children was often denied to or difficult to obtain for disabled children. Letters in the official files on disability in the Roosevelt and Truman administrations show that parents had to sometimes take extraordinary steps to ensure that their disabled children received an education. And, as noted above, even when parents found a school, the school might be far from home, forcing separations of parents and children. Indeed, in 1937 the U.S. Office of Education estimated that of the approximately two million disabled children in the country only one in every ten benefited from a special education program.[23] These circumstances led many parents to appeal directly to the president of the United States. Taken together, these constituent letters—focused on the difficulties that parents faced in accessing educational opportunities for their disabled children—show how families experienced and navigated local- and state-level discrimination on a national scale. While these files do contain a reasonable number of letters from disabled children about their experiences in schools and rehabilitation facilities, many of the individual points of the larger image contained in these files reflect the experiences of parents and descriptions generated by school officials and community members. These records require that one constantly ask questions about the disabled children who lived the experiences being narrated for them and through others. What is obscured or misrepresented in each of the varied presentations? The letters from parents and school officials, when read alongside the letters from disabled children in these same files and memoirs found elsewhere, have the potential to expand what we know about lived experiences of disability and to map how certain elements of these lived experiences were minimized, amplified, distorted, or ignored.

Like the dearth of educational opportunities, difficulties in securing health care for disabled children led many family members to write to the president. In the spring of 1948, President Truman received a number of letters about a nineteen-year-old boy in Asheville, North Carolina, who had been injured and paralyzed in a fall. Doctors feared that if he did not receive special treatment and regain use of his hands and arms he would not live much longer.

The doctors in the area knew of only one organization that provided such treatment: the Veterans Administration (VA). When the young man's family and even his U.S. senator had failed to have him admitted to a VA facility, his family turned to President Truman. In this particular case, the family was willing and able to pay for the son's treatment but still lacked access to the needed treatments. Numerous parents, however, appealed to the president when they were unable to afford available medical care for their children.[24] For example, Norman Robert Ehret and his mother of Pennsylvania wrote to Truman in 1948, appealing for financial assistance so that Norman could receive treatment for cerebral palsy to enable him to walk and talk.[25]

Disabled adults also expressed frustrations about a lack of access to health care and prosthetics. In 1946, a man from Washington State sent a letter to the president, asking for his aid in securing prosthetic hooks after having both hands amputated. The man had been told that the government had claimed priority on all of the prosthetic hooks being made at the time. He appealed directly to the president because his prolonged wait for prosthetics prevented his rehabilitation and limited his ability to care for himself.[26]

American medicine improved dramatically between World War I and the end of World War II. In May 1945, the Technical Information Division of the Office of the Surgeon General of the U.S. Army reported that the improved survival rate of injured soldiers during World War II as compared to World War I meant "that already more than sixty thousand men have returned from this war who would have died but for the advances in military medicine since World War I."[27] Given these improvements, why did so many Americans with disabilities still find themselves unable to secure appropriate health-care services?

While the military, the VA, and veterans themselves put significant pressure on the medical establishment to improve treatments and build better prosthetics and assistive devices for disabled people, these changes took time to filter down to civilians. Many disabled people could not afford any form of assistive technology, much less the newest and best. Moreover, in the immediate postwar years, the economic chaos of reconversion and the return of millions of veterans—hundreds of thousands of whom now had disabilities—led to more than shortages of consumer goods. American health care, like the economy more broadly, had been transformed to support the war effort. Like the man who appealed to the president for help in securing prosthetic hooks in May 1946, Americans confronted war-related health-care disruptions into the early postwar years. For example, the wartime service of many American physicians created physician shortages in American communities. War needs and material shortages disrupted the production of prosthetics, braces, and other assistive devices, and efforts to prioritize the needs of disabled veterans further limited access to these devices for civilians.

While access to education and health care were tied up with American ideas about economic security, the opportunity to work also came to be central to postwar thinking about security. Employment discrimination, therefore, figured prominently in letters to the president from disabled Americans. For instance, John R. Wade of Washington, DC penned a letter to President Truman in October 1945. He wrote that disabled people wanted homes and to "make decent wages." Wade described in detail the difficulties that a disabled worker could face when employed by an able-bodied man. An able-bodied boss, he wrote, "expects [a handicapped person] to produce more work than an able-bodied person. If not, he will cut his wages or let him go." Despite these unfair expectations, Wade argued, employers often dismissed disabled applicants without real consideration, saying "'I'm sorry, no openings,'" while easing the sting by taking the applicants' information and asking "a hundred questions" but still throwing the disabled applicants' materials "in the trash can" once the applicant left.[28] Like Wade, George C. Nielson from New York wrote to the president in 1949 expressing his concern about the employment opportunities available to disabled people. Despite his college education and several years of experience in business, Nielson could not find employment because of a polio-related disability. He argued that employers were passing over qualified disabled people. Despite their service in industry during the war, disabled Americans, Nielson asserted, had been relegated to "the scrap heap" in the postwar era.[29]

In mid-twentieth-century America, work provided a means to secure health care and access to the benefits of the welfare state. Moreover, work also shaped one's ability to serve as a breadwinner, as John Wade put it, to have "a home and a wife."[30] For many Americans, work represented more than the security of state protections against old age and unemployment, access to health care, and ability to maintain a certain standard of living. Work was also bound up in ideas about masculinity and good citizenship. It is not surprising then that Wade connected his ability to have a "dandy" of a wife with his job.[31] Within the files of Presidents Roosevelt and Truman, historians can locate rich and detailed letters about Americans' experiences of and with disability. While any single letter in these files provides detail about an individual life and experience, collectively these letters illuminate an image much larger and clearer than just the individual points combined. These letters exist, and exist in the archive as they do, because of the particular circumstances of the United States at the time. That reality, however, might guide other historians who are searching for disability in various archives to seek similar moments and to consider to whom disabled people and their families might have directed appeals.

Federal efforts to address disability also created important records about experiences of disability. These documents, however, present the most significant challenges to historians of disability in that they often obscure the perspectives of disabled people. Many federal programs sought to mitigate, prevent, or cure disability and to train disabled people to better meet socially constructed ideas of fitness for citizenship. These documents constitute a vast record of changing state perceptions of disability, of the perspectives and actions of state officials and a range of professionals who administered programs and worked directly with disabled Americans, and of the programs in their broader context within the federal government. To be sure, disabled Americans' voices are captured here, too, but in many cases their experiences must be read "against the bias grain," as historian Marisa J. Fuentes suggests in her efforts to elucidate the experiences of enslaved women in eighteen-century Bridgetown, Barbados. Just as fabric gains more elasticity in this way, Fuentes approaches documents and archives from new directions, deeply contextualizing fragmentary evidence, shifting the perspective of a document's author to center the subject, and considering what might be learned from absences.[32] These approaches allow historians of disability to understand more about disabled people's lives, even from records produced by efforts to contain, reshape, and erase disabled people and disability.

In addition to establishing old-age pensions, unemployment insurance, and Aid to Dependent Children, the Social Security Act of 1935 included several programs that sought to address disability and grew out of an understanding of disability as a threat to economic security. The act extended public assistance to blind people living in poverty and increased appropriations for the vocational rehabilitation program, which aimed to provide educational and vocational assistance to prepare disabled people to enter or reenter the workforce. The idea that disability and ill health created significant economic insecurity shaped the state's investment in various public health programs, including funding for general public health work and Maternal and Child Health Services. The Social Security Act also initiated federal support for a number of programs that focused on "crippled" children—the vast majority of whom had orthopedic disabilities. The Social Security Act provided federal grants to states for recording information about the prevalence of childhood disability, locating disabled children, and extending health care to them, including medical, surgical, and rehabilitative care. It also provided funding to establish facilities and clinics for diagnosis and treatment. The U.S. Children's Bureau administered the program, Services for Crippled Children (SCC), and states developed and implemented plans, after approval by the Children's Bureau. By 1943, the federal government invested over $4.3 million in the program annually. That level of funding provided, for example, over 1.4 million days of hospital care in 1941. The program served more than one out of every three hundred American children by 1948, identifying, enumerating, and providing medical services to disabled children across the nation.[33]

The Children's Bureau noted that the purpose of the program was "for each child served . . . to attain for him the maximum physical restoration possible and to aid him in adjusting to life at home and in the neighborhood and in taking advantage of opportunities for education and vocational training." Additionally, the program aimed "to reduce the chances that children will be crippled" through medical visits and early diagnosis, treatment, and public health education. These efforts ranged from the promotion of cod-liver oil and exposure to sunlight to prevent rickets to funding for diagnosis and treatment during polio or meningitis epidemics.[34] State actors and reformers who led the charge for the SCC described the program as an investment in reducing dependency.

While records about the SCC provide direct documentation of state and medical perceptions of disability and its intersection with race, gender, class, and sexuality, they can also illuminate the lives of disabled children. For example, in November 1939, Dr. R. C. Hood, who directed the U.S. Children's Bureau Crippled Children's Division, recommended that a Louisville, Kentucky mother seeking suggestions for her four-year-old child who had "been diagnosed as a birth injury" consider a hospital in New Jersey or a specialist in Maryland. Hood wrote that "facilities for the treatment and care of children with this type of disability are extremely limited in the United States." Beyond the hospital and physician referenced in the letter, Hood noted that the director of the Crippled-Children Commission in the Kentucky State Department of Health might have other suggestions, though he admitted, "I do not know of any special institutions in Kentucky that are providing treatment for children suffering from birth injuries." Even this letter, written by the physician who directed Children's Bureau programs for disabled children, referring a mother to others, might allow us to refocus and center the disabled child. Without the mother's letter, we are left with just a few clues about this child's experience. The fact that at age four the child's mother was seeking treatment suggests that perhaps the family had only recently received this diagnosis, framed here as more of an identity than condition—the child was diagnosed "as a birth injury," not with a birth injury. The child's age and request for information raises questions about what had changed. Had the child received relatively little care, or had the child's disability only been noticed by the parents with development? Had the parents only recently learned of the SCC? Had they read or heard about new treatments? Two details emerge relatively clearly from this one letter. Given that the child's mother wrote to a federal agency in search of medical assistance, it seems highly unlikely that physicians had figured prominently in the child's life, or at least in a way that satisfied the parents. Given the Children's Bureau response, it would seem that, whether a physician in Maryland or New Jersey could help this particular child or not, other families in similar situations undoubtedly would have struggled to locate and afford distant treatment for their children and navigate the emotional consequences of forced separation during treatment that took place states away. The letter describes a child who had been assigned a medicalized identity and yet the care that identity seemed to call for was beyond reach.[35]

Throughout the first half of the twentieth century, the federal government documented disability and intervened in disabled people's lives in direct and indirect, large and small ways. New Deal public works programs built institutions to cure and treat, contain, educate, and rehabilitate disabled people. The federal government invested significant resources into public health initiatives aimed at preventing disability and into efforts to detect disability at the borders. From veterans' pensions to veteran and civilian rehabilitation, the SCC, aid to blind people living in poverty, and myriad other programs, the federal government monitored, interacted with, and served disabled people. The rich documentation of efforts to contain or mitigate disability, at times, can overwhelm the voices of disabled people who were the objects of these policies, but historians can still center disabled people with these sources by richly contextualizing the moments when we can access those voices and shifting the perspective when those voices are absent.

The particular historical context of the first half of the twentieth century and the particular structure of the U.S. state at that time shape the sources examined briefly in this chapter. For example, the confusion sparked by the shared system of federal and state responsibility for disabled citizens' welfare prompted many letters that disclosed and recorded disabled people's experiences. The confusing federal-state dynamics left many Americans without a sense of who could or would help them at the local or state level, so they turned to the federal government to find solutions to the problems that they confronted, sometimes appealing directly to the president. Moreover, citizens turned to the federal government for support when they believed that the states were failing at a given job, like educating disabled children. The New Deal no doubt heightened this tendency as the Great Depression and New Deal transformed citizens' expectations of the federal government. The confusion that prompted disabled people and their families to write to officials also shapes how and where these records appear in the archives. While the records about disability in the first half of the twentieth century in the United States are numerous, the historical context of their production has created a diffuse archive, with records spread across record groups and archival sites.

Despite the importance of this particular historical context in shaping many of these sources (and perhaps because of the importance of context), disability's presence in the modern U.S. federal archive offers lessons that transcend the moment. As a socially constructed identity, disability is a fluid concept. Locating it in any archive requires an understanding of the particular context. What constituted disability at that moment? Who defined disability? What words described it? For example, within Works Progress Administration records, some records about disabled people's experiences appear in a file labeled "unemployables," a label shaped by changing ideas about work and bodies and the economic circumstances of the Great Depression. Understanding what shaped disability, who defined it, how people talked about it, when and in what circumstances it was considered a "problem," and who responded to this problem help to provide direction when disability was ubiquitous and yet is often absent from finding aids.

In the case of how the modern U.S. state captured the experiences of disabled Americans, a massive collection of sources spread across National Archives sites show, often in very personal terms, how individuals experienced state and national disability policies as well as how individuals, families, and sometimes even communities experienced disability itself. So much remains obscured about disabled people's experiences in this period, yet many points that would illuminate a national portrait of the experiences of disability are captured in a variety of federal records. Piecing together that portrait will allow us to better center disability histories and disabled Americans who have often been simultaneously highly visible, as the objects of policy and concern, and invisible, as Americans whose individual stories are central to understanding United States history.

Notes

1. Laura Curley to Franklin D. Roosevelt (hereafter FDR), September 19, 1938, Folder OF 836 Physically Handicapped Persons, 1938, Official File (hereafter OF) 836, Box 2, Franklin D. Roosevelt Papers, Franklin D. Roosevelt Presidential Library, Hyde Park, NY (hereafter Roosevelt Papers).

2. See, for example, Rachel Louise Moran, *Governing Bodies: American Politics and the Shaping of the Modern Physique* (Philadelphia: University of Pennsylvania Press, 2018); Molly Ladd-Taylor, *Fixing the Poor: Eugenic Sterilization and Child Welfare in the Twentieth Century* (Baltimore: Johns Hopkins University Press, 2017); Sarah Rose, *No Right to Be Idle: The Invention of Disability, 1840s–1930s* (Chapel Hill: University of North Carolina Press, 2017); Douglas C. Baynton, *Defectives in the Land: Disability and Immigration in the Age of Eugenics* (Chicago: University of Chicago Press, 2016); Audra Jennings, *Out of the Horrors of War: Disability Politics in World War II America* (Philadelphia: University of Pennsylvania Press, 2016); Thomas C. Leonard, *Illiberal Reformers: Race, Eugenics and American Economics in the Progressive Era* (Princeton: Princeton University Press, 2016); Beth Linker, *War's Waste: Rehabilitation in World War I America* (Chicago: University of Chicago Press, 2011); Barbara Young Welke, *Law and the Borders of Belonging in the Long Nineteenth Century United States* (Cambridge: Cambridge University Press, 2010); and John Fabian Witt, *The Accidental Republic: Crippled Workingmen, Destitute Widows, and the Remaking of American Law* (Cambridge: Harvard University Press, 2004).

3. The U.S. National Archives and Records Administration manages over forty-five locations, including regional sites and presidential libraries. "About the National Archives of the United States," National Archives, archives.gov/publications/general-info-leaflets/1-about-archives.html (accessed August 31, 2022); and "Plan a Research Visit," Franklin D. Roosevelt Presidential Library and Museum, fdrlibrary.org/research-visit (accessed August 31, 2022).

4. Curley to FDR, September 19, 1938, Folder OF 836 Physically Handicapped Persons, 1938, OF 836, Box 2, Roosevelt Papers. For a discussion of material culture and disability history, see Katherine Ott, "Disability Things: Material Culture and American Disability History, 1700–2010," 119–35, in *Disability Histories*, eds. Susan Burch and Michael Rembis (Urbana: University of Illinois Press, 2014).

5. For more on polio, Warm Springs, and Roosevelt, see, for example, David M. Oshinsky, *Polio: An American Story* (New York: Oxford University Press, 2005); Daniel J. Wilson, *Living with Polio: The Epidemic and Its Survivors* (Chicago: University of Chicago Press, 2005); and Daniel J. Wilson, "Experiencing Polio in the Era of FDR," *Bulletin of the History of Medicine* 72 (Fall 1998), 464–95.

6. Curley to FDR, September 19, 1938, Folder OF 836 Physically Handicapped Persons, 1938, OF 836, Box 2, Roosevelt Papers.

7. Curley to FDR, September 19, 1938, Folder OF 836 Physically Handicapped Persons, 1938, OF 836, Box 2, Roosevelt Papers.

8. See Welke, *Law and the Borders of Belonging in the Long Nineteenth Century United States.*

9. Douglas C. Baynton, "Disability and the Justification of Inequality in American History," in *The New Disability History*, eds. Paul K. Longmore and Lauri Umansky (New York: New York University Press, 2001), 33.

10. Gerald Markowitz and David Rosner, "Death and Disease in the House of Labor," *Labor History* 30, no. 1 (1989), 115–16.

11. See Linker, *War's Waste* for a discussion of World War I, and Jennings, *Out of the Horrors of War* for a discussion of World War II.

12. See, in particular, Rose, *No Right to Be Idle*, and Baynton, *Defectives in the Land.*

13. Congress, House, Debate over H. R. 230, 78th Cong., 2nd sess., *Congressional Record* 90, pt. 5 (June 20, 1944), 6324–28.

14. Congress, House, Debate over H. R. 230, 78th Cong., 2nd sess., *Congressional Record* 90, pt. 5 (June 20, 1944), 6324–28.

15. Congress, House, Committee on Labor, Subcommittee to Investigate Aid to the Physically Handicapped/Subcommittee on Aid to the Physically Handicapped, *Hearings*, Parts 1–25, 78th–79th Congresses (Washington, DC: Government Printing Office, 1945–46). For a more in-depth history of the committee, see Jennings, *Out of the Horrors of War.*

16. Congress, House, Extension of Remarks of Representative Augustine B. Kelley of Pennsylvania, 78th Cong., 2nd sess., *Congressional Record* 90, pt. 11 (September 12, 1944), A3980; and "Lauds American Federation of Handicapped," *Del Rio News Herald* (Del Rio, TX), August 22, 1944, 4.

17. Congress, House, Committee on Labor, Subcommittee to Investigate Aid to the Physically Handicapped, *Hearings*, Part 15, Amputees, 79th Cong., 1st sess. (Washington, DC: Government Printing Office, 1945), 1791.

18. Congress, House, Representative Kelley of Pennsylvania paying tribute to Mildred Scott, 81st Cong., 1st sess., *Congressional Record* 95, pt. 16 (October 11, 1949), A6220–A6222.

19. Memorandum (Regarding September 17, 1940 letter from Katharine Grant Sterne to Franklin D. Roosevelt), Folder OF 836 Physically Handicapped Persons, 1940, OF 836, Box 2, Roosevelt Papers.

20. Lydia Dierks to FDR, November 4, 1938, Folder OF 836 Physically Handicapped Persons, 1938, OF 836, Box 2, Roosevelt Papers. For more analysis of letters written to Roosevelt from people with polio-related disabilities, see Wilson, "Experiencing Polio in the Era of FDR," 464–95.

21. Mrs. Vurl Thomas to Harry S. Truman (hereafter HST), March 25, 1948, Folder 443 (1948–Mar. 1949), OF 443, Box 1289, Harry S. Truman Papers, Harry S. Truman Presidential Library, Independence, Missouri (hereafter Truman Papers).

22. Mrs. E. C. Rowland to HST, December 31, 1948, Folder 443 (1948–Mar. 1949), OF 443, Box 1289, Truman Papers.

23. William J. Ellis, "The Handicapped Child," *Annuals of the American Academy of Political and Social Science* 212 (November 1940), 143.

24. A series of memorandums and letters about the Langston case, dating from April 26 to May 11, 1948, Folder 443 (1948–Mar. 1949), OF 443, Box 1289, Truman Papers.

25. Norman Robert Ehret to HST, June 7, 1948, Folder 443 (1948–Mar. 1949), OF 443, Truman Papers.

26. Memorandum to Civilian Production Administration, May 9, 1946, Folder 443 (1945–47), OF 443, Box 1289, Truman Papers.

27. Technical Information Division, Office of the Surgeon General, U.S. Army, "The Physically Disabled," *Annals of the American Academy of Political and Social Science* 239 (May 1945), 10.

28. John R. Wade to HST, October 1, 1945, Folder 443 (1945–47), OF 443, Box 1289, Truman Papers.

29. George C. Nielson to HST, August 31, 1949, Folder 443 (Apr.–Nov. 1949), OF 443, Box 1290, Truman Papers.

30. John R. Wade to HST, October 1, 1945, Folder 443 (1945–47), OF 443, Box 1289, Truman Papers.

31. John R. Wade to HST, October 1, 1945, Folder 443 (1945–47), OF 443, Box 1289, Truman Papers.

32. See Marisa J. Fuentes, *Dispossessed Lives: Enslaved Women, Violence, and the Archive* (Philadelphia: University of Pennsylvania, 2016).

33. Katherine B. Oettinger, "Title V of the Social Security Act: What It Has Meant to the Children," *Social Security Bulletin* 23 (August 1960), 39–50; U.S. Children's Bureau, *Facts About Crippled Children, 1943* (Washington, DC: Government Printing Office, 1943); and U.S. Children's Bureau, *Services for Crippled Children Under the Social Security Act: Development of a Program, 1936–39* (Washington, DC: Government Printing Office, 1941).

34. Children's Bureau, *Facts About Crippled Children, 1943.*

35. R. C. Hood to Mrs. John Davin, November 10, 1939, Folder 4-15-1-3-1 Birth Injuries (Spastic Paralysis), Central Files, 1937–40, U.S. Children's Bureau, Box 788, Record Group 102, National Archives at College Park, Maryland.

CHAPTER 7

There Are No Invalids in the Archive

Hidden Sources and Ideological Obscurations in the History of International Blind Activism

MARIA CRISTINA GALMARINI

A few years ago, I set out to reconstruct the untold history of the World Council for the Welfare of the Blind. Since this agency had been one of the few post–WWII international organizations of disability advocacy to include members from both Cold War blocs, I thought that the best way to recover its story was a transnational approach grounded in archival research in multiple countries. I believed this methodology would enable me to write a complete and multisided narrative of the global blind movement, one that accounted for the perspectives of diverse actors not only across the political divide of the time but also within the category of "the blind" itself. What I discovered, however, was that both the Western and the Eastern archives were marked by erasures, which—albeit different in nature—shared deep ideological roots and ultimately led to emphasize only certain (ableist) dimensions of blindness and certain (politically inflected) notions of blind activism.[1]

In the West, the World Council's members had performed erasures that pertained to the very existence of this agency and were triggered by the end of the Cold War. From the mid-1960s until its dissolution in 1984 and merger with the International Federation of the Blind (IFB) to form the World Blind Union (WBU), the World Council had not only included socialist countries among its members but also elected Eastern activists in prominent positions of leadership and celebrated the socialist, state-centered approach to disability activism. But after 1989/1991, this aspect of its history appeared if not outright problematic then certainly immaterial to the present and the future. The World Council came to represent a model of activism that was considered outdated and irrelevant to contemporary developments in disability advocacy, which by the 1990s prioritized liberal ideas of equality and civil rights over socialist emphasis on welfare and blind people's employability. While a large bulk of sources about the (socialist-free) IFB had been collected in the Jacobus tenBroek fund at the National Federation of the Blind, the WBU did not make any effort to preserve the historical memory of its other, now almost illegitimate predecessor, that is, the World Council.[2] The few surviving records about it are still scattered across multiple countries, and no one seems interested in locating them and bringing them together in one place. In the end, the political atmosphere of the early 1990s, which celebrated the correctness of long-standing anticommunist political stances and promoted jubilation for (neo)liberal democracy's victory over communism, had unwittingly led to blind activists' distancing from the socialist-friendly World Council, and, as we know from many other fields of human activity, the victors tend to write the history.[3]

In Russia and Eastern Europe, instead, the centralized nature of the socialist countries' national blind organizations had allowed for the creation and preservation of fuller archives than in the West. Specifically, the collections of the All-Russian Union of the Blind (*Vserossiiskoe Obshchestvo Slepykh*, or VOS) and the East German Union of the Blind and Low-Sighted (*Blinden- und Sehschwachen-Verband*, or BSV) contain myriad primary sources on these agencies' involvement in the World Council. Yet, their archives suffer from erasures too. Since Eastern blind activists followed their state authorities in regarding international campaigns as a means to show socialist superiority in disability welfare, they carefully omitted from their record any evidence that might have portrayed the socialist systems, themselves as activists, and their very blind constituency in nontriumphant ways. A discourse of achievement and success marked the thousands of pages I read, but no failures, difficulties, or problems ever appeared in them. There was no trace in these archives of ordinary blind people who had failed to rehabilitate, had not conformed to the image of model blind persons that the activists hoped to project, or had protested the lack of real inclusion in their societies. Paraphrasing the title of Valerii Fefelov's memoirs about his life as a mobility-impaired man in the Soviet Union, one might say that "there are no invalids" in the Eastern archives.[4] They have all been purged, leaving on display only the "able disabled" and the "supercrips."[5]

The Eastern and Western archives thus present a two-edged pruning: while Western sources nearly erase the World Council altogether as an agency that appreciated socialist approaches, Eastern ones obfuscate unrehabilitated blind people and their unresolved problems. The effect has been a shrinking of the imaginary of disability politics and its historical growth. On one hand, historiography grounded in Western sources has emphasized a narrative in which blind activists felt inspired by the American civil rights movement, learned from it how to speak in the language of political opposition to discriminatory laws, and finally achieved justice in 1990 with the issuance of the Americans with Disabilities Act (ADA). In this storyline, the only legitimate disability activists were those who joined grassroots social movements and engaged in political fights for blind people's rights.[6] On the other hand, while no scholarly work has been so far written on the international blind movement that is based in the Eastern archives, memoirs literature about socialist blind activism either dismisses the archival record as mere propaganda or falls into the trap of celebratory chronicles that recite only tales of success and glory.[7] The latter approach is especially dangerous: by reproducing a documentary record that conceals blind people's setbacks in rising above their disability, this approach ultimately promotes an ableist conceptualization of blindness as a personal tragedy and a social burden that must be overcome by the individual with the help of the state. Yet, discounting the socialist archives as just repositories of lies is no solution either, because this method does not critically address why "supercrips" were showcased and "invalids" made invisible under socialism.

This chapter interweaves a reconstruction of the World Council's history with the story of my own research and methodological struggle to uncover it. The frustration of selective sources and ableist repositories has been identified by other disability scholars too. Gracen Mikus Brilmyer, in particular, has drawn attention to both disability silences in the archives and "the prevalence of . . . stereotypes, tropes, and limited perspectives" of disability descriptions in legal and medical records. Further, Brilmyer has emphasized the "affective impacts" of "witnessing such representations (or lack thereof)" on disabled researchers themselves.[8] Others have denounced the inaccessibility of disability archives. As Susan Burch and Michael Rembis write in their introduction to the volume *Disability Histories*:

> Bureaucratic policies that restrict [] access to the sources most readily associated with disability . . . hamper [] efforts to study disability and disabled people in history. Many libraries, archives, and special collections [are still] physically and financially inaccessible to disabled and nondisabled researchers.[9]

Drawing on this literature as well as other, non–disability-related theoretical works in archival studies, here I trace the lineage of erasures and distortions contingent on specific institutions and places during the Cold War.[10] I also encourage disability historians to harness the generative power of what is *not* in the archives or, in Brilmyer's words, "what archives sometimes cannot give us."[11] When we deal—as I do in this chapter—with activists' archives, recognize these individuals as purposeful creators of their own histories, focus on the gaps left by their erasures, and identify the ideological principles by which they have selected what to keep and what to exclude, we take the first steps toward the writing of a more nuanced history of the international blind movement. We see not only that political ideologies structure narratives of disability in the archives but also that disabled people themselves have the power to control these narratives. Most importantly, perhaps, we begin to perform a more critical analysis of blindness under socialism and juxtapose its construction and experience with those of other disability groups.[12] Instead of simply delegitimizing socialist actors and the records they left, this history helps scholars assess both the positive contributions and the ableist limitations of the socialist approach to disability.

The World Council for the Welfare of the Blind: A Brief History

First conceived during an International Conference of Workers for the Blind held in August 1949 in Oxford (England), the World Council was officially born at the Founding General Assembly of July 1951 in Paris. It presented itself as an agency working for the welfare of the blind and the prevention of blindness through international collaborations. In particular, following practices of international standard-setting pursued in the interwar period by the League of Nations' Health Organization and the International Labor Office, the organization's founders focused on the issue of minimum living standards for blind people. They understood that their real power was purely consultative but hoped that the use of international forums and campaigns would bring blindness to the attention of single governments as a problem of national policy and facilitate the adoption of uniform standards in all countries.[13]

Its original membership system would later expose the World Council to sharp criticism, because it led to a higher number of sighted members than visually impaired. Indeed, at the head of the World Council was an executive committee composed of around twenty-five to thirty representatives, who could be nominated not only by national unions *of* the blind, but also by any type of relief institutions *for* the blind. In addition, honorary members were included in the executive committee as persons (either sighted or blind) who had rendered outstanding service in blind welfare, while associate members were admitted based on donations.[14] Clearly, this system reflected a logic of tutelage of the sighted over the blind. Yet, in the aftermath of a devastating war, it was embraced by several European activists who wished to gain American philanthropic support and explicitly called for a "Marshall Plan" for the blind of postwar Europe.[15]

In line with these aspirations, in its first decade of existence the World Council saw the United States and Britain share responsibility for the world's blind. For instance, the new international agency had its headquarters in the offices of the American Foundation for Overseas Blind in Paris and received substantial funding from the United States, but it was also dependent on the financial support of two British groups—the Royal National Institute for the Blind and the St. Dunstan's Institute.[16] In terms of personnel too, North America and Great Britain constituted the World Council's backbone: the Canadian colonel Edwin Albert Baker, who had been blinded by a sniper's bullet in 1915 while fighting in Belgium and offered rehabilitation at St. Dunstan's, was elected as the organization's first president, while the British-born but U.S.-naturalized Eric T. Boulter was chosen as its first general secretary.[17]

Boulter is a particularly interesting figure, standing at the center of both the World Council's Anglo-American origins and its later transformation into a truly global organization of blind advocacy. He was a blind veteran like Baker, but belonged to a younger generation of disabled ex-servicemen, those who had been injured during the Second World War. After losing his sight in Normandy, Boulter went to the United States to receive medical care and, upon recovery, was invited to work at the American Foundation for Overseas Blind. His World Council's career was impressive: he first served as general secretary for eight years (1951–59); then he was elected as deputy president and finally as president. While holding these positions, he also continued to work for the American Foundation for Overseas Blind and indeed represented it on the World Council's executive committee. In 1969, Boulter retired and returned to England, but he continued to have an impact on the agency's activities as honorary life member and liaison with the United Nations and UNICEF. It was largely thanks to his efforts that the socialist countries of Eastern Europe slowly joined the World Council: besides Yugoslavia, which had been among the original members, Poland entered the organization at the end of 1956; Czechoslovakia and Hungary became members in 1959 and 1962; while the German Democratic Republic and the Soviet Union joined the group in 1967 and Bulgaria in 1968.[18]

Eastern Europe's entry, at the height of the Cold War, into a disability organization originally founded by Western actors as a type of "Marshall Plan" is one of those surprising historical processes that pique scholars' curiosity. Running counter to common narratives about both Cold War international organizations and the role of disabled people in them, the World Council's Eastern expansion raises important questions about East-West collaboration during the Cold War and the ways in which socialist activists might have contributed to the growth of the international blind movement.[19] Indeed, it was precisely this unexpected story of collaborations and encounters that had initially triggered my interest in the World Council and motivated me to go on a transnational quest for its historical records. This search, as shown in the following sections, turned out to be rather complicated and frustrating, but, in the end, it was at least as revealing as the content of the archive itself.

Searching for a Vanishing Archive

Embarking on a search for the World Council's archive, my point of departure was the World Blind Union (WBU), the international agency of blind advocacy that, according to its own website, had been "formed in 1984 through the Union of the International Federation of the Blind (IFB) and the World Council for the Welfare of the Blind (WCWB)."[20] WBU's then CEO, Penny Hartin, told me that the organization's office in Toronto had not kept any records pertaining to the World Council's history.[21] However, she shared with me the contacts of some activists who might know more or mobilize their networks of colleagues and friends to assist me in finding out. It was in this manner that Rodolfo Cattani (Italy), Pedro Zurita (Spain), Fred Schroeder (USA), Mokrane Boussaïd (France), and many others became my accomplices. Through them, I identified three repositories that promised to include primary sources about the World Council: the UNESCO archive in Paris, the American Foundation for the Blind Helen Keller Archive at the American Printing House for the Blind in Louisville (Kentucky), and the private archive of the European Blind Union (EBU) in Paris. Unfortunately, as I discovered when I visited them, these collections not only held less than what I hoped to find but (ironically) were also quite difficult to access.

UNESCO had never been the official repository of the World Council's documents and only includes some administrative files about it because the World Council used to have category B consultative status with it. These files—about one inch in a folder covering the period 1951–77 and two and a half inches in two other folders from the post-1971 period—provided me with useful nuts-and-bolts information, but not much to clarify the World Council's role in the development of blind advocacy. The AFB Helen Keller Archive in Louisville, instead, holds multiple boxes of primary sources pertaining to the American Foundation for Overseas Blind and Eric Boulter. However, when I perused them in spring 2021, they were still badly organized and not conducive to effective research. Finally, EBU's office on Rue Gager-Gabillot in Paris is the depository of some records about the World Council's European Regional Committee (ERC). Originally shipped to Paris from Berlin, where the ERC's Secretariat was located until 1984, these documents thinned out throughout the 1990s and 2000s as EBU's offices changed location multiple times. Now, the records have turned into a set of around ten folders that occupy one shelf of a closet, a small private archive strictly guarded by EBU staff members. If a scholar wants to study it, they need to sign legal paperwork concerning their use of the materials, give up their computers, and take notes by hand on paper provided by EBU employees. No photocopying or scanning is allowed.

More than providing the proverbial smoking guns of Cold War blind activism, these archives told me stories of documents that had been disposed of, shipped around the world, and simply gone missing. For instance, I discovered that Eric Boulter had accumulated files pertaining to the World Council in his New York office since the very foundation of this institution in 1951. When in January 1970 he retired and decided to move back to his native Britain, Boulter went through all his files and prepared "four cartons, each weighing approximately 40 pounds," to be sent the World Council's office in Paris by sea parcel. He also put together a "small shipment of files to be contained in one box weighing approximately 9 pounds" and sent it to the new World Council president, the Swede Charles Hedkvist. These materials included not only records about the World Council's General Secretariat, but also about other disability organizations such as the Conference of World Organizations Interested in the Handicapped and the International Council of Educators of Blind Youth. They also comprised the proceedings of a conference on rehabilitation arranged by the World Veterans Federation, the reports of an African conference on blind people's welfare, a set of UNESCO's resolutions, sources on the World Council's General Assemblies of 1954, 1959, and 1964, and issues of the organization's *Newsletter* from 1956 to 1961. Finally, the shipments to Paris and Stockholm contained statics, miscellaneous reports, short and long memos, correspondence about the World Council's foundation, the registration of its Paris office with French authorities, and its relations with the United Nations. What Boulter retained in New York, at the headquarters of the American Foundation for the Blind, were only records of membership fees and other transactions related to the World Council's bank account in the United States.[22] While these financial documents made their way into the Louisville archive, the papers sent to Paris have gone irretrievably lost. Lack of time and financial resources hindered my ability to track the documents shipped to Charles Hedkvist in Stockholm.

Certainly, inadequate storage facilities and the rotating nature of the positions of president and general secretary are significant reasons why only vanishingly few documents have survived about the World Council and are scattered around the world. However, this organization's archives in the West are not simply fragmented, but also purposefully unbalanced in what they include. Throughout the 1990s, their creators (who often were themselves blind activists) made specific choices in their purges of nonessential records, letting the political zeitgeist of the present in which they lived drive the selection of what past to preserve. To them, the World Council's advocacy model appeared both unfashionable in its insistence on state-supported welfare and problematic in its admiration of socialist blind organizations. This selectiveness—and its ideological underpinnings—was clear when I turned to the Russian and East German archival collections and juxtaposed the Western erasures to the lengthy paper trail left by the East.

What the Eastern Archives Reveal . . .

The historical records of the All-Russian Society of the Blind (VOS), which for the period between 1923 and 1969 are preserved in the State Archive of the Russian Federation in Moscow, contain abundant information on the World Council. This includes not only evidence of Soviet interactions with Western activists but also rich materials on the history of the World Council itself. Primary sources become somehow less bountiful for the period after 1969. This was the time when VOS began to keep its own archive on the top floor of its Central Administration building on Novaia Ploshchad'. Here, inclement weather conditions damaged the documents and caused the loss of much material. In addition, when Boris Zimin wrote his memoirs of VOS's international work, he took out of the archive entire folders. Nobody at VOS could tell me whether he saved the archive in his own home or threw everything away after having created his own historical narrative.

Fortunately, the gaps in VOS's archive can be filled by consulting the records of the East German Union of the Blind and Low-Sighted (BSV) held at the German Central Library for the Blind in Leipzig. Because this association's president, Helmut Pielasch, was involved in multiple international initiatives (as the World Council's deputy president, general secretary of its European branch, and president of the International Blind Sports Association), BSV's collection has thousands of pages of meeting transcripts and provides a fuller record of decision-making documents than any other blind organization I have researched. Walking into the storage room where BSV's archive is located and looking at the stacks of well-organized folders, I was able to find vast documentation on the World Council.

Together, the sources in Moscow and Leipzig helped me find an answer to the question that had originally triggered my interest, namely why the socialist blind unions had been integrated in the World Council and elevated to leadership positions within it. As I discovered, expansion to the East was related to two important changes in the World Council of the late 1950s and early 1960s: the first was a growing displeasure among Western blind activists with the presence of too many sighted experts and philanthropists within their organization; the second was the emergence of two competing approaches to this problem, each entailing a completely different attitude toward the socialist model of blind-led, but state-supported disability advocacy.

The first approach suggested breaking away from philanthropy by leaving traditional organizations *for* the blind and founding completely new agencies *of* the blind. In the United States, this idea was advanced with particular strength by Jacobus tenBroek, a blind professor of political science at the University of California, Berkeley, who in 1940 had founded the National Federation of the Blind in antagonism to the American Foundation for the Blind. He claimed that the World Council "was not the way to a progressive future for the blind," but rather an agency that would "simply further paternalism."[23] His views were shared by several nonsighted activists from developing countries, who felt that participation in international advocacy was denied to them by the strong service organizations that dominated the World Council.[24] In 1969, this group of dissenting activists left the World Council and founded the International Federation of the Blind (IFB). Crucially, they barred the Soviet Union and Eastern Europe from participation in their new organization.[25] According to the Italian Rodolfo Cattani, this exclusion was "because they did not consider them to be democratic" and, in line with the anticommunism prevalent in U.S. public culture at the time, could not accept agencies in the IFB that were supported and financed by the state.[26]

The second approach, instead, proposed to solve the issue of sighted leadership over the affairs of the blind precisely by involving the socialist camp more closely in the institutions of international blind advocacy. The Soviet and East European unions, as the argument went, would reform the World Council from within through their principled rejection of philanthropy and their support for blind self-determination. For instance, the Belgian blind advocate and Esperantist Achille Dyckmans believed that VOS was a model of genuine blind self-advocacy. In his opinion, the "path" undertaken by the Russians should be followed by all blind activists of the world regardless of the political "vision" that they espoused and the location in which this vision was implemented.[27] Agreeing with Dyckmans, World Council members such as the U.S.-based Eric Boulter, the Danish Hans Cai Seierup, the British John Colligan and John Jarvis, and the Swedish Charles Hedkvist articulated admiration not only for VOS's prioritization of blind people's agency, but also more broadly for the Soviet approach to social legislation, pensioning, and the employment of nonsighted people in the industrial economy. In the early 1960s, when the Cold War became hot over the issue of divided Berlin and the Cuban missile crisis, these men pursued collaboration strategies that ultimately brought about the socialist bloc's full integration in the World Council, the election of Bulgarian, Russian, and East German representatives in its executive committee, and the appointment of VOS's chairman Zimin as its president for the period 1974–79.

The World Council of the 1970s thus emerged as an international institution that recognized the legitimacy of the socialist blind unions and celebrated their leaders as embodiments of progress in disability advocacy. Although some Western activists disagreed with specific features of the socialist policies—especially blind children's segregated education in special schools and adults' employment in separate specialized workshops—they neither contested their Eastern colleagues' genuine commitment nor dismissed their experience in struggling for blind people's equality. In fact, activists from the United States and Northern Europe welcomed socialist input in debating new mainstreaming trends and notions of accessibility. As the Swiss Ami Mermod argued, the socialist model "can help to facilitate employment, to stimulate the sense of responsibility of managers and directors as well as to make our companions happy in their field of activity and their employers satisfied with their production."[28] Agreeing with Mermod, the chairman of the World Council's Committee on Professional and Urban Employment, the West German Horst Geißler, asked VOS to send one of its representatives to take part in the work of this group. As he explained in a letter to Zimin, "thanks to your rich experience, you could provide great help."[29]

At that time, disabled people in North America and Western Europe were chronically underemployed and their status as "workers" was often contested, especially in the face of technological advancements. According to the Italian activist Giuseppe Fucà, only around 15 to 20 percent of the blind were integrated in the national economy of the most technologically advanced parts of the world.[30] The Scandinavian countries reported that around 11 percent of their blind citizens had a job.[31] In Britain and Luxembourg respectively 12 and 10 percent of the total blind population was calculated to be gainfully employed in the late 1960s, while statistics compiled by the American Foundation for the Blind estimated that "less than a quarter of blind adults and no more than 10 percent of all blind persons" were employed.[32] With these numbers, Western activists addressed questions about effective job placement that were at the core of how they defined progress in disability advocacy. Regardless of their geographic positions and political inclinations, most of them believed that it was by combating perceptions of people with disabilities as unproductive citizens and nonworkers that they could challenge the disability stigma—a notion that in turn derived from early-twentieth-century constructions of the ability to work as a marker of health, vitality, and morality. Creating employment opportunities was thus imagined to be one of the key roles of any blind advocacy movement, and Western activists took Soviet declarations to have solved the problem of blind people's employment very seriously.[33]

This situation, however, changed in the mid-1980s due to a combination of factors.

First, Mikhail Gorbachev's perestroika in the Soviet Union unleashed a wave of political and socioeconomic crises that affected all East European countries and changed the configuration in which their blind activists operated. It became increasingly difficult for them not only to travel abroad to meet their Western colleagues, but also to host international conferences at home. For instance, a congress on blind people's social rights had been planned to take place in Moscow in September 1987, but it was moved to Paris "owing to unforeseen events."[34] Although the socialist activists remained members of the European Blind Union (EBU), their international commitment dwindled, and their attention shifted to domestic problems. Second, the growth of the European Economic Community (EEC) made collaboration increasingly difficult between the Eastern and Western members of EBU. Indeed, the EEC began to promote programs whose impulse was to harmonize disability policies among those European countries that were supposed to become integrated, but these programs worked to the disadvantage of the non-EEC members of the European continent.[35]

Finally, in 1989, the collapse of Eastern Europe's communist governments added to the crises generated by perestroika and the hierarchies created by the EEC, and gave the final blow to socialist activists' engagement in the international blind movement. While not "the end of history"—in Francis Fukuyama's words—the end of power blocs competition and the supposed final victory of capitalism strongly contributed to devaluing the experiences and perspectives of people such as Zimin and Pielasch.[36] Following North American trends, Western experts and NGOs now grounded disability advocacy in the civil rights approach exemplified by the ADA. They emphasized (neo)liberal legality in the field of labor, the reduction of welfare dependence, and the priority of individual political rights over collective economic ones.[37] The adoption of an independent-organization model became vital as the international community gave the palm of real disability advocacy only to those activists who were involved in human rights organizations and worked outside political parties and state agencies.[38] Suddenly, the socialist paradigm of disability activism ceased being a viable option. The EBU's Berlin-based Secretariat was replaced by a "permanent office" in Paris, where a new generation of leaders carried out "new executive tasks," and where the European states with "stronger economies" could provide advice and financial assistance to the others.[39] The former socialist countries were out of the "Common House of Europe" and, to enter it, had to adapt to its rules, including those on disability-related matters.[40]

It was in the wake of these changes that the staff of the new permanent office of EBU in Paris and the WBU's headquarters in Toronto selected which historical records to keep and which to dispose of. The history of how socialist blind activists had been seen in the 1960s and '70s as embodiments of progress and how their social policies had stimulated debates over issues of deinstitutionalization, mainstreaming, and access to regular labor markets was now considered irrelevant. Communism was gone and with it its old model of disability.

. . . And What the Eastern Archives Make Invisible

While the ideological erasure of socialism from the Western archives has produced a distorted historical narrative of the international blind movement, a critical disability analysis of the Eastern archives and their creators (the act of cripping them) reveals ideological obscurations there too. Indeed, as socialist disabled activists gave maximum visibility to the "super blind," they also made ordinary blind people invisible, both internationally and domestically. Locating this seeming paradox in the broader context of Soviet ideology is crucial not only to making better sense of it, but also to understanding some of the ableist limitations of the socialist model of disability.

Health, bodily ability, and concepts of production occupied a central place in communist ideology. Conversely, disabled bodies that differed from those of idealized workers-citizens did not have much positive space in the visual culture of the socialist bloc. Carole Poore has argued that "the realm of disability" was "stigmatized" because the ideal communist worker was "young, strong, manly, and healthy."[41] This did not mean that impaired bodies were completely denied. On the contrary, as Elena Iarskaia-Smironova and Pavel Romanov have shown, disabled people were everywhere in Soviet visual discourse. Yet, rather than being represented in their everyday realities, they were "bestowed meanings" that symbolically produced and reproduced "socialism at particular periods of Soviet history."[42]

One "meaning" imparted to disabled people pertained to the Soviet rejection of philanthropy. Disabled men, women, and children (including the blind) were to prove that charity had no place in socialist societies because the state took full care of its most vulnerable citizens. At least in theory, there were no helpless, begging "invalids" on the Soviet streets because vocational rehabilitation was provided to all, and nobody was excluded from participation in productive labor and the building of socialism. A second "meaning" was related to public health services. The socialist countries were said to have reduced blinding eye diseases such as trachoma and others. Congenital blindness—which activists both East and West tended to associate with poverty and lack of hygiene—was declared "a rare occurrence" in the Soviet Union, while most new cases supposedly came from the "natural" process of aging.[43] In other words, the very socialist investment in regimes of labor, health, and hygiene determined this system's politics of visibility in relation to people with physical disabilities. The "invalids"—the problematic, passive, unrehabilitated, unproductive, and resourceless subjects that deviated from the norm of model socialist subjectivity—became invisible in order to sustain the "truths" proclaimed by the state.[44]

The need to confirm certain "truths" also explains why blind athletes from the Soviet Union and other socialist countries participated in international sports competitions (such as the First European International Sport Competitions of the Blind in 1977 and the Olympic Summer and Winter Games for the Disabled in 1976 and 1980),[45] while mobility-impaired people did not. As émigré dissident writer Valerii Fefelov recounted in his memoirs, when the organizers of the Stoke Mandeville Games invited the Soviet Union to take part in this competition, a Soviet official responded that "there are no invalids in the USSR."[46]

This "denial of the very existence of citizens with disabilities" was more than an absurd attempt to portray Soviet society as untainted by "defect" and made up exclusively of healthy and able-bodied people.[47] It was also an effort to preserve an image of social progress in the perception of foreign audiences. The Soviet government could not allow the international community to see the inadequate prostheses and wheelchairs that the state provided to its mobility-impaired citizens (if it provided them at all). Soviet authorities were also aware that their paraplegic athletes had minimal chances to successfully compete against Western Paralympic champions and their better assistive technology, while athletic activities for blind people required less infrastructural investment to flourish. In short, blind sportsmen who became "able disabled" and won medals at international events could be utilized to celebrate and legitimize the order of socialism, but helpless crips on heavy wheelchairs and ineffective protheses would have told a different story. They would have undermined the official discourse of a state that attributed "invalidity" only to the capitalist world and claimed for itself the capacity to turn disabled people into happily integrated individuals, successfully reforged, restored, and transformed.

The blind activists of VOS and BSV supported the ableist stance of their governments. Certainly, by participating in the visual economy of international work as visibly impaired persons (wearing black glasses and carrying white canes), they chipped away at disability stigmas. Sighted audiences recognized them as being blind, while also discerning the geopolitical significance of their work. Through this intersecting visual economy of disability and diplomacy, socialist activists contested perceptions of blind people as irrelevant nonworkers, instead presenting them as central assets to their governments' foreign policy projects. However, in their international collaborations, socialist activists displayed only those successful blind persons who had overcome adversity and become able disabled—while simultaneously losing any right to fail and be different. Besides victorious athletes at international sports competitions, these included also master chess players, virtuoso musicians, performers of feats of industrial labor, high-skilled mathematicians, and computer programmers, but never the many ordinary blind who struggled with access and social integration in their everyday lives.

This visual economy has turned the collections of VOS and BSV into eminently ableist archives. Like the Soviet press and literature that glorified disabled heroes who rose above their physical impairments but silenced the voices of others, most of the primary sources preserved in the repositories of VOS and BSV string together one success story after the other.[48] By putting ordinary blind people out of sight, these primary sources give visibility only to those few disabled whose healing and rehabilitation confirmed the correctness of the socialist approach. Socialism had overcome invalidity—or so it declared—and those blind people who overcame it too appear in these archives as the best ambassadors of social progress. The others are not hidden and made invisible per se, but as the tragic spinoff of an ideology that mandated the erasure of the "invalid" status and localized access to specific spaces.

* * *

Telling the history of my quest for the World Council's historical records, in this chapter I have analyzed two different but complementary archival erasures and reflected on the ways in which both have reduced the horizons of imaginable disability politics. First, the obfuscation of the socialist contributions to the growth of international disability advocacy, which marks the archives of the blind based in the West, creates the impression that only liberal democracies had autochthonous and legitimate disability movements. Second, in the archives of former socialist countries, efforts to preserve materials have overlooked those communities of disabled people who could not or did not want to become able disabled; and references to invalidity as a social problem have been minimized or fully excluded. This omission mirrors not only the ableist limitations, but also the ideological convictions of socialist blind activists. Indeed, admitting to the existence of "invalids"—especially in their interactions with the West— would have equated to recognizing problems in their advocacy and, more broadly, in their sociopolitical system.

Identifying both acts of archival erasure allows us to see blind activists as conscious creators of their own archives, deciding what papers should be preserved for posterity. In addition, recovering sources that have been ignored and silenced in the past is not simply a methodological exercise or case study in historical preservation. It is also a potentially generative step toward the expansion of contemporary activists' political imaginary because it reveals that there was—and still could be—a more complex and robust range of disability movements than a disability politics centered exclusively on the neoliberal model and its prioritization of legal equality over economic and social security.

Notes

Parts of the analysis of source materials have appeared in my book *Ambassadors of Social Progress: A History of International Blind Activism in the Cold War* (Ithaca, NY: Cornell University Press, 2024), to which I refer for deeper discussions of some of the events and processes described here.

1. "East" and "West" are contested terms in humanities scholarship, often indicating not just places but positionalities. In this chapter, I use them and the dichotomy they imply specifically in relation to Cold War history.

2. https://nfb.org/sites/nfb.org/files/images/nfb/publications/resources/tenbroek_finding_aid.html.

3. For a discussion of how the victors wrote the history of the international women's movement after 1989, see Kristen Ghodsee, *Second World, Second Sex: Socialist Women's Activism and Global Solidarity during the Cold War* (Durham, NC: Duke University Press, 2019). Emblematic of how this rewriting was done

in the literature on disability activism are D. Tobis, *Moving from Residential Institutions to Community-Based Social Services in Central and Eastern Europe and the Former Soviet Union* (Washington, DC: World Bank, 2000); Egle Sumskiene, Violeta Gevorgieniene, and Rasa Geniene, "Implementation of CRPD in the Post-Soviet Region: Between Imitation and Authenticity," in *The Routledge Handbook of Disability Activism*, edited by Maria Berghs et al. (New York: Routledge, 2020), 385–97; Jitka Nelb Sinecká, "Peeping over the Wall: Communism, Goffman and the Deinstitutionalization of People with Autism in the Czech Republic," in *The Imperfect Historian: Disability Histories in Europe*, edited by Sebastian Barsch, Anne Klein, and Pieter Verstraete (Frankfurt: Peter Land, 2013), 215–33; Daniel Holland, "The Current Status of Disability Activism and Nongovernmental Organizations in Post-Communist Europe: Preliminary Findings Based on Reports from the Field," *Disability & Society* 23, no. 6 (2008): 543–55; Disability Rights Advocates, *Invisible and Neglected: Status of the Human Rights of People with Disabilities in Central Europe* (Oakland, CA: Disability Rights Advocates, 2001).

4. V. A. Fefelov, *V SSSR invalidov net!* (London: Overseas Publications Interchange, 1986).

5. On the "able disabled," see Sharon L. Snyder and David T. Mitchell, "Introduction: Ablenationalism and the Geo-Politics of Disability," *Journal of Literary & Cultural Disability Studies* 4, no. 2 (2010): 113–25. For an application of the concept to the East European context, see Natalia Pamula, "'Maternal Impressions': Disability Memoirs in Socialist Poland," *Aspasia* 13 (2019): 95–112.

6. See James J. Megivern and Marjorie Megivern, *People of Vision: A History of the American Council of the Blind* (Bloomington, IN: American Council of the Blind, 2003); Floyd W. Matson, *Blind Justice: Jacobus tenBroek and the Vision of Equality* (Washington, DC: U.S. Government Printing Office, 2005); and Matson, *Walking Alone and Marching Together: A History of the Organized Blind Movement in the United States, 1940–1990* (Baltimore: National Federation of the Blind, 1990). Histories of the larger international disability movement also omit the East. See Nora Groce, *From Charity to Disability Rights: Global Initiatives of Rehabilitation International, 1922–2002* (New York: Rehabilitation International, 2002) and Gildas Brégain, *Pour une histoire du handicap au XXe siècle: Approches transnationales* (Europe et Amériques) (Rennes: Presses Universitaires de Rennes, 2017).

7. The exception is my own *Ambassadors of Social Progress*. For examples of literature that dismisses the archival record, see Martin Jaedicke, "Zur Geschichte des BSV—einige Thesen und Probleme," *Wissenschaftliche Blätter zu Problemen des Blinden- und Sehschwachenwesens* 2 (1990), 3–9; and Helmut Schiller, 100 Jahre DZB: *Die wechsvolle Geschichte der ersten deutschen Blindebücherei* (Leipzig: Verlag Deutsche Zentralbücherei für Blinde, 1994). Among the better-known memoirs denouncing the Soviet approach to disability broadly is Ruben Gallego, *White on Black* (Orlando, FL: Harcourt, 2006). For examples of celebratory chronicles, see Boris V. Zimin, *Razvitie mezhdunarodnoi deiatel'nosti VOS* (Moscow: Logos, 1995); Marat V. Biriuchkov, *Istoriia obshchestvennogo dvizheniia nezriachkh Moskvy* (Moscow: VOS, 1990); Biriuchkov, *Siluety* (Moscow: Molodaia Gvardiia, 2000); Biriuchkov, *Izbrannoe: ocherki, stat'i, esse* (Moscow: Rossiiskaia gosudarstvennaia biblioteka dlia slepykh, 2015); and Willi Finck, *Zwischen Licht und Schatten: Kriegsblinde in der DDR—Geschichtliches*

zur politischen, organisatorischen und sozialen Lage Kriegs-und Wehrdienstblinder in Ostdeutschland (1945–2004) (Rostock: Ingo Koch, 2005).

8. Gracen M. Brilmyer, "'I'm Also Prepared to Not Find Me. It's Great When I Do, but It Doesn't Hurt If I Don't': Crip Time and Anticipatory Erasure for Disabled Archival Users," *Archival Science* 22 (2022), 168.

9. Susan Burch and Michael Rembis, "Re-Membering the Past: Reflections on Disability Histories," in *Disability Histories*, Susan Burch and Michael Rembis eds. (Urbana: University of Illinois Press, 2014), 4.

10. See, for instance, Jarrett Drake, "Blood at the Root," *Journal of Contemporary Archival Studies* 8 (2021), 1–24.

11. Gracen M. Brilmyer, "Toward a Crip Provenance: Centering Disability in Archives Through Its Absence," *Journal of Contemporary Archival Studies* 9: 1, Article 3 (2022), at https://elischolar.library.yale.edu/jcas/v019/iss1/3.

12. For a historical approach that takes Soviet deaf activism seriously, see Claire Shaw, *Deaf in the USSR: Marginality, Community, and Soviet Identity* (Ithaca, NY: Cornell University Press, 2017). For examples of nuanced anthropological work on mobility impairment in the postsocialist context, see Sarah D. Phillips, *Disability and Mobile Citizenship in Postsocialist Ukraine* (Bloomington: Indiana University Press, 2011); and Cassandra Hartblay, *I Was Never Alone or Oporniki: An Ethnographic Play on Disability in Russia* (Toronto: University of Toronto Press, 2020).

13. UNESCO archives, BRX/ONG.1/24.1, questionnaire compiled by John Jarvis dated April 7, 1960; briefing note entitled "World Council for the Welfare of the Blind," no date or page number; "Constitution of the World Council for the Welfare of the Blind (revised July 1959)"; and "Conseil d'administration."

14. UNESCO archives, BRX/ONG.1/24.1, questionnaire compiled by John Jarvis dated April 7, 1960; briefing note entitled "World Council for the Welfare of the Blind," no date or page number; "Constitution of the World Council for the Welfare of the Blind (revised July 1959)"; and "Conseil d'administration."

15. *International Conference of Workers for the Blind* (New York; Paris: American Foundation for Overseas Blind; London: National Institute for the Blind, 1951), 103.

16. The salary of the general secretary and his office was borne by American sources until 1959 and then met from British sources until 1969. See *Proceedings of the World Assembly of the World Council for the Welfare of the Blind held at Vigyan Bhavan, New Delhi, India, October 8–17, 1969* (Bombay: National Association for the Welfare of the Blind, 1969), 78.

17. Euclid Herie, *Journey to Independence: Blindness—The Canadian Story* (Toronto: Dundurn Press, 2005); and UNESCO archives, BRX/ONG.1/24.1, briefing note.

18. Bernard Lacy, *An International Adventure: A Brief History of the American Foundation for Overseas Blind, 1915–1965* (New York: n.p., 1965); and Zimin, *Razvitie*.

19. Deaf people from the Soviet Union and Eastern Europe were represented internationally, too. Compared to other disabilities (such as mobility impairment and intellectual disability), blindness and deafness enjoyed a privileged political status under socialism. This was due to several reasons, including the belief that sensory disability had greater rehabilitative potential and that its "fixing" did not

require major investments in the built environment. For a discussion of deafness in post–WWII international politics, see Claire Shaw, "'Just Like It Is at Home!' Soviet Deafness and Socialist Internationalism during the Cold War," in *Re/imaginations of Disability in State Socialism: Visions, Promises, Frustrations*, edited by Kateřina Kolářová and Martina Winkler (Frankfurt: Campus Verlag, 2021), 27–61. To the best of my knowledge, scholars of Russia and Eastern Europe have not yet offered any systematic discussions of the gaps marking the socialist archives of other disabilities. For the larger context of disability and internationalism in the twentieth century, see Galmarini, *Ambassadors of Social Progress.*

20. https://worldblindunion.org/about/history/.

21. Personal correspondence dated April 19, 2018.

22. American Foundation for the Blind Helen Keller Archive at the American Printing House for the Blind, AGN 202, folder "World Council for the Welfare of the Blind, President Hedkvist," Boulter's letter to Hedkvist dated March 9, 1970; Noel Fontaine's letter to Annie Dvoretsky dated March 13, 1970; and Fontaine's letter to Hedkvist dated January 23, 1970.

23. Frederic K. Schroeder, "History of the Independent Living Movement of the Visually Impaired." Paper presented at the International Conference of the World Blind Union in Seoul, South Korea, December 2, 2019, 2.

24. Rienzi Alagiyawanna, "The Relationship between Organizations of and for the Blind," in *Proceedings of the World Assembly of the World Council for the Welfare of the Blind held at Sao Paulo, Brazil, August 7–16, 1974* (Paris: World Council for the Welfare of the Blind, 1975), 280–81; and Fatima Shah, "Report on Cooperation Between WCWB and IFB," in *Proceedings of the World Assembly of the WCWB held in Antwerp, Belgium, August 1–10, 1979* (Paris: World Council for the Welfare of the Blind, 1979), 58–62.

25. Archive of the Central Administration of VOS (hereafter TsP VOS), f. 422, o. 1, d. 2765,11. 130–31, "A Charter for the Blind of the World," issued in New York in August 1964.

26. Interview with Rodolfo Cattani on September 9, 2019. See also Zimin, *Razvitie*, 29.

27. Central Museum of VOS, uncatalogued document, announcement about the World Meeting of the Blind written by A. Dyckmans, dated December 1957. See also State Archive of the Russian Federation, f. 422, o. 1, d. 1053,1. 16 and 1. 17, Dyckmans's letters to Charov, cultural attaché of the Soviet consulate in Brussel, respectively dated January 16, 1958 and December 12, 1957.

28. TsP VOS, f. 422, o. 1, d. 2518,11. 112–14, Mermod's paper titled "Blind and Weak-Sighted Industrial Workers," presented at an ERC meeting in Copenhagen in 1970, at 1. 114.

29. TsP VOS, f. 422, o. 1, d. 2523,11. 6–7, Geißler's letter to Zimin dated December 30, 1969, at 1. 6.

30. Giuseppe Fucà, "Berufsausbildung und Umschulung der Blinden in Italien," in *Internationales Symposium über Probleme der beruflichen Rehabilitation Sehgeschädigter vom 22. bis 26. Mai 1967 in Berlin* (Leipzig: Dt. Zentralbücherei f. Blinde, 1967), 97–101.

31. Hans Cai Seierup, "Aufgabe und Bedeutung der speziellen Betriebe und Werkstätten bei der beruflichen Rehabilitation Blinder," in *Internationales Symposium* (Leipzig, 1967), 148.

32. J. C. Colligan, "The Employment of the Blind in Professional and Administrative Work," in *Proceedings* (Bombay, 1969), 168–75; Léon Schuller, "Die Rehabilitation Blinder in Luxembourg," in *Internationales Symposium* (Leipzig, 1967), 93–94; and Eric Josephson, "Demographic and Social Aspects of Blindness," in Leslie L. Clark ed., *Proceedings of the International Congress on Technology and Blindness* (New York: American Foundation for the Blind, 1963), vol. 1, 484.

33. Bengt Lindqvist, "Widening and Diversifying Job Opportunities for the Visually Handicapped," in *Proceedings* (Paris, 1975), 173–80; and *Training and Employment Opportunities for the Visually Handicapped: A Survey* (Stockholm: World Council for the Welfare of the Blind, the National Swedish Labour Market Board in collaboration with the International Labour Office, 1973). See also Carol Poore, *Disability in Twentieth-Century German Culture* (Ann Arbor: University of Michigan Press, 2007), 172; and Richard Scotch, *From Good Will to Civil Rights: Transforming Federal Disability Policy* (Philadelphia: Temple University Press, 2001).

34. Archive of the European Blind Union (hereafter EBU), folder "II Generalversammlung Varna 1987," "Report of the Commission on Rehabilitation and Social Rights to the General Assembly of the EBU, 3rd–4th June 1987."

35. See, for instance, EBU, folder "II Generalversammlung Varna 1987," "Report on the Activities for the 3 Year 1984–1987 of the Commission for Liaising with the EEC."

36. Francis Fukuyama, *The End of History and the Last Man* (New York: Free Press, 1992).

37. Katharina Heyer, *Rights Enabled: The Disability Revolution from the US to Germany and Japan, to the United Nations* (Ann Arbor: University of Michigan Press, 2015).

38. Besides the literature cited in note 3, see also Majda Bećirević and Monica Dowling, "The Complex Role of Nongovernmental Organizations in Advancing the Inclusion of Children with Disabilities in Bosnia-Herzegovina and Bulgaria," in *Disability in Eastern Europe and the Former Soviet Union*, edited by Michael Ransell and Elena Iarskaia-Smirnova (London: Routledge, 2014), 226–44.

39. EBU, folder "Third General Assembly of EBU, Lisbon, 11–13 October 1990," "Report of a Meeting of the EBU Commission for Liaising with the EEC, held in Brussels on 6 and 7 March 1990."

40. Eugène Loeff, "EBU Work under the New Conditions of a Common House of Europe," *Review of the European Blind*, 1991: 1, 14–21.

41. Poore, *Disability in Twentieth Century German Culture*, 232. See also Dora Vargha, "Polio and Disability in Cold War Hungary," in *The Oxford Handbook of Disability History*, M. Rembis, C. J. Kudlick, and K. Nielsen eds. (Oxford: Oxford University Press, 2018), 369–83.

42. Elena Iarskaia-Smirnova and Pavel Romanov, "Heroes and Spongers: The Iconography of Disability in Soviet Posters and Film," in *Disability in Eastern Europe and the Former Soviet Union*, edited by Michael Rasell and Elena Iarskaia-Smironova (London: Routledge, 2014), 93.

43. Boris V. Zimin, *To Live and to Work* (Moscow: VOS, 1983), 9; and Zimin, *Élévation du bien être des aveugles en U.R.S.S.* (Moscow VOS, 1972), 4.

44. People with nonphysical disabilities were subjected to a different visual regime. As Natalia Pamula has suggested, "the impossibility of curing an intellectual or developmental disability was, probably, the reason behind its silencing." "'Maternal Impressions,'" 96. On the socialist states' thrust to normalize disabled bodies through rehabilitation or remediate them through prosthesis and surgeries, see also Frances Bernstein, "Rehabilitation Staged: How Soviet Doctors 'Cured' Disability in the Second World War," in *Disability Histories*, edited by Susan Burch and Michael Rembis (Urbana: University of Illinois Press, 2014), 218–36; and Pamula, "Violent Inclusion: Disability and the Nation in Polish 1950s and 1960s Young Adult Literature," *East European Politics and Societies and Cultures* 34, no. 4 (November 2020): 858–78.

45. EBU, folder "1978," "Report on the activities of the Sports Commission at the Presidium of the ERC on the period from 1976 to 1978"; and folder "1981," "Report of the Sports Commission" to the 10th General Assembly in 1981. See also Arvo Karvinen, "Poznan 1977—Highlights of Sports of the Blind in Europe," *Review of the European Blind*, 1978: 1, 8–12.

46. Fefelov, *V SSSR invalidov net!*, 34.

47. Sarah D. Phillips, "There Are No Invalids in the USSR!": A Missing Soviet Chapter in the New Disability History," *Disability Studies Quarterly* 29: 3 (2009), https://dsq-sds.org/article/view/936/1111.

48. Anna Krylova, "'Healers of Wounded Souls': The Crisis of Private Life in Soviet Literature, 1944–1946," *Journal of Modern History* 73 (June 2001), 307–31; and Lilya Kaganovsky, *How the Soviet Man Was (Un)Made: Cultural Fantasy and Male Subjectivity under Stalin* (Pittsburgh: University of Pittsburgh Press, 2008). Beate Fieseler has noted this trend also outside literature. See her article "The Bitter Legacy of the 'Great Patriotic War': Red Army Disabled Soldiers under Late Stalinism," in *Late Stalinist Russia: Society between Reconstruction and Reinvention*, Juliane Fürst ed. (London and New York: Routledge, 2006), 46–61.

CHAPTER 8

Silence and Stigma

How Archival Restrictions Threaten Histories of the Mentally Ill in the United States

SARAH HANDLEY-COUSINS

My relationship with Daniel Folsom began in 2013, though he'd already been dead for about 130 years. I found Folsom in the pages of the patient case files of the New York State Lunatic Asylum at Utica, the foremost government-funded mental institution in the state during the nineteenth century. I was researching my first book, and I hoped to include a chapter on the experiences of Civil War soldiers who had experienced war trauma. Daniel's story immediately jumped out from the patient case files, and he was a kind of companion for nearly a decade as the project wound its way from dissertation to manuscript to published book. While Daniel's life story was perfectly demonstrative of the experiences of many soldiers who struggled with their mental health, there was another reason why his story stuck with me.

Here's what I can say, legally and with certainty, about Daniel. He was a young tinsmith from St. Lawrence County, New York who enlisted to fight in the United States army in the spring of 1861. He had a good service record, sick barely four days in two years of hard service.[1] Sometime after the battle of Fredericksburg, Folsom seemed different to his comrades, and when he returned home to upstate New York in the summer of 1863 he couldn't focus on his work. By fall, he was extremely depressed and thinking about suicide. He tried to die by cutting himself. His father had him committed to the Utica Asylum, where he slowly improved. He was discharged recovered the following fall.

When Daniel was discharged, he would have been about twenty-five years old, a young man with his entire life ahead of him. But his patient record from Utica, detailing just one year in his life, is really the only source I can use to describe Daniel's life. It's not because the sources are so limited. To the contrary, I have several more sources about Daniel in my possession. From just a few searches on genealogical databases, I can construct a clear outline of Daniel's life over the course of a couple of decades—marriage, several children, successful careers. I could order more, richer sources, such as his service record and pension files, from the National Archives this afternoon and have them in my hands within a few weeks. But even if I had access to those additional sources, sharing anything from them in written work would pose legal, ethical, and methodological problems.

To begin to untangle this, let me start by saying that Daniel Folsom's name isn't actually Daniel Folsom. That's a pseudonym I assigned him when I transcribed his patient case file. Because Daniel was institutionalized in New York State, his patient case files—and all others in the New York State Archives and Library—are restricted under the Mental Hygiene Law. Section 33.13 allows for "qualified researchers" to access patient records with "the approval of the institutional review board or other committee specially constituted for the approval of research projects," with the major qualification that "the researcher shall in no event disclose information tending to identify a patient."[2] In order to access restricted patient case files like Daniel's, I had to apply to be considered for qualified researcher status from the state archives and Office of Mental Health, then go through an institutional review board (IRB). In both processes, I had to promise repeatedly that I would protect any confidential material, use pseudonyms for all patients, and obscure any identifying information.

To be clear, this option was absolutely critical to making my research possible, so I happily consented. Once I had IRB clearance, I gathered case files, carefully assigned each subject a pseudonym, and began weaving their stories into my research. The records provided incredible insight into the experiences of profoundly mentally ill soldiers and veterans, insight that certainly would not be available in other sources. The problem, however, arose when I tried to contextualize the patient case files. The case files were medical documents, created by doctors who wielded incredible power over patients. They captured soldier-patients at their most vulnerable, pathologizing their agonized cries and desperate actions. I had hoped to place those fraught moments within the greater frame of these men's lives. But when I gathered outside details—marriages, families, careers—I found myself in a confidentiality trap. Details, even without names included, could serve to identify the patient. If I did include details, I would need to cite them. If I cited them, I had to either alter the citation with the man's pseudonym, or risk exposing their identity.

With those additional details, I could reconstruct the full and nuanced life of a real person. I could include some of the mundanities that make up human lives. I could sketch out a picture of Daniel's life that showed him as a patient but also as a husband, father, business partner, and community member. I could show that he lived a typical, even happy, life after his release from Utica in 1863. But without them, I could only present the one year that Daniel spent as an inmate in an asylum. Those details created a very different image: Daniel as a trapped and suffering young man.

New York is not the only state that restricts archival material relating to mental health and institutions.[3] While New York's law makes it onerous to access records, at least there's a process in place. Massachusetts records are completely sealed, without any avenue to access, even for researchers.[4] Other states are more cryptic. In Pennsylvania, access to restricted records can depend entirely on the archive, the archivists, and the researcher. While I was given access to state hospital records of patients who had been deceased for at least fifty years, a colleague was told a similar collection of records in a different institution was restricted under federal HIPAA law. Some states have no laws specifically restricting access, but fear that providing access will be considered a privacy violation anyway. One researcher, for instance, was granted access to nineteenth-century patient case files of a mental institution in Virginia one day only to have them literally yanked out of her hands the next. In her 2016 book *Privacy and the Past: Research, Law, Archives, Ethics*, historian of medicine Susan Lawrence recounted the experience of her graduate student, Marilyn, who had spent several days in research on the register of an Iowa poor farm at rural residential facility when she was told to cease and desist by an alarmed administrator. In both cases, archivists and administrators cited patient privacy and declared the materials restricted, even when no such restrictions were actually in place.[5]

On the surface, restrictions have the appearance of being a patient-centered approach to mental health records. After all, our own medical records contain some of the most intimate details of our lives: descriptions of our bodies and details of private, vulnerable moments. Indeed, how would Daniel Folsom feel about me publishing notes his doctor scribbled down about his mental condition? To publish those details can certainly feel invasive. Yet, most disabled people did not leave behind rich archival collections, making medical records vital to the historian's ability to reconstruct their lives. Between the annotations of body temperature and medications administered, medical records like Daniel's can be imaginatively read and interpreted to offer up glimpses into his life.

In this way, Daniel's patient records exemplify the unique source needs of an entire historical discipline. Despite some notable exceptions, for example, prominent disabled figures like Franklin Roosevelt and Helen Keller, many disabled Americans, especially those who lived before the twentieth century and who were institutionalized and/or barred from equal access to education, did not produce significant historical records for themselves. Further, the stigma of a mental or physical disability caused many disabled individuals who did produce documentation during their lifetimes to choose not to discuss them or to consciously obscure them in their legacies.[6] The result is that in many cases, the most significant documentation of disabled lives exists in medical documents, patient case files, and bureaucratic paperwork. In the face of such research challenges, historians of disability often have no choice but to rely on creative reading of documents of oppression and control; as historians of slavery such as Marisa Fuentes have demonstrated, it is necessary to read documents written by those in positions of power creatively to unearth traces of the lives of the powerless.[7] Kim Nielsen, in her examination of the life of institutionalized physician Anna Ott, explains that while Ott left "shallow footprints," Nielsen had to piece together fragmentary sources to recreate a "shadow biography." Ott's archival exclusion wasn't incidental, Nielsen argues, but rather the result of oppression and ableism. Defying that kind of archival erasure requires prodding documents to reveal "the stories they hide, the people erased, the details baked invisible but apparent in the seasoning and the powers glossed over."[8] Yet, in order for historians to perform that difficult work and resurrect disability history from the archive, they must have access to those records—records kept locked up in by archival restrictions.

In New York State, materials from psychiatric facilities are restricted by the Mental Hygiene Act, initially enacted in 1927 and revised several times over the ensuing decades. The bill was conceived of as a reform, repealing the previous state law regarding the commitment of the mentally ill called simply the Insanity Law, which was largely concerned with the creation and maintenance of large state hospitals.[9] The reform of the Mental Hygiene Act was influenced, in name and in content, by the work of the mental hygiene movement, inspired by the life and work of former asylum patient Clifford Beers. Beers struggled with his mental health during college, and after his graduation from Yale in 1897 eventually attempted death by suicide.[10] His family had him committed to a series of asylums, first private ones like the Hartford Retreat, and when they could no longer afford those, state-run hospitals like the Connecticut Hospital for the Insane. His unhappy experiences in these institutions convinced him that the system of care and treatment of the mentally ill was in desperate need of reform. After his release, Beers channeled his desire for reform into the publication of a memoir of his time in the institution, *A Mind That Found Itself*, in 1908, then into the foundation of the National Committee for Mental Hygiene a year later.

The mental hygiene movement proved to be a quintessential Progressive-Era reform. Beers and his partner, psychiatrist Adolf Meyer, hoped to marshal cutting-edge scientific research and methods into preventing mental illness through education, research, and public health measures.[11] Ultimately, despite Beers's galvanizing experience while committed, the organization wasn't terribly effective in improving the lives of people inside asylums. Exposés and memoirs, including Beers's own, criticized institutions, but actual reform was a losing battle. By the 1920s, funding sources like the Rockefeller Foundation were more interested in general prevention than fighting with institutional bureaucracy for limited improvements, and psychiatrists, eager to establish themselves as medical professionals, sought distance from the asylum system. Instead, mental hygiene ceded ground to the eugenics movement, which offered clear-cut causes and cures for mental illness with its theory of biological origins.[12] Nonetheless, the mental hygiene movement continued to have an impact, especially in New York, where the NCMH was based. In 1926, the New York State Legislature passed the Mental Hygiene Act, a reform of the 1909 Insanity Law. The act created a bureaucratic organization within a department of mental hygiene, filled with medically trained civil service workers and led by commissioners and deputy commissioners, which would oversee the running of the state's mental institutions and work toward the public prevention of mental illness.

The Department of Mental Hygiene maintained this structure for fifty years, over which time both psychiatry and the federal government were evolving in their approach to care. Over the next several decades, the state commissioned studies of its mental health policies and institutions, used federal funds to build new psychiatric facilities, and struggled to implement community care programs like transition programs and clinics. Despite years of studies underscoring the need for community-based care options that could help people function outside of the walls of state hospitals, by the late 1960s, there had been little improvement. That became a serious liability when both popular and scholarly attitudes toward psychiatry took a sharply critical turn in the 1960s and '70s. Scholar-activists like Michel Foucault, Thomas Szasz, Albert Deutsch, and Erving Goffman began to criticize psychiatry and state hospital systems, while the general public was horrified by the system of "care" depicted in the novel *One Flew Over the Cuckoo's Nest*.[13] The mad pride movement formed in New York with organizations like the Mental Patients Liberation Project amid the broader disability rights movement, and argued that institutions were a tool of social control. National exposés, especially the television report on the Willowbrook State School, shone a spotlight on the neglect of institutionalized patients, and in a series of lawsuits, courts began ruling that patients could not be committed against their will if they were capable of living independently, rulings that also underscored the patient's right to treatment.[14]

Over the same decades, the concept of patient privacy and informed consent was also undergoing a transformation. For much of American history, physicians were more concerned with building and maintaining professional prestige than with the rights of patients. In 1847, the American Medical Association's (AMA) first code of ethics included a lengthy passage on the obligations that patients had to their doctors that included admonishments to be quiet, deferential, and obedient.[15] The AMA revised the code in 1957, producing the *Principles of Medical Ethics*, which more clearly articulated the physician's responsibilities and duties to the patient, including a requirement to "safeguard patient confidences and privacy within the constraints of the law."[16] While this was a step forward, physicians were still largely responsible to their own commitment to professional ethics rather than to the law. Confidentiality between physician and patient depended on state statutes until the passage of the Health Insurance Portability and Accountability Act (HIPAA) in 1996, which included a later provision known as the Privacy Rule that safeguarded the dissemination of patient information without consent.[17]

Human subject research was not explicitly included in the AMA's statements on ethics and privacy. Just as patient privacy ultimately had to be shielded with federal legislation, medical research also required congressional intervention to ensure the safety and protection of patients. After years of trying to get the attention of authorities within the Centers for Disease Control, whistleblower Peter Buxton went to the press in 1972 about the ethical breaches of the four-decade-long Tuskegee syphilis study, during which public health researchers from the CDC studied, but did not treat, the disease course of syphilis in impoverished Black men from Tuskegee, Alabama.[18] While it was hardly the only unethical medical study conducted in the twentieth century, the scale of the Tuskegee study made an immediate impact on research concerning human subjects. Within two years, Congress passed the National Research Act, which established guidelines for human subject research, including the use of institutional review boards to ensure that human subject research is closely monitored and supervised. At the end of the decade, the National Commission for the Protection of Biomedical and Behavioral Research published its study of human subject research ethics, the Belmont Report, which established ethical best practices for researchers.[19]

It was within this larger context that New York expanded its legal protection of psychiatric patient rights, added into the Mental Hygiene Act in 1972 as subsection 33.13, requiring the strict confidentiality of patient records. Influenced by coverage of the maltreatment of patients of psychiatric facilities, the activism of disabled people themselves, and the move toward increased privacy and confidentiality, the subsection was an important patients' rights–centered reform.

While it wasn't the intention of the laws' authors, archival collections of patient records were caught up in these new laws. In 2005, Susan Lawrence described the confusing implications HIPAA had on archival materials. For instance, not every medical record fell under the law's purview. Records produced by a now-closed institution that never used computers, for instance, wouldn't be protected under the law, but anything produced by an institution that still existed would be, no matter how old. The law wasn't concerned with all existing patient data, but with the current and future digital transmittal of data. "What matters is where those medical documents were on 14 April 2003," writes Lawrence, "when the Privacy Rule went into effect. If they were held in a covered entity, they are covered."[20] In other words, if a university with a teaching hospital also had medical library with archival materials, it was considered covered by HIPAA's patient confidentiality requirements. But even within covered archives, determining exactly what was confidential patient material and what wasn't was confusing: personal letters concerning individuals who weren't treated in the facility wouldn't seem to be covered, but just their existence in a restricted collection might make an archivist nervous to release them.[21] After years of confusion and frustration as historians tried to navigate restricted records and clunky institutional review boards, in 2013 the Department of Health and Human Services released the HIPAA Omnibus Final Rule, which allowed research into records if the patient had been deceased for at least fifty years. While this can be tricky for some collections (where archivists are faced with the huge task of confirming death dates for all patients included), in general this means that for nineteenth- and early-twentieth-century records, HIPAA is no longer a valid restriction.[22]

Yet, historians still encounter archives that use HIPAA as a reason why they can't allow historians to conduct research in psychiatric records. Kylie Smith, historian of psychiatric nursing at Emory University, found that archives in the Deep South where she conducts research still claim they cannot release psychiatric records because of HIPAA restriction. "Because both Alabama and Georgia's large state hospitals were the subjects of exposes or court cases," Smith shares, "government departments became very risk averse and have now hidden behind HIPAA to refuse access to researchers to any records that do exist."[23] In 1959, the *Atlanta Constitution* published a multipart exposé of the Milledgeville State Hospital in central Georgia, which resulted in a Pulitzer Prize for the author and a public relations nightmare for the state.[24]

While institutions like Milledgeville (now called Central State Hospital) with histories of patient abuses are not exactly eager to facilitate historical research into their dark pasts, the real reason archives often decide not to allow research access is fear of litigation. When doing research in Alabama, Smith was told she would need a lawyer to access any records from state mental facilities, even administrative and operational materials that contained no patient details at all. At the Georgia State Archives, Smith was doing research in the correspondence of institutionalized patients—which are not medical records and don't contain material that would apply to any interpretation of physician-patient privilege—when an archives employee noticed the box was marked with a red "restricted" sticker and took the materials away. When Smith pointed out that HIPAA wouldn't apply to those records, archives employees pointed her to the Georgia legal code, which included a small clause stating that any material containing any medical information was restricted. She would have to appeal to the chief state archivist for access, which she has done—with the help of an attorney. "Because there has been so much public attention" to their histories of maltreatment, Smith explains, archives "are just saying, 'oh, no one can see anything.'"[25]

Another scholar, Jonathan Jones of the Virginia Military Institute, also ran into appeals to HIPAA, even though his research on Civil War veterans surely meant that all subjects had been deceased for over fifty years. While researching opiate addiction among veterans of the American Civil War, Jones faced no restrictions whatsoever in researching in North Carolina's Dix Asylum records, but when he tried to conduct research in Pennsylvania, he was told repeatedly that HIPAA and state law entirely prohibited access, with no pathway to achieving access. Discouraged, Jones gave up on using Pennsylvania records in his research at all, though they "would have been major sources for [his] research on the history of opioid addiction, as many individuals ended up being committed, generating surprisingly robust paper trails in the asylums."[26] Deciphering the state's policy on mental health archives is difficult. The Pennsylvania State Archives website doesn't include a section on archival restriction to explain the specific laws that supposedly restrict its records. According to a 2015 article in the *Pittsburgh Post-Gazette*, a state archivist explained that archives employees could do targeted research for a patron interested in one person and provide materials, but couldn't allow a patron to browse for themselves, and that while they could share medical information, they were absolutely restricted from sharing anything related to mental health. Even then, it's internally inconsistent: the register for one Pennsylvania mental hospital is restricted, while a similar register from another institution isn't.[27]

Nicole Lee Schroeder, a postdoctoral fellow at Kean University, is a historian of disability in early American history who has also experienced the complicated system of policies in Pennsylvania. While trying to access the Pennsylvania Hospital Historic Collections at Penn Medicine, the University of Pennsylvania Health System, Schroeder found the mental health records completely closed. In a statement on its website, the Pennsylvania Hospital Collections has two statements. One explains that it is reconsidering its access policy for medical records. The other matter-of-factly declares that state law "prohibits the use of all patient mental health records."[28] Schroeder points out that while she could understand some restriction of more recent materials, her research ends in the 1840s, meaning the relevant records are around two hundred years old. "There is no personal information I might disclose about my chapters that could be traced back to those living today," she explains. She sees this restriction as "arbitrary," but also stemming from the desire that institutions have to control the dissemination of their own unflattering histories. "As a functioning hospital, Pennsylvania Hospital has a reputation to uphold," she writes. "That reputation does not stand as strong when historians begin to unpack the degree of neglect, abuse, experimentation, and collective harm perpetrated by hospital administrators, medical students, and professors against disabled individuals."[29]

Two themes arise in researchers' experiences with archival restriction: their confusing and arbitrary nature, and their fixation with protecting mental health records in particular. Jones conducted extensive research in the records of the Virginia Western Lunatic Asylum at the Library of Virginia, and while he was limited to records from before 1920, the collection was robust and vital to his project. A few months after Jones's last trip to the archive, his dissertation advisor Diane Miller Sommerville traveled to research in the same collection for a project on the history of postpartum depression in the nineteenth century. Sommerville researched for one day undisturbed, but when she began to go through the collections on the following day, an alarmed archivist pulled the records out of her hands and told her they included confidential patient information and were restricted. Now, the Library of Virginia website states that while HIPAA opens records fifty years after a patient's death, a state law passed in 2019—after Jones and Sommerville accessed those records—restricts medical records for 125 years after their creation.[30] But even with that clarification, that law doesn't seem to be applied consistently. The records of the Home for Needy Confederate Women includes patient records for women who lived in the facility during the twentieth century, but has no restrictions. The manuscript collection of Virginia physician George Taylor Klipstein includes patient names and occasional diagnoses, according to the finding aid, but also has no restriction.[31] The medical records that seem the most carefully restricted, based on my research in the state of Virginia's finding aid database, are from the Eastern State Hospital and the Western State Hospital, both institutions for the treatment of the mentally ill.[32]

Restrictions also create a barrier of access for researchers for whom travel would be expensive and onerous. Emily Cock, lecturer in early modern history at Cardiff University in Wales, reached out to the New York State Archives to see if it could help her confirm whether a politician she was researching may have spent time in the Utica Asylum in the 1840s. She had a newspaper article that suggested that he was committed for a time, but it was sensational and politically biased, so she hoped for some independent confirmation. While most archives are happy to perform this kind of research assistance for far-off historians—including the New York State Archives—head of researcher services Jim Folts responded that he couldn't provide her that information because of the restriction of mental health records. She could, Folts advised, appeal the denial, but cautioned her that all other appeals for access to clinical records had been denied.[33] It didn't look promising. Cock was left with the option of leaving the politician's story out of her work entirely, or relying on the biased newspaper article. "I'm necessarily left with sensational newspaper clippings as my main evidence," she writes, "and at this point [I have] no way of verifying or refuting their claims."[34]

While Cock wasn't able to travel to New York to perform research in person, scholars who are able to be physically present in the archive do have an option for accessing restricted materials: applying for approval through an institutional review board. In my work on disabled Civil War veterans, I have gone through the process of gaining qualified researcher status to gain access to these manuscript collections. First, I needed to complete several hours of virtual trainings on human subject research. When I earned the certification at the end of that process, I had to create a profile on IRBNet, a platform used by researchers to facilitate the institutional review board process. There, I was asked to create and submit a document package that included a nine-page site-specific research protocol (SSRP), which asked for explanations about how I would protect subject privacy, such as "explain how the research presents no more than minimal risk to the subjects' privacy," and "explain why the research could not be conducted without the Private Identifiable Information." While these inquiries are clearly important for research projects that concern living subjects, they are an awkward fit for historical research. My research presents no more than a minimal risk to the subjects' privacy because, well, they're all dead, and have been for a century or more. The research can't be conducted without access to the Private Identifiable Information because it's the subject of my research; I can't learn more about the way that doctors and veterans experienced and understood war trauma without access to patient records.

Along with the SSRP, I uploaded numerous forms to IRBNet and submitted it all for consideration to an institutional review board, which in my most recent application was housed in the Nathan Kline Institute for Psychiatric Research. The board read through my materials and invited me to a virtual meeting to discuss my application. The meeting was collegial, and the researchers on the board were interested in my research—but they also were unwavering in their commitment to subject confidentiality and unconcerned with the age of the records. There was concern about how I would store photographs if I took pictures of records in the archives (was it too risky to use my phone to snap pictures?) and how I would transfer data from a device to my computer while avoiding cloud storage. I had to make several edits and changes to my SSRP to more clearly articulate the potential risk to subjects (would a descendant be able to identify them?) and provide further details on the research personnel (just me). With these changes, my application was approved and I was given permission to access the restricted collections.

Getting access to the records is only one part of the battle. I had done research in some of the same collections in 2013, when I was researching my first book. Archives staff were incredibly helpful, and the records were a critical component of that project. But IRB policy also requires that the principal investigator have their application reapproved annually. The first couple of years went smoothly enough, but at some point, the IRB responsible for my research moved from the Office of Mental Health to the Nathan Kline Institute. Suddenly, I found myself working with an ever-changing cast of administrators, all unaware that my project involved historical research rather than psychiatric research. More than once I received an email saying the point of contact assigned to my case had changed, only to find when I reached out to that individual that they too had left Nathan Kline, leaving me with no idea who to go to next. Finally fed up with this frustrating annual exercise, I declared my research complete, thinking it would stop the yearly reviews. This created yet another complication. The director of research compliance now requested I either destroy my records or store them locally in an encrypted folder on an encrypted computer. In addition, I was asked to remove any identifiable material (such as names) from the records, making it all but impossible to do any further contextual research on the patients.[35] Even now, the records are safely locked up in an encrypted folder on my desktop.

While my experience with the New York State Archives was onerous and irritating, I was fortunate that a process existed that allowed me to get access. Starting in 2008, Central Connecticut State University professor Matthew Warshauer and his graduate student Michael Sturges found themselves embroiled in a long, confusing, and infuriating struggle with the state of Connecticut to get (and keep) access to the records of a local asylum in order to research institutionalized Civil War veterans. Despite assurances they would not publish any identifying information, Warshauer and Sturges were repeatedly dissuaded from researching in the asylum's records, even when they consulted an attorney and invoked Connecticut's freedom of information law. The records remained in the hands of the institution, now the Connecticut Valley Hospital, and thus (not unlike my experience in New York) the researchers had to request permission from a series of Department of Mental Health and Addiction Services (DMHAS) individuals with no experience with historical research. One tried to convince Warshauer and Sturges that the records wouldn't even be useful to them, even though the researchers had strong evidence that they would find Civil War patient records in the collections. Ultimately, the DMHAS employee admitted that the real concern was that in order to find the soldiers, the pair would need to browse through hundreds of patient case files, which they felt was a privacy concern. Only after a lengthy legal process did the DMHAS allow Warshauer and Sturges access. But even as they were doing their research, someone tacked an amendment on to a state house bill, which was pushed through quickly without seeking comment from Warshauer, Sturges, or anyone other than employees of the DMHAS. The law, which went into effect in October 2011, closed essentially any and every possible record that could be considered to have confidential information.[36]

While New York is not nearly as tightly locked down as Connecticut now is, most people are still barred from research there. The qualified researcher process is only open to scholars, meaning genealogists are barred from access. Genealogist Linda Stuhler spent years running an independent blog project called *The Inmates of Willard: 1870–1900*, devoted to providing resources for researchers trying locate information about family members who lived in the asylum, inspired by her own attempts to learn more about her institutionalized great-grandmother. Frustrated that New York State would not allow genealogists access to the records in the state archives, Stuhler set about compiling everything she could and making it accessible to the public. The website is full of useful sources for historians and genealogists alike, with a subpage for nearly every institution in the state, government reports, digitized newspaper articles, and even copies of census reports. She also gave researchers step-by-step instructions on how to use the one option open to family researchers: a form that family members could fill out to authorize the Office of Mental Health to release family medical information. The form can only be completed with the help of a physician, who must provide a statement that shows a "demonstrable need for the information" in order to diagnose or treat a condition in the living family member.[37]

Stuhler was particularly concerned by the fact that New York would not provide a burial register for the institution's cemetery, where graves were marked only with numbered stone discs. Stuhler even worked with state senator Joseph Robach to pass legislation that would have helped researchers access restricted materials. She was endlessly frustrated that the privacy change to HIPAA had taken effect in 2013, and the Office of Mental Health was still dragging its feet, fixated on the possibility, she notes, "that New York State could be sued."[38] Robach's bill ended up becoming an amendment to the Mental Hygiene Law, passed and signed into law in 2015, which allowed the Office of Mental Health to release basic information—name and birth and death dates—about a patient who had been dead for at least fifty years for the sole purpose of marking a grave.[39] In conjunction with a group of volunteers called the Willard Cemetery Memorial Project, the Office of Mental Health began marking graves in 2014.[40] Even though Stuhler had long advocated for marking the graves, the passage of the amendment to the Mental Hygiene Law seemed like just another roadblock for any meaningful research. The law was strict and limited: only the barest amount of identifying information would be released, and only for the purpose of memorials and grave markers. Researchers had no greater access to restricted material. "The law only helped the NYS Office of Mental Health to continue to keep the records and photographs of deceased patients away from the public," Stuhler wrote on her blog in 2020. If she had written the bill herself, she said, it would have opened all the records, writing that "there is no good reason why these long-deceased souls need to be punished and stigmatized in death for an illness or intellectual disability that they lived with in life."[41]

Stuhler's frustrated final blog post highlights a central truth of archival restrictions: they are founded on, and continue to reinforce, stigma. While some of the impetus behind archival restriction is certainly the desire to protect the reputation of the institution from facing the sins of its past, the stated intention of nearly all restrictive laws and policies is to respect and protect patient privacy. But when state bureaucrats, archivists, and modern researchers point to the importance of protecting identifiable information, they aren't protecting the identity of the subjects themselves, all of whom have been deceased for decades. In reality, the need for privacy is premised on the descendants of the institutionalized person, who, it is assumed, would be humiliated if it was revealed that they had a mad person in the family tree. In turn, this assumption bolsters stigma by treating records as if they themselves are illicit, as archivists literally snatch records out of the hands of senior scholars and require professional historians to go through arduous processes to be considered "qualified." When restrictions allow access to records but require strict confidentiality, it's difficult or impossible to reconstruct the full lives and experiences of institutionalized people. As I encountered when I first wrote about Daniel Folsom, while I could use his real name to dig deeper and trace his life in other records, I couldn't use that research without potentially revealing his identity. Strict confidentiality requirements result in life stories limited to the asylum, which results in an inaccurate picture of disabled lives and reinforces the idea that inmates were marginal people with marginal experiences.

Further, archival restrictions buttress the assumption that there is no larger history to be drawn from the lives of individual disabled persons, and that mental illness is a private problem, without larger meaning, relevance, or importance. The records of institutions tasked with the care or education of the disabled are often considered unimportant, meaning their records are neglected or even discarded. This was an issue identified by the Disability History Association from its earliest days. In 2008, disabled historian and then DHA president Catherine Kudlick described her experience conducting research on schools for the blind in Paris, France. She described barely organized collections kept in dirty storage rooms, with records so neglected that they crumbled in her hands. Kylie Smith shared that just recently journalists researching institutions in the South have reported seeing "trash cans with patient records in them or strewn on the floor."[42] The shame and stigma of being disabled or having a disabled family member also means that it's difficult to locate disability in other types of sources, such as diaries and manuscript collections. It's precisely because of the scarcity and precarity of sources that disability historians by necessity rely on institutional records held in larger archives.

Centering the institution, a tool and a site of oppression, in disability history can be understood as problematic, but the paucity of other types of sources simply makes research in institutional records necessary. And with skilled reading and interpretation, those records are not only tremendously fruitful, but make that historical inquiry possible. Disability historians doing work across both time and space rely on the records of a variety of institutions to reconstruct the lives of disabled people, well beyond the asylum-as-institution. Historians of disability and enslavement, for example, must use the records created and maintained by oppressors; historians of disability before the mid-nineteenth century read the records of poor houses and courts. Others rely on the records of schools, hospitals, and medical schools—all institutions invested in the control and oppression of disabled people. Yet, as Kim Nielsen noted in her research on Anna Ott, an inmate in a mental institution, with careful reading disability historians use institutional records in thoughtful ways to make up for the otherwise silent archive. Nicole Schroeder notes that while she doesn't want to center the institution in her work, "disability studies researchers and historians know that these are some of the most fruitful places to find disabled voices." For historians with disabilities, like Schroeder, restriction becomes another barrier to access alongside inaccessible reading rooms and arduous, underfunded travel. "I feel that disabled people are barred from engaging in their own histories," she writes. "When spaces like the Pennsylvania Hospital Historic Collections bar researchers from unpacking complex . . . histories because of arbitrary laws in Pennsylvania protecting medical histories, they bar disabled people from accessing our collective histories."[43] Kylie Smith underscores that all of this is further exacerbated when trying to research the lives of disabled people of color: "The voice of the Black disabled person is almost entirely absent in the archive. How do you do disability history with people who have been eradicated from the process, and then from the archive? It makes the disability-centered approach . . . really difficult."[44]

Restrictions, then, are a profound problem for disability history as a discipline. They are particularly damaging to work that seeks to illuminate and analyze the lives of those who were institutionalized, who were so often warehoused and rendered invisible in other source materials. And unfortunately, the path to access isn't clear. It's possible that advocacy from major historical organizations would help. The American Historical Association has used its platform to advocate on behalf of historians for various issues relating to archives, including concerns about access.[45] It's also possible that legal pressure, like that from the nonprofit activist group Reclaim The Records, could convince state governments and individual libraries to open access to materials. However, the experiences of Linda Stuhler in New York State and Matthew Warshauer and Michael Sturges in Connecticut show that getting lawyers and politicians involved won't necessarily solve the problem—and, in fact, may end up making the problem worse. In the meantime, historians dedicated to illuminating the lives of asylum inmates will do what we've always done: read the sources to which we do have access with creativity and compassion, crafting histories as an act of resistance to forces of silence and stigma.

Notes

1. Daniel Folsom, pseudonym, case files, Utica State Hospital Patient Case Files, 1843–1898, New York State Archives, Albany, NY.

2. New York State Mental Hygiene Law 33.13. https://www.nysenate.gov/legislation/laws/MHY/33.13/.

3. Restrictions also exist outside of the United States. In the British National Archives, for instance, individual patient files—where they exist—can be accessed seventy-five years after a patient's death, but can be accessed sooner with a freedom of information request. Other repositories, such as Surrey History Centre, restrict access for a century. In Canada, most archives open records of those who can be

proven to have died ninety to one hundred years ago. For researchers or family members to access records before one hundred years have passed, they must provide multiple forms of proof of a patient's death, included a document signed by a funeral director. When historian Alanna Knight went through this process to gain access to her grandmother's records from the Queen Street Hospital in Toronto, she was ultimately granted access to the records, but when she received them, they were still partially redacted.

4. There is currently a bill winding its way through the Massachusetts State Legislature that would open all records over ninety years old in custody of the state secretary. As of December 2021, this bill is in the hands of the state senate Ways and Means Committee. https://malegislature.gov/Bills/192/SD2425.

5. Susan Lawrence, *Privacy and the Past: Research, Law, Archives, Ethics* (New Brunswick: Rutgers University Press, 2016), 2–3.

6. See, for instance, Sarah Handley-Cousins, "Wrestling at the Gates of Death: Joshua Lawrence Chamberlain and Nonvisible Disability in the Post-Civil War North," *Journal of the Civil War Era* 6 (2016), 220–42.

7. For a discussion of different ways of reading documents of oppression to unearth histories of oppressed peoples, see Marisa J. Fuentes, *Dispossessed Lives: Enslaved Women, Violence, and the Archive* (Philadelphia: University of Pennsylvania Press, 2016). Saidiya Hartman and Sasha Turner have also significantly contributed to this discussion, and before them, Michel-Rolph Trouillot.

8. Kim Nielsen, *Money, Marriage, and Madness: The Life of Anna Ott* (Urbana: University of Illinois Press, 2020), 6–7.

9. Frank P. Hoffman, *The Insanity Law of the State of New York: A Compilation of Statutes Relating to the Insane and to Institutions for Their Care and Treatment; to Which are Appended the Official Orders and Regulations of the State Commission in Lunacy* (Troy: Stowell & Son, 1909).

10. Clifford Beers, *A Mind That Found Itself* (New York: Longmans, Green and Co., 1908); Gerald Grob, *Mental Illness and American Society, 1875–1940* (Princeton: Princeton University Press, 1983), 147.

11. Grob, *Mental Illness and American Society*, 149; Bonita Weddle, "Mental Health in New York State, 1945–1998: A Historical Overview," *New York State Archives* 70 (1998), 3–4.

12. Grob, *Mental Illness and American Society*, 166.

13. Weddle, "Mental Health in New York State," 18–20.

14. Weddle, "Mental Health in New York State," 22.

15. Jay Katz, *The Silent World of Doctor and Patient* (Baltimore: Johns Hopkins Press, 1984), 21; American Medical Association, *Code of Medical Ethics* (Chicago: American Medical Association Press, 1847), 96–97.

16. The principles have been revised twice since 1957, once in 1980 and again in 2001. "Principles of Medical Ethics (2001)." In *Encyclopedia of Bioethics*, third edition, edited by Stephen G. Post, 2666–67 Vol. 5 (New York: Macmillan Reference USA, 2004). *Gale eBooks* (accessed March 11, 2022).

17. Susan Lawrence, "Access Anxiety: HIPAA and Historical Research," *Journal of the History of Medicine and Allied Sciences* 62 (2007), 425–27.

18. James H. Jones, *Bad Blood: The Tuskegee Syphilis Experiment* (New York: The Free Press, 1993), 204.

19. Department of Health, Education, and Welfare, "The Belmont Report: Ethical Principles and Guidelines for the Protection of Human Subjects of Research," April 18, 1979. https://www.hhs.gov/ohrp/regulations-and-policy/belmont-report/read-the-belmont-report/index.html/.

20. Lawrence, "Access Anxiety," 431–32.

21. Lawrence, "Access Anxiety," 434–35.

22. Department of Health and Human Services, "Modifications to the HIPAA Privacy, Security, Enforcement, and Breach Notification Rules under the Health Information Technology for Economic and Clinical Health Act and the Genetic Information Nondiscrimination Act; Other Modifications to the HIPAA Rules," *Federal Register* Vol. 78 No. 17, January 25, 2013.

23. Kylie Smith, correspondence with the author, January 28, 2022.

24. Edward J. Larson, *Sex, Race, and Science: Eugenics in the Deep South* (Baltimore: Johns Hopkins Press, 1996), 159. It should be noted that many archivists are concerned about social justice in the archive, including as it pertains to disability. See, for example, Sara White, "Crippling the Archives: Negotiating Notion of Disability in Appraisal and Arrangement and Description," *American Archivist* 75 (2012), 109–24.

25. Kylie Smith, correspondence with the author, January 28, 2022. In a disturbing twist, while Smith was unable to access these records, she recently found literally hundreds of stolen patient case files, along with other asylum artifacts, for sale on eBay. See her essay with Aparna Nair, "We're Historians of Disability. What We Just Found on eBay Horrified Us," *Slate*, July 21, 2022.

26. Jonathan Jones, correspondence with the author, January 26, 2022.

27. Joe Smydo, "Vanished Mental-Health Archives Stymie Genealogists," *Pittsburgh Post-Gazette*, February 15, 2015.

28. Pennsylvania Historical Collections, https://www.uphs.upenn.edu/paharc/collections/.

29. Nicole Lee Schroeder, correspondence with the author, February 9, 2022.

30. Jonathan Jones, correspondence with the author, January 26, 2022; A Guide to the Records of Western State Hospital, 1825–2000, Virginia Heritage.

31. Guide to the George Taylor Klipstein Manuscript Medical Account Books, 1881–1918, Virginia Heritage, https://ead.lib.virginia.edu/vivaxtf/view?docId=gmu/klipstein.xml;query=patient;brand=default.

32. Interestingly, another finding aid that includes restrictions is made up of records from medical training sessions in which the patient information seems likely to be fictional. The finding aid states that they are restricted, essentially, just in case. A Guide to the Blue Ridge Sanatorium Records, Virginia Heritage, https://ead.lib.virginia.edu/vivaxtf/view?docId=oai/lib.virginia.edu/repositories/7/resources/153.0ai_ead.xml;query=blue%20ridge%20patient;brand=default; A Guide to the Records of the Western State Hospital, 1825–2000, Virginia Heritage, https://ead.lib.virginia.edu/vivaxtf/view?docId=lva/vi00937.xml;query=patient%20restricted%20;brand=default; A Guide to the Records of Eastern State

Hospital, 1770–2009, https://ead.lib.virginia.edu/vivaxtf/view?docId=lva/vi03031.xml;query=patient%20restricted%20;brand=default.

33. Emily Cock, correspondence with the author, January 24, 2022.

34. Emily Cock, correspondence with the author, January 24, 2022.

35. Challace Pahlevan, correspondence with the author, September 7, 2016.

36. Matthew Warshauer and Michael Sturges, "Difficult Hunting: Accessing Connecticut Patient Records to Learn about Post-Traumatic Stress Disorder during the Civil War," *Civil War History* 59 (December 2013). One interesting aspect of Warshauer and Sturges's experience was that the DMHAS at one point suggested removing all the patient names from the records before giving them to the researchers. Warshauer had to explain that the names were necessary to gathering contextual information about the inmate's life, including their experience in the military during the Civil War. While administrators might see this as a simple fix, it shows a lack of understanding of historical research methods.

37. While Stuhler is no longer updating the site, citing her frustration and exhaustion with the issue, the Inmates of Willard website is still available for researchers. https://inmatesofwillard.com. You can see Form OMH-11 on the Office of Mental Health's website. http://www.omh.ny.gov/omhweb/forms/omh11.pdf.

38. Linda Stuhler, "Something That Needs to Be Said," January 5, 2020. *Inmates of Willard, 1870–1890*. https://inmatesofwillard.com/2020/01/05/something-that-needs-to-be-said-1-5-2020/.

39. Senate Bill S840, https://legislation.nysenate.gov/pdf/bills/2015/S840.

40. Dan Barry, "Restoring Lost Names, Recapturing Lost Dignity," *New York Times*, November 28, 2014. While it's not clear in the bill itself, the article—published a year before the bill was signed—stated that descendants need to authorize the release. According to the *New York Times*, at one point the Office of Mental Health was using hundreds of volunteers to search for family information on Ancestry.com to locate patient family members in order to gain permission to list their names and birth and death dates on a grave marker. This seems to have been the case with the ninety-six Willard patients who were buried at a nearby Catholic cemetery, who were memorialized only after the Office of Mental Health contacted their descendants in 2017. See Jennifer Burke, "Willard Psychiatric Center Residents Honored at Ovid Cemetery," *Catholic Courier*, December 5, 2017. A legal advocacy group called Reclaim The Records is currently trying to get the records of all state-run institutions opened. www.reclaimtherecords.com.

41. Stuhler, "Something That Needs to Be Said." There is currently a renewed attempt to increase descendants' access to New York's mental health records, led by historian Alexandra Lord. See www.alexandramlord.com.

42. Kylie Smith, correspondence with the author, January 28, 2022.

43. Nicole Lee Schroeder, correspondence with the author, January 29, 2022.

44. Kylie Smith, correspondence with the author, February 9, 2022.

45. See, for example, the American Historical Association, "AHA Issues Statement Concerning Access to French Archives," November 2020.

CHAPTER 9

Recovering the Past to Understand the Present

Cripping School Segregation in New York City

FRANCINE ALMASH AND JAN VALLE

Introduction

Historical discussions of race and disability have tended to treat the two as separate issues. As stated by Jasmine E. Harris, "This approach has ignored the ways in which states have relied on disability as a tool of subordination, leading to the invisibility of disabled people of color in civil rights movements and an incomplete theoretical and remedial framework for contemporary justice initiatives."[1]

This chapter describes the process of articulating historical inquiry on disabled youth of color in the context of the fight to desegregate New York City public schools during the era of community control. Archival and other resources on disabled youth are rife with silences and gaps; biased distortions and full erasures characterize the representations of institutional structures, political movements of the time, and students' voices. The chapter revisits the New York City school boycotts led by Brooklyn minister Milton Galamison, focusing specifically on the 1965 boycotts of segregated middle schools that primarily included students from New York City's "600" schools for "socially maladjusted" and "emotionally disturbed youth." In an attempt to reach back into urban schooling's institutional history, a process of historical excavation is employed, a sideways journey into known history to offer a new and substantive imaginary of the time.

This chapter addresses the archival culture particular to records on disabled, delinquent, Black and Brown students. Through critical discourse analysis (CDA) and primary resource document analysis, it illustrates how records relating to Black student protests in Harlem treat students from community junior high schools and 600 school students as two separate groups. Through an examination of reporting about the 1965 boycott in both the white and Black press, the chapter illustrates how racism and ableism conspire to create a distorted view of student participation in the protest. While student participation by those in community schools is well documented as an act of resistance, no such historical records exist celebrating the 600 school students who participated in the same boycott. As a result, disabled students who were part of the fight for desegregation have been effectively removed as participants in this liberatory movement for education in New York City.

The Age of Delinquency: Historical Roots of the 600 Schools

In 1946, the New York City Board of Education announced a plan to open five specialized schools, known as the "600" schools, to address the academic and social needs of delinquent and troubled youth. By the 1960s, the goal of the 600 schools shifted from rehabilitation and reform to removal and isolation, partially in response to an influx of Black and Puerto Rican students into New York City schools. Moreover, the number of 600 schools tripled over two decades, functioning as a tool to justify the racial segregation of students labeled "socially maladjusted" and/or "emotionally disturbed" by public school personnel.

The historical roots of the 600 schools, a collaboration between the Board of Education and the juvenile court system, can be traced to the Children's Court Act of 1924 that released judges from the limitations of formal legal proceedings when dealing with the city's youth. Minors who found themselves before the court had their acts addressed as civil rather than criminal violations.[2] By the 1930s, studies by the New York State Crime Commission emphasized the relationship between criminal behavior and problem behavior at school. According to the commission's report, though problem children made up a small percentage of the school-going population (approximately 2 percent out of nearly a million children), they were disproportionally represented among the criminal ranks.[3] The belief was that children in "slum" neighborhoods developed patterns of behavior based on their family and neighborhood backgrounds, then brought those behaviors into the classroom.

Throughout the 1930s, New York City's Juvenile Aid Bureau (formerly the Crime Prevention Bureau) reported a spike in juvenile crime. However, this perceived increase in criminal behavior was due to the decision to surveil "potential delinquents" who comprised 90 percent of the bureau's caseload.[4] Prevention and the problem of the "potentially delinquent" child was reflected in Board of Education policies, which saw an increase in special classes and programs intended to get to the root of problem behavior and save the "delinquent child"—and society—from himself.

Antidelinquency efforts were supported by a variety of sources, including politicians and social scientists, and by the 1940s, theoretical constructions of criminality shaped both public and educational policies.[5] Economic and political shifts after World War II, including increased automation, expanded the white-collar labor market while reducing the need for blue-collar labor. Education standards also shifted as literacy standards increased and a greater emphasis was placed on reading.[6] Higher standards meant wider gaps in achievement. At the same time, the sensationalist press fueled the perception that the city was gripped by a youth crime wave; New York in the 1950s was dubbed the "decade of delinquency" for Black youth.[7] Moreover, white middle-class families pushed to uphold the moral and intellectual "normalcy" of their own children, advocating for the categorical creation of "learning disabilities" when they struggled at school. With this definitional shift, they provided a path to higher achievement and differentiated their children from low-achieving, low-income, Black and Brown children.[8]

Reverend Milton Galamison and the Era of New York City School Boycotts

In the 1960s, as the civil rights movement grew, so did frustration over the city's inability (or unwillingness) to address segregation in its schools. A grassroots movement emerged in New York, led by Milton Galamison, a minister and activist in Brooklyn who was part of a coalition of parents and community leaders. Galamison's most famous school boycotts are documented in well-known published histories about New York City's fight for school desegregation and community control that led to the 1968 citywide teachers strike. His Freedom Day Boycott, held on February 3, 1964, called for a citywide plan for integration. As one of the largest civil rights demonstrations ever held, this boycott included the participation of 460,000 public school students. A second boycott, less successful, followed on March 16, 1964.[9]

While these two boycotts are discussed as pivotal moments leading up to the demand for community control of the schools and the subsequent 1968 teachers "strike that changed New York," there is often little mention of the subsequent boycott that Galamison carried out early the following year specifically targeting the 600 schools. On January 19, 1965, Galamison began Operation Shutdown, a boycott of 31 of the city's 139 junior high schools, all of which had more than 85 percent Black and Puerto Rican enrollment.[10] Among the schools on Galamison's list were the city's fifteen 600 schools, which had grown by that year to enroll approximately five thousand students. The boycott started with three junior high schools and one 600 school. In response to students from the

600 schools staying out of school in protest, James Donovan, president of the Board of Education, accused Galamison of using "sick" kids for political gain and threatened to jail him for violating compulsory attendance laws.[11] Donovan made good on his promise, but the boycott continued.

The 600 schools, however, proved to be a controversial issue for Operation Shutdown as those within the Black community began to publicly question whether students placed in 600 schools were the right ones upon which to focus the movement. Galamison continued to include the 600 schools in his school integration plan, but after seven weeks, with resources exhausted, he called an end to the boycott.[12] Galamison also expressed frustration that "the press was making the '600' schools the whole issue," losing sight of the original purpose of the protest.[13] Though the boycott ended sooner than planned, it was the first time the question of the suspension and transfer of Black and Puerto Rican students out of mainstream schools had received such public attention. Galamison's efforts put the Board of Education on the defensive. The Board conceded that the schools needed improvement.

Critical Discourse Analysis of the 600 Schools Boycott in the *New York Times*

During the seven-week boycott of the 600 schools, the *New York Times* regularly reported on the unfolding events. This section of the chapter draws upon critical discourse analysis (CDA) to uncover the presence of power relations and ideological assumptions in two *New York Times* newspaper articles about the 600 school boycott that appeared in 1965: "90% Boycott Hits Problem School: 136 Students Out in 'Rights' Protest by Galamison" (January 20) and "Teachers at a '600' School Resist Boycott There" (January 26).[14] Using CDA offers a discourse level of analysis of these texts to make transparent the power relations circulating within this historical context.[15] The section draws from Norman Fairclough's linguistic features of discourse to critically analyze headlines, lexical choices, and quotations from sources in each article.[16] Both articles are written by Martin Tolchin, a white journalist working for the *New York Times.* Given the prestige of the *Times*, it is reasonable to assume that Tolchin was afforded the power and privilege typically ascribed to journalists of his caliber.

Headlines

Headlines are significant in their purpose to attract a reader's attention and capture the essence of an article in a few words. In the first headline, "90% Boycott Hits Problem School: 136 Students Out in 'Rights' Protest by Galamison" (January 20, 1965), the 600 school is unnamed but designated as a "problem school," thereby implying that the most relevant feature of the story is the problematic nature of the school and its students rather than identification of the school itself.[17] Use of the verb "hits" suggests aggression upon a vulnerable population assumed to inhabit a school for problem students. Of significance, the placement of quotation marks around "rights" serves to delegitimize the protest as rights-based in nature. The second headline, "Teachers at a '600' School Resist Boycott There" (January 26, 1965), is largely innocuous, although the somewhat awkward placement of the word "there" at the end of the headline implies some urgency about active teacher resistance on site at the school.[18] It is unclear if "teachers" refers to all faculty or some or few; yet inserting qualifying words such as "some" or "few" would certainly lessen the impact of the headline.

Lexical Choices

In "90% Boycott Hits Problem School: 136 Students Out in 'Rights' Protest by Galamison," students who attend the 600 school are referred to as "violent," "disruptive," "problem students," "predominately Negro and Puerto Rican," and "mostly inveterate truants"—in other words, deserving of segregation.[19] Galamison is portrayed as resistant to such wholesale characterization of these youth, arguing that "not all of the students were volatile, aggressive, and impulsive-ridden as reported by the Board of Education" but rather victims of improper screening by the Board of Education.[20] The conflation of negative descriptors and race/ethnicity validates stereotypes and assumptions about these two groups already circulating among white New York City residents of this era—a subset of which we might assume to be readers of the *New York Times*. It is noteworthy that the word "truants" is modified by the adjective "inveterate" (meaning a long-established habit unlikely to change), suggesting that placement at a 600 school is unlikely to modify their deeply entrenched behavior. The following passage is quoted in full for analysis:

> A 14-year-old boy wearing a light blue sweater huddled in a doorway a block from the antiquated red brick schoolhouse in the Williamsburg section. It was lunchtime, and hot meals were being provided by the school. Nevertheless, he preferred to stay on the streets.[21]

Here, the journalist paints a picture for the reader of a typical 600 school student. Of note, the boy is described as "huddled in a doorway"—evoking imagery of a vagrant aimlessly loitering. Given that one of Galamison's claims for the boycott of 600 schools is inadequate facilities, it is of interest that the journalist supports this claim in his description of the school as "antiquated." The reason for the boy's decision not to eat the hot meal offered by the school is assumed to be his preference to "stay on the streets" rather than accept what is offered to him by the school. This last sentence reinforces white fear of dangers on "the streets" and the Black and Brown youth who populate them. Moreover, it is implied that despite best efforts to reach "those" students (i.e., placement in a 600 school), they can be expected to reject the care that schools offer to them.

In "Teachers at a '600' School Resist Boycott There," Tolchin describes students at another 600 school as "disturbed," "violent," and "disruptive," adding that these are "children who have interfered with the learning of others."[22] This language implies that "good" students deserve protection from students who ought to be segregated. The sentence immediately following identifies these students as mostly "Negro" and Puerto Rican, reinforcing the same conflation of race/ethnicity with the negative descriptors noted in his prior article. Racial stereotyping is further evident in the description of Galamison arriving at Junior High School 139 in Harlem "in his black Lincoln Continental"—conjuring a stereotypical racial image readily recognizable to white readers.[23] Moreover, James B. Donovan, president of the Board of Education, is reported to have described boycott leaders as "exploiting the disturbed children, most of whom are inveterate truants who need little excuse to stay home from school."[24] In a single statement, the president of the Board of Education accuses the leaders of the boycott of using "disturbed" children for their political purposes (rather than the stated reason for the boycott as a protest of gross educational inequities in the 600 schools) and ascribes inveterate truancy and innate lack of interest in education to most of the students.[25] Of significance, there is no acknowledgment of any connection between truancy and the abysmal education the students were receiving; rather, the "cause" of truancy was located squarely in Black and Brown bodies. It is of further interest that the journalist describes the 600 school as "the antiquated schoolhouse on 113 East Fourth Street," again seemingly lending credence to Galamison's claims of inadequate educational facilities.[26]

Quotations from Sources

In "90% Boycott Hits Problem School: 136 Students Out in 'Rights' Protest by Galamison," James B. Donovan, president of the Board of Education, is quoted as a source:

> Whether or not the boycott continues, the offense has been committed. This is no more a civil rights demonstration than if someone urged children to demonstrate their civil rights by seeing how many homes they could set fire to.[27]

Speaking from his high status as president of the Board of Education, Donovan's ideological position is evident in his appraisal of the boycott as an "offense" rather than a "civil rights demonstration." His use of exaggeration in likening the boycott to children demonstrating their civil rights by setting fire to homes suggests explicit disregard for Galamison as well as implicit association of 600 school students with criminal acts. In contrast to the exercise of power inherent in Donovan's words, Galamison is described as striving "vainly" to keep order among the students. Observing the scene, the journalist reports that he says to a sixteen-year-old student, "Look, baby, take your hat off. You know better than that."[28] Juxtaposing these words with Donovan's words serves to construct Galamison as weak in comparison and inept at controlling students—a primary objective of 600 schools.

Several students are also quoted as sources. They are characterized as "delighted by any excuse not to attend school"—implying that they are neither interested in nor aware of the purpose of the boycott—thereby confirming the ideology of those who criticize Galamison and his followers for exploiting students as props in their political game. (It is worth noting that most students would be delighted by a reason not to attend school.) Below are direct quotes from students:

> Nobody is going. Why should I go?
> Why are we boycotting? Because I hate teachers.
> We follow the majority. The majority wins.[29]

An argument could be made that these statements reflect a lack of understanding of the boycott on the part of these students; however, such flippant responses are typical of adolescents responding to an unfamiliar adult—particularly if interviewed as a group. It is of interest that these source quotes are immediately followed by a statement of the daily truancy rate at 30 percent as reported by the Board of Education. James Donovan, president of the Board of Education, is quoted as referring to the boycott as "a reprehensible act" in which boycott leaders encouraged truants not to come to school.[30] It is also worth noting that the journalist writes that the students "stayed out" of school rather than describing students as engaging in a boycott.

In "Teachers at a '600' School Resist Boycott There," Galamison, described as the leader of the Citywide Committee for Integrated Schools, is not quoted as a source; however, the article refers to his "claims" about the 600 schools: inferior education from poorly trained teachers, improper screening of students, and the lack of adequate textbooks and facilities.[31] Of note, the journalist quotes a fourteen-year-old boy from the recently boycotted Public School 617 who is distributing leaflets to students: "Take it home and let your mother read it to you. I go to a 600 school. I should know about them."[32] This is a student who is aware and engaged in the mission of the boycott and whose behavior does not reflect the descriptors regularly attributed to 600 students.

The article goes on to quote the principal, Joseph Del Barto, as telling his teachers, "If they give leaflets to any kid, take them away from him."[33] Teachers are described as grabbing students by the arms, slapping some students on the back and shoulders, and snatching the leaflets. The instinct of the teachers to readily engage in such behaviors certainly raises questions about the everyday interactions between teachers and students at 600 schools. The Board of Education, quoted as a source, speaks to "an inquiry about using physical force with the pupils":

> The rule against using force in any way except for the purpose of restraint of a pupil or self-defense is well-established. The director of the 600 schools, Sidney I. Lipsyte, has been acquainted with this report and will look into these facts very closely.[34]

The sentence immediately following this quote is a statement about the "2000 violent, disruptive children" who attend 600 schools—as if to remind the reader who these students are and why physical force is warranted.

The 600 Schools Boycott: Publications from the Black Community

Let's contrast the reporting by the *New York Times* against two important publications from the Black community through the use of primary source document analysis: *The Call to Conscience* and the *Amsterdam News*. *The Call to Conscience* was a publication of the Harlem-based Charter Group for a Pledge of Conscience, a multiracial community group that fought against racism and played a role in the fight for community control of public schools.[35] The *Amsterdam News* is the oldest continuously published Black newspaper in New York.

The Call to Conscience: Harlem Student Protesters in Operation Shutdown

The February/March 1965 issue of *The Call* featured an article titled "A Freedom School in Manhattan: A Report by Its Principal, Dr. Annette Rubinstein," describing the actions of Harlem-based youth (not attending a 600 school) who participated in Operation Shutdown. In contrast to the *New York Times* reporting on the 600 school students discussed elsewhere in this chapter, the tone of Rubinstein's article describes the student protests as joyful, liberating, and empowering.[36] Students participating in the boycott attended a Freedom School run by the Harlem Parents Committee. Whereas the 600 school students' participation in a Freedom School is barely mentioned, Rubinstein describes the Harlem students' routine in detail as a daily program of morning classes and lunch (alternately provided by members of the Harlem Parents Committee, teachers, and mothers who belonged to the group EQUAL) before students left to join picket lines, sit-ins, and other protest activities. In this case, students staying out of school and participating in protests is characterized as an important part of their educational experience. Contrast that with the 600 school students for whom staying out of school was equated with harm—to the students and the community.

When the Harlem students defy authority, *The Call* describes it as an act of heroism. This can be seen in Rubinstein's account of an incident when the students refuse to heed the warnings of an attendance officer who urges them to return to school:

> To the utter delight and amazement of the teachers present, the entire group maintained a courteous absolute silence until he had finished, and then spontaneously began to sing, "We shall not be moved." After the "truant officer" had thanked them for their courtesy and left, a young eighth grader said meditatively, "I think deep in his heart he was glad we acted that way."[37]

Additionally, described as "among the highlights of the school's last days" was mass attendance by the Freedom School students at a Congress of Racial Equality (CORE) meeting held at the City College of New York (CCNY) addressed by CORE cofounder James Farmer. CCNY students who walked the picket line with student protesters were so impressed with their conviction that they invited the young people to share a picnic lunch.

CCNY students were not the only ones the student protesters made an impression on. Farmer told the group:

> We have rejected the concept that youngsters should not participate in civil-rights demonstrations. They are not being forced to do anything against their will. In fact, most of the motivation for the civil-rights struggle has come from the youth.[38]

The young protesters are told in no uncertain terms that they *belong*. They are brave and defiant while their counterparts from the 600 schools are disruptive and disturbed.

Amsterdam News: Jackie Robinson on the 600 School Student Protests

After making history as the first Black player in Major League Baseball, Jackie Robinson used his notoriety as a professional athlete to call attention to the civil rights movement. Among his contributions after retiring from sports was a regular column in the *Amsterdam News*. In February of 1965, he used his platform to address Galamison's boycott. In a column titled "There Must Be a Better Way," Robinson called the Reverend out for his decision to focus on segregation in the 600 schools:

> We heartily approve of and admire the campaign and program which Dr. King has set in motion in Selma, Alabama. We have mixed emotions about the technique being called into play by Dr. Galamison.[39]

Though Robinson's tone is kinder than Donovan's calling the students "sick kids," he shared Donavan's criticism that engaging students who attend the 600 schools in the boycott was taking advantage of them. "Why use these especially disadvantaged children as pawns in the struggle to accelerate desegregation on our schools?" he asked. "There must be a better way."[40]

While Robinson was not opposed to children participating in acts of civil disobedience or being put on the frontlines of the movement, he was opposed to *those* children doing it. Dr. King is to be admired, but Galamison is not. Again, in contrast to the students in Harlem who refused to go to school and were unmoved by the threats of a truant officer, who were celebrated for their actions, Robinson had harsh criticism of what he called

> [Galamison's] highly questionable method of dragging out of the classrooms thousands of socially damaged children who have no idea how to meet scores of other problems they face daily—and much less an idea why they are being told not to go to school.[41]

Recovering the Past to Understand the Present

"History repeats itself" is a phrase we hear often. In this view, the past exists as a series of episodic lessons that we must learn from, we are told, lest we be doomed to repeat them. History, however, particularly at the intersection of race and disability, is not a repetition but a continuum. The violence and segregation against raced and disabled bodies does not appear and reappear throughout the past. Rather, race and disability have historically reinforced each other as categories used to justify violence and segregation—from the Middle Passage to the long fight for civil rights to our current educational practice.

It is worth noting that in archival collections the 600 schools are not represented as an important part of New York City history. Nor are they discussed as a part of the history of disability and special classes and schools for disabled students in the context of school segregation in published historical records. Yet, in a 1972 meeting with the Harlem Parents Committee, Milton Galamison reflected back on the 1965 boycott, referring to it as "the last big boycott effort" of the desegregation era, specifically naming the 600 school students as key actors in the movement. Even then, years later, he recalled the criticism before anything else: "You can imagine what this was like. 'Now they're gonna bring those 600 kids out into the street. You know, the crazy children.'"[42] In spite of reporting at the time that characterized the 600 school boycotters as "violent," "disturbed," and "disruptive" (Tolchin) or "socially damaged children" (Robinson) who barely understood their actions, Galamison paints a different picture:

> Frankly the 600 youngsters conducted themselves better than the high school and junior high school youngsters because they were accustomed to being sheltered and more regimented. And . . . we had no trouble with the 600 school children at all.[43]

Finally, Galamison confirms that the students who participated in the boycott deserve to be remembered the same way as the students in Harlem and other young people who participated in liberatory acts of resistance. As he put it, "People might be inclined to say, maybe nothing had happened. But it isn't true that nothing had happened because what started as an issue in New York is now a national issue."[44]

Conclusion

Archives and record keeping shape our collective history, reflecting societal and organizational memory and reinforcing the erasure of the people and events that society prefers to forget.[45] This rewriting of the past is not reflective of the life cycle of records, but status and power.[46] History is rife with archival silences and intentional obfuscations enforced by the powerful, such as attempts to erase state-sponsored violence from collective memory by excluding records from "official" collections. We recognize the role that archives play in shaping history not as neutral collections, but as sites with the power to deny marginalized groups the ability to determine their own social memory and history.[47] The 600 schools are a story about disability. The boycott and the 600 schools exemplify the way race and disability inform each other. They also tell us something about how disability continues to be used to segregate schools and the importance of a clear and rigorous understanding of racism, ableism, and their historical relationship to one another. In the largest school system in the country, one that continues to be defined by segregation, we argue that it is important to remember the 600 schools, but *how* we remember them matters, too.

If you look closely enough, conflicting depictions of the 1965 boycott exist in the written record. In Daniel Perlstein's work, we find the standard narrative about these events. He describes the boycott this way: "Galamison and other boycott organizers were harshly criticized for threatening to turn uncontrollable, delinquent black youth loose on the city."[48] Reinforcing a distorted historical memory of the event, Perlstein portrays the 600 school students just as Galamison said people would. Yet, a more accurate picture of the 600 school student protesters exists in the written record. It's not hidden in the background, you don't have to dig for it; you just need to be willing to shift your focus as did teacher and community control advocate Joseph Laspro. As a member of the dissident group within the United Federation of Teachers (UFT), the New Coalition, Laspro had an altogether more radical view of these all-but-forgotten youth. As he put it, "The great majority of our children will become so-called 'disruptive children.' Perhaps then, a more appropriate epithet for these youth will be 'revolutionaries.'"[49]

Notes

1. Jasmine E. Harris, "Reckoning with Race and Disability," *Faculty Scholarship at Penn Carey Law*, 2021.

2. Carl Suddler, "'The Child Is Never Basically Bad': Creating Crime through Prevention," in *Presumed Criminal: Black Youth and the Justice System in Postwar New York* (New York: NYU Press, 2019), 13–38, https://muse.jhu.edu/chapter/2665965; Cheryl Nelson Butler, "Blackness as Delinquency," *Washington University Law Review* 90, no. 5 (2013): 1335–97.

3. Harry M. Shulman, "Crime Prevention and the Public Schools," *Journal of Educational Sociology* 4, no. 2 (1930): 69–81, https://doi.org/10.2307/2961178.

4. Suddler, "'The Child Is Never Basically Bad,'" in *Presumed Criminal.*

5. Suddler, "'The Child Is Never Basically Bad,'" in *Presumed Criminal.*

6. Christine Sleeter, "Why Is There Learning Disabilities? A Critical Analysis of the Birth of the Field in Its Social Context," *Disability Studies Quarterly* 30, no. 2 (June 1, 2010), https://doi.org/10.18061/dsq.v30i2.1261.

7. Suddler, "'The Child Is Never Basically Bad,'" in *Presumed Criminal.*

8. Sleeter, "Why Is There Learning Disabilities?"

9. Clarence Taylor, *Knocking at Our Own Door: Milton A. Galamison and the Struggle for School Integration in New York City* (Columbia University Press, 1997).

10. "Galamison Planning Prolonged Boycott of 31 Junior Highs," *New York Times*, November 14, 1964; Martin Tolchin, "90% Boycott Hits Problem School," *New York Times*, January 20, 1965.

11. Tolchin, "90% Boycott Hits Problem School."

12. Video, Milton Galamison at the Harlem Parents Committee Meeting, March 2, 1972. Babette Edwards Education Reform in Harlem collection, 1964–2006. Schomburg Center for Research on Black Culture.

13. "Rev. Galamison Sets More School Closings," *New York Amsterdam News*, January 30, 1965.

14. Tolchin, "90% Boycott Hits Problem School"; Tolchin, "Teachers at a '600' School Resist Boycott There."

15. Critical discourse analysis emerged in the 1980s and '90s as a method to identify social relations and power structures within language. CDA tells us that it is within the social practice of language that power relations and ideologies become reproduced. It is the work of CDA to extract actual meaning that is often invisible within discourse. See the work of Carmen Rosa Caldas-Coulthard, "Discourse

Analysis," in *Exploring Language and Linguistics*, edited by Natalie Braber, Louise Cummings, and Liz Morrish (Cambridge University Press, 2015), 219–45; Michael Alexander Kirkwood Halliday, *Language as Social Semiotic: The Social Interpretation of Language and Meaning* (London: Edward Arnold, 1978); Norman Fairclough and Ruth Wodak, "Critical Discourse Analysis: An Overview," in *Discourse and Interaction*, edited by Teun A. van Dijk (London: Sage, 1997), 67–97.

16. Norman Fairclough, *Language and Power* (3rd ed.) (New York: Routledge, 2015).

17. Tolchin, "90% Boycott Hits Problem School."

18. Tolchin, "Teachers at a '600' School Resist Boycott There."

19. Tolchin, "90% Boycott Hits Problem School."

20. Tolchin, "90% Boycott Hits Problem School."

21. Tolchin, "90% Boycott Hits Problem School."

22. Tolchin, "Teachers at a '600' School Resist Boycott There."

23. Tolchin, "Teachers at a '600' School Resist Boycott There"; Fon Gordon, "Driving 'Jim Crow': Cars and Race in the United States," *Technology's Stories*, September 28, 2020, https://doi.org/10.15763/jou.ts.2020.09.28.05.

24. Tolchin, "Teachers at a '600' School Resist Boycott There."

25. Tolchin, "Teachers at a '600' School Resist Boycott There."

26. Tolchin, "Teachers at a '600' School Resist Boycott There."

27. Tolchin, "90% Boycott Hits Problem School."

28. Tolchin, "90% Boycott Hits Problem School."

29. Tolchin, "90% Boycott Hits Problem School."

30. Tolchin, "90% Boycott Hits Problem School."

31. Tolchin, "Teachers at a '600' School Resist Boycott There."

32. Tolchin, "Teachers at a '600' School Resist Boycott There."

33. Tolchin, "Teachers at a '600' School Resist Boycott There."

34. Tolchin, "Teachers at a '600' School Resist Boycott There."

35. Gerald Meyer, "James Baldwin's Harlem: The Key to His Politics," *Socialism and Democracy* 25: 1 (2011), 273–81.

36. Annette Rubinstein, "A Freedom School in Manhattan: A Report by Its Principal, Dr. Annette Rubinstein," *A Call to Conscience* 1, no. 3 (March 1965).

37. Rubinstein, "A Freedom School in Manhattan."

38. Rubinstein, "A Freedom School in Manhattan."

39. Jackie Robinson, "There Must Be a Better Way," *New York Amsterdam News*, January 30, 1965.

40. Robinson, "There Must Be a Better Way."

41. Robinson, "There Must Be a Better Way."

42. Video, Milton Galamison at the Harlem Parents Committee Meeting.

43. Video, Milton Galamison at the Harlem Parents Committee Meeting.

44. Video, Milton Galamison at the Harlem Parents Committee Meeting.

45. Brien Brothman, "The Past That Archives Keep: Memory, History, and the Preservation of Archival Records," *Archivaria*, January 1, 2001, 48–80.

46. Brothman, "The Past That Archives Keep"; Achille Mbembe, "The Power of the Archive and Its Limits," in *Refiguring the Archive*, eds. Carolyn Hamilton et al.

(Dordrecht: Springer Netherlands, 2002), 19–27, https://doi.org/10.1007/978-94-010-0570–8_2; Rodney G. S. Carter, "Of Things Said and Unsaid: Power, Archival Silences, and Power in Silence," *Archivaria*, September 25, 2006, 215–33.

47. Carter, "Of Things Said and Unsaid."

48. Daniel H. Perlstein, *Justice, Justice: School Politics and the Eclipse of Liberalism* (New York: Peter Lang Publishing, 2004), 105.

49. Jerald E. Podair, *The Strike That Changed New York: Blacks, Whites and the Ocean Hill-Brownsville Crisis* (Yale University Press, 2003), 163.

PART III

Decolonizing

CHAPTER 10

Settler Ableism

Indigeneity, Unsettling the Archive, and Accountability in History

SARAH WHITT (CHOCTAW NATION OF OKLAHOMA), TRACI BRYNNE VOYLES, AND SUSAN BURCH

Buried within an archival file labeled "Canton Asylum," a letter written in 1940 by Dr. Riley Guthrie to the daughter of Prairie Band Potawatomi healer O-Zoush-Quah sought an intervention in the name of comfort and treatment. "Your mother . . . has long hair which we believe should be barbed in order to add to her comfort and wellbeing." The physician continued, "We believe that [cutting off her long hair] would be of benefit to her and would make her much more comfortable and contented."[1] The word "comfortable" appears regularly in archived Asylum reports about O-Zoush-Quah. According to hospital staff, she was usually "quite comfortable mentally." Repeated assurances that staff "take good care of" O-Zoush-Quah and "make her comfortable" follow references to her good physical health.[2] As many institutionalized people and scholar-activists who study their lived experiences know, comfort is a euphemism for docile.

Potawatomi women like O-Zoush-Quah and her daughters had always worn their hair long. Photos of the mother and her young girls show all of them with carefully parted dark hair pulled back into single braids or buns.[3] O-Zoush-Quah would have spent her early years brushing the girls' hair; the older daughters might have brushed hers as well. Long strokes, fingers and strands cascading down, in the daily ritual of care and kinship.

When staff sought to bob the Potawatomi woman's hair to ease their own management of her, they also resisted doing the care work that a family—particularly other women—would provide. Casting the shearing as a means to make her comfortable contributed to the process of erasure that institutionalization wrought on the whole family. O-Zoush-Quah's daughters pleaded for the right to provide her with the intimate, domestic kind of care that would have affirmed her valued place in their world.[4] Hospital employees consistently described their efforts, including cropping the Potawatomi woman's hair, as treatment. In actuality, order and management drove this and many other interventions in the locked wards. Power propels this archived moment: asylum personnel and physicians claimed authority over O-Zoush-Quah as well as her family. Context deepens its meaning. The Bureau of Indian Affairs assumed that the medicine woman was incompetent and imposed Western medical diagnoses and treatments. They detained her in federal psychiatric facilities, far away from her family, her home, from the land that held her medicine and her ancestors.[5]

O-Zoush-Quah refused the eradicating forces of institutionalization. Her actions, if not her direct perspective, rise through staff reports about the healer. Speaking Potawatomi—in whispers, sometimes in screams—she tore at the clothing that itched her skin, lunged for nurses' keys that would unlock the ward doors, and refused the staff who tried to enforce her compliance. The same personnel called her "irritated" and "excited" when she defied them, when she was not "comfortable."

The experiences of institutionalization that O-Zoush-Quah and her family lived were profound and also unexceptional. Since settler conquest unfurled on Turtle Island, Native nations and their ancestral lands, air, water, and fellow beings have been harmed by, struggled against, adapted to, and sought to survive settler colonialism and ableism in their many manifestations.

Many disability historians who study North America have demonstrated that disability is a shape-shifting category as well as a lived experience, taking different forms and meanings across times and places.[6] Building on this insight, we ask: What happens when we center Indigenous perspectives? What happens when we examine these historical phenomena through the lens of settler colonialism? One result is greater recognition that the concept and term "disability" is non-Indigenous, settler; it is rooted in particular worldviews and cultural practices. It also clarifies that the concept of ableism would benefit from closer historical scrutiny and attention to both Indigeneity and settler colonialism. Carefully considering ableism as a central feature of settler colonialism recenters our understandings of the relationships between disability, Indigeneity, settler colonialism, and the archives.[7] Historicizing settler ableism insists that we engage with absences and presences, and commit to practices for generating accountable ways of doing history.[8]

With this in mind, we turn our attention to the system of settler ableism and its impacts on human and other-than-human beings. Focusing on the particular ways in which ableism and settler colonialism have been enmeshed as power structures in what settlers call the United States, we ask how, in specific times and places, individual colonists and colonial institutions have deployed settler ableism to enact power over Native peoples and others. Examples in this chapter illustrate ways that settler ableism shapes judgments and experiences as well as documentation and tellings of the past. This work is an invitation for renewed attention to historical specificity, to power, and to archives.

Access, perspective, and process guide this chapter. Robust citations are intended to invite further study and conversation and to recognize sources beyond the printed page. The format reflects an intentional practice of collaboration. Some sections convey our collective exploration of key themes. Drawing on our individual situated knowledge, other sections—marked with our names—offer focused critiques of research methods, archival experiences, and practices of re-storying.[9]

Settler Colonialism and Settler Ableism

When Bureau of Indian Affairs agents forcibly removed O-Zoush-Quah and countless others to psy institutions, boarding schools, and outing systems, they drew on ableist ideas that ranked and organized living beings according to culturally and historically specific values and beliefs that include productivity, competitiveness, capacity, self-management, independence, linear time and progress, and mobility.[10] Western biomedicine and settler political structures buttressed and sustained these interventions, providing justifications and means to separate kin and dismantle past and future Indigenous lifeways. By design, intrusive settler processes stripped O-Zoush-Quah and her family of self-determination and daily care relations. Physically uprooting the medicine woman from her home/land/ancestors in a process of displacement aligned with broader settler colonial aims of Indigenous dispossession. As O-Zoush-Quah and many others before and after her have lived it, diagnosis served as a useful mechanism of settler ableism. And settler ableism served the broader project of settler colonialism.

In our usage, "settler colonialism" refers to a set of power relations that seeks to colonize Indigenous peoples and claim their homelands as settlers' own through intersecting forces of racism, sexism, heteropatriarchy, environmental degradation, dispossession, and capitalism. Settler colonialism emerged out of the intersecting convergences of a set of global historical power forces—capitalism, imperialism, anti-Blackness, nationalism—all of which hold complicated consequences for the meanings and lived experiences of humans and other beings; it is a historical *and* an ongoing structure of power relations.

In these converging, intersecting, and seething systems of power, beings of all types matter. We are interested in the entrapment and representation of people and their other-than-human kin at the intersections of settler colonialism and ableism.[11] The consequences of these ostensibly social power relations for the more-than-human world hold our attention as well. Settler ableism targets humans *and* broader communities of beings in their respective ecological systems.[12] This system targets human-nonhuman relationships, particularly those associated with Indigenous peoples whose relationships to the nonhuman world emphasize balance, care, and reciprocity over capitalist settler values of extraction, profit, and occupation.[13] Critical attention to the contexts and consequences of settler colonialism has direct implications for historical understandings of settler ableism. Indigenous peoples' experiences in different historical contexts, in turn, reveal both the malleability and the pervasiveness of settler ableism.

As a category within an ableist system, disability is shaped by settler colonialism and the discourses, ideologies, and practices that have emerged from, within, and in between episodic land grabs in the West. Settler colonial social ordering and the labels accompanying ideas of disability do not align well with Indigenous cosmologies, which assert the power inherent in the diversity and specificity of all humans, animals, elements, and sentient and nonsentient beings. For example, viewed from a Choctaw perspective, the collective's capacity for equilibrium, balance, and longevity informs the meaning, place, and expectations of people and their kin.[14]

This fundamentally different view of people and relations changes the questions historians ask of archival sources, like those referencing O-Zoush-Quah during her involuntary institutionalization. Queries like whether O-Zoush-Quah (or anyone else who shared the locked wards with her) "was or wasn't disabled" are rooted in Western biomedicine and settler colonial values. But this is an incomplete and skewed approach to lived stories. Other questions, like whether someone was targeted by settler ableism, and what the consequences were of that targeting, point us to different truths, insights, and histories.

Applying an Indigenous studies lens to discussions about ableism highlights the settler structures that foreclose not only the possibility of normative personhood for Indigenous peoples—but of life at all. "We are the land, and the land is us," as the common refrain goes in Indian Country. For Indigenous peoples, settler ableism is always-already debilitating; it is implicated in many structures of white supremacy and is predicated, first and foremost, upon Indigenous dispossession.[15] Historical processes, shifts, and transformations, including the rise of manufacturing, expansion of Western biomedicine, and the proliferation of institutionalization, would not be possible without settler-citizens' systematic appropriation of Indigenous lands. Settler ableism is a structural precondition and consequence of the emergences of a range of social and environmental injustices with which Native as well as non-Native people continue to grapple.[16]

The systematic appropriation of Indigenous lands, a central feature of settler colonialism, has wrought devastating consequences for Indigenous peoples in ways that reach beyond the loss of territorial holdings. Indigenous cosmological ideas of collectivity extend beyond human communities to encompass the nonhuman world and all its complexities. Potawatomi philosopher Kyle Powys Whyte points to the fact that settler colonialism carries ecological consequences by design, as a form of oppression that "violently disrupts" Indigenous peoples' relationships to their homelands as a means of targeting Indigenous ecological relationships.[17] Indigenous relations to the nonhuman world, in turn, have been described by Hupa, Yurok, and Karuk scholar Cutcha Risling Baldy and Diné scholar Melanie K. Yazzie as "radical relationality," in which nonhuman entities such as lands and waters are "relative[s] with whom we engage in social (and political) relations premised on interdependency and respect."[18] This offers a stark contrast to settler orientations to the nonhuman world, which regard its lands, waters, and beings as resources for capitalist extraction and exploitation.[19]

Traci Brynne Voyles: Settler ableist discourses have enacted violent disruptions by constructing Native relationships to their lands as deviant and abnormal. The guiding logic of dispossession, across multiple centuries and manifesting in myriad ways, has been that Native peoples used their lands in ways that settlers recognized as deficient. The Natives "inclose noe land, neither do they have any settled habytation, nor any tame cattle to improve the land by, and soe have no other but a natural right to those countries," opined Massachusetts Bay Colony governor John Winthrop in 1629, laying out an early legal apologia for dispossession.[20] Inclosing land, establishing permanent townsites, and taming cattle—demonstrably English ideas about how to live on the land—became in Winthrop's framing the pathway to "civil" as opposed to "natural" rights to land. Wampanoags' disinterest in fences, towns, or domesticated livestock, in Winthrop's eyes, justified colonists' imposition on their homelands.[21]

Two and a half centuries later, another settler politician from Wampanoag land in the settler state of Massachusetts, Henry Dawes, used similar logic to endorse his 1887 General Allotment Act (known colloquially as the Dawes Act), which sought to force white agricultural practices on Native peoples and divide up the remaining land among settlers.[22] Native peoples, Dawes asserted, "have got as far as they can go because they own their land in common." Until they "consent to give up their lands, and divide them among their citizens so that each can own the land he cultivates," he stated, "they will not make much progress."[23] Native peoples' inefficiency at exploiting their land bases, to Dawes's settler ableist way of thinking, pointed to an inherent flaw that could only be rectified by forced assimilation—a full eradication of Indigenous peoples' ways of being in favor of white relationships to land. Dawes's perspective represented a broad, enduring way of thinking among white settlers: that Native polities were fundamentally underdeveloped as societies, and that the absence of capitalist ambition in the stewarding of land indicated inadequacies in how Native peoples thought and behaved.

These kinds of examples saturate the settler archive, spanning centuries of settler colonial violence against Native peoples, and rely on deeply ableist logics, propping up an image of settler land uses as unquestionably rational against ideas of Native land relations as inferior, problematic, and illogical—in short, as representing defective capacity. As Cherokee literary critic Sean Kicummah Teuton puts it: "Since early settler colonial history . . . European thinkers were swiftly led to target non-Europeans and especially communally defined tribal peoples as innately intellectually inferior. Rather abruptly race became inextricably tied to mental deficiency."[24] Wardship status itself, the legal precedent set in 1831 by Supreme Court Chief Justice John Marshall characterizing sovereign Native nations as "domestic dependent nations" and their relationship to the U.S. settler government as resembling "that of a ward to his guardian," turns on "settler ableist rhetoric" that infantilizes of Native peoples in comparison to settlers.[25]

Tracing settler ableism's long reach reframes historic constructions that cast colonizers as rational adults and Natives as innately deficient inferiors. In the 1850s, California settlers criminalized Natives' use of fire to manage forests and other ecosystems and linked this practice to settlers' regard for Indigenous peoples generally as incompetent and childlike.[26] Federal agents in the 1930s saw Diné sheepherding practices as evidence that they did not understand their own homeland and its limitations as a rangeland.[27] Throughout what settlers now call northern California, Native peoples' long and successful reliance on acorns and other cultivated food sources earned them an epithet from settlers that referenced digging in the dirt—a deployment of racist framing that specifically linked Native peoples' dietary and ecological practices to a presumption about their lack of sophistication and an incapacity to sustain themselves through other, more "civilized," food sources.[28]

It is important to note that these and other examples targeted not only Indigenous peoples' ecological cosmologies and their specific practices of managing local environmental conditions (their "radical relationality" with the nonhuman world) but also the *collectivism* of Indigenous societies. Individual white settlers and settler institutions, including archives, have long represented this kind of collectivism, which extended between humans in a community but also to the nonhuman world, as a central deficiency of Indigenous cosmologies and ecological practices. O-Zoush-Quah's intimate ties to her family, for example, provided a rationale for her incarceration at Canton; her isolation from her family, as well as her separation from their land, was seen by her captors as an integral part of her "treatment." In this instance, settler ableism manifested as an attempt to cleave an individual medicine woman from her home and her family under the pernicious rubric of care, specifically targeting her connections to land and people.

Historian Caroline Lieffers contends that "as American power and the American nation extended westward and beyond, scientists, physicians, anthropologists, and other so-called experts moved across the landscape too, recommending agricultural practices, medical interventions, and regimes of racial and ethnological comprehension that sorted landscapes and people by degrees of productivity, health, normalcy, and civility, and sought, ostensibly, to improve them."[29] Invoking self-serving judgments of "depending people, incompetent cultures and races, and unused lands," white settlers justified ongoing erasures and replacement.

Lands on Turtle Island were, of course, never "unused" and any discussion of American expansion must necessarily acknowledge this while accounting for the complicated, contested, and contingent process of Indigenous land dispossession and physical conquest. This history of settler invasion is *not* one of humanitarian impulses or benevolence, despite rhetoric, beliefs, and reams of archived documents that claim the contrary. This, not coincidentally, is also one of the defining features of settler colonialism in the United States; as historian and theorist Lorenzo Veracini suggests, these discourses help obscure the settler order: "the more it goes without saying, the better it covers its tracks."[30] The primary objective of settler colonialism similarly is Indigenous elimination; settler institutions, ideologies, and ideas about Indigenous peoples ultimately function in pursuit of Indigenous disappearance.

The ranging ways in which settler ableism has manifested—how it has buttressed other systems of power and been sustained by them; how its consequences have been lived, preserved, and taught; and how its insidious "common sense" has been inscribed and enshrined in archives—have never been universal, ahistorical, or static. Attention to the particularities of time, place, and experiences enables a more precise understanding of settler ableism as a historical force. Recognizing most archives as manifestations of settler ableism and other historical forces changes the way researchers engage with these sites of knowledge.

The archives reinforce the context and the legitimacy of settler ableism through selective processes of inclusion, labeling, categorizing, and indexing of institutional documents. Susan Burch's experience conducting archival work on the Canton Asylum and people detained there extends this point. As her account reveals, accounting for context and structure is not the only challenge to fully perceiving settler ableism in the past; the archive, too, poses barriers, pitfalls, false starts, and trap doors. And as Sarah Whitt reminds us, a nuanced approach, taken with a commitment to Native sovereignty, agency, and intergenerational care, can help us navigate these archival traps where necessary—and, when we need to, bypass them altogether.

Settler Ableism and the Archive

Susan Burch: What the entire archived Canton Asylum records conspicuously do not acknowledge is the impact of place in O-Zoush-Quah's and other institutionalized people's stories: medical reports systematically uncouple people from the space holding them, the material realities of their lives. Canton Asylum's locked wards, the hallways and bedrooms, are rendered invisible; staff members' medical gaze appears in institutional files as objective and unplaced.

For O-Zoush-Quah and countless others, confinement within a psychiatric institution becomes itself justification for sustained detention and an eclipsing lens through which they are judged and documented. The process of institutionalization and institutional reporting—by design—edits out moments of agency and personhood.[31] Compounded constraints—inherent in carceral institutions and sustained in archival practices—narrows historians' window into historic sites (like Canton Asylum) and experiences (like O-Zoush-Quah's). This contributes to skewed histories that serve settler colonialism.

O-Zoush-Quah cannot be located in the National Archives catalog using a name search; materials referencing her, and her children's petitions on her behalf, are held across different boxes in the National Archives and Records Administration in Washington, DC, organized by series name "Canton Asylum for Insane Indians" and by the BIA unit that oversaw her nation's reservation (Potawatomi); some are nested within the series number 722.1, which refers to Asylums—Insane Indians. Her archival presence is fundamentally affiliated with a medicalized settler institution, then with the category of psy, then as Indigenous (generic).[32] This example is a microcosm of an archival universe predicated on settler ableism.

Settler ableism influences what is seen as important in the archives, what is rendered knowable, what is obscured based on the perceived value and worth of the person, and who can (literally) access its holdings. In the National Archives—as just one example—most people (and especially Black and Indigenous people, other communities of color, and disabled people) are grouped according to institutions that were designed to manage them. The very terms used to define materials, to organize and manage them, are imbued with ideas about control, worth, authority, and settler ableist concepts of normalcy, capacity, and personhood.[33] The category of disability and all its linguistic kin (such as deficiency, incompetency, wardship, and the like) function as settler ableist guideposts in the archive.

The archive is thus a vital space for exploring the ways that settler ableism tracks, defines, creates, and polices normativity, as well as a place where the consequences for abnormality can be indexed. It is not a place, generally, where the full humanity of individual and collective people can be recognized—for that, we will often need a different kind of method and a different rubric for what counts as "archive." As we riffle through stacks of paper, we might also run our fingers through soil, over fabric and carefully threaded stitches, over the grainy photographs of our own ancestors' faces, or over the furrowed skin of our grandmothers' hands.[34]

Archives from a Different Center

The Jensen family quilt holds many stories: absences and presences, Indigeneity and settler ableism, and continuance. For O-Zoush-Quah, her daughters, and

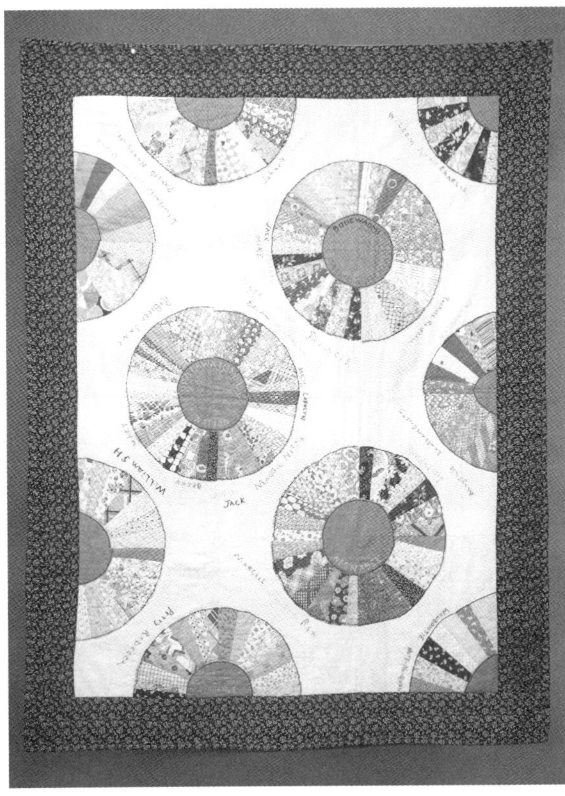

Figure 10.1. In this four foot by six foot quilt, bright calico fabrics circle blue plates that spread across twelve squares. Family members' names are sewn around each circle. Prairie Band Potawatomi healer O-Zoush-Quah, and her daughter, Pah-Kish-Ko-Quah, made this quilt during the mother's incarceration at Canton Asylum, c. 1910–30. Used with permission by Jack Jensen.

many other Potawatomi women, quilt-making as a cross-generational practice fused lessons about kinship, home, childrearing, and history.[35]

To alleviate the relentless monotony and other harms to their mother imposed by her medicalized exile, O-Zoush-Quah's children asked asylum staff to provide her with patchwork supplies. Mirroring their mother's act of quilting inside Canton, her daughter Pah-Kish-Ko-Quah created additional quilt squares from her home in Kansas. Across walls, miles, and decades, the mother and daughter assembled the parts for a quilt that would hold family relations, memories, and future generations of kin.

For O-Zoush-Quah's descendants, this quilt is an animate archive. Running his hands across the stitched fabric, O-Zoush-Quah's great-grandson Jack Jensen imagines her and his grandmother (Pah-Kish-Ko-Quah) creating the squares, compiling them. Looking at the quilt, Jack Jensen was reminded that his great-grandmother was medicine—someone to whom others turned when seeking blessings and healing. Her quilt's creation challenged the archival reports he had read. Holding the fabric archive, Jensen understood that his ancestors continued to claim his great-grandmother; they refused the U.S. government's assertion that it knew what was best for her. O-Zoush-Quah's own refusals to staff domination and institutional erasure filled her physical absence from Jensen's daily life with new forms of presence. Remembering his ancestor and being remembered by her, Jensen tended to the quilt and his great-grandmother, countering institutionalization's cross-generational harm that was enacted in the name of Western medicine and care.

The quilt that O-Zoush-Quah and Pah-Kish-Ko-Quah made is an archive of care and comfort. Family members on the outside intentionally advocated for her to have quilting materials. Staff may have agreed in part because craftwork kept people busy and therefore easier to manage. But the Potawatomi kin understood that piecework offered their mother more than distraction from the numbing infinity of time on the inside. Quilting was a practice that ancestors had passed down for generations, that O-Zoush-Quah had taught them before she was forcibly taken away. Elders' hands over younger ones, stitches and memories, combined efforts that provided comfort—as padded baby hammocks, buffers from harsh winds and cold ground, and shelter during illness. As she waited for her parent to return, Pah-Kish-Ko-Quah collected her mother's pieces, adding her own cloth squares and stacking them together. Pah-Kish-Ko-Quah was archiving the quilt pieces—her family's history—guided by kinship obligations, expectations, care, and reciprocity.

Archival Silences

Sarah Whitt: What do we do with the fragments?

I pose this question as a historian and as a Choctaw woman whose engagement with Indigenous histories has sometimes been facilitated or impeded by colonial archives and the keepers of those records. This issue, of course, is not uniquely mine; others have also had to find ways to access archival records and weave together the fragments of those narratives into a cohesive whole. But when it comes to Indigenous people—especially Indigenous women who lived at the turn of the twentieth century—there just never seems to be enough of what you want, or need, to reanimate the worlds they inhabited. So, you have to get creative.

I was looking for a way to get closer to the young Indigenous women held at the House of the Good Shepherd when I came across the Reading postcard during an internet search. I purchased it on eBay for $2.97—a paltry sum, given its value to me, a twenty-first-century historian. Although it has been in my possession for several years, many of my questions remain unanswered about this artifact, a truly mysterious object. Why would anyone—Edna—ever send a friend such a thing? *Will come to make settlement*, she scribbled before signing her name. Did she plan to settle a debt with Florence, or to settle permanently in Reading?

I wonder if Edna knew what the Reading house was. I wonder if she would've cared.

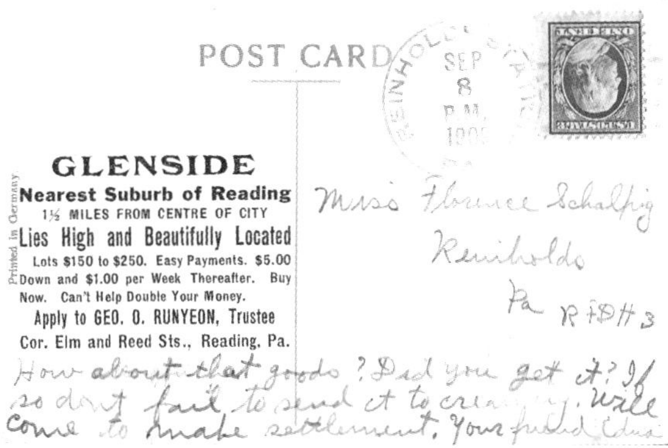

Figure 10.2. A 3 × 5-inch postcard with an image of the House of the Good Shepherd in Reading, Pennsylvania.

Around 1915, at least three young Indigenous women were sent from the Carlisle Indian Industrial School, the United States' most notorious off-reservation Native American boarding institution, to the Good Shepherd Home, situated eighty miles to the east of Carlisle in Reading, Pennsylvania. Sent from one alien environment to another, their transinstitutionalization, or the movement from one institution to another, highlights the importance of settler colonialism to histories of forced confinement in Progressive-Era institutions—histories that are often understood and analyzed through the lens of state power alone.[36] Their experiences similarly reflect how ableist attitudes, grounded in the American project of nation-building, seized upon American Indian people in complex ways at the turn of the twentieth century.

The young women—Carrie (Red Cliff Chippewa), Agnes (Menominee), and Gertrude (Sioux)—ranged in age from fifteen to twenty, and records reflect that they were incarcerated at the Good Shepherd Home at the direction of Carlisle superintendent Moses Friedman. A fourth young woman, Myrtle (Omaha), was also cleared for transfer to the Good Shepherd Home, but it is ambiguous at the time of this writing whether she was sent. Other letters of correspondence relating to two additional Carlisle enrollees, Charlotte (Chippewa) and Lillian (Sioux), similarly reveal that Friedman and his successor, Carlisle superintendent Oscar Lipps, were making arrangements in 1914 and 1915 for the young women's transfer from Carlisle to the Good Shepherd Home; inconsistent record keeping makes it unclear as to whether this was done. A seventh woman named Edna (tribal affiliation, if any, unknown), who claimed to be a Carlisle affiliate, was confined to the Good Shepherd Home by the Cumberland County court system for the crime of prostitution in 1927. The young Carlisle women's "transgressions" were diverse—refusing subordination to white heads of household, perceived uncleanliness, "incorrigibility."[37] In the context of a residential school designed to subordinate Indigenous people to U.S. authority, Carlisle officials viewed these and similar behaviors as threatening to institutional order. But the circumstances around each young woman's confinement also register Carlisle officials' attempts to control Indigenous bodies and suppress Indigenous lifeways, and reveal the settler ableist impulses that underlay Carlisle's administration. As the Indigenous women's experiences of forced confinement make clear, the ideology of settler ableism and its attendant practices have wide-ranging implications for diverse populations assigned an inferior social status, including, but not limited to, people with disabilities.

The young Indigenous women sent to the Reading house had not accepted their assigned place in the racial, class, and gendered hierarchies in which they were situated at the bottom. They were, as their Carlisle disciplinary records suggest, too threatening in their refusals; simply put, they were too enlivened. Even our received understanding of this history—the impulses that inform the exclusion of Indigenous perspectives from the colonial archive, and the historical narratives that make sense of this chimerical era—are influenced by settler ableist assumptions about the worth of the women's lives and experiences.[38]

The silences endemic to the stories of Indigenous women's confinement are tremendous. They echo and reverberate into the narratives of the present and index the ways in which settler agents wielded institutionalization as a powerful way to control, subdue, or eliminate Indigenous peoples viewed as threatening in their corporeality or otherwise lacking against settler ableist rubrics of normalcy. Carrie (Red Cliff Chippewa), for example, was removed from Carlisle in 1914 at the age of seventeen and sent to the Reading house as punishment for being a "menace."[39] Despite the fact that Carlisle's superintendent kept Carrie on the rolls as an Outing Program laborer, a designation that enabled the institution to continue to receive federal monies for her "education" even though she was physically confined elsewhere, a portion of Carrie's per-capita payment from the Red Cliff agency was redirected to the convent to pay for her "care."[40] This was often the way Carlisle superintendents described similar arrangements of forced confinement: as beneficial, uplifting. Their rhetoric of benevolence dominates the archive; their structures of supremacy hide in plain sight.

Menace. Incorrigible. Unclean. In the coded rhetoric of white supremacy, the words U.S. officials chose to describe the Indian girls and women they confined to the Good Shepherd Home were meant to underscore their deviance, their inability to achieve "proper" femininity by virtue of their racialized status as Indian women. "Care," in these scenarios, thus also signaled a kind of benign violence: as institutionalization came to replace other forms of elimination, U.S. officials cloaked their settler grammar in the ableist language of reform.

In another letter, written by Carlisle's Outing matron Lida Johnston, Carrie was described by a nun named Sister Corsini as having made "excellent progress" after being confined there for nearly a year, yet Carrie was disallowed from returning home as a result of the conditions on the reservation. According to this correspondence, Sister Corsini even went so far as to say that Carrie was "thinking of becoming a Sister at the institution."[41] Concluding this letter, Johnston wrote that "[Carrie's] worst features seem to be laziness and uncleanliness."[42] This comment, meant to rationalize her ongoing confinement, also underscores how Indigenous pathologization is central to the architecture of white supremacy.[43] Nowhere is Carrie's supposed "infraction," the reason she was sent to the Reading house, explained beyond her characterization by Carlisle officials as "incorrigible and practically unmanageable."[44] In the eighty pages of documents contained in Carrie's Carlisle file, three short letters are written in her own hand. In a letter dated August 14, Carrie wrote to Lipps from the convent: "I'm doing the best I can. I don't know whether I'll ever go home. If I do, I [don't] know what I'll be, but I hope I'll be a good girl after I get out, as that's what I'm aiming for."[45]

Tanana Athabascan feminist theorist Dian Million observes that "peace after state and civic violence is rarely accomplished by silencing victims. If a victim's or a group of victims' experience has no voice, the experience returns through continuing discord."[46] Million's observation is instructive in considering the consequences of silenced voices and obscured stories in relation to histories of forced institutionalization and ableist rubrics of normative personhood, both of which remain relevant to Indigenous women, Indigenous people, and the struggles our nations face today.[47]

Deconstructing archival silences is a process of careful storying. Applied to the history of Indigenous women's confinement at the Reading house, this statement is doubly true. As Haitian American philosopher Michel-Rolph Trouillot explains, "any historical narrative is a particular bundle of silences, the result of a unique process, and the operation required to deconstruct these silences will vary accordingly."[48] He describes his own practice as a historian recuperating silenced histories, using the Haitian Revolution as a powerful case in point. He writes, "That silencing . . . is due to uneven power in the production of sources, archives, and narratives. But if I am correct that this revolution was unthinkable as it happened, the insignificance of the story is already inscribed in the sources, regardless of what else they reveal. There are no new facts here; not even neglected ones. Here I have to make the silences speak for themselves."[49]

There are some substantial methodological quandaries at play in attempts to recuperate silenced histories. In the colonial archive, Indigenous women's perspectives—like Carrie's—are few and far between. Nonetheless, reading across the grain helps us to understand a little bit about their lives and the structures of supremacy that they negotiated in the early years of the twentieth century. Occasionally, we hear from the women themselves. In other instances, silences overwhelm the archive, and we are left with many more questions than answers. It is here that I am reminded of Trouillot's call to action. Here, I am compelled to make the archival silences speak by listening critically.

What does it mean to listen to the archive, to make the silences speak? This methodology—reading in between the lines and across the grain, turning the colonial archive inside out and against itself—is an act of care, a radical act of listening. Administrative marginalia, rhetorical inconsistencies, fingerprints, ellipses—all may be recuperated as powerful traces of the Indigenous women's agency and as profound sources of historical knowledge and understanding about their experiences. Engaging the archive in this way yields unexpected results; it also constitutes a form of "talking back," deconstructing the value systems and language of settler oppressors.[50]

Consider the following: In 1915 a young Lakota woman named Lillian was accused by her Outing patrons of nearly causing the "double murder" of their twin infants, and was being considered for confinement at the House of the Good Shepherd as punishment.[51] According to a report from Outing matron Lida Johnston, Lillian had placed a worm in the napkin of one of the infants under her care, in what one Carlisle official described as "the most fiendish attempt to commit a crime that has ever been perpetrated by a student of this school."[52]

Read another way, the documents contained in Lillian's file cast doubt on the veracity of this settler ableist narrative, opening space to access what Saidiya Hartman refers to as "impossible stories."[53] Hartman refers to this move as a critical mining of the archive; a means of "exploiting the capacities of the subjunctive (a grammatical mood that expresses doubts, wishes, and possibilities)."[54] Lillian hated it at her patrons' home, and longed for her kin: as she wrote in a letter to her father Andrew, "I am getting very poor because I am sick . . . I am very lonesome out in the country . . . I never to stop thinking of you."[55] Other records kept in Lillian's file, preserved by Carlisle officials as evidence of Lillian's "incorrigibility," unselfconsciously reveal that she was brutalized at the hands of her ostensible "protectors." As nurse Emma Clay wrote to Lipps after a field visit to Lillian's Outing home, she was going to "lock Lillian in her room and whip her until she told me the truth."[56] Placing these events centrally in a recapitulation of the past, Lillian's actions might be explained as an attempt to be sent back home—a strategy of intentional misbehavior that others with similar aims also employed.[57]

Letters of correspondence reflect that Superintendent Lipps wanted to transfer Lillian to the Good Shepherd Home against the wishes of her father, where labor under the Catholic sisters would be prescribed as the "cure" for her misbehavior. But in spite of Lipps's insistence that Lillian's confinement would be uplifting and reformative, other documents show that U.S. officials wanted to be rid of young Indian women like Lillian, whose behavior was viewed as threatening to the maintenance of settler power and control. Pine Ridge Indian agent John R. Brennan wrote to Lipps in a letter dated June 30, 1915: "It came nearly being a double murder, and I believe the discipline of your school and the hideousness of the crime will justify this action."[58] He concluded this petition to keep Lillian away from his agency by appealing directly to Lipps's sense of power over the Indian people under his jurisdiction: "Your civil authority could take the evidence of all concerned and pass sentence, which would seem legal to the parents of Lillian."[59]

Lillian's father fought to have his daughter released from Carlisle, but his petitions were not immediately successful. The archival record is ambiguous: it is unclear whether she was sent from Carlisle to the Good Shepherd Home, a fact that tells us little about what Lillian's days looked like for the next two years, and even less about how she survived them. Like the postcard that beckoned settlers like Florence and Edna with cheap land—Buy Now! Can't Help But Double Your Money!—while concealing Indigenous presence, the Indigenous women's experiences as told through the colonial archive reflect U.S. officials' use of confinement as a tool of settler control. The circumstances that inform Lillian's experiences—the rhetoric of supremacy employed by Carlisle officials, the language of monstrosity used to legitimize her potential incarceration, Lipps's attempted usurpation of Lillian's father's authority as her kin and legal guardian—demonstrate the efficacy of settler ableist attitudes and unrelenting attempts to undercut tribal nations' claims to self-determination.

This story is not the one I hoped the archive would tell.

But folded between the officials' letters, between their pathologizing language and settler agendas, Lillian's presence is palpable. We witness her determination to survive her Outing home in the letter to her father, explaining that she is doing everything in her power to remain healthy, and writing to remain connected to her relatives back at Pine Ridge: "Come to close with love to you all at home and a kiss," she wrote.[60] Lillian's method of resistance, of refusing her assigned role in her Outing household, is both risky and bold.

The rushed cursive of the Outing matron, recapitulating Lillian's "crime," affirms the power inherent in her original refusal to "obey." Even as the archive attempts to consign Lillian to a footnote in the master historical narrative of Carlisle's institutional history, it unwittingly affirms the strength of her presence; the archive also reflects other Indigenous women's powerful attempts to direct the outcome of their lives, however circumscribed their actions might have been. But this is not the narrative presented in the young Indigenous women's "student" files. Instead, this is an act of re-storying; an attempt to critique the settler ableist impulses that characterize the colonial archive, and which inform our received understanding of the struggles of tribal nations, while remaining attentive to Indigenous scholars' calls to resist damaging, and damage-centered, narratives.[61] It is a radical act of refusal and care that is culled from the spaces in between the typewritten words on archival documents while respecting the limits of what we can know as observers of the past.

The archive, as it proves time and again, is inadequate to the task of remembering—but that has never stopped us from trying to resist its investment in forgetting.

Imagining and telling stories that actively counter settler ableism redirects how we "make" history. Re-storying as a principle and a practice calls for a radical redefinition of archive, including where, what, how, and for whom knowledge is recognized, cared for, and made accessible.[62] This path demands that we follow historical and archival clues in different ways. We might reevaluate what we choose to find in the archive, how the choices are made, what we are trained to look for and to dismiss—what's seen as important and trivial. The invitation rises for us to linger longer when we confront that archival moment of "I can go *this* far but no further with that source." Intentional, careful efforts to fill absences with presence challenge us to reconsider who inhabits and belongs in the histories we tell. And it provokes us to reflect on and respond to the ways power dynamics function—in and out of archives, and across the pasts before us.

Notes

1. Riley M. Guthrie to Julia Darling, June 28, 1940, Box 3, Canton Asylum, CCF 1907–39, Record Group (hereafter RG) 75, National Archives and Records Administration (NARA)-DC.

2. For example, Letter to Rebecca J. Butler, September 28, 1938, Box 3, Canton Asylum, CCF 1907–39, RG 75, NARA-DC; Riley Guthrie to Rebecca B. Butler, February 26, 1940, Box 3, Canton Asylum, CCF 1907–39, RG 75, NARA-DC; Riley Guthrie to Julia Darling, May 16, 1940, Box 3, Canton Asylum, CCF 1907–39, RG 75, NARA-DC; Riley M. Guthrie to Julia Darling, June 28, 1940, Box 3, Canton Asylum, CCF 1907–39, RG 75, NARA-DC; "Mrs. Maggie Hale,"

Admissions report #39216, St. Elizabeth's Hospital, January 15, 1934, Box 4, Canton Asylum, CCF 1907–39, RG 75, NARA-DC.

3. O-Zoush-Quah and Jensen family photographs, 1890s to 2019. Personal collection of Jack Jensen, Houston, Texas.

4. For more on the violence of settler archives, including erasure, see Marisa J. Fuentes, *Dispossessed Lives: Enslaved Women, Violence, and the Archive* (Philadelphia: University of Pennsylvania Press, 2016); Michel-Rolph Trouillot, *Silencing the Past: Power and the Production of History* (Boston: Beacon, 1995); Saidiya Hartman, "Venus in Two Acts," *Small Axe* 12, no. 2 (2008): 1–14; Ashley Glassburn Falzetti, "Archival Absence: the Burden of History," *Settler Colonial Studies* 5, no. 2 (2015): 128–44.

5. In 1908, the Bureau of Indian Affairs (BIA) forcibly committed O-Zoush-Quah to the Canton Asylum—a U.S. federal psychiatric facility in South Dakota designed specifically to confine American Indians. When the asylum closed in 1933, she was among the seventy-one people the BIA transferred to the other federal psychiatric institution—St. Elizabeth's—in Washington, DC. Across her confinement, O-Zoush-Quah's family fought the government's violent intervention in their lives, writing letters to administrators to seek her release; they also wrote to their incarcerated kin. Ultimately, O-Zoush-Quah would spend the remainder of her life—thirty-four more years—in the locked wards.

6. See, for example, Kim Nielsen, *A Disability History of the United States* (Boston: Beacon Press, 2013); Siobhan Senier, "'Traditionally, Disability Was Not Seen as Such': Writing and Healing in the Work of Mohegan Medicine People," *Journal of Literary & Cultural Disability Studies* 7, no. 2 (2013): 213–29; Rabia Belt, "Mental Disability and the Right to Vote," PhD dissertation, University of Michigan, 2015; Alison C. Carey, *On the Margins of Citizenship: Intellectual Disability and Civil Rights in Twentieth-Century America* (Philadelphia: Temple University Press, 2009); Laurel Daen, "Beyond Impairment: Recent Histories of Early American Disability," *History Compass* 17, no. 4 (2019): e12528–38; Greta Lafleur, "'Defective in One of the Principle Parts of Virility': Impotence, Generation, and Defining Disability in Early North America," *Early American Literature* 52, no. 1 (January 1, 2017): 79–107; Geoffrey Reaume, "'Keep Your Labels Off My Mind!' or 'Now I Am Going to Pretend I Am Crazy but Don't Be a Bit Alarmed': Psychiatric History from the Patients' Perspectives," *Canadian Bulletin of Medical History* 11, no. 2 (Fall 1994): 397–424; James Trent, *Inventing the Feeble Mind: A History of Intellectual Disability in the United States* (Oxford: Oxford University Press, 2016); Jonathan Metzl, *The Protest Psychosis: How Schizophrenia Became a Black Disease* (Boston: Beacon Press, 2010); Natalia Molina, *Fit to Be Citizens? Public Health and Race in Los Angeles, 1879–1939* (Oakland: University of California Press, 2006); Leslie J. Reagan, "Monstrous Births, Birth Defects, Unusual Anatomy, and Disability in Europe and North America," in *The Oxford Handbook of Disability History* (Oxford: Oxford University Press, 2018), 385–406; Jenifer Barclay, *The Mark of Slavery: Disability, Race, and Gender in Antebellum America* (Urbana: University of Illinois Press, 2021).

7. Scholar Jess L. Wilcox Cowing coined the term "settler ableism." Jess Cowing, "Occupied Land Is an Access Issue: Interventions in Feminist Disability Studies and

Narratives of Indigenous Activism," *Journal of Feminist Scholarship* 17 (Fall 2020): 9–25; Cowing, "Review of 'Holding Up the Sky,' or Naming Maine as Wabanaki Homelands," *Disability Studies Quarterly* 41, no. 4 (2021). In our historicizing of settler ableism, we also draw on work by other Indigenous+ disability historians. See Caroline Lieffers, "Imperial Mobilities: Disability, Indigeneity, and the United States West, 1850–1920," in *Global Histories of Disability, 1700–2015* (New York: Routledge, 2022), 93–108; Anne Gregory, "Competency, Allotment, and the Canton Asylum: The Case of a Muscogee Woman," *Disability Studies Quarterly* 41, no. 4 (2021); Laura Jaffee, "Student Movements Against the Imperial University: Toward a Genealogy of Disability," *Berkeley Review of Education* 10, no. 2 (2021); Kelsey Henry, Anna Hinton, and Sony Coráñez Bolton, "Origins, Objects, Orientations: New Histories and Theories of Race and Disability," *Disability Studies Quarterly*, 43, no. 1 (Fall 2023), https://dsq-sds.org/index.php/dsq/article/view/9719/8026.

8. See, for example, Jeff Corntassel, Chaw-win-is, and T'lakwadzi, "Indigenous Storytelling, Truth-telling, and Community Approaches to Reconciliation," *ESC: English Studies in Canada* 35, no. 1 (2009): 137–59; Sins Invalid, https://www.sinsinvalid.org/; Geoffrey Reaume, "Posthumous Exploitation? The Ethics of Researching, Writing, and Being Accountable as a Disability Historian," *Untold Stories: A Canadian Disability History Reader* (2018), 26–39; Marisa Fuentes, *Dispossessed Lives: Enslaved Women, Violence, and the Archive* (Philadelphia: University of Pennsylvania Press, 2016); Amy Lonetree, *Decolonizing the Museum: Representing Native America in National and Tribal Museums* (Chapel Hill: University of North Carolina Press, 2012); Saidiya Hartman, *Wayward Lives, Beautiful Experiments: Intimate Histories of Riotous Black Girls, Troublesome Women, and Queer Radicals* (New York: W.W. Norton and Co., 2019); Eve Tuck and K. Wayne Yang, "Unbecoming Claims: Pedagogies of Refusal in Qualitative Research," *Qualitative Inquiry* 20 (2014): 811–18; Katherine Ott, "Collective Bodies: What Museums Do for Disability Studies," in *Re-Presenting Disability* (New York: Routledge, 2013), 289–99. For more on the concept of *present absence*, see Toni Morrison, "Unspeakable Things Unspoken: The Afro-American Presence in American Literature," The Tanner Lecture on Human Values, University of Michigan, October 7, 1988, 123–63; Avery F. Gordon, *Ghostly Matters: Haunting and the Sociological Imagination* (Minneapolis: University of Minnesota Press, 1997); Kathryn W. Shanley, "Talking to the Animals and Taking Out the Trash: The Functions of American Indian Literature," *Wicazo Sa Review* 14, no. 2 (1999): 32–45; Shanley, "Indigenous Intellectual Sovereignties: A Hemispheric Convocation," University of California, Davis, April 8–10, 1998.

9. We join the many other scholars and activists who have been thinking and teaching about re-storying. See, for example, Henry Yu, Sarah Ling, and Denise Fong, "Re-Storying and Restoring Pacific Canada: Alternative Pasts for a Changing Present," in *Oral History, Education, and Justice* (New York: Routledge, 2019), 13–31; Carla Rice, Eliza Chandler, Jen Rinaldi, Nadine Changfoot, Kirsty Liddiard, Roxanne Mykitiuk, and Ingrid Mündel, "Imagining Disability Futurities," *Hypatia* 32, no. 2 (2017): 213–29; Lisa Kahaleole Hall, "More Than 'Two Worlds': Black Feminist Theories of Difference in Relation," *Critical Ethnic Studies* 4, no. 1 (2018): 64–83; "Restorying Autism," https://www.restoryingautism.com/the-project;

Pemina Yellow Bird, "Wild Indians: Native Perspectives on the Hiawatha Asylum for Insane Indians," National Empowerment Center, http://www.power2u.org/downloads /NativePerspectivesPeminaYellowBird.pdf; Alice Wong, *Disability Visibility Project*, https://disabilityvisibilityproject.com; Saidiya Hartman, *Lose Your Mother: A Journey Along the Atlantic Slave Route* (New York: Macmillan, 2008); Chris Anderson and Jean O'Brien, eds., *Sources and Methods in Indigenous Studies* (New York: Routledge, 2017); Eli Clare, *Brilliant Imperfection: Grappling with Cure* (Durham, NC: Duke University Press, 2017); Critical Design Lab, https://www.mapping-access.com/lab; Adria L. Imada, "Family History as Disability History: Native Hawaiians Surviving Medical Incarceration," *Disability Studies Quarterly* 41, no. 4 (2021), https://dsq-sds.org/article/view/8475/6289.

10. For more on Indigenous people and settler institutions, see, for example, Sarah Whitt, "'Care and Maintenance': Indigeneity, Disability, and Settler Colonialism at the Canton Asylum for Insane Indians (1902–1934)," *Disability Studies Quarterly* 41, no. 4 (2021), https://dsq-sds.org/article/view/8463/6299; Gregory, "Competency, Allotment, and the Canton Asylum"; Brenda J. Child, *Boarding School Seasons: American Indian Families, 1900–1945* (Lincoln: University of Nebraska Press, 1998); Whitt, "False Promises: Race, Power, and the Chimera of Indian Assimilation, 1879–1934," PhD dissertation, University of California, Berkeley, 2020; Carol Devens, "'If We Get the Girls, We Get the Race': Missionary Education of Native American Girls," in Frederick E. Hoxie, Peter C. Mancall, and James H. Merrill, *American Nations: Encounters in Indian Country, 1850 to the Present* (New York: Routledge, 2001), 156–71; Marilyn Irvin Holt, *Indian Orphanages* (Lawrence: University Press of Kansas, 2001); Melinda Garcia, Gayle Skawen:nio Morse, Shelby Loft, and Meredith Alberta Palmer, "Competent Discernment: A Case Study," in *Understanding Indigenous Perspectives in Psychology* (Cognella Academic Publishing, 2020); Margaret Jacobs, *A Generation Removed: The Fostering and Adoption of Indigenous Children in the Postwar World* (Lincoln: University of Nebraska Press, 2014); K. Tsianina Lomawaima, *"To Remain an Indian": Lessons in Democracy from a Century of Native American Education* (New York: Teachers College Press, 2006); Susan Burch, *Committed: Remembering Native Kinship in and beyond Institutions* (Chapel Hill: University of North Carolina Press, 2021); Margaret Jacobs, *White Mothers to a Dark Race: Settler Colonialism, Maternalism, and the Removal of Indigenous Children in the American West and Australia, 1880–1940* (Lincoln: University of Nebraska Press, 2009); Kevin Whalen, *Native Students at Work: American Indian Labor and Sherman Institute's Outing Program, 1900–1945* (Seattle: University of Washington Press, 2016); Robert A. Trennert Jr., *The Phoenix Indian School: Forced Assimilation in Arizona, 1891–1935* (Norman: University of Oklahoma Press, 1988); Beth H. Piatote, *Domestic Subjects: Gender, Citizenship, and Law in Native American Literature* (New Haven, CT: Yale University Press, 2013).

11. Stacy Alaimo, *Bodily Natures: Science, Environment, and the Material Self* (Bloomington: Indiana University Press, 2010); Traci Brynne Voyles, "Man Destroys Nature? Gender, History, and the Feminist Praxis of Situating Sustainabilities," in *Sustainability: Approaches to Environmental Justice and Social Power*, Julie Sze, ed. (New York: NYU Press, 2018).

12. We draw in part on disability and environmental humanities scholar Sunaura Taylor's wise insights in this claim, and extend the critique to consider historical context and settler colonialism. See Taylor, *Beasts of Burden: Animal and Disability Liberation* (The New Press, 2017). We also note that a range of studies have explored how settlers use, abuse, exploit, and draw in animals as justification and/or proxies for colonization and other forms of racist violence and control; see, for example, Virginia DeJohn Anderson, *Creatures of Empire: How Domestic Animals Transformed Early America*, first edition (Oxford; New York: Oxford University Press, 2006); Tyler D. Parry and Charlton W. Yingling, "Slave Hounds and Abolition in the Americas*," *Past & Present* 246, no. 1 (February 1, 2020): 69–108, https://doi.org/10.1093/pastj/gtz020.

13. On Indigenous relations to the nonhuman world, we draw from a range of scholars including scholars exploring Traditional Ecological Knowledge (TEK), Indigenous environmental history, Indigenous ethnobotany, and Indigenous environmental justice. See, for example, Nicholas James Reo and Kyle Powys Whyte, "Hunting and Morality as Elements of Traditional Ecological Knowledge," *Human Ecology* 40, no. 1 (February 2012): 15–27, https://doi.org/10.1007/s10745-011-9448-1; Kyle Powys Whyte, "On the Role of Traditional Ecological Knowledge as a Collaborative Concept: A Philosophical Study," *Ecological Processes* 2, no. 1 (April 5, 2013): 7, https://doi.org/10.1186/2192–1709–2-7; Robin Wall Kimmerer, *Braiding Sweetgrass: Indigenous Wisdom, Scientific Knowledge and the Teachings of Plants*, first edition (Minneapolis: Milkweed Editions, 2013); Winona LaDuke, *All Our Relations: Native Struggles for Land and Life* (Chicago: Haymarket Books, 2015); Joshua L. Reid, *The Sea Is My Country: The Maritime World of the Makahs, an Indigenous Borderlands People*, The Henry Roe Cloud Series on American Indians and Modernity (New Haven, CT: Yale University Press, 2015), https://ebookcentral.proquest.com/lib/lmu/detail.action?docID=3421613; Clint Carroll, *Roots of Our Renewal: Ethnobotany and Cherokee Environmental Governance*, First Peoples: New Directions in Indigenous Studies (Minneapolis: University of Minnesota Press, 2015); Zoe Todd, "Fish, Kin and Hope: Tending to Water Violations in Amiskwaciwâskahikan and Treaty Six Territory," *Afterall: A Journal of Art, Context and Enquiry* 43, no. 1 (Spring 2017): 102–7; Melissa K. Nelson and Daniel Shilling, *Traditional Ecological Knowledge: Learning from Indigenous Practices for Environmental Sustainability* (Cambridge University Press, 2018); Gwyneira Isaac et al., "Native American Perspectives on Health and Traditional Ecological Knowledge," *Environmental Health Perspectives* 126, no. 12 (December 2018): 125002, https://doi.org/10.1289/EHP1944; Dian Million, "'We Are the Land and the Land Is Us': Indigenous Land, Lives, and Embodied Ecologies in the Twenty-First Century," in *Racial Ecologies*, eds. LeiLani Nishime and Kim D. Hester Williams (Seattle: University of Washington Press, 2018), 19–33; Dina Gilio-Whitaker, *As Long as Grass Grows: The Indigenous Fight for Environmental Justice, from Colonization to Standing Rock* (Boston: Beacon Press, 2019).

14. For more information on Indigenous perspectives on disability, see Carol Locust, *American Indian Beliefs Concerning Health and Unwellness*, Native American Research and Training Center Monograph Series (Tucson: University of Arizona, 1985); Lilah Morton Pengra and Joyzelle Gingway Godfrey, "Different

Boundaries, Different Barriers: Disability Studies and Lakota Culture," *Disability Studies Quarterly* 21, no. 3 (Summer 2001): 36–53; Senier, "'Traditionally, Disability Was Not Seen as Such,'" 213–29; Yellow Bird, "Wild Indians: Native Perspectives on the Hiawatha Asylum for Insane Indians"; Pearl Yellow Old Woman-Healy and Stacey Running Rabbit, "Raising Our Children with Disabilities in Akomi-moksin," *Disability Studies Quarterly* 41, no. 4 (2021), https://dsq-sds.org/article/view/8467/6290; Mary-Ellen Kelm, *Colonizing Bodies: Aboriginal Health and Healing in British Columbia 1900–50* (Vancouver: UBC Press, 1998).

15. Cowing, "Occupied Land Is an Access Issue," 9–25; Laura Jaffee and Kelsey John, "Disabling Bodies of/and Land: Reframing Disability Justice in Conversation with Indigenous Theory and Activism," *Disability and the Global South* 5, no. 2 (2018): 1407–29, https://dgsjournal.org/vol-5-no-2/; Susan Burch, "Disorderly Pasts: Kinship, Diagnoses, and Remembering in American Indian-US Histories," *Journal of Social History* 50, no. 2 (Winter 2016): 362–85; Emily J. Hutcheon and Bonnie Lashewicz, "Tracing and Troubling Continuities between Ableism and Colonialism in Canada," *Disability & Society* 35, no. 5 (2020): 695–714; Siobhan Senier and Clare Barker, "Introduction," *Journal of Literary & Cultural Disability Studies* 7, no. 2 (2013): 123–40; Caroline Lieffers, "Imperial Ableism: Disability and American Expansion, c. 1850–1930," PhD dissertation, Yale University, 2020.

16. See, for example, Sean Kicummah Teuton, "Disability in Indigenous North America: In Memory of William Sherman Fox," in *The World of the Indigenous Americas*, edited by Robert Warrior (Hoboken, NJ: Taylor and Francis, 2014), 569–93; Jaffee and John, "Disabling Bodies of/and Land," 1407–29; Maile Arvin, *Possessing Polynesia: The Science of Settler Colonial Whiteness in Hawaiʻi and Oceania* (Durham, NC: Duke University Press, 2020); Meredith Alberta Palmer, "Rendering Settler Sovereign Landscapes: Race and Property in the Empire State," *Environment and Planning D: Society and Space* 38, no. 5 (2021); J. Kēhaulani Kauanui, "'A Structure, Not an Event': Settler Colonialism and Enduring Indigeneity," *Lateral* 5, no. 1 (2016); Ned Blackhawk, *Violence over the Land: Indians and Empires in the Early American West* (Cambridge: Harvard University Press, 2006); David A. Chang, *The Color of the Land: Race, Nation, and the Politics of Landownership in Oklahoma, 1832–1929* (Chapel Hill: University of North Carolina Press, 2010); LaDuke, *All Our Relations*; Phillip J. Deloria, "From Nation to Neighborhood: Land, Policy, Culture, Colonialism, and Empire in U.S.–Indian Relations," in *The Cultural Turn in U.S. History: Past, Present, and Future*, edited by James W. Cook, Lawrence B. Glickman, and Michael O'Malley (Chicago: University of Chicago Press, 2008), 343–82.

17. Kyle Whyte, "Settler Colonialism, Ecology, and Environmental Injustice," *Environment and Society* 9, no. 1 (September 1, 2018): 125, 126, https://doi.org/10.3167/ares.2018.090109. See also Kyle Whyte, "Indigenous Experience, Environmental Justice and Settler Colonialism," SSRN Scholarly Paper (Rochester, NY: Social Science Research Network, April 25, 2016); Million, "We Are the Land and the Land Is Us," 19–33.

18. Melanie K. Yazzie and Cutcha Risling Baldy, "Introduction: Indigenous Peoples and the Politics of Water," *Decolonization: Indigeneity, Education & Society* 7, no. 1 (2018): 3.

19. We draw from a range of scholars to understand the stark discrepancies between settlers' perspective on nonhuman beings as "resources" and Indigneous worldviews that center relations; in particular, we emphasize Whyte, "Settler Colonialism, Ecology, and Environmental Injustice," 125–44; Whyte, "Indigenous Experience, Environmental Justice and Settler Colonialism"; Zoe Todd, "From a Fishy Place: Examining Canadian State Law Applied in the Daniels Decision from the Perspective of Métis Legal Orders," *TOPIA* 36 (November 2016): 43–57, https://doi.org/DOI: 10.3138/topia.36.43; Melanie K. Yazzie, "Decolonizing Development in Diné Bikeyah," *Environment and Society* 9, no. 1 (September 1, 2018): 25–39, https://doi.org/10.3167/ares.2018.090103; Andrew Curley, "Infrastructures as Colonial Beachheads: The Central Arizona Project and the Taking of Navajo Resources," *Environment and Planning D: Society and Space* 39, no. 3 (June 1, 2021): 387–404, https://doi.org/10.1177/0263775821991537.

20. Quoted by Traci Brynne Voyles, *Wastelanding: Legacies of Uranium Mining in Navajo Country* (Minneapolis: University of Minnesota Press, 2015), 31.

21. Jenny Hale Pulsipher, *Subjects unto the Same King: Indians, English, and the Contest for Authority in Colonial New England* (Philadelphia: University of Pennsylvania Press, 2014).

22. Significantly for our analysis, the Dawes Act specifically sought to colonize the collectivism of Native societies as well as and along with Native relations to land, in favor of solitary ownership of plots of property that were to be worked by individuals.

23. Quoted by Carroll, *Roots of Our Renewal.*

24. Teuton, "Disability in Indigenous North America," 574.

25. Cowing, "Occupied Land Is an Access Issue," 12. These forms of infantilization run rife through settler history. In 1819, Henry Clay, the Speaker of the House of Representatives, lamented the conditions of "the poor children of the forest," invoking both Natives' presumed immaturity *and* implying settlers' maturity. Quoted by Jeffrey Ostler, *Surviving Genocide: Native Nations and the United States from the American Revolution to Bleeding Kansas* (New Haven, CT: Yale University Press, 2019), 183.

26. Traci Brynne Voyles, *The Settler Sea: California's Salton Sea and the Consequences of Colonialism* (Lincoln: University of Nebraska Press, 2021), 48.

27. Marsha Weisiger, *Dreaming of Sheep in Navajo Country* (Seattle: University of Washington Press, 2011); Voyles, *Wastelanding.*

28. James J. Rawls, *Indians of California: The Changing Image* (Norman: University of Oklahoma Press, 1984); Blackhawk, *Violence over the Land*; Jack Norton, "If the Truth Be Told: Revising California History as a Moral Objective," *American Behavioral Scientist* 58, no. 1 (January 2014): 83–96; William J. Bauer, "Family Matters: Round Valley Indian Families at the Sherman Indian Institute, 1900–1945," *Southern California Quarterly* 92, no. 4 (December 2010): 393–421. For primary source examples of the racist vitriol spewed against Natives of northern California and the Great Basin, see Mark Twain, *Roughing It* (Penguin, 2008 [1872]); Robert Heizer, *The Destruction of California Indians* (Lincoln: Bison Books, 1993).

29. Lieffers, "Imperial Ableism," 4.

30. Lorenzo Veracini, *Settler Colonialism: A Theoretical Overview* (Palgrave Macmillan: 2010), 15.

31. Susan thanks Eli Clare, Meredith Palmer (Tuscarora, Haudenosaunee), Alison Kafer, and Lisa Kahaleole Hall (Kanaka Maoli) for their insights on agency, personhood, institutionalization, and the archives.

32. See, for example, *Guide to Records in the National Archives of the United States Relating to American Indians* (National Archives and Records Service, General Services Administration, 1981), 55. See also Susan Burch, "'Dislocated Histories': The Canton Asylum for Insane Indians," *Women, Gender, and Families of Color* 2, no. 2 (2014): 141–62; Burch, *Committed*.

33. For more on disability-related terminology, ableism, and history, see, for example, Penny Richards and Susan Burch, "Documents, Ethics, and the Disability Historian," in *The Oxford Handbook of Disability History*, edited by Michael A. Rembis, Catherine Jean Kudlick, and Kim E. Nielsen (Oxford: Oxford University Press, 2018); Corinne Kirchner and Liat Ben-Moshe, "Language and Terminology," in *Encyclopedia of American Disability History* (New York: Facts on File, 2009); Eli Clare, "Freaks and Queers," in *Exile and Pride* (Durham, NC: Duke University Press, 2015), 81–118; Laurel Daen, "Beyond Impairment: Recent Histories of Early American Disability," *History Compass* 17, no. 4 (April 2019).

34. For more on material culture and history, see Katherine Ott, "Disability Things: Material Culture and American Disability History, 1700–2010," in *Disability Histories*, edited by Susan Burch and Michael Rembis (Urbana: University of Illinois Press, 2014), 119–35. For some context on the specific politics of archival research in Native American and Indigenous studies, including with regard to material culture, see Alyssa Mt. Pleasant, Caroline Wigginton, and Kelly Wisecup, "Materials and Methods in Native American and Indigenous Studies: Completing the Turn," *Early American Literature* 53, no. 2 (2018): 407–44.

35. Francis Jensen, interviews by Susan Burch, April 7 and 8, 2014, Holton, Kansas; Jack Jensen, interviews by Susan Burch, April 22 and 23, 2017; October 3, 4, and 5, 2019, Deer Dancer Ranch, Texas.

36. See Liat Ben-Moshe, *Disability Incarcerated*.

37. See "Gertrude B. P. Student File," RG 75, Series 1327, Box 47, Folder 2327, NARA, Carlisle Indian School Digital Resource Center (hereafter CISDRC), Dickinson College; "Carrie P. A. Student File," RG 75, Series 1327, Box 107, Folder 4533, NARA, CISDRC; "Lillian C. Student File," RG 75, Series 1327, Box 119, Folder 4814, NARA, CISDRC.

38. Attention to settler ableism helps us understand the impacts of this particular history of confinement, as well as its long reach: Lori Record and Michelle Jones, two women incarcerated at the Indiana Women's Prison, assert in an article that Good Shepherd Homes—some of the first women's prisons in the United States—were Magdalene Laundries, and the very architecture of the Reading house confirms this fact. The Indigenous women's confinement to the Good Shepherd Home thus also registers global interconnections. In recent years, the general public has become increasingly interested in the experiences of women confined to laundries in Ireland, thanks in part to the global film industry. But the history of Indigenous and other

women's confinement to Magdalene Laundries remains virtually unexplored on Turtle Island. Unlike the women in Ireland, Indigenous women who were institutionalized in similar facilities in the United States have never received an apology. Indeed, they have never even had their experiences acknowledged at all. See Sarah Whitt, "Wash Away Your Sins," *American Indian Culture and Research Journal*, vol. 46, no. 3 (2023) 1–20.

39. "Carrie P. A. Student File," NARA CISDRC, 15.

40. Carlisle's Outing Program was a system of labor exploitation in which Carlisle enrollees were placed in the homes of white Americans to perform domestic and farm work. Devised by Captain Richard Henry Pratt, Carlisle's founder, in 1879, the philosophical foundations of "Outing" were simple: Pratt believed that by placing Indigenous people in the homes of white Americans to perform often unremunerated menial labor, "civilization" and self-sufficiency would be rapidly accomplished. In additional to facilitating the exploitation of Indigenous laborers, however, the Outing system also enabled Carlisle officials to profit from Indigenous confinement in external institutions: although Carrie was physically absent from Carlisle, her designation as being "under the Outing" meant that she was retained in enrollment ledgers and thus counted in Carlisle's quarterly reports. Federal monies were sent to Carlisle on her behalf, while she paid for her own confinement at the Good Shepherd Home with per-capita funds from the Red Cliff agency. For more information about the Outing Program at Carlisle and elsewhere, see, for example, David Wallace Adams, *Education for Extinction: American Indians and the Boarding School Experience*, 1875–1928 (Lawrence: University of Kansas Press, 1995); Jacqueline Fear Segal, *White Man's Club: Schools, Race, and the Struggle of Indian Acculturation* (Lincoln: University of Nebraska Press, 2007); Whalen, *Native Students at Work*. For more information about the ways in which Indigenous institutionalization directly benefited the settler society, often monetarily, see Sarah Whitt, "'An Ordinary Case of Discipline': Deputizing White Americans and Punishing Indian Men at the Carlisle Indian Industrial School, 1900–1918," *Western Historical Quarterly*, vol. 53, no. 1 (2023) 51–70.

41. "Carrie P. A. Student File," NARA CISDRC, 9.

42. "Carrie P. A. Student File," NARA CISDRC, 9.

43. See Ann Laura Stoler, *Carnal Knowledge and Imperial Power: Race and the Intimate in Colonial Rule* (Berkeley: University of California Press, 2002).

44. "Carrie P. A. Student File," NARA CISDRC, 59.

45. "Carrie P. A. Student File," NARA CISDRC, 58.

46. Dian Million, *Therapeutic Nations: Healing in an Age of Indigenous Human Rights* (Tucson: University of Arizona Press, 2013), 2.

47. Dian Million, "Indigenous Perspectives on the Environment," talk hosted by the University of Washington, October 13, 2021, https://youtu.be/YsyGJ1RQZIg.

48. Trouillot, *Silencing the Past*, 27.

49. Trouillot, Silencing the Past, 27.

50. hooks, *Talking Back: Thinking Feminist, Thinking Black* (Boston: South End Press, 1999).

51. "Lillian C. Student File," NARA CISDRC.

52. "Lillian C. Student File," NARA CISDRC, 31.

53. Hartman, "Venus in Two Acts," 10.

54. Hartman, "Venus in Two Acts," 11.

55. "Lillian C. Student File," NARA CISDRC, 16.

56. "Lillian C. Student File," NARA CISDRC, 27.

57. American Indian girls and women in the Outing system regularly used strategic misbehavior as a way to get sent back to Carlisle from undesirable Outing home scenarios. Kevin Whalen has documented similar tactics at the Sherman Institute in his text *Native Students at Work: American Indian Labor and Sherman Institute's Outing Program, 1900–1945*. Brenda Child's foundational text *Boarding School Seasons* also discusses student resistance at length.

58. "Lillian C. Student File," NARA CISDRC, 12.

59. "Lillian C. Student File," NARA CISDRC, 27.

60. "Lillian C. Student File," NARA CISDRC, 17.

61. Eve Tuck, "Suspending Damage: A Letter to Communities," *Harvard Educational Review* 79, no. 3 (Fall 2009): 409–27.

62. Sandy Grande, "Aging, Precarity, and the Struggle for Indigenous Elsewheres," *International Journal of Qualitative Studies in Education* 31, no. 3 (2018): 168–76; Gracen Brilmyer, "Archival Assemblages: Applying Disability Studies' Political/Relational Model to Archival Description," *Archival Science* 18 (2018): 95–118; Colette Leung, "Profile: The Living Archives Project: Canadian Disability and Eugenics," *Canadian Journal of Disability Studies* 1, no. 1 (2012): 143–66; Sara White, "Crippling the Archives: Negotiating Notions of Disability in Appraisal and Arrangement and Description," *Society of American Archivists* 75/1 (Spring-Summer 2012): 109–24; Kelly L. Hernández, "The Rebel Archive," in *City of Inmates: Conquest, Rebellion, and the Rise of Human Caging in Los Angeles, 1771–1965* (Chapel Hill: University of North Carolina Press, 2017).

CHAPTER 11

Hall of Miracles

Central American Disability Archives

HEATHER VRANA

About a hundred crutches of all sizes cover the walls of a quiet corner in the picturesque tourist town of Antigua, Guatemala. Some are wooden, others are made of aluminum and rubber. A few are sticks and branches carefully carved and sanded into shape. A knot of plastic, wood, and glass rosaries hangs from the hewn cradle that used to nestle into a warm armpit. Many crutches are figures purchased in order to be left in gratitude. But others are worn with use: the tip that ground against stone, dirt, and pavement and the crutch pads wrapped with stuffing and fabric to soften the point of contact with the body. Around the crutches are other votives, like braces, prescription glasses, sunglasses, shoes with prosthetics, canes, photographs in black and white and color, plaques, and still more rosaries. This is the Pasillo de Milagros, or Hall of Miracles.

A historian might stumble into this small passageway on a weekend respite from the capital city where most government archives are located. Guatemala City is like most other Central American capitals. It is dusty, labyrinthine, and wrenching for its full display of inequity. Some neighborhoods resemble Miami, with manicured gardens and the bitter stink of fertilizer, their glassy modern apartment buildings set between restaurants that serve global fare and posh versions of local dishes. In other neighborhoods, homes are precariously stacked along ravines. In the rainy season, they threaten to slide down into sweet rivers of sewage. People with visible disabilities are common in a place where the thirty-six-year civil war ended only a generation ago and where adequate health care is out of reach for many people.[1] But the omnipresence of disabled people, disability, and disabling life conditions has not buoyed an interest in disability history or archives.

Connecting the scarcity of U.S. disability archives to the newness of the field of disability history, Douglas Baynton noted that "archives have neither sought out disability-related materials nor catalogued their own collections to make such material easily located."[2] In Central America, not only is disability history just now emerging, but national access to information laws and social stigma and its sequelae, especially the prevailing assumption that disability does not have a history, structure what can and cannot be known about disability in state archives. Guatemalan and, more broadly, Central American archives of disability reflect the exclusions and confinements that characterized disability's pasts in the region. In Nicaragua, El Salvador, Honduras, Costa Rica, and Panama, as elsewhere in Latin America, the logics of the state, the church, and biomedicine overdetermine what can be known about disability.[3] These logics continue to shape disability's present. Yet, some archives, like the Hall of Miracles, offer a peek at crip worldmaking. This chapter argues that these archives can alter our understandings of care, cure, and faith in disability studies. While focused on Guatemala, it points to some other Central American state and nonstate archives when they are pertinent.

State Archives: No Archive No History

Guatemala's major state archive is the Archivo General de Centro América (AGCA). It occupies half of a building in the historical center of the capital. The other half of the building is the National Library and Hemeroteca Nacional, a collection of newspapers and broadsides from the 1840s. AGCA's collection extends from the colonial Captaincy General of Guatemala to the twentieth century. Its documents are organized in a confusing tangle of systems, for instance, by government ministry, institution, department, municipality, or even theme. Some indices are printed and remain incomplete and out of date. Others are digitized but can only be accessed on desktop computers in the reading room, which fills with dust in the dry season. A barely legible photocopy of the index for the elusive Valenzuela Collection used to circulate among graduate students. Countless documents remain piled up and uncatalogued in the building's recesses.

In the Ministry of Public Health Document Collection (Fondo Documental Ministerio de Salud Pública (1822–1956)) there are thousands of patient case files from the national psychiatric asylum. I learned about them one morning when I skimmed a set of printed indices in the reading room. It was a revelation.[4] The files are organized alphabetically by the last name of the person who was reduced to a patient on the pages therein. The folders are red or blue and labeled "Asilo de Dementes," "Asilo de Alienados," or "Hospital Neuro-Psiquiátrico," following changes in the hospital's name. On the outer cover of older files, there is space for the patient's name, date of entry and discharge, and dates of other hospitalizations; more recent files only ask for a name and file number, a line that is always blank. Inside the folders are intake surveys, Rorschach tests, intelligence tests, letters between administrators, and sometimes letters or statements written by the patients themselves. Despite the ruse of standardization, each file is different, each one with incomplete forms or missing pages. Some, like those of the young person who suffered "sexual aberrations" and the woman who wrote long letters to her doctor to explain herself, are thick. Others, like most files for teenagers and prisoners who were incarcerated in the asylum, are sparse. Some pages are annotated: "se fugó" indicates a patient who ran away; a solemn cross, a patient who died in the asylum. Some made these escapes long before their family members wrote to inquire about them.

Archive making is an act of governance. Archives are, in Ann Laura Stoler's words, "commitments to paper."[5] In colonial archives, Stoler models how to attend "to the principles and practices of governance lodged in particular archival forms."[6] In the AGCA case files, these principles and practices are those of medical governance: symptom, diagnosis, family antecedents, and referral. As Eli Clare writes, case files reduce, they document, they prove, they "lay claim to the truth. They lie."[7] They are only small cracks in the locked doors of asylums and hospitals. They tell more about repression than resistance, and they expunge most of a person's life. But their pages also tell of determination against forced acquiescence. Félix, a man living in the Asilo de Dementes in August 1923, reported to hospital workers that "the spirits [*almas*] complained to him" and he was not hungry and would not eat "because spirits [*espíritus*] do not eat." He also said he was never sad. Yet Félix died in the hospital on November 22, 1924. Did Félix starve to death? He was not sad, but what did he feel? Like Clare, "[a]ll I can do is mourn and rage."[8] We have an obligation not to turn away from this violence and instead to explain its origins and impacts.[9]

Who should have access to case files, and what should they be permitted to do with them? In Guatemala, access is precarious. The legislature passed the Access to Public Information Law (Ley de Acceso a la Información Pública) in 2008. This law included guidelines that guaranteed an individual's right to locate and read information about oneself and immediate family members *and* the protection of personal data. Otherwise, access to protected information would require petitioning the government by writing a letter, which the director of the archive would deliver to her superiors. This is how the process was explained to me—all vague nouns and passive verbs. What to make of these maneuvers by Guatemala's legislature, which is so committed to covering up the past that it approved a genocide denial petition in 2014? What to make of the fact that the legislature, as I was told it sought to protect citizens' privacy, held a hearing on a general amnesty law for perpetrators of political violence during the civil war? Or of a government that was willing to fire AGCA's director for her efforts to preserve the Historical Archive of the National Police (AHPN)? Susan Reverby's discovery that Guatemalan physicians and bureaucrats willingly complied with the deliberate exposure of asylum patients and prisoners to gonorrhea and syphilis between 1946 and 1948 has left officials wary of other discoveries.[10] Impunity reigns. The case files record the state's failure to care for its citizens. Recent efforts by the government to restrict access to its archives under the pretext of protection should be eyed with suspicion. It is too soon to tell what a new dawn of democracy under President Bernardo Arévalo will mean for Guatemalan archives.

Other state archives of disability are shaped by the assumption that disability does not have a history or that its history is not worth knowing. The first assumption holds that disability is only medical, its meaning or meanings unchanging, transhistorical, above the vicissitudes of politics, culture, or economy. The second assumption means that no major Central American archive to date has an archival heading or collection of documents entitled "disability" (here *discapacidad*). To locate documents about disabled people or ideas about disability, I *research around* disability by looking for adjacent keywords, not unlike how Stoler reads along the archival grain to note colonial anxieties and omissions. These keywords might include public health, labor, social security, charity, beneficence, asylums, schools, orphanages, or in some cases terms like blindness or deafness, tuberculosis, syphilis, *locura*, and goiter. Often, I use outdated terms like "cripple" (*minusválido*) and "invalid" (*inválido*).

Asking an archivist for documents about "discapacidad" is only successful when the archivist can think in the institutional, social, or medical terms listed above. I have not yet experienced this. In January 2019, when I signed out each folio at AGCA, an archivist made sure that I noted "Public Health" ("Salud Pública") in the ledger. She corrected me when I wrote "disability" ("discapacidad") or "Insane Asylum" ("Asilo de Alienados"), even as I was researching disability (in general) and the Insane Asylum (in particular). She may have believed disability is without history or that disability's history is not worth knowing, or maybe she was ashamed of disability and thought it better to focus on health. Maybe her insistence that I did not write the word "discapacidad" can be explained by the term's anachronism. It simply was not used in Guatemala until the 1990s.

Within the AGCA's Ministry of Public Health Document Collection, items related to disabled people and disability as a social and political phenomenon can be found in Correspondence, the Books of Hospital Admissions, Records (*Memorias*) of the Hospital General and its Dependencies, and in a few other places where records of donations or special charity events have been collected. Another way into the massive stacks at AGCA is through the card catalog (called the *Catálogo* or *Fichero Pardo* for Joaquín Pardo, its creator) that stretches down a long hallway on the second floor. The *Fichero Pardo* includes the category "inválidos" in its drawers on legislation (1812–14); inheritance courts in Chiapas for widows of soldiers who belonged to the Military Monte Pío (1788) and similar concerns in Nicaragua (1779); those exonerated of paying tribute (1603–1819); and aid for injured soldiers (1838).[11] For the

Pardo Catalogue, *inválido* clearly means war wounded. Its categories reflect the distinct valorization of veterans compared to other disabled people that many historians have identified elsewhere. Other disabled people can be found under the term *locos* and *dementes*, joined on one card with little additional information ("Dementes. Locos Enajenados (1750–1818)").[12] Only two cards appear under this thematic category. Any other reference to disabled people must be located through the hospitals, asylums, hospices, and jails where they lived out what may have been the most difficult parts of their lives.

On the other side of the building in the National Library, disability archives include monthly or weekly public health periodicals and thousands of pages of statistical health indicators, from epidemic diseases to sanitation and nutrition programs. Like case studies, these texts tend to view disabled individuals as only their diagnosis or even as an omen for national reproductive and productive futures. They collect and disseminate family planning and vital statistics to measure the impacts of nutrition campaigns, education, vaccination programs, dietary supplements, and home visits.

The AGCA, National Library, and Hemeroteca Nacional reflect the exclusions and confinements of disability's pasts. Case files exist *because of* loss, violence, and congregation. Their archival forms perpetuate the principles and practices of medical governance, especially symptom, diagnosis, inheritance, and referral. They can be used to perpetuate the same principles and practices in the present. What is the purpose of disability history that is written from case files? Are they marshaled to construct a history of ideas or a hagiography of a famous doctor, or to discuss the experiences and thoughts of the "mad people" they claim to record?[13] How shall they be used now that the legislature has limited researchers' access to them?[14] Case studies (and public health periodicals and statistics) exemplify how medical governance generated state archives of disability and how state archives acted out—continue to act out—medical governance. State archives disorganize disability, parse lives into case histories, impose key words, create chronologies, and lose track of or discard pieces of paper along the way.

The modernist building that houses the three major state archives of disability squats at the edge of the capital's main plaza facing the colonial-era Cathedral and the National Palace, its architecture and location reflective of its governing function.[15] On hot days, it offers shade to people who seem down and out, whose lives could be read in the endless folders of case files inside, but for the grace of God and the Guatemalan legislature.

Miracle and Cure in the Hall of Miracles

By contrast, the Hall of Miracles is tucked away within the ruins of Iglesia de San Francisco at the end of a cobblestone street in sleepy Antigua.[16] First constructed in the late sixteenth century, the church's expansive grounds have long been a place of refuge and pilgrimage. Some of its first visitors were drawn to the hospital and school built by a Franciscan missionary to the poor and the sick, Hermano Pedro de San José Betancur. Earthquakes ruined the original building. Every effort at reconstruction has been thwarted by still more earthquakes and other natural and human disasters. In 1980, Hermano Pedro was beatified and thereafter could intercede on behalf of people who prayed in his name. Two years later, someone moved his mortal remains to a small museum with artifacts of his life. When Hermano Pedro was canonized in 2002, Pope John Paul II and seven hundred thousand believers congregated in the capital. But Hermano Pedro's remains stayed in Antigua, where they have been a destination for believers since at least the nineteenth century.

It is easy to be captivated by this little corner in a tourist trap so far removed that it is often called "Guatelandia" (a play on Disneylandia, or Disneyland). Antigua is quaint and sometimes feels frozen in time, dominated as it is by crumbling ruins, bougainvillea, and a centuries-old street grid. But the old presses against the new. Genteel seventeenth-century mansions tilt into breweries, a palimpsest that evokes the former Kingdom of Guatemala's cosmopolitan past. So do the offerings in the Hall of Miracles that come from El Salvador, Mexico, Nicaragua, and the United States, and some from even farther afield. The Hall of Miracles is a sacred place. It is also a solitary place even as its walls testify to its importance in Central American, Mexican, and U.S. Latino disability cultures. It could be a place of pilgrimage for disability scholars, too, as it is a miraculous archive, "so extraordinary as to appear supernatural; remarkable, astonishing."[17]

To call the Hall of Miracles an archive is to make it both like and unlike state archives. It is not subject to access to information laws. But sometimes photography is prohibited. It has no finding aid. It is always being renewed and reorganized. Like state archives, its archival forms reflect certain principles and practices of governance. Instead of symptom, diagnosis, inheritance, and referral, its principles are the articles of faith, miracles, and salvation; its practices, the sacraments, votives, and prayer.

Miracles—miracle cures, miracle drugs, miracle workers—occupy a dubious place in disabilities' pasts. From its early usage, the word miraculous was associated with cure and things that were "not explicable by natural laws," including freakery and sin.[18] But in her pursuit of disability as a metaphor in sacred texts, Sharon V. Betcher calls for an understanding of the Holy Spirit that "promotes Spirit not as the power to rescue and repair according to some presupposed original state or ideal form, but as the energy for unleashing multiple forms of corporeal flourishing."[19] Her intervention reminds us to take seriously religious understandings of disability.[20]

Votives left for Hermano Pedro can help translate disability conditions and meanings across time, space, and faith. There are so many prosthetics and orthotics on the walls of the Hall of Miracles. While some crutches may be replicas or figurative votives, many of the items on the wall were designed for and used by someone. These items are personal, designed for each individual.[21] They link past to present. They counter analyses of disability limited to metaphor.[22] Katherine Ott writes, "People come back into the story when attention is given to objects."[23] We encounter things that other people touched, moved, believed in, and left behind.

For instance, there is one small rigid leg brace hanging among the crutches. We might look at the molded plastic and ask how and where was it manufactured. Look at its size and imagine it was for an infant. Notice its shape and consider how social class limited access to custom orthotics, or research orthotics manufacturing in Guatemala, more generally. But objects' meanings and their uses only seem easy to interpret; instead, they are unstable and opaque. We cannot know precisely how a person used an item, only its intended use.[24] How did this child feel when they wore the brace? The shape of the brace kept the child's knee from bending while they wore it—was this the point? When and where did they use the brace? For how long? It is tempting to squint at its broken-in leather straps and frayed padding and determine it was worn often. But infants usually grow quickly. How did it get so worn? Doesn't the presence of the item in the Hall of Miracles suggest it was no longer needed? An inscription in black marker on the brace's calf is only partially visible without touching and moving the miracle—which is forbidden—but it thanks Hermano Pedro for interceding on behalf of Lupita's knee. Ott writes that items "owned and used by people with disabilities and those that are used upon them or that are encountered in life create possibilities, impose limits, assert political and ideological positions, and shape identity."[25] We can read much of this into Lupita's brace—possibility, limitation, and ideological position.

Attending and giving significance to objects that, in some ways, are extensions of people's bodies can crip the archive.[26] AGCA Ministry of Health documents could allow me to report how many infants were treated in a given month at the Hospital Roosevelt or tabulate how many children were fitted with orthotics at the Hospital de Rehabilitación. But a crip reading of the Hall of Miracles as an archive of "disability things" curated by disabled people reminds us to think about individuals not populations, it challenges our distinctions between faith and science, and it plainly demonstrates how people draw unpredictable meanings from their lives.[27] That some of the Hall of Miracle's "disability things" were made by medical experts, police, or bureaucrats and later reimagined as objects of faith reminds us that disabilities' meanings are not universal and their materiality is never immutable. Lupita's brace was made by technicians and likely fitted by a doctor, but Lupita wore it for a time and later, she, or more likely her family, made it a votive. It became evidence of—not a metaphor for—a miracle. This distinguishes the Hall of Miracles from other material archives.

These "disability things" became more than material as they were carried to the Hall of Miracles. Honoring the many meanings of these "things"—great comforts, costly acquisitions, endured aids, expressions of faith—can push historians to resist the fantasies of positivism that link the discipline of history to violent carceral and eugenic practices. If faith in the miraculous can be reclaimed and reworked, then it might point us to new ways of approaching disabilities' pasts and present. Kevin Lewis O'Neill connects Christian piety to efforts to create feelings of security amid gang violence and the United States' War on Drugs in Guatemala. O'Neill writes, "[R]eligion is a social fact deeply bound to the practice and to the construction of security, to the very idea of what it means to be secure."[28] But faith is more than piety. It is the "willingness to give one's heart to an understanding of a world that could be without asking for objective proof of the mind" or, if you like, to "act as if."[29] An embroidered rectangle hangs by a mass of wooden crutches. It reads, "Thank you Hermano Pedro for helping me [*ayudarme*] to walk again, Fernando Saquimux from Totonicapán, 2009."[30] Saquimux offered a prayer to Hermano Pedro with a promise of faith in exchange for aid toward restoration. Then he left a token of faith, maybe even before the cure occurred. Eli Clare persuasively describes the ideologies and ambivalences of cure. He writes, simply, that "the desire for cure, for the restoration of health, is connected to loss and yearning . . . . We wish. We mourn. We make deals."[31] Saquimux's prayer to Hermano Pedro for intercession with God, for healing, care, or cure, can be understood as just such a wish and a deal.[32]

Most disability studies and history scholarship has taken a negative stance toward cure. An "anti-cure" approach holds that cure, in the present and over time, not only individuated and isolated but reduced disabled people to problematic bodies. Cure pursued and maybe even demanded an end to nonnormative conditions. It thus sought the extermination of difference by "correction" and the dogged maintenance of "normal" according to standards defined by and in the image of those with the power to do so. This is especially bolstered by the social model of disability. But others, like Courtney W. Bailey, argue anti-cure interpretations create a "disabled normate" who must transcend their disability without seeking cure, a cousin to dominant culture's "supercrip."[33] To be sure, anti-cure approaches are not compatible with all disabilities and not all people with disabilities accept them. Other scholars draw an effective distinction between ideologies and practices of cure. Clare writes, "As an ideology, cure presents an inflexible set of values. But as a multifaceted and contradictory practice, it multiplies into thousands of different technologies and practices."[34]

In fact, even the ideology of cure is not singular nor inflexible. It certainly cannot be reduced to a singular meaning across time, place, communities, or people. It also is possible to understand cure outside of a medical model.

Again, Clare writes, "What begins as loss or pure suffering frequently becomes ordinary and familiar over time." He adds, "This transformation is another response to body-mind loss."[35] Perhaps a prayer to Hermano Pedro made loss more familiar, more livable, so the cure that was sought and found was not medical (or not only medical) and did not refer to a well-unwell binary. Prayer grants meaning to body-mind loss.

So much of this thinking is speculative because artifacts of gratitude are not quite treatises on cure. Offerings mention *curación* (recovery) or *superando* (overcoming). The plaques often use the verb *salvar*, too. What does it mean to be saved? In this case, the verb *salvar* means not only "to save" or "to save from," but is also associated with overcoming an obstacle, making something less bad or unfortunate, and offering aid. So, to be saved may not mean to be healed, but to be salved or eased, to be aided. *Salvar* shows us how to rework and reclaim the miraculous and to consider healing beyond biomedical cure. It is an opportunity to believe, for those who left the *milagros* and for others who see them.

Robert A. Orsi has urged scholars "to withhold from absence [of the gods] the intellectual, ethical, and spiritual prestige modernity gives it, and to approach history and culture with the gods fully present to humans."[36] Can we take seriously a range of Eucharistic practices and start to understand what Orsi calls "real presence"? Feeling the real presence of God through prayers to Hermano Pedro can fill with meaning the sometimes-disappointing, sometimes-painful experience of human embodiment. The rituals of pilgrimage and leaving a *milagro* may *salvar*. This speculation resonates with Jennifer Scheper-Hughes's analysis of lived religion across five centuries in Mexico, where Cristo Aparecido (Christ Appeared) has long been revered for miraculous healings.[37] But I am not aware of disability history scholarship that takes such an approach to Catholic belief.[38] Healing is also about a testament of faith and expresses a relationship to belief and the church. If one were to pray and then not-heal, could one's faith be thrown into crisis? Who does not leave a votive? Who did not become healed or could not believe in their own healing? These questions require disability studies scholars to seriously consider religious understandings of disability rather than continue to assert that they were displaced by medical interpretations by the nineteenth century.

To be sure, miracles are complicated. So is cure. Both cut right to the value that is—or is not—ascribed to certain ways of being in the world. But miracles also offer another approach to disability where the ability of medical cure to *salvar* is unpredictable or unrealistic. Disability and miracle offer the opportunity to express belief and gratitude. Perhaps prayers were answered when comfort, not cure, was sought. And perhaps the prayer itself was a comfort. Maybe comfort is an alternative to cure.

The repetition and the sheer volume of offerings suggests an army of believers, of faith shored up. There are many single and pairs of children's shoes. One orthotic is made of steel and leather with shoes attached to the uprights at a mechanical ankle joint. It is older than the others and covered in a film of dust. To whom did it belong? Did it offer comfort? Did its prayer? Other votives are carefully drawn or painted on paper and framed. Some of these are very general and offer thanks for favors or support (*favores*). One rugged dark-stained wooden cross reads "Thank you for saving me. Memento from Jessica" in white lettering. There are many framed sets of small portrait photographs. These collections are assembled from identification photographs that are taken in commercial photo studios and commonly used in the government-issued Personal Identification Document (DPI). One set includes the faces of more than two hundred "people who have received *favores* from Hermano Pedro," as the only accompanying text notes. The frame includes no other information—no names, no years, no description of the aid sought or received. Do pilgrims to the Pasillo recognize the names or faces of their neighbors or kin on *milagros*? The community of the church can be an important social support network for disabled believers, too.

Rigid braces like Lupita's and others with hinges in very small sizes, children's shoes, photographs, and tiny rosary bracelets attest to the social relations of families, especially children and parents. In Guatemala, where caring for disabled family members can easily exceed a family's finances and where the state has not provided sufficient employment opportunities or social security for disabled people, a family's desire to pray for their child's cure is not only spiritual, but also an appeal for help vis-à-vis structural problems. Related, a few plaques thank Hermano Pedro for saving mothers from cancer and an operation, which speaks to the blurred boundary between illness and disability. To be disabled in Guatemala is very expensive. Perhaps the Hall of Miracles is also an archive of that.

Conclusion: Pilgrimage to the Hall of Miracles

After weekdays at AGCA, I return to Guatelandia as a pilgrim. The damp ruins that were never rebuilt and the accretion of centuries of burnt copal defy the state's governance. Past the crumbling fountain and its pigeons and behind the wall of Hermano Pedro's penitential garments is the Hall of Miracles. Although sometimes the offerings on its ochre walls are rearranged, they are never removed.[39] It is a relief to return to this archive of comfort—in addition to or sometimes as an alternative to cure—and care. The Hall of Miracles is miraculous and astonishing because it exists as an archive created by disabled people. It is also astonishing for how it calls up so many of the methodological and theoretical discussions of disability studies and disability history, like cure and rehabilitation, prosthetics, aging, dependency, family, stigma, and trauma. It asks its readers to accept miracles. It also demands that we consider how and why archives are tended and curated.

The Hall of Miracles, the case files at AGCA, government public health publications at Guatemala's National Library and similar collections in San Salvador and Managua, indeed all Central American archives of disability, determine what we can know about disability's history. To read well the Hall of Miracles requires a range of literacies—material history, Catholicism, histories of technology and medicine, disability history, Guatemalan history, Spanish language. It may require a willingness to accept and even extend the religious model of disability.[40] It may also require redefining this model, at least insofar as most "models of disability" prove unstable outside of the United States and Europe.[41] Like most archives, the Hall of Miracles presents new questions even as it makes possible our answering of others.[42] For instance, why is political violence invisible in the votives? Has Hermano Pedro ever healed any war wounded (*lisiados de guerra*)? What might this disunion of politics and faith teach us about how people survived the region's deadly Cold War?

There is a final element to acknowledge. A hall (*pasillo*) is a place to move through, a space that implies and encourages mobility. But accessing the Hall of Miracles—indeed most archives in Central America—is difficult. Alongside other contributors to this volume who discuss this matter with greater nuance and detail, I must note that archival research itself is far from equitable. The reading room of the Archivo Histórico de Centro América in Guatemala City where researchers can access asylum records requires walking up two flights of stairs. Gaining permission to photograph a document requires walking down a long hall at least twice. Using the restroom means descending two flights of stairs, then ascending again to return to the reading room. El Salvador's old National Library had a popular Braille collection before the building was demolished to make room for a more modern facility. Now the National Library boasts 24/7 access and numerous videogaming systems and iPads, but how well the former patrons of the Braille collection have been welcomed into the new space is uncertain. Even more, the infrastructure of the urban centers where most archives are located creates serious barriers to access. As disability history in Latin America grows, more and more disabled researchers will travel to the region to do archival research. How might an ethics of care transform archives of disability?

Imperfect as they are, these records are important. They are also under threat, as Central American state archives are precariously funded, so key positions in archives and libraries are unfilled and visiting hours are restricted. The haphazard restrictions on access to these materials mandated by national access to information laws demand a sense of urgency. Laws like Guatemala's are on the books in El Salvador, Honduras, Nicaragua, Costa Rica, and Panama. Also, the restriction of political speech in Nicaragua and El Salvador (albeit to a lesser extent), all but guarantees disability archives and critical writing about disabled Central Americans will continue to be threatened.

Yet the Hall of Miracles stands as evidence that Central American archives of disability can challenge the separation of medical, religious, and social models of disability that has dominated much of disability history and studies scholarship. Archival research of disability history in Central America can be liberatory and change the way that all historians of the region think about its past. It can also expand the way that disability scholars think about the region. The Hall of Miracles and other archives like it can enrich the methodologies that already help us to understand the many varied and shifting meanings of disability. It has the potential to show archivists how to be custodians for many different embodied and experienced pasts. Many material archives challenge the natural and the normative. Miraculous material archives like the Hall of Miracles should encourage us toward astonishing ways of approaching the past that are "not explicable by natural laws." Disability's meanings are not universal, and its materiality is never immutable, according to the Hall of Miracles. Miraculous material archives of disability urge scholars toward a "usable past." They invalidate the argument against presentism. They upend the positivist anti-theory claim that hounds the discipline of history. Central American disability archives can offer a new way to gather and assemble, even ephemerally—especially ephemera of—crip lives for the future.

Notes

This essay benefited from conversations with Gabriela Soto Laveaga and Elizabeth O'Brien and the other participants of the Erasures workshop at Harvard in April 2022, KJ Cerankowski, and David Kazanjian.

1. On Pentecostal responses to social precariousness of poverty (and to some extent disability), see Kevin Lewis O'Neill, "On the Importance of Wolves," *Cultural Anthropology* 33, no. 3 (2018): 499–520 and O'Neill, *Secure the Soul: Christian Piety and Gang Prevention in Guatemala* (Berkeley: University of California Press, 2015).

2. Baynton's letter of endorsement for a National Historical Publications and Records Commission grant to fund a disability history collection at the University of Toledo is quoted in Diane F. Britton, Barbara Floyd, and Patricia A. Murphy, "Overcoming Another Obstacle: Archiving a Community's Disabled History," *Radical History Review* 94 (Winter 2006): 213–27.

3. All archives present challenges in translation, erasures and absences, access, and organization. Of the vast scholarship on archives in the humanities, I find Michel-Rolph Trouillot, Antoinette Burton, Jacques Derrida, and Tiya Alicia Miles to be helpful models in thinking through archive problems. Joan W. Scott's "The Evidence of Experience," *Critical Inquiry* 17, no. 4 (Summer 1991): 773–97 is also an important guide.

4. Historians do not make discoveries. This grandiose framing of discovery in archival research eliminates the labor and technique of archivists and other caretakers who collect, pare down, clean, preserve, organize, locate, and move documents for researchers. Instead, revelation points toward "the disclosure or communication of truths which would not otherwise be known, at least in the same way" and a distinction between truths revealed through reason and those from God. See "Revelation," *The Concise Oxford Dictionary of World Religions*, John Bowker, ed. (Oxford: Oxford University Press, 2000).

5. Ann Laura Stoler, *Along the Archival Grain: Epistemic Anxieties and Colonial Common Sense* (Princeton: Princeton University Press, 2008), 14.

6. Stoler, *Along the Archival Grain*, 29.

7. Eli Clare, *Brilliant Imperfection: Grappling with Cure* (Durham, NC: Duke University Press, 2017), 112–15.

8. Clare, *Brilliant Imperfection*, 114.

9. On using psychiatric case files for historical research, see John Harley Warner, "The Uses of Patient Records by Historians: Patterns, Possibilities and Perplexities," *Health and History* 1, no. 2/3 (1999): 101–11; Warwick Anderson, "The Case of the Archive," *Critical Inquiry* 39, no. 3 (Spring 2013); David Wright and Renée Saucier, "Madness in the Archives: Anonymity, Ethics, and Mental Health History Research," *Journal of the Canadian Historical Association* 23, no. 2 (2012): 65–90. The emerging field of Mad studies also has a great deal to teach historians about the ethics of researching the lives and experiences of people medicalized by psychiatry.

10. Foreign researchers and journalists are complicit in the spectacular and damning gaze cast toward disabled people in the country's psychiatric institutions, even as these exposés may seek to spur reform. Seemingly every year, a new documentary film crew infiltrates the national insane asylum and posts a spectacularly tragic video on YouTube. Why do some people seem compelled to watch these videos? Rosemarie Garland Thomson considers this in *Staring: How We Look* (New York: Oxford University Press, 2009).

11. See Enrique Gordillo, "Guía del 'Catálogo Pardo' del Archivo General de Centro América," Dirección General de Investigación, Universidad de San Carlos. https://digi.usac.edu.gt/bvirtual/informes/puihg/INF-2002-051.pdf (accessed October 8, 2024); Jorge Luján Muñóz, *Guía del Archivo General de Centro América* (Guatemala: Ministerio de Educación, 1982); Pedro López Gómez, *El Archivo General de Centro América (Ciudad de Guatemala): Informe* (Madrid: ANABAD, 1991).

12. Of course, no one lived a life according to key words. But the key words by which one's life is reduced are significant.

13. On defining "mad history," see Geoffrey Reaume, "Mad People's History," *Radical History Review* 94 (Winter 2006): 170–82.

14. When I was prohibited from requesting case files, a beloved archivist quietly passed me one *legajo* of case studies at a time. Why? I will always be grateful to him.

15. One beautiful analysis of the architecture and space of archives is Daniel Nemser's "Eviction and the Archive: Materials for an Archaeology of the Archivo General de Indias," *Journal of Spanish Cultural Studies* 16, no. 2 (2015): 123–41.

16. The Pasillo de Milagros is not unique; indeed, it is exemplary of healing spaces (including pasillos, santuarios, and capillas) in Catholic Latin America.

17. "miraculous, adj., adv., and n." OED Online. March 2022. Oxford University Press. https://www-oed-com.lp.hscl.ufl.edu/view/Entry/119063?redirectedFrom=miraculous (accessed March 24, 2022). To astonish is to stun, bewilder, and even dismay, which the Pasillo de Milagros may do to certain secular approaches to disability.

18. "miraculous, adj., adv., and n." OED Online. March 2022. Oxford University Press. https://www-oed-com.lp.hscl.ufl.edu/view/Entry/119063?redirectedFrom=miraculous (accessed March 24, 2022).

19. Sharon V. Betcher, *Spirit and the Politics of Disablement* (Minneapolis: Fortress Press, 2007), 50.

20. Thank you to Liz Roberts and Gabriela Soto Laveaga for pushing me to try to think like a believer.

21. Katherine Ott, "Prosthetics," in *Keywords for Disability Studies*, Rachel Adams, Benjamin Reiss, and David Serlin, eds. (New York: New York University Press, 2015), 140.

22. Katherine Ott, "The Sum of Its Parts," in *Artificial Parts, Practical Lives: Modern Histories of Prosthetics*, eds. Katherine Ott, David Serlin, and Stephen Mihm (New York: New York University Press, 2002), 3; Danielle Peers and Lindsay Eales, "Moving Materiality: People, Tools, and This Thing Called Disability," *Art/Research International* 2, no. 2 (2017). For an introduction to "thinking with things," see Laurel Thatcher et al., *Tangible Things: Making History through Objects* (Oxford: Oxford University Press, 2015).

23. Katherine Ott, "Disability Things: Material Culture and American Disability History, 1700–2010," in *Disability Histories*, eds. Susan Burch and Michael Rembis (Urbana: University of Illinois Press, 2014): 129.

24. On how disabled people and caregivers hack existing items for better use, see Laura Mauldin, "Care Tactics," *The Baffler* no. 64 (July 2022). https://thebaffler.com/salvos/care-tactics-mauldin?utm_source=substack&utm_medium=email.

25. Ott, "Disability Things," in *Disability Histories*, eds. Burch and Rembis, 119.

26. Thank you to KJ Cerankowski for this insight.

27. On the phrase "disability things," see Ott, "Disability Things," in *Disability Histories*, eds. Burch and Rembis, 119–35.

28. Kevin Lewis O'Neill, *Securing the Soul: Christian Piety and Gang Prevention in Guatemala* (Berkeley: University of California Press, 2015), 11.

29. Understanding faith as "willingness to give one's heart to an understanding of a world that could be without asking for objective proof of the mind" comes from Jenny Ann Martinez, who generously shared this idea with me.

30. The text of an offering at the Pasillo de Milagros, Iglesia de San Francisco, Antigua, Guatemala in March 2022. Thank you, Michael Tallon. The needlepoint offering from a man suggests that sometimes *milagros* were left on behalf of others, though I have not been able to find Saquimux and ask who made it.

31. Clare, *Brilliant Imperfection*, 57.

32. The growing group of Pentecostals (neo-Pentecostals) in Guatemala take a different approach to disability, which is worthy of investigation and discussion. While disability healing stories in the New and Old Testaments conflate sin and disability, how believers experience or place faith in intercession probably exceeds this association.

33. Courtney W. Bailey, "On the Impossible: Disability Studies, Queer Theory, and the Surviving Crip," *Disability Studies Quarterly* 39, no. 4 (Fall 2019).

34. Clare, *Brilliant Imperfection*, 76. See also Eunjung Kim, *Curative Violence: Rehabilitating Disability, Gender, and Sexuality in Modern Korea* (Durham, NC: Duke University Press, 2017).

35. Clare, *Brilliant Imperfection*, 58.

36. Robert A. Orsi, *History and Presence* (Cambridge: Harvard University Press, 2018), 8.

37. Jennifer Scheper-Hughes, *Biography of a Mexican Crucifix: Lived Religion and Local Faith from the Conquest to the Present* (New York: Oxford University Press, 2010).

38. Theologian Sharon V. Betcher takes a different approach. Betcher, "Saving the Wretched of the Earth," *Disability Studies Quarterly* 26, no. 3 (Summer 2006). Many scholars of disability outside of the United States and Europe have studied religious understandings of disability, see especially Jenifer Barclay, "Differently Abled: Africanisms, Disability, and Power in the Age of Transatlantic Slavery," in Jennifer Byrnes and Jennifer Muller, eds., *Bioarchaeology of Impairment and Disability: Theoretical, Ethnohistorical, and Methodological Perspectives* (New York: Springer Publishing Company, 2017): 77–94, and Siobhan Senier, "Traditionally, Disability Was Not Seen as Such: Writing and Healing in the Work of Mohegan Medicine People," *Journal of Literary and Cultural Disability Studies* 7, no. 2 (2013): 213–29.

39. I have been a pilgrim to this archive for more than a decade and it never seems to change very much, although a few new items have been added. I know because I always ignore the "no photography" sign. I need to bear witness and I am only ever very alone there. On those who cared for similar relics in twelfth-century England, see Ruth J. Salter, *Saints, Cure-Seekers and Miraculous Healing in Twelfth-Century England* (Woodbridge: York Medieval Press, 2021).

40. See text and notes for Orsi and Scheper-Hughes above.

41. Indeed, there is a distinction to be drawn about histories of disability "written in geographic or temporal contexts that do not assume medicine's social and cultural authority to label, to frame." Julie Livingston, "Comment: On the Borderland of Medical and Disability History," *Bulletin of the History of Medicine* 87, no. 4 (Winter 2013), 564. Beth Linker's essay, "On the Borderland of Medical and Disability History: A Survey of the Fields," *Bulletin of the History of Medicine* 87, no. 4 (Winter 2013), 499–535, leads an extended discussion of histories of medicine and disability in the journal issue.

42. Curiously, there is an ex-voto thanking Hermano Pedro for a functioning Yamaha piano, which was brought all the way from Tapachula, Mexico. What is disabling? What is healing?

CHAPTER 12

Cripping the Settler Archive

Disability in Women's Memoirs of the Indian Service

JESS L. WILCOX COWING

When Minnie Braithwaite Jenkins visited her home in Williamsburg, Virginia, between 1901 and 1902 after working as a boarding school instructor in the federal Indian Service, now the Bureau of Indian Affairs (BIA), her family celebrated her adventurous life and assumed that the dangers she faced in remote Arizona were directly connected to the proximity to Diné and Hopi reservations.[1] In *Girl from Williamsburg* (1951), Jenkins writes: "The boys had a great time feeding me. They were proud of the little cousin who had survived life in the wilds among the Indians, although I repeatedly assured them that the dangers I had experienced had not been *from the Indians*."[2] Here, Jenkins refers to the stories she told her family about working as the only teacher for one hundred Diné and Hopi youth, nursing the school through an epidemic, surviving sandstorms, and living with the effects of fatigue and illness. Jenkins's memoir chronicles her time as an instructor, first at the Blue Canyon School in Arizona beginning in 1899, and later at the Fort Mohave School outside of Needles, California until 1906. Jenkins is one of six white women who worked in the Indian Service and who later published accounts of their work in remote boarding schools in the early twentieth century.[3] In addition to Jenkins, Estelle Aubrey Brown published *Stubborn Fool: A Narrative* (1952), which examines her time as an instructor, matron, and clerk in the early twentieth century. Both born in the 1870s, Brown and Jenkins entered the Indian Service around the turn of the century.

Brown and Jenkins provide firsthand accounts of the labor conditions for white women in low-level and low-paying positions in the Indian Service. Most work on white women's boarding school memoirs and experiences either uncritically celebrates their white savior "pioneering spirit" and "charitable work," or focuses solely on assimilation measures that caused generational harm and trauma for Native people.[4] A significant amount of work by Native scholars and writers documents the legacy of settler assimilation projects that deliberately targeted Native children and young people for genocidal termination and cultural destruction in the nineteenth and twentieth centuries.[5] Brenda Child's *Boarding School Seasons: American Indian Families 1900–1940* and K. Tsianina Lomawaima's *They Called It Prairie Light: The Story of Chilocco Indian School* are necessary reading for understanding the intergenerational impact on Native families.[6] The work of the Native-led organization the National Native American Boarding School Healing Coalition continues to build programs for boarding school survivors and advocate for a U.S. truth and reconciliation process.[7] Building on and informed by the work of such Native scholars and activists, this chapter explores federal boarding schools as specifically disabling sites of overwork and manufactured illness. Boarding schools targeted Native youth and also generated dangerous and disabling conditions for under-resourced, mostly white federal staff. Native scholars and writers have thoroughly documented the conditions of Native youth incarceration during the historic boarding school era. Coming to this work as a white settler descendant, I am interested in how the project of colonization assumes and generates disabling conditions and institutions for all those subjected to its destructive daily grind.

Historians have written about the white women who taught in boarding schools through the Indian Service as supplements to the historiographies of the administration of boarding schools. Most significantly, David Wallace Adams's comprehensive study of the administration of federal Indian education in *Education for Extinction* cites memoirs, including those of Jenkins and Brown, to detail daily practices in boarding schools. Yet, literary historians' scholarship has not substantially focused on the women of varying age and class backgrounds who taught in the Indian Service in the early twentieth century, and even fewer have done so as records of disability history. This chapter draws from disability history and crip methodologies to interpret Jenkins and Brown's witnessing and experiences of institutional disability with the knowledge that, as scholar Patricia A. Carter explains, "these [women] were not heroines, but average women with common biases and foibles."[8]

A disability history framework alongside a crip methodology identifies how the structures of school buildings and limited resources in isolated geographical settings created an unsustainable living situation for everyone housed in the physical space of a boarding school. Feminist disability scholars Jina B. Kim, Sami Schalk, and Julie Avril Minich have argued for disability as a methodology, a practice to move beyond disability representation and to interrogate the systemic ways in which disability is generated and normalized.[9] Building on the work of Kim, Minich, and Schalk, I consider federal boarding schools as one historical site that necessitates a disability methodology to better understand how long-term residency and work generated lasting effects on the youth and the employees' quality of life and access to wellness, broadly defined. Brown and Jenkins include many medical examples of the experience of Native youths as well as their own experiences, but they also gesture to the disabling impact of care work and survival as necessary upkeep for a chronically underfunded institution. Brown and Jenkins describe the boarding schools where they lived and worked as constantly lacking in supplies and frequently in disrepair. Medical emergencies and staff shortages in these rural and isolated boarding schools resulted in chronic disablement, and for these women generated distress and extra work that waxed and waned.

This chapter focuses on the low-level white women employed as teachers, cooks, laundresses, and matrons, who were charged with enforcing federal assimilation goals. These women perpetuated the harm of BIA directives on Native youth and their families even as they also experienced disabling impacts of enforcing ableist-racist assimilation policies. Brown and Jenkins are just two of the many women who worked for the BIA from various class and economic backgrounds and across a range of ages from young, unmarried women to aging women. These women's stories are part of a larger archive of settler-authored boarding school histories, except that unlike official administrative records, they come from white low-wage women with the least amount of power in the BIA. In addition to offering insight into the gendered class and labor dynamics that factored into white women's decisions to live far away in unfamiliar cultural contexts in the early twentieth century, these memoirs additionally record and witness the day-to-day physical and cognitive impact of upholding white supremacist assimilation ideologies. Jenkins and Brown's memoirs are critical resources for understanding boarding schools as part of a legacy of disability that state violence and carceral sites themselves engendered and exacerbated. There is much work remaining to unpack how the BIA relied on ableism to justify the existence of assimilation sites such as residential boarding schools. Throughout this chapter, I read Jenkins and Brown's memoirs as archival documents offering insight into the daily operations of isolated boarding schools in the Southwest. I do not interpret Jenkins and Brown's memoirs as reliable sources for understanding Native students' perspectives or experiences, as these memoirs are written from the perspective of white staff with power over Native youth in their charge. Instead, I interpret their memoirs as sources to better understand how the federal government relied on a range of women and other low-level staff to operate boarding schools. In dialogue with archival records from the Bureau of Indian Affairs, and read through feminist disability theory, Jenkins and Brown's accounts of boarding schools offer an archive of disability history. Their memoirs help explicate the combined disabling impact of federal assimilation policies both on the people who executed them and on the Native children and young people subjected to them.

Why the Indian Service?

Jenkins and Brown's memoirs have historical significance as little-known texts in a longer tradition of overlooked women's writing about gender and self-reliance in the late nineteenth and early twentieth centuries. This chapter offers an example of feminist disability literary reading practices to *crip*, or read against the grain, genre conventions and settler depositories such as the National Archives and Records Administration and archival records from sources such as the Government Printing Office.[10] A crip reading invites looking beyond the ways that lesser-known texts adhere to standard categories and generalizations, or to recognize how a well-known text offers innovative ways of understanding disability—such as physical variance and neurological difference—that few readers or scholars have written about before. A crip reading of archival material in settler depositories means to critically examine the categories into which documents are labeled and resist taking them at face value to, instead, consider how their categorization reveals the social values and ableist biases of the original archivists. In other words, a crip reading—informed through Native/Indigenous studies and Native-authored accounts of boarding school experiences—shows how the federal government justified the assimilation of Native youth through assertions that they required physical and cognitive training. This work can support both scholars and Native people directly impacted by the legacy of these policies in their research and advocacy. White women's memoirs of boarding schools, when read for disabling impacts of assimilation directives alongside BIA administrative records, crips or critiques the structural harm of underfunded, isolated assimilation sites that boarding schools epitomized.[11]

White women such as Brown and Jenkins participated in what I call settler ableist justifications for assimilation training in boarding schools.[12] Indian education reformers and BIA administrators justified assimilation training for Native youth and families as an ableist rehabilitation mandate that imposed white, Christian norms of living and self-sufficiency on Native people perceived to lack the physical and intellectual abilities to become self-reliant and productive members of U.S. society. Instructors such as Brown and Jenkins were the people charged with the day-to-day policies of the federal government's aim to assimilate Native youth through forced Christian-centric English language training and immersion in white, middle-class cultural norms.

Low-level white women engaged in direct assimilation directives including corporeal punishment and cultural erasure techniques in classrooms even as they also experienced sexist, disabling working conditions. Both Brown and Jenkins described their frustration with opportunities available for young women on the East Coast and their yearning for adventure and learning experiences that would challenge them and overcome limited options in their home communities. Brown explained that "[i]f a girl failed to get a husband, she could teach a rural school—if she could spell. She could be a country dressmaker—if she could sew. Failing these, she could be a burden, for which no qualifications were necessary."[13] Young, unmarried white women similarly seeking meaningful occupations made up the bulk of the boarding school instructors employed by the Indian Service. According to Cathleen D. Cahill, "the Indian School Service in particular" was an "early example of a feminized federal agency" where there was "an insidious effort to disrupt the affective bonds between Native children and their parents" as "the boarding schools tried to substitute Indian Service employees as fictive kin for an entire generation of Indian children."[14]

Many factors led young white women to work in the Indian Service, and as Patricia A. Carter has noted, the women who author the available accounts of firsthand experience all describe some need to leave their home communities in order to lead independent and self-sufficient lives.[15] Brown grew up in rural New York State and began working at age fifteen as a teacher. Jenkins grew up in a well-connected family in Williamsburg, Virginia, where she was able to rely on family and hired household staff for her day-to-day needs. Yet, both Brown and Jenkins arrived at their first Indian Service jobs without ever having meaningfully interacted with Native people and without almost any reported training or experience with federal assimilation policies. Brown explained that not many people from her home community knew what the Indian Service was, and she herself had never heard of it until she learned that "the quickest way to enter government service was, at that time, as a kindergartner [teacher] in the Indian Service."[16] To the extent that Brown was familiar with mission projects for Native people, she thought of charity drives and her mother's "mission society" to collect clothing and "dress" that "had to be pretty much on its beam ends before it was fit to send to the missionaries for the Indians."[17] Jenkins described how she decided to "go West to teach the Indians" after "many disappointments," including being denied entry to chemistry classes at the College of William & Mary before women were admitted in 1918.[18] Neither Brown nor Jenkins reported having training before accepting these positions, and Brown recalled that "[n]o such test" assessing her "fitness to teach children of a savage race" was administered in her civil service exam.[19]

At the time of Jenkins and Brown's federal employment, the federal government had charged white women with the education mandates for assimilating Native people beginning with the forced training of Native men incarcerated by Colonel Richard Henry Pratt at Ft. Marion in Florida in 1878 where nineteenth-century author Harriet Beecher Stowe once visited. Some of the same Native men at Ft. Marion were later detained at the Hampton Normal and Agricultural School.[20] Indian education reformers at the turn of the century substantially comprised educated and typically elite northeastern white women who had begun to publicly critique the federal government's treatment of Native people. These progressive reformers advocated for a change in policy and practices that would support Native people through offering services and training in boarding schools and teams dispatched to reservations, what scholars now recognize as assimilation, and what this chapter refers to as assimilation training. Helen Hunt Jackson voiced the "progressive" views of some Indian education reformers in her 1899 text, *A Century of Dishonor: A Sketch of the United States Government's Dealings with Some of the Tribes.* Jackson argued that the United States had wrongfully oppressed Native people and tribes, and used the framework of liberal democracy and sentimentalism as a means of restoring her idea of justice. For example, Jackson "recommend[s] . . . the establishment of more schools" because "if a boarding and industrial school, similar to those at Hampton and Carlisle, could be established in Southern California, it would be of inestimable value, and would provide opportunities for many children who, owing to the isolation of their homes, could not be reached in any other way."[21] Moreover, in Josephine Richards's address published in the National Education Association's 1900 proceedings, she deputized white women as the primary cultural "protectors" and social "makers" charged to forcibly socialize young Native women into normative modes of settler domesticity.[22]

Brown and Jenkins wrote in the style of white women trained to understand their work as an honorable and necessary service for Native children and their families—a respectable, if risky, occupation for an unmarried, educated woman who wanted to expand her life experiences and escape the limiting options available to women in the early twentieth century.[23] Brown showed a willingness to examine her own participation in the assimilation of Native children and young people and how her work in the Indian Service challenged her initial lack of knowledge about Native/Indigenous peoples and relations with the U.S. government through assimilation and termination policies. Jenkins also criticized the Indian Service, but her reflections are more focused on personal health issues and the common overwork women experienced.

Overwork and Exhaustion

Brown and Jenkins account for the gritty overwork and inadequate resources of remote early twentieth-century boarding schools through personal narratives that critique the agenda BIA administrators outline in annual reports. Both Brown and Jenkins offer language and frameworks for biomedical understandings of illness as well as the emotional and social hardships that shape Native youths' physical, emotional, and cognitive health in a congregate setting. Brown and Jenkins write about the debilitating expectation for highly gendered caretaking—supporting young people's emotional and developmental needs, monitoring food supplies and storage, and managing acute virus and illness crises—beyond their job descriptions as educators. Brown engaged in more sustained critical analysis of the mission and rhetoric of assimilation training in boarding schools based on her more than ten years working for the BIA. Jenkins's memoir focuses on her personal development and process of learning about Native peoples' distinct cultures and connections even as she rarely critiqued her own participation in enacting oppressive federal assimilation policies. Universal curriculum guides and BIA correspondence of the late nineteenth and early twentieth centuries justify assimilation goals through top-down management strategies that do not consider the variance in geographical sites.[24] Many of the boarding schools that needed instructors in the early twentieth century were remote schools in the Southwest and not yet easily accessible by train. Because the aim of boarding schools was to impose white settler lifeways on Native youth and families, superintendents in boarding schools dismissed tribal history and knowledge of reservation life. Brown wrote that "[d]uring my time at Crow Creek the subject of improving reservation conditions was not mentioned in my hearing."[25] Moreover, school administrators and missionaries dismissed Native/Indigenous knowledge of local food sources, protective measures against harsh weather conditions, and practices that offered stable shelter.[26] School administrators' unwillingness to acknowledge or learn local Native/Indigenous knowledge meant that teachers from other parts of the country, such as Brown and Jenkins, had little information on how to adapt to unfamiliar settings or how to support Native youth in their care. Jenkins tells her family that "[t]he government did not provide for us at all . . . and we could not provide for ourselves because our salaries were so inadequate."[27]

The work of caring for all of the Native youth during two epidemics takes a toll on Jenkins's health. She writes: "I had had to work under so many handicaps that my strength was inadequate for the demands made upon it."[28] She explains that the "catastrophe" of the epidemics "was the last straw. I threw myself upon one of the children's beds and wailed."[29] In the chapter entitled "Stress and Strain," Jenkins describes how months of working at the Blue Canyon School made her feel like she was "in a state of constant fatigue."[30] The near constant work during the epidemics affected her stamina, something that becomes apparent after a walk through a canyon to look for "watercress."[31] She writes: "Doctor had been telling me that I should collapse under the load of work I was carrying, and this trip down the canyon that I could have made so easily and so pleasantly six months before showed me, as nothing else could, my weakened condition. I was now teaching one hundred and seventeen pupils, and if I were to last out the term, I should indeed have to be careful."[32] Jenkins then connects her workload to her job security at

Blue Canyon, recalling how other staff members warned her about the school administration's pattern of pushing out young teachers through untenable and disabling work conditions. Jenkins writes: "Mildred, as well as others, had repeatedly told me that those in charge would let the number of pupils grow until I succumbed. Then they would report to Washington that I was unable to do the work."[33] She notes how the doctor "was uneasy and was giving me iron. 'When you go home,' he said, 'don't you dare to come back here. You'd never leave alive!'"[34]

Understaffed facilities and lack of adequate infrastructure meant that disabling health conditions affecting daily operations were a baseline reality for both staff and Native youth at boarding schools. Brown and Jenkins both detailed how the small number of staff led to arduous labor and disabling health impacts for women and the Native youth housed on school grounds. In the chapter "Officials," Jenkins describes the labor of preparing for the beginning of a school year at the Blue Canyon School for Diné youth. According to Jenkins: "It did not matter to what department an employee was appointed. At our school, whether doctor, farmer, or industrial teacher, he was almost sure to be engaged in putting up more buildings."[35] Similarly, upon arrival at the Crow Creek Indian School in South Dakota, a supervisor informed Brown that she should expect duties in addition to her role as a "kindergartner."[36] Mr. Hillyard, the superintendent, told Brown: "Employees in the Service are given duties in addition to their regular work."[37] As Jenkins described, federal boarding schools often lacked the physical capacity to support the number of people typically housed on school grounds and "shelter was the prime necessity."[38] Schools typically held one hundred or more forcibly enrolled Native children and young people, a cook, sometimes a doctor, one to three teachers, and support staff such as laundresses and dorm matrons. Brown learned that she was one of three total teachers for two hundred students. And Jenkins reports that for one hundred students, she was the only teacher, and there were around three or four other staff members to assist with cooking, cleaning, and maintenance (all of which Jenkins reports doing as well).[39]

As Brown and Jenkins both narrate, job titles did not account for the level of shared and extra labor imposed on the women to make up for sickness and leave as well as general overwork. In preparation for the beginning of a new year at the Blue Canyon School, Jenkins recalls how "Ada, the school cook" was tasked with cooking "for a hundred persons with equipment for thirty" and in the process "collapsed from overwork."[40] Jenkins was then "notified to close the schoolroom and go to the kitchen" to continue Ada's work.[41] Jenkins manages to complete Ada's tasks with the help of a Diné man who was more familiar with the kitchen. However, she accomplished this "[b]y arising at four in the morning and working until ten at night."[42] Most boarding schools had men in professional-class positions such as doctors and superintendents, whereas mostly white women staffed lower-wage jobs at the support level, including as seamstresses, laundresses, dorm matrons, and cooks. Brown observes, after a year at the Crow Creek Indian School, that "I began to understand Miss Swinton and the other overworked industrial employees. Miss Swinton's physical and mental angles had been sharpened by endless tasks . . . . Years and work had fretted her spirit to acidity, sharpened her tongue to acrimony."[43]

Critiquing the BIA

Brown and Jenkins both describe their own and others' emotional distress as crucial narratives for conveying life in boarding schools. Yet, Brown critiques the prevalence of Native youths' physical and mental ailments as problems the Indian Service created through a centralized bureaucracy out of touch with the day-to-day concerns of boarding school staff. Jenkins also provides a description of similarly debilitating experiences without directly criticizing the Indian Service, as further analyzed later in this chapter. At the end of her first year of teaching at Crow Creek Indian School, Brown reflected on her observations, writing: "As time passed and I learned how that school was conducted, I was indignant for the first time, but by no means for the last. Crow Creek was an isolated Federal institution that had to maintain itself. There were only a few white people. Who did the work? The children."[44] Brown regularly addresses the reader, which emphasizes the emotional quality of learning unsettling details about how boarding schools relied on forced child labor. She describes in detail the daily minutiae of operating the school through relying on forced labor of Native youth. Following BIA directives for gender-appropriate vocational training, "the older girls made all the clothing worn by two hundred pupils, with the exception of the boys' Sunday uniforms . . . . [B]olts of material were sent in under contracts that supplied identical fabrics to all schools."[45] In addition to sewing clothing and uniforms, Native girls were also responsible for items that "frequently" had "to be mended."[46] Brown learns how "the small girls from the kindergarten darned stockings four hours daily except on Sunday . . . . The little pioneers sat patiently darning with their inflamed finger joints, with no outcry for hands pricked at unaccustomed tasks."[47]

Reflecting on her own role in their forced labor and the employment the staff there relied on, Brown considers how "[w]e had set their feet on the long, hard road to civilization."[48] She notices details of how overwork and forced labor affected the youngest Native youth detained at the school, referring to the young girls with descriptors such as "pioneers" to qualify her "indignant" awareness of child labor with the language of assimilation.[49] Brown continues to detail how forced labor also included general maintenance for the school building, including cleaning and janitorial work. Addressing the reader again,

Brown asks: "Who kept the shabby, desolate buildings in a semblance of cleanliness?" Repeating her rhetorical style of accounting for the way she learned about the daily school operations, she answers, "The children."[50] According to Brown, "Children were forever scrubbing."[51] She wonders what impact that had on the boys she saw scrubbing the floors of their dorms, writing: "I wished I might know their thoughts as, on hands and knees, they wielded brush and soap before the white man's goddess of sanitation."[52] Brown's narrative chronicles a long time period and moves beyond reflections of her own personal development, whereas Jenkins, as discussed later, remains fixated on her own experiences. Brown connects her observations to federal management and questions the purpose of assimilation practices and how they might affect the Native youth detained on school grounds.

Brown additionally addresses readers with a plea to learn through her memoir and critique federal assimilation mandates. For instance, Brown's foreword is a plea for her audience to read about an aspect of U.S. policy and practice that few have learned or seriously considered. She calls her text "an American story" that "is known to few Americans."[53] Brown dedicates her memoir to John Collier and his dog, Collier being one of the appointed Commissioners of Indian Affairs (COIA) during Brown's employment. She then writes in her foreword: "[T]he hound of heaven—Voice of Conscience—to the author was so real that she worked for years to build a doghouse to shut it up in. Readers will also know this hound, since they listen, or should listen, to its voice."[54] Her foreword anticipates a familiar and contemporary audience, assuming that at the time of publication, or in the years after, readers might have personal knowledge as colleagues or administration officials about the circumstances of her employment, writing: "You will recognize many of these people, may know personally one or more of them."[55] Brown continues to implore readers to take the subject of her narrative seriously, with a tone of self-critique and reflection that does not yet emerge in the narrator's voice in the early chapters. She introduces her narrative as a cautionary tale with some distance from the subject matter, even though the story contains "real people" including some who "hide behind pseudonyms."[56]

In the last sentence of the foreword, Brown addresses her own role in a shameful history she participated in. Brown writes in a third-person style that creates distance between herself as the narrator and the boarding school assimilation she implicitly critiques. Brown does not introduce *Stubborn Fool* as *her* story, but rather generates a third-person narrator through whom she addresses the general public from behind a rhetorical veil as "the woman who lived it."[57] Yet, her writing also serves as a kind of public testimony, a way to say that she was a witness and a complicit actor or, as she puts it, a woman "who found much of it infamous, and who freely confesses her own shabby part in it."[58]

The Disabling Impact of Boarding Schools' Congregate Settings

In addition to overworked women, the colonizing mission of boarding schools also relied on the forced labor of Native youth under the guise of "training" and "apprenticeship." Inadequate facilities generated exhaustion and overwork as well as recurring illness and its disabling impacts on Native youth. Brown and Jenkins both suggest that the effects of illness become a norm for people housed in boarding schools. Brown links disability to the result of disease transmission in congregate settings, a reality that surprised her in her first few days at Crow Creek Indian School. Brown explains that she "expected Indian children to be shining with health."[59] Instead, she describes how "the faces" she saw on her first day in the classroom "shone," but "with mercuric ointment generously spread over their scrofula sores."[60] Scrofula had transmitted so thoroughly among the Native youth at Crow Creek that Brown identifies her students through their visible "scrofula sores," expressing dismay that they "refused to acknowledge ownership" of the names on her class roster.[61] Instead, she recalls how "[t]he sores helped. I separated the children with visible sores and so came to identify Sophia Ghost Bear by the running sore on the right side of her neck."[62]

Jenkins also expresses discomfort on her first day of teaching because the Native youth in her charge draw pictures of "animals in the most intimate of corral animal life."[63] Upon her arrival at the Blue Canyon School, Jenkins observes that "[n]one of the boys had sufficient clothing and they were a ragged and pitiful lot."[64] She blames this on "The Government," which "might furnish them at least sufficient clothing."[65] Yet, Jenkins's narrative suggests an emotional attachment to Native youth as children who needed proper guidance because of what white staff attributed to their growing up "in the corral among animals."[66] Jenkins consistently describes her students in favorable terms. Fanny, a young Native girl (likely Diné or Hopi), becomes one of her most trusted students. (Fanny assists Jenkins in hiding a student who might be given away in an arranged marriage.) Jenkins describes Fanny as "blind" and she refers to Fanny through disability as an identifier, as in "Little Blind Fanny," or just "Little Fanny."[67] Fanny knew lessons "by heart," but could not identify words on charts and so Jenkins accommodates her by asking Fanny to select a classmate to point to the right words on the chart for her.[68] It is not clear what the origins of Fanny's blindness are, whether a congenital condition or the result of an illness sustained from the boarding school environment, and Jenkins never specifies. Nonetheless, Jenkins lightly critiques the federal government's provisions for students and otherwise largely focuses on how the Diné and Hopi youth are "appreciative" of her instruction and in need of "a teacher to love."[69] In other words, Jenkins and Brown lament what they describe as workplace challenges and what Jenkins refers to as "distress," but what reads instead as their struggles to anticipate the debilitating environment of boarding schools with a lack of adequate resources from the Indian Service.[70]

The BIA's enforcement of assimilation practices in boarding schools relied heavily on discouraging boarding school staff from treating Native people as equals and learning about their lives and tribal practices, as Jenkins and Brown's narratives reveal. Brown explains the lack of preparation before beginning her work: "Later, when the Indian Bureau sent me to Crow Creek, it did not even tell me the name of the tribe it was sending me to teach. History had taught me—as it was to teach future generations of American schoolchildren—a highly one-sided and inaccurate version of the so-called massacre of General Custer and his Seventh Cavalry."[71] Brown recalls being aware that the history she learned was heavily biased, "one-sided and inaccurate," and expresses a desire to have known more about the Native youth she would be teaching and perhaps their tribal nations' experience in her "one-sided and inaccurate" history.[72] Brown and Jenkins arrive at their jobs with ignorant and racist understandings of Native lifeways as well as a lack of knowledge of Native history and genocidal devastation enacted through federal assimilation and termination policies that preceded their appointments as Indian Service employees.

In addition to discouraging boarding school staff from learning about the Native people they lived with, the BIA also relied on an ableist enforcement of settler norms of health. Periodic epidemics and disease transmission were regular occurrences for everyone housed in boarding schools since their establishment in the late nineteenth century. Moving away from the rhetoric of termination in the nineteenth century, the discourse of assimilation in the early-twentieth-century boarding school era focused intensely on how to manage Native people's lifeways. By the early twentieth century, administration of boarding schools in the BIA had become more centralized, and the Bureau tasked higher-up administrators with standardizing a curriculum and set of standards and procedures for all federal boarding schools. Part of the standardization of boarding schools included a focus on disease management that was heavily based on racist and ableist interpretations of Native people's unhealthy and "primitive" lifestyles. For example, COIA Thomas Morgan's 1890 curriculum guide stipulates that physicians assigned to boarding schools should provide "simple, appropriate talks" focused on health, hygiene, and proper "assimilation of food" in addition to "ventilation" and "hygienic conditions."[73] And in a letter on the state of Indian education for 1915, E. B. Meritt,

Assistant Commissioner of Indian Affairs, reports that "[t]he health of pupils in Indian schools receives constant oversight" and students need physician certification before enrolling in off-reservation schools.[74]

Yet Brown and Jenkins describe a near total lack of guidance from the BIA in disease prevention and management, requiring that they perform a substantial amount of nursing and health care in their jobs as instructors at boarding schools. In the "Epidemics" chapter, Jenkins recalls how an outbreak of smallpox shut down the school after Christmas one winter. Staff decided to quarantine students in dug-out caves near the school in lieu of finding a place to quarantine them in the school building.[75] After the laundry attendant resigned, the doctor's wife washed all the clothes of infected and healthy students in the school to sanitize as much as they could. Jenkins reflects that "[n]aturally, I supposed the pay for the laundress position was paid to her. More than forty years later, when she visited me, she told me that she had received no remuneration whatever for her labor, nor was one word of thanks given her in the superintendent's annual report."[76] The small staff, Jenkins, the doctor and his wife, and the principal and his wife, quarantined and gender-segregated the children. Jenkins describes a scene when Diné and Hopi parents gathered at the school to ask who had brought the smallpox, citing how many people had died from it in the past. She writes: "In time past, thousands had died with smallpox—so many that the dead could not be buried and were thrown into a deep pit, the Indians told [the doctor]."[77]

After the smallpox epidemic spread, the school was shut down and eventually, Jenkins writes, "many of the children came down with pneumonia and grippe" and school operations ceased as the site became a hospital.[78] Jenkins writes that along with the school superintendent and the doctor, she "was nurse from seven in the morning until nine at night"[79] in addition to taking on nursing and seamstress tasks for sick staff.[80] Jenkins references how parents had demanded their children return home after sickness at other boarding schools and states that "[t]he parents, however, did not lose their heads and demand to carry their children home, as they had done at other schools."[81] The staff decided "that in the last extremity, a child should be removed from the building before death. But to give the child Christian burial a coffin would be needed."[82] The school went to the lengths of commissioning coffins from a local farmer. When the school ran out of medicine, they sent for one girl's parents to come get her so that she would not die at school. She left for her family and the reservation, and after treatment, she recovered. In one of the passages of the whole narrative most critical of the BIA, Jenkins explains how shortly after the epidemics "[a]n order had come out from Washington that the Department of the Interior had decided that all Indian hair was to be cut. No reason was given for this order."[83] Later they find out that this order was sent in error, after an agent was sent to cut the hair of Native people on a nearby reservation, including elders and war chiefs. Jenkins reflects that "the revocation of the order did not give back the hair to War Chief, nor did it modify the keen sense of injustice that it had caused. This was one more wrong the Government had inflicted upon them. We blamed the Department for this as we blamed it for our shortage of clothes, shoes, and other supplies."[84]

Jenkins and Brown's memoirs contain descriptions of a disorganized government program to apply universal mandates to early-twentieth-century federal boarding schools that had the effect of generating disabling conditions for both staff and incarcerated Native youth in the service of settler nationalism and colonization. Jenkins and Brown offer an on-the-ground recollection of the people they lived with and the administration they lived under with haphazard oversight from the federal government, even as they both subscribe, to varying degrees, to the mission of training Native youth and Native people to adopt white settler lifeways as the uncontested norm for a healthy quality of life. Their memoirs help readers understand the degree to which illness and disabling conditions at remote boarding schools generated a difficult quality of life for everyone who lived and labored within those spaces. Brown and Jenkins both explain the process of applying to work in the Indian Service in addition to analyzing gendered labor divisions as well as pay and labor inequity among staff, including structural failures of the BIA to provide staff training and resources. They describe the lives of the people most directly charged with the day-to-day mandate of assimilating Native youth and young families. Most significantly, Brown and Jenkins detail the myriad reasons these women sustained their lives through work in the Indian service in addition to critiquing the mission of assimilation and total rehabilitation that they were charged to dutifully carry out.

Notes

1. The word "Indian" in this sentence is used because it is part of a name for a federal office, the Indian Service. Throughout the chapter I only use the word "Indian" for clarification when it is part of a title of an office or division of what we now call the Bureau of Indian Affairs. In other places I use the words "Native" to refer to Native people within the United States, as this chapter focuses on boarding schools within the United States. Sometimes I also use the word "Indigenous" to gesture to other settler nations that also have histories of boarding schools, such as Canada.

2. Minnie Braithwaite Jenkins, *Girl from Williamsburg* (Richmond, VA: The Dietz Press, Incorporated, 1951), 248.

3. Mary Ellicott Arnold and Mabel Reed, *In the Land of the Grasshopper Song: Two Women in the Klamath River Indian Country in 1908–09* (Lincoln: University of Nebraska Press, 1957, reprinted 1980); Gertrude Golden, *Red Moon Called Me: Memoirs of a School-teacher in the Government Indian School* (San Antonio: The

Naylor Company, 1954); Flora J. Gregg Iliff, *People of the Blue Water: A Record of Life among the Walapai and Havasupai Indians* (New York: Harper and Bros., 1954; reprinted Tucson: University of Arizona Press, 1985). For more on the four other women who published firsthand accounts of their work in the Indian Service, see Patricia A. Carter, "'Completely Discouraged': Women Teachers' Resistance in the Bureau of Indian Affairs Schools, 1900–1910," *Frontiers: A Journal of Women Studies* 15.3 (1995): 53–86, and Jessica Wells Cantiello, "School Pictures: Photographs in the Memoirs of White Teachers of Native American Children," *a/b: Auto/Biography Studies* 29.1 (2014) Issue 1: Framing Lives, 79–106, accessed July 4, 2022, https://www.tandfonline.com/doi/full/10.1080/08989575.2014.921984.

4. With the exception of Patricia A. Carter, who argues for white women teachers' resistance in boarding schools and qualifies that interpretation with the biases of early-twentieth-century white women and the assimilation policies of the BIA. See Carter, "'Completely Discouraged.'"

5. For example, Brenda Child, *Boarding School Seasons: American Indian Families 1900–1940* (Lincoln: University of Nebraska Press, 1998); Margaret L. Archuleta, Brenda J. Child, and K. Tsianina Lomawaima, eds., *Away from Home: American Indian Boarding School Experiences 1879–2000* (Phoenix: The Heard Museum, 2000); K. Tsianina Lomawaima, *They Called It Prairie Light: The Story of Chilocco Indian School* (Lincoln: University of Nebraska Press, 1994).

6. For more on the legacies of boarding schools, see Archuleta, Child, and Lomawaima, eds., *Away from Home*, and Christine Diindiisi McCleave and the National Native American Boarding School Healing Coalition, "Indian Boarding Schools: The First Indian Child Welfare Policy in the U.S.," National Native American Boarding School Healing Coalition (blog). October 30, 2020.

7. https://boardingschoolhealing.org/.

8. Carter, "'Completely Discouraged,'" 58.

9. Jina B. Kim, "Toward a Crip-of-Color Critique: Thinking with Minich's 'Enabling Whom?,'" *Lateral: Journal of the Cultural Studies Association, Forum: Emergent Critical Analytics for Alternative Humanities* 6 (1) (2017), https://doi.org/10.25158/L6.1.14; Julie Avril Minich, "Enabling Whom? Critical Disability Studies Now," *Lateral: Journal of the Cultural Studies Association, Forum: Emergent Critical Analytics for Alternative Humanities* 5 (1) (2016), https://doi.org/10.25158/L5.1.9; Sami Schalk, "Critical Disability Studies as Methodology," *Lateral: Journal of the Cultural Studies Association, Forum: Emergent Critical Analytics for Alternative Humanities* 6 (1) (2017), https://doi.org/10.25158/L6.1.13. Schalk, Kim, and Minich provide approaches to critical disability methodologies that critique systems of oppression through race, ethnicity, and identity formation.

10. Disability studies scholars often use the term "to crip" as a way of arguing how the presence of disability or disabled knowledge disrupts conventional norms and ways of living. Applying a historical context, I draw on Alison Kafer, Robert McRuer, and Sami Schalk's work expanding what disability scholars refer to as "crip theory" to analyze boarding schools as sites of disablement and examples of how colonization generates mass disablement. See Alison Kafer, *Feminist, Queer, Crip* (Bloomington: Indiana University Press, 2013); Robert McRuer, *Crip Theory:*

Cultural Signs of Queerness and Disability (New York: New York University Press, 2006); Sami Schalk, *Bodyminds Reimagined: (Dis)ability, Race, and Gender in Black Women's Speculative Fiction* (Durham, NC: Duke University Press, 2018).

11. See Kafer, *Feminist, Queer, Crip*, McRuer, *Crip Theory*, and Schalk, *Bodyminds Reimagined* on expanding the understanding of crip theory.

12. Jess L. Cowing, "Occupied Land Is an Access Issue: Interventions in Feminist Disability Studies and Narratives of Indigenous Activism," *Journal of Feminist Scholarship* 17 (Fall): 9–25 (2020), 10.23860/jfs.2020.17.02, and Jessica Cowing, "Settler States of Ability: Assimilation, Incarceration, and Native Women's Crip Interventions," PhD diss., College of William & Mary, 2020.

13. Estelle Aubrey Brown, *Stubborn Fool: A Narrative* (Caldwell, ID: Caxton Printers, Ltd., 1952), 15.

14. Cathleen D. Cahill, *Federal Fathers and Mothers: A Social History of the United States Indian Service, 1869–1933* (Chapel Hill: University of North Carolina Press, 2011). For an "early example of a feminized federal agency," see page 263 and for "[i]n an insidious effort to disrupt the affective bonds between Native children and their parents," see page 54.

15. Carter writes that "[a]ll [white women who author the memoirs of Indian school service] stressed the importance of testing the limits of self-reliance." See Carter, "'Completely Discouraged,'" 68.

16. Brown, *Stubborn Fool: A Narrative*, 17.

17. Brown, *Stubborn Fool: A Narrative*, 18.

18. Jenkins, *Girl from Williamsburg*, 4. For more on Jenkins's activities at William & Mary (she was then named Minnie Braithwaite), see "Minnie Braithwaite Lecture," *Gender, Sexuality, and Women's Studies*, William & Mary, accessed June 2022, https://www.wm.edu/as/gsws/research/braithwaitelecture/index.php.

19. Brown, *Stubborn Fool: A Narrative*, 48.

20. An account of Stowe's visit is published in *The Christian Union.* See "The Indians at St. Augustine," in Richard Henry Pratt, *Battlefield and Classroom: Four Decades with the American Indian, 1867–1904* [1964], edited by Robert M. Utley, foreword by David Wallace Adams (Norman: University of Oklahoma Press, 2003), 154–66. Native men from Ft. Marion were moved to the Hampton Normal and Agricultural School, a historically Black college in Virginia, and it was the perceived "success" of the Indian Education Program at Hampton that justified the first federal off-reservation boarding school, the Carlisle Indian Industrial School in Pennsylvania.

21. Helen Hunt Jackson, *A Century of Dishonor: A Sketch of the United States Government's Dealings with Some of the Tribes* (New York: Harper and Bros., 1889), 468. https://www.nps.gov/articles/000/a-century-of-dishonor-by-helen-hunt-jackson.htm.

22. Josephine Richards, "The Training of the Indian Girl as the Uplifter of the Home," NEA (National Education Association) 1900, 701–4.

23. Brown and Jenkins both received pushback for their decisions to join the Indian Service because of the remote locations and perceived dangers involved. Jenkins writes that her mother goes so far as to attempt to block her application and that the local placement office offers her a remote position that it assumes she

won't take because "[a]ll appointments to it have been declined." Jenkins, *Girl from Williamsburg*, 4.

24. For examples, see the annual reports from the Commissioners of Indian Affairs from the years 1890–1924.

25. Brown, *Stubborn Fool: A Narrative*, 42.

26. Carter, "'Completely Discouraged,'" 80, note 1.

27. Jenkins, *Girl from Williamsburg*, 248.

28. Jenkins, *Girl from Williamsburg*, 214.

29. Jenkins, *Girl from Williamsburg*, 214.

30. Jenkins, *Girl from Williamsburg*, 218.

31. Jenkins, *Girl from Williamsburg*, 224.

32. Jenkins, *Girl from Williamsburg*, 225.

33. Jenkins, *Girl from Williamsburg*, 225.

34. Jenkins, *Girl from Williamsburg*, 225.

35. Jenkins, *Girl from Williamsburg*, 152.

36. Brown, *Stubborn Fool: A Narrative*, 33.

37. Brown, *Stubborn Fool: A Narrative*, 35.

38. Jenkins, *Girl from Williamsburg*, 152.

39. Brown, *Stubborn Fool: A Narrative*, 149.

40. Jenkins, *Girl from Williamsburg*, 152.

41. Jenkins, *Girl from Williamsburg*, 152.

42. Jenkins, *Girl from Williamsburg*, 153.

43. Brown, *Stubborn Fool: A Narrative*, 45.

44. Brown, *Stubborn Fool: A Narrative*, 45.

45. Brown, *Stubborn Fool: A Narrative*, 45.

46. Brown, *Stubborn Fool: A Narrative*, 45.

47. Brown, *Stubborn Fool: A Narrative*, 46.

48. Brown, *Stubborn Fool: A Narrative*, 45–46.

49. Brown, *Stubborn Fool: A Narrative*, 45.

50. Brown, *Stubborn Fool: A Narrative*, 46.

51. Brown, *Stubborn Fool: A Narrative*, 46.

52. Brown, *Stubborn Fool: A Narrative*, 46.

53. Brown, *Stubborn Fool: A Narrative*, 7.

54. Brown, *Stubborn Fool: A Narrative*, 7.

55. Brown, *Stubborn Fool: A Narrative*, 7.

56. Brown, *Stubborn Fool: A Narrative*, 7.

57. Brown, *Stubborn Fool: A Narrative*, 7.

58. Brown, *Stubborn Fool: A Narrative*, 7.

59. Brown, *Stubborn Fool: A Narrative*, 41.

60. Brown, *Stubborn Fool: A Narrative*, 41. Scrofula was a form of tuberculosis that circulated through federal boarding schools.

61. Brown, *Stubborn Fool: A Narrative*, 41.

62. Brown, *Stubborn Fool: A Narrative*, 41.

63. Jenkins, *Girl from Williamsburg*, 39.

64. Jenkins, *Girl from Williamsburg*, 33.

65. Jenkins, *Girl from Williamsburg*, 33.

66. Jenkins, *Girl from Williamsburg*, 33.
67. Jenkins, *Girl from Williamsburg*, 38, 56.
68. Jenkins, *Girl from Williamsburg*, 207.
69. Jenkins, *Girl from Williamsburg*, 38.
70. Jenkins, *Girl from Williamsburg*, 39.
71. Brown, *Stubborn Fool: A Narrative*, 48.
72. Brown, *Stubborn Fool: A Narrative*, 48.
73. Morgan's 1890 Annual Report of the Commissioner of Indian Affairs (ARCIA) included the first guide and curriculum for all boarding schools. Thomas Morgan, Commissioner of Indian Affairs, "Appendix. Rules for Indian Schools," in *Report of the Commissioner of Indian Affairs for the Year 1890*, Washington, DC: Government Printing Office, 1890, CXLVI-CLXXXLVI.
74. "Indian Education During Fiscal Year 1915," furnished by the Commissioner of Indian Affairs at the request of the Commissioner of Education, letter from E. B. Meritt, Assistant Commissioner of Indian Affairs to Hon. P. P. Claxton, Commissioner of Education, October 23, 1915, National Archives and Records Administration, Record Group 75, CCF, 1907–39, General Service, Box 1531, folder 115432–15, page 5.
75. Jenkins, *Girl from Williamsburg*, 199.
76. Jenkins, *Girl from Williamsburg*, 200.
77. Jenkins, *Girl from Williamsburg*, 201.
78. Jenkins, *Girl from Williamsburg*, 206.
79. Jenkins, *Girl from Williamsburg*, 210.
80. Jenkins, *Girl from Williamsburg*, 207.
81. Jenkins, *Girl from Williamsburg*, 211.
82. Jenkins, *Girl from Williamsburg*, 212.
83. Jenkins, *Girl from Williamsburg*, 214.
84. Jenkins, *Girl from Williamsburg*, 216.

PART IV

De-Centering

CHAPTER 13

Deafness and Silences in the Archives

OCTAVIAN E. ROBINSON, MEREDITH PERUZZI, JAMES MCCARTHY, WILLIAM T. ENNIS III, BRIAN H. GREENWALD, AND JOSEPH J. MURRAY

Introduction

Among the earliest historical records to mention deaf people come from no less than Aristotle and Plato, who noted that deaf people were "incapable of reason" and could not be taught. For much of recorded history, the historical remnants of deaf people have been the product of the hearing gaze, in the care of—and controlled by—hearing people. Much of what the historical record preserves about deaf people was produced and curated by hearing people. The exclusion of deaf people from the archive, both as subjects and as actors, reflects multiple realities about the value of deaf people in the larger societies in which they reside. The heterogeneity of deaf people and manifestations of deafness as a low-incidence disability complicates our understanding of what counts in writing from the deaf perspective. What is in the archive about deaf people, then, is primarily what hearing people have thought of deafness and their responses to deaf people's biosociality. Audism, ableism, and linguistic chauvinism intersect to exclude deaf people from the archive by rendering them objects of the hearing gaze. Because deaf people live within the same world as hearing people, the historical record is also shaped by the larger forces of whose stories matter for inclusion.

This chapter looks at the deaf experience of the archives. It begins with silences and absences of deaf people in the archive and moves on to a consideration of how deaf people and signed languages are excluded and included in the archive. Finally, it looks at a specific archival collection, the Gallaudet University Archives, as a case study in both how deaf-centered archives can be realized, but also how deaf centered archives replicate the power relations and silences found in archives more generally.

Silences and Absences

Michel-Rolph Trouillot, a Haitian American academic and anthropologist, framed the lack of stories about marginalized groups in mainstream historiography as a collection of "silences." In Trouillot's first silence, the significance of an event in the life of someone recording it determines whether that event is even worth writing down; even legendary diarists fail to note every event that happened to them. While English diarist Samuel Pepys wrote of a deaf person in 1666, many thousands more deaf people lived and died without their existence ever having been recorded by those who encountered them. And what of deaf writers themselves? Education for deaf children did not begin in earnest until formal deaf education methods were developed in Spain during the seventeenth century.[1] Without widespread education for deaf children, the literacy required to leave behind a written record was more likely to occur among the privileged classes who became deaf later in life, like Pierre Desloges, who wrote the first published defense of sign languages for deaf people in 1779.[2] Our lack of knowledge of deaf people from prior to this period stems not from their not remembering or wanting to record their lives, but often from the lack of ability to keep their own records. Instead, glimpses of deaf people's lives are recorded by hearing people, who in turn may judge an encounter with a deaf person as unworthy of note. And when written about, those records are filtered through the hearing gaze, which reflects contemporary attitudes about disability, deafness, language, and intellect.

The Archives Emerge/Deaf History and the Archive

The history of deaf people burst into public view with the 1984 work of hearing psychologist Harlan Lane and his book *When the Mind Hears: A History of the Deaf.* Professional historians and histories did not approach deaf narratives in a monograph format or center questions about deafness until John Van Cleve and Barry Crouch's germinal work, *A Place of Their Own: Creating the Deaf Community in America*, was published in 1989. After Van Cleve and Crouch—both hearing authors—for about two decades, deaf history led the field of disability history as a category of inquiry.[3] Prior to the publication of *A Place of Their Own*, deaf people themselves compiled histories and historical accounts of places, figures, and institutions dear to locally and nationally organized communities of deaf people. Some of those brief accounts are in newspapers produced by deaf people, transmitted through oral literature traditions, and published as reference books such as Jack Gannon's *Deaf Heritage.*[4] Hearing people adjacent to deaf people, such as children of deaf adults, signed language interpreters, and linguists also attempted to describe histories of deaf people.[5] Prior to the 1980s, few concerted efforts to catalog deaf history as a resource for future research existed. In the grander scope of history, deaf-run archives were and remain rare.

Our inspiration for this chapter derives from a desire to refocus how archives, both deaf and nondeaf, address deaf people in history, and by extension, focus on signed languages as the natural languages of deaf people. All of the authors of this chapter identify as Deaf; our work stems from our lived experiences as historians, archivists, researchers, and museum professionals. We have used, created, curated, exhibited, and archived; we work in the fields of deaf studies, history, linguistics, policy, library and archival science, and museum studies.

In our work, we often engage in the complex dual role of both the privileged and the subaltern. In deaf-focused archives, such as those at Gallaudet University and the Rochester Institute of Technology in the United States or Døvehistorisk Selskab and Doof Verleden Vlaanderen in Denmark and Flanders in Europe, we may find ourselves overwhelmed with resources. These collections, which we from here on call "deaf archives," have usually been established and maintained by deaf people, and they are supportive of the work of deaf researchers. In nondeaf archives, though, we struggle to find ourselves. Hearing archivists commonly overlook the lives and works of deaf people as a subject of collection. Archivists often misidentify or mislabel materials about deaf people and signed languages because they do not understand the cultural background or value of materials to tag them in ways that render deafness, signed languages, or deaf histories apparent to researchers. In archives, deaf people are either hypervisible or invisible.

Several elements inform our thinking about the archives. We examine not only what is present in archives, but what is absent; the influence of colonialism and the global North on archives and their silences; and the intersections of power and privilege as they apply to deaf people. As deaf communities frequently engage in transnational work, we include a perspective on the complicated intersection between hegemony and counterculture within deaf communities—both within and across constructed borders—and how power structures can be both reified and challenged through archival practice. Disability, as a category, shapes the archives physically, politically, linguistically, and curatorially. From a deaf perspective, this chapter illuminates internalized ableism and audism, as well as the audist and ableist power structures of archives. We examine what the *perseverance* of deaf history means for both deaf archives and nondeaf archives.

Audism in the Archives

Returning to the silences defined by Trouillot, it is the second silence that highlights a pressing problem for those looking to research deaf history: who determines the worthiness of a primary-source record for inclusion in an archive? Hearing people have typically been in charge of archival collections.

Reflective of social attitudes toward disabled populations, those collections likely omit, mislabel, disregard, or otherwise erase deafness from the archive. Only after long and tedious hours of combing through thousands of records can researchers locate deaf histories in nondeaf archives.

Even when deaf people are included, their presence may be primarily mediated through the medical gaze. The silences here are the silencing of a cultural and linguistic community. In the nineteenth and twentieth centuries, state-funded schools for the deaf (and later, other state agencies such as employment bureaus) marked deaf people as citizens worthy of investment and as potential contributors to the workforce and national projects. Many of those schools for deaf children would become the loci of the culturally deaf community, but to secure access to those schools, a deaf child must first have received a medical diagnosis. That official diagnosis, combined with the medical expertise of the child's educational team, including doctors, speech pathologists, and deaf education experts—who were sometimes treated as de facto medical authorities—means many records in those schools were mediated through the medical gaze. Doctors, audiologists, speech pathologists, and teachers used the language of diagnosis and rehabilitation to describe deaf pupils. The pipeline to deaf schools was heavily influenced by medical professionals. This is apparent in school records that describe deaf children in medical terms—not only in terms of deafness but in how deafness became adjacent to disabilities—particularly cognitive and linguistic disabilities. However, those schools, despite being grounded in efforts to "restore the deaf to society" and being heavily shaped by pathology, became centers of cultural flourishing and community formation. They especially served as spaces for counternarratives, resisting tropes of pity, tragedy, and burden to celebrate joy, resilience, and agency. This fostered a sense of pride and identity, along with group belonging. As deaf spaces, white deaf schools became a place where deaf people claimed their histories by preserving records and artifacts—segregated deaf schools were usually less tended by their teachers.[6] The hegemonic operation of deaf schools, though, means that the medical and the cultural are closely intertwined in school archival records.

Remaining school collections are the survivors of audist attitudes that devalue deaf materials. Former Gallaudet archivists recounted the heartbreak at the state of early-eighteenth- and nineteenth-century materials at the Institut National de Jeunes Sourds (INJS), the Paris institution for deaf children that is heralded as the wellspring of Western deaf education. Former Gallaudet University archivist Ulf Hedberg recounted a visit to a deaf school that had left two centuries of paper records in a damp hot space—likely including the writings of canonical figures in deaf history. In the 1980s, the Pennsylvania School for the Deaf dumped all its historical papers in the middle of the gymnasium. Gallaudet archivists rented a truck and drove to Philadelphia immediately to rescue the papers before they were thrown out as part of the school's retrofitting project.[7]

Deaf histories and archives carry on because of the commitment of individuals and community members to the perseverance of deaf materials—however haphazardly, however poorly resourced. The care of such archives is often contingent upon individuals and reliant on informal methods of preservation, which may not always reflect best practices. Over the last two centuries, deaf individuals from many schools and associations for the deaf squirreled away documents and artifacts in attics, closets, and basements. In many cases, these tangible cultural artifacts, despite the best intentions of those safeguarding them without formal training in best practices, are maintained haphazardly. For example, one of this chapter's coauthors recalls seeing books from the 1870s left on top of a radiator at a deaf school museum, damaging at least one rare edition. In another case, one elderly man rescued material from being tossed out and stored it in his guest room—without appropriate mechanisms such as humidity control, heating, air conditioning, and acid-free boxes. Old tin-canned flammable film from the mid-twentieth century has been left in parked cars in the hot southern sun for months at a time. In the experience of the authors, these episodes are common.

Outside of deaf schools, deaf organizations have often acted as community archives. These archives are inherently fragile and limited, with access to these materials reliant on personal networks. Many such collections have been kept in the personal homes of organizational officers, delivered to their successors with each subsequent election. The authors have encountered numerous stories of records lost when the hearing descendants of an officer or organization member threw away the records after their family member's demise, not recognizing the value in keeping such materials.

For example, the National Fraternal Society of the Deaf (NFSD) ceased operations in 2010. NFSD was an insurance organization established by deaf people in 1901, at a time of widespread discrimination by insurance companies against insuring deaf people. Over the years, the insurance function remained as the local chapters across the country evolved into important social and political arenas for local (predominantly white) deaf communities. Often chapter materials were passed on from organization officer to officer, with secretaries or presidents storing such materials in their homes. Unfortunately, NFSD's closure meant that while the national headquarters' archives were deposited at the Gallaudet University Archives, the status of materials from local chapters varied widely, precipitating the loss of a vast quantity of materials on local deaf communities in the United States. These exclusions are often unintentional and largely the result of unexamined complicity in the imposition of dominant, hegemonic narratives concerning the value of disabled ways of knowing and being.

Signing the Archive Public

Language is central to identity, to the formation of knowledges and experiences, to understanding our internal and external worlds. Before written sources were collected, the long tradition of deaf people preserving their own history took place in the form of sign language narratives, passed through the generations, that serve as testimony or record of deaf peoples' lives. We need to value and honor those efforts.

Signed languages and deaf ways of languaging, including protactile, are central to understanding deaf people's relationships to the world and their surrounding communities.[8] Technologies capable of capturing signed languages did not exist until the early twentieth century. Many signed languages did not develop written systems until the early twenty-first century; most still do not have one. Without direct capture of deaf people's experiences through their most natural languaging modality, any precinematic accounting of deaf people in the archive is inherently incomplete. With the advent of twentieth-century film technologies and twenty-first-century developments in making film technologies widely accessible to signing deaf people, the signed archives emerged. The ability to access deaf people's historical experiences through their natural language and oral traditions, which involve stories passed on over generations of deaf people, highlights both agency and vulnerability. These oral traditions can be conceived of as metaphorical "signed archives," a repository of histories and stories in signed languages that await discovery and cataloging by historians.

The signed archives is a matrix where signed stories, interviews, anecdotes, video-logs, and the like create a body of historical information about the lives of deaf people. Some are within organized collections, the Gallaudet University and the National Technical Institute for the Deaf (NTID) archives being two prominent examples, but most float around as home videos hidden away in private homes or in the infinity of cyberspace, uncatalogued. The ubiquitous influence of storytelling in deaf communities is often a crucial feature in the historical research of deaf lives and experiences. While these stories face the same issues as other oral cultures, particularly in the areas of phenomenology and power dynamics, they also serve as important signposts for deaf historians looking for information and themes of importance to deaf communities.[9] Signed archives serve as primary sources, as spoken oral histories do, or as supplements to historians working in combination with traditional archives and print records. One chapter coauthor, William T. Ennis III, found such oral histories to be essential in his research on eugenics in deaf communities. His research on the eugenic impact of deaf lives in the late nineteenth and early twentieth centuries was buttressed by anecdotal evidence that provided not only context but also inspiration: a conversation with his father led to a deep dive into traditional archives. The backstory of a simple anecdote in

Ennis's research presents an opportunity to further explore the concept of signed community archives.

Literary critic Mahmoud Abdelhamid M. A. Khalifa writes that the archives are one way of preserving identity.[10] One cannot preserve identity without also preserving an important vehicle for said identity: natural ways of languaging. For deaf people, this means the technology to capture signed languages, making such technologies broadly accessible and available, and the infrastructure to catalog and maintain such records. But, as Khalifa further asserts, the archives "enables the subaltern to speak by digging up and even making up archives. . . . [T]his quest reflects the trauma that motivates digging up the past as recovered memory and the desire to keep traces of the past as tokens of a marginalized identity seeking redress."[11]

Pathos, Culture, Biosociality, Complicated Models

Archives are political. Wendy Duff and Verne Harris's influential 2002 paper, "Stories and Names," reminds us that text and context are not readily separable; the context of a record is not bounded by static and unchanging well-defined boundaries.[12] Archivists' understandings of deafness as pathological or biosocial/cultural, of languages and modalities, of sensory orientations, all influence how records are created and intervened upon. In our visits to deaf and nondeaf archives, we interrogate, in the same vein, the norms of archival practice and our assumptions about archival interventions, including decisions about record creation and how records came to be in a particular repository. Those interrogations reveal quite a bit following T. R. Schellenberg's 1956 attempt to define an archive as that collection of an institution's records deemed worthy of inclusion in an archive—which then went on to say that the use of an archival record is always different from the reason for the record's creation. In other words, the user of an archival record matters very much in an archival context. For deaf historians and scholars, our usage of (and frustrations with) the archive informs how useful the deaf archive is to understanding histories of deafness, signed languages, and deaf people. If we take this as a starting point, then the next questions to ask are, what is the role of context in the life of a record and what is its true utility to the user? Dominique Daniel adds: If context matters, to what extent? Does the archival intervention constitute a context that itself needs to be documented in the life of a record? If a record's context is ever-evolving, how does that affect the underlying principles of provenance and original order in archiving?[13] These questions, as articulated by Duff and Harris and Daniel, challenge hegemonic narratives that are reinforced by the archetypal archivist as an "impartial craftsperson," a dispassionate observer of history that unerringly judges the (discrete and well-defined) traces left by human activities as worthy or unworthy of inclusion in the historical record.[14]

This so-called neutrality is the target of Howard Zinn's 1977 accusation of archives as complicit in upholding the narratives of the oppressor while claiming to do only what is objective, as well as of a turn toward informational justice, in which the claim to neutrality becomes less an overarching tenet governing the library and archival sciences than merely one value among many held by practitioners.[15] In turn, the new focus on narratives counter to histories kept by the dominant group provides the roots for a shift toward what Zinn himself referred to as "history from below," which challenges the archiving of the subject and replaces it with the agency of those being recorded to author their own narrative.[16]

That agency itself is often challenged by archival "silences," gaps in the historical record that often spring from two separate but related phenomena. As we have noted, a "silence" arises from the convenient elision of inconvenient narratives from the archival record.[17] But another "silence" derives from the deliberate use of silence by marginalized communities to repress painful memories.[18] Overcoming those gaps requires either additional work to demonstrate the value of multiple perspectives, if not simple divestment from traditional archiving in favor of community-based archive development, or the willingness to vulnerably share lived experiences that are painful to survive the first time, much less multiple times in the retelling.[19]

Participatory archiving, which arose in the 1990s as a response to traditional archiving's historically exclusionary practices, is most strongly characterized by radical hospitality to multiple perspectives and multiple ownerships, responding to and challenging the idea of a static, unchanging, and well-defined context for an archival record.[20] This is especially important in the context of the historical focus on the individual in archiving being used to dispossess Indigenous peoples, requiring the transformation of the archive into a space that is negotiated and agreed upon by different communities sharing stewardship of common resources.[21]

That radical hospitality becomes important in the recognition that the traditional representation of an archival record is incomplete and "biased because it represents a particular worldview and is constructed to meet specific purposes."[22] To meet those "specific purposes," information must necessarily be elided, and the record's disposition and provenance simplified. Traditional archiving's principle of *respect des fonds*, in which provenance and original order are venerated as a measure of a record's true historicity and evidentiary utility, seldom survives when faced with real-world activities that generate records that change over time and pass through multiple hands. This becomes doubly true when acknowledging that the kind of intellectual and authorial control requisite in traditional archives often ignores important questions of silences such as what voices are (not) being heard and what ways of knowing are (not) being privileged. This makes the deaf archive all the more important for deaf communities and historians. An archive centered in deaf ways of being and languaging orients us to important insights.

The Deaf Archives

What is a deaf archive? The deaf archives organize collections around the ways deaf people understood themselves to be, kin by a common touch of nature.[23] Deaf archives categorize deaf people beyond pathology, conceptualizing deaf peoples as cultural communities, sociolinguistic minorities, or social groups with shared sensory orientations and impairments. There are few centralized collections devoted to gesture, signing peoples, communities formed around signed languages and shared sensory orientations, and common political consciousnesses.

The deaf archive then becomes subject to the biases and lenses of deaf and hearing people who seek to research material gathered and stored in archives. Through the deaf archive, we preserve materials that celebrate a shared sensory orientation and experience centered on signed languages. Because some of us are members of the deaf community, we may be more familiar with cultural nuances, or quite simply, more familiar with tools on where to start looking. But not all deaf archives follow best practices in the field, due to ideological or systemic barriers that discourage promising deaf archivists from obtaining training. Adding to the complexity of archival access is the transmission of primary source material by cultural heritage bearers. Ninety-five percent of deaf people are "one generation thick,"[24] born to hearing parents and having hearing children unfamiliar with the tangible cultural value of deaf community records.

Despite material being lost every year, most centralized archives of deaf materials are housed in publicly funded institutions that serve deaf people. These include Gallaudet University, the Rochester Institute of Technology Archives (courtesy of its relationship with the National Technical Institute for the Deaf, or NTID), and California State University at Northridge (courtesy of its relationship with the National Center on Deafness, or NCOD). There are also collections housed in numerous residential schools for the deaf across the United States, and many deaf organizations have material that has been passed down through generations. Community organizations led by deaf people have also emerged in different countries around the world, seeking to preserve deaf histories. National Deaf History Societies have emerged in Great Britain, Denmark, Sweden, and Norway.

The archives at Gallaudet University stands as a giant among deaf collections. The Gallaudet University Archives is home to the world's largest collection of material, correspondence, photographs, and ephemera related to deaf people. Preserving deaf identity is part of the Gallaudet University Archives mission, which "is responsible for the institutional memory of the University and also strives to preserve the memory of the global Deaf Community."[25] There are few places with comparable collections.

The presence of such archives suggests that deaf people have achieved some sort of status. It may be that occupying a substantial space within an institution's library and archival storage space signals some degree of social value assigned to deaf people's histories. These archives live on in publicly funded spaces, although the quality of their management varies widely, and some might point to the existence of such archives as a symbol of belonging (or value). However, the mere existence of such archives is not a marker that deaf people have "arrived." Those archives are heavily dependent on individual efforts for perseverance; in all cases, we cannot neglect the role of deaf people within each institution, nurturing collections and advocating for space, funding, resources, and preservation. Deaf archivists and librarians like Joan Naturale at NTID/RIT and Tony Ivankovic at CSUN were critical in securing space and growing the deaf collections.

National organizations like the National Association of the Deaf, founded in September 1880, did not have physical office spaces; instead, the archives traveled with the volunteers who served as association officers, hidden away in private homes vulnerable to weather, time, and simple human carelessness. When interest in deaf histories emerged in the latter half of the twentieth century, those documents moved into school museums, libraries, and more organized archival collections. Some school museums are informal affairs, organized by school staff who double as deaf history enthusiasts; in these archives there are usually a few items of particular significance to the school's history and, by extension, deaf America. In others, professional archivists work alongside volunteers, as Gary Waite did at the American School for the Deaf. At the museum on campus, Thomas Hopkins Gallaudet's glasses are proudly on display. Reminiscent of religious relics, deaf archives treasure items having belonged to canonical figures in deaf history.

Although deaf people are a small minority within the larger world, and deaf archives represent pockets of resilience for deaf material culture and histories, those archives are not necessarily representative of bottom-up history. Those archives still maintain multiple silences. Even in deaf-led spaces, the status quo preserves. Deaf archives are reproductions and refractions of the societies in which they exist. Not only are the archives exclusive, they are also dependent on broader social values and understandings of deafness as something to be cherished and understood.

Deafness might be found in all sorts of archives but here we talk about deafness as a communal and cultural sensibility: thinking about deaf people as people who coalesced around particular sorts of schools, associations, institutions, and ways of languaging/being in the world. Deaf archives are often located in institutions where a significant number of deaf people are involved. Deaf archivists and museum curators painstakingly collect, preserve, organize, and display materials they believe are relevant to deaf histories. Those political, cultural, and social understandings of deafness shape our definition of "deaf archives." To be clear, while many of our archives contain documents that are mediated by the medical gaze, deaf archives are not medical in nature. The archives showcase our relationships, our socialities, our cosmopolitanism, our transnational relationships, our politics, and our various educational methods.

In general, the deaf archives grant less attention to the pathological condition, that of hearing loss. There are some artifacts or collections related to the notion of "cure"—recipes to cure deafness to collecting crude hearing aids. Jaipreet Virdi's work in some ways crips the archives, teasing out collections to find artifacts on hearing aids when these collections had not cataloged these items within their own medical collections.[26] Raising the consciousness of those archives to add deaf collections within their own collections shifts from the medical gaze to acknowledgment of the community's cultural capital and worth.

The Silences of Deaf Archives

Given deaf people's status in society, generally, one might view the establishment of such archives and their public funding as a space where one finds subaltern voices. While the temptation might be present to cast deaf archives as a neutral site of data collection, it is important to remember that these deaf archives are sites of status and incomplete data; they enact and effect their own silences. While intended to highlight deaf people as a cultural community, the reading of deafness as a *trait* and thus the determination of what is allowed admission and what is not is telling. This reminds us that data is not objective, and archives are not objective.

Who, then, is granted admission? Deaf archives have explicit biases—modality, linguistic, racial, gendered, classed, abled. Although there is a spectrum of linguistic modalities and identities for deaf people, the archive overwhelmingly favors the written modality, as there are no common written systems for signed languages. The written systems of the dominant language(s) used in various localities dominate even in deaf-led/held/managed archives. What does this mean for the voice of signing deaf people, who were "monolingual" or monomodal, but eloquent in their signed language? What did expectations and norms surrounding print literacies mean for deaf people and for how information/data filtered into the archives? What does it mean to not have signed languages captured in their original form, to be missing the knowledges inherent in signed languages before video technology? Until the ubiquity of video camera technology of the ascendant twenty-first century, signed records were largely the realm of those who could afford and manage such devices (excluding disabled or poor deaf people).

Archives overwhelmingly favor the written word and material remnants, but video technologies have changed rapidly and are now broadly available and accessible. However, with the greater availability of video technology, issues with digital media preservation and organization have arisen. One major issue is organizing and searching signed language–based medias; although schemas are under development, they have not been standardized. The bias in archival records toward print English means that the perspectives of print-literate deaf people dominate the archives, even deaf-centered ones. Signed languages are often mistakenly believed to be less complex and competent for communication as opposed to the spoken and written modalities of dominant languages such as English, or to be replications of these languages in a signed form.[27] Those language attitudes are refracted in archival practices, which privilege the print records of print-literate deaf people. Archival treatment of sign languages should recognize these languages as distinct from their surrounding spoken and writing languages, and deaf people, as all other multilinguals, have varying degrees of competence in the different languages they use. And the archives should aim to include even those deaf people who are not print-literate.

Like any social institution, deaf archives are refractions of the broader society in which those archives reside. Mirroring archival silences again, archives have not sought to collect and preserve materials of *all* deaf people. If the deaf persons were not in organizations or schools, their lives would be less likely to appear in the archive. And if those organizations or schools excluded Black deaf people, as many did, the archives would skew more toward the non-Black deaf experience.

Efforts to preserve deaf histories have led to contestations over ownership of deaf materials. Some community history enthusiasts have insisted on keeping the records of local deaf clubs and organizations, refusing to turn them over to state, local, or institutional archives. This reluctance to turn over materials is symptomatic of a larger academy-community divide where members of the deaf community do not have trust in professionally managed archives to provide equitable access to deaf historical materials or to care for deaf histories in the same way that deaf people might. Some institutional archives are working on participatory models to foster trust and relationships with local communities and to teach people how to preserve their own materials.

A Case Study of a Deaf Archive

The questions of silences perhaps become most apparent in the archive closest to deaf orientations to history, where the archives are housed in an institution that centers deaf people and are led by deaf archivists: the Gallaudet University Archives. While conventionally understood as a deaf archive, its commitment to the record and contexts of deaf lives is complicated by the cultural nature of its focus on deafness. Rather than simply the medical binary of deaf/hearing, the boundaries to be negotiated include identity, language, and modality preferences by deaf people who acquired deafness at different stages in their life; DeafBlind, DeafDisabled identities; temporal and contextual settings that shape people's view of deafness as a medical condition; additional intersectional identities related to race, ethnicity, sexuality, and gender; and so on. Consequently, the makeup of the collections begs the question of how archivists' commitment to recording those deaf lives should be judged.

This case study complicates the boundaries between traditional and participatory, and often finds itself negotiating the tensions between oral/literate, traditional/nontraditional, and hegemonic/countercultural, among other binaries. Established sometime around 1980, the Gallaudet University Archives were effectively spun off from the Gallaudet University Library to accommodate a growing volume of material that did not meet the traditional definition of circulating materials or ready-reference materials.

Today, the Gallaudet University Archives comprises some fifty thousand individual items occupying four miles of linear footage, in addition to another five thousand square feet of nontraditional materials. The materials include desks, printing presses, film projectors, several generations of telecommunication devices for the deaf (TDDs), and more. All told, the Archives occupies a volume estimated conservatively at approximately fifteen thousand cubic feet. Collection development in the Archives could be charitably described as "broad"; for at least two decades, anything related to the history of deaf communities and cultures was accepted. Some objects were added to the collection simply because they had once been owned by a deaf person or were created by someone rumored to have difficulty hearing.

The scale and variety of the Archives' holdings alone would recommend them for study, but the cultural contexts in which the Archives swim offer some even more interesting observations through the lenses of the binaries mentioned above.

Oral/literate: Though the Archives have nominally operated according to traditional principles, including *respect des fonds*, the archival intervention is often challenged by the lack of a written counterpart to American Sign Language (ASL); as such, film and video represent a large proportion of the Archives' holdings. Unfortunately, film degrades, and the Archives often must determine what should be preserved (via digitization) and what may risk decay or obsolescence.

Further, written English often does not fully capture the complexity of signed languages or the histories of the various deaf cultures and communities of North America and the world due to modality differences and the kinetic, spatial, and temporal dimensions of signed languages. Signed language is not universal. There are many local variations, regional and national signed languages. The sign languages used within a country may vary according to race, ethnicity, membership in Indigenous communities, national origin, and other factors. Linguists are still building corpuses of various signed languages. The temporal, spatial, visual, and tactile natures of signed languages cannot always be translated into two-dimensional form via writing systems. Most signed languages do not tend to be mutually intelligible with each other or with their spoken counterparts. This leads to questions about what is described fully, accurately, or usefully; it also lends itself to troubling questions about what is prioritized in the case of media on the verge of becoming irretrievably lost to decay.

Traditional/nontraditional: Although the Archives is ostensibly traditional, it is nontraditional in one significant aspect. While most university archives are largely university repositories, the Gallaudet Archives has extensive community-based collections. Since the Archives' primary focus is on documenting as extensively as possible the history of its parent institution, Gallaudet University, operational records of all kinds, from building blueprints to travel expense reports, are prioritized when allocating space and assigning staff time. Beyond that, the Archives has sought to position itself as the primary depository of any and all records associated with the development and growth of deaf cultures in the United States and around the world.

However, the vast majority of collection development and growth for the Gallaudet University Archives has come through soliciting and encouraging donations of records, memorabilia, ephemera, artwork, and other documents from Gallaudet alumni. These alumni are predominantly white; many are former faculty, staff, or administrators; and a not-insignificant number of donated records come from middle-class and wealthy alumni who also are associated with multigenerational deaf families. Consequently, the Archives reflects a particular kind of white, wealthy, well-educated deaf history displaying a continuity strongly tied to the presence of a small number of family names. Although its approach to collection development has not been traditional, the result very much is. Here, we recall Michel-Rolph Trouillot's and Arita Balaram's reminders that archival silences come about from exclusions.

Hegemonic/countercultural: The Gallaudet University Archives occupies a length along this axis, characterized by a series of points interspersed between the extremities. First, it documents an alternative "hidden" history that counters the dominant narrative. For example, although many hearing people may agree that deafness is primarily a physiological matter, the proprietors of the Archives—and indeed most individuals affiliated with the Archives' parent institution—assert that taking this view of deafness reduces deaf culture and history to a nonfunctional organ.

Further, though a hearing individual may come to agree that the state of being deaf is not the same thing as "hearing loss," they still may be surprised to note that, in fact, the Archives does not accept *any* material related to deafness as a physiological phenomenon other than in a peripheral way. The notion of there being a "deaf culture" is made further countercultural simply because of its basis in separate languages that formed spontaneously among deaf people. The dominant narrative, in this case, was first adopted at the Second International Congress on the Education of the Deaf, hosted in 1880 in Milan, Italy, which specifically sought to suppress—often violently—the emergence and use of signed languages among deaf pupils in favor of spoken language.[28]

In reaction to this tendency to suppress sign languages, individuals like George Veditz began documenting the sign language used by deaf Americans in the early twentieth century. Since his time, the study of what is today known as American Sign Language (ASL) and the more than two hundred other signed languages around the world has grown considerably; there are grammars and formal linguistics of ASL, and many a doctoral thesis has been written on the topic. However, in recent years, some critics claim Gallaudet researchers, advocates, and sign-language activists have hegemonized ASL into a prescriptive form approved by white, well-educated elites associated with the university.

Additionally, even transnational communication among deaf people—particularly International Sign (IS)—is often perceived as dominated by ASL users, or signers from the global North. Though IS is a pidgin that relies heavily on iconicity, much of its lexicon was originally borrowed from Western signed languages, particularly those in the French family, including ASL. Over time, IS has become closer to a true international pidgin, allowing users to rely on signs from their native languages to communicate, but the perception remains.[29]

It should here be made explicit that the common thread found through examining the Gallaudet University Archives on the axes described by the three binaries listed above is, quite simply, exclusion. Each discussion of the three binaries includes arguments both for and against the Archives' placement on one end or another of each axis. This suggests that further discussion is needed on a fourth binary.

Neutrality/bias: Early Gallaudet archivists would probably claim that the Archives' collection-development policy is "neutral" in that it doesn't discriminate; all materials related to deaf culture and history are welcome. This is probably the closest the Archives comes to truly traditional conceptions of neutrality in which value judgments are not applied to a record's worthiness for inclusion in the historical record.

In practice, however, the policy is anything but neutral. Because of systemic racism, institutional misogyny, and deeply rooted homo- and transphobia, the only individuals who are comfortable entrusting the accretion of their lives to the Archives have tended to be white, cisgender men—as have the proprietors of the Archives themselves. Further, they tend to be ASL users and are usually affiliated with the institution as staff, faculty, former members of the board of trustees, or alumni. As such, the archival silences in the Gallaudet University Archives are overwhelming.

To give examples, there are virtually no records related to deaf people from Latin America, deaf Canadians in the collection vastly outnumber deaf Mexicans, and the Chicano/a/x experience filtered through a deaf lens is nonexistent, as far as the Archives is concerned. Representation improves somewhat when examining the Black deaf experience; part of that is probably related to the 1952 lawsuit brought by Louise B. Miller against Gallaudet University for using an ostensibly "neutral" policy as cover for refusing to educate Black deaf children from the District of Columbia in the on-campus primary school.[30]

Taken as a whole, the portions of the collection originating from outside the United States have tended to either be fragmentary or sourced from a *respect des fonds* perspective, collecting records from entities enabling international cooperation between deaf communities, such as records from the World Federation of the Deaf, Deaf History International, the International Committee of Sports for the Deaf, the International Congress on Education of the Deaf, and others. These records are often donated by former organization members who see the Archives as the safest possible site for these records, regardless of other local alternatives. This relocation of international records to the United States shows the unique position of the Gallaudet University Archives in a world with few other options for professionally maintained deaf archives accessible to deaf researchers. This represents yet another lens through which to view the tensions between the traditional/nontraditional binary experienced by the Gallaudet University Archives.

The remainder of international representation in the Archives is largely either fragmented and the result of individual donations, or consists of complete runs of publications by groups, associations, or schools of the deaf located in other countries. The fragmentary nature of the Archives' international collections outside such materials speaks to the continuing problem of adopting a "neutral" position. Rather than seeking out materials valuable to deaf cultures and histories other than those in the United States, the additional barriers of geographic distance and shipping costs have a further adverse impact on representation in the Archives, silencing cultures other than those originating in English-speaking North America.

The experience of DeafBlind individuals is another example of an archival silence. DeafBlind individuals have long been recognized as an integral part of the community—at least where access is easily provided—but not addressed as a coherent group with shared needs and the power to have those needs addressed. Because of this, for example, a recent researcher—himself a DeafBlind man—had to hire an assistant, incurring additional expense, to manually comb through thousands of pages of school newsletters to find and identify DeafBlind individuals of significance in the history of American deaf education. This was because the Gallaudet University Archives did not find them to be equally as worthy of note as, say, deaf artists, deaf Lutherans, or deaf basketball players from a specific class at a particular school for the deaf.

The Archives' unique focus and approach notwithstanding, it continues to be vulnerable to the same biases, oppressive silences, and otherization as any other repository. Duff and Harris argue that although radical hospitality to multiple viewpoints and authority is necessary for archives to fulfill their responsibilities to the historical records, boundaries drawn around the work are necessary for it to be meaningful. Those boundaries mean that "others" must be created and, in their argument, catered to.

So, who does the Gallaudet University Archives serve? It documents Gallaudet history, deaf histories, and deaf cultures. Does that suggest that it does so to serve a purpose that does not align with those activities? Who, then, are its users intended to be? On occasion, determining users requires specifying who the record creators and keepers are and proceeding by elimination. For participatory archives, this has been approached in the past by using linear models that begin with the creator of a record and end with people who are completely disengaged from participation in the process of record keeping. In Gregory Rolan's discussion, those models—"ladders" with specific archiving roles and levels of engagement forming each rung—take note of the bottom-up nature of participatory-archiving initiatives, reflecting the work by citizens to seize control of their narratives from authorities.[31] This kind of model often falls prey to radicalism, which often takes the form of an argument that because only two or three "rungs" of the ladder—often those who have the time, funding, or educational background to be actively engaged in the archival intervention in a significant way—actually matter to the initiative because of their active participation, the existence of the remaining rungs amounts to a kind of tokenism. This argument essentially states that if a marginalized individual is unable to participate equally in an archival initiative due to barriers presented by race, class, or ability—among others—the only value they can offer, from the perspective of those who *are* actively engaged, is as an identity to appropriate.[32]

Instead, various continuum models have been proposed to address the multiple axes of activity and engagement often found in those initiatives.[33] This is especially important in the context of community-based archival interventions, which often focus first on providing safe spaces for community record-keeping activities—enacting a boundary in so doing—then on drawing specific boundaries between certain activities within that space, such as those that should be undertaken by trained archivists (who may or may not be members of the community represented) versus those that can be undertaken by any participant. In a continuum model, the primary determinant of the level and nature of someone's engagement with an archival record is the individual's distance from the act of the record's creation. This becomes fairly broad—past a certain point in the archival intervention, the "user" becomes virtually anyone and, because of their interaction with the record, becomes complicit in the record's evolution.[34]

This perspective on the never-ending, ever-created nature of all archival records becomes important to the Gallaudet University Archives because it, perhaps uniquely, plays an outsize role in shaping, and being shaped by, deaf cultures and histories of all stripes. It is often consulted in matters as wide-ranging as the outcome of a sporting competition or the profession of someone's great-great-grandfather. By the same token, its past failures in reaching out to underrepresented communities represent a danger to those communities; no archive exists for the Latin deaf experience. The lives of deaf undocumented migrants vanish under the ever-growing load of sashes, pins, graduation photos, and theses on the handshape for the number eight.

The new director of the Archives, hired in 2021, has developed a plan in which the Archives becomes responsible not only as a depository but as an active participant in the preservation of deaf histories and cultures beyond its threshold. Staffers will be sent into local communities to train groups in topics related to digital preservation of their family photos, arrangement and description of the financial records of their local deaf club, or the collection of oral histories. In this way, the Archives hopes to cultivate a sense of shared responsibility among the various deaf cultures of the world to preserve their histories in ways that make sense to them.

This responsibility also extends to making the archives, and by extension, deaf people's histories, visible to larger society.[35] The Archives, independently and alongside the university's National Deaf Life Museum, has embarked on several digital and physical exhibitions with the aim of translating the deaf experience to nondeaf people. This work also includes consultation with journalists on aspects of deaf culture that have become part of larger society, such as the football huddle,[36] or providing materials for the History Through Deaf Eyes Exhibition at the Smithsonian Institution.[37] Currently the Archives is placing archival materials in thematic digital collections outside of Gallaudet, in disability history and other areas. The story of deaf people is not a story separate from but interwoven with other histories. For example, Hume LePrince Battiste was a Black deaf man who passed as Indigenous in order to enroll as a Gallaudet student during the Jim Crow era. His story of race and passing is echoed across the United States, but we are able to tell his story today because the small nature of Gallaudet—and of deaf archives—means that he was better recorded than many in similar positions elsewhere. It is especially unique that he chose to pass as Indigenous in contrast with Samuel Codes Watson, a Black student who passed as white in 1850s Michigan. Watson flew under the radar, but Battiste could not; Watson attended a large institution, and Battiste did not.[38] Their stories are nonetheless parallel, and the unique nature of Battiste's position in the small deaf community means that his story can more clearly evoke the experiences of hearing Black Americans who passed, but whose stories were lost to archival silences.

Deaf archives keep materials that other archives might interpret as insignificant, for example, printouts of TTY phone conversations and handwritten pocket notes, a typical deaf languaging practice where deaf people communicate with others by writing on scraps of paper. Olof Hanson's exchange of notes with suspected deaf peddlers and hearing fakirs at the police station, which asked a series of questions like "do you know Mr. . . . ," "which school did you go to? The one at Berkeley?," or "do you lipread?" gives us insight into how deaf people communicated with hearing people, the value of print literacy in being an active participant in local politics, the friction involved in passing as disabled-nondisabled, the fraught relationship deaf people had with claiming an able-bodied identity while protecting their status as disabled citizens, and the intimacy of deaf networks across the United States where Hanson could use personal knowledge of social relationships to determine if a peddler was friend or foe to deaf people. Those conversations are often on scraps of paper that other archives likely would see as insignificant, hastily scribbled on torn small pieces of paper in pencil asking seemingly quotidian questions. Another example might be Gallaudet's "Archiving Alumni" project, which records oral histories from Gallaudet alumni celebrating their fiftieth anniversary reunion. Some stories are told from our perspective that seem interesting and engaging, but which are covered in newspapers with considerably less impact. Those narratives tell us about homes for the aged deaf, dedicated cemeteries, and of course schools and clubs that illustrate the different nodes of the deaf cultural community network in the United States. What this spotlights is that there are many parallel histories occurring through, under, between, and beside what we typically think of as "American" history—not just of the deaf community, but of other marginalized communities as well. The development of a shared responsibility becomes especially important when considering the precariousness of much of the material infrastructure of deaf lives. Since the advent of the ADA, many schools for deaf people—once the nucleus of deaf life and the wellspring of deaf culture in the United States—have either been shut down or scaled back significantly in the face of decreased funding and increased numbers of students taking advantage of ADA-mandated accommodations in their local public schools. This loss has in turn created generations of young deaf individuals disconnected from the social organizations—deaf clubs, fraternal groups, and sports leagues—that represented other centers of twentieth-century American deaf life. In the absence of these institutions, another way to maintain the material records of deaf communities needs to be found.

At the same time, the Archives' current collection is being evaluated for its true value to future users and digitized to enable access to stories that may have been hidden in yearbooks, obscured by boxes, or stored in corners. Gallaudet University's history as a white-dominated institution contains many unfortunate incidents, traditions, and practices; once revealed, these revelations may create wounds seen as difficult to heal. The Archives' role in maintaining the secrecy of these past transgressions—and in exacerbating the pain felt by younger generations and excluded communities when those transgressions are discovered—has long been considered a matter of maintaining a sort of neutrality, an "agenda-free" approach to documenting history. It has become increasingly clear that this was never the case.

Participatory archiving, as a praxis for addressing many of the risks inherent in maintaining a bias cloaked in a narrowly defined kind of "objectivity," holds a great deal of promise for the Gallaudet University Archives, deaf communities, and marginalized communities generally. Though technical questions remain—particularly around accessibility for all members of the community and for outsiders—the move toward inclusion of multiple perspectives and multiple kinds of history can leave room for the processing of trauma while enabling a new kind of growth.

In spite of the limitations of the deaf archive and the need to embrace accountability for inclusion and access, deaf people claim the deaf archives as special places of joy, belonging, and resistance. People, places, events, and objects important to our cohesive identity as a community bound by a shared sensory orientation and approach to languaging are memorialized, celebrated, and preserved. Deaf archives are stalwart nodes of a sociocultural network that is otherwise slowly dissipating due to eugenicist policies and technological innovation. There, we find evidence of ways of languaging unique to deaf people, networks shaped by shared sensory orientations, and kinship. We also find evidence of how deaf people and communities are reflections, refractions, and reproductions of their sociocultural political environments. Deaf archives are complex and multilayered in their service to deaf communities, but are nonetheless often a source of pride.

Notes

The order of authorship belies the actual labor processes involved in collaborative knowledge production.

1. Susan Plann, *A Silent Minority: Deaf Education in Spain, 1550–1835* (Berkeley: University of California Press, 1997).

2. Renate Fischer, "The Study of Natural Sign Language in Eighteenth-Century France," *Sign Language Studies* 4 (2002): 391–406.

3. Catherine J. Kudlick, "Disability History: Why We Need Another 'Other,'" *American Historical Review* 108, no. 3 (2003): 763–93.

4. Jack Gannon, *Deaf Heritage: A Narrative History of Deaf America* (Washington DC: Gallaudet University Press, 2012).

5. Harry Best, *The Deaf: Their Position in Society and the Provision for Their Education in the United States* (New York: Thomas Crowell Publishing, 1945); Anthony Aramburo, "Sociolinguistic Aspects of the Black Deaf Community," in *The*

Sociolinguistics of the Deaf Community, edited by Ceil Lucas (New York: Academic Press, 1989), 103–22.

6. Susan Burch and Hannah Joyner, *Unspeakable: The Story of Junius Wilson* (Chapel Hill, NC: University of North Carolina Press, 2007).

7. Michael Olson and Ulf Hedberg, Gallaudet University archivists, personal communications.

8. Annelies Kusters et al., "Beyond Languages, Beyond Modalities: Transforming the Study of Semiotic Repertoires," *International Journal of Multilingualism* 14, no. 3 (2017): 219–32, https://doi.org/10.1080/14790718.2017.1321651/; Terra Edwards, "Rechanneling Language: The Mutual Restructuring of Language and Infrastructure Among DeafBlind People at Gallaudet University," *Journal of Linguistic Anthropology* 28, no. 3 (2018): 273–92, https://doi.org/10.1111/jola.12199/.

9. Michael Chapman, "The Problem of Identity: South Africa, Storytelling, and Literary History," *New Literary History* 29, no. 1 (1998): 85–99, http://www.jstor.org/stable/20057469; R. Kenneth Kirby, "Phenomenology and the Problems of Oral History," *Oral History Review* 35, no. 1 (2008): 22–38.

10. Mahmoud Abdelhamid M. A. Khalifa, "Feverish Souls: Archives, Identity, and Trauma in Fihris and Ḥiṣn Al-Turāb," *Arab Studies Quarterly* 42, no. 4 (2020): 287–307, https://doi.org/10.13169/arabstudquar.42.4.0287/.

11. Khalifa, "Feverish Souls," 306.

12. Wendy Duff and Verne Harris, "Stories and Names: Archival Description as Narrating Records and Constructing Meanings," *Archival Science* 2, no. 3 (2002): 263–85, https://doi.org/10.1007/BF02435625/.

13. Dominique Daniel, "Archival Representations of Immigration and Ethnicity in North American History: From the Ethnicization of Archives to the Archivization of Ethnicity," *Archival Science* 14, no. 2 (2014): 169–203, https://doi.org/10.1007/s10502-013-9209-6/.

14. Duff and Harris, "Stories and Names," 264.

15. Alexandrina Buchanan and Michelle Bastian, "Activating the Archive: Rethinking the Role of Traditional Archives for Local Activist Projects," *Archival Science* 15, no. 4 (2015): 429–51, https://doi.org/10.1007/s10502-015-9247-3/; Kay Mathiesen, "Informational Justice: A Conceptual Framework for Social Justice in Library and Information Services," *Library Trends* 64, no. 2 (2015): 198–225, https://doi.org/10.1353/lib.2015.0044/.

16. Arita Balaram, "Crafting New Narratives of Diasporic Resistance with Indo-Caribbean Women and Gender-Expansive People across Generations," *Societies* 11, no. 1 (2021): 2, https://doi.org/10.3390/soc11010002/.

17. Michel-Rolph Trouillot, *Silencing the Past: Power and the Production of History* (Boston: Beacon Press, 1995).

18. Balaram, "Crafting New Narratives of Diasporic Resistance," 2.

19. Balaram, "Crafting New Narratives of Diasporic Resistance," 2.

20. Duff and Harris, "Stories and Names," 268.

21. Sue McKemmish, Tom Chandler, and Shannon Faulkhead, "Imagine: A Living Archive of People and Place 'Somewhere Beyond Custody,'" *Archival Science* 19 no. 3 (2019): 281–301, https://doi.org/10.1007/s10502-019-09320-0/.

22. Duff and Harris, "Stories and Names," 275.

23. Joseph J. Murray, "One Touch of Nature Makes the Whole World Kin: The Transnational Lives of Deaf Americans," (unpublished doctoral dissertation, University of Iowa, 2007).

24. Robert Hoffmeister, "One Generation Thick: What Is Our Heritage and How Will We Pass It On?" Paper presented at the first Building Bridges Conference, Gallaudet University, May 2, 1997.

25. "Archives Goals," Gallaudet University Archives, Gallaudet University, November 2022, accessed June 10, 2024, https://gallaudet.edu/archives/archives-goals/.

26. Jaipreet Virdi, *Hearing Happiness: Deafness Cures Through History* (Chicago: University of Chicago Press, 2020).

27. Jon Henner and Octavian Robinson, "Unsettling Languages, Unruly Bodyminds: Imaging a Crip Linguistics," Preprint, 2021, https://psyarxiv.com/7bzaw/.

28. John Vickery Van Cleve and Barry Crouch, *A Place of Their Own: Creating a Deaf Community in America* (Washington, DC: Gallaudet University Press, 1989); R.A.R. Edwards, *Words Made Flesh: Nineteenth Century Deaf Education and the Growth of Deaf Culture* (New York: New York University Press, 2012).

29. Annelies Kusters, "The Tipping Point: On the Use of Signs from American Sign Language in International Sign," *Language & Communication* 75 (November 2020): 51–68.

30. Sandra Jowers-Barber, "The Struggle to Educate Black Deaf Schoolchildren in Washington, DC," in *A Fair Chance in the Race of Life: The Role of Gallaudet University in Deaf History*, edited by Brian Greenwald and John Van Cleve (Washington, DC: Gallaudet University Press, 2008), 113–31.

31. Gregory Rolan, "Agency in the Archive: A Model for Participatory Recordkeeping," *Archival Science* 17, no. 3 (2017): 195–225, https://doi.org/10.1007/s10502-016-9267-7/.

32. Rolan, "Agency in the Archive," 203.

33. Rolan, "Agency in the Archive," 205.

34. Danielle Allard and Shawna Ferris, "Antiviolence and Marginalized Communities: Knowledge Creation, Community Mobilization, and Social Justice through a Participatory Archiving Approach," *Library Trends* 64, no. 2 (2015): 360–83, https://doi.org/10.1353/lib.2015.0043/.

35. Brian H. Greenwald and Joseph J. Murray, eds., *In Our Own Hands: Essays in Deaf History, 1780–1970* (Washington, DC: Gallaudet University Press, 2016).

36. Stephen Whyno, "From Inventing the Huddle to Trying a New Helmet, Gallaudet Is Home to a Proud Football Tradition," *Associated Press*, October 31, 2023.

37. Douglas C. Baynton, Jack R. Gannon, and Jean Lindquist Bergey, *Through Deaf Eyes: A Photographic History of an American Community* (Washington, DC: Gallaudet University Press, 2007).

38. Meredith Peruzzi, "Reframing Hume LePrince Battiste's Impact," *Gallaudet Today*, 2020; Micah Walker, "He Passed as a White Student at UM—but Was Actually College's First Black Enrollee," *Detroit Free Press*, October 19, 2019, https://www.freep.com/story/entertainment/2019/10/19/samuel-codes-watson-unviersity-michigan-tylonn-j-sawyer/3992118002/.

CHAPTER 14

The Spoken Word Is Not Neutral

Oral History, Disability, and Nonverbal Communication

OSNAT KATZ AND SAMUEL GOLDSTONE-BRADY

Introduction

Oral history has proven to be a potent methodology for research by, with, and about marginalized people, as well as those silenced by the documentary record and textocentrism. For disabled people in particular, oral history has been used as a method of curating previously hidden histories and has also been identified as a potent source of advocacy for disabled activists.[1] More importantly, oral testimony captures the reality of disabled, neurodivergent, and D/deaf people's lives—their barriers, joys, and pain. These records reinforce the diversity of human experiences captured in historical research.

Yet access to and representation within oral history methodology and oral history collections is not equal across different groups of disabled and neurodivergent people. A narrow focus on orality, "neurotypical communication," and methodological goals all combine to make oral history practice exclusionary for those who do not communicate verbally. In turn, this exclusionary practice leaves such groups of disabled people out of oral history collections and renders their experiences unrecorded. Further, this creates concern for disabled and neurodivergent researchers, who may find oral history methodology difficult or inaccessible in other ways.

This chapter highlights how oral history methodology can be exclusionary, and ways in which oral history methodology may be modified to include a wider range of disabled people. It begins with the authors' own perspectives relating to the experiences of carrying out oral history projects and defines some of the concepts in question. Then, a literature review outlines the history of this methodology, alongside the focus on orality and narrative, which champions neurotypical communication. The next sections outline accommodations that can be made for disabled participants and researchers engaging with oral history research. Existing accessibility modifications used by researchers are explored, such as sign language oral history interviews and close questioning in certain circumstances. The chapter then suggests further possible alterations stemming from the authors' experiences of oral history data collection, with a focus on written interviews and remote interviewing.

Lastly, new considerations within oral history methodology may challenge the construction of oral history collections. Traditionally, oral history collections consist of recordings of the oral history interviews accompanied by written transcripts. A changed methodology, one that is more inclusive of disabled people, might also include video footage and transcripts that recorded nonverbal vocalizations, such as squeaking and groaning. By facilitating a more inclusive oral history archive, archivists, researchers, and interviewees can include a wider variety of perspectives and lived experiences of disabilities. We invite readers to consider how such changes to oral history methodology challenge the archiving and use of sources, and who is not included within current methodologies. We should stress here that this chapter is not meant to be an exhaustive guide to cocreating inclusive oral histories; it is borne out of our own interests and experiences. We aim for this chapter to be a starting point for further reflection and innovation rather than the last word in inclusionary oral history practice.

Authors' Perspectives and Concepts

Interest in this topic arose due to the authors' personal use of and interest in oral history as a methodology, alongside their own identities and experiences.

Osnat Katz used remote oral history methodology for her research into the social and cultural history of space science in the United Kingdom. She began conducting remote interviews in March 2020 and concluded interviewing in 2023. Katz is a disabled and neurodivergent researcher with a formal diagnosis of autism. Her neurological differences affect her pervasively; she finds skills prioritized in oral history methodology, such as active listening or building rapport, to be difficult, nonintuitive, and tiring, as they require a great deal of mental focus. Further, her autism also causes auditory processing difficulties. While training as an oral historian, she felt isolated by training set up for neurotypical people in the way it assumed the effortlessness of building rapport. Further, Katz is involved in running an online peer support group for autistic people. This aids her in making more explicit the ways in which autistic people use and play with language. The members of the peer support group make use of spoken English in voice chats, but also communicate via text, GIFs, and emotes. Members of the group are also encouraged to "stim"—to use syllables and language in ways that relax them or express energy, such as repeating a syllable over and over again. These different forms of communication and use of language are thus used by Katz and her peer group as both methods of interaction and relaxation, highlighting uses of language by certain groups of disabled people in ways oral history does not capture.

Samuel Goldstone-Brady used oral history methodology for his research into the social, political, and technological history of sporting wheelchairs. This data was gathered between October 2020 and March 2021, conducted remotely due to the COVID-19 pandemic. His experiences interviewing wheelchair users with a range of impairments and experiences facilitated reflection on the ability of oral history methodology to include different groups of disabled people. Brady's interviewing included instances of flexibility with oral history methodology, which is explored later in the chapter. Goldstone-Brady identifies as a neurodivergent researcher, with a formal diagnosis of dyslexia. During his experiences conducting verbal interviews, Goldstone-Brady found certain aspects of the process impacted by his dyslexia, such as rapid question formulation and notetaking.

Reflexivity is paramount in any research, especially research concerning marginalized groups. Disabled and neurodivergent people are underrepresented in the mainstream academic community, and research focusing on these groups often originates from the perspectives of abled or neurotypical researchers. In their study of the independence of individuals with intellectual disabilities, Judy Verseghy, Lynda Atack, and Janet Maher noted the need for reflexivity when conducting interviews with disabled participants, partially due to their own outlook as nondisabled people.[2] Their research required unexpected flexibility in their interviewing methodology, alongside further reflection on their assumptions and biases when conducting research with disabled participants. This process of reflexivity has direct practical benefits, as improved research design for disabled participants allows researchers to gather more and higher-quality records, alongside improving the participatory experience for those involved. Participatory research with autistic adults, for instance, has generated a wealth of practical benefits, including research that is more valuable and meaningful to certain groups of autistic people.[3] Accommodations made for disabled participants are also important for researcher accessibility to oral history methodology, and this chapter is also cognizant of the needs of disabled and neurodivergent people as researchers.

In this chapter, the authors refer to the idea of "neurotypical communication." As a broad definition, this refers to verbal communication and the interpretation of nonverbal cues deemed "normal" by Western mainstream social standards in a variety of locations and situations. This neurotypical communication consists of clear, moderately paced speech adhering to standard grammar, with eye contact and culturally appropriate use of body language. This style of communication is often able-bodied and neurotypical, as any deviation from these norms is perceived as "strange" or "wrong" to Western, abled social standards. Deviation from such neurotypical communication has facilitated the othering of disabled or neurodivergent people. As we explore later in the chapter, orality and intelligence possess a cultural link. This link furthers stigmas surrounding the intellectual or communication capabilities of certain disabled people. Such groups have thus been excluded from this form of history-making.

In both a literal and epistemological sense, nonverbal disabled people are thus silenced by oral history methodology. Silencing, according to Michel-Rolph Trouillot, appears at four points in the historical record: in silencing of sources, in silencing within the archives, in silencing within narratives, and silencing in what Trouillot describes as the making of history itself—the way in which narratives are interwoven to create a picture of overarching historical significance.[4] From this perspective, nonverbal disabled people are silenced in the act of making history, as the act of creating oral history records has distinct limits. This in turn creates silences in oral history collections, creating inequalities in the application and representative power of oral history for a range of disabled people.

The authors therefore conceive oral history archives or collections as collecting a particular type of oral history record. In the authors' experiences, oral history collections usually store text-based transcripts, derived from a researcher or heritage worker's transcription of the audio interview.[5] Collections often also contain the audio record of the interview. Older oral history collections are often physical, stored on audio media formats such as cassettes, CDs, or DVDs. Recent oral histories will likely have been recorded as audio files, copies of which are accessible for public or researcher use. In many cases, oral histories are available online in some fashion, and older formats may also be digitized to ensure preservation, often making oral history records accessible. Nevertheless, many of these records are created using methodologies that may not take different forms of communication, or barriers to neurotypical communication, into account. While oral history collections may include other groups of disabled people, the use of oral methodology cannot include those who are nonverbal, creating a difference in power and representation for these disabled and neurodivergent people.

Literature Review

Oral history, as it is practiced by Western academics today, derives from multiple roots. In nineteenth-century America, anthropologists worked with Indigenous people to record their stories onto phonograph cylinders.[6] In the late 1930s, the Federal Writers' Project gave work to unemployed writers through sending them out to collect the life stories of Americans across the country, while after 1948 Allan Nevins made use of tape recorders to record the voices and memories of "notable" people.[7] Conversely, the roots of oral history in the United Kingdom differ, deriving more from studies of folklore and a desire to capture the voices of marginalized people. As such, these roots combine many contradictory perspectives on who may record and who may be recorded. For example, while Francis la Flesche was the first Native American anthropologist, he also brought singers of sacred songs from Oklahoma to Washington, DC to avoid neighbors objecting to his recording of ceremonial songs. Meanwhile, Polish American anthropologist Paul Radin approached Native American converts for his song recordings because he knew that traditional adherents would not record for him.[8] Issues of power, authority, and permission are thus deeply rooted within oral history.

Another issue that must be grappled with is the origins of modern oral history practice within Western colonialist perceptions of orality. These perspectives have delegitimized and continue to delegitimize the histories and traditions of Indigenous groups, who have often been silenced in the Western historic canon. Drawing from the perspective of the Ngati Porou, an Indigenous community in Aotearoa (New Zealand), Nēpia Mahuika outlines how Indigenous oral histories were delegitimized by settlers, as the label of "tradition" rendered them unreliable.[9] Moreover, Indigenous oral histories traditionally went beyond strict orality, as they intertwined with everyday life.[10] The colonial focus on strict orality results in the invalidation of other ways of communicating significance, such as paying attention to the geography of a place, and it delegitimizes the experience of people who do not speak in a normative or neurotypical way.[11]

The ethical implications of oral history practice have been explored in scholarship, particularly the complexities surrounding power and authority. Ultimately, it is the interviewer who seeks out the interviewees, records them, interprets the transcript, and publishes the interview.[12] Academic oral historians seek out interviewees to "consume" their experiences and "regurgitate" their interpretations as published work—interpretations that may differ significantly from how interviewees understand their narration of their experiences. Hence, there is an inherent power imbalance in interviewing. In the alternative, oral historians speak of a turn toward empowerment, often by centering a call for advocacy as part of the research.[13] This makes oral history scholarship particularly powerful for research concerning disabled people, who have often been rendered invisible in traditional sources and archives. Jan Walmsley's scholarship in particular has been vital in establishing methodological alterations for participants with learning disabilities and using oral history as a method of empowerment and advocacy.[14] Similarly, Karen Hirsch highlighted the potency of oral history for disabled people's activism, as this methodology could be used to "give the disability community its history."[15]

Modern academic oral history methodology has been employed for research conducted with or by many different groups of disabled people. For example, researchers have worked with amputees and those with spinal cord injuries, the D/deaf and hard of hearing community, intellectually disabled people, and developmentally disabled people.[16] Yet, this methodology is potentially inaccessible for people with other experiences of disability and impairment, whether as interviewee or interviewer. It excludes people who are nonspeaking, have speech-related impairments, or who use nonnormative forms of speech. This exclusionary paradigm limits the use of oral history as a tool of advocacy or knowledge production for such groups of disabled people. As oral history methodology values the spoken word above all else, disabled people who are nonspeaking or who use nonnormative forms of speech are excluded from this form of historical research.

The origins of oral history, and its use in activism, have led to oral history centering the spoken word and the meanings conveyed in neurotypical communication. Alessandro Portelli argued that the supposed shortcomings of oral history were its methodological strengths in his 1979 article, "What Makes Oral History Different."[17] Portelli emphasized the importance of orality for oral sources, as it allowed narrators to infuse their spoken narratives with emotion. This is because, unlike written sources, oral accounts allow the quirks of verbal communication—tone of voice, pace of speech, pauses and volume—to create greater context and meaning for the words spoken.[18] If interviewees hesitate between responses or during speech, for example, the researcher may interpret certain emotional responses to particular topics or moments in time. This is the key advantage of oral history over other types of testimony, as researchers can gain extra depth of meaning from their participants' responses in ways not possible from traditional records such as written documents. This also applies to elements of communication not recorded by the audio record, such as body movement, eye contact, and hand articulation.[19] These practices in oral history can be used to generate rich data. However, they presume neurotypicality and ablebodiedness in both interviewer and interviewee.

As Portelli points out, oral history sources are narrative sources, particularly as they are descended from the oral folk tradition, where a community's stories may be passed down by speech.[20] Accordingly, the narrative focus in interviewing practice has been concerned with participants being "able to tell a good story"—this concept manifests as the participant "taking control of the interview and [talking] freely," and being "articulate" and "able to verbalize."[21] This also preserves facets of local dialect and pronunciation, which add extra information and nuance to testimonies.[22]

Unsurprisingly, focus on the spoken word presents the largest barrier for the inclusion of some groups of disabled people within oral history methodology, as the different ways in which disabled people speak may not be recognized by or intelligible to the abled majority. The centering of the spoken word inherently accentuates a preference for, or exclusive acceptance of, neurotypical communication. Oral history methodologies thus encourage interviewees to engage in active listening or undertake multiple sessions with the participant to build rapport and to eliminate comprehension difficulties. Yet, there is an assumption this all takes place within the parameters of what is considered normal spoken conversation. For some autistic people, for instance, communicating within these parameters can be difficult, tiring, or even distressing, due to the degree of extra effort needed to engage in this type of communication. Adjustments therefore make oral history methodology more accessible and create a more suitable research environment for certain disabled researchers.

Some autistic people are partially or completely nonspeaking, using text, emotes, GIFs, or augmentative and alternative forms of communication.[23] Those who do speak may speak more slowly, more quickly, or with fewer vocal inflections; these mark the speaker as having atypical speech. In certain settings, this communication preference may be mocked and is often underrepresented in formal academic research or heritage collections.

As an autistic oral history interviewer, Katz has direct experience with the privileging of the spoken word and how this impacts her practice. She speaks differently from neurotypical people; in particular, she speaks more slowly, repeats phrases, and often makes unconscious vocal stims. She cannot speak at all when fatigued. Being conscious of the need to build rapport with her neurotypical interviewees, she "masks" as neurotypical by consciously changing her speech patterns and preparing her questions so that she does not find herself in a nonspeaking state during an interview. Her unmasked autistic communication goes unrepresented in the oral history archive because her unmasked communication will not build rapport. Indeed, masked communication that neurodivergent interviewers must engage in is not noted by oral history guidance, rendering such experiences invisible. Moreover, autistic masking has negative consequences including exhaustion, which Katz experienced during her data collection period, and burnout.[24] It should be noted that neurotypical interviewers also face physical, psychological, and emotional stresses, although these are often based on the content or context of the interview as opposed to the act of interviewing itself.[25]

A neurotypical interviewer who is unprepared for differences in communication between autistic people and neurotypical people may interpret autistic people as being more combative or unwilling to engage with the interviewer. In some circumstances, this may be interpreted as the interviewee being inarticulate, and therefore silent. Oral historians may not necessarily jump to this conclusion instantaneously, as silence is also a valuable source of data.[26] Moreover, some neurotypical people can associate what they consider to be inarticulateness with a lack of comprehension or intelligence.[27] Researchers need the ability to read different types of silences accurately. It should be noted that these concerns are not limited to neurodivergent or disabled researcher participants—neurotypical people may also be difficult to read—but the social perceptions of neurodivergence may complicate how silences are interpreted.

Neuronormative oral history privileges neurotypical communication. For certain disabled interviewers and participants, this creates additional barriers to doing oral history, ultimately limiting which groups of disabled people are included in oral history archives. This may limit how representative oral history collections of disabled people's testimonies can be: the only disabled people who are recorded are those who can articulate their thoughts and experiences in ways that mesh with existing approaches to oral history methodology. To be more direct and critical: most oral history only includes disabled people when their impairments do not impact their ability to speak. Despite the oral nature of oral history, it is vital to recognize the limits of this form of research and inquiry for certain groups, and to work toward adjustments that can better serve a broader range of ability groups.

Existing Adjustments

Adjustments to oral history methodology and practice are not a new concept. These adjustments challenge the definition of the oral history archive by introducing alternative formats and approaches to interviewing; they also challenge who is included within such archives. The adjustments listed in this section provide examples of how researchers may make interview formats accessible. Project leaders should aim to make reasonable adjustments where possible. Appropriate adjustments will depend on the individual needs of both the interviewer and the interviewee, alongside the circumstances of the interview itself.

D/deaf histories have been created using oral history interviews with D/deaf participants, despite what Donna F. Ryan identifies as a lack of contact between professional oral historians and D/deaf community oral historians by the late 1990s.[28] Research published by Gallaudet University uses oral history to preserve and share a range of D/deaf histories, including the experiences of D/deaf Hungarian Jews during the Second World War.[29] An example of this practice in the wider heritage sector would be "History of Place," a United Kingdom–based heritage project that ran between 2016 and 2019, researching "800 years of deaf and disability history relating to 8 buildings."[30] One aspect of this project included the recording of seven oral history interviews with people who were previously members of the St Savior's Deaf Church in Acton, London. These interviews were conducted in British Sign Language (BSL) by both the interviewees and interviewers, with verbal audio translations voiced by interpreters simultaneously. Aside from the use of BSL, the interviews are otherwise typical to mainstream oral history methodology. However, the interviews were recorded as videos of both the interviewee and interviewers and are now hosted on the History of Place website. The video recording ensures that the sign language of the interviewee and interviewer is preserved for those who communicate using BSL. This approach further challenges what an oral history collection may be, presenting interviews solely as a series of videos. Similar use of video recording was used for Ryan and John S. Schuchman's research into the experiences of D/deaf Jewish Hungarian survivors of the Holocaust, which also allowed for the interviews to be translated into American Sign Language from Hungarian Sign Language.[31] Unfortunately, the lack of subtitles and possible difficulties in understanding audio in the History of Place videos hamper the experience for those who do not understand BSL or rely solely on audio information. This, however, does indicate that those producing and disseminating interviews should remain cognizant of different access needs throughout the interview and archiving process.

Brad Rakerd suggests several recommendations to the interview process that result in a more accessible end record.[32] Many of these recommendations are also beneficial in the initial interviewing process. His suggestions include improving the audio quality of recordings to ensure clarity, ensuring that speakers' lips are visible to aid in comprehending language, and providing semantic context in the formation of questions to assist with the understanding of speech. These proposals allow those with hearing loss—as well as those with informational processing impairments—to access the oral accounts. Rakerd also suggests providing interviewees with more time to process their thoughts, which benefits interviewee, interviewer, and audience alike. He also writes that when asked to "speak clearly," interviewees would often adopt a moderate rate of speech and tone of voice, which improves audio comprehension and improved communication during the interview process. Rakerd's work benefits nondisabled people, showing that accommodations made for marginalized communities can make oral histories more inclusive of and more significant for all.

The literature of other fields, such as medical or sociological research, suggests similar practices when interviewing participants with learning disabilities or other forms of neurodivergence.[33] Tim Booth and Wendy Booth, for example, recounted their experiences of interviewing "Danny Avebury," an interview participant with a learning disability who was described by the researchers as "inarticulate."[34] Danny was reportedly not forthcoming with responses in ways interviewers trained to communicate with neurotypical participants might expect. Booth and Booth state, for example, that "[d]uring three interviews running to almost two-and-a-half hours of recorded conversation he uttered only 10 complete sentences, including four 'don't knows' and a 'can't remember.'"[35]

Accordingly, the researchers reassessed their approach based on how the participant engaged with the interviewer, paying closer attention to the form and content of their questions. For Booth and Booth, this resulted in relying on closed questioning, instead of open-ended questioning as favored by most oral interviewing styles, primarily delivered in a yes/no format.[36] This encouraged the participant to respond to the researcher's questions in a way that suited his capabilities and created a usable record. Nevertheless, there are disadvantages to this specific form of interviewing. First, the approach necessitates the researcher barraging the participant with questions, so that the participant can lead the interviewer to the "right" questions.[37] Second, this could allow for the researcher's perspective to overshadow the perspective of the participants in the record—which may be of particular concern if non-disabled and neurotypical people are the only parties facilitating the interview and looking over the testimony.[38] Booth and Booth note that these concerns can be addressed by attentive and patient interviewers who are familiar with their participants.[39] Similarly, Paul Cambridge and Rachel Forrester-Jones describe the importance of rapport-building, careful location selection, and multiple sessions in order to build familiarity for interviewees with learning impairments.[40] Nevertheless, adapting oral history methodologies is feasible, particularly when other parties such as relatives, friends, or caregivers can support the interviewee if needed. This flexibility can be applied broadly to oral history methodology, allowing oral historians to include participants of differing communication abilities.

Methodological flexibility demonstrated by adaptations made for D/deaf people and those with learning impairments demonstrate the adjustments that can be made to better include disabled and neurodivergent interviewers and interviewees. These adjustments could benefit those who are partially or completely nonspeaking, such as some autistic people. At the same time, there are specific experiences of autism and other impairments that should be considered. The next section considers these by drawing on the author's experiences of interviewing. However, it should be noted that these suggestions may also be of benefit to other disabled or neurodivergent people.

Further Adjustments—Written Interviews

A possible adjustment is using a written interview format, formulated like a traditional oral history interview. For Samuel Goldstone-Brady, his PhD research featured oral history as the primary method of data collection. Some of the participants involved in the research were unable to take part in video-based oral interviews, due to personal preference and/or their oral communication abilities. In early 2021, multiple possible participants suggested a written interview format. The first instance of written interviews in his data collection was with athlete and sports chair designer Ed McGuire. McGuire was approached because of his work collaborating on the StrikeForce, an electric wheelchair specifically made for powerchair football. Like athletes who created chairs for manual wheelchair sports, McGuire's insight and experiences as an athlete and designer of electric wheelchair sport made him an ideal research participant. However, McGuire declined to participate in an oral-based interview, as his cerebral palsy impacts his verbal speech. Over email prior to the written interview, he wrote:

> Absolutely, I would love to help! . . . my speech is hard to understand. Yet, I know people who can understand/interpret my speech just fine. If we did zoom, well, that would be kind of pointless because you would do all the talking and I would just nod my head.[41]

McGuire later said this is particularly so in the case of speaking with strangers. Honoring McGuire's request, the two agreed on a written interview format. Additionally, Brady's research supervisors recognized the inaccessibility of existing methodologies and agreed to a flexible interview format.

In this scenario, Goldstone-Brady drew up a list of questions for McGuire. To elicit the feeling of a normative spoken interview, he wrote these questions in a conversational style. They were formatted in the exact same way as the verbal oral histories Goldstone-Brady conducted. The file was sent to McGuire, who would then answer these questions in his own time, which was necessary given the time difference between McGuire in the United States and Goldstone-Brady in the United Kingdom. Once all questions were answered, the file was then sent back to Goldstone-Brady. At this point, Goldstone-Brady reviewed McGuire's responses and wrote further questions to follow up on anything arising from the initial wave of answers. This was an attempt to replicate the process of in-the-moment follow-up questions occurring as part of spoken communication. The file was then returned to McGuire, who provided answers for the new questions. After this, Goldstone-Brady made edits to ensure the written interview matched the style of the other participants' interviews. However, the content was not altered, in order to preserve McGuire's testimonial voice. The resultant file was then returned to McGuire one final time. Once the finalized interview was agreed upon by McGuire, a completed interview had been generated.

Initially, this seems like a practical approach to address the needs of participants concerned about being understood clearly. However, it may be a methodologically unsound suggestion for the purpose of replacing an oral interview. A written interview limits the spontaneity of instantaneous communication. Follow-up questions to McGuire's statements were asked hours or days after the initial prompt, and answered further on. This limited the extent to which any answer was reactive, as might be expected by standard oral history interviews. Delay between responses may affect how participants make connections between memories and thoughts. In McGuire's case, the interview was spread out over the course of four days, meaning the interview had not faded to obscurity in the minds of interviewer or interviewee. However, other participants or researchers may find that their interviews take more time. The use of instant communication messaging (e.g., social media platforms) may address this issue, as this spontaneity can help replicate the pattern of neurotypical spoken conversation. On the other hand, providing interviewees with extra time to formulate responses may benefit people with learning or processing disabilities, limited energy, fatigue, or poor health.

The main advantage of the written interview format lies in the accessibility it provides for those who choose to communicate nonverbally. In this circumstance, a written interview provided comfortable and easy access for both the interviewee and interviewer, and made the oral history process more accessible for McGuire. Oral historians need to take care to not cause undue distress, harm, or inconvenience to their participants, and offering alternative formats can make a huge difference to the comfort of some interviewees. Further, this process allowed Brady's research to include a wider range of participants, as previously his research had focused primarily on those with spinal cord injuries or mobility impairments. By taking a new approach, it was possible to preserve McGuire's voice, perspectives, and experiences in a way that is still accessible for other researchers.

McGuire's interview will be archived alongside the other oral history interviews conducted for the research by the National Paralympic Heritage Trust, allowing his story to be placed among others in the history of sporting wheelchair technology. Without accessibility arrangements in place, McGuire would have been unable to agree to an interview, leaving his perspective and work out of the wider data collection. This may suggest that disability-inclusive approaches to oral history archives may simply be hybrid collections. Such collections could feature a range of interview format types, including typical oral history interviews and those that were recorded as entirely written or video interviews.

It is also worth considering other ways in which this approach impacted the process of conducting oral histories. The written interview was less time intensive for the interviewer as other aspects of the process, such as audio or video editing, or transcription, were negated. This may be an appealing approach for disabled or neurodivergent researchers who may have limited energy. However, another drawback noted by Goldstone-Brady was that the written interview resulted in a shorter overall transcript as compared to the verbal oral histories. This is likely due to the difference in written and spoken language, as the written word allows for ideas and narratives to be communicated much more efficiently and without noncommunicative utterances (for example, umm, ahh, err, etc.), while also requiring more work from the interviewee if long responses are requested. Alternatively, this may occur because the written interview does not necessarily fall into the confines of a time limit. Oral interviews were often structured in one- or two-hour blocks, to fit with participants' schedules. A written interview, however, does not conform to the same time constraints—in theory, an interviewee could type their responses over the course of an entire day or over the course of five minutes. Without the social cues established by back-and-forth verbal communication, or the establishment of time commitment, the written format may easily result in shorter interviews. This may present a challenge to the written format due to a perceived diminishing of content, which is a valid concern for data gathered for research.

Further Adjustments—Remote Interviewing

Researchers should also consider remote interviews for possible advantages for autistic interviewees and interviewers. Remote interviewing became common practice during the COVID-19 pandemic, when national lockdowns forced people to turn to video calling platforms like Zoom or Microsoft Teams for communication and research. These platforms present some built-in accessibility features, such as automatically generated live captioning and the ability to input live (human-written) captions. Moreover, the widespread use of video calling platforms allow immunocompromised and other disabled people to protect themselves from COVID-19.

Oral historians were quick to develop guidance for researchers forced to alter their interviewing methodologies to the digital sphere, although they did acknowledge that this was a temporary solution that was not ideal for what is considered proper oral history research.[42] Issues with remote interviewing have been noted in prior years. Both Paul Hanna and Aaron Payne reflected on remote interviewing methodology, as telephone or Skype interviews were perceived to be less effective. This was due to technical difficulties, and a lack of communicative subtleties that accompany face-to-face communication.[43] While remote interviewing may not be a perfect replacement for in-person interviewing, the approach does offer distinct advantages for disabled and neurodivergent interviewers and interviewees. Remote interviewing allows interviewers and interviewees to meet without the challenges of travel while also facilitating an easier way to record interviews.

However, associated costs and logistics may limit the recording of interviews. Needing to record both interviewer and interviewing signing, for example, was a problem reported by Payne, with the researchers ultimately deciding to only focus the camera on the interviewee.[44] However, because of the nature of the equipment setup and screen capturing, video calling platforms allow for interviews to be recorded with less effort than conventional recording.

Another potential feature of benefit for autistic people may be chat and text functions, which provide more communication options. Written communication, text language, and emotes can all be used on the chat functions of platforms like Zoom. Utilizing these tools allows for remote interviews to address a range of communication preferences. Other aspects of remote interviewing may also have appeal for disabled people in doing oral history. Some autistic people and people with ADHD are easily overstimulated in crowded spaces. Remote interviewing allows both interviewees and interviewers to participate in a setting that is comfortable to them. However, remote interviewing introduces additional complications. Interviewers and interviewees require access to equipment, such as computers, cameras, and microphones, as well as access to recording software. While interviewers and interviewees may already own such equipment, especially as it became a necessity during the pandemic, it is an important barrier to inclusion. Disabled and neurodivergent people are disproportionately impacted economically and may have limited access to or familiarity with WiFi, computers, and recording equipment.

Indeed, it is possible that the perceived limitations of remote interviewing may benefit some disabled interviewees and interviewers. For instance, one noted disadvantage to remote interviewing is the reduced or lack of ability to perceive body language or make eye contact. This is often seen as a critical part of the interview process, allowing researchers to draw further detail from participants' responses, and assisting interviewees in connecting with researchers. These concerns also exist with other alternative approaches to interviewing, such as phone interviews or written interviews. However, for some neurodivergent people, these markers of neurotypical communication may be a barrier to participation. Some autistic people, for instance, find making and maintaining eye contact difficult, if not stressful. Aside from causing discomfort for either party in the interview, differences in eye contact may be misinterpreted by interviewers or interviewees. For instance, if an interviewee is not making eye contact with the interviewer, an interviewer may interpret this lack of eye contact to indicate apprehension or negative emotions linked to the conversation. Conversely, an interviewee might have difficulty approximating eye contact because of webcam positioning. Remote interviewing does not allow for eye contact naturally, and it may be preferable to some participants or researchers for those reasons. As a caveat, both neurotypical and neurodivergent people can experience "Zoom fatigue"—fatigue from video conferencing caused by close-up eye gaze, cognitive load, and regulating one's body movements and facial expressions on camera.[45] While remote interviewing may be more accessible, it may also induce fatigue more quickly than in-person or phone interviews, especially if it is mandated that cameras be kept on.

Conclusion

Although written interviews do not replace spoken oral history, the authors feel that commitment to including disabled voices and experiences is more important than strict adherence to form. The approaches outlined by the authors, combined with existing adjustments described by other researchers, highlight the ways in which oral history methodology can be altered to better accommodate different groups of disabled and neurodivergent people. There is no universal methodology that works for all interviewees and interviewers, and this goes beyond contextual, logistical, or temporal considerations. The practical act of interviewing and being interviewed is a different experience depending on the impairment of the individual, and research methodology should be flexible enough to be adjusted accordingly. For those who cannot communicate verbally, extra considerations can be made, allowing historians and other researchers to include nonverbal communication in their records.

Changes in oral history methodology alter what an oral history archive may look like. In the use of signed communication or remote interviews, an oral history may be visual, consisting of videos with captions and visual descriptions. Alternatively, oral history collections may be hybrid, consisting of a collection of traditional (audio and transcript), written (instant messages, emails, or written documents), and visual (images and videos) interview media. Such variety not only creates diverse and engaging collections but ensures accessibility and representation. Format-diverse collections acknowledge and demonstrate a consideration of access needs based on different types of impairment and providing a range of material types. Therefore, oral history collections can be made more inclusive and representative using different or new methodological approaches.

Yet, oral historians must also consider who else may be included in disabled people's oral history archives. Do these collections just pertain to disabled people or others involved in their daily interactions, such as family members, friends, social workers, medical professionals, and equipment providers? Would including such perspectives impinge on the activist role of collections, diminishing the extent to which collections are emphasizing disabled people's own experiences? Answers to these questions may change with the focus, purpose, and scope of individual projects, teams of researchers, and participant availability.

Beyond making the act of recording the interview accessible, issues of power, authority, ownership, and interpretation will still impact these interviews as much as a neurotypical spoken interview. The act of translating nonverbal communication, for instance, may be a point of contention between interviewer and interviewee, specifically in cases where visual imagery such as GIFs or emotes are used in place of text. These factors are complicated by the positionality of disabled and neurodivergent people in research and wider society. Ultimately, these issues demonstrate the political and epistemological importance of having disabled and neurodivergent people involved at multiple stages of the process of doing oral history.

Notes

1. Karen Hirsch, "Culture and Disability: The Role of Oral History," *Oral History Review* 22, no. 1 (1995): 1–27.

2. Judy Verseghy, Lynda Atack, and Janet Maher, "Key Considerations When Interviewing Individuals with Expressive Language Difficulties," *Qualitative Research* 20, no. 6 (December 1, 2020): 960–70.

3. Sue Fletcher-Watson et al., "Making the Future Together: Shaping Autism Research through Meaningful Participation," *Autism* 23, no. 4 (2019): 943–53.

4. Michel-Rolph Trouillot, *Silencing the Past: Power and the Production of History* (Boston: Beacon Press, 2015), 20–27.

5. While it is a selective bibliography, Gloria Rhodes noted a similar concept of what an oral history collection "is." Gloria L. Rhodes, "Oral History Centres and Collections: A Selective Bibliography," *Reference Reviews* 27, no. 8 (January 1, 2013): 4–8.

6. Martin Clayton, "Ethnographic Wax Cylinders at the British Library National Sound Archive: A Brief History and Description of the Collection," *British Journal of Ethnomusicology* 5 (1996), 68.

7. Lynn Abrams, *Oral History Theory*, second edition (Abingdon: Routledge, 2016), 4.

8. Judith Grey, "Returning Music to the Makers: The Library of Congress, American Indians, and the Federal Cylinder Project," *Cultural Survival Quarterly Magazine*, December 1996.

9. Nēpia Mahuika, *Rethinking Oral History and Tradition: An Indigenous Perspective* (Oxford: Oxford University Press, 2019), 169.

10. Mahuika, *Rethinking Oral History and Tradition*, 170. The intersectional restriction to oral history for disabled Indigenous people may also be considered. Medical discrimination, for instance, left many Aboriginal Australians in New South Wales with a hearing impairment. This not only suggests intersectional struggles disabled Indigenous populations face, but also a lack of access to their own histories if only recorded orally. Karen Flick and Heather Goodall, "Angledool Stories: Aboriginal History in Hypermedia," in *The Oral History Reader*, eds. Robert Perks and Alistair Thomson, first edition (New York: Routledge, 1997), 424.

11. Mahuika, *Rethinking Oral History and Tradition*, 17.

12. Abrams, *Oral History Theory*, 163; Kathryn Haynes, "Other Lives in Accounting: Critical Reflections on Oral History Methodology in Action," *Critical Perspectives on Accounting, The Contours of Critical Accounting*, 21, no. 3 (March 1, 2010): 226–27.

13. Abrams, *Oral History Theory*, 81–83, 168–78; Adeline R. Rafael, "Advocacy Oral History: A Research Methodology for Social Activism in Nursing," *Advances in Nursing Science* 20, no. 2 (December 1997): 32–44.

14. Sheena Rolph and Jan Walmsley, "Oral History and New Orthodoxies: Narrative Accounts in the History of Learning Disability," *Oral History* 34, no. 1 (2006): 81–91; Jan Walmsley and The Central England People First History Project Team, "Telling the History of Self-Advocacy: A Challenge for Inclusive Research," *Journal of Applied Research in Intellectual Disabilities* 27, no. 1 (2014): 34–43.

15. Hirsch, "Culture and Disability," 27.

16. Rolph and Walmsley, "Oral History and New Orthodoxies," 81–91; Kristin Snoddon, *Telling Deaf Lives: Agents of Change* (Washington, DC: Gallaudet University Press, 2014). There are many examples of oral history interviews with amputees or spinally injured people. In the study of disability sport, for instance, author Sam Brady's research took place primarily with wheelchair users with spinal cord injuries, or amputees. Additionally, other interviews conducted by the National Paralympic Heritage Trust also contained many wheelchair and prosthetic users, alongside those who are visually impaired.

17. Alessandro Portelli, "What Makes Oral History Different," in *The Oral History Reader*, eds. Perks and Thomson.

18. Portelli, "What Makes Oral History Different," in *The Oral History Reader*, eds. Perks and Thomson, 70–72; Andrea Hajek, *Oral History Methodology* (London: Sage Publications, Ltd. 2021). https://doi.org/10.4135/9781446273050135504183.

19. Nien Yuan Cheng, "'Flesh and Blood Archives': Embodying the Oral History Transcript," *Oral History Review* 45, no. 1 (April 1, 2018): 127–42.

20. Portelli, "What Makes Oral History Different," in *The Oral History Reader*, eds. Perks and Thomson, 72–73; Abrams, *Oral History Theory*, 4–5; Abrams, *Oral History Theory*, 3.

21. Tim Booth and Wendy Booth, "Sounds of Silence: Narrative Research with Inarticulate Subjects," *Disability & Society* 11, no. 1 (March 1, 1996): 57.

22. Hajek, *Oral History Methodology*; Portelli, "What Makes Oral History Different," in *The Oral History Reader*, eds. Perks and Thomson, 74.

23. This also acknowledges the use of low-tech augmentative and alternative communication methods, such as drawing or using photographs, and high-tech augmentative and alternative communication devices, such as mobile phones or tablets, or speech generating devices.

24. Laura Hull et al., "'Putting on My Best Normal': Social Camouflaging in Adults with Autism Spectrum Conditions," *Journal of Autism and Developmental Disorders* 47, no. 8 (August 1, 2017), 2519.

25. Christine Garnaut and John R. Gold, "Interrogating Voices from the Past: Making Use of Oral Testimony in Planning Historical Research," *Planning Perspectives* 36, no. 6 (November 2, 2021), 1302; Emma L. Vickers, "Unexpected Trauma in Oral Interviewing," *Oral History Review* 46, no. 1 (March 1, 2019): 137–38; Martha Norkunas, "The Vulnerable Listener," in *Oral History Off the Record: Toward an Ethnography of Practice*, eds. Anna Sheftel and Stacey Zembrzycki, Palgrave Studies in Oral History (New York: Palgrave Macmillan US, 2013), 81–96.

26. Alexander Freund, "Towards an Ethics of Silence? Negotiating Off-the-Record Events and Identity in Oral History," in *Oral History Off the Record*, eds. Sheftel and Zembrzyck, 233.

27. Booth and Booth, "Sounds of Silence," 56, 67.

28. Donna F. Ryan and John S. Schuchman, eds., *Deaf People in Hitler's Europe* (Washington, DC: Gallaudet University Press, 2002), viii.

29. Ryan and Schuchman, *Deaf People in Hitler's Europe*; Snoddon, *Telling Deaf Lives*.

30. History of Place website, https://historyof.place/.

31. Ryan and Schuchman, *Deaf People in Hitler's Europe*, 168. It should be noted that this process requires three instances of translation: Hungarian Sign Language into American Sign Language, into written American English. This may present some methodological challenges, as the original meaning of the Hungarian D/deaf subjects may be lost.

32. Brad Rakerd, "On Making Oral Histories More Accessible to Persons with Hearing Loss," *Oral History Review* 40, no. 1 (January 1, 2013): 67–74.

33. Jan Walmsley, "Life History Interviews with People with Learning Disabilities," *Oral History* 23, no. 1 (1995): 71–77; Jan Walmsley and Dorothy Atkinson, "Oral History and the History of Learning Disability," in *Oral History, Health and Welfare*, eds. Joanna Bornat et al. (London: Routledge, 2000).

34. Booth and Booth, "Sounds of Silence," 59–60.

35. Booth and Booth, "Sounds of Silence," 60.

36. Booth and Booth, "Sounds of Silence," 61.

37. Booth and Booth, "Sounds of Silence," 63.

38. Booth and Booth, "Sounds of Silence," 63; Sari Knopp Biklen and Charles R. Moseley, "'Are You Retarded?' 'No, I'm Catholic': Qualitative Methods in the Study of People with Severe Handicaps," *Journal of the Association for Persons with Severe Handicaps* 13, no. 3 (September 1, 1988): 155–62.

39. Booth and Booth, "Sounds of Silence," 64–66.

40. Paul Cambridge and Rachel Forrester-Jones, "Using Individualised Communication for Interviewing People with Intellectual Disability: A Case Study of User-Centred Research," *Journal of Intellectual and Developmental Disability* 28, no. 1 (2003): 5–23.

41. Paraphrased from an email sent by McGuire to Goldstone-Brady on January 10, 2021.

42. For instance, see Oral History Society Guidance, Version 5, April 2020. Version 7 available at https://www.ohs.org.uk/covid-19-remote-recording/.

43. Paul Hanna, "Using Internet Technologies (Such as Skype) as a Research Medium: A Research Note," *Qualitative Research* 12, no. 2 (April 1, 2012): 239–42; Aaron Payne, "The Challenges of Producing an Oral History of the Deaf: Cued Speech in New South Wales 1965–1990," *Oral History Association of Australia Journal*, no. 35 (2013): 3–8. https://search.informit.org/doi/10.3316/informit.766320764485206.

44. Hanna, "Using Internet Technologies (Such as Skype) as a Research Medium"; Payne, "The Challenges of Producing an Oral History of the Deaf."

45. Jeremy N. Bailenson, "Nonverbal Overload: A Theoretical Argument for the Causes of Zoom Fatigue," *Technology, Mind, and Behavior* 2, no. 1 (February 23, 2021).

CHAPTER 15

Ephemeral Madness

The Patient-Theorists of Psychiatric Archives

LIANA KATHLEEN COLE

Vanda Vieira-Schmidt is a contemporary artist living in a German inpatient psychiatric facility. Her "World Rescue Project" is made of more than half a million sheets of paper with individual drawings on them, and Vieira-Schmidt continues to add to the piles every day. In the documentary film *Between Madness and Art: The Prinzhorn Collection*, Vieira-Schmidt explains that the drawings include codes, symbols, and designs that she telepathically directs to a computer in the German Ministry of Defense, who alone can interpret them. Vieira-Schmidt tells the viewer that the purpose of her World Rescue Project is to achieve world peace and reduce international conflicts. The artist will sometimes fax a drawing to an international figure, directing artistic energy against enemies who—in her explanation—have allied with the devil to use uranium and computers to make their victims' hearts and veins burst. Vieira-Schmidt's other projects similarly use art as a process to enact global change. "I draw so humanity can live in peace," Vieira-Schmidt tells the interviewer in the film. She explains that she once redesigned beautiful new inner organs for adults and children using primary colors and geometric shapes because she heard that the old organs were "obsolete." She also once felt an unbearable heat from what she called star explosions, so she channeled the explosions onto the paper and painted over them; only then did she feel cool air.[1]

A psychoanalytic reading of Vieira-Schmidt's art might begin with her diagnosis of paranoid schizophrenia. Within the ambit of twentieth-century psychoanalytic interpretations, her beliefs and art would represent her pathology, and the trained viewer could play detective to interpret her diagnosis. This has traditionally characterized the reception of psychiatric patients' creative expression; since the earliest concerted efforts to archive or curate patient art at the turn of the twentieth century, patient expression often serves as evidence of madness, or is held up as an example of *art brut*—outsider, raw, or free from modern cultural influence. It has been defined by its deficits. To counter this, this chapter proposes a reexamination of art and writing by psychiatric patients that situates disabled, Mad, and institutionalized creators not as outsiders or as fodder for a pathology-based interpretation, but as experts with political drives, personal desires, and complex messages. The artistry and expression in these works is often made invisible in the service of making the artist's perceived deficits hypervisible; the result is that work by patient-artists gets archived in patient files or displayed in outsider art exhibits. Shifting away from pathology and toward expertise in scholarship, archival work, and therapeutic practices related to art by Mad creators will help us break down these archival barriers and move toward disability justice.

Though there may not be evidence of a telepathic link between Vieira-Schmidt's mind and the German Ministry of Defense, her artwork is still an active, political process that engages deeply with her material conditions. All of her art responds to physical, material, or geopolitical desires—a desire for peace, a desire for new inner organs, a desire for cool air during a star explosion. Recognizing Vieira-Schmidt as a theorist of these forces also positions her as a creator within a particular historical and institutional context; a reading of Vieira-Schmidt's art that focuses on perceived pathology would also likely miss the ways that she uses her art to bend the walls of the institution she lives in and engage politically and artistically with world powers. Vieira-Schmidt's work—and work by other institutionalized creators—has the power to theorize, transform, and speak back to her institution. Further, Vieira-Schmidt joins a long lineage of disabled institutionalized women who use the materials around them—sometimes quite literally, as is the case with artists like Judith Scott or the women fiber artists in the Prinzhorn Collection—to make transformative change. Recognizing this potential requires viewing her art as an engaged response to institutional contexts rather than an expression of individual pathology.

Seeing patient art as a way to theorize the institution also gives us insight into the experiences of Mad and disabled people throughout history. I focus here on the United States and Germany in the late nineteenth and early twentieth centuries; these locations had particularly established models for psychiatric institutionalization, often shared psychoanalytic practices, and were both interested in documenting/archiving those institutions. Because my interest is partly in how academics have interpreted this artwork over the years, Germany and the United States are particularly interesting case studies given their relevance to *art brut* criticism. However, it is my hope that this framework is applicable beyond this era and geographical boundary, and that reevaluating the role of patient art and writing brings us closer to the goals of disability justice in all eras of archival scholarship.

To understand how some patients used creative expression to theorize or transform their institutions, this chapter explores two categories of writing and art made by psychiatric patients: patient-authored periodicals (one unpublished newsletter from the Oregon State Hospital in the 1920s and one published house organ from the Alabama Insane Hospital at the end of the nineteenth century) and fiber art by women from the Prinzhorn Collection (Germany, 1919–22). The creators of these pieces are many things—writers, poets, journalists, artists, seamstresses, Mad, not Mad—but are united by their shared status as hospital patients and creatives.

Insiders and Outsiders: Methods and Archives

Psychiatric hospitals have historically been the sites of prolific textual and artistic production; the institutions produced paperwork and annual reports while patients produced newspapers, letters, memoirs, and artwork.[2] Within the remaining archives of these institutions, however, the voices of those who experienced the hospital as patients are largely subsumed by institutional efforts to tell stories of progress, charity, and cure; psychiatric archives are a stark example of the simultaneous visibility and invisibility of disabled people in archives. Asylum archives in the United States can be difficult to track down, having been scattered or destroyed after what is commonly (but often erroneously, considering the mass incarceration of disabled and Mad people today) called deinstitutionalization, a period in the 1970s when total psychiatric institutions largely emptied in favor of community-based care. This is a long and complicated history, but in short, the patients' rights movement of the 1960s and '70s built on the momentum of civil rights achievements and the work of anti-asylum scholars and activists, journalists, authors, and filmmakers who had exposed the horrors of asylum life over the last century. Today, total psychiatric hospitals have been replaced, more or less, by cottage systems and group homes that allow for more freedom of routine and flexible diagnoses, but these have come under harsh criticism for leaving some patients homeless and underserved, particularly poor patients and patients of color, who more often end up imprisoned than in a hospital.[3]

One exception is the Oregon State Hospital, a public psychiatric hospital that has been in operation since 1862. Though this chapter looks at only one example from this archive, the comprehensiveness of the Oregon State Archive's records from the OSH preserves the answers to some important questions: How were patients' writings included (or not) in the bureaucratic process? What types of writing did doctors deem worth preserving and why? And, most importantly, how do these writings theorize the hospital (in other words, how do patients use writing to think through, transform, contextualize, and politicize their institutional conditions)? The OSH has made efforts on many fronts to be an ethical steward of these difficult histories; the hospital itself now houses a museum of the history of mental health, and the State Archives in Salem contain nearly 190 cubic feet of neatly ordered patient files from the facility. Typical patient files in this collection include paperwork, financial records, carbon copies of letters sent to the patients' families by physicians, letters received by the physicians from the families, and any other legal or medical records from the time of the patients' hospitalization. A minority of patient files also include writing done by the patients themselves; these include poems, religious writings, intercepted letters, and more. These writers are notable precisely because they were not published; their creative expression remained in the textual ecosystem of the hospital.

In this attempt to frame institutionalized artists and writers as theorists of their own environs, it is also worth considering how this method runs counter to the ways that we typically talk about noninstitutionalized artists. If the purpose is, in part, to truly study these artists as artists, then why treat their creative expression differently than that of noninstitutionalized artists? Here we might turn to Nicole Fleetwood's work on art made in U.S. prisons today: though her context is quite different, her work does an exemplary job of taking these artists seriously as artists *and* situating their work within a particular institutional context. Fleetwood relates an anecdote about moderating a talk with a formerly incarcerated artist when an audience member remarked that we rarely accord significance to the settings in which nonincarcerated artists work. "The formerly incarcerated artist agreed," Fleetwood writes,

> but also made clear that when a piece of art is made in prison, it is impossible not to acknowledge the significance of the institutional context. He noted that his artwork changed significantly when he went to prison because of the setting, the regulation of time, the constant presence of correction officers, and the limited access to materials—all of which altered his aesthetic horizons. For him, penal time, penal matter, and penal space led to a more deliberate, repetitive, and sometimes even mechanical process—one that produced labor-intensive, time-laden works that he would not have made outside punitive captivity.[4]

Fleetwood's observations about the significance of "penal time, penal matter, and penal space" do not lessen the significance of the art as art; rather, they help to counter the tendency "to consider art by incarcerated people as existing outside of art discourses or institutions [which] rehearses the violent erasure of being imprisoned."[5] This insistence on recognizing the setting does, however, ask the viewer to reckon with the fact that the artist is creating within a context where time, materials, and space have a very different meaning; it brings outside viewers one step closer to recognizing the creativity, critiques, and transformations that these artists enacted in their pieces.

Rather than assume that these artists share intrinsic qualities that one might ascribe to madness, I group them by shared genres and consider how they each use that genre to theorize or transform their institutional context. On the rare occasion that I use the term "patient" to refer to a person outside of their artistry, it is done deliberately and is not intended to reinforce the potentially dehumanizing or subjectivizing effects of the term, but rather to capture the material conditions under which they created their work. My choice to use the language of "madness" is similarly fraught, but I do so to distance this work from the clinical language of mental illness, to echo the strides made by the Mad Pride movement, and to honor the language that many patient-writers used to talk about their experiences in the late nineteenth and early twentieth centuries.[6] While some of the artists whose work is explored in this chapter self-identify as mad/Mad, some do not; as I demonstrate, the act of narrating one's own identity can be transformative, particularly in the context of an institution where one's identity is so often defined by authority figures, and I do my best to mirror the language the writers use to describe themselves.

Focusing on the institutional setting of asylum art also diverts critical focus away from the idea that there is something intrinsic to madness that shapes the creative process; this often manifests in the trope of the Mad genius. While the trope has a much longer history, it was mobilized in the context of asylum art in the mid-twentieth century by the French painter Jean Dubuffet and the English art critic Roger Cardinal, who conceptualized *art brut*/outsider art. Dubuffet coined the term *art brut* (sometimes translated as "raw art") in 1945 out of contempt for the culture of European art and art criticism, seeing the scene as stifling to creativity. Cardinal formulated this as the central question in his influential 1972 book *Outsider Art*: "Can art be conceived that is not 'cultural'? Does such a rigorously *different* art exist?"[7] Outsider artists are typically divided into three categories, each representing a type of distance from the European art world: "primitives," institutionalized "lunatics," and children.

Madness is particularly interesting to critics like Cardinal and Dubuffet because, according to the psychiatrists they cite, Mad artists create in an "autistic theater" "wherein creator, work, and audience are identical."[8] Further, Cardinal argues, "madness as the most extreme mental attitude may be expected to produce an art whose essence is alien to the established norms of culture."[9] Though Cardinal's work intends to celebrate the art of these institutionalized artists, arguments like this ultimately reproduce the logic of the asylum, wherein people with psychiatric and mental disabilities were separated from society at large, out of touch, and dangerous to the status quo. By arguing that Mad creators are not in conversation with their surroundings, that there is something essential to madness that situates the Mad creator outside of culture, Cardinal (and other outsider art critics before him) participates in placing the artist outside of time, place, and—perhaps—personhood.[10] The resulting archives—wherein artwork and writing is often placed inside a folder of medical records, if it is saved at all—therefore imply that anything created by that person is evidence of their madness, that the institution is a necessary societal good, and that the person's artistry is more akin to medical records than to artwork.

Patient-Authored Newsletters

There is something notable about patient-authors adopting the format of a newspaper; the genre is destined to be seen, to circulate, and to connect the writers with the larger world from which they've been isolated. Patient-authors use these newsletters to direct the public in how they might engage with hospital patients, support their well-being, and challenge preconceived notions of madness. By the end of the nineteenth century, the genre invoked a professional journalistic authority, suggesting that the material contained within was a reliable public record, something worth saving. A number of hospital periodicals, or "house organs," circulated in the late nineteenth century. One of the most accessible today is *The Meteor*, a serial publication written, edited, and printed by patients at the Alabama Insane Hospital in Tuscaloosa between 1872 and 1881. Like a meteor, the newspaper appeared at irregular intervals throughout the near-decade that it ran. Its contents were primarily written by one anonymous patient-editor, though each edition usually includes a few anonymous contributors as well. The writers cover typical nineteenth-century concerns such as gardening, Christianity, dancing, and manners, but the content is primarily taken up with patients' musings on insanity and institutional life.

The writers frequently theorize institutional life quite explicitly, typically with a striking sense of humor. For example, because the hospital shares a campus with the University of Alabama, the editor calls them the "two Poles of the great intellectual Magnet of the State," with a few distinct differences:

> The inmates of the University come to acquire ideas. We to get rid of them. They receive encomiums for proficiency in military tactics. The slightest proclivities in that direction, at our house, insure rebuke. If a student is insubordinate or irregular in his deportment, he is sent home. The more obstreperous our behavior, the closer we are held.[11]

These moments of transformation through creative expression are not always explicit critiques or threats to the hospital system. As Benjamin Reiss argues in *Theatres of Madness: Insane Asylums and Nineteenth-Century American Culture*, direct resistance is hard to find in asylum house organs, since they were usually closely supervised by staff. Presumably, the light jokes at the expense of staff were approved for print and therefore not deemed threatening to institutional authority. Less explicit moments of critique, or "jagged or offkey pieces" in Reiss's words, were "more perverse and unsettling than direct critique, because it could not quite be pinned down."[12] Sometimes, those supervisors even incorporated the writing and publication process into their therapeutic agendas, and thus it became an arena in which patients might demonstrate what the doctors would consider to be healthy behavior and rhetoric.[13] In these situations, writers transformed their experience of the hospital in a concrete way by using writing to help secure freedom.

One of the most creative ways that the editor of *The Meteor* used the publication to transform his hospital experience was by embracing what we might now call crip time—that is, a flexible or irregular way of moving through time, which the editor likened to meteors—in the hospital's publication schedule.[14] For example, after a long hiatus, the editor opens the final issue in 1881 with a statement on the regularity of the publication:

> The editor, who was also the printer, disgusted with the long succession of years that still found him at the Hospital, determined to strike a halt in the regular issue, and to print a number only when inclined to do so. Fortunately he had repeatedly warned his readers that any job dependent on the will of a Hospital patient was likely to be irregularly achieved, so that his readers were not surprised when from a quarterly, our paper changed to a semi-occasionally.[15]

The publication itself became a vehicle for the editor's protest against the hospital's excessive regulation of his time.[16] He also mobilized his reader's preconceptions about his identity as a "Hospital patient," adopting and using this identity in a somewhat tongue-in-cheek manner to insist on his agency to disrupt the regulation of his time. To recognize the wholeness of these authors is to remember that they were many things in life—siblings, artists, lovers, workers—but used this venue to embrace and theorize one identity category in particular: that of the Mad hospital patient.

Most people who experienced the hospital as a patient did not have this outlet for publication; we know from the few remaining intact psychiatric hospital archives that many patients spent time writing inside the hospital, and that only some of this writing is included in their patient files. One motivation for a doctor to include a sample of a patient's writing in her case file was as evidence of her insanity. In the Oregon State Archive, one patient's file includes her letters to a priest, to an unnamed loved one, to the governor, and to the Pope about her religious revelations.[17] This is reflected across numerous other patient files; it is common to find (presumably intercepted) letters to the president, to the United States Department of Justice, and to family members detailing abuse and maltreatment at the hospital; each letter is marked "FILE" and many are referenced in the patients' case notes as evidence of paranoia. Yet another patient's letters are included in her file alongside carbon copies of letters sent between her doctor and her husband; the doctor reports to the husband that she has been writing letters to other men around Portland and asks the husband what he would like done with those letters.[18] While we do not have access to the husband's response, the letters rest in her case file, presumably as evidence of pathological promiscuity. Each of these examples demonstrates that writing—letter-writing in particular—was a contested site of power and expression in the hospital. Further, it supports the claims made in asylum memoirs by writers like Elizabeth Parsons Ware Packard that writing in the hospital was closely surveilled, letters were intercepted, and that writing was not seen as a neutral or entirely therapeutic activity by administrators.[19]

On occasion, a patient's creative expression aligned with the hospital's goals; one patient's file, for example, includes poems that reflect her journey through the hospital, which follows a path that ultimately credits the hospital with her restoration and inner peace.[20] The most prolific patient-author I found at the Oregon State Archives, however, was not so well aligned with the hospital's goals. This patient wrote under the pseudonym Neleh Eldré.[21] The file contains a range of writing by Eldré, nearly all of which was completed in the weeks before she was brought to the Oregon State Hospital; it seems that these writings were confiscated upon her arrival and placed in her file. The pages include prose about her devotion to Christian Science, details about her psychic abilities, speculations about her potential pregnancy (which she says is an "exception to the rule" as she has been menstruating since conception), assertions about her engagement to the Prince of Wales, countless loose pages that sort Bible verses by theme, and two issues of a handwritten and hand-drawn newsletter called *Ravings: A Rag Devoted to Humanity, Published Wherever We Happen to Be*. Eldré's mother brought her to the hospital in December 1928, citing delusions, erratic behavior, and a recent arrest in California. Eldré was released in April 1929, at which time she "ridiculed" her past delusions and looked forward to rejoining the work force as a dress seller. A few letters are included in Eldré's file from after her release in which she states that she is feeling much better with the help of her stay and a recent (unnamed) surgery.[22]

Eldré's writing is funny, personable, and occasionally moving in its resilience. Eldré valued her own writing; the front page of *Ravings* reads "this is not a free circulating sheet. Let's see the color of your money 1 at a time!" and the first edition concludes "Ravings—Finished for this issue. If you haven't had 50 cents worth, bring youre copy back. We'll give you a dirty story in exchange for the Rag if its in good sanitary condition. Maybe that will please yuh!" The second edition of *Ravings* details Eldré's arguments against the vivisection of animals, points in support of sex work and sex workers, comments on political figures, and references her personal trials. The archived file includes earlier drafts of these columns, which she seemingly spent much time and care copying over into the newspaper format.

The letters exchanged between Eldré and the physicians after her stay evidence the dissonance in how she valued her papers and how the hospital viewed them. After she was released, Eldré wrote back to Dr. Looney (yes, really) asking "if among the various papers and things which I believe you have in your files regarding me you may have a California automobile drivers license" as well as permits to sell dresses, adding "am I not entitled to have returned to me any other papers and writings taken from my effects?" To the first question, the assistant physician replied that he had thoroughly examined her file and had not found the license or permits; however, they are both included in the file just a few pages later. Perhaps they were filed separately at the time, but they now rest just behind his letter as if to say to the contemporary reader that Eldré was right. The assistant physician did not answer her question about her writings, however, which prompted Eldré to write again. He replied that "I am instructed by the Superintendent to write and state that your papers, writings, etc. can not be sent you as they are a part of the institutional records, and to make copies of the same would be an endless job."[23] This response demonstrates that the hospital sees itself as the owner of her writings, both for the sake of preserving the institutional record and for the ease of bureaucratic labor. Beyond the material ownership of the papers, Eldré's file poses a challenge to a contemporary reader looking to believe her account and honor her story; Eldré herself did not believe parts of her account by the end of her stay.

In the face of such a complex set of writings, we as contemporary readers should set aside the impulse to read Eldré's writings as evidence of her pathological deficits and instead recognize Eldré as someone who was responding to equally complex material conditions. Though she wrote quickly and prolifically and made claims that her family and doctors felt did not match up with the facts of her life (such as her engagement to the Prince of Wales), if we recognize Eldré's writing as transformative and engaged with her material surroundings, we would not see these sheets as manic ravings, but rather as a way to materially connect to the world around her. The very fact that she intended *Ravings* to circulate while she herself remained institutionalized demonstrates a reaching toward connection and community, which she enacted through humor, religion, and the insistence on the material value of her writing.

The archive itself is similarly complex, as the bureaucratic impulse is both the reason Eldré never repossessed her writings and the reason that scholars and descendants of former patients today can access them. Ultimately, no amount of careful reading or scholarly reclamation can right the wrongs done to Eldré. Whether she wanted to repossess her writings because they were evidence of a period of her life that she wished to bury or because she wished to pursue publication of those writings, these papers should have been hers to claim. What we can learn from them now—about bureaucratic practice, power in these hospitals, or creative expression—is only secondary to the violence against patient autonomy that they represent. We might begin to honor her legacy by recognizing the transformative and theoretical power of her work, situating it alongside other writers in the genre, and considering the ways that she used *Ravings* to put a value on her own writing and imagine her ideas in circulation beyond the hospital walls. While *The Meteor* and *Ravings* offer obvious ways for their authors to remain in conversation with the outside world (and have therefore generally escaped the grasp of outsider art theorists), visual art has not had the same luxury.

Fiber Art in the Prinzhorn Collection

Katharina Detzel's man stands a head taller than her own height. Her arm reaches around his back to hold him up, and his feet turn inwards as they fall against the floor. He is made of mattress ticking and stuffed with straw, and he sports a long straw beard, tiny wire spectacles, a canvas penis, and a bald head. His arms are asymmetrical, with one ending just below the bicep and the other ending at the elbow. In a photograph, Detzel wears a checked dress and looks at the camera with the slightest hint of a smile. The man's effect—from his life-sized scale to the tiny spectacles perched on his Kilroy-esque nose to Detzel's careful attention to his anatomy—is just as artistically impressive as it is playful. This photograph was taken some time between 1914 and 1919 at a German psychiatric hospital and subsequently donated to the Prinzhorn Collection. Everything else that we know about Detzel's man, we know from her patient file.[24] According to the file, Detzel had apparently created this man overnight on April 13, 1914 from materials that she could access in her isolation cell. Nurses and doctors entered her cell the next morning to find the straw man dangling from a lamp, and Detzel explained that men had come into her cell that night, hanged this (straw) man, and threatened to do the same to her; she asked to be removed from isolation and placed with fellow patients so as to be protected from the intruders. Instead, however, doctors kept Detzel in isolation but removed her access to clothes, blankets, and mattresses. Detzel's paper trail ends in 1941; she spent some time outside the asylum, but remained institutionalized when the Nazis came into power and began enacting the systematized murder of psychiatric patients.

A quick Google search of Detzel's name shows that, about once a year since 2012, the image gets posted to blogs, content mills, Reddit, and Tumblr under headlines like "50+ Insanely Creepy Vintage Photos That Will Probably Give

You Nightmares."[25] Each time, the photo is accompanied by a caption that claims that Detzel would "pummel [the straw man] when she was angry or dance with when she felt happy. This male gave her the surrogate love she needed in the institute."[26] In this (almost Freudian) interpretation, Detzel uses the man to fill a social/emotional/sexual lack. Certainly, the isolation of the institution may have produced this need, and by creating the man, Detzel fulfills it. This focus on individual behavior and need, however, limits the ways that Detzel's man might speak back to—and indeed transform—her institutional setting, keeping the viewer's critique focused on Detzel's individual psyche rather than the system in which she created her art. Historian Monika Ankele interprets Detzel's action of creating and hanging the man as a way to identify the isolation cell "as a life-threatening space where—even though she was unsupervised and unprotected—she was not necessarily alone. Detzel used the situation of the room and its material culture to confront and thus to interact with the doctors, hoping to impact their actions and decisions."[27] The fact that the doctors responded by removing Detzel's textile materials—and, therefore, the potential to create another man—demonstrates that her creative actions were, in some way, threatening to the administrators and the physical environment they sought to control.

If we began from the assumption that Detzel's work has the power to theorize and transform her environment, we become less concerned with speculations about her individual needs and deficits—speculations that seem to have shaped the popular caption associated with the image. For example, let us again notice the fact that Detzel's man's arms end before the elbow. This might draw our attention to the asylum version of what Fleetwood called "penal time" or "penal matter," reminding us that Detzel had limited time, privacy, light, and material with which to create the man—perhaps she ran out of material or time before finishing the arms. Perhaps it was simply an aesthetic choice. No matter the reason, Detzel's man also participates in Tobin Siebers's *disability aesthetics*; her man challenges expected body boundaries, "return[ing] aesthetics forcefully to its originary subject matter: the body and its affective sphere."[28] While we cannot know the many factors at work behind Detzel's creative process—whether she created her man out of a desire for "surrogate love," to convince the administrators to move her out of isolation, or to simply create—we can acknowledge the many ways that her art exposes, transforms, and speaks back to her institutional setting.

The history and reception of Detzel's man is, in some ways, in keeping with the reception of the Prinzhorn Collection as a whole, but also demonstrates an important departure. In brief, beginning in 1919, Heidelberg Clinic psychiatrists Hans Prinzhorn and Karl Wilmanns solicited art by psychiatric patients across Germany. They collected about five thousand drawings, textiles, and writings, which became known as the Prinzhorn Collection. The collection was not housed with typical archival care: pieces were glued onto cheap pasteboard, obscuring the images and text on their backing (this has since been remedied to some extent by more recent archivists and curators), and there was no proper record of dates of acquisition, only the name of the institution and the artist's diagnosis.[29] Further, Prinzhorn published his own interpretation of the pieces in his 1922 *Artistry of the Mentally Ill*, highlighting the work of ten male "schizophrenic masters." Throughout, Prinzhorn carefully avoided the word "art" (*Kunst*) to refer to the patients' work and chose instead the term *Gestaltung*, which Roger Cardinal translates as something nearer to "forming" or "shaping."[30] To his credit, Prinzhorn's interpretation of the work did not read the pieces in search of some presumed pathology on the part of the artist, but recognized the fact that it would be impossible to read the pieces without any preconceptions. He wrote that

> our material itself will be the basis for our discussion; the pictures will not be measured or judged by any fixed, outside standard. Instead, we shall try to comprehend and analyze the pictures visually, as free of prejudice as possible. No matter how hard we shall try to be unprejudiced, however we are under no illusions about the possibilities of an approach free of all preconceptions.[31]

Regardless, in the text, Prinzhorn oscillates between praising the work on its own merit and suggesting that artistic production is a pathological trait of schizophrenia.

Since Prinzhorn publicized the collection, it has served many and varied purposes. In 1937, when the Heidelberg Clinic was under new leadership, some visual art from the collection was lent to the Nazis and displayed alongside that of modern artists at the Degenerate Art Exhibit (*Entartete Kunst*) to suggest the insanity of modern artists. Beginning in 1939, many of Prinzhorn's former patients were murdered in *Aktion T4*, the program initiated by the Nazis designed to kill sick, disabled, elderly, and Mad people in psychiatric and medical facilities. After the war, the collection was immortalized by Jean Dubuffet's *Collection de l'Art Brut* in the 1950s and '60s and theorized in Roger Cardinal's 1972 *Outsider Art*; Dubuffet, Cardinal, and other proponents of *art brut* used the Prinzhorn Collection (with specific attention to the Ten Masters) to represent art by untrained artists, untainted by modern society. Many of these artists were trained, however, if not in fine art, then in an artisan trade. Far from creating in an "autistic theater" (as Cardinal calls it), their art engaged deeply with material economies, contemporary politics, and their institutional contexts. Psychiatrists like Prinzhorn, eugenicists like the Nazi collectors, and *art brut* theorists all, to a degree, removed the artists' work from its historical, institutional, and material context so that they might make some claim about the pathology of the artists. This decontextualization seems to feature in almost every realm where creative work by psychiatric patients is received. Denying asylum art its historical and cultural context does not simply produce a faulty interpretation, but, as the Prinzhorn Collection demonstrates, can invoke life-and-death stakes for the creators.

As evidenced by that copied/pasted caption across the internet, Detzel's man has been subjected to the same ahistorical, pathologizing reception as the rest of the Prinzhorn Collection; little attention has been given to the fact that she is one of many institutionalized women fiber artists throughout history. Fiber art, in the hands of women artists, is so often a collective, material, and functional form of expression. In revisiting and historicizing Detzel's work, I do not aim to reify the mad-male-genius trope as the outsider art critics did. Detzel was not one of Prinzhorn's Ten (male) Masters, and her medium of choice situates her alongside craftswomen working in common rather than male painters working alone—she created her man precisely so that she might be transferred from her isolation and be closer with other patients. While over five hundred artists are represented in the original Prinzhorn Collection, only eighty of these have been identified as women.[32] Many of these women, like Detzel, chose fiber art as their medium of choice.

This choice reflects the fact that many of these women were trained in sewing and embroidery, of course, but also suggests something about the process and product. The process behind creating fiber art (whether one is cross-stitching, embroidering, weaving, knitting, crocheting, sewing, or quilting) is often repetitive, detail-oriented, done in communal circles, and grounded in a fundamentally tactile experience—all elements of what we might now call self-soothing techniques. These artists were likely drawing on their familiarity with the medium, but they were also practicing a creative act that had the power to self-soothe and build resilience. Further, fiber art is often wearable and functional, though (perhaps because it was done so primarily by women) it is often classed as a "craft" rather than an "art." Regardless, it has the power to transform one's material relationship to her environment by providing warmth, protection, or wearable aesthetic expression.

One woman's fiber art in the Prinzhorn Collection has garnered particular interest over the decades: Agnes Richter's embroidered jacket. Richter was a seamstress who was admitted to the Heidelberg Psychiatric Hospital in 1893; her jacket is made from repurposed institutional linen and is covered in embroidered script. The words, numbers, and fragmented phrases overlap each other, are stitched in a variety of colors, and are written in *deutsche schrift*, a now-antiquated script. The lettering itself is largely illegible, but bold and colorful; Richter repeatedly stitched over her letters. The jacket shows signs of wear, with sweat-stains and some unusual tailoring that was possibly made to accommodate Richter's hunched back. Whatever the language on Richter's jacket translates to, the *meaning* of the jacket seems to transcend its linguistic expression. In her stitching, Richter tapped into her training as a seamstress. She perhaps self-soothed in a chaotic environment through repetitive stitching. She wore her jacket as an expression of self as colorful, irregular, and illegible in an institution that was designed to regulate and control her behavior. She wrote and rewrote her life narrative in defiance of a system that attempted to write it for her.

The jacket is the namesake of Gail Hornstein's 2009 *Agnes's Jacket: A Psychologist's Search for the Meanings of Madness*, which examines patients' art and narratives. Hornstein argues that Richter's jacket is more than just a static art object, but that

> wearing her jacket on the ward must have made her seem different from other patients, strange and special. Was she reassuring herself or showing off, shouting, "I have something important to say!" but preventing those who threatened her from knowing what it meant? In Islamic countries in the seventh century, prayers and quotations from the Qu'ran were embroidered directly into the decorative patterns of ceremonial robes. Only those few who knew how to read the sacred texts could tell what the designs meant.[33]

Like Detzel's man, Richter used her jacket to transform her relationship to her institutional environment. As Hornstein points out, the jacket signaled that Richter was an individual with a unique set of insights and knowledge. While I am wary of Hornstein's next logical step—which is to frame Richter's jacket as a code that one might translate with the help of "someone fluent in the language of madness"—I support her methods. Hornstein attempts to undo some of her psychiatric training, which taught her that "psychotic patients were supposed to be too 'narcissistic' and 'unrelational' to allow others into their inner worlds," and instead take seriously first-person madness narratives, which she says "were proposing alternative ways of understanding madness and coping with it."[34] It is this type of reframing that can reorient scholarship, archival practices, art curation, and therapeutic techniques toward better honoring patients' experience, expertise, and creative contributions.

Conclusion

Outside of hospitals, Mad and disabled people have continued this powerful history of creative expression and self-narration in the service of liberation. Groups like the Hearing Voices Network (HVN) have demonstrated that reading narratives and viewing art with a radical openness to a person's own explanatory model of madness requires an almost anti-interpretive stance. The HVN is a networked group of people who work to destigmatize and de-pathologize the experience of hearing voices; it is largely run by people who hear voices for people who hear voices. They frame voice-hearing not as a problem in and of itself, but as a neutral experience that may—like many other life experiences—create some associated complications and distress in a person's life. The HVN provides community for voice-hearers and support in tackling those challenges. One of the first methods for de-pathologizing voice-hearing is (in the words of HVN founders Marius Romme and Patsy Hage) to acknowledge that there are benefits to explanatory models that do not fit the accepted psychiatric pathologization. Synthesizing Romme and Hage's view, Gail Hornstein writes:

> Thinking that voices come from the collective unconscious or a spirit or a reincarnated being is likely to make a person feel connected to others. Taking a biological view, on the other hand, usually leaves people feeling isolated, pessimistic, and frightened. Believing that they have a brain defect or a chemical imbalance or a mental illness implies that they are powerless to do anything about their situation and must turn themselves over to the ministrations of physicians.[35]

Hornstein provides a model for how to approach this variety of explanatory models as both a scholar and a practitioner. When she embeds herself in the group and begins listening to members' life stories, she realizes that

> the last thing that people who've had their deepest feelings turned into symptoms need is someone else analyzing them. No matter how empathetic I might be, every description is interpretive, and whatever I write imposes a frame on the event that wasn't there originally. In the politics of the mental health world, every framing is political; there's no neutral ground to stand on.[36]

I say that my stance is *almost* anti-interpretive for a reason similar to Hornstein's; my readings are guided by questions borne out of disability justice, medical humanities, and my own interests in seeing a shift in how scholars talk about patient art and narratives. No framing is neutral, and my introduction and analysis of each of the works in this essay has been in service of these interests. While scholars might strip away some of the more harmful effects of past interpretive models, it is necessary to remain as transparent as possible about the factors that guide our current readings. Recognizing artists and writers as theorists of their psychiatric settings has the potential to make for scholarship, archives, exhibits, and therapeutic practices that are more attuned to the agency and expression of the people they proport to serve.

Notes

1. Christian Beetz, *Between Madness and Art: The Prinzhorn Collection* (Icarus Films, 2007).

2. I have written elsewhere about asylum paperwork; see Liana Glew, "Documenting Insanity: Paperwork and Patient Narratives in Psychiatric History," *History of the Human Sciences*, February 2022.

3. For more on disability and incarceration, see *Disability Incarcerated: Imprisonment and Disability in the United States and Canada*, edited by Liat Ben-Moshe et al. (Palgrave Macmillan US, 2014).

4. Nicole R. Fleetwood, *Marking Time: Art in the Age of Mass Incarceration* (Harvard University Press, 2020), 12.

5. Fleetwood, *Marking Time*, 6.

6. This body of literature is wide-ranging and requires only that the author center the experiences of Mad individuals; I consider it to include the many first-person memoirs by Mad people (such as the excerpts included in Dale Peterson's *A Mad People's History of Madness*), literary theorizations of madness (such as Therí A. Pickens's *Black Madness :: Mad Blackness*), and examinations of madness in artistic and political identity formations (such as La Marr Jurelle Bruce's *How to Go Mad without Losing Your Mind: Madness and Black Radical Creativity*). See La Marr Jurelle Bruce, *How to Go Mad without Losing Your Mind: Madness and Black Radical Creativity* (Duke University Press, 2020); Dale Peterson, *A Mad People's History of Madness* (University of Pittsburgh Press, 1982); Therí Alyce Pickens, *Black Madness :: Mad Blackness* (Duke University Press, 2019).

7. Roger Cardinal, *Outsider Art* (Praeger Publishers, 1973).

8. Cardinal, *Outsider Art*, 22.

9. Cardinal, *Outsider Art*, 15.

10. There is a large body of scholarship critiquing (and supporting) the category of outsider art and the role of psychiatric patient-artists within that category; Jonathan Eburne, for example, notes in his book *Outsider Theory* that the critical praise of art created by psychiatric patients has "at times eclipsed the working conditions of the artists themselves, who often lived and died in obscurity, poverty, or institutional confinement," but that the category of "outsider" does offer a dynamic field on which to play out the relationships between "normal and pathological ideas, between acceptable and inadmissible concepts." Jonathan Eburne, *Outsider Theory: Intellectual Histories of Unorthodox Ideas* (University of Minnesota Press, 2018). Disability scholars have also critiqued the category of outsider art; see, for example, Hiram A. Durán, "Disability Artistry Is Not Outsider Art," *Craig Newmark Graduate School of Journalism Capstone*, December 2019; Rachel E. Adams, "Bound and Unbounded" (Avidly, 2014), https://avidly.lareviewofbooks.org/2014/12/05/bound-and-unbounded/; and Jesse Prinz, "Against Outsider Art," *Journal of Social Philosophy*, vol. 48, no. 3, 2017: 250–72.

11. "Magnetism," *The Meteor* (first edition, section 1, 1872).

12. Benjamin Reiss, *Theaters of Madness: Insane Asylums and Nineteenth-Century American Culture* (University of Chicago Press, 2008), 26.

13. Reiss notes that the *Opal*, a literary journal written and edited by patients at the Utica (New York) State Lunatic Asylum in the mid-nineteenth century, was not received like other writing done by psychiatric patients; it was not held up by physicians as evidence of insanity. He suggests that this might reflect "its authors' successful internalization of appropriate modes of conduct and rhetoric." Reiss, *Theaters of Madness*, 34.

14. Alison Kafer, *Feminist, Queer, Crip* (Indiana University Press, 2013).

15. "The Meteor," *The Meteor* (eighth edition, section 21, 1881).

16. The regulation of time in asylums has been theorized in Michel Foucault's 1965 *Madness and Civilization* and Erving Goffman's 1961 *Asylums*, and we may again recall Fleetwood's remarks in *Marking Time* on how "penal time" influences art in prisons. Michel Foucault, *Madness and Civilization: A History of Insanity in the Age of Reason* (Pantheon Books, 1965). Erving Goffman, *Asylums: Essays on the Social Situation of Mental Patients and Other Inmates* (Aldine Transaction, 2007).

17. Patient File: "M.W." (Salem: Oregon State Hospital, Oregon State Archive, 1933).

18. Patient File: "W.R." (Salem: Oregon State Hospital, Oregon State Archive, 1920).

19. E. P. W. Packard, *The Prisoners' Hidden Life, or, Insane Asylums Unveiled: As Demonstrated by the Report of the Investigating Committee of the Legislature of Illinois, Together with Mrs. Packard's Coadjutors' Testimony* (A. B. Case, 1868).

20. Patient File: "P.N." (Salem: Oregon State Hospital, Oregon State Archive, 1928).

21. It is with some hesitation that I include unpublished writing from a patient's file, and there is a small amount of scholarship about ethics and privacy surrounding psychiatric records (Barbara Brookes and James Dunk, "Bureaucracy, Archive Files, and the Making of Knowledge," *Rethinking History*, vol. 22, no. 3 (September 2018): 281–88). While these files are older than seventy-five years and thus fall outside of HIPAA protections, I've chosen to use the pseudonym with which the writer has signed her writing rather than the name on her file, a decision I've made out of support for self-narration and self-identification. While I wish to work toward destigmatizing experiences of mental illness, I am also sensitive to the fact that this woman may not have wished to use her legal name and legacy for the same goal.

22. Patient File: "Neleh Eldré" (Salem: Oregon State Hospital, Oregon State Archive, 1928).

23. Patient File: "Neleh Eldré."

24. While a copy of the physical file is available in German at the Heidelberg University Hospital, I am indebted to Monika Ankele's English language summary of the file in "The Fabric of Seclusion: Textiles as Media of (Spatial) Interaction in Isolation Cells of Mental Hospitals," included in the 2020 volume *Material Cultures of Psychiatry.* Monika Ankele, "The Fabric of Seclusion: Textiles as Media of (Spatial) Interaction in Isolation Cells of Mental Hospitals," in *Material Cultures of Psychiatry*, edited by Monika Ankele and Benoît Majerus (Columbia University Press, 2020), 140–57, https://doi.org/10.14361/9783839447888-010. Kreisirrenanstalt Klingenmünster, patient file Katharina Detzel, copy of the file in the Collection Prinzhorn, Heidelberg University Hospital, original file in the Pfalzklinik Landeck Nr. 2554.

25. *50+ Insanely Creepy Vintage Photos That Will Probably Give You Nightmares*, https://www.bygonely.com/insanely-creepy-vintage-photos/, no date, accessed November 20, 2021.

26. The copied/pasted caption also claims that Detzel was murdered by the Nazis (not entirely verifiable, as far as I can tell) and that she wrote a play about

her treatment in the institution. The furthest back I can trace this caption is a Dutch blog from 2012 hosted on Blogspot and titled "formal: Contemporary art." Beatrice, "formal: Katharina Detzel," *formal* (blog), July 22, 2012, http://kuunst.blogspot.com/2012/07/katharina-detzel.html. The blog cites a Dutch magazine called *Deviant* from December 2006, NR 51, https://www.tijdschriftdeviant.nl/teksten/deviant51/05.pdf.

27. Ankele, "The Fabric of Seclusion," 150.

28. Tobin Siebers, *Disability Aesthetics* (University of Michigan Press, 2010), 2.

29. Bettina Brand-Claussen et al., *Beyond Reason: Art and Psychosis: Works from the Prinzhorn Collection* (Hayward Gallery, 1996), 9.

30. Cardinal, *Outsider Art*, 18.

31. Hans Prinzhorn, *Artistry of the Mentally Ill: A Contribution to the Psychology and Psychopathology of Configuration* (Springer Science and Business Media, 2013), 6.

32. Brand-Claussen et al., *Beyond Reason*.

33. Gail Hornstein, *Agnes's Jacket: A Psychologist's Search for the Meanings of Madness. Revised and Updated with a New Epilogue by the Author* (Routledge, 2017), xiii.

34. Hornstein, *Agnes's Jacket*, xvi.

35. Hornstein, *Agnes's Jacket*, 36.

36. Hornstein, *Agnes's Jacket*, 27.

CHAPTER 16

Privileged, Oppressed, and Liberated

Unearthing the Archives of a Multigenerational White Deaf Family

LEALA HOLCOMB, TARA HOLCOMB, AND THOMAS K. HOLCOMB

> Those who believe as I do, that the production of a defective race of human beings would be a great calamity to the world, will examine carefully the causes that lead to the intermarriages of the deaf with the object of applying a remedy.
>
> —Alexander Graham Bell, 1883

> Sign language, which many students tend to learn because of its flexibility, often relegates the deaf people who use it to a lower class and limits their work opportunities in life.
>
> —Addison Neal Smith, Director of the AGB Association for the Deaf, 1973

> When today's parents are told that their deaf children should or must learn ASL as part of a deaf culture, they increasingly respond that their children actually are part of a hearing culture—that of their families, friends and the world at large.
>
> —Meredith Sugar, Director of the AGB Association for the Deaf, 2016

Introduction

The quotations above illuminate the grand narrative on the perils of signing deaf people[1] and how they are cut off from "*hearing culture . . . and the world at large.*"[2] Experts on deafness, who are not deaf themselves, have been persistent across generations in spreading rhetoric equating deaf communities with a great calamity, a lower class, limitations, and isolation. Professionals such as doctors, speech-language pathologists, audiologists, and teachers systematically propagandize these audist[3] views while working with deaf children and their families, including ours.

Polarizing Perspectives

The archives reveal polarizing perspectives on what it takes for a deaf person to lead a fulfilling life and be a contributing member of the society. Professional journals depict the hardships that deaf people face. They struggle to achieve typical language milestones, interact with hearing people, access general education settings, obtain jobs, and maintain relationships with hearing people, especially family members. In a nutshell, they are isolated, impoverished, and marginalized in the eyes of professionals. The following articles in professional journals exemplify how negative perspectives are espoused about what it means to be deaf:

"Physiological Peculiarities of Deafness" in 1854[4]
"Should Hard of Hearing Marry" in 1919[5]
"Hearing Loss in the 21st Century and Beyond: A New Era of 35 Precision Diagnosis and Treatment Using Genomics" in 2023[6]

Practically all of these articles were authored by hearing individuals. By contrast, periodicals from deaf communities present vibrant lifestyles developed and fine-tuned by deaf people where they create their place in society on their terms. Here, rich community activities abound with athletic tournaments, religious functions, and literary societies, all of which are organized by deaf people themselves. Some of these are centered within deaf communities, and others are aligned within the larger society populated by nonsigners. The following articles illustrate the realities of deaf people's lives throughout the generations from their perspectives:

"Deaf Mutes Give Readings Before Literary Society" in 1917[7]
"Humor among the Deaf" in 1969[8]
"Youth Leadership Camp Celebrates Its 30th Anniversary" in 1998[9]
"Deaf Creators and Influencers to Support" in 2021[10]

Deaf Archives

While professional journals have a long history and are well preserved, as evidenced by the oldest professional journal, *American Annals of the Deaf*, first released in 1847, deaf periodicals are not as easily accessible due to several factors. Most of these publications were homegrown, made possible by volunteers and leaders within deaf communities. Because they were of community origins, they were often stored at the homes of deaf club leaders and officers, typically in basements, and were frequently lost or even discarded over the years. This is likely because most offspring of deaf people are not deaf and do not realize the value in preserving these artifacts. Additional challenges include the limited number of deaf scholars who could put together manuscripts for public perusal. There is also the issue of not having the technology to preserve artifacts in American Sign Language (ASL) until recently. Interestingly, the significant investment made by the National Association of the Deaf from 1910 through 1920 to video-record deaf people's narratives in ASL indicates deaf people's awareness of the need to preserve their cultural and linguistic heritage through visual media.[11]

Between the professional journals and the homemade releases are the publications put out by the state-sponsored schools for the deaf.[12] These publications include official banners by the schools highlighting their efforts in preparing their graduates to become contributing members of society. This was especially important as these schools were publicly funded and therefore accountable to the taxpayers. Another type of publication by these state schools was annual yearbook productions produced by high school students under staff supervision. These yearbooks often spotlighted the curriculum designed to prepare deaf students for employment (e.g., vocational training) or college. Ordinary scholastic activities typical of any educational settings such as interscholastic athletic competitions, homecoming games, and formal dances were also featured. These publications are easily mined as they are typically well preserved in a school's archival collections. Students' records are also informative as they often contain information related to the age of onset and etiologies of their deafness as well as their academic performance. It is also noteworthy that information about hearing levels is rarely included in the membership roster of deaf organizations as they are of no interest to deaf people per the norms of Deaf culture in not prioritizing or elevating hearing status.[13]

Deaf Family Archives

We engage with Michelle Caswell, Alda Allina Migoni, Noah Geraci, and Marika Cifor's[14] concept of symbolic annihilation to illustrate how minoritized communities perceive the absence or misrepresentation of their experiences in archival collection policies, in descriptive tools, and within collections themselves. Caswell et al. encourage us "to conceive of and build a world in which communities that have historically been and are currently being marginalized due to white supremacy, patriarchy, capitalism, gender binaries, colonialism and ableism are fully empowered to represent their past, construct their present and envision their futures as forms of liberation." This chapter presents counternarratives that challenge the typical assumptions or representations of deaf people in professional journals, illuminating the actual lived experiences of deaf individuals from our own perspectives. Through these counternarratives, we reclaim the power to represent our past, construct our present, and envision our future, showcasing how we experience privilege, oppression, and liberation as white deaf people.

Here, we take the opportunity to mine our family archives as a five-generation deaf family. Specifically, our family consists of a single lineage of great-grandparents, grandparents, parents, children, and grandchildren, most of whom are deaf or hard of hearing. Beyond this single lineage are relatives such as aunts, uncles, and cousins who are hearing, many of whom could sign. Our family archives include unpublished autobiographies, published books, newspaper clippings from mainstream publications, deaf periodicals, school yearbooks, family photo collections, family videotapes, and professionally made videos. Anna Woodham and her coauthors[15] explain that people "are increasingly interested in understanding 'behind the scenes' heritage" and that "growth in popularity of family history . . . ha[s] arguably given personal family histories a new significance." Through our family archives, we can enable the larger society to better understand what we see as valuable to ourselves as deaf individuals, to our multigenerational deaf family, and to our deaf communities. As we mined our family archives, we attempted to explore the following questions:

> What were the lived experiences of our white deaf family members in the United States across five generations?
>
> How did historical events impact members of our deaf family and contribute to our experiences of privilege, oppression, and liberation?
>
> What does inclusion mean to the deaf members of our family?
>
> What is the significance of analyzing deaf family archives and what are the challenges in the archival process?

In the subsequent sections, we present our findings, beginning with the first generation of deaf members in our family from 1890 and concluding with the deaf children in the current generation.

The First Generation (1890–1920)

Samuel D. Stakley (1892–1970)

Sam and his younger sister, Eulalia, were born deaf to hearing parents in Pennsylvania. A local church group close to the farm where Sam's father worked helped send both deaf children to an exclusive, private oral program ten hours' drive from home. While Sam and Eulalia were away for seven years, their parents adopted Elizabeth to have a "perfect child who could hear."[16]

After Sam and Eulalia returned home, their parents were disappointed that both children still could not speak well enough to communicate with practically anyone. Eventually, they learned about the Western Pennsylvania

School for the Deaf (WPSD)[17] in Pittsburgh, an hour away, and enrolled both children there.[18] At that time, two different educational systems existed for deaf students in the United States—private oral schools where signing was completely banned and state schools where signing was allowed only with older deaf students after every attempt had been made to develop their speech during the elementary years.

When the United States entered the First World War in 1917, many non-disabled men joined the military. During this time, manufacturing companies including the rubber industries in Ohio[19] aggressively recruited white deaf people but did not hire Black people.[20] As white deaf people flocked to Akron, deaf communities there flourished, with deaf-owned co-op stores, semi-pro football teams, recreational clubs, and more.[21] Seeing white deaf people thriving in Akron on their own terms, hearing people there "accepted the deaf as normal people and [did] not look on them as abnormal as was a common practice in many places."[22] Learning about job opportunities in Akron, Sam and both of his sisters moved there to work for the Goodyear Company. Sam's youngest hearing sister, Elizabeth, also became proficient in signed language through her involvement in deaf communities. In 1923, Sam married Hazel Pike, a highly social deaf woman.

Without legal protections in place for disabled employees, Sam and other deaf workers had to prove their worth by being hardworking, productive, and loyal workers. As such, their contributions to the company were so highly regarded that in 1918 there was a special issue in the monthly newsletter about skilled deaf employees.[23] During the Great Depression, Sam's appreciation of his job deepened as "often he was lucky to work at least one day a week."[24] He was one of the first people to own a car and taught his hearing coworkers and neighbors how to drive due to his continued employment.[25]

In his older years, with white hair and full beard, he received many requests to play the role of Santa Claus for children at public events.[26] At his funeral, the reverend remarked: "The Stakley house is always open to friends. Without exception when I have been there, friends have dropped in for a moment, coming and going in a spirit of friendship."[27] In contrast to the messages he received while growing up, finding deaf communities and learning signed language opened up his world in ways that he did not expect.

Hazel Pike (Stakley) (1896–1977)

Hazel's hearing mother gave birth to thirteen children, of whom three were deaf. All three deaf children attended the North Carolina School for the Deaf (NCSD) in Morganton at a young age and stayed in the dorms. NCSD, like all other state deaf schools, emphasized oral approaches without the use of signed language with younger students in the classroom. Hazel, like most of her peers, did not develop intelligible speech. Hazel cherished the dorm life where she could freely sign and have meaningful interactions with her deaf peers. After graduating in 1922, Hazel was able to attend Gallaudet College because she was white; Black deaf students were denied entrance between 1905 and 1950.[28] World War I was going on during Hazel's time there, and she had "fun passing notes back and forth with the homesick soldiers"[29] who camped out on campus.

After her time at Gallaudet College, Hazel migrated to Akron and was hired to work at Goodyear, where she met and married Sam. During the Great Depression, women faced pressure to quit working so that unemployed men with families could have their jobs. Her daughter Mabs wrote, "Many women refused, but my mother resigned."[30] Over this period, Hazel and Sam became amateur entertainers and magicians, responding to great demand for shows from the public. The couple sewed their own clothes, built their own stage, and traveled to different states to perform.[31] They were especially renowned for their artistic renditions of Yankee Doodle songs, among others delivered in signed language.

Throughout her life, Hazel was known as someone who "would always welcome anyone to her house, teaching everyone to sign."[32] To supplement the family's income, she ran a boarding house and expected hearing boarders to be included in the household by using their hands to communicate. During this time, Hazel and Sam gave birth to Mabs (deaf) and Lois May (hearing), creating a second generation of deaf people in our family. Hazel and Sam recalled multiple occasions in which well-meaning hearing people gave them the name of a new church with the promise that their children would be cured of deafness if only they would attend.[33] They largely rejected this audist view, however, and celebrated the existence of deaf children like Mabs and hearing children like Lois May who could sign.[34]

The Second Generation (1920–1950)

Majoriebell (Mabs) Stakley Holcomb (1924–2014)

Like Hazel, Mabs began her schooling as a residential student at age six, but at the Ohio School for the Deaf in Columbus, several hours south of Akron. Mabs's teachers spent hours daily teaching her to speak and lipread, with limited results: "We were expected to pronounce correctly the name of each object she pulled out of the basket."[35] Mabs was notorious for teaching deaf peers from hearing families how to sign. She said, "We had to secretly sign in the bathroom, behind the teacher's back, or under the table."[36] To prevent Mabs from signing in class, the teachers told her to "stop flapping your arms like a windmill" and to "sit on your hands."[37] Despite having not developed any usable hearing or speech skills, Mabs, like Hazel, was able to read and write very well due to early access to signed language. On the basis of Mabs's high literacy skills, the teachers told her: "You are hard of hearing, not deaf, because you are not dumb."[38]

In spite of blatant audism by hearing staff, Mabs, like Hazel, deeply valued her experience at school, as she bonded with her deaf peers and had a rich and fully accessible social life in the dorm. She delighted in participating in extracurricular activities such as cheerleading, Girl Scouts, and theater.[39] Mabs and her friends frequented museums and theaters in the afternoons and on weekends. Her younger hearing sister, Lois, often expressed disappointment that she could not attend and enjoy the dorm experience even though she could sign just as well as her sister and friends. Mabs's close relationship with Lois contributed to her "penetrating insights as to how communication with hearing people could be encouraged and developed to the fullest."[40]

Mabs continued her intellectual pursuits at Gallaudet College from 1943 to 1947, where she met her future husband, Roy.[41] After graduating with college degrees, they were not allowed to work with young deaf children because they were deaf and used signed language. However, they managed to secure teaching jobs at the secondary level in various states over the years. Along the way, they befriended hearing neighbors, attended local deaf clubs, visited community museums and arts, and played bridge card games with their deaf and hearing colleagues. They often wrote articles in school papers about their out-of-state trips and social activities, hoping to inspire other deaf and hearing people to lead larger lives.[42]

It was not always smooth sailing for deaf people at that time. Their lives were indeed harder without disability rights laws in place. When Mabs and Roy enrolled in a master's program at the University of Tennessee in Knoxville to study Special Education, there were no support services. They managed to pass their classes by copying their hearing classmates' notes, reading textbooks carefully, and frequently quizzing each other to prepare for tests. During this period, they became the parents of two deaf children, Sam and Tom, representing the third generation of deaf people in the family. After graduating, the family moved to Indianapolis, where the deaf school there was reputed to be the best in the nation although signing was still not allowed with young deaf children.[43]

Aligning with the larger white feminist movement, Mabs became a lifelong activist for women's rights. She insisted that women had the right to work, own a bank account, and not be expected to be solely responsible for household chores.[44] She wrote, "I have been on lecture tours proclaiming that deaf women have always done well, but need to be recognized for their endeavors."[45] She coauthored a book titled *Deaf Women: A Parade Through the Decades* and helped found an organization called Deaf Women United to promote expanded opportunities and leadership among deaf women.[46] While

Mabs was outspoken against sexism, there was nothing in our archives about the experiences of people of color in the United States.

Mabs and Roy finally settled in Fremont, California in 1977. Mabs taught at a local college until her forced retirement in 1985 due to partial paralysis from brain surgery to remove a tumor.[47] She moved into an assisted living facility, where she was known for unapologetically roaming throughout the building on her motorized wheelchair. The hearing residents often shared their delight in chatting with her through paper and pen, and visitors seemed to always occupy her living room. Mabs died in 2014.

Roy K. Holcomb (1923–1998)

In contrast to Mabs's experience, Roy struggled to feel included in his community, as he was the only hard of hearing person in his family and his entire town. He was the eldest of eight children in Alexander, a poverty-stricken community in Texas, where his hearing parents worked side by side pulling cotton in the fields.[48] Roy was able to acquire speech because he was born with hearing, but he struggled in public school as his hearing deteriorated over the years.

At age nine, his parents discovered the Texas School for the Deaf (TSD) in Austin and immediately sent him there. For the first time, Roy had his own bed and three hot meals each day in the dorm. Like most deaf students everywhere, he learned signed language from his deaf peers, as none of his teachers in the elementary department signed. He wrote in his unpublished autobiography:

> All children caught using sign language instead of their speech were given a demerit for every sign that they were caught giving. For every sign given, they had to sit on a long bench after school for one hour in order to have it removed from their records.[49]

At TSD, Roy quickly became a poster child because he could speak well and was showcased to visitors and prospective families. Roy was appalled by the shameless audism of hearing staff at the school:

> I was born with some hearing and I was able to speak . . . . What people must understand is that the person who is born totally deaf has a more difficult time learning language and speaking . . . . They have tried to make deaf people imitations of hearing people . . . . They said "deaf people you talk or you don't communicate at all."

After TSD, Roy went to Gallaudet College and worked every weekend in Washington, DC and summers in resort communities at Lake Placid so that he could send money home to support his hearing family.[50] He repeatedly said attending a residential deaf school and then Gallaudet were the best things that had happened to him, as they allowed him to escape poverty.

Even though Roy had considerable privileges as a white Christian male who could hear and speak relatively well, he still faced audism. For example, Roy had his teaching certificate formally revoked by the state of California on the grounds of not having prerequisite normal hearing.[51] Not receiving any offer to move up from a teaching post to an administrative position for many years was another indication of the unjust barriers for aspiring deaf leaders. Undeterred, Roy went on to earn one master's degree after another. It took him four master's degrees from three different universities[52] and unwavering persistence before he became one of the first deaf administrators in the nation. None of the deaf schools were willing to offer him an administrative position, and only one public elementary school with a small deaf program in California did.

Unlike in pre-1880 days when signing deaf teachers and leaders were involved in establishing and operating deaf schools, throughout much of the twentieth century hearing professionals were dead set against deaf individuals becoming administrators. They were concerned that the use of signed language would be promoted with young deaf children, and indeed, they were right. As Roy rose up in the ranks, he was outspoken about the importance of signed language for deaf children's language and literacy development and overall well-being.[53] He believed all deaf children deserved the kind of life that his wife, Mabs, had with her signing family, rather than his own and his peers' traumatic experiences with families and teachers who refused to use their hands to communicate.

In 1964, Roy's observations were validated by Congress, which concluded in a federal study on the state of deaf education that "oralism is a dismal failure."[54] Roy spent the rest of his career working as an administrator in several states, leading institutional reforms to liberate deaf children from policies that restricted them to surviving solely through oral means.[55] In the wake of the nationwide impact of his work, Roy became known as the "Father of Total Communication."[56] Total Communication was defined as embracing any and every type of method to communicate effectively with deaf children.[57] It was through this argument that Roy successfully persuaded some hearing professionals to break free from rigid oral-only approaches.

In the meantime, ASL was formally recognized as a bona fide language by linguists in the early 1960s, and the Registry of Interpreters for the Deaf was established in 1964. In mainstream settings, Roy hired ASL/English interpreters to work in the classrooms and made free signing classes available to everyone to increase the inclusivity of the environment. Yet, during these times, many hearing professionals contested Roy's pro-signing model by continuing to insist that ASL had no place in deaf children's environment.[58] They were relentless in their beliefs that oral-only approaches were the best route for deaf children to be included in society.[59] As a result, two opposing philosophies remained in place: one espousing the oral-only methods and the other embracing Total Communication. Unfortunately, Roy's career was cut short due to Parkinson's disease, leading to his death in 1998.

The Third Generation (1950–1980)

Thomas (Tom) K. Holcomb (1959–present)

While their deaf children were growing up in Indianapolis, Mabs and Roy made sure that they were part of the neighborhood by providing signing classes in the garage with promises of ice cream and fun games for hearing neighbors.[60] Mabs wrote, "Sam and Tom would ride their bicycles around the neighborhood and bring us the news of what was happening: houses being remodeled, garage sales, and car accidents."[61] Tom has recollections of these positive experiences with hearing neighbors while he was growing up.

While Tom could sign freely at home and with his neighbors, he was restricted to communicating orally in the classroom at the Indiana School for the Deaf due to anti-signing policies. Similar to the roles that Hazel and Mabs had in teaching ASL at their deaf schools, Tom also introduced ASL to many of his deaf peers. Consequently, Tom got his "hands slapped a lot," while Sam did not because he attended classes with older children in a different building where signing was allowed.[62]

When Roy finally secured his first administrative job at a public school in California in 1968, the whole family moved west. The rubella epidemic had caused a jump in the number of babies being born deaf, leading the California School for the Deaf in Riverside to reject new students due to full capacity.[63] Tom ended up attending the public school, where he was a beneficiary of Roy's progressive experiments to bring ASL to mainstream settings. Tom and other deaf students were mainstreamed into some hearing classes with interpreters. Some hearing students who had benefited from instruction in ASL in classes such as math were reverse mainstreamed into deaf classes. This new model garnered a lot of media attention as well as visitors from all over the world.[64]

In 1973 Roy accepted a job offer in Delaware and relocated the family to the East Coast. The local schools remained adamant about having deaf students sit in the front row and exclusively lipread, calling it the best inclusion model. For this reason, Mabs and Roy decided to send Tom to the Model Secondary School for the Deaf (MSSD), a residential school in Washington, DC where ASL was embraced. Tom found that the quality of day-to-day access and learning at MSSD significantly surpassed that of his previous public school, where he relied on interpreters and peers and teachers who were novice signers.

Similar to the positive experiences that Hazel and Mabs had in the North Carolina School for the Deaf dorms, Tom became very active in extracurricular activities, becoming president of the student body government. He played tennis against students from hearing schools. He was also involved in school plays and once played the role of the Artful Dodger in the musical *Oliver*.[65] In *Oliver*, there was a collaboration with hearing students from a local public school's drama club who sang the songs off stage while the deaf students signed on stage.

Tom attended Gallaudet University to continue enjoying a fully accessible program with signing professors and peers, and then later earned a doctorate in curriculum and instruction from the University of Rochester using interpreters. It was in the thriving deaf communities in Rochester that Tom met a deaf woman, Katherine, and they had three deaf children, Tara, Leala, and Cary. A newspaper posted an interview with Tom when he was thirty years old in which he described what it was like being deaf:

> Yes, we're different, but that's not making us less. We have a beautiful community, culture and language, so in a sense we are doubly blessed with two languages and two communities that we can take advantage of. Different life, yes. Hard life, no. It is a fact of life that I'm deaf and if I could change, hearing would not be on top of my list.

When the journalist asked what would be on top of the list, Tom responded, "Taller. I've always regretted not being 6-foot just like my father and being a basketball star."[66]

Tom married twice, first to Katherine, and then to Michele, a hearing daughter of deaf parents. Tom and Michele had a hard of hearing child, Troy. To their pride and joy, these four children were the fourth generation of deaf lineage in the family. Tom spent the rest of his career as a college professor, teaching and doing scholarly work on inclusive practices that are deaf-centered.

To this day, the majority of inclusion efforts in education continue to focus on having deaf children interact only with hearing children, and only through lipreading, hearing, and speaking.[67]

Katherine Leatrice Greene (January 27, 1956)

Katherine and her deaf brother, Tracy, were born into a hearing nonsigning family that focused on training them to hear and speak. They attended a private oral school for deaf children in Atlanta, Georgia from 1961 to 1967 where signing was prohibited at all times. An audiologist report from 1961 stated, "Kathy does not like to use her personal hearing-aid . . . . My impression is that this is basically a problem of adjustment to her hearing-aid, rather than any flaw in the instrument itself."[68] Even though Katherine was in speech therapy during all school hours, her speech was comprehensible only to her mother and not anyone else—including her own father. Yet, Katherine, like many of her deaf peers, was led to believe that she could hear and speak well enough, as she was constantly praised for her efforts. She faced reality when she ordered burgers and fries at a fast-food restaurant only to realize the cashier could not understand her.

When Katherine was sixteen years old, her brother by chance bumped into some signing deaf people at a bowling alley and befriended a deaf teenager. Tracy shared his excitement with Katherine, and without their parents' knowledge, they began sneaking out to interact with their new deaf friends.[69] After learning ASL, Katherine realized how hard she had been working to communicate with hearing people and how much she had missed out. She chose to enroll at the Rochester Institute of Technology, where the National Technical Institute of the Deaf (NTID) was housed.[70] For the first time, she experienced direct access in some of her classes where teachers and peers signed for themselves. In other classes, Katherine was able to benefit from interpreters. Katherine signed in a video, "My parents believed speech would help me access society, but they were wrong. ASL opened up my world."[71]

After Katherine met Tom and had given birth to deaf children, they found it necessary to educate people over and over again that having deaf children does not mean those children would have the difficult childhood painted by hearing professionals. For example, when Tara was born, her parents received a letter from an audiologist providing her test results and opening with "*Unfortunately*, Tara has a hearing loss."[72] This triggered painful memories for Katherine of hearing professionals shaping her hearing parents' negative outlook on deafness and insisting on the need to focus solely on speech. In protest, Katherine sent the letter back to the audiologist and asked her to rewrite it without any audist language.

In 1991, Katherine and Tom moved to Fremont, California to be closer to Mabs and Roy in their declining health. This was around the same time that the Americans with Disabilities Act (ADA) was passed. Deaf communities now had greater access than ever to public and private sectors through interpreters and captioning. However, with the passage of the Individuals with Disabilities Education Act (IDEA) in 1975 and its reauthorization in 1990, hearing professionals also had greater systemic support to steer deaf children into attending public schools with hearing peers based on their inclusion model. Consequently, these children were often the only deaf person in the whole school. While accommodations such as the frequency modulation (FM) system, Computer Assisted Real-Time Translation (CART) services, and interpreters were increasingly available, these accommodations often proved to be inadequate in preventing language deprivation, academic underachievement, trauma, low self-esteem, and isolation among deaf students.[73]

In the first decade of the twenty-first century, the deaf education system had evolved to include three main educational philosophies that differed substantially from one another: (1) spoken English only; (2) Total Communication, which had been misapplied by hearing professionals to primarily using spoken English with sign support; and (3) ASL/English bilingualism, in which proficiency in both ASL and written English were expected from all deaf students. While some deaf schools were increasing deaf leadership in their administration and implementing ASL/English bilingualism, most mainstream schools primarily used spoken English with sign support and called this approach Total Communication. In environments that claimed to practice Total Communication, many deaf children were once again left behind and struggled to develop or access spoken language.[74] Roy's original premise was to convince hearing professionals and families of the value of providing access to communication and education vis-à-vis ASL for every deaf child. Our family felt Roy's ideation of Total Communication was hijacked by hearing professionals to fit their beliefs regarding the superiority of speech.[75]

When reflecting on school placement, Katherine and Tom shared similar feelings to Roy when he described the pitfalls of public schools when inclusion efforts were led by hearing professionals:

> In the past many deaf people have been hurt by mainstreaming, often to the extent that the term "mainstream" was a dirty word. Much harm is being done in schools where beautiful stories are told on mainstreaming by those in charge but where the end results are miserable . . . . Mainstreaming should not be attempted merely for the sake of mainstreaming . . . .[76]

For these reasons, Katherine and Tom decided to enroll all three children in an ASL/English bilingual school, the California School for the Deaf, Fremont (CSDF). CSDF was reputed to provide some of the most accessible and rigorous academic instruction in the nation, with at least 50 percent of staff members being deaf themselves.

After spending ten years as a stay-at-home mom, Katherine got her master's degree in deaf education from San Jose State University, which had some signing professors and also provided interpreters for nonsigning professors. Throughout her twenty years of work as an elementary school teacher and librarian at CSDF, Katherine was fierce in her passion about providing deaf students with full access to language through ASL.

The Fourth Generation (1980–2010)

Leala Holcomb (1987)

Leala represents the fourth generation of deaf people in our family, which includes Tara, Leala, Cary, and Troy. Leala identifies as nonbinary (not identifying as a woman or a man) and uses gender neutral pronouns (they/them/

theirs). When Leala was young, Tom and Katherine used ASL rhyme and rhythm, engaged in language play, and brought books to life through storytelling.[77] A newspaper article in 1989 noted the rich interactions between two-year-old Leala and their older sibling and other hearing peers: "[T]hey sign to each other, their hands and arms moving quickly. Even Leala signs about 1,000 words . . . and will go up to hearing children in the store and start signing . . . ."[78]

In the 1990s, Leala and their siblings became the first generation in the family to benefit from direct communication with their teachers and peers through ASL starting in preschool.[79] Their school, CSDF, championed the belief that deaf students could become proficient in both ASL and English and fully access the general education curriculum. Deaf students were empowered to decide whether to pursue speech therapy or use hearing aids. Leala opted for hearing aids and speech classes, while their siblings chose not to. Thanks to CSDF's diverse deaf role models—deaf individuals who varied in their use of hearing aids and speech—none of the siblings felt inferior about their skills, choices, or preferences.

Growing up, Leala had rich social experiences that were common to deaf students attending deaf schools. Leala played on hearing and deaf sport teams, participated in after-school organizations, and was the homecoming royalty. They also enjoyed attending plays that Tom directed about complex issues in society.[80] One dealt with deaf people's real experiences with AIDS. Another explored the dynamics of hearing/deaf relationships through humor. At ten years old, Leala joined Tom on a work trip to Japan where they interacted with Japanese deaf people using Japanese Sign Language. Leala sent a fax message to their mother: "We went to a Deaf Japan school. I joined the class!"[81] As a high school senior, Leala went to Greece as part of their international studies class and interacted with local deaf Greeks and learned their signs.[82] Inspired by these adventures, Leala chose to major in International Education at Gallaudet in 2005 and took three years of Spanish courses.

Traveling and meeting deaf people from all over the world was, and continues to be, a popular activity for deaf college graduates who have the privilege to do so. Leala did the same after graduating from Gallaudet, hitchhiking from Mexico to Argentina for over a year, visiting deaf clubs and schools along the way. They communicated with local hearing people in written Spanish and with local deaf people using gestures and local signs. Through networks with deaf people globally, Leala was eventually invited to work in several countries, including Vietnam, Hong Kong, Morocco, the Philippines, Malawi, and Rwanda, to boost local deaf perspectives on improving deaf education. Leala found that, similar to the situation in the United States, inclusion practices as implemented by hearing professionals focused on speech therapy and assimilation, which made accessing language, communication, and academic subjects very difficult for deaf students.

In 2011, Leala pursued a master's degree through a program that was entirely online, while teaching deaf preschoolers. Leala became fascinated with the practice of signed rhyming activities to support language development, leading them to obtain a doctoral degree in education from the University of Tennessee. Leala's oldest sibling, Tara, obtained a doctorate in clinical psychology with a focus on childhood trauma among deaf individuals due to linguistic and communication neglect. Leala's younger sibling, Cary, is a behavioral support staff person working with deaf students. Leala's youngest sibling, Troy, is currently in college.

Leala is partnered with a hearing person, Damon, who has two children (one deaf and one hearing) from a previous marriage. When ASL became a widely popular foreign language course offered in high schools in the 1990s, Damon learned the language for fun and ended up majoring in ASL and theater in college. Interestingly, ASL is now the third most studied language in the United States.[83] Tara and Chad, a deaf man from a hearing family who embraced signed language, are raising three deaf children together, continuing the unbroken lineage of five generations in our deaf family.

The Fifth Generation (2010–2024)

Catie Holcomb (2014)

Catie[84] represents the fifth generation, as she is the youngest child of all the siblings and cousins. In 1990s, the Food and Drug Administration approved cochlear implants to be surgically implanted in young deaf children, leading the majority of parents to elect this procedure for their deaf children.[85] An ongoing apocryphal narrative spread by hearing professionals concerns the outright rejection of cochlear implants by deaf communities.[86] While this was true in the 1970s and '80s when cochlear implants were experimental and resulted in additional disabilities, complications, or trauma in some deaf children, the procedure has become progressively safer and thus has greater acceptance today.[87] Regardless of whether parents choose to implant their children or not, there is a shared consensus that ASL plays an important role in preventing language deprivation and broadening the child's connections to deaf communities and the wider world.[88]

Tara and Chad decided not to implant their children for several reasons. They knew the surgery itself was not without risk and that this medical procedure must be followed by lengthy and intensive therapy for listening and speech development, with highly variable outcomes. Because both of them had overall fulfilling lives without relying on hearing and speech, it was not their priority to invest in exhaustive therapy. They knew their deaf children would be able to thrive with their access to ASL, a robust bilingual deaf school, and multilingual/multimodal role models from diverse backgrounds. While Catie's schoolmates all signed, they varied widely in their use of hearing aids, cochlear implants, and spoken language. Similar to Leala's experience growing up, whether anyone could hear or speak was rarely a topic of discussion, and these variables were never used to measure success in school or life. Catie herself enjoys wearing hearing aids and has chosen to attend speech classes at an ASL/English bilingual deaf school. She tests her parents' lipreading skills by speaking English phrases she learned in speech class, often in jest.

Yet, when Catie did not "pass" the initial hearing screening at her birth, medical professionals gave Tara and Chad packets of information about cochlear implants and oral-only education as the best solution for all the problems associated with deafness. Among several communication choices, ASL was presented as one option, with the implication that signing deaf communities were exotic, small, and isolated from mainstream society. It appeared as if her parents had to choose one for Catie—speaking or signing, deaf world or hearing world. Those messages befuddled Tara and Chad, as they were in direct contrast with their lived experiences as deaf individuals who have always enjoyed being part of both deaf and hearing communities. Nonetheless, they were able to largely ignore those systemic-driven audist messages as they intentionally chose to live in a community where the local early intervention center focused on full access to language and healthy identity formation through ASL and English.

At present, Catie's experience is similar to Leala's in that she is thriving at the deaf school and developing proficiency in both ASL and English. She adores sports, and participates in city leagues in flag football, basketball, and baseball with deaf and hearing peers. She especially enjoys meeting new children at the playground, the pool, and sporting events, easily making new best friends, hearing or deaf, along the way. She communicates with nonsigning children via various means: lipreading, mouthing words, writing, texting, reading, signing, and gesturing, in flexible ways that reflect her full access to languages multimodally. This is not to deny those painful moments where she is met with cruelty or ignorance by other, hearing children, but to recognize her ability to assert herself and connect with peers who value her identity as a deaf child.

Catie, too, is part of the generation who grew up during the COVID-19 pandemic. With long periods of at-home quarantine with her two working parents, she spent more hours than Tara and Chad would admit on online games. While playing, she chats with her hearing and deaf peers in ASL in video calls and in English through game chat boxes. One day she signed to Tara, to her surprise, "I know some words in Spanish like 'Hola' [hello], 'Soy

Catie' [I am Catie], and 'Soy de EU' [I am from the United States]."[89] Catie had learned those Spanish phrases from other Spanish-speaking children in game chat boxes. Although Catie enjoys reading books and can comfortably write sentences in English, she often argues with her mother that "writing in ASL word order is far better!" and that she "doesn't care if they think it is wrong" because her online hearing friends understand her just fine. Due to the monolingual bias in the United States, Catie's freedom in using multiple languages in various contexts is often perceived as ASL impairing English development; this perception, unfortunately, has been used as a tool to further reinforce anti-signing efforts. Fortunately, Catie has no qualms about asserting her place in the world as a deaf multilingual child with the expectation to be included, respected, and connected in all aspects of her life.

Discussion

In this section, we reflect on our research findings in response to our research questions. We also share insights from our experiences with archival processes as deaf family members who advocate for the rights of deaf people to exist on our own terms in society. Our research questions were as follows:

What were the lived experiences of our white deaf family members in the United States across five generations?
How did historical events impact members of our deaf family and contribute to our experiences of privilege, oppression, and liberation?
What does inclusion mean to the deaf members of our family?
What is the significance of analyzing deaf family archives and what are the challenges in the archival process?

We are three deaf family members, not trained archivists or professional historians. Our interest lies in the lived experiences of our white deaf family members in the United States across five generations and understanding how historical events have shaped our experiences of privilege, oppression, and liberation. We sought to understand how deaf people, especially in our family, define inclusion and how these perceptions differ from those of hearing people. To find answers, we relied on informal, family-based archival work of signed and written artifacts that we kept within our households. This process deepened our understanding of the archival processes involving public and private heritage, including its challenges and limitations as well as its value in preserving deaf people's history, culture, and language. While the counternarratives presented here are centered on the experiences of one white deaf family spanning five generations, these stories may resonate with those of others in deaf communities, as evidenced by artifacts found in the broader literature produced by deaf people.[90]

Inclusion on Whose Terms?

Exploring the experiences of a multigenerational deaf family through family archives offers an insider perspective on the persistent dominance of hearing norms as well as the ways in which deaf people have resisted. Through these family archives, we found that social and educational solutions developed by hearing professionals, often touted as inclusive practices for deaf children, tend to more closely resemble assimilation. These assimilation efforts are designed to make deaf children conform to the behaviors, thoughts, and speech patterns of the dominant group,[91] operating under the false premise that reliance on signed language leads to isolation from hearing culture and the broader world.[92]

Our family archives provide compelling evidence to the contrary, showing that deaf individuals do not regard mimicking or being surrounded exclusively by hearing people as the ultimate goal of inclusion. As a deaf family, our intentional use of family artifacts to counter the negativity associated with the deaf experience addresses the fundamental question of the purpose and value of a "family archive" as discussed by Woodham et al.[93] This approach has symbolic significance and legitimates the ongoing advocacy efforts of deaf communities. In essence, it affirms our existence, values, and beliefs as part of a collective goal embraced by many deaf people.

According to our family archives, deaf communities benefit from spaces tailored to their social, cultural, and linguistic needs, grounded in shared identities and experiences. Despite society's increasing acceptance of and respect toward minoritized groups, these spaces remain indispensable and should not be disregarded or dismantled. The cultures, languages, arts, and experiences that thrive within these spaces should be perceived and understood as valuable contributions to the strength and beauty of society's fabric, rather than as existing separately in isolation.

Family and Community Archival Processes

Archival work originating from minoritized communities often arises in response to the painful realities of erasure or misrepresentation in society, a concept known as symbolic annihilation.[94] Signing deaf people rarely see our experiences represented in a positive light in professional journals or media. In the dark clouds of symbolic annihilation, the autonomy and authenticity of family- and community-driven archival processes offer a silver lining for us as a deaf family. This approach allowed us to deliberate on the deaf-centered values that have been passed down in our family since the 1890s. We reflected on our collective memories while examining artifacts together, constructing narratives that resonated with our self-perceptions and experiences as deaf individuals. This advantage aligns with the rising interest in family- and community-based archives that operate independently of professional archivists, emphasizing more personalized and direct control over historical narratives.[95]

For example, artifacts in our family records indicate that the use of ASL, involvement in deaf communities, and active participation in deaf-led events have not isolated deaf people. For our multigenerational deaf family, these activities have enriched our lives and strengthened our confidence, pride, identity, purpose, and sense of belonging as multilingual and multicultural individuals. Our archives have repeatedly highlighted how deaf communities have become a source of healing and respite for many deaf individuals, including some members within our family who were raised by hearing parents opposed to the idea of signed language.

Yet, aspects of deaf people's lives such as ASL, deaf communities, and deaf cultural events are undervalued by society due to audism, leading to their neglect in preservation efforts. Official archives like the census or government documents can validate the existence of specific groups by preserving artifacts that show the value of their lives. However, there is a scarcity of archives that document the experiences of multigenerational deaf families. For instance, the U.S. census does not even collect information about ASL, rendering our family's language invisible in governmental records. The exclusion of our language, culture, and contributions to society from official archives can reinforce persistent narratives that paint signing deaf individuals as isolated from society and burdened with hardships. By maintaining and sharing collections that showcase signing deaf individuals leading fulfilling lives, we address the systemic erasure of our existence and affirm our place in society as active participants.

Challenges of Archival Work When the Medium of Language Is Signed

Reflecting on the barriers we have encountered in archival work, we recognize challenges related to ASL artifacts, as only recently has it become feasible to access them through video mediums. Before the 1960s, artifacts were primarily available through printed English or photographs—methods that are not the most effective or authentic means of capturing the deaf experience. Nonetheless, deaf individuals in our family who developed strong skills in both ASL and English managed to produce valuable written records. Additionally, extensive photo collections have yielded useful data for analyzing the earliest years of our deaf family.

As technology advanced, our family members leveraged available tools to document family gatherings, dinners, and birthdays. In the 1960s, Roy and Mabs began using the emerging technology of 8mm recording to capture family events. Due to the high cost of developing film at the time, the number of available films for review was limited. By the 1980s, videotaping became more affordable and accessible, allowing Tom and Katherine to record numerous family activities on VHS tapes. Over time, VHS tapes became outdated, necessitating their transfer to DVDs. Eventually, DVDs also became obsolete, prompting the digitization of some videos for archival purposes, with storage shifting to the cloud for easier access.

These processes were tedious, challenging, and expensive. Interestingly, research shows that digital data like videos are often accessed less and used less in the act of remembering the past compared to physical objects, due to their perceived instability and inconvenience.[96] We found that viewing and locating specific quotations in videos was difficult due to the lack of textual searchability inherent in video formats. The most useful videos were those previously edited by family members to highlight key moments. In contrast, written texts can be easily scanned, labeled, bookmarked, highlighted, and annotated in Word documents, facilitating efficient information retrieval and analysis. Despite these challenges, the importance of these videos for archival purposes cannot be overstated. They document ASL, an essential language of deaf communities, and provide deeper insights into the lived experiences of deaf people.

Conclusion

Alexander Graham Bell's concerns about the potential propagation of a "defective race" through intermarriage among deaf individuals seem to have been realized within our multigenerational deaf family. However, rather than resulting in the great calamity that Bell feared, our family's history demonstrates the rich and fulfilling lives that deaf individuals can lead despite the oppression they may encounter. While our family's relative comfort may be attributed in part to privileges associated with our race and socioeconomic status, it starkly contrasts with the prevailing narratives, exemplified by quotations from former directors of the Alexander Graham Bell Association found at the beginning of this chapter, which dictated the restrictive prerequisites for the inclusion of deaf individuals in society. Our archival work is in line with the broader ethos of the disability community, encapsulated by the slogan "nothing about us without us," which holds relevance for the deaf population. Powerful counternarratives can be realized through family archives that challenge audist ideologies and practices in a pursuit of meaningful inclusion and respect for deaf people in modern society.

Notes

Epigraph 1: Alexander Graham Bell, *Upon the Formation of a Deaf Variety of the Human Race* (U.S. Government Printing Office, 1884).

Epigraph 2: *Washington Post*, May 20, 1973.

Epigraph 3: Meredith Sugar, "AG Bell: Dispelling Myths about Deafness," *Baltimore Post-Examiner*, April 2, 2016.

1. Our use of "deaf" in this chapter includes all deaf and hard of hearing people who use signed language, regardless of their hearing levels or abilities.

2. Meredith Sugar, "AG Bell: Dispelling Myths about Deafness," *Baltimore Post-Examiner*, April 2, 2016.

3. Audism refers to the systematic oppression of deaf people and signed language through prejudice, discrimination, and bias.

4. George Wing, "Physiological Peculiarities of Deafness," *American Annals of the Deaf and Dumb* 8, no. 1 (1854): 146–47.

5. Fred De Laud, "Should the Hard of Hearing Marry?," *Volta Review* 21 (1919): 754.

6. A. Eliot Shearer, "Hearing Loss in the 21st Century and Beyond: A New Era of 35 Precision Diagnosis and Treatment Using Genomics," *Volta Review* 123 no. 1 (2023).

7. *Akron Beacon*, "Deaf Mutes Give Readings before Literary Society: Employees in Silent Division at Goodyear Turn from Athletics to Debate and Also Enter Factory School to Further Their Education" (Akron, Ohio), February 21, 1917.

8. *Deaf American*, "Humor among the Deaf," December 1969.

9. *Deaf Life*, "Youth Leadership Camp Celebrates Its 30th Anniversary," September 1998.

10. Marlene Valle, "Deaf Creators and Influencers to Support," *NADmag* 21, no. 2 (Fall 2021): 18–19.

11. Magdalena Zdrodowska, "To Document Is to Preserve: Moving Pictures and Sign Language," in *Documentary and Disability*, edited by Catalin Brylla and Helen Hughes (London: Palgrave Macmillan, 2017).

12. Beth Haller, "The Little Papers: Newspapers at Nineteenth-Century Schools for Deaf Persons," *Journalism History* 19, no. 2 (1993): 43–50.

13. Thomas K. Holcomb, *Introduction to Deaf Culture* (Oxford University Press, 2023).

14. Michelle Caswell et al., "'To Be Able to Imagine Otherwise': Community Archives and the Importance of Representation," *Archives and Records* (2016): 1–22, doi:10.1080/23257962.2016.1260445, 2.

15. Anna Woodham et al., "We Are What We Keep: The 'Family Archive,' Identity and Public/Private Heritage," *Heritage & Society* 10, no. 3 (2017): 204.

16. Marjoriebell Holcomb, personal communication in 2000.

17. Deaf schools are typically operated and funded by the state government.

18. Marjoriebell Stakley Holcomb, *The Sounds of Silence* (self-published, 1992), 183.

19. Akron Stories, 2023. https://www.akronstories.com/.

20. Carol A. Padden and Tom L. Humphries, *Inside Deaf Culture* (Harvard University Press, 2006).

21. *Akron Beacon*, "More and More Deaf 'Hear' about Akron: City Gains National Fame for Employment of Handicapped," 1952.

22. Holcomb, *Sounds of Silence*, 22.

23. *Wingfoot Clan* [Goodyear Company newsletter]. Volume 7. May 11, 1918.
24. Holcomb, *Sounds of Silence*, 185.
25. Marjoriebell Stakley Holcomb, *The Brewster/Stakley Lineage* (self-published, 1990, ISBN 0–915035–47–2) 91, 93.
26. Holcomb, *Brewster/Stakley Lineage*, 93–95.
27. Holcomb, *Brewster/Stakley Lineage*, 93–95.
28. Edna Edith Sayers, "White Nation, Black Deportation, Deaf Education," *American Annals of the Deaf* 165, no. 2 (2020): 136–56.
29. Marjoriebell Stakley Holcomb, *The Pike Clan* (self-published, 1980, ISBN 0–915035–48–0), 54.
30. Holcomb, *Pike Clan*, 56.
31. Holcomb, *Brewster/Stakley Lineage*, 91.
32. Holcomb, *Brewster/Stakley Lineage*, 103–4.
33. Holcomb, *Sounds of Silence*, 198.
34. Holcomb, *Sounds of Silence*, 198.
35. Holcomb, *Sounds of Silence*, 198.
36. Leala Holcomb, "5 Generations of Deaf Family," YouTube video, 1:33:07. Posted by Leala Holcomb, January 14, 2014, https://www.youtube.com/watch?v=SRRQpxwawM0&t=73s/.
37. Holcomb, "5 Generations of Deaf Family."
38. Holcomb, "5 Generations of Deaf Family."
39. Family collection: A photo of Mabs Holcomb in cheerleading outfit.
40. Holcomb, *Sounds of Silence*, 1.
41. Family collection: A photo of Mabs Holcomb selected in "Who's Who" of college students; Family collection: A photo of Roy and Mabs Holcomb at Gallaudet.
42. Family collection: A photo of Roy and Mabs Holcomb in front of a car.
43. ISD Hoosier. Mr. and Mrs. Holcomb as new faculty members at ISD giving demonstration on communicating with deaf children. November 1961.
44. Holcomb, *Sounds of Silence*.
45. Holcomb, *Sounds of Silence*, 163.
46. Marjorie Holcomb and Sharon Wood, *Deaf Women: A Parade Through the Decades* (Berkeley, CA: Dawn Sign Press, 1989).
47. Family collection: A photo of Mabs Holcomb in a wheelchair.
48. Marjoriebell Stakley Holcomb, *The Holcomb Heritage* (self-published, 1989, ISBN 0–915035–49–9), 71.
49. Roy Holcomb, *Autobiography* (unpublished).
50. Holcomb, *Holcomb Heritage*, 71.
51. Private letter from the state of California to Roy Holcomb; *Argus*, "Job Loss: Was It Prop. 13 or Politics?," Fremont, California, July 20, 1979; *Oakland Tribute*, "Holcomb Firing Probe Promised," March 4, 1981.
52. University of Tennessee (1957/1960), Ball State University (1967), and California State University, Northridge (1968).
53. Family collection: A scrapbook of Indiana days.
54. Homer D. Babbidge Jr., *Education of the Deaf. A Report to the Secretary of Health, Education, and Welfare by His Advisory Committee on the Education of the Deaf*, 1965.

55. Dan Cloud Leadership Award; Gallaudet honorary degree.

56. *Deaf Life Magazine*, vol. VI, December 1998; Holcomb, *Holcomb Heritage*, 73; Gallaudet honorary doctorate.

57. Holcomb, *Introduction to Deaf Culture*; J. A. Pahz and C. S. Pahz, *Total Communication: The Meaning Behind the Movement to Expand Educational Opportunities for Deaf Children* (Springfield, IL: Charles C Thomas, Publisher, 1978).

58. Holcomb, *Autobiography*; *Washington Post*, "Deaf Children Taught to Speak with Hands and Voice," May 20, 1973.

59. Edward L. Scouten, *Turning Points in the Education of Deaf People* (Interstate Printers & Publishers, 1984).

60. Family collection: A photo of Sam and Tom Holcomb in garage; *Indianapolis Star*, "Educators of Deaf Seeking Break Through," April 10, 1968.

61. Holcomb, *Sounds of Silence*, 141.

62. Family collection: A photo of Tom Holcomb in classroom with headphones.

63. Donald D. Johnson and Robert L. Whitehead, "Effect of Maternal Rubella on Hearing and Vision: A Twenty-Year Post-Epidemic Study," *American Annals of the Deaf* 134, no. 3 (1989): 232–42; Richard S. Silverman, "Deafness and Rubella: Infants in the '60s, Adults in the '80s," *American Annals of the Deaf* (1980): 963–67.

64. Holcomb, *Autobiography*.

65. Family collection: *Oliver* program book.

66. *Democrat and Chronicle*, "A Silent World of Harmony," Rochester, New York.

67. Charlotte Enns, Jonathan Henner, and Lynn McQuarrie, eds., *Discussing Bilingualism in Deaf Children: Essays in Honor of Robert Hoffmeister* (Routledge, 2021).

68. Family collection: A letter from an audiologist, 1961.

69. Katherine Greene, personal communication, July 2024.

70. NTID is a federal program to provide postsecondary support for deaf people seeking technological education.

71. Holcomb, "5 Generations of Deaf Family."

72. Family collection: A letter from an audiologist, 1961, emphasis added.

73. Wyatte C. Hall, "What You Don't Know Can Hurt You: The Risk of Language Deprivation by Impairing Sign Language Development in Deaf Children," *Maternal and Child Health Journal* 21, no. 5 (2017): 961–65; Tom Humphries et al., "Language Acquisition for Deaf Children: Reducing the Harms of Zero Tolerance to the Use of Alternative Approaches," *Harm Reduction Journal* 9 (2012): 1–9.

74. Laura Mauldin, "Lessons Learned: How Studying Cochlear Implantation Reveals the Context in Which d/Deaf Identities Are Formed," in *Deaf Identities: Exploring New Frontiers* (2019), 96; David R. Meek, "Dinner Table Syndrome: A Phenomenological Study of Deaf Individuals' Experiences with Inaccessible Communication," *The Qualitative Report* 25, no. 6 (2020): 1676A–1694.

75. Kenneth R. Alexander, "Forgotten Aspects of Total Communication," *American Annals of the Deaf* (1978): 18–21; Karin Allard and Deborah Chen Pichler, "Multi-Modal Visually-Oriented Translanguaging Among Deaf Signers," *Translation and Translanguaging in Multilingual Contexts* 4, no. 3 (2018): 384–404; Thomas K. Holcomb, "Deaf Epistemology: The Deaf Way of Knowing," *American Annals of the Deaf* 154, no. 5 (2010): 471–78.

76. Holcomb, *Autobiography*.

77. Family collection: Home footage of Tom Holcomb signing ASL rhyme and rhythm.

78. *San Jose Mercury News*, "Fremont Becomes Hub of Deaf Activity," June 13, 1984.

79. CSDF was a pioneer in promoting the use of ASL and bilingual pedagogy (rather than oralism or contrived Signed English systems) with young deaf children.

80. Family collection: Sign Theatre program books.

81. Family collection: Fax documents from Leala Holcomb.

82. Family collection: Pictures of Leala Holcomb in Greece.

83. Modern Language Association, 2016.

84. A pseudonym is used to honor the minor's privacy.

85. Jaipreet Virdi, *Hearing Happiness: Deafness Cures in History* (University of Chicago Press, 2020).

86. Mauldin, "Lessons Learned," 96.

87. Noel L. Cohen and Ronald A. Hoffman, "Complications of Cochlear Implant Surgery in Adults and Children," *Annals of Otology, Rhinology & Laryngology* 100, no. 9 (1991): 708–11.

88. Kathryn Davidson, Diane Lillo-Martin, and Deborah Chen Pichler, "Spoken English Language Development Among Native Signing Children with Cochlear Implants," *Journal of Deaf Studies and Deaf Education* 19, no. 2 (2014): 238–50; Neil S. Glickman and Wyatte C. Hall, eds., *Language Deprivation and Deaf Mental Health* (Routledge, 2018).

89. Tara Holcomb, personal communication, January 2023.

90. Padden and Humphries, *Inside Deaf Culture*.

91. Paul Statham and Nancy Foner, "Assimilation and Integration in the Twenty-First Century: Where Have We Been and Where Are We Going? Introduction to a Special Issue in Honour of Richard Alba," *Journal of Ethnic and Migration Studies* 50, no. 1 (2024): 4–26.

92. Sugar, "AG Bell."

93. Woodham et al., "We Are What We Keep," 207.

94. Michelle Caswell, "Seeing Yourself in History: Community Archives and the Fight Against Symbolic Annihilation," *The Public Historian* 36, no. 4 (2014): 26–37.

95. Caswell et al., "'To Be Able to Imagine Otherwise,'" 1–22.

96. Daniela Petrelli and Steve Whittaker, "Family Memories in the Home: Contrasting Physical and Digital Mementos," *Personal and Ubiquitous Computing* 14 (2010): 153–69.

PART V

Accessing

CHAPTER 17

"It Felt Like Everything"

Disability, Affect, and the Creation of Archival Interdependence

GRACEN MIKUS BRILMYER

Introduction

It means everything to write this chapter with and alongside the voices of my communities, of disabled people. Throughout my whole life my health and disabilities have fluctuated—I've had varying levels of pain, mobility, cognition, and mental capacity. But more importantly, my relationship with an identity as Disabled, as sick, as chronically ill, as neurodivergent has changed and continues to change. My identity has been shaped through relationships with friends, mentors, collaborators, and community members—many of whom were disabled, some of whom worked in the field of disability studies, some who I came to know well, others who I only shared space with occasionally. Through these crip communities in Chicago, the Bay Area, Los Angeles, Montréal, and online, I attended and also became involved in organizing events, art, activism, and community-based projects. Witnessing performances by Sins Invalid and AXIS Dance Company; attending and organizing meetings around access and technology with the Bay Area Accessibility and Inclusive Design meetup and Accessibility Camp Bay Area; advocating for access to museum and academic events for and with d/Deaf and hard of hearing comrades; volunteering for, attending, and/or witnessing powerful conversations around disability and disability justice at events such as *Disability Incarcerated*, *Disability as Spectacle*, *Sick Fest*, and *Bay Area Day of Mourning*; organizing mask distribution for protests and broader mask access projects with COVID-cautious comrades; collaborating on and experiencing community care work and contributing to long-distance care networks; and building community through emails, social media, phone calls with friends of friends, academic connections, and other disabled people—all of these experiences, conversations, knowledges, and people have shaped my identity as Disabled and facilitated my deeper, constantly growing understanding of disability as political, historical, cultural, and relational. I've experienced what Stacey Park Milbern and Leah Lakshmi Piepzna-Samarasinha call *crip doulaing*—"crip mentoring and assisting with birthing into disability culture/community, different kinds of disability, etc. . . . Naming disability as a space we can be born into, not alone but supported and welcomed by other disabled people."[1] Throughout my life, I have been around disabled people who have shaped and continue to shape who I am, without whom this chapter would not be possible. In other words, disabled communities have deeply impacted who I am, and for me, community is a central aspect of being disabled.

This chapter uses interviews with disabled archival users located in the United States and Canada to think through some facets of our relationships to archival representation. It first covers the existing literature around disability and the value of community as well as how archives have been found to affectively impact some historically marginalized communities. It then covers my approach to research, which leads to three key themes from disabled archival users. First, although interviewees described being familiar with dominant (often problematic) forms of the representation of disability, many noted meeting this type of misrepresentation and erasure with a critical and political lens. Second, using such lenses, they could understand harmful and partial records as evidence of past harms documenting the history of disability. Therefore, lastly, the people who I spoke to had complex affective responses to historical documentation—feeling the violences of the past while also sometimes feeling excited to see disabled people historically present. This research demonstrates the necessity for disabled people to see themselves in history and underscores how disabled people can feel a deep sense of community not only with current communities—which is so vital to our existence—but also with disabled people across time, thus illustrating an *archival interdependence*.

Literature Review: Disability, Community, Archives, and Affect

Disability and the Value of Community

For many d/Deaf, disabled, neurodivergent, mad, and sick people,[2] community is a central part of survival. Aimi Hamraie and Kelly Fritsch state that disabled people's "collective experiences and histories have taught us that we are effective agents of worldbuilding and dismantling toward more socially just relations."[3] And many have emphasized the importance of cross-disability solidarity, comprising communities of many identities. In defining disability justice, Patty Berne and the Sins Invalid family list ten principles, one of which is a:

> *Commitment to Cross Disability Solidarity.* We value and honor the insights and participation of all of our community members. We are committed to breaking down ableist/patriarchal/racist/classed isolation between people with physical impairments, people who identify as "sick" or are chronically ill, "psych" survivors and those who identify as "crazy," neurodiverse people, people with cognitive impairments, and people who are a sensory minority, as we understand that isolation ultimately undermines collective liberation.[4]

Though understanding the ways different disabilities and illnesses impact people as well as our united work toward collective liberation, Mia Mingus reminds us, "*It means something to be disabled. Never forget that.*"[5] As "unequivocally . . . disabled people are everywhere,"[6] it's important to think about our relations to each other. We come to find one another online, in support groups, through shared (and differing) experiences and identities, and we develop culture, languages, technologies, support systems, art, and other maker-cultures.

Reflecting on our communities and countering the dominant narratives surrounding "independence"—a myth whereby one can (and "should") exist without the support of others—disabled writers have emphasized the *value of community* for disabled people. Eva Feder Kittay identifies the paternalistic stance that can come with "dependence" as well as the moral and other stigmas that come with relying on others.[7] Conversely, Piepzna-Samarasinha describes how collective care can help counteract the ways traditional medical systems of so-called care can be abusive, ableist, transphobic, homophobic, sexist, racist, and also financially unattainable. They describe queercrip scholar Loree Erickson's care collective where "disabled and nondisabled friends and community members . . . work shifts each week to help her with dressing, bathing, and transferring . . . [as well as] the admin work of emailing, scheduling, and training potential care shifters."[8] They emphasize that "Loree's care collective is not just a practical survival strategy to get her the care she needs; it's a site of community and political organizing, where many people learn about disability politics (both the theory and the nitty-gritty) in action for the first time."[9]

Such community systems of care highlight the concept of *interdependence*, which as Mingus highlights, "moves us away from knowing disability only through 'dependence,' which paints disabled bodies as being a burden to others, at the mercy of able-bodied people's benevolence."[10] She critiques "[t]he myth of independence [that] reflects such a deep level of privilege, especially in this rugged individualistic capitalist society and produced the very idea that we could even mildly conceive of our lives or our accomplishments as solely our own."[11] In other words, the concept of independence is rooted in capitalism, liberalism, individualism, and ableism. Likewise, as Ki'tay Davidson points out, "No one is actually independent; we are all actually interdependent. The difference between the needs that many disabled people have and the needs of people who are not labeled as disabled is that nondisabled people have had their dependencies normalized."[12] And, furthermore, others have underscored how inextricable we are to each other, to systems, and to social arrangements.[13] Mingus highlights the interconnectedness of people's lives, in general:

> Someone made the clothes you're wearing now, your shoes, your car or the mass transit system you use; we don't grow all our own food and spices. We can't pretend that what happens in this country doesn't affect others, or that things like clean air and water don't bound us all together. We are dependent on each other, period.[14]

Moreover, as Audre Lorde writes, "Only within that interdependency of different strengths, acknowledged and equal, can the power to seek new ways of being in the world generate, as well as the courage and sustenance to act where there are no charters."[15] Especially as top-down systems to accessibility and care do not work for many disabled people—specifically disabled queer, trans, and people of color—interdependence highlights new forms of support and care for survival. Interdependence points toward how disabled people can rely not only on medical, government, and bureaucratic systems but also on each other, communities, and collective access.

Archives, Representation, and Affect

Many disabled people have highlighted how representation for disabled people matters. For example, #CriticalAxis, a The Disabled List project that collects and analyzes disability representation in media, critiques commercials, design, and other media that depict disability or accessibility. #CriticalAxis's essays highlight multiple issues around disability representation such as inspiration, accessibility, exploitation, and humor.[16] Addressing the lack of complex representation of disability, Vilissa Thompson founded the hashtag #DisabilityTooWhite to draw attention to issues around disability rights and representation, as well as disability issues in the Movement for Black Lives. These examples, among many others, show how complex representation is important for disabled people—being able to see themselves in media (portrayed not only in negative or stereotypical ways) as well as having multiple axes of their identities addressed.[17]

Turning more toward historical representation, recent work in archival studies has shown the impact of archives on historically marginalized and minoritized communities. Michelle Caswell, Marika Cifor, and Mario H. Ramirez utilize George Gerbner's notion of "symbolic annihilation"—whereby members of historically marginalized or minoritized groups are underrepresented or misrepresented in mainstream media—to frame the impact of archival representation on those communities. Through empirical data collected through focus groups consisting of users of community-based archives, they note that participants' "responses indicate a sense of alienation, isolation, and misrepresentation in mainstream repositories that is consistent with the concept" of symbolic annihilation. They describe the affective impacts of how marginalized groups essentially feel erased in history through the ways in which they are underrepresented and misrepresented in archives. In contrast, Chloe Brownlee-Chapman, Rohhss Chapman, Clarence Eardley, Sara Forster, Victoria Green, and Helen Graham have begun to investigate the value for and of disabled people being involved in archival processes to document and complicate historical narratives.[18] Building the Living Archive of Learning Disability History, a collaborative project between disabled people, researchers, designers, health workers, and allies, they illustrate how when disabled people are at the center of archival projects, awareness can be raised around disability history with nuanced narratives. Along these lines, Wendy Duff, Jefferson Sporn, and Emily Herron describe how the involvement of survivors of state-enforced sterilization in a community-based archive project could reflect an ethics of care and combat symbolic annihilation.[19] So, while some archives can produce a sense of alienation for marginalized archival users, the involvement of those communities can also have positive impacts for archival representation.

Using the aforementioned literature as a foundation, this multiyear research project has investigated the ways that archival materials impact disabled people. In previous publications that use the same interviews as this chapter, I have outlined multiple facets of disabled people's relationships to archives. First, the accessibility of archival spaces deeply shapes disabled interviewees' experiences of materials. Participants described how the inaccessibility of archives—such as stairs, reading room configurations, required academic affiliation, and hours of operation—and the ways access is treated shaped feelings around how disabled people are devalued by institutions.[20] Through constantly navigating both subtle and blatant inaccessibility in archives, the conversations illuminated the ways that space and place shape feelings of belonging (or unbelonging)[21]—complicated by other axes of identity—which also opened space to consider the other disabled people who might not be able to access archives.[22] Second, in another publication, this research has shown the ways that these disabled interviewees were deeply familiar with the ways that disabled people are represented through stereotypes, tropes, and limited perspectives. Yet, they nonetheless felt an inherent violence in such records and in the absence of disabled people in history; they remarked on an anticipated absence of subjectivity as well as a complete lack of records about disabled people. They described how their past experiences with such violence, disappointment, and harm led to them expecting—and preparing themselves—to encounter future harms, absences, and other archival unknowns.[23]

Building on these previously published findings, this chapter places focus and further elaborates on disabled people's relationships to historical documentation. Although there are profound positive impacts of disabled communities being involved with archiving projects, I investigate the contrary: the plethora of historical documentation around disability—such as institutional, medical, criminal, and sideshow records—that can be partial, problematic, or violent, or erase the agency of archival subjects. Through understanding the violence experienced by disabled people in history alongside how living disabled people feel through it, expect it, and bear witness to it, this chapter further investigates how and if disabled people feel symbolic annihilation through the ways that they are represented in archival material. This research brings together the aforementioned facets—how disabled people have a long history of being misrepresented in archival material, the ways in which some marginalized communities feel a sense of erasure in archival material, and how community is a vital aspect of many disabled people's lives—in order to investigate disabled people's relationships to their representation, misrepresentation, or erasure in archives. I look to disabled people's affective responses to disabled people in history—even in their absence—as well as how both archives and records on disability shape disabled people's experiences of themselves and their communities.

Research Approach

This chapter uses conversations from semi-structured interviews with disabled archival users with a wide array of disabilities, identities, and experiences who were located in the United States and Canada. Participants (a) identified as disabled, (b) conducted research in any type of archive and found records that they considered to be about disability, and (c) were at least twenty-one years old at the time of recruitment. The archives with which interviewees worked varied greatly; some would be considered mainstream archives and special collections while others identified disability-specific collections or framed themselves as a disability-centered archives. In other words, the themes described below are not limited to mainstream archives; however, most of the archives participants spoke about were located in North America and Europe. Additionally, participants described a wide variety of records: although many described problematic, violent, and limited representations of disabled people, other interviewees referenced literature, media, and cultural objects that didn't always depict disability in an explicit or problematic way.

The interviews were conducted during 2018 and 2019 via video and phone and in person. I utilized this wide range of methods in order to prioritize each interviewee's accessibility needs and comfort as well as to communicate with participants located across North America. Each interview was audio recorded with the consent of the interviewee, and then each recording was transcribed. The transcripts were then coded in an iterative manner to locate themes within and across interviews.[24] While many of the themes described below (and in other pieces from this research) are shared across some or many interviews, I recognize the differences within and across them as well. As I describe some commonalities across the conversations that follow, I try to honor the differences across each person's experiences—in life, in varying moments in their lives, and in different archives—since disabled people have their own experiences of disability, intersecting identities, politics, and opinions that shape their experience of the world. It is because of these specificities that the following themes emerge in multiplicity and might not be applicable to all disabled people, archives, or contexts.

Through a consent form, each participant had the initial opportunity to choose if they wanted to be cited anonymously, by name, or by an alias, and we went over the consent form before the interviews so that they could ask any questions or get clarification on the research. I also had each participant describe their positionality, and I use these descriptions accordingly. I continue to get their consent for using their words in all published materials: each participant had an opportunity to read this chapter, change the way that they are cited, edit their quotes, and give feedback on the chapter as a whole.

Importantly, community is central to this research. Margaret Price and Stephanie L. Kerschbaum outline the importance of centering disability from the beginning of a research project; they describe how emphasizing disabled people's narratives as well as access remakes research as "One of our purposes in telling stories is to offer them as opportunities to reflect deeply on the beauty, complexity, and pain of research."[25] Likewise, I do this research with and for disabled communities, and through this research I am building community with them. While centering the words of sick and disabled people to tell our own histories, this chapter also illuminates how, by even doing this research, I am in community with disabled people, and these communities are expanding further through these new connections, conversations, and networks with disabled people. As I'm describing the relationships of the interviewees to historical documentation of disability, I'm simultaneously describing my relationships to each of them, all of them as a cohort,[26] and all of us to history.

Emerging Themes from Conversations

As highlighted in previous publications, many people who I spoke to described how although they were familiar with prominent stereotypes of disability and have come to expect it, they still felt an inherent violence in witnessing themselves misrepresented or underrepresented in history.[27] Building on these relationships to archival material, the first theme in this chapter illustrates how many participants talked about bringing a critical and political lens to both their misrepresentation and erasure in archival material. Second, using such critical lenses, many described feeling nonetheless excited to see disabled people in history, because, although they are often misrepresented or represented in partiality, such documentation has the potential to be activated as evidence of the ways in which disabled people have been—and continue to be—treated and misunderstood. Lastly, through these records, they described their complex affective responses, including a prominent feeling of connection to disabled people in the past. All of these themes are twofold: throughout all three, participants remarked both on the *presence* of limited or problematic representations as well as the *absence* of documentation about disabled people in history. And they highlighted how both misrepresentation and erasure occur through the creation of records and their contents as well as through archives, archival processes, and interventions.

Theme 1: Criticality of Misrepresentations and Erasure

When participants spoke about witnessing problematic or limited representations, many described how they could grapple with and *problematize the misrepresentation and erasure of disability in records.* First, many interviewees described how they complicated problematic representations of disability that reinforced certain stereotypes. Stefan Sunandan Honisch, sessional lecturer in the Department of Theatre and Film at the University of British Columbia and a biracial disabled scholar, educator, and musician, for example, recounts his experiences with tropes around blind musicians and how he complicates them:

> It wasn't simply that the tropes ceased to become important or that I was unable to engage on a human level with those photographs—because I always have the sense that I was dealing with something staged or artificial—but there was also a sense of conflict [for me] . . . as a disabled researcher.[28]

Honisch's words identify an acute awareness of tropes of disability, which led to his recognition and critical engagement with them. White, disabled nonbinary scholar Jess Waggoner identifies their critical lens to reframe limited records through locating the common disconnect between medical history and what might constitute disability history. They ask:

> What kind of *framing with care* do we need to use in order to transform something from medical history to disability history? Because I've seen there are moments where I encounter something that called itself "disability history" or archives and I'm like, "this is just a medical archive." It's clinical, it's diagnostic. It's not really leaving a lot of room for agency, but I think that the researcher could possibly transform this into a disability archive. But I'm troubled sometimes by—not the ambiguity. I'm fine with the ambiguity—I'm troubled by the sort of uncritical naming of something that still feels pretty medical to me as "disability."[29]

Their words highlight not only their awareness of a disconnection between discourses but also how they bring a critical lens for reshaping or reframing records with a sense of care.

Others described how they grappled with partial or incomplete narratives, when research did not immediately yield records on disabled people. White, queer, disability rights activist and author Corbett O'Toole states, "What I came away with is that *we're there*; a lot of times disabled people are between the lines or are in situations we don't wish they were, in like institutionalized situations. But we're there and there's a lot of information about us and what, to me, what the challenge has been [is] how to take that information and make it useful and available to other people in a contemporary context."[30] And Cody Jackson, a white, disabled, gay graduate student, describes how "it's a bit of an emotional kind of laborious process because I tried to take a look at young gay men who committed suicide. And so I take a look at those kind of unfinished narratives, and I try to figure out if there's an ethical way that we could entangle ourselves in those archival moments."[31] Similarly, Honisch describes identifying the subtlety of problematic discourses or tropes of disability:

> When that kind of discourse isn't obviously at work, then as researchers, we have to expand perhaps even more effort to ask critical questions. Are there [. . .] forms of exclusion at work, or what dynamics of power and privilege need to be unpacked? And whose experiences are being validated, whose aren't? Which is all just to say that I think that the value in those more ambiguous sources . . . may very well lie in the extra effort, and the more subtle critical work that they ask us to do, or perhaps even demand that we do.[32]

Addressing the partiality of the documentation around the deaths of disabled people after an earthquake at Agnews Developmental Center, a California psychiatric and medical facility, O'Toole states, "[T]he historical record was there, but the fact that this history is completely ignored in the earthquake history is that kind of classic, 'incarcerated people don't get to be part of our mainstream history.'"[33] Such histories aren't always readily apparent in records, so participants, as Black disabled professor of English Therí Pickens points out, often look for the subtleties and also address the lack of critical frameworks to address the specificities of disabled experiences:

> I found some places where disability was not heralded as, not called as such, where it was talked about in terms of blood, cause that's how pseudoscience wanted to talk about in the 19th century. . . . What was also fascinating was that there were all of these folks itching to talk about disability and trying not to do so from the standpoint of pity, but they didn't quite have the vocabulary to describe how pervasive the experience was. . . . I think that's also the absence of something that is uniquely Black, about the experiences

> of blackness and disability. So the critical armature, even if it existed for some people, it's too white.[34]

Adding to the ways in which interviewees were critical of the absence of disability, Pickens highlights the lack of ways of identifying how disability and race intersect and inform one another throughout history and impact archival erasure. Through encountering the partiality of records around disability and interpretations of them—the representation stereotypes, the absence of perspectives of disabled people, or the lack of complex ways to address how race, gender, class, size, and nationality inform how disability is understood—interviewees described their engagement with records. These quotes illustrate how many interviewees critically approached stereotypical representations of disability in history as well as how records can be incomplete.

Participants not only talked about being aware of stereotypes, tropes, and such limited perspectives of disability in the historical record, but also spoke about taking a *critical lens toward the absence of records about disability*. Self-described "half-Indian, half-Polish, half-deaf, 100% archivist," Michelle Ganz spoke about identifying items not obviously about disability as she processes materials: "There's sort of a collection of almost keywords that are always in my head, and as I'm scanning any collection and kind of assessing for keywords within the collection. . . . I note it in the finding aid, you know, 'here's the item that relates to this topic[,]' [words like] 'Deaf,' 'Disabled,' the slur words that go along with 'deaf' and 'disabled,' anything that catches my eye as 'othered.'"[35] Blind historian Alida Boorn spoke about the sparse description of a disabled person in a record, "for him, it's just, well, 'here's this guy. He had rheumatic fever. He survived, he carried on and he was blind,' and basically that said . . . well, yeah, here he was blind and he did this work anyway. And that's about it, period. I'm going, 'well that's not a lot.'"[36]

Pickens spoke about training a critical lens on the nuances of erasure, stating, "Sometimes I think the integrity of talking about disability, whether it's present in the archival record officially or not, requires saying something about what kind of erasure we're dealing with. Like whether it's a deliberate erasure by the people or persons who left things behind or whether it's erasure based on our archival methods or whether it's an erasure because people didn't know or didn't have a critical vocabulary."[37] Similarly, Travis Chi Wing Lau, a gay, disabled poet and scholar of color, reflecting on the six people forcibly vaccinated in Newgate Prison, speaks about identifying records never created about disabled people:

> I think about those unnamed bodies, those unnamed *criminal* bodies. And there's really no specific case details about who those people were, but I wouldn't be surprised if there were women or people of color, as the sort of experimental matter by which a practice became popularized and justified

> to the English elite. . . . What do we do with the fact that disabled people frequently are the very matter by which medical knowledge advances? That was my first instinct was to say what do we do with that?"[38]

Expanding on archival work, Lau states, "[Y]ou would often have to extrapolate sort of the number of bodies *not* represented, how the data itself is a distortion of what was a much larger phenomenon. So yes, it's been weird [to] just sort of toggle between the individual experience of, say, a person whose smallpox case was ideal for vaccination and this population-level record in which thousands of bodies are being conflated into a single piece of evidence that justifies the use of vaccination."[39] Considering how identifying and addressing the partiality of disability histories is often painful and arduous, many interviewees described how they applied a critical lens to the lack of complex representations and ways to engage with them.

This theme outlines the ways in which participants described how they approached disability in records: interviewees noted how they complicate problematic or stereotypical representations of disability, how they recognize when narratives are incomplete, and how they also detect the palpable absence of disabled people in archives. Such strategies included engaging with tropes to locate forms of agency, developing critical vocabularies for talking about disability in history, and recognizing when disabled people are "between the lines" or histories need to be extrapolated from sparse documentation.

Theme 2: Evidence and Political Potential

Through their critical approaches to records on disability, interviewees described how such misrepresentations—although often inaccurate to the lived experience of disabled people—could still serve as evidence of past violences, which, with a political lens, could be activated to tell histories of violences against disabled people. Pickens talked about the complexity between the absences within a record and their potential as she draws on Du Bois's concept of "double consciousness," where one is "always looking at one's self through the eyes of others."[40] She states, "To encounter it [a Black disabled woman in archives] is I think to feel this strange mix of *being seen and unseen* because you're cognizant of what's on the [record], what you see in front of you, what you're touching: literal evidence."[41] Waggoner similarly comments on how "even though I see these really horrible ablest—often entangled with sexism and racism—representations, it still feels like it resonates on a bunch of different levels because it's also like *evidence of that we were there in history and also like evidence of that violence*."[42]

When harmful records were understood as evidence of disability history, participants noted how that made room to be able to bring such harmful histories to light. Megan Suggitt, a disabled, white undergraduate student, conveys the importance of records about a former asylum, Huronia Regional Centre: "I feel like people need to be aware of this history. And the thing with disability history is people are erased, disabled lives are erased and [addressing the history] is not done in a meaningful manner. Like you need to actually acknowledge what happened. It is history. You need to maintain that history so people are aware that this happened."[43] Ganz also addresses how records have the potential to tell crucial pieces of history: "There's a lot of people who want to go back and change records to update them to less hurtful language. And for me that goes against everything we're supposed to be doing because it's changing the truth, and the truth may be hurtful, but we need to acknowledge it in order to move forward."[44] Similarly, disabled, white lawyer Lili Siegel spoke about not wanting the violence to get left behind in overly positive narratives of disability, stating that "while I think that it's important to do the history of disabled pride, I don't want the ways in which it's hard and the ways in which people do suffer to be left behind. But I feel like if I'm going to be the disability rights person, I feel like I have to be just that. And it's hard to make room for nuance."[45]

And when harmful pasts are brought to light, some participants noted that they could be politically activated in the present moment. For example, Lau posits the use of gaining historical context about the ways that disabled people have been and still are treated: "Especially thinking about the history of incarceration and institutionalization of disabled people, it, on a very simple level, makes us all have to say that this is not a recent thing. This is very far back in history."[46] He continues, speaking about the potential to activate records, "I think about how those stories get sort of flattened into those glimpses in the record but require in some ways the imagination to revive or to bring into our present."[47] Boorn describes a personal connection to archival material and excitement while researching early sunglass production: "I was going blind and [researching] sunglasses . . . finding it from the archives, it was very exciting because I was getting to tell the story using the advertisements in the newspapers."[48] Likewise, Honisch spoke of the political possibilities of historical material: "I think that raising those questions in terms of societal and cultural attitudes as a whole, that's a valid and important critical undertaking. Engaging with those archival sources becomes a dance between getting at the political possibilities, and the potential disruptions that certain ways of reading or interacting with those sources might bring about."[49] And Suggitt, speaking about working with the Centre's survivors, says, "I love hearing about survivor's stories. I feel like their history is more knowledgeable than government history, but . . . we also need to maintain those records so we acknowledge the history and why it was built and because . . . if you erase that aspect, you're still erasing what Huronia represented."[50] Such powerful quotes demonstrate a connection that participants felt to those in the past: when framed as evidence, records—even those that portrayed disabled people in harmful or stereotypical ways—could be activated, not only to tell histories of disability, but also to address the politics of disability in the present moment.

Theme 3: Historical Harms and Relationships with History

The previous two themes—the ways in which participants critically read the partial nature of disability in records and can therefore activate them as evidence of past harms—point to a notable complexity around representation, misrepresentation, and erasure in history. As such, participants described a particular affective tension: between witnessing problematic representations and glaring absences, and being able to foreground how those violences or inaccuracies can also be seen as meaningful evidence of our histories.

Through witnessing past violences and framing them within the politics of disability, participants described *feeling connected* to disabled people in the past. Jackson reflects broadly on disabled people represented in historical records and his relation to them: "Particularly with archives, I think it just kind of reminds me that there were disability activists before me doing this work. And I have ancestors and people in the past that I can look to who have done this work and put their bodies on the line."[51] Siegel articulates how archival materials have facilitated a shift in her personal and political understanding of disability and discrimination:

> I think that when I first learned about the disability rights movement and the ways in which it sprang out of a history of eugenics . . . it has a weight that I hadn't ever thought of it with, where I felt like I got why people were so upset, for the first time. I hadn't really let myself feel much by way of like anger. . . . And then I learned about the history more, and it was like, "wow, maybe they do hate me." It was good that I grappled with some of that, but it also really is painful.[52]

Her words highlight how such documentation opened up access not only to learn about the history of disability and the disability rights movement, but also to *feel* the history as it informs her present-day experiences. O'Toole states that even while looking at horrific records

> what I came away feeling like was *I was really grateful that the public record existed* like the basic public record so that other people could find what I found . . . and I was grateful for the absolute bean-picking bureaucracy of everybody who goes in and has to get registered so we know some basic information, some self reported basic information about these people. So that part felt really good. I mean, I really felt like having that information in the record was really important to me because *I felt like there were ways in which I could connect with them*. That felt really relevant.[53]

And Honisch recalls, "There were moments in certain photographs when I did feel a kind of connection that, it's not like it made me forget about the tropes and about the importance of maintaining a certain critical engagement."[54] Witnessing disabled people in the past, and the activism, discrimination, and mistreatment that they experienced, allowed for participants to feel connected to disability history.

It was through such connections that many spoke about the affective duality of the painful nature of witnessing violences of the past, while also feeling excitement to witness disabled people—even though problematically represented—in history. Waggoner talked about finding woodcut illustrations of disabled women that were produced for promotional materials for a rehabilitation center. They describe feeling connected to people in the past:

> There is this excitement of *we were here* like, *absolutely*. And that we took up space. . . . I'm excited that the document exists. . . . And to see those and be drawn to them in that way, but then to also be like, "this is part of an advertisement," that you should send your "problem girl" here, police or parents or families or whatever . . . so definitely complicated around that. Excited to see it, excited that it's there in an archive, *but felt really weird about it*.

Likewise, Honisch describes the excitement of seeing disabled people in history, reflecting on how "[m]isrepresentation isn't simply a straightforward opposition between invalidating disabled people's lived experience and representing them according to stereotypes. There is also a certain satisfaction or *something like an 'aha moment' that comes from seeing other disabled people historically present*."[55]

Lau spoke about the complexity of wanting to see disabled people in history even though they are often problematically represented. He states, "It's a desire I sometimes don't know what to do with because I feel its problematic nature." Pickens similarly articulates the emotional complexity she feels when conducting archival research:

> This [experience of looking for disability] was sort of enmeshed in something that I think violates the laws of physics. I was in like six different places at the same time. You know what I mean? Like it felt like this confluence of emotions; this anger, this fear, this excitement, this beauty, this difficulty, and then this sort of hope. If someone would but understand this piece of paper and this archive and its importance, then maybe I won't have to fight these battles anymore . . . . *It felt like everything*.[56]

These words all show the deep entangled emotions that come with researching disability history. Through witnessing disabled people in historical records, the people who I spoke to not only felt a deep connection with disabled people in the past—histories of institutionalization, incarceration, and discrimination—but also experience affective complexities, feeling excitement and gratitude alongside harm, pain, anger, and many other emotions.

Extending the Conversations

These themes illustrate some of the complex ways in which disabled people—as diverse communities with multiple intersecting identities, politics, and opinions—find, relate to, and are impacted by archival representation, misrepresentation, and erasure. Building on previously published work—where interviewees described having experienced the harms of witnessing the violence of the past and expecting disabled people to be erased in history[57]—this chapter shows how they approach problematic representations and absences in archival material with contemporary critical lenses. Through this critical and political connection to the past, they can frame such representations as evidence of the ways that disability is perceived and understood and therefore value connecting to disabled people across time. While recognizing how limited and stereotypical records on disability (as well as the lack thereof) can be harmful to disabled people, this research also underscores the excitement that can accompany such harms for disabled researchers and the value of seeing yourself in history.

In a way, interviewees expressed a similar affective impact to Caswell et al.'s description of archival symbolic annihilation, where they feel represented in problematic ways and also feel erased in history. As I've outlined previously through these same interviews, "Disabled people are so deeply familiar with the ways in which they are misunderstood in society—through stereotypes and tropes—and witness how that is reflected in archives."[58] They therefore can feel an inherent, or familiar violence around the ways that disabled people have been (and continue to be) treated as well as how it is reflected within records. However, because we might expect to be erased—either through the partiality of records created about us or the lack of records entirely—when we see ourselves in history, the affective impacts are complex.

This research, then, complicates archival symbolic annihilation for disabled researchers. While *feeling* the harms of the past, participants simultaneously understood how records can also serve as evidence of the oppression and objectification of disabled people. Records therefore contain "political possibilities," as Honisch states, where "the researcher could possibly transform this into a disability archive," as Waggoner notes. Participants described how they might also "[come] away feeling . . . really grateful that the public record existed," as O'Toole said, an "excitement of *we were here*," as Waggoner described, and an avenue to, as Suggitt and Ganz point at, "acknowledge what happened." Therefore, this research highlights the dual affective nature of problematic representation and erasure for disabled people: to feel, as Pickens states, a "confluence of emotions; this anger, this fear, this excitement, this beauty, this difficulty, and then this sort of hope." Whereas Caswell et al. describe those marginalized by mainstream archives as essentially feeling erased in history through the ways in which they are misrepresented or underrepresented, participants in this research, as Honisch describes, didn't feel "simply a straightforward opposition." They could often simultaneously feel the harm of the treatment of disabled people—as well as their misrepresentation and erasure in records—*alongside* a complicated excitement or gratitude for evidence because such records are *illustrative* of how we have been treated across time. And this felt different for each of them in different archives and witnessing different records.

Additionally, the political activation and complex affective relationships to history underscore the *necessity* for disabled people to see themselves in history. To not only feel excitement, gratitude, or hope, but also to feel connected to—as Jackson puts it—disabled ancestors, those "who have done this work and put their bodies on the line," even if represented in limited or painful ways. O'Toole described feeling grateful for how "there were ways in which I could connect with them [disabled people in the past]." Waggoner illustrated how, although the records they found were problematic, they nonetheless felt the value that "*we were here*." And Honisch described the "satisfaction or that 'aha moment' that comes from seeing other disabled people historically present." As these quotes illustrate, many interviewees felt a sense of connection with disabled subjects of records. The different ways they witnessed disabled people across time evoked a sense of excitement to be able to see pieces of their identity in records. And, despite how—and because—disabled people can be hard to find in records, being able to witness disability in archives created a sense of connection with disabled people across time, highlighting the value and importance of witnessing disabled people in history.

I'm drawn to think about how these themes echo and extend writing around interdependence. Mingus describes how "[i]nterdependency is both 'you and I' and 'we.' It is solidarity, in the best sense of the word. It is inscribing community on our skin over and over and over again. It is truly moving together in an oppressive world towards liberation and refusing to let the personal be a scapegoat for the political."[59] Through their excitement around and desire for evidence of disabled people, many participants expressed their communion with disabled people in the past, even through their limited and problematic representation or even absence. Through the ways in which, as O'Toole states, "disabled people are between the lines or are in situations we don't wish they were," some disabled people who use archives can identify the traces of us in history, because, as Mingus writes, "the truth is: we need each other. We need each other. And every time we turn away from each other, we turn away from ourselves. We know this. Let us not go around, but instead, courageously through."[60] Along these lines, this research demonstrates the power of turning toward and going through archives—of witnessing and relating to disabled people in archives and of finding power, solidarity, and community within those moments.

Extending interdependency further, I recognize that this research connects disabled people in community not only in the present moment, but also across time. Thinking about the history of sick and disabled people of the past, Piepzna-Samarasinha states, "Disability justice allowed me to understand that me writing from my sickbed wasn't being weak or uncool or not a real writer but a *time-honored crip creative practice*."[61] Likewise, records serve as evidence of disabled existence throughout time. The deep connection that interviewees felt to disabled people represented in records underscores what I might call an *archival interdependence*: interdependence, care, and community that disabled people can feel not only with current communities but also with disabled people and practices in the past in archival materials. Thus, this research highlights the expansive temporal nature of interdependence. Disabled people feel in community with those in the past, describing not only a sense of identity through records—experiencing the importance of how "we were there"—but also feeling in community with them—to have ancestors and to feel connected to them.

Further, considering the multiple and expansive temporal aspects of both archives and disability, an archival interdependence not only points backwards to our histories of oppression, resistance, and resilience, but also forward toward our collective liberation. Piepzna-Samarasinha writes, "I passionately believe in recording sick and disabled QTBIPOC [Queer, Trans, Black, Indigenous, People of Color] stories, and because I believe the stories I have witnessed and participated in over the past decade of building ways of creating care [are] both a core part of disability justice work and the work of making the next world, the world we want."[62] Lorde also points to future-building, positing that "[w]ithin the interdependence of mutual (nondominant) differences lies that security which enables us to descend into the chaos of knowledge and return with true visions of our future, along with the concomitant power to effect those changes which can bring that future into being."[63] Along similar lines, interviewees illustrated their desires for the future activation of records. O'Toole described "how to take that information and make it useful and available to other people in a contemporary context," so that, as Suggitt emphasizes, "people are aware that this happened." And, as Pickens tells us, "If someone would but understand this piece of paper and this archive and its importance, then maybe I won't have to fight these battles anymore." Within their critical approaches to the past were also imaginings of the future—where people could be aware of disability histories, learn about the nuances around disability, and could therefore better understand disabled people in the present and into the future. In other words, the very records that advocate for the eradication or institutionalization of disability can also serve as evidence to be politicized for our contemporary and future liberation. This chapter, then, describes not only multifaceted affective responses to the representation of disabled people in the past, but also the need for, commitment to, and interdependency with disabled people across time and toward a more just future. Disabled communities, as this research shows, are connected not only through cross-disability solidarity, but also across time and space—through learning about past oppressions, struggles, activism, resilience, and existence of disabled people, even through their absence in historical records.

Conclusion

By approaching archives through a notion of interdependence, this chapter thinks through some facets of what might be called an *archival interdependence*. These conversations have helped me to show how the representation of disability is frequently perceived as having limits, whether intentional—through how records were created for the containment and criminalization of disabled people—unintentional—through documentation practices around medical history and disability—or through archival decision making—their description and placement in archives. Yet, archival interdependence prompts a rethinking of those limits and their impacts while at the same time gesturing toward disabled communities that can be located across time. The unique lenses that disabled people bring to archives—to locate, interpret, complicate, and affectively experience records on disability—create a constellation of contexts for how we understand disabled people in history. Through shedding light on the archival interdependence of disabled people with our histories, this research opens space for more questions.

Historical representations also make room for recognizing problematic histories and enacting interventions. For example, Chris Bell's use of HIV/AIDS criminalization law and case records not only illuminates the violence on Black disabled and queer bodyminds, but also makes space for Bell to coconstruct and respond to public narratives constructed in an archives. He states in reference to one legal case, "The politics of containment are alive and well as *evidenced* in: the Cox and Carriker cases, [and] the questionable laws in Atlanta."[64] Bell intersperses personal narratives with such laws and legal cases of HIV/AIDS criminalization in order to reflect, respond to, and complicate such records. His mode of engagement with archival records and histories of containment is but one instance of refiguring historical narratives through disabled subjectivity, agency, and pleasure.[65] To draw on Lorde, Mingus, Piepzna-Samarasinha, and many others who write toward more just futures through interdependence, I wonder how else might archives make room for future disabled people's interventions and imaginings with histories.

Further, interdependence, as many note, is not just collective care between disabled people, but expands broadly to include people who don't identify as disabled in supporting disabled people. How might archival interdependence fit into archival practice? Through understanding disabled people's complex relationships with their misrepresentation in archival material, might we extend archival interdependence to the responsibility of archivists to address harmful or problematic descriptive language? What might collective care and solidarity with disabled people look like for records about disability? I am interested in asking how archivists might work with disabled communities to further foster archival interdependence and forge new solidarities with multiple archival subjects, users, creators, donors, and communities.

This chapter not only illustrates the archival ways in which disabled people are in community with one another, but also lays the foundation to better understand the nuances of archival erasure. This research demonstrates the necessity for disabled people to see themselves in history as well as the need for a political activation of archival material through the development of robust critical and theoretical frameworks for archivists and archival users alike. And by connecting disabled lived experiences to disability theories, this research shows how theory does not only exist in academe, but is experienced, felt, and theorized by disabled people in everyday life. By centering archival interdependence in response to these themes, this work is just the beginning of elevating the people who are impacted by representations of disability, who interpret records and histories in unique ways, and who are invested in cocreating more just futures.

Notes

1. Leah Lakshmi Piepzna-Samarasinha, *Care Work: Dreaming Disability Justice* (Arsenal Pulp Press, 2018), 240–41.

2. These words come from the communities who have reclaimed them and use them as identity and community identifiers. For example, see Richard A. Ingram, "Doing Mad Studies: Making (Non)Sense Together," *Intersectionalities: A Global Journal of Social Work Analysis, Research, Polity, and Practice* 5, no. 3 (December 29, 2016): 11; La Marr Jurelle Bruce, *How to Go Mad without Losing Your Mind: Madness and Black Radical Creativity* (Duke University Press, 2021); Margaret Price, *Mad at School: Rhetorics of Mental Disability and Academic Life* (University of Michigan Press, 2011); Therí Alyce Pickens, *Black Madness: Mad Blackness* (Duke University Press, 2019); Johanna Hedva, "Sick Woman Theory," *Mask Magazine*, January 19, 2016, http://www.maskmagazine.com/not-again/struggle/sick-woman-theory; H-Dirksen L. Bauman and Joseph J. Murray, "Deaf Studies in the 21st Century: 'Deaf-Gain' and the Future of Human Diversity," in *The Oxford Handbook of Deaf Studies, Language, and Education*, Vol. 2, eds. Marc Marschark and Patricia Elizabeth Spencer (Oxford University Press, 2010), 0, https://doi.org/10.1093/oxfordhb/9780195390032.013.0014.

3. Aimi Hamraie and Kelly Fritsch, "Crip Technoscience Manifesto," *Catalyst: Feminism, Theory, Technoscience* 5, no. 1 (April 1, 2019): 2.

4. Sins Invalid, *Skin, Tooth, and Bone: The Basis of Movement Is Our People: A Disability Justice Primer*, first edition (Sins Invalid, 2016), 18.

5. Mia Mingus, "Access Intimacy, Interdependence and Disability Justice," *Leaving Evidence* (blog), April 12, 2017, https://leavingevidence.wordpress.com/2017/04/12/access-intimacy-interdependence-and-disability-justice/, emphasis in original.

6. Mingus, "Access Intimacy."

7. Eva Feder Kittay, "17. Dependency," in *Keywords for Disability Studies* (New York University Press, 2015), 54–58.

8. Piepzna-Samarasinha, *Care Work*, 45.

9. Piepzna-Samarasinha, *Care Work*, 45.

10. Mingus, "Access Intimacy."

11. Mingus, "Access Intimacy."

12. Ki'tay Davidson, quoted in Talila "T.L." Lewis, "A Primer: Disability Justice in the Age of Mass Incarceration," 2017, https://affectconf.com/talks/tl/.

13. For example, see Eva Feder Kittay, "Centering Justice on Dependency and Recovering Freedom," *Hypatia* 30, no. 1 (2015): 285–91; A. J. Withers, *Disability Politics and Theory* (Fernwood Publishing, 2012); Barbara Arneil, "Disability, Self Image, and Modern Political Theory," *Political Theory* 37, no. 2 (April 1, 2009): 218–42, https://doi.org/10.1177/0090591708329650.

14. Mingus, "Access Intimacy."

15. Audre Lorde and Cheryl Clarke, *Sister Outsider: Essays and Speeches*, reprint edition (Crossing Press, 2007), 111.

16. Liz Jackson and Alex Haagaard, "#CriticalAxis: A Community Driven Project from The Disabled List," May 25, 2021, https://www.criticalaxis.org.

17. For example, see Jan Grue, "The Problem with Inspiration Porn: A Tentative Definition and a Provisional Critique," *Disability & Society* 31, no. 6 (July 2, 2016): 838–49, https://doi.org/10.1080/09687599.2016.1205473; Alice Wong, "Stella Young, Inspiration Porn, and the Objectification of Disabled People," *Disability Visibility Project* (blog), October 16, 2014, https://disabilityvisibilityproject.com/2014/10/16/stella-young-inspiration-porn-and-the-objectification-of-disabled-people/; Christopher M. Bell, ed., *Blackness and Disability: Critical Examinations and Cultural Interventions* (Michigan State University Press, 2012); Douglas Baynton, "Slaves, Immigrants, and Suffragists: The Uses of Disability in Citizenship Debates," *PMLA* 120, no. 2 (2005): 562–67; Elizabeth Bearden, *Monstrous Kinds: Body, Space, and Narrative in Renaissance Representations of Disability*, illustrated edition (University of Michigan Press, 2019); Laura Briggs, "The Race of Hysteria: 'Overcivilization' and the 'Savage' Woman in Late Nineteenth-Century Obstetrics and Gynecology," *American Quarterly* 52, no. 2 (2000): 246–73; Evette Dionne and Alice Wong, "Why We're Running a Series about Access," *Bitch Media*, November 1, 2021, https://www.bitchmedia.org/article/access-issue-intro.

18. Chloe Brownlee-Chapman et al., "Between Speaking Out in Public and Being Person-Centred: Collaboratively Designing an Inclusive Archive of Learning Disability History," *International Journal of Heritage Studies* 24, no. 8 (September 14, 2018): 889–903, https://doi.org/10.1080/13527258.2017.1378901.

19. Wendy Duff, Jefferson Sporn, and Emily Herron, "Investigating the Impact of the Living Archives on Eugenics in Western Canada," *Archivaria* 88 (November 17, 2019): 122–61.

20. Gracen Brilmyer, "'Weren't . . . Designed with Lived Experiences of Disability in Mind': The Affect of Archival (In)Accessibility and 'Emotionally Expensive' Spatial (Un)Belonging," *Archivaria*, in press.

21. Brilmyer, "'Weren't . . . Designed with Lived Experiences of Disability in Mind.'"

22. Gracen Brilmyer, "'Many of Whom Have Never Been and Are Like Me and Feel Alienated by It': Access Intimacy in Archives," in *Disability Intimacy: Essays on Love, Care, and Desire*, ed. Alice Wong (Vintage, 2024), 229–42.

23. Gracen Mikus Brilmyer, "'I'm Also Prepared to Not Find Me. It's Great When I Do, but It Doesn't Hurt If I Don't': Crip Time and Anticipatory Erasure for Disabled Archival Users," *Archival Science*, October 18, 2021, https://link.springer.com/article/10.1007/s10502-021-09372-1.

24. Johnny Saldana, *The Coding Manual for Qualitative Researchers*, third edition (Sage Publications, 2015); Barney G. Glaser and Anselm L. Strauss, *The Discovery of Grounded Theory: Strategies for Qualitative Research* (Transaction Publishers, 2009); Anselm Strauss and Juliet Corbin, *Basics of Qualitative Research: Grounded Theory Procedures and Techniques*, second edition (SAGE Publications, Inc., 1990).

25. Margaret Price and Stephanie L. Kerschbaum, "Stories of Methodology: Interviewing Sideways, Crooked and Crip," *Canadian Journal of Disability Studies* 5, no. 3 (October 31, 2016): 18–56, https://doi.org/10.15353/cjds.v5i3.295.

26. After all ten interviews were complete, I emailed each participant to get their consent to connect them as a cohort. Currently, eight out of ten participants have been connected with one another via email.

27. Gracen M. Brilmyer, "'It Could Have Been Us in a Different Moment. It Still Is Us in Many Ways': Community Identification and the Violence of Archival Representation of Disability," in *Sustainable Digital Communities*, eds. Anneli Sundqvist et al., Lecture Notes in Computer Science (Springer International Publishing, 2020), 480–86, https://doi.org/10.1007/978-3-030-43687-2_38; Brilmyer, "'I'm Also Prepared to Not Find Me.'"

28. Stefan Sunandan Honisch, interview by author, July 18, 2018.

29. Jess Waggoner, interview by author, August 16, 2018.

30. Corbett Joan O'Toole, interview by author, July 17, 2018.

31. Cody Jackson, interview by author, July 5, 2018.

32. Stefan Sunandan Honisch, interview by author, July 18, 2018.

33. Corbett Joan O'Toole, interview by author, July 17, 2018.

34. Therí A. Pickens, interview by author, September 6, 2018.

35. Michelle Ganz, interview by author, August 14, 2019.

36. Alida Boorn, interview by author, August 7, 2019.

37. Therí A. Pickens, interview by author, September 6, 2018.

38. Travis Chi Wing Lau, interview by author, August 16, 2019.

39. Travis Chi Wing Lau, interview by author, August 16, 2019.

40. William Edward Burghardt Du Bois, *The Souls of Black Folk* (Courier Corporation, 1994), 8.

41. Therí A. Pickens, interview by author, September 6, 2018.

42. Jess Waggoner, interview by author, August 16, 2018.

43. Megan Suggitt, interview by author, July 6, 2018.

44. Michelle Ganz, interview by author, August 14, 2019.

45. Lilith Siegel, interview by author, August 23, 2018.

46. Travis Chi Wing Lau, interview by author, August 16, 2019.
47. Travis Chi Wing Lau, interview by author, August 16, 2019.
48. Alida Boorn, interview by author, August 7, 2019.
49. Stefan Sunandan Honisch, interview by author, July 18, 2018.
50. Megan Suggitt, interview by author, July 6, 2018.
51. Cody Jackson, interview by author, July 5, 2018.
52. Lilith Siegel, interview by author, August 23, 2018.
53. Corbett Joan O'Toole, interview by author, July 17, 2018.
54. Stefan Sunandan Honisch, interview by author, July 18, 2018.
55. Stefan Sunandan Honisch, interview by author, July 18, 2018.
56. Therí A. Pickens, interview by author, September 6, 2018.
57. Brilmyer, "'I'm Also Prepared to Not Find Me.'"
58. Brilmyer, "'I'm Also Prepared to Not Find Me.'"
59. Mia Mingus, "Interdependency (Excerpts from Several Talks)," *Leaving Evidence* (blog), January 22, 2010, https://leavingevidence.wordpress.com/2010/01/22/interdependency-exerpts-from-several-talks/.
60. Mingus, "Interdependency (Excerpts from Several Talks)."
61. Piepzna-Samarasinha, *Care Work*, 17, emphasis added.
62. Piepzna-Samarasinha, *Care Work*, 35.
63. Lorde and Clarke, *Sister Outsider*, 111–12.
64. Christopher M. Bell, "I'm Not the Man I Used to Be: Sex, HIV, and Cultural 'Responsibility,'" in *Sex and Disability*, eds. Robert McRuer and Anna Mollow (Duke University Press Books, 2012), 224, emphasis added.
65. Bell has referred to such interventions as "recovery work" and "detective work" to "uncove(r) the misrepresentation of black, disabled bodies and the missed opportunities to think about how those bodies transform(ed) systems and culture." Bell, ed., *Blackness and Disability*, 3–4.

CHAPTER 18

Transnational Disability Praxis

Archiving Survival, Resistance, and Resilience Amid Ongoing Emergencies

SONA KAZEMI, HEMACHANDRAN KARAH, EFRAT GOLD, AND MARY JEAN HANDE

The project described in this chapter, currently in development, represents an ambition to create a digital living archive designed toward maximizing accessibility transnationally across various ages, disabilities, bodyminds,[1] languages, and other differences. It is an outgrowth of Sona Kazemi's informal Instagram[2] archive that emerged from conversations with disabled people in Iran who became disabled through war and state violence, and is imagined as a platform for disabled people transnationally to contribute, discuss their lives and how they survive, and create opportunities for community connections and solidarity. Informed by the principles of disability justice,[3] we are imagining how we might create a public resource available to anyone with internet access. This chapter summarizes our considerations, reflections, and struggles as we strive toward creating an interactive digital archive and multilingual dictionary of disability and care; resources that can provide a platform upon which community, linguistic ethos, activism, solidarity, and justice can flourish complementarily. First, we conceptualize and introduce the project. Following the introduction, we discuss the project's ambitions and goals in more detail, provide a brief description of Kazemi's (2017) transnational disability theory and praxis,[4] and flesh out the history of the project. Then we discuss traditions within radical archiving that we draw from and hope to further build on before explaining what we mean by "cripping the archive" in this project. We end with a discussion of the barriers to carrying out this project as well as our hesitations in creating this resource.

Conceptualizing the Project

During early COVID lockdowns, Kazemi began having livestreamed conversations on her Instagram channel with acid attack and torture survivors in Iran. After each conversation, more survivors would reach out, wanting their stories livestreamed and describing various aspects and elements of their lives. Kazemi began to notice a desire from those she spoke with to convey both their ongoing systemic neglect, poverty, and marginalization as well as the innovative informal strategies of survival that people adopt and experience community through. Although such informal infrastructures of care are present everywhere alongside formal institutional arrangements, little has been done toward understanding and documenting how informal infrastructures work and are maintained. Our interest in pursuing this project lies in providing a platform for diverse disabled and older people to share our/their methods of survival and resilience. Integrating concepts of mutual aid and radical archiving practices, we envision this project as a living space where community can build and grow, and as a form of sharing stories, thus creating accessible new framings for scholars, activists, and community members. Through discussions based on Kazemi's Instagram channel, we realized that this is a type of digital oral history archive that, among other things, documents disabled survival through informal care infrastructures. As people discussed their care communities and strategies, the idea emerged to create a multilingual dictionary of care that articulates how disability is understood, expressed, communicated, and accommodated across languages and emotional registers. Informed by the terms emerging from the oral histories, we imagine creating a resource that draws connections and understandings rooted in the language used by disabled people to describe varied experiences of disability.

Given the disproportionate impact of the pandemic on older people (who may or may not be disabled) around the world, we want to feature their experiences as well, highlighting the "aging-disability" nexus[5] as we think through transnational relations and practices, and how processes and relations of violence and disaster impact older and disabled people in different and similar ways. This works toward building solidarity across generations and disability status, tracing how the need for care and support marginalizes some and not others. In developing this project, we address the lack of transnational representations, multilingual expressions of disability, and global connections, and we work to build solidarity across difference. By focusing our oral history archive transnationally and foregrounding informal infrastructures of care, we imagine materializing this project in a way that fosters new language, connections, and solidarities across borders, linguistic boundaries, and other barriers.

History of the Project

This project is the outgrowth of two existing research projects: a social media archive and radio program based on Kazemi's interviews with various disabled people, torture survivors, burn survivors, and acid attack victims in the Middle East and elsewhere; and a digital archive project called *Recovery Project: Actions of Survival, Archives of Resilience* led by Kazemi, Hemachandran Karah, and a few other scholars.[6] In this latter community-engaged project, the team conducted ninety surveys and nineteen interviews with people on the frontline of COVID-19 with a focus on their unique mental health and resilience strategies, and asked them what stories/images/discourses represent their experiences. With this data, the team created an "Archive of Resilience," using discourse, narrative, and rhetorical analysis to discuss how these images and stories contribute to resilience (or don't and disrupt understandings of resilience). The project endeavored to build a community-engaged archive of pandemic testimonies, collected from those affected. During the *Recovery Project*, Kazemi and Karah realized that formal modes of investigation (i.e., questionnaires) miss the role of informal care infrastructures, such as those emerging from Kazemi's conversations with acid attack and torture survivors in Iran and others excluded from state and institutional supports, such as migrants.

Oral Archive and Dictionary of Disability and Care

The potential of this project to contribute to growing interest in radically rethinking archival knowledge and challenging expert authority over contested histories is exciting, not only because it provides new insight into the survival of disabled and mad people but also because the project is designed to include community partners at every stage. We imagine this resource to not only promote inclusion of disabled people but to consider many types of technological accessibility needed to create an oral archive and dictionary of disability and care. Creating this resource will require intensive consultation with an advisory board of disabled people, civil society members, grassroots organizations, scholars, activists, and community partners across the world to develop our project as an accessible teaching, research, and community-building tool.

As we develop this resource, the needs and priorities of scholars and participants need to be identified in order to best incorporate disability stories and disability justice into an accessible digital oral history archive and multilingual dictionary. The archive and dictionary are designed to enhance solidarity across difference, which is an important function of community pedagogy. Solidarity is essential for marginalized communities' sense of well-being and as a catalyst for change. Further, attitudes and perceptions of disability vary widely between places, cultures, classes, and other forms of difference. We aim to build a resource that facilitates learning with openness and curiosity, connecting across difference, and sharing strategies of disability justice organizing and survival through informal networks.

Our project can become a valuable pedagogical tool, creating a multilingual dictionary of care, a digital archive that can prompt novel approaches to studies of resilience, community-based care practices and discrimination, and a community-driven resource aimed at including people with diverse disabilities in meaningful ways. An accessible archive of oral histories offers disabled people a place to share their experiences where they are respected, validated, documented, and included in analyses about their lives and perceptions. As the work of philosopher and critical educator Paulo Freire demonstrates in *Pedagogy of the Oppressed*, the experience of unpacking a stressful experience in the immediate circumstance itself lightens the burden of that stress.[7] This life-affirming effect is also discussed in all leading work in trauma theory, including Babette Rothschild's pathbreaking *The Body Remembers*.[8] The point is not to replace psychotherapy, but to draw upon the beneficial effects of sharing strategies for survival as one piece of a constellation of resources that considers the well-being of disabled people.

The narratives and contributions collected will form a living archive that prioritizes transnationally accessible content and is designed toward challenging oppression, ableism, ageism, and stigma by sharing diverse stories and contributions from disabled, mad, and older people, highlighting themes of survival and resilience. We engage the academic fields of historiography, medical humanities, linguistics, care work, narrative, disability studies, aging studies, as well as Deaf, Mad, and anti-ableist, anti-ageist politics as we work with transnational social justice movements. Our goal is to build cross-cultural relations that are geared toward social justice intersectionality and promote solidarity between diverse community-based social movements transnationally.

The growing field of disability studies has built a powerful platform from which disabled people and our allies are fighting ableism and exploring disability and madness as legitimate and valuable ways of being in and perceiving the world. However, the need for this project stems from a gap in disability studies—namely, that disabled people in the non-Western world remain underrepresented in the field (with notable exceptions, including the work of Shaun Gretch in global disability studies). Disability exists everywhere in the world, and part of the struggle of creating a transnationally inclusive disability studies is finding ways to communicate across different frameworks, histories, and languages of disability—a theme more fully addressed through the project's multilingual dictionary. We will potentially take into account the evolution of local and institutional histories of differences in the making of concepts and languages of disability. Our resource will promote a culture of equity, access, and accommodation transnationally, providing a historical record of the ways that disabled people survive around the world and communicate their survival strategies across difference. As archives represent a type of cultural memory and record of what has existed, this project also involves writing disabled people and their survival into recorded history (i.e., cripping histor(iograph)y).[9] This transnational archive will be a necessary resource toward more inclusive and equitable relations. In creating a platform where stories of survival and care can be shared, we highlight the role of mutual aid networks that disabled people create and rely upon but that are chronically under-resourced and ignored as sources of support and survival in the lives of many. Inspired by Roy Porter and in the tradition of doing history from below, we purposefully consider the distortions produced by expert-centered accounts as we create a living archive that features stories of individuality, community, and the messy realities of being a disabled person navigating diverse social, political, and economic realities.[10]

This exploratory project will be unique in its global reach and multilingual focus, leading to the creation of a public resource that does not yet exist. Although disabled people are regularly excluded, isolated, and disconnected from one another and society, we approach in the opposite manner, by emphasizing the lives, relations, multiplicity, and strength of disabled people, and helping disabled and scholarly communities further connect across contexts and regions. The expansive goals of our project are crucial in recognizing systemic and cultural barriers faced by disabled people. An accessible digital archive can directly serve participants and their broader communities by making raw data available and amplifying the strategies and tactics utilized by participants to broaden global disability and community-based care networks. Contributors are invited to share what they wish through a variety of creative works (such as poetry, photography, film, and fiction), visual arts, and more traditional written and audio/video narratives. We will curate contributions, commentary, curriculum, teaching texts and resources, along with strategies for integrating marginalized knowledge into various disciplines, community social justice struggles, notes from the field (e.g., war zone activism, underground shelters, grassroots prototyping infrastructures, mutual aid projects, informal caregiving tactics, and clandestine grassroot organizing details under authoritarian states), and historical discussions concerning disability into an accessible website. This will raise consciousness about the global reach/interconnections of localized informal responses, allowing participants, communities, and scholars to identify and analyze gaps in formal support that make informal strategies necessary.

Dictionary of Care

To understand the narratives we have collected/plan to collect, we embark on what we call a "Dictionary of Care." The proposed dictionary need not be a mere glossary of terms linked to caring but an evolving corpus of narrative performances shaped by disability, caregiving, and survival. In other words, we can say that oral histories will be analyzed for language/terms/concepts that can inform the dictionary. Creating a multilingual dictionary of care and aligning that with some data practices can help the research field but may also help individuals who seek care and community online.

In one sense, the dictionary will host the newly developed vocabulary linked to care, and therefore, it will complement the archive and even act as a tool of knowledge expansion. In other words, it is supposed to value and enhance the digital archive of informal infrastructure. Almost all dictionaries are gathered based on formal curation methods. For example, dictionaries involving language and meaning, grammar, society, and disciplines such as psychoanalysis all rely on formal curation methods. However, this is not how our multilingual dictionary is conceived. It derives its reason for being from ground practices, grassroots realities, and language crossovers that transpire amid care relationships. When care happens, it also gives rise to novel relationships, kinships, nomenclatures, narrative universes, connective modalities, cosmologies, and objects of care such as prosthetics. Our multilingual dictionary based on Kazemi's oral history archive is geared to such possibilities.

We will curate a multilingual dictionary of care based on the following themes emerging from Kazemi's existing archive:

(1) Multisensory registers of care

Senses such as touch were highlighted during COVID, when so many were unable to access physical intimacy. Registers link to touch, and other sensory modes do not vanish altogether. In fact, they come back alive as disabled people creatively deploy institutionally invalidated senses such as touch. There is an urgent need to capture such animations. In terms of formal networks, touch may be associated with people knowing each other and establishing some form of intimacy. In a care relationship, touch may involve sentiments such as gratitude that are local to a particular cultural arrangement. There is no one way of defining gratitude. A formal dictionary definition in English concerning gratitude may not be able to capture the significance with which it emerges in a care relationship that takes place in a totally alien language. This situation may be an opportunity for us to explore how dictionary definitions evolve across cultural settings and eventually live alongside local meanings.

(2) Kitchen speaks

Most societies depend upon culinary interventions for healing, nourishment, and resilience. Such culinary interventions do not remain static; they travel via community channels through a special cluster of registers and lexicons (words and idioms). One may call this "kitchen speak."

(3) Emotional registers

Emotional registers form the bedrock of formal institutions. For example, notions of romantic love vary greatly between Indian and Western traditions. Due to a culture of cerebralization, such registers remain grossly invalidated. By cerebralization we mean rendering human notions intellectually astute so that they are devoid of commonplace language and feeling. Making a notion only intellectually appealing can be hugely self-serving and caters much less to everyday living. A multilingual dictionary of care can meaningfully account for emotional registers that make possible informal infrastructures of care in the first place. Registers are meanings that are local to disciplines, institutions, and cultures. For example, there are registers for physics, religions, and literature, meaning they have their own vocabularies.

(4) Folk intuitions

Folk intuitions are idiosyncratic beliefs. They shape all human decisions, yet they remain underanalyzed. All the same, folk intuition is shaped by an archive of diction that is orally transmitted. A glossary of diction linked to folk intuition may therefore add value to an oral history archive as a method.

(5) Narrative moments of imperilment

Care infrastructures sometimes crumble. Along with them crash human theories, institutions, frameworks, and expressions. Due to the culture of political correctness, scholars tend to look away from such moments of imperilment. Without exploring imperilment lexicon, we are unlikely to comprehend community resilience and zest for survival. For example, one does not have to feel pity for people in abject poverty. They know how exactly to flourish in a situation where there are very limited means. Instead of pity, one can work with the human propensity for resilience even amid abject poverty.

(6) Histories of objects of care

Layers of history that reflect the social relations of care and caring adhere to various objects and should be included in a dictionary of care. Sometimes objects are used for entirely different purposes than originally intended, such as screen reader technology, which might be used to learn English in service of care. Other more everyday items like cradles and chulhas are also critical objects of care. Mothers might fashion cradles for their infants out of various materials, including castaway items, that capture their ingenuity, creativity, and care for their children who can be secured above floor level and kept safe from harm in the workplace. Chulhas — makeshift stoves — can serve their original purpose of cooking food or, as they are in certain parts of India where communities do not have access to protective shelters, can be used for life-sustaining heat in cold weather. Finally, objects of care may also be found in proverbs, sayings, statements of will, mantras, prayers, and directives that can travel across generations.

To put it ambitiously, in gathering a dictionary of care in tandem with an oral history archive, we may also come up with insights that can potentially shape a novel field such as care lexicography. Community-based lexicography (i.e., the practice of compiling a dictionary) thrives already.[11] Care shapes our narrative universes via lexical, syntactic, performative, affective, analytical, resilient, intermedial, and interpersonal means. Care lexicography is bound to thrive on such insights if we could render it more accessible!

Cripping Expertise

The accessible digital archive conceptualized in this project stems from our interest in radically rethinking archival knowledge and practices, while theorizing archives as contested ideological sites and imaginings that house traces of presences and absences.[12] The need to radically rethink archival knowledge and practice has been taken up around the world, with calls to decolonize queer and crip archives through social justice–informed praxis.[13] Achille Mbembe theorizes archives not as a set of objective data, but rather as a status; a product of human judgment of what is deemed worthy of preserving, and, relatedly, what is not.[14] Expert authority over contested and marginalized histories often conflicts with the lived experiences of those most marginalized and affected by particular conditions and relations. As demonstrated through Indigenous reconciliation efforts in Canada, there is growing need to make marginalized histories public, and to both challenge and rethink "expert" authority over contested realities.[15] The status of being archive-able, that is, deemed worthy of preservation in a recognized archive, is one that has historically been afforded only to officials, professionals, and others with relative privilege and power. This has helped comprise and propel the "expert" into the status of expert—if their documents and artifacts were not deemed worthy of archive-ability, their expertise could more easily be questioned and unsettled. Consider, for example, the victims of state terror in Iran who have long resisted the selective amnesia imposed on their public memory by the Islamic state's practice of denying having ever committed mass atrocities against them since the 1979 revolution.[16] As these instances indicate, so-called expert authority has led to the creation of archives that have historically been recorded from privileged positions, thereby masking the oppression and inequality underlying much of what becomes recorded as archival knowledge.[17] This has led to the continuation of officially recognized knowledge to become synonymous with the knowledge of the oppressor.

In recent decades, radical archiving practices are challenging more traditional practices, where archives are increasingly coming to present an exciting opportunity to reimagine the creation, curation, and record-keeping practices of subjugated knowledges, as created through the realities of ongoing oppression and marginalization. Beyond challenging the types of data and artifacts that can be found in an archive, radical approaches challenge the very notion of status that archives have historically upheld and contributed to, presenting an insurrection of knowledge by those lacking the traditional status of archive-ability—a status increasingly challenged by initiatives such as the Disability Visibility Project initiated by Alice Wong. The politics of display and "museumization of disabled bodies"[18] and ways of recording, acknowledging, and honoring histories of extreme marginalization are increasingly prescient (as demonstrated by Indigenous residential school legacies, social justice–informed curations/exhibits of madness and disability, and exiled Iranian and Syrian dissidents who hold commemoration events in their host land remembering their ongoing struggles for freedom and democracy against the authoritarian states at home). Further, widespread use of technology and the internet has allowed for the creation of user-led living digital archives such as the Digital Archive of Literacy Narratives (DALN), which asks users to share their memories and experiences of literacy, providing a continuously changing cultural platform that creatively records people's literacy practices and compositions of meaning. These novel archiving approaches and practices stem from radical rereadings of epistemic knowledge that seek to address power imbalances through transformative questioning of what archives are, what they do, who they represent, and who they are intended for.

Traditionally, archives have been understood and approached as physical repositories of documents and artifacts, generally recorded and preserved by so-called experts wielding authority over a particular subject matter or repository. In practice, this has translated to the selective recording of only *some* histories, *some* artifacts, and *some* knowledges. As a result, much archival knowledge represents a type of history recorded from above—reflecting the ideologies, biases, status/class, interests, and limits of those with relative authority. Historian Roy Porter challenged this oversight in the field of history, calling instead for "doing medical history from below."[19] The idea of doing history from below has encouraged new sources of data, insight, and politics while displacing the expertise of traditional archivists and historians. As a repository often intended for future audiences, archives present a unique opportunity to reflect on the types of knowledge that can be preserved for the future; what seems important in the moment is not always what's important in a different era and/or context. While there is no way to predict what will be important to future users, our project imagines a creative way to address the lack of transnational representation of disability, survival, and care networks of disabled people.

Transnational Disability Model

The digital archive mobilizes Sona Kazemi's transnational disability theory and praxis,[20] which is rooted in dialectical historical materialism.[21] Following this theory, we conceptualize disability/madness/injury in a transnational context at the intersections of gender, age, race, sexuality, citizenship, and legal status. In contributing to intersectional and transnational approaches to disability, we move away from the mainstream disability studies content emerging from the English-speaking so-called global North—namely the United States, United Kingdom, Canada, and Australia. We (re)theorize disability by trying to unveil the ways in which representations of Western subjects in disability rights and cultural movements have disallowed a focus on disablement caused by violent historical processes and relations in different global contexts (e.g., war, extreme poverty, imperialism, forced migration, theocracy, nationalism, gender-based violence, and torture). Besides being rooted in the material world, a transnational model works toward envisioning and prefiguring a world that, first, is beyond nation-state borders and universalizing disability identities—meaning, disability is co-terminus with the problem of citizenship; second, decenters whiteness and the West as its inseparable norms;[22] third, is where diverse groups of people are organized with intersectional and community-oriented initiatives beyond state-sponsored efforts; and fourth, demystifies the social relations of disability beyond the immediate narrative that the subject evokes. In other words, transnational disability theory allows us to grasp both the social organization of disablement and the situated knowledges of, and resistance to, these social relations. We believe that our transnational, intersectional, and materialist approach to disability offers a spectrum of standpoints that disabled people's movements can make use of. In developing this project, we center the transnational characteristics of the social/political/economic conditions that structure how disabled people and disability communities access each other, health services, and technologies, particularly in times of crisis or emergency.

Cripping

As part of "cripping the archive," we engage in an act of collective witnessing. This collective witnessing is a multilayered process that involves "cripping historiography," whereby disabled and mad people's lives are multilingually documented and honored. As discussed above, this is similar to the idea of "history from below" first articulated by Roy Porter, who in the 1980s suggested that so much of history was missed by not considering the patients' view or the histories of the oppressed—a move that allowed for a drastic widening of the analytic gaze within the field of history.[23] In his foundational work, *Crip Theory*, Robert McRuer uses "cripping" as a verb to expose the ableism involved in a certain process, structure, or attribute. McRuer reclaims the term "crip" as both a verb and a noun to describe a new politics and consciousness around disability.[24] We approach cripping historiography by writing disabled people back into their own histories and exposing the embedded ableism in documenting peoples' histories. Alison Kafer also uses the term "crip" in her book *Feminist, Queer, Crip*, explaining that she finds it more radical, expansive, and fluid than "disability."[25] As Kafer notes, however, the term has some limitations. For instance, it is sometimes used only to refer to physical disabilities or in opposition to cure. The term is slowly being taken up by disability justice activists, but it is not a term that is commonly used by disabled people, particularly outside of the predominantly English-speaking world generally construed as the global North.[26]

Cripping Informal Care

Care work, and particularly informal care work, is often taken for granted, made invisible and unpaid. For many, as Rachel Gorman explains, experiences of madness or disability is just "struggle" or "life."[27] Nevertheless, informal care practices are increasingly being politicized, particularly since the beginning of the COVID pandemic, when informal caregiving became further strained and caregiver burnout became an undeniable reality across the world. As precarious communities cobbled together resources, support networks, and survival strategies, mutual aid societies proliferated around the world and in diverse communities,[28] popularizing community care organizing principles and practice.[29] Disability justice activists have been quick to comment that many of the mutual aid practices are not new in disability communities, and that in fact, mutual aid networks and practices have been a core dimension of organizing and survival in disability communities for decades.[30] Nevertheless, disability justice activist Leah Lakshmi Piepzna-Samarasinha notes that mutual aid or informal care is "cripped" or practiced differently in disabled versus nondisabled communities, characterized by small acts such as checking in on people or "showing up" in disabled spaces and relationships (as opposed to "showy" or heroic displays of support) and geared toward "long-haul" community building and practices of reimagining care and support.[31] This archive project works toward cripping informal care in response to disabling violence and emergencies. This includes making the invisible care labor and technologies visible, storied, and politicized as a means of both survival and resistance for disabled people globally.[32]

Advisory Board as Continuous Community Engagement

A project with the ambition of creating a transnational community and scholarly resource that does not yet exist requires ongoing reflection and community feedback along the way, allowing our team to make changes in approach, direction, or philosophy as needed. To this end, we imagine the assembly of a transnational, multidisciplinary, social justice–oriented advisory board. Informed by our commitment to community pedagogy, our team aims to be meaningfully engaged with disability justice communities and to support the goals of these communities toward political empowerment, representation, transnational mobilization, and conscientization.[33] The advisory board aims to include representatives from grassroots and/or advocacy groups and people with or without an institutional affiliation from across the world who are engaged in supporting marginalized people who access grassroots support and health services. The composition of the advisory board will ensure that we are in ongoing dialogue with multilingual grassroots communities, scholars, and disability groups from around the world.

With our focus on informal infrastructures, we anticipate that advisors who are not institutionally affiliated may be central to this endeavor, yet will likely require structural supports such as monetary compensation or access to digital technologies to be able to participate. These individuals will likely not have previous experience working with formal research teams and may find difficulties in participating or critiquing the project design and plans. We might better engage the expertise of these members through informal individual conversations or by other personalized means that best fit the person and context. By engaging them this way, we hope to support ongoing and creative actions toward flattening hierarchies between researchers and community organizations, which facilitate relationship building, idea sharing, collective decision making, and meaningful engagement toward mutually beneficial outcomes.[34]

Clearly, we will also need ongoing feedback from scholars who would use this resource for teaching and research purposes so that we can consistently work toward improving our prototype and eventual platform, making it a valuable and usable tool informed by diverse academic communities. To this end, the advisory board will also include selected academics who are not formally a part of the research team.

Engagement with our ethical guidelines for inclusion in the advisory board is informed by Bridget Pratt's priority-setting framework for participatory research, which attends to considerations of power and difference.[35] This helps us to recognize and attend to power dynamics related to identity, language, institutional privilege, etc. within the advisory board and research team more broadly. As we develop the archive, the advisory board will serve as a touchstone to ensure these resources are developed centering disabled grassroots community-based values, goals, and social justice politics and traditions. Our engagement activities will be iterative and dynamic, ensuring that the advisory team adequately supports the archival content and strategic community outreach activities we are currently engaged in. We plan to meet with the advisory board regularly to receive guidance and feedback on the project's evolving goals and be informed as we innovatively approach accessibility and universal design, as well as ensuring ethical engagement with participants. Following the traditions of disability studies, access always remains alive as a question, an ongoing practice, and a consideration that requires our presence and attention.[36]

Ethical Risks and Commitments

The highly public and transnational character of this archive requires us to be reflexive and mindful of the potential risk for this type of subaltern storytelling. Participants whose activism may be criminalized and prosecutable in their counties may be hesitant about the risks involved or want to participate anonymously.

We plan to work with those wanting to participate through ethical and creative deployment of digital technologies. For example, wherever necessary we may anonymize contributors who may experience torture and annihilation in their places of domicile. Given our commitment to cripping the archives, we consider inclusion through a multisensorial sensibility. For example, a person who is on a ventriloquial rant about state excesses may face total annihilation. Her voice therefore may be protected by layers of voiceover speech modulations. Such multisensorial blurring may contribute creative ways of preserving multivocality in times of crisis.

Because we imagine the archive to facilitate relationship building and independent interactions among participants, there are also risks to researchers and other participants that might arise from these interactions. Such ethical and social dilemmas have already arisen in Kazemi's current archival work. As part of her efforts to raise awareness about disability rights and gender inequality in Iran, Kazemi decided to connect with disabled women who have been attacked by acid by going live and interviewing them on Instagram. This gave her an opportunity to foreground the material reality of ableism and sexism that exists in Iran and attempt to convey what people with disabilities or visible physical differences, like a burn scar, actually go through on a daily basis. The results were shocking. One acid survivor revealed that her landlord asked her to vacate her apartment after the acid attack, due to the stigma attached to such incidents. Another disabled woman said that the disability allowance that she receives from the Social Welfare Organization in Iran (*Behzisti*) is barely enough to buy four cartons of eggs, while she has other expenses to take care of, including uninsured medications. The more live conversations Kazemi had with disabled Iranian women to highlight their problems and build a culture against ableism and sexism, the more frustrated and useless she felt. Witnessing other people's pain and not being able to change much in their lives is synonymous with suffering.

Further, while doing this work, it is easy to find oneself giving directions and providing unsolicited advice to vulnerable populations with whom one conducts research, for a variety of reasons. During her encounters with disabled people and burn survivors, Kazemi found many of them messaging her privately and asking for mostly financial help. Given that disabled people deal with poverty almost everywhere in the world, disabled people in Iran are no different, not to mention the economic and social difficulties imposed on the country's economy by the Iranian state's imperialist adventures in the Middle East region and its deep corruption. Therefore, it is completely understandable that disabled people are hit the hardest with horrific social, political, and economic obstacles.

We are mindful of the complex feelings of guilt, frustration, and helplessness that such cries for help might arouse in those directly engaged in the project. We are mindful that we must remain careful not to view our roles in this project as saving or rescuing other disabled people. "Saving" rhetoric is especially problematic since it exacerbates extant power imbalances between activists with relative privilege in the Western world and potential disabled participants elsewhere in the world that derive from vastly different circumstances and cultures. We imagine the goal of this project as building solidarity. Developing community-based principles and ethical guidelines with our advisory board and engaging regularly with the board regarding such inevitable ethical dilemmas will help address tensions as they arise.

While our aim is to create a space that can manifest material change, we must use a deft hand in facilitating organic connection and networking between contributors. Where there is much need, there is also messiness and complexity. At times even the participants' activism strategies may be different and contradictory. For instance, Kazemi observed that some of her interviewees believed that working with the system is the only way through and that working with government-run medical facilities is better because they are cheaper. Others, however, articulated that government facilities are awful and useless. They believe that working with doctors in private medical settings is the best way. Proponents of these two very different approaches to activism regarding the same issue often get into arguments online when they are live on Instagram.

These disagreements and conflicts are unavoidable and part of any collective or community-based project. Moderating, setting boundaries, and starting some structuring through these conflicts as we are thinking about building spaces for connection and solidarity building is an essential component of this larger project. Sometimes, differences and contradictions are not solvable or resolvable. We just have to hold on to the tension to come up with thoughtful, insightful, and complex ways of proceeding in relation.

Further, as Kazemi observed in her social media activism, oppressive jokes circulate a lot. Many of those who crack such jokes are not bad people. These jokes are used as a "rhetorical tool" to mediate the harsh and brutal realities these individuals must navigate in their lives. Disability studies scholar Hemachandran Karah, who is blind, says: "I crack blind-related jokes to handle realities that don't accommodate me. Materiality of accommodation and the rhetoric around accommodation don't go together at all." Mary Jean Hande says that she sees this in the organizing work that she does. "We [humans] are full of contradictions," she states. "We have regressive tendencies, so we see this from time to time."

The value of creating an online space like the one we imagine is in bringing people together who struggle with very different challenges. People will come with their own consciousness in approaching these stories, and they transform their own consciousness as they emerge and change in the course of the oral history building. We acknowledge that curating, mediating, and moderating these interactions will not be an easy task.

Conclusion

This archival project is unprecedented and politically necessary in its attempts to connect diverse communities of disabled people in places in the world that are currently largely ignored by most disability theorists and activists. Messiness and contradiction are inevitable in a project that engages directly and reflexively with complex and widely diverse communities. Yet, we understand that social justice, meaningful community engagement, and transformative change is messy work, and that by embracing and working through these contradictions within this project, we are contributing to the transnational disability studies praxis.[37] Breaking from traditional archival approaches that seek to create order, this project instead takes up an approach informed by social justice that challenges exclusionary practices of what gets the status of being archivable and centers self-representation in accounts of disabled life, kinship, and survival. We are enthusiastic about connecting with other coconspirators interested in cripping the archive in the subversive and revolutionary ways found in the pages of this book. To this end, we suggest tools and methods that acknowledge the informal characteristics of care that thrive beyond formal institutional boundaries.

Notes

1. Margaret Price, "The Bodymind Problem and the Possibilities of Pain," *Hypatia* (2014): 1–17.

2. https://www.instagram.com/drsonakazemi/.

3. Disabled activists and cultural workers based in California have articulated ten principles of disability justice: intersectionality, leadership of those most impacted, anticapitalist politic, commitment to cross-movement organizing, recognizing wholeness, sustainability, commitment to cross-disability solidarity, interdependence, collective access, and collective liberation. For more detail, see https://www.sinsinvalid.org/blog/10-principles-of-disability-justice/.

4. Sona Kazemi, "Toward a Conceptualization of Transnational Disability Theory and Praxis: Engaging the Dialectics of Geopolitics, Third World, and Imperialism," *Critical Disability Discourse Journal* (2017): 31–63.

5. Katie Aubrecht, Christine Kelly, and Carla Rice, *The Aging-Disability Nexus* (Vancouver: University of British Colombia Press, 2020).

6. Amy Shuman, Margaret Price, and Amrita Dhar.

7. Paulo Freire, *Pedagogy of the Oppressed* (New York: Continuum, 2000).

8. Babette Rothschild, *The Body Remembers: The Psychophysiology of Trauma and Trauma Treatment* (New York: W. W. Norton and Co., 2000).

9. Sona Kazemi, *Disabling Relations: Wounded Bodyminds and Transnational Praxis* (Philadelphia: Temple University Press, forthcoming).

10. Roy Porter, "The Patient's View: Doing Medical History from Below." *Theory and Society* (1985): 175–98.

11. See Gregory D. S. Anderson and Anna L. Daigneault, "Living Dictionaries: An Electronic Lexicography Tool for Community Activists." *Proceedings of eLex* (2021): 339–60.

12. Jenny Rice, *Awful Archives: Conspiracy Theory, Rhetoric, and Acts of Evidence* (Columbus: The Ohio State University Press, 2020); L. White, "Hodgepodge Historiography: Documents, Itineraries, and the Absence of Archives." *History in Africa* (2015): 309–18.

13. Achille Mbembe, "Decolonizing Knowledge and the Question of the Archive" [lecture]. Wits Institute for Social and Economic Research (2015); C. Birdsall, M. Parry, and V. Tkaczyk, "Listening to the Mind: Tracing the Auditory History of Mental Illness in Archives and Exhibitions." *The Public Historian* (2015): 47–72; E. Gagen, "Facing Madness: The Ethics of Exhibiting Sensitive Historical Photographs." *Journal of Historical Geography* (2021): 39–50.

14. Achille Mbembe, "The Power of the Archive and Its Limits," in *Refiguring the Archive*, by C. Hamilton et al., eds. (Amsterdam: Kluwer Academic Publishers, 2002), 19–26.

15. Dian Million, *Therapeutic Nations: Healing in an Age of Indigenous Human Rights* (Tucson: University of Arizona Press, 2013); Karen Stote, *An Act of Genocide: Colonialism and the Sterilization of Aboriginal Women* (Black Point, NS: Fernwood Publishing, 2015).

16. Kazemi, "Disabling Relations: Injured Bodyminds and Active Witnessing."

17. Bill Adair, Benjamin Filene, and Laura Koloski, *Letting Go? Sharing Historical Authority in a User-Generated World* (Walnut Creek, CA: Left Coast Press, 2011); Mbembe, "Decolonizing Knowledge and the Question of the Archive"; White, "Hodgepodge Historiography."

18. Sona Kazemi, *Toward a Conceptualization of Transnational Disability Theory and Praxis: Entry Point, Iraqi Chemical Attack on Iran* (PhD dissertation, Toronto, University of Toronto, 2018), 164.

19. Porter, "The Patient's View," 65.

20. Kazemi, "Toward a Conceptualization of Transnational Disability Theory and Praxis," 31.

21. Karl Marx and Friedrich Engels, *The German Ideology, Including Theses on Feuerbach* (New York: Prometheus Books, 1932/1998).

22. See the works of Mel Y. Chen, *Animacies: Biopolitics, Racial Mattering, and Queer Affect* (Durham, NC: Duke University Press, 2012); Parin Dosa, "Creating Alternative and Demedicalized Spaces: Testimonial Narrative on Disability, Culture, and Racialization." *Journal of International Women's Studies* (2008): 79–101; Nirmala Erevelles, *Disability and Difference in Global Contexts: Enabling a Transformative Body Politic* (New York: Palgrave MacMillan, 2011); Helen Meekosha, "Decolonizing Disability: Thinking and Acting Globally." *Disability & Society* (2011): 667–82; Christopher B. Bell, "Introducing (White) Disability Studies: A Modest Proposal," in *The Disability Studies Reader*, second edition, by L. J. Davis, ed. (New York: Routledge, 2006); Rachel da Silveira Gorman, "Disablement in and for Itself: Towards a "Global" Idea of Disability." *Somatechnics* (2016), 6(2): 249–61.

23. Porter, "The Patient's View."

24. Robert McRuer, *Crip Theory: Cultural Signs of Queerness and Disability* (New York and London: New York University Press, 2006).

25. Alison Kafer, *Feminist, Queer, Crip* (Bloomington: Indiana University Press, 2013).

26. Kafer, *Feminist, Queer, Crip.*

27. Rachel Gorman, "Mad Nation? Thinking through Race, Class, and Mad Identity Politics," in *Mad Matters: A Critical Reader in Canadian Mad Studies*, by Brenda A. LeFrançois, Robert Menzies, and Geoffrey Reaume (Toronto: Canadian Scholars Press, 2013).

28. D. Béhague and F. Ortega, "Mutual Aid, Pandemic Politics, and Global Social Medicine in Brazil." *The Lancet* (2021): 575–76; F. McLafferty Bell, "Amplified Injustices and Mutual Aid in the COVID-19 Pandemic." *Qualitative Social Work* (2020): 410–15.

29. For more concrete examples, see Cassie Thornton, *The Hologram: Feminist, Peer-to-Peer Health for a Post-Pandemic Future* (London: Vagabonds, Pluto Books, 2020); and https://tmapscommunity.net/.

30. Alexia Arani, "Mutual Aid and Its Ambivalences: Lessons from Sick and Disabled Trans and Queer People of Color." *Feminist Studies* (2020): 653–62.

31. Leah Lakshmi Piepzna-Samarasinha, *Care Work: Dreaming Disability Justice* (Vancouver: Arsenal Pulp Press, 2018); *How Disabled Mutual Aid Is Different Than Abled Mutual Aid*, Disability Visibility Project (2021).

32. Mary Jean Hande and Christine Kelly, "Organizing Survival and Resistance in Austere Times: Shifting Disability Activism and Care Politics in Ontario, Canada." *Disability & Society* (2015): 961–75.

33. Conscientization is the idea that through continual shifting between reflection and action people can develop critical understandings of the world and their place in it. Paulo Freire, *Pedagogy of the Oppressed* (London: Penguin Classics, 2017).

34. See Lucy Costa, "Democratic Patient-Led Councils, the Rise of Patient Engagement, and the Erosion of Advocacy." *Matters of Engagement* (2020), https://mattersofengagement.com/democratic-patient-led-councils-the-rise-of-patient-engagement-and-the-erosion-of-advocacy-with-lucy-costa/; Valerie Francisco-Menchavez and Ethel Tungohan, "Mula Sa Masa, Tungo Sa Masa, From the People, To the People: Building Migrant Worker Power through Participatory Action Research," 17, no. 2 *Migration Letters, Special Issue: Participatory Methods in Migration Research* (2020): 257–64; Bridget Pratt, "Constructing Citizen Engagement in Health Research Priority-Setting to Attend to Dynamics of Power and Difference." *Developing World Bioethics* (2018): 45–60; Susan Woelders and Tineke Abma, "Participatory Action Research to Enhance the Collective Involvement of Residents in Elderly Care: About Power, Dialogue and Understanding." *Action Research Journal* (2019): 528–48, for discussions on the ethical and practical dimensions of engaging marginalized mad, older, patient, and migrant communities in participatory research.

35. Pratt, "Constructing Citizen Engagement in Health Research Priority-Setting to Attend to Dynamics of Power and Difference," 45–60.

36. Tanya Titchkosky, *The Question of Access: Disability, Space, Meaning* (Toronto: University of Toronto Press, 2011).

37. Kazemi, "Toward a Conceptualization of Transnational Disability Theory and Praxis," 31.

CHAPTER 19

Accessibility Widely Defined

Making the University of Massachusetts Archives' Disability Collections Available to Everyone

SHUKO TAMAO AND AARON RUBINSTEIN

A Historian Meets an Archivist to Make the Archives Accessible

My opportunity to create accessible archives came out of the blue. On an early summer day in 2013, I had a meeting with Robert S. Cox, the head of the University of Massachusetts Archives, who was busy expanding disability-related archival collections. During the meeting, he mentioned the recent acquisition of the papers of Judi Chamberlin, who became a disability rights activist after being sent to a state-run psychiatric hospital against her will.[1]

Although I had never heard of Chamberlin before, I told him that these papers sounded like an interesting addition to the Archives and he suggested I process them. At the time, I was a master's student in public history at the University of Massachusetts Amherst and was vaguely thinking about doing a project collecting memories of institutionalization told from the perspective of people who had been committed as patients. I immediately said yes to his offer, and by the end of my summer internship, I had managed to make twenty bankers boxes worth of material available for public use.

This processing project was a dream for a fledgling scholar in the history of disability. I discovered that the Judi Chamberlin Papers contained a vivid first-person narrative about a woman who had gone from being an "ordinary 1960s housewife" to becoming an internationally regarded disability rights activist. After experiencing a series of stays in psychiatric hospitals in New York City, culminating in an involuntary commitment to Rockland State Hospital, Chamberlin became politically conscious. She first embraced feminism, then became one of the leading figures in what came to be called the psychiatric survivors movement, a civil rights effort organized around the activism of ex-patients in psychiatric institutions. By 1990, when the Americans with Disabilities Act (ADA) became law, Chamberlin had grown into a civil rights activist and advocate for a coalition of people with disabilities, including physical and mental disabilities.

Because I found her story so powerful, I became interested in learning about other disability rights activists. Since my first archival encounter with this subject was so rich and detailed, I assumed that first-person accounts of disabled people were ubiquitous in the archives. However, while collecting primary sources for my dissertation, I realized that my experience at the UMass Archives had been extraordinary. Collections in North American archives focused on people with disabilities either simply did not exist or were impossible to use for publication purposes. I found that institutional records essentially objectified their "patients" through the lens of medical model explanations that depicted disability in terms of pathology. These records were often subject to the Health Insurance Portability and Accountability Act (HIPAA) of 1996 and other privacy protection measures. I also explored the possibility of examining manuscripts of well-known people with disabilities but ultimately left the archive empty-handed and discouraged because layers of copyright restrictions guarded the use of the materials. As a result, I learned to rely less on archives. I found that I had to turn to other sources instead: biographies, material object analysis of everyday things, and first-person accounts gathered through oral history interviews that I conducted myself. I also used an extensive body of oral history conducted by Fred Pelka and others on behalf of the Oral History Center at the University of California Berkeley's Bancroft Library. My experience with conducting research in archives had left me frustrated. I thought if I—a nondisabled researcher with archival experience and funding opportunities—had difficulty finding the voices of disabled people in archival collections, what would the experience be like for the public, especially for people with disabilities who had no scholarly background?

According to Susan Burch, for any historically marginalized community, knowledge of the experiences of their peers in the past is crucial to building group identity and strengthening their sense of belonging.[2] The communities of disabled people—including those who are regarded as disabled—have a long history of being dehumanized because the nondisabled world has systematically erased their identities.[3] On the other hand, as Fred Pelka pointed out, these communities have rich histories of resisting the process of dehumanization.[4] In order to acknowledge their humanity, the archives should represent the varied past experiences of community members by making their histories accessible to the public. In doing so, we should be aware that there are multiple kinds of barriers that prevent such improved availability. Since the enactment of the ADA, libraries have increasingly focused on making their built and digital environments accessible. However, these efforts could go further in building disability-centered archives so that people with disabilities can have better access to them and so that the broader public can have more opportunities to learn about disabled people's lived experiences. Archives need to envision accessibility beyond their existing infrastructure by creating barrier-free collections in order to promote a better understanding of the past, regardless of a researcher's or research subject's disability.[5]

In this chapter, "accessibility" and "barrier-free" refer to the degree of ease with which researchers and disabled people can access information that would help them to interpret disability beyond medical model explanations. In archival and historical practices, there are many barriers to creating a truly accessible archive. In order to remove them, we need to envision best practices by examining what archivists and historians have done to locate the voices of disabled people in archives. This chapter gives special consideration to what the Robert S. Cox Special Collections and University Archives Research Center (SCUA) has done to increase accessibility to its disability-related collections. It also discusses the remaining tasks the SCUA and other archives should do to create truly accessible archives. Assistance was given in writing this article from Aaron Rubinstein, the current head of SCUA, who provided an overview of SCUA's disability collection and helped in identifying invisible barriers present in archives.

What Are Accessible Archival Collections?

A 1975 survey conducted by a library and information science scholar reported that due to the lack of accessibility, disabled people were not using libraries or library services to which they were entitled.[6] Since the enactment of the 1990 Americans with Disabilities Act (ADA), the built environment of libraries has become more accessible. Accessibility has largely been framed in terms of the physical environment—can patrons physically enter the building where information is located? We tend to think of accessibility in terms of ramps and elevators. However, a greater emphasis needs to be placed on accessing the contents of libraries and archives as well as on the inclusivity of those contents.[7]

In tracing recent systemic changes in the ways people with disabilities access information, the popular discussions focus on policy changes associated with infrastructure. The ADA prohibited discrimination based on disability in employment and mandated accessibility requirements for every public facility. As a result, libraries became more accessible by creating barrier-free built and digital environments. Desks, bookshelves, and bathrooms became accessible for people with physical disabilities. Elevators and doors have Braille signs for people who are blind or low vision. More libraries became mindful of the subtle aspects of their built environment by paying attention to how lighting, noise level, and airflow affect people with sensory sensitivities. In terms of the accessibility of information, however, progress has been slower.[8]

Have libraries and archives been putting sufficient effort into the way they collect and present information? Accessing vital information is crucial to the survival of any historically underrepresented communities, but do archives even have the kind of histories, memories, and stories that these communities want to access? From a disability studies standpoint, do archival collections preserve and disseminate the kind of information that helps us defy ableism? Essentially, the archives have prioritized the voices of powerful elites who are regarded as reliable and thus worthy of consideration, while dismissing the voices of disabled people that have been labeled as undesirable for preservation. For example, the power imbalance between the two becomes apparent when comparing the volume of archival records available, which is disproportionately weighted on clinical records, hospital administrative papers, court case records, and so on. This imbalance is the most obstinate barrier for those who wish to know about the lives of disabled people.

In archives, harmful mindsets and practices—what I call "invisible barriers"—still exist. Despite such improvements as providing wider digital access to books and other library holdings and allowing researchers to review needed information from home, many intangible barriers still exist. This section examines these systemic obstacles from the perspective of historians, paying special attention to the inaccessibility of first-person voices from within the community of disabled people. It also examines the search for valuable primary sources beyond institutional repositories and look at what archives can do to help such researchers who have been struggling to find sources from within archival collections.

For historians, accessible collections are ones in which they can easily locate and access records detailing the lived experiences of disabled people—especially their first-person narratives—with few legal or institutional restrictions acting as barriers to those records being made public. However, in countries where English is the primary language, there have been few archival collections centered on disabled people.[9] To tackle this deficit, historians have looked beyond archival collections to locate the voices of disabled people. For example, Susan Burch, Isabelle Lawrence, and other contributors to this book, as well as Katherine Ott, Geoffrey Reaume, Darby Penney, Jaipreet Virdi, and other scholars have used material objects as their points of inquiry. Robert Bogdan, Rosemary Garland-Thomson, and others have examined photographs of disabled people in popular media.[10] Extensive oral history interviews of disability rights activists by Fred Pelka, as well as Sam Goldstone-Brady, Osnat Katz, and Nicki Pombier in this book, have collected recent narratives in order to tackle the lack of voices of disabled people.[11] Kim Nielsen and Michael Rembis have examined biographies to locate voices from earlier periods that can no longer be collected by interviews.[12]

Although many historians have learned to conduct research outside of archival collections, archives still remain their first stop when searching for primary sources related to their interests. Because gathering primary sources is such an essential activity for historians, any obstacles preventing historians from using them can cause a great deal of angst.[13] A lack of information and legal and ethical restrictions have complicated the research process for many scholars. However, this frustration has also led them to develop innovative interpretations of what primary sources are available at archives. For example, they have learned to locate missing voices by looking at the records cataloged in nonmedical contexts or by reading available medical records against the grain.

An innovative interpretation of primary sources started when historians of medicine began adapting the "history from below" approach, analyzing the practice of medicine from the perspective of patients.[14] In the 1960s, French philosopher Michel Foucault analyzed how modern medicine created a system that treats patients as subordinates to doctors. He theorized that these experts dominated the production of knowledge, including how architects designed hospital buildings and how doctors conducted therapy.[15] In 1985, British social historian Roy Porter proselytized that instead of examining stories told from the vantage points of medical breakthroughs, heroic doctors, and anti-folklore, social historians of medicine should explore existing primary sources that were not necessarily cataloged as "medicine" in the archives: "proverbs, sayings, folklore, superstitions, remedies, traditional wisdom about diet, the calendar, omens, animals, natural pharmacy, the religious propitiations of *ex-votos*, pilgrimages, shrines, prayers, and so forth." He even suggested that "the testimony of the doctors themselves" could be used after some decoding.[16]

Influenced by Porter and others, social historians of medicine began interpreting archival sources with this new perspective, decoding doctors' testimony to reconstruct patients' narratives. Geoffrey Reaume, a Canadian historian of madness, "read against the grain" of 431 clinical files of people admitted to the Toronto Hospital for the Insane between 1870 and 1940.[17] However, this method would test any historians' interpretive ability; clinical records rarely mention patients' criticism of hospitals because the people responsible for keeping such records typically wished to avoid recording any negative remarks about their institutions. An exception to this silence, Reaume conjectures, was when doctors used patients' own words to portray them as "unreliable," a depiction that was frequently made about people with psychiatric diagnoses or labels.[18]

While recent works tend to focus on reconstructing the individual lives of disabled people, New Zealand historian of madness Catharine Coleborne and a team of archivists demonstrated that a large set of data allows us to consider power dynamics not only within psychiatry or colonialism but also within the archival practice. She and her team conducted a macrolevel analysis of four thousand clinical records from multiple asylums in Australia and New Zealand between 1864 and 1910. They argue that archives could remedy the historical absence of disabled people's voices by presenting this kind of collective data as a record of the lives of diverse groups of people.[19]

Historians have found valuable primary sources by thinking outside of the archival box. In their desire to locate the voices of disabled people, they have started asking the question: what constitutes a "worthy" human being? Historians have investigated how the label of "undesirable" when attached to people with disabilities has excluded many from participating in the civic sphere.[20] As an extension of the larger public discourse, most archives still disregard the lives of disabled people and still collect only "credible" records made by influential individuals and institutions. Thus, archives should create collections that are geared not only toward researchers but also toward the disability community at large so that they can connect to much-needed primary sources. The next section demonstrates what the UMass Archives has done to make its disability-related collections accessible to everyone.

Accessibility Is a Social Change

The disability-related collections at the Robert S. Cox Special Collections and University Archives Research Center (SCUA) at the University of Massachusetts Amherst have their roots in the philosophy of African American activist thinker W. E. B. Du Bois. Since the acquisition of Du Bois's papers in 1973, SCUA has focused on collecting papers and records that align with his commitment to social change. The Du Bois papers demonstrate his lifelong achievements as a thinker, writer, and organizer, exemplifying the diversity of movements he engaged with because he identified how interconnected social issues were. For example, he believed that it was impossible to fight racism without fighting for economic justice or understanding the history of Africa and the impact of European colonialism. Using Du Bois's intersectional insight as a model, the former SCUA head Robert S. Cox and Curator of Collections Danielle Kovacs developed the basic philosophies that underpin SCUA's approach to collection development: "rather than focus on individual movements, the archival center therefore focuses on the connections between and among movements and the flow of people, organizations, and ideas." Under this approach, the collections are curated to capture the "whole lives, whole communities."[21] Based on this principle, SCUA has collected a wide array of materials that illustrate the diversity of social change movements within America, which include Black liberation, conscientious objectors, spiritual revolutionaries, the labor movement, the antinuclear movement, and beyond.

The growth of SCUA's disability-related collections derived from this commitment to gather the voices of social change movements. Cox and Kovac's fundamental goal of capturing "whole lives, whole communities" calls for documenting people and their communities in their entirety, rather than concentrating only on those aspects of people's lives that fit into a single category or topic from a dominant perspective. Several years into implementing this holistic approach to collection development, it became clear that their acquisition activity also needed to focus on connections between different movements. In addition to paying attention to the embodied nature of people's experiences, their collection development began to capture the intersecting nature of these movements and networks, creating a robust archive of interconnected collections. SCUA's strength in materials related to disability history, disability rights activism, and the lived experiences of disability grew out from this web of connections.

SCUA's disability-related collections include the papers of pioneering figures in the disability rights movements, such as Judi Chamberlin, Paul Khan, George Ebert, Elmer Bertels, Darby Penney, Denise Karuth, and Fred Pelka. They also include a wide range of organizational and institutional records, including Clarke School for the Deaf, International Center for the Disabled, Belchertown State School, Boston Center for Independent Living, and White Light Communications, a media company producing content by and for psychiatric survivors. This intersection of materials ranging from personal to political as well as from scientific to institutional creates opportunities for weaving together a more holistic picture of disability experiences and a richer biography of people.[22] This has only been possible through partnerships with activists and through dialogues with the disability community.[23]

Digitization is a critical step in removing barriers to increase the accessibility to archival collections. In 2017, SCUA won a $250,000 grant from the Council on Library and Information Resources (CLIR) as part of the Digitizing Hidden Collections program. It took SCUA multiple grant cycles to convince the committee that its disability-related collections were valuable materials ideal for digitization. SCUA argued that disability history and the experience of people with disabilities is a truly hidden story and that these collections are

Figure 19.1. Judi Chamberlin wearing political button, c. 1985. Judi Chamberlin Papers (MS 768). Special Collections and University Archives, University of Massachusetts Amherst Libraries (https://credo.library.umass.edu/view/full/mums768-b019-f025-i001).

a body of rare historical records that has great potential to influence a wide variety of the Archives' patrons because of SCUA's intersectional approach in collection development. The grant allowed SCUA to digitize over thirty thousand objects from nineteen different collections, representing the full range of its disability-related holdings. This was an unprecedented opportunity to make a significant swath of the history of disability open and available online. However, this opportunity also revealed several critical questions about the nature of the accessibility of online primary sources relating to the experience of disability: how should SCUA address the potential physical and technological barriers to access?

In creating accessible collections, barriers present in physical and technological access were an easier issue to address. Earlier in the process of applying for the CLIR grant, SCUA had identified several fundamental issues with the accessibility of its digital collections site Credo. To remedy these, SCUA redesigned the user interface of Credo, placing accessibility as the core design principle. Each component developed for the renovated site went through a series of tests to ensure ADA/WCAG compliance—website accessibility guidelines complying with the ADA—and to meet the screen reader user experience (UX) standards for blind or low-vision users. At the end of development, the UMass Assistive Technologies Center ran a full audit of the site, giving both technical and UX feedback, improving the interface accessibility of Credo.

The digitization project helped enhance overall technological access to SCUA's digital collections site. As the next stage toward fulfilling this vision of accessibility, SCUA and other archives need to tackle systemic, invisible barriers present in their collections. The next section identifies three principal invisible barriers that keep the disability community from connecting with crucial information and also recommends actions archives can take to address these barriers.

Remaining Barriers in the Archives

Bias in Archival Standards

In order to ensure that the archival practice is consistent for every project, archival science has developed clear standards. Through the process of adhering to these rules, however, archival institutions have produced powerful biases in the way they choose certain kinds of historical records to preserve while rejecting others. As a result, this practice has created a selection imbalance in collections that has also influenced the ways researchers conduct their research—with the result that archives have tended to favor the narratives of influential figures and institutions over the experiences of those who are regarded as less powerful.[24] In the traditional archival practice, it is common for archives to select the kinds of material that conform with their collecting policies, which reflect the institutional priorities and identity, while excluding materials that do not concur with these preferences.

When archives only acquire collections that match with their policies, they run the risk of favoring certain narratives that fit their institutional identity.[25] For example, if an archive collects papers of independent living activist Paul S. Kahn, it might not process his other identities as a playwright, painter, and world traveler. The archive patrons would only find his legacy of disability rights activism because the archive had solely focused on his disability-related organizing work to the exclusion of other facets of his life.[26] Historians may wish to explore a nuanced representation of disability identity in order to investigate the complex ways that disability forms, changes, and interacts with the lives of others. Thus, it becomes critical for collections to present the individual's experience of disability as one part in the body of that person's life work, spanning multiple directions.[27] We believe that SCUA's holistic collection approach has the potential to defy the persistent biases within the scholarship or even within the community where white voices and the experiences of visible disabilities, for example, still dominate discussions.

To remedy this imbalance in collection development, more scholars in archival science are now practicing "reparative metadata."[28] By arguing that "[t]he power to describe is the power to make and remake records and to determine how they will be used and remade in the future," they revisit the existing descriptive practices embedded in collection and item descriptions in finding aids, databases, and digital collections. These seemingly "neutral" item descriptions could contain biased language and harmful labels rooted in ableist or Western-centric assumptions.[29] For example, until 2021, the Library of Congress kept the cataloging subject headings of "Alien" and "Illegal aliens." After activists and librarians campaigned to drop this dehumanizing terminology, the headings changed to "Noncitizens" and "Illegal immigration."[30] In a digital collection, online descriptions that reflect the principle of reparative metadata will directly connect to the wider community of disabled people, other disadvantaged communities, and the larger public, and more librarians, archivists, and community members are creating readily available online resources to make the practice of reparative metadata the guiding principle for everyone.[31]

Uneven Collection Development

Like any other educational and cultural organization, archives operate within the existing social order, and this means they have the choice of either challenging or sustaining colonialism, racism, ableism, and other forms of inequalities present in society.[32] Truly accessible archives will question existing mindsets about disability by including collections that detail disabled people's experiences. These collections should cover a wide range of time periods, spaces, and personal backgrounds. They should also show the multiplicity of ways that people have interacted with their disabilities or diagnoses. Thus, in addition to disclosing the differences between disabled and nondisabled communities, archives should develop a body of collections that capture the diversity of the voices within the disability community.

Current work in disability studies has increasingly examined race, explaining how the experience of being disabled or of being regarded as disabled differs depending on a person's race.[33] However, most of the existing archival collections about disability, including SCUA's collections, skew toward white voices. This imbalance is partly because the leaders in the disability rights movement, such as the psychiatric consumer-survivor movement, have been disproportionately white.[34] In order to facilitate ongoing scholarly innovation, archives need to develop more collections related to disabled people of color. As an extension of this effort to diversify narratives, archives should also endeavor, for example, to collect the voices of nonnative speakers of English in the North American context as well as the testimony of Deaf people who used sign language as their mode of communication.[35]

Archives should challenge the community of disability studies scholars, too. Since the emergence of disability studies in the 1980s, scholars have critiqued the narrative of disabled people overcoming adversity, arguing that this amounts to a form of "inspiration porn," a biased narrative that does not embody the typical everyday life of a disabled person.[36] However, Beth Linker has pointed out that many scholarly works still focus on stories of the "healthy disabled," celebrating their accomplishments and achievements while stories of chronic pain, declining health, and needing constant medical intervention are often sidelined from the inquiry.[37] To respond to Linker's suggestion, archives should embrace a more nuanced and holistic approach, one that engages more in community outreach and in building trust with community members in an effort to make every voice count in the process of building accessible archives.

Prioritizing Process in Digitization

When digitizing disability-related collections, the process poses a unique set of challenges associated with increased visibility. While digitization appears beneficial for everyone, this enhanced accessibility is exactly the reason why archives might hesitate to digitize certain materials.

Increased accessibility associated with digitization potentially can be harmful for some people. For example, disability-related archival collections often contain personal health information, a kind of data under the purview of privacy protection laws. The original intention of the 1996 Health Insurance

Portability and Accountability Act (HIPAA) was to protect patients from growing concerns about insurance companies denying clients' coverage by referring to their genetic information.[38] The Institutional Review Boards (IRBs) regulate biomedical and behavioral experiments to protect research subjects from abuse.[39] In addition, state privacy laws also apply to the patient records of state-run institutions. Archives make decisions based on these policies. When SCUA was processing Judi Chamberlin's papers, it withdrew most of her organization's member list, which had asked members to identify their psychiatric diagnoses.

When prioritizing digitization, archives must weigh risk and benefit, and records that are more than a hundred years old are generally deemed "safe" to digitize.[40] However, the material that archives choose to digitize and the way archives describe that material are still influenced by how the wider society interprets the lives of people with disabilities. As a result, some state archives still guard old patient records despite those records having already been digitized.[41] Historian Sarah Handley-Cousins, who is gathering primary sources about disabled Civil War soldiers, has gone through an arduous IRB process to use state hospital records. She has witnessed how these privacy protection measures have prevented descendants of committed soldiers from accessing their ancestors' information, as she discusses in chapter 8 of this book ("Silence and Stigma").[42]

Protection of privacy in digitized collections creates a paradox. While it is important to respect personal privacy, especially of people who have had their humanity disregarded through institutionalization, these protective measures also function as barriers, erasing the very existence of disabled people. The current system has numerous barriers to fulfilling these goals. To solve this, we need to promote more cross-disciplinary, pan-institutional, and multi-community discussions in order to share ideas about privacy protection and ethical data access so that we can create more accessible digital archives.

Conclusion

Fully accessible archives should operate under the principle of "nothing about us without us." Making archival records accessible will help the larger public, especially communities of disabled people, to interact with new aspects of the past and present that they never imagined before. The author's experience in processing the Judi Chamberlin Papers opened the door to becoming a well-balanced historian who can identify multiple perspectives in the past by critically examining archival practices. The effort will also help archivists understand how to better document and represent the lives of people with disabilities. It will help historians connect with new primary sources that can spark new avenues of inquiry. Ultimately, accessible and inclusive archives help everyone because such an approach can lead to a user-centered understanding of medicine and to a more expansive interpretation of the human condition by revealing the contested nature of health, human rights, autonomy, and independence.

Inspired by the philosophy of W. E. B. Du Bois, SCUA employs a holistic, inclusive approach in collecting papers and records that facilitate social change. Using this approach as a guiding principle, SCUA is passionate about its efforts because in addition to race, class, gender, and sexuality, disability is a newer point of inquiry that intersects with other viewpoints, helping everyone arrive at a nuanced, uniting understanding of the past and present. We believe that this intersectional approach will stimulate a wide range of future activism and social change movements.

In order to achieve this goal, however, archives still need to tackle invisible barriers addressed in this chapter in addition to any potential barriers that have yet to be identified. These systemic barriers, ranging from the technological to the ethical, would have proven less problematic if more educational and cultural institutions had adopted a more holistic approach to gathering information using "nothing about us without us" as an operational principle. Hopefully, this chapter will help interested individuals and organizations become part of this spearheading effort.

Acknowledgment

Lastly, throughout this process of chronicling our effort, the authors of this chapter as well as the SCUA staff feel even more indebted to the foundational work done by SCUA's former head, Robert S. Cox. We inherited the digitization project of the Archives' disability-related collections after his death at age sixty-one in May 2020, when the world was experiencing the shutdown associated with COVID-19. For Shuko Tamao, the last conversation with Cox, while he was in hospice care, was to communicate how she had successfully defended her PhD dissertation. Aaron Rubinstein succeeded Cox as the new head of SCUA, and he has been leading the digitization project along with Danielle Kovacs and other staff members. We hope that our effort in collecting and disseminating these historically underrepresented voices will go beyond the academy, facilitating a wide range of collaborations with the communities of disabled people to create truly accessible archives.

Notes

1. Chamberlin's prolific work spans over four decades, and it would be impossible to introduce her life, work, and contribution in detail here. However, the University of Massachusetts Archives' Judi Chamberlin Papers are available to everyone through

free and accessible digital collections. The Archives also have papers of other psychiatric survivor-consumer activists and disability rights activists available via the Credo digital collections depository: "Chamberlin, Judi, 1944–2010—Special Collections & University Archives," accessed June 21, 2024, http://scua.library.umass.edu/chamberlin-judi-1944-2010/; "Visibility for Disability: Digitization Sponsored by the Council on Library and Information Resources," accessed June 21, 2024, https://credo.library.umass.edu/search?q=%27Digitization%20sponsored%20by%20the%20Council%200n%20Library%20and%20Information%20Resources.

2. Susan Burch, *Committed: Remembering Native Kinship in and beyond Institutions* (Chapel Hill: University of North Carolina Press, 2021), 105.

3. Burch, *Committed*; Kim E. Nielsen, "The Perils and Promises of Disability Biography," in *The Oxford Handbook of Disability History*, eds. Michael A. Rembis, Catharine Kudlick, and Kim E. Nielsen (New York: Oxford University Press, 2018), 21–40; Darby Penney, Peter Stastny, and Lisa Rinzler, *The Lives They Left Behind: Suitcases from a State Hospital Attic*, reprint edition (New York: Bellevue Literary Press, 2009).

4. Judi Chamberlin, *On Our Own: Patient-Controlled Alternatives to the Mental Health System* (Lawrence, MA: National Empowerment Center, 1977); Judith Heumann and Kristen Joiner, *Being Heumann: An Unrepentant Memoir of a Disability Rights Activist* (Boston: Beacon Press, 2021); Fred Pelka, *What We Have Done: An Oral History of the Disability Rights Movement* (Amherst: University of Massachusetts Press, 2012).

5. Angela McCarthy et al., "Lives in the Asylum Record, 1864 to 1910: Utilising Large Data Collection for Histories of Psychiatry and Mental Health," *Medical History* 61, no. 3 (July 2017): 358–79, https://doi.org/10.1017/mdh.2017.33; Michelle Kowalsky and John Woodruff, *Creating Inclusive Library Environments: A Planning Guide for Serving Patrons with Disabilities* (Chicago: American Library Association, 2016), http://ebookcentral.proquest.com/lib/buffalo/detail.action?docID=4805360; J. J. Pionke, "Disability and Accessibility Related Library Graduate School Education from the Student Perspective," *Journal of Education for Library and Information Science* 61, no. 2 (April 2020): 253–69, https://doi.org/10.3138/jelis.2019–0036.

6. Linda Baldwin Alexander, "ADA Resources for the Library and Information Professions," *Journal of Education for Library and Information Science* 46, no. 3 (2005): 250, https://doi.org/10.2307/40323848; Linda Lucas Walling, "Educating Students to Serve Information Seekers with Disabilities," *Journal of Education for Library and Information Science* 45, no. 2 (2004): 137, https://doi.org/10.2307/40323900.

7. This gap between what patrons want and what libraries imagine patrons want often surfaces when well-intentioned libraries attempt to serve disadvantaged communities. For example, see a case study about bookmobiles: Jennifer Cummings, "'How Can We Fail?' The Texas State Library's Traveling Libraries and Bookmobiles, 1916–1966," *Libraries & the Cultural Record* 44, no. 3 (2009): 299–325.

8. Kowalsky and Woodruff, *Creating Inclusive Library Environments*, 3–5.

9. Douglas C. Baynton, "Disability and the Justification of Inequality in American History," in *The New Disability History: American Perspectives*, eds. Paul K.

Longmore and Lauri Umansky, *The History of Disability Series* (New York: New York University Press, 2001), 33–57; Burch, *Committed*; McCarthy et al., "Lives in the Asylum Record, 1864 to 1910," 358–79, https://doi.org/10.1017/mdh.2017.33; Geoffrey Reaume, "From the Perspectives of Mad People," in *The Routledge History of Madness and Mental Health*, ed. Greg Eghigian (New York: Routledge, 2017), 277–96.

10. Robert Bogdan, *Picturing Disability: Beggar, Freak, Citizen, and Other Photographic Rhetoric* (Syracuse: Syracuse University Press, 2012); Rosemarie Garland-Thomson, "The Politics of Staring: Visual Rhetorics of Disability in Popular Photography," in *The New Disability History: American Perspectives*, eds. Paul K. Longmore and Lauri Umansky (New York: New York University Press, 2001), 335–74; Shuko Tamao, "Picturing the Institution of Social Death: Visual Rhetorics of Postwar Asylum Exposé Photography," *Journal of Medical Humanities*, December 3, 2021, https://doi.org/10.1007/s10912-021-09723-0.

11. Pelka, *What We Have Done*.

12. Kim E. Nielsen, *The Radical Lives of Helen Keller*, illustrated edition (New York: New York University Press, 2009); Michael A. Rembis, *Writing Mad Lives in the Age of the Asylum* (New York: Oxford University Press, 2024).

13. Nielsen, "The Perils and Promises of Disability Biography," 24.

14. E. P. Thompson, *The Making of the English Working Class* (New York: Vintage, 1966).

15. Michel Foucault, *Madness and Civilization: A History of Insanity in the Age of Reason* (London: Routledge Classics, 1961); Michel Foucault, *The Birth of the Clinic: An Archaeology of Medical Perception* (London: Routledge Classics, 1963); Michel Foucault, *Discipline and Punish: The Birth of the Prison* (New York: Vintage Books, 1975); Michel Foucault, *Psychiatric Power: Lectures at the Collège de France, 1973–1974* (New York: Palgrave Macmillan, 2006).

16. Roy Porter, "The Patient's View: Doing Medical History from Below," *Theory and Society* 14, no. 2 (1985): 176, 183.

17. Geoffrey Reaume, *Remembrance of Patients Past: Life at the Toronto Hospital for the Insane, 1870–1940* (Toronto: University of Toronto Press, 2009); Reaume, "From the Perspectives of Mad People," 285.

18. Reaume, "From the Perspectives of Mad People," 285.

19. McCarthy et al., "Lives in the Asylum Record, 1864 to 1910," 359.

20. Audra Jennings, *Out of the Horrors of War: Disability Politics in World War II America* (Philadelphia: University of Pennsylvania Press, 2016); Paul K. Longmore, *Telethons: Spectacle, Disability, and the Business of Charity* (Oxford, New York: Oxford University Press, 2016); Kim E. Nielsen, *A Disability History of the United States* (Boston: Beacon Press, 2012), 100; Sarah F. Rose, *No Right to Be Idle: The Invention of Disability, 1840s–1930s* (Chapel Hill: University of North Carolina Press, 2017).

21. "What We Collect—Special Collections & University Archives," accessed March 16, 2022, http://scua.library.umass.edu/overview/collection-policy/.

22. Nielsen, "The Perils and Promises of Disability Biography."

23. The disability community is a diverse entity of multiple racial, gender, class, and sexuality groups. In a later section, we discuss how archives should represent this diversity by collecting a variety of voices within the community.

24. Randall C. Jimerson, "Archives for All: Professional Responsibility and Social Justice," *American Archivist* 70, no. 2 (2007): 252–81.

25. Kelvin L. White and Anne J. Gilliland, "Promoting Reflexivity and Inclusivity in Archival Education, Research, and Practice," *Library Quarterly: Information, Community, Policy* 80, no. 3 (2010): 117–18, https://doi.org/10.1086/652874.

26. "Kahn, Paul S.—Special Collections & University Archives," accessed March 18, 2022, http://scua.library.umass.edu/kahn-paul-s/.

27. Nielsen, "The Perils and Promises of Disability Biography."

28. Tonia Sutherland and Alyssa Purcell, "A Weapon and a Tool: Decolonizing Description and Embracing Redescription as Liberatory Archival Praxis," *The International Journal of Information, Diversity, & Inclusion (IJIDI)* 5, no. 1 (February 20, 2021): 60–78, https://doi.org/10.33137/ijidi.v5i1.34669; Jessica Tai, "Cultural Humility as a Framework for Anti-Oppressive Archival Description," *Journal of Critical Library and Information Studies* 3, no. 2 (2021), https://doi.org/10.24242/jclis.v3i2.120.

29. Wendy M. Duff and Verne Harris, "Stories and Names: Archival Description as Narrating Records and Constructing Meanings," *Archival Science* 2, no. 3 (September 1, 2002): 272, https://doi.org/10.1007/BF02435625.

30. Kay Shawnda, "ALA Welcomes Removal of Offensive 'Illegal Aliens' Subject Headings," Text, News and Press Center, November 12, 2021, https://www.ala.org/news/member-news/2021/11/ala-welcomes-removal-offensive-illegal-aliens-subject-headings.

31. Alexis A. Antracoli et al., "Archives for Black Lives in Philadelphia: Anti-Racist Description Resources," October 2019, https://www.google.com/url?sa=t&rct=j&q=&esrc=s&source=web&cd=&cad=rja&uact=8&ved=2ahUKEwi8u5HEz876AhXhjokEHdIYBiMQjBB6BAgUEAE&url=https%3A%2F%2Farchivesforblacklives.files.wordpress.com%2F2020%2F11%2Fardr_202010.pdf&usg=AOvVaw14vRV9k8hW4Ue5espqlsVu; "Terminology," Densho: Japanese American Incarceration and Japanese Internment, accessed October 7, 2022, https://densho.org/terminology/; National JACL Power of Words II Committee, "Power of Words Handbook: A Guide to Language about Japanese Americans in World War II Understanding Euphemisms and Preferred Terminology," April 2013, https://jacl.org/https://jacl.org/s/POW-Handbook-Rev2020-V4.pdfpower-of-words; Walter Cronkite School of Journalism and Mass Communication, Arizona State University, "Disability Language Style Guide, National Center on Disability and Journalism," accessed October 7, 2022, https://ncdj.org/style-guide/.

32. Burch, *Committed*, 6; Catharine Coleborne, *Madness in the Family: Insanity and Institutions in the Australasian Colonial World, 1860–1914* (Basingstoke, UK: Palgrave Macmillan, 2010), 144; Tiya Miles, *All That She Carried: The Journey of Ashley's Sack, a Black Family Keepsake* (New York: Random House, 2021), 17, 27.

33. Jenifer L. Barclay, *The Mark of Slavery: Disability, Race, and Gender in Antebellum America* (Urbana: University of Illinois Press, 2021); Christopher M. Bell, "Introducing White Disability Studies." In *The Disability Studies Reader*, edited by Lennard J. Davis, second edition (New York: Taylor & Francis Group, 2006), 275–82; Burch, *Committed*; Stefanie Hunt-Kennedy, *Between Fitness and Death: Disability and Slavery in the Caribbean*, first edition (Urbana: University of Illinois

Press, 2020); Ayah Nuriddin, "Psychiatric Jim Crow: Desegregation at the Crownsville State Hospital, 1948–1970," *Journal of the History of Medicine and Allied Sciences* 74, no. 1 (January 2019): 85–106; Martin Summers, *Madness in the City of Magnificent Intentions: A History of Race and Mental Illness in the Nation's Capital* (Oxford, New York: Oxford University Press, 2019); Kylie M. Smith, "No Medical Justification: Segregation and Civil Rights in Alabama's Psychiatric Hospitals, 1952–1972," *Journal of Southern History* LXXXVII, no. 4 (November 2021); Esmé Weijun Wang, *The Collected Schizophrenias: Essays* (Minneapolis: Graywolf Press, 2019); Alice Wong, ed., *Disability Visibility: First-Person Stories from the Twenty-First Century* (New York: Vintage, 2020).

34. Linda J. Morrison, *Talking Back to Psychiatry: The Psychiatric Consumer/Survivor/Ex-Patient Movement* (New York: Routledge, 2009), 78; Sami Schalk, *Black Disability Politics* (Durham, NC: Duke University Press, 2022), 56.

35. Douglas C. Baynton, *Forbidden Signs: American Culture and the Campaign against Sign Language* (University of Chicago Press, 1996); Burch, *Committed*, 7, 61; McCarthy et al., "Lives in the Asylum Record, 1864 to 1910," 367.

36. Stella Young, *I'm Not Your Inspiration, Thank You Very Much*, 1402326644, https://www.ted.com/talks/stella_young_i_m_not_your_inspiration_thank_you_very_much/transcript.

37. Beth Linker, "On the Borderland of Medical and Disability History: A Survey of the Fields," *Bulletin of the History of Medicine* 87, no. 4 (2013): 526.

38. Anne T. Gilliland and Judith A. Wiener, "Digitizing and Providing Access to Privacy-Sensitive Historical Medical Resources: A Legal and Ethical Overview," *Journal of Electronic Resources in Medical Libraries* 8, no. 4 (October 2011): 385, https://doi.org/10.1080/15424065.2011.626347.

39. Ryan Spellecy and Kristin Busse, "The History of Human Subjects Research and Rationale for Institutional Review Board Oversight," *Nutrition in Clinical Practice* 36, no. 3 (2021): 560–67, https://doi.org/10.1002/ncp.10623.

40. Gilliland and Wiener, "Digitizing and Providing Access to Privacy-Sensitive Historical Medical Resources," 390; David Wright and Renée Saucier, "Madness in the Archives: Anonymity, Ethics, and Mental Health History Research," *Journal of the Canadian Historical Association* 23, no. 2 (2012): 68–69, https://doi.org/10.7202/1015789ar.

41. IRBs are not designed for humanities research. In 2018, oral history projects conducted by humanities and journalism became no longer subject to IRB approval.

42. Sarah Handley-Cousins and Shuko Tamao, "Email Correspondence with Handley-Cousins," February 14, 2022.

CHAPTER 20

File/Life

Remediating the Pennhurst Archive with Community Archivists

NICKI POMBIER

Introduction

Pennhurst State School and Hospital is a now-shuttered institution, once operated by the state of Pennsylvania, that warehoused thousands of people with disabilities throughout the twentieth century. From 1908 to 1987, more than ten thousand women, men, and children lived in Pennhurst. Their experiences would offer an authoritative account of Pennhurst's history. Who were these people? Where is their trace? One source is the documentation generated by the institution itself. In 2019, Temple University's Institute on Disabilities (the Institute) secured a program grant from the Pew Center for Arts & Heritage to embark on a multiyear process designed to unlock historical, personal, and emotional knowledge of Pennhurst through a collaborative inquiry into, and creative response to, a limited set of residents' files. This community-led inquiry became File/Life: We Remember Stories of Pennhurst.

When an individual was admitted to Pennhurst, a file was opened, and in that file the institution's story for this person unfolds, from application for admission to discharge or death certificate. There are court transcripts, psychological evaluations, hospital logs, lists of personal items, field notes from social workers, and letters from relatives, but not much in the first person from the person whose file this is, save for quotes documented by Pennhurst staff, medical professionals, or social workers, kept in institutional logs or evaluations. Many files include two photographs, one taken of the person in profile and one camera-facing with their number pinned or held to them like a mugshot. Only in these photographs do the people in the files look back at us. File/Life is a project of trying to meet their gaze and find the lives within these files.

Every person admitted to Pennhurst had a file. Every person at Pennhurst had a life. File/Life asks how these files can be opened with care, without exploitation. How can that care resuscitate the people in these files to a public from whom they were hidden by design? What do we have to learn from the thousands who lived in Pennhurst, and how can an archive of case files from a century ago hold a mirror to the present, revealing not just how far we may have come, but how far yet we have to go? How can the telling of Pennhurst's story be part of a process of repairing the harm of institutionalization and point us toward a future of true, radical inclusion, of freedom for, and with, people with Intellectual and Developmental Disabilities (IDD)?

File/Life centers a team of community archivists representing the intersectionality of the disability community, including former Pennhurst residents, self-advocates with IDD, support staff, family members, and multidisciplinary artists with participatory practices. The project culminated in an interactive, multisensory public sharing in 2023. I am a collaborating artist on the File/Life team, participating in my capacity as an oral historian, writer, and a parent to a child with IDD. In this chapter, I describe the methodological and ethical questions of this work, in the context of the Institute's documentation and interpretation of the trajectory of the IDD Rights Movement in Pennsylvania through arts-based programs.

As a project centered on collaborative creative inquiry, working with an archive of sensitive files, File/Life engages with but does not enact archival practices. We are a group of community archivists in the sense that we are building community; we are grappling with an archive, responding to its materials and their meanings. We are striving to make something new. As an oral historian, I work in the realm of memory, and to remember is an act of creation, not retrieval. While the Pennhurst archive begins with a thingness—more than ten thousand total patient files—meaning is not retrieved, is only ever made. Our approach of creatively interpreting archival materials in File/Life draws inspiration from the scholarship of Saidiya Hartman. Her "intimate histories" of Black young women at the turn of the twentieth century liberates them from archival documents that frame them as a problem. Instead, Hartman shows that what the case file deems as deviant was in fact a form of freedom, a "refusal to be governed."[1] In this spirit, we seek to untether those who lived in Pennhurst—or loved or lost someone who did—from the reductive, rhetorical, and often real violence of the case file. Rather, we attend to them with collective care, imaginative inquiry, and an insistence on seeking and honoring the people the files both introduce and obscure as part of a shared commitment to a better present and a better story for the future.

This includes noticing and acknowledging the limits of what we can know: what Gracen Brilmyer, Director of the Disability Archives Lab at McGill University, calls the "unknowable and fluctuating," the complexity of lived experience of disability that defies or is denied by the file.[2] What silences are present in the Pennhurst archive, and how can our group work to imagine the unknowable and reveal the systems of power and oppression that would finally silence the lived experience of people institutionalized at Pennhurst? How can we do this in such a way that centers the intersectional, multifaceted ways of knowing represented by our community archivists? Can we work in a way that reflects principles of narrative allyship across ability, working to further the interests of people with IDD, optimizing their autonomy in the storytelling processes and products, telling stories with and not "about" them?[3] If we succeed, this project may serve as a useful case study for analysis using Brilmyer's critical disability archival framework, which proposes that work grappling with archival absences must be accountable to and in solidarity with people with disabilities.[4] This is the bar we have set.

The Pennhurst Files

March 17, 2022, Harrisburg, Pennsylvania. The State Archives building is windowless, a solitary brutalist block, seventeen stories tall. A small group of community archivists walks and rolls in when the Archives open, promptly at 9:00. We are here to see a subset of the Pennhurst patient files, the contents of thirty-six boxes of the earliest records (1908–61), organized in numerical order by patient number. We will have access to nonrestricted files, people who were discharged before March 1947 or who died before March 1972. We leave our belongings in small lockers and with our pencils, notebooks, and "investigating the archives" worksheets, we settle in, open the files, and begin.

Forty-four years earlier, to the day: March 17, 1978. Philadelphia, U.S. District Court for the Eastern District of Pennsylvania. U.S. District Judge Raymond J. Broderick issues an order "directing the County and Commonwealth defendants to provide adequate community living arrangements and services for the residents of Pennhurst."[5] Evidence from the Pennhurst files was key to the decision to close the institution. A team from Temple University had analyzed records from a sample set of 124 people, painting a picture of Pennhurst as "such a dangerous, miserable environment for its residents that many of them actually suffered physical deterioration and intellectual regression during their stay at the institution."[6]

March 17, 1978, became a research baseline for the Temple University Developmental Disabilities Center Evaluation and Research Group, which later became the Institute. On that date, when Judge Broderick declared them free, 1,154 people were institutionalized at Pennhurst. Every year after, from 1979 to 1986, a team of researchers from the Institute met with each of those 1,154 people face to face to ask: are they better off living outside of Pennhurst? The data showed an unequivocal "yes" by every measure.[7]

The Institute has its own history, then, of attending to the Pennhurst files, listening to people who lived there, and trying to gather the information that would enable analysis and understanding of their experience after Pennhurst finally closed.

Established in 1974, the Institute is one of sixty-seven University Centers for Excellence in Developmental Disability Education, Research and Service nationwide. Its advocacy, education, policy, and research programs have the mission of working with and learning from people with disabilities and their families to generate knowledge, change systems, and promote self-determination.[8] In 2019, the Institute received a program grant from the Pew Center for Arts & Heritage to build a collaborative, inclusive, arts-based process to "unlock historical, personal and emotional knowledge" of the Pennhurst files and work toward creating an interactive, multisensory, multidisciplinary installation to "illustrate the untold story and ongoing impact of institutionalization."[9] Building on more than a decade of producing work centering people with IDD in documenting and interpreting their history to a broader public, under the leadership of Lisa Sonneborn, Director of Media Arts and Culture, the Institute launched File/Life.

History, Intellectual and Developmental Disability, and Institutions

The history of IDD in the United States is not synonymous with the history of institutionalization, but these histories are intertwined and inextricable.[10] Institutions like Pennhurst were, for much of the twentieth century, sites of carceral warehousing where tens of thousands of people with disabilities were consigned, controlled, exploited, experimented on, abused, and isolated. Rarely discharged, except by death and often abandoned even then, they were buried in untended graves or delivered to the anatomical board. Institutions like Pennhurst were also, simultaneously, sites lauded by the state as models for the care and confinement of a problem that the state itself created. People with IDD have always existed. But in the nineteenth century, industrial capitalism created a category of people—disabled people—who, defined by their exclusion from the labor force and the "menace" that presented, became a social problem to be solved by segregation and prevention.[11] The creation of institutions at the turn of the twentieth century aimed to achieve both of these solutions, materially separating people from "main street" and implementing systemic eugenic policies. They segregated people within institutions by sex, refused requests for discharge until women were past childbearing age, and sterilized many without consent. Contained on large campuses set apart from cities or towns, institutions were owned, operated, and overseen by the state, administered largely by a class of political elites, and quickly became overcrowded. Placement in institutions was at least as much about the economic precarity of families—rendered poor by structural inequalities of industrial and racial capitalism—as it was about perceived intellectual or developmental limitations. In fact, institutions grew into an industry that created a professional class of medical experts and human services administrators while exploiting the unpaid labor of people confined there in a system of peonage that was legal until it was ruled unconstitutional in 1973.[12]

To be placed at Pennhurst was to become a subject of the state; it was a life sentence. Some people successfully gained freedom, released to their own custody, and some people escaped. Some families successfully fought to regain custody of their family members, and some tried and failed. Some did not try. Many people died. Everyone placed there persisted in living in some way; life continued in Pennhurst, under conditions that are difficult to witness. Indeed, it was the work of witnesses—those who told the world beyond Pennhurst's walls about the world within them—that sparked important early efforts first to reform and finally to close institutions like Pennhurst, catalyzing the deinstitutionalization movement.[13]

Who gets to tell this history? Telling this history in ways that elicit and center the perspectives and experiences of people with IDD challenges common narrative modes, including my practice of oral history, which is audist and ableist in many ways.[14] Yet doing so is critical to generating a history that does not replicate, reify, or leave untroubled ableist frames or logics.[15] Here we can see critical disability history as a decolonizing practice, as Susan Burch enumerates in her research with archival materials from the Canton Asylum for Insane Indians. "When a wide range of sources is seen as valid, including those that are invalidated by pathologization, our understanding and telling of history changes."[16] Scholarship from Indigenous thinkers whose work points the way to decolonizing oral history also resonates with a critical disability history and is especially relevant when working with people whose lived experience may be expressed in ways that a recorder, or a formal interview, might miss.[17] Including and beyond oral history, people with IDD are among the most overlooked in scholarship as sources of expertise, knowledge, or historical experience.[18] The very systems that codify and value historical knowledge often do not account for the ways of knowing or modes of expression that many people with IDD possess. To this day, there is controversy over what to do about institutions that remain open, where nearly a thousand Pennsylvanians with IDD live.[19] The perspectives of people with IDD must continue to be centered as witnesses to history, actors on the present, and authors of their futures. Narrative allyship can be a critical force for bringing them into historical and cultural discourse.[20]

Community Archivists

How can nondisabled people with access to narrative power work ethically with people with IDD so that their experiences, perspectives, and desires are centered? How can such allyship be attentive to and work against entrenched power dynamics that harm people with IDD, including how their history is told? For the past decade, the Institute has been bringing together disabled and nondisabled people through arts-based processes in the theory that these can make actionable the belief that people with IDD are equal collaborators and historical actors. My reflections on what this process has been with File/Life are limited in their particulars out of protection for the group's confidentiality at the stage of our work together at the time of writing. While the members of our planning team will be named, as they were publicly known at the time of writing, I will honor the agreements developed with our community archivists, protecting their anonymity while striving to share what we have begun to learn together.[21]

The team's planning artists are David Bradley, María Teresa Rodríguez, Margery Sly, and me. We have collaborated in past work with the Institute, beginning File/Life with a shared understanding of the complexity of this history, a shared commitment to working as allies with collaborators with IDD, and relationships with one another that run deep. Together, we have experience in archiving, theater, oral history, participatory documentary filmmaking, media art, civic engagement, and teaching.

Through an intensive process of outreach to the IDD community and listening sessions, the Institute recruited an intersectional group of seven community archivists, including people with IDD and family members. Two community archivists lived at Pennhurst themselves. Our group is multiracial, multigenerational, of mixed genders and sexualities, urban and suburban, and includes a range of classes and professional and educational backgrounds. Lisa Sonneborn serves as the project's producer. Biany Perez, a therapist and social worker, plays a foundational role in designing a trauma-informed approach to this project. Finally, Each+Every, an Ohio-based graphic design firm specializing in participatory design, worked with us to develop an interactive, multisensory installation.

From October 2021 through December 2022, we visited the State Archives in Harrisburg, toured the grounds of Pennhurst, and held eight daylong workshops, facilitating exploration of and response to files selected from the Archive. From September 2021 into early 2022, supporting artists worked with the community archivists to help them create and realize their visions for our spring 2023 installation.

In process and product, our group was guided by our dedication to uplifting, protecting, and honoring the humanity of the people whose files we work with; being led by the wisdom, lived experiences, interests, questions, and imaginations of the community archivists; and our commitment to working in community together. In these ways, we speculated that the public sharing we cocreate might, in the lineage of Saidiya Hartman, "elaborate, augment, transpose and break open archival documents," to free from the case files the people we seek within them.[22]

Dignity: Honoring the People We Meet and Those We Can't Know

Each time we came together, we began with silence in honor and remembrance of the people whose lives we were trying to learn and those we were not able to know. We endeavored to never lose sight of the fact that each file we touched represents a real person. The nature of our team makes that impossible to forget. When we met at the State Archives in March, one of the community archivists who lived at Pennhurst spoke up, asking if their files were going to be seen. They are a private person, they said, and didn't want anyone to be able to read through their business. We clarified the limits on the files we could access, which predate their file, but the stakes of this work hung in the air, as real as the person who asked. In this moment and its aftermath, we encountered the impact of what Gracen Brilmyer calls the "politics of sickness in archives," where the archive itself is a source of both physical and metaphorical harm.[23] Archives enact metaphorical harm in the systems of oppression their records represent and can replicate. Physical harm comes from both the risks associated with accessing archival records (toxins, airborne pollutants) and the barriers that make such access impossible for many disabled people. How many of the thousands of people who lived at Pennhurst have been to the State Archives? In this project, we brought two. Their response to the very fact of access—in this case, wanting to protect the privacy of their own records—kept our group alive to the politics of sickness in the Pennhurst archive. The harmful systems underpinning and authoring the files we worked with have a cost that is not metaphorical, and while historical, is not past. This knowledge, embodied in our collaborator's protection of their file, was now activated in our project, reinforcing our guardrails against forgetting that we are working with real people's records, without their consent. To paraphrase Susan Sontag, we must tread with care when trafficking in the pain of others.[24] That knowledge came alive in our group. This is one example of what becomes possible when archives are made accessible to the communities whose histories they contain.

One of our core ethical questions was whether and how to permission ourselves to work with the files that we have legal access to. Margery Sly, Director of Special Colleges at Temple University, emphasized in many of our planning conversations that archivists are often working in the tension between maximizing access and protecting privacy. How do we protect the privacy of the people whose files we worked with? Restricted to files from the first half of the twentieth century, it was more than likely that the people they belonged to were long passed, but that does not mean their family members or descendants are not alive; neither does it automatically confer their consent to us to "make use" of their stories. The ethical stakes here were especially pronounced because people in institutions were subjected to so much control and intervention without their consent. Beyond legal restrictions that HIPAA and Medicaid placed on which files we could access, we did not want to reproduce, in this archival afterlife, conditions of control over their lives, including through the involuntary use of their "data."[25]

There is a larger context for the ethical treatment of these files, which are themselves a kind of "remains" particular to and beyond Pennhurst. The involuntary experimentation on people living at Pennhurst in the name of medical research was a well-documented phenomenon, especially during and after World War II.[26] This research was largely funded by the state and conducted under the purview of the University of Pennsylvania. Our group knew we needed protocols that reflected our ethical responsibility to the people whose records comprise the Pennhurst files. Margery Sly suggested modeling the Protocols for Native American Archival Materials. Their emphasis on reciprocity, centering consultation and concurrence with leadership in tribal communities, the development of different ways of thinking about public accessibility, and the need for special treatment of particular materials were a valuable resource in our effort to build collaborative creative processes for grappling with, and sharing stories from, the Pennhurst files.[27] Indigenous perspectives on oral history are also instructive, emphasizing methods for working with memory and lived experience that reflect the cultural and political modes and priorities of Indigenous communities.[28] The community we were accountable to was our community archivists, and their priorities, concerns, and storytelling guided us.

As we developed a vision for bringing File/Life to a public, we asked: How could we honor people who lived at Pennhurst without exploiting them, when they are not here to give their consent? How do we protect the privacy of the people we "meet" in these files, while also stewarding into the public a portrait of what they have to teach? In many ways, the files include information that is "both none-of-our-business and our responsibility."[29] Susan Burch writes into this tension, reflecting on the particular challenges that arise when institutional documents are severed "literally and symbolically" from the tribes and relatives of the people whose lives the files trace, who are the descendants to and rightful owners of this history and its materials. "What and how much to reveal remains an ethical challenge for those with access to these sources and the intimate information they contain."[30] With File/Life, we were able to make the Pennhurst archives directly accessible to people who can claim, if not these specific files, then this history as their lineage, whether as family members or people with IDD, or, for two community archivists, as former residents of Pennhurst. We were not able to develop a process for seeking contact with relatives of people whose files the community archivists explored. To the best of our ability, we redacted identifying information from any files that community archivists chose to include in the exhibit. Our ethical compass for decisions about what to share, and how, derived from the File/Life community archivists. Those who lived at Pennhurst chose not to work with their own files and instead to tell their own stories. Those working with files from the Pennhurst archives wanted to bear witness to the people whose stories they encountered and to the files themselves. In the words of one community archivist, "The ink on these pages is what makes this person a reality to me. If I hadn't found his file, it would probably still be buried in an archive somewhere." The scale of history brought to the scale of one: The files do this. They make specific and irrefutable the individual, and, when seen not as defining documents but clues to be decoded, to be understood as ableist not authoritative, then perhaps we can take the power back from the archive, can bring out into history the people Pennhurst confined.

Guided by Community Archivists

The work of this project is to center, insist on, and imagine the humanity of the people in these patient files, the contents of which make people both incredibly real and frustratingly obscured. When we first looked at a file together as a group, one of the community archivists pounded their fist on the table, saying: "We object." What they meant was this: we object to the placement of this person in Pennhurst in the first place. This objection to the very premise of admission in the first place shows the power of the kind of story this particular group made possible. By questioning the authority of the file from the outset—challenging its very existence before trying to understand the "data" it presents—the community archivists invoked an alternate patient, the one who might have been, had this person never been admitted in the first place. They were not only looking for what was between the lines, behind the words, outside the frame of the file, but were asking: should this file have ever been created?

Our orientation weekend in October 2021 set the project firmly on the path of this kind of questioning. We began by defining for ourselves what we mean by "archive": the noun and the verb. Margery Sly gave us the "Classic Coke" description of what an archive is and what an archivist does, and then we held a facilitated discussion with the community archivists. Together, we posited that our work as community archivists could rewrite, remake, expand,

and connect history to the present. It could bring people together and reclaim who gets to write history, down to the very language that is used. This work could "talk back" to the files and allow us to share our understandings of the feelings and experiences of the people we meet in the patient files. Our community archivists readily defined this charge to trouble the power of the archive, intuitively setting our project on a path lit by the scholarship of many who have identified the need for such strategies and argued for the authority of ways of knowing that fall outside the academy. It is in fact these ways of knowing that, because they fall "outside our efforts," can reveal the limits of conventional "techniques of retrieval."[31] If the study of institutions often privileges or is predicated on institutional traces such as the case files generated by Pennhurst, what might our group reveal instead, if our attention to the institutional trace is not meant to retrieve data but subvert it?[32]

One phrase that emerged from the community archivists in our first orientation session is "living archive." This captured our group's intention to anchor our exploration of the Pennhurst files in an unwavering commitment to the human life, in all its nuance and complexity, behind each file. It also encompassed the dynamism of our process, that we were coming together not to represent the archive to the public, but to creatively respond to the archive. Each community archivist responded from a place of lived experience that was the unique source of our collective authority in interpreting the files to a public. The notion of a "living archive" is not new, and its meaning for our group reflects much of what has been developed by, for instance, Aboriginal communities in both claiming authorship with colonial archives about them and creating community archives of their own. The "living Aboriginal archive" might contain both "tangible and intangible records," which include art, dance, and storytelling, and as such are transmitted not as data but through "interaction and connection between people."[33] Art, movement, and storytelling are not incidental elements of our project design, not modes for generating content, not tools for creating an exhibit, but rather are key strategies for eliciting, through interpersonal exchange, connection, and interaction, the many kinds of knowledge and modalities of expression represented in our intersectional group of community archivists. At the end of our orientation session, David Bradley led us all in a thirty-second dance of sorts, drawing on what the choreographer Liz Lerman calls the "spontaneous gesture" of the ordinary motions David had seen each of us making throughout the day: from wheeling forward to open a file to the final pound of a fist on the table.[34] In this way, we ended our first day as a group enacting together a nonverbal vocabulary of witness: seeing one another, as we began to look for the people in the files.

A "living archive" also reflects our group's conviction that this history is not the past; that we have a duty to the living, including protecting their privacy.

Here is where the composition of our group was a core strength. Two community archivists have lived experiences as former Pennhurst residents, which kept alive the stakes of protecting privacy, as described above. It also meant that our group could speak back to history with our own histories. During our orientation, historian Dennis Downey gave an overview of some historical context intended to help anchor our group's responses to the files. He outlined the eugenic thinking underpinning institutionalization, the changes over time in how people were managed there, some of the atrocities that were revealed, the age of advocacy spurred by those revelations, and finally the key legislative measures resulting in its closure. At several points during his orientation talk, one of our community archivists offered their own memories of living there. In my field notes, I marked my discomfort when the lived history came into encounter with the "capital H" history, wanting to clear the room entirely of the latter to allow the authority of the former. I worried that a description of historical atrocities would be triggering to our colleagues who had lived there. I did not yet know what their experiences had been, or whether or how to ask. But at the end of our first day of orientation, this community archivist said, "I feel good. I told my story. Tomorrow [at the site visit to Pennhurst], as long as I'm with a group of people who've been through the system or people who want to know about Pennhurst—that's all I need."

The next day, we went to the Pennhurst ruins. A brief note on the present site is important. After Pennhurst closed in 1987, two decades of contestation over its use ensued. In 2008, the Pennhurst Memorial and Preservation Alliance (PMPA) was formed to "advocate for the sensitive reuse of the site." PMPA secured membership in the International Coalition of Sites of Conscience in January of 2009 and dedicated a historical marker to Pennhurst in 2010. In that same year, under private ownership, the site began operations as Pennhurst Asylum, a haunted attraction that brings in several million dollars in annual revenue.[35] Currently, PMPA has installed its Traveling Exhibit on Pennhurst and Disability History on the premises of the Pennhurst Asylum, a sequence of twelve banners describing "The Pennhurst Story: Tragedy to Disability Rights" in text and archival images. The Asylum offers ticketed historical day tours of the grounds, alongside its popular "Haunted Attraction" and "Paranormal Investigations."[36]

We secured permission from the Pennhurst Asylum for our site visit. Dennis Downey came with us to give a historical guide of the ruins. Throughout the day, one of the community archivists who had lived there began to speak up. "All of Pennhurst is on my mind now," they said. They began describing their own experiences, situating their memories against or alongside the history Dennis Downey narrated. The community archivist described the relationships they built with certain staff and how they had used the strength of their charm to work the system and get what they needed. They described their experience of Pennhurst closing, how sudden it seemed, and how long it took to gain independence from state control even after leaving Pennhurst. They asked questions about what had happened to the place after it closed, and about how their experience compared to that of earlier residents. At the end of the day, they said that it didn't hurt to be there because they were with us, and that they were happy to share the story about their life, and to teach us where they're coming from.

The lived experience represented in our group drove the project, not only in speaking back to the history but also in choosing what to highlight in the files. When we went to the State Archives, we were each charged with choosing the files we wanted to work with over the course of the project. Another community archivist who had lived at Pennhurst chose files where they found stories of escape, which became the central stories they worked with during our group activities in workshops that spring. Three other community archivists also chose to work with stories of escape. One community archivist, a young person with IDD, interviewed one of the community archivists who lived at Pennhurst about their own experiences escaping Pennhurst. "What did freedom feel like?" they asked. This became a core question in the File/Life exhibit. We thought about the risks of lifting from the archive a disproportionate number of stories of escape as we planned the public showing. So many thousands never escaped. But perhaps this focus on stories of escape is where and how our community archivists were working into the archive's silences, toward speaking the speculative, toward freedom. Black feminist scholarship, theory, and practices show the necessity and power of speculative work in addressing archival erasures of Black voices.[37] "The reform pictures and the sociological surveys documented only ugliness," Hartman writes, as she looks for archival traces of "what it meant to live free" for the generations twice removed from slavery.[38] To render into or as history what eluded the archive, Hartman had to interpret from the margins the fugitive modes of freedom she sought and saw: the good and decent, the beautiful, the radical, the intimate. In so doing, she insists the subaltern into the record on terms that center their dignity, animating "elusive figures" who reveal and defeat the racist traces left by reformers, sociologists, and the state.[39] In the carceral conditions of institutions like Pennhurst and in the ugliness of the case files, escape is powerful evidence of subjectivity and one of the few legible actions expressing desire. We lifted this up not as an act of revision or wishful history, but to insist the desire for freedom out of the archive and into the present. "What did freedom feel like?" Escape, freedom: disability, institutionalization, and incarceration are braided together and the links to justice intertwined.[40] Disability justice is abolitionist.

As we delved into the patient files, the lived experience represented across the members of our community archivists continued to provoke and prompt a range of questions, backstops, moments to talk back to other histories, and propositions for the present. Our intersectional group brought diverse connections to the history of institutionalization, including young people with IDD, who may themselves have been sent to Pennhurst if they were born in another era, and people like me, with experiences as caregivers for people with IDD, for whom the traces of family in the files are especially fraught. The stakes were alive for all of us, and the lived connection we made with the files was at the beating heart of the project.

Building Community: We Cannot Do This Alone

Looking at the files is difficult. Gracen Brilmyer has written about the challenges posed to disabled archivists when their research materials include language and frames that make plain painful attitudes and violent policies toward people with disabilities. The impact can come both from taking in the misrepresentation of people with disabilities through stereotypes and dated language and through contending with the temporal difference between researcher and subject. On the one hand, disabled researchers indicate a sense that "this might have been me" in another era and, on the other, they understand the many differences between themselves and their subjects across time and disabled identity, indicating a desire to "counter or complicate the violence of the stereotypical representations" and a wariness of presentism, or applying contemporary frameworks to archival materials.[41]

This is the line File/Life has tried to tread. Each file representing an individual admitted to Pennhurst suggests a cascade of relationships—parents, siblings, extended families—meaning that there were touchpoints for traumatic recognition for everyone in our group. How we each experienced, made sense of, negotiated, resisted, or otherwise engaged with these files, from our respective positions, was both a strength of the project design and a continual question: how can we take care of ourselves and one another?

How do we deal with the difficult language of the archive? With File/Life, we tried to put the Pennhurst files in dialogue with the range of lived experiences represented by the community archivists, talking back to words with our bodies, with our own language, with whatever we could create. In our workshop sessions, we experimented within the safety of our community, not yet concerned about what to make for the public. In one session, a community archivist stood at the front of the room while one supporting artist read aloud details from a Pennhurst file; the community archivist responded to the words in the file with their own questions, which another supporting artist transcribed in real time, filling the screen behind the community archivist with their own words and questions, in place of the text from the file. "I want to know: did she have any feelings against her grandmother for sending her to Pennhurst? Did she experience remorse, fear? Did she tell anyone what she felt?" Here the community archivist, standing before the rest of us, spoke back to the harmful language of the archive, replacing it with their own words and wonderings. In a way, they gave the lie to the authority of the file, replacing its diagnoses and prognoses and declarations of deficiency with questions the file raises and does not answer. The file does not have all the answers.

In another session, one of the community archivists worked with a transcription of their own life story to create an erasure poem; when a supporting artist took a stab at making his own erasure poem with the community archivist's story, they said, "Nope, that doesn't sound right. It's not your story." In a third session, a community archivist created a head-sized hole in a poster and asked others to put their faces there in turn, while leading the rest of us in a chorus of the archive's worst words. I couldn't do it; I couldn't look people in the face while the words were in the air: feebleminded, moron, cretin, idiot, imbecile, retard. And why shouldn't the stakes of that language, its cruelty and violence, be that real, always? In another session, artists from Each+Every led us in a collaging exercise with photocopied pages from one woman's file. As I sat gleefully scribbling on a photocopy of her intake application, a community archivist sat near me, hesitant. They said they didn't think they could really write on the files. Yes, I assured them, you can do whatever you want with the file. They took a red marker, found a page from a social service report, and made long, sweeping marks up and down and back and forth until the whole page was covered, transformed from report to canvas, no longer Pennhurst's but ours. We can't know what the person whose file this was would think of this act or activity, she whose life is not contained by the file yet whose life was constrained by the words on its pages. We can only try to do right by her with our questions—What did she want? What did she feel? What did she say?—and hope that what we make might transform her file in some way and remember her life as more than simply whatever her file had to say.

As we began planning how to design an exhibit to share File/Life with the public, the questions we asked in our workshops took on new meanings. How can we ensure that our responsibility is always to the dignity of the humanity of the people in the files? We sought to be intentional, imaginative, and vigilant in how we handled not only the identities of people in the files, but the language itself, much of which is offensive, often racist and classist, and emphasizes deficiency and lack. This was especially important in a social context when the status of people with IDD was fragile, when the COVID-19 pandemic heightened the ongoing presence and prevalence of eugenic thinking about the value of disabled lives.[42] The files are replete with offensive language. There are words that remind us of the connection between disability and incarceration: people are referred to as inmates; they are committed, detained, or in custody; they are released or paroled. There are words that remind us of the medicalization of disability: people are referred to as their diagnoses—Mongoloid, moron, cretin, epileptic, feebleminded, mentally retarded. There are words that show us attitudes toward what people were worth, or capable of: untrainable, defective, prognosis strictly guarded. There are words that remind us that institutions are part of economic systems: people are referred to as clients or consumers, and do real labor for little or no pay. There are words that are outright racist, antisemitic, and xenophobic: ape-like, Jewish-looking. Should we even share such language? So much language is freighted with history that is largely unknown. Sharing the files publicly is an opportunity to ask the public to confront the roots of stigma that is still embedded in common language, detached from its historical context, words like idiot and imbecile. In the words of one community archivist: let all who lay eyes on these documents be changed.

Over the course of our time together, we supported one another in not only learning from what we found in the files, but in responding with our own imaginations, interpretations, and experiences, individually and together. To do this responsibly, community was critical. "We cannot do this alone," Debbie Robinson said of the self-advocacy movement.[43] Susan Burch writes of the importance of communal gatherings in remembrance of the Canton Asylum, where descendants of people who had been incarcerated there can meet one another and both experience and create new bonds of kinship.[44] Visiting the grounds of Pennhurst is not something I would have wanted to do alone. As we engaged with this difficult history and painful archive, building our community was central to cultivating our knowledge of one another and our capacity to take in and interpret the files and imagine the stories that we wanted to tell. Through our workshops, we sought to make connections between the past and the present and to discover what kinds of creative "superpowers" each community archivist possessed, to use David Bradley's term. Our charge as supporting artists was to nurture the intelligence, ways of knowing, creativity, and insights of everyone in the room, through cocreation. We hoped our process would reveal something new in and of the Pennhurst patient files. The Institute's engagement in arts-based, cross-ability collaborative work to document and interpret the history and present of IDD demonstrates that the kind of story generated by centering the knowledge of people with IDD has a narrative truth that holds nuance, resists easy resolution, is oriented toward justice, and creates many points of contact that make it accessible, in the sense that it touches many. It is not THE history, nor is it a simple compilation; it's a story that alchemizes experiences across language and time; it is a story that has not ended.

File/Life: The Exhibit

From April 20 to 23, 2023, the results of this two-year process were on view for the public at the Arch Street Meeting House in Philadelphia.[45] The location is historically significant. Quaker conscientious objectors to World War II who were given work placements in Pennhurst and other institutions were among the first early witnesses to atrocities taking place against people with IDD.[46]

Making File/Life fully accessible was a critical part of the planning and creative process. All the video content is open captioned, ASL interpreted, and audio described. An ASL interpreter was available on site every day. We hosted several community conversations, which were captioned through Computer Assisted Real-Time Translation (CART). For blind or low-vision visitors, all display materials included QR codes that linked to digital content, all content was available in Braille, and visitors could also use Aira, a visual interpreting service that gives live, on-demand access to visual information. Arch Street Meeting House had designated areas for service animal relief. Relaxed tours of File/Life were available every day for an hour before the exhibit opened to the public. File/Life was awarded the 2024 Virginia and Harvey Kimmel Family Award for Accessible Experience from ArtReach.

Inside the Arch Street Meeting House, the File/Life exhibit filled two rooms. Visitors first entered an anteroom featuring the community archivists' displays, anchored around eight-foot-tall portraits of people who lived at Pennhurst (Figure 20.1). Each community archivist designed their own display with selected pages from the files they worked with and other photos, objects, and ephemera of their choosing. Each display had a tablet where visitors could browse digitized files and watch video interviews the community archivists

Figure 20.1. Overview of one room in the File/Life exhibit at Arch Street Meeting House in Philadelphia, April 2023. Photo by Alex Catanese.

conducted with one another. Two panels had archival photos of Pennhurst, historical context and timeline, information about the archives, and a description of the File/Life process. Beyond these displays, visitors interacted with additional materials from the Pennhurst files at a designated "story table," where they could create "alternative files" by generating poetry erasing, redacting, replacing, or reimagining words from the files into poems.

The second room was where visitors experienced the stories created by the community archivists, projected onto a large cube in the center of the room (Figure 20.2). Each community archivist's work was represented in video vignettes, cocreated by supporting artist María Teresa Rodríguez and woven together into an approximately hourlong film. The vignettes showed the community archivists' stories in the form of embroidery, erasure poetry, reenactment, research, searches for and visits to gravesites, prayers, oral history, photo montage, interviews with one another, coloring books, animation, and visual art. Interspersed between the vignettes were quiet moments when visitors were prompted to respond to questions connecting to themes of belonging, bearing witness, freedom, justice, inclusion, and a good life. These prompts were drawn from the community archivists' research and embedded throughout the exhibit, asking visitors to respond via QR code and projecting their answers on two sides of the cube in real time. In the center of the cube, visible as a shadow, was a single file cabinet from Pennhurst.

Figure 20.2. File/Life stories and visitor responses are projected onto a cube in the Arch Street Meeting House in Philadelphia, April 2023. Photo by Alex Catanese.

No single file can stand in for more than ten thousand people, or for the complexity of one. File/Life is an invitation to open this history to the lives the files cannot contain and to let the care and imagination of people with a connection to this history show us new throughlines to the present. Let all who lay eyes on these documents be changed.

Outro

Bedtime is hardest. Released from the grip of day, Jonah and I lie entwined in the bluedark of his bedroom. He'll coo to me, stroke my face, mutter I love you so much, so so so so much. My beloved son. My mind roils, the line between archive and imagination unsteady. I see bed after bed from image after image, an image common in the visual parlance of institutional histories. I wonder if this image is so repeated for its efficiency. What does it say? Black and white photos of bed upon bed, always empty. Empty to protect privacy? Protect reputation? What would it say if the beds were all full, as they were, always full. Bedroom, a room of beds, the terrible scale of it. The merciful silence of photos. What I've read in testimonies of the sounds, of the smells. Archives of grief.[47] Who there to coo to him, was there ever a sweetness of touch? What I've read in testimonies of what happened after dark. Resist generalizing, hold close the knowledge of all you don't know, hold space for the ways they might have cared for each other, ways they fought for themselves. Think of Hartman's *Wayward Lives*, the labor of imagination it takes to see—to seek—the people embedded in files, to read against the grain of language that says more about the beliefs and attitudes of the time than the personhood of the observed. Understand you are intellectualizing, and that too is a lifeline, it steadies the line between archive and imagination, between your son and the people you read about. Let him in, let them in, there are beds enough in your heart.

Notes

1. Saidiya Hartman, *Wayward Lives, Beautiful Experiments: Intimate Histories of Riotous Black Girls, Troublesome Women, and Queer Radicals* (New York: Norton, 2019), xv.
2. Gracen Brilmyer, "Towards Sickness: Developing a Critical Disability Archival Methodology," *Journal of Feminist Scholarship* 17 (2020): 33.
3. Nicki Pombier, "A Different Story: Narrative Allyship Across Ability," in *Disability Alliances and Allies*, Research in Social Science and Disability, vol. 12, eds. Allison C. Carey, Joan M. Ostrove, and Tara Fannon (Bingley: Emerald Publishing Limited, 2021), 225–57.
4. Brilmyer, "Towards Sickness," 28.
5. Halderman v. Pennhurst State School and Hospital, 533 F. Supp. 631 (U.S. District Court for the Eastern District of Pennsylvania 1981).

6. James W. Conroy, "Pennhurst Longitudinal Study and Public Policy: How We Learned That People Were Better Off," in *Pennhurst and the Struggle for Disability Rights*, eds. Dennis B. Downey and James W. Conroy (University Park: Pennsylvania State University Press, 2020), 154.

7. Conroy, "Pennhurst Longitudinal Study and Public Policy," 156–65.

8. "Our History," Temple University Institute on Disabilities, accessed October 12, 2022, https://disabilities.temple.edu/about/our-history.

9. "Media Arts and Culture," Temple University Institute on Disabilities, accessed October 12, 2022, https://disabilities.temple.edu/advocacy/media-arts-culture.

10. The Social History of Learning Disability (SLHD) Research Group at the Open University has done extensive inclusive research with people with IDD, documenting and interpreting the histories and legacies of large-scale institutions in the United Kingdom. "Research Projects," Open University Social History of Learning Disability, accessed October 11, 2022, https://www.open.ac.uk/health-and-social-care/research/shld/research-projects-0.

11. Liat Ben-Moshe, Chris Chapman, and Allison C. Carey, *Disability Incarcerated: Imprisonment and Disability in the United States and Canada* (New York: Palgrave MacMillan, 2014); Martha Russell, *Capitalism and Disability* (Chicago: Haymarket Books, 2019).

12. Allison C. Carey, *On the Margins of Citizenship: Intellectual Disability and Civil Rights in Twentieth-Century America* (Philadelphia: Temple University Press, 2009); Dennis B. Downey and James W. Conroy, "Introduction," in *Pennhurst and the Struggle for Disability Rights*, eds. Downey and Conroy; Steven Noll, *Feeble-Minded in Our Midst: Institutions for the Mentally Retarded in the South, 1900–1940* (Chapel Hill: University of North Carolina Press, 1995); Steven Noll and James Trent, eds., *Mental Retardation in America: A Historical Reader* (New York: New York University Press, 2004); James Trent, *Inventing the Feeble Mind: A History of Mental Retardation in the United States* (Berkeley: University of California Press, 1994).

13. Liat Ben-Moshe, *Decarcerating Disability: Deinstitutionalization and Prison Abolition* (Minneapolis: University of Minnesota Press, 2020); Burton Blatt, *Exodus from Pandemonium* (Boston: Allyn and Bacon, Inc., 1970); Burton Blatt, *Souls in Extremis: An Anthology of Victims and Victimizers* (Boston: Allyn and Bacon, Inc., 1973); Gunnar Dybwad, *Challenges in Mental Retardation* (New York: Columbia University Press, 1964); Steven J. Taylor, *Acts of Conscience: World War II, Mental Institutions, and Religious Objectors* (Syracuse, NY: Syracuse University Press, 2009).

14. Brian Greenwald and Jean Lindquist Bergey, "Deaf Interviews: Documenting Narrative History in American Sign Language" (Keynote Address, Oral History in the Mid-Atlantic Region Annual Conference, Monmouth University, West Long Branch, New Jersey, April 23, 2019); Pombier, "A Different Story"; Alice Wong, "Disability Visibility Project at StoryCorps," The Disability Visibility Project, accessed October 12, 2022, https://disabilityvisibilityproject.com/how-to-participate/oral-histories-at-storycorps/.

15. In many ways, first-person experiences of people with IDD have driven the history of deinstitutionalization in Pennsylvania. See, for instance, Mark Friedman and Nancy K. Nowell, "The Rise of Self-Advocacy," in *Pennhurst and the Struggle for Disability Rights*, eds. Downey and Conroy, 124–49; Judith A. Gran, "From PARC

to Pennhurst: The Legal Argument for Equality," in *Pennhurst and the Struggle for Disability Rights*, eds. Downey and Conroy, 104–23; Roland Johnson, *Lost in a Desert World: An Autobiography as Told to Karl Williams* (Philadelphia: Speaking for Ourselves, 1999); J. Gregory Pirmann, "Living in a World Apart," in *Pennhurst and the Struggle for Disability Rights*, eds. Downey and Conroy, 39–57.

16. Susan Burch, *Committed: Remembering Native Kinship in and beyond Institutions* (Chapel Hill: University of North Carolina Press, 2021), 9.

17. Nēpia Mahuika, *Rethinking Oral History and Tradition: An Indigenous Perspective* (New York: Oxford University Press, 2019).

18. Dorothy Atkinson, "Autobiography and Learning Disability," *Oral History* 26, no. 1 (1998), 73–80; Sara E. Green and Donileen R. Loseke, eds., *New Narratives of Disability: Constructions, Clashes, and Controversies*, Research in Social Science and Disability, vol. 11 (Bingley: Emerald Publishing Limited, 2020); Pombier, "A Different Story"; Jan Walmsley, "Interviews with People with Disabilities," in *The Oral History Reader*, eds. Robert Perks and Alistair Thomson (London: Routledge, 2009), 184–97.

19. At the time of this writing, in March 2023, Pennsylvania's Office of Developmental Programs still operates two residential centers for individuals with IDD, Ebensburg State Center and Selinsgrove Center. Two other residential centers, Polk State Center and White Haven State Center, were slated for closure in early 2023. Their status is undetermined at the time of writing. Many of those who are currently institutionalized have been so for most of their lives. At the Selinsgrove Center, for instance, in 2017 over 70 percent of its residents had lived there for forty years or longer.

20. Pombier, "A Different Story."

21. I use they/them pronouns when referencing individual community archivists for the purposes of anonymity.

22. Hartman, *Wayward Lives, Beautiful Experiments*, xiv.

23. Brilmyer, "Towards Sickness," 30.

24. Susan Sontag, *Regarding the Pain of Others* (New York: Picador, 2003).

25. Patricia Galloway, "Providing Restricted Access to Mental Health Archives within Government Archives: The Subject Stakeholder," in *American Archivist*, vol. 84, no. 1 (2021): 166.

26. James W. Conroy and Dennis B. Downey, "The Veil of Secrecy: A Legacy of Exploitation and Abuse," in *Pennhurst and the Struggle for Disability Rights*, eds. Downey and Conroy, 58–75; Taylor, *Acts of Conscience*.

27. The Protocols for Native American Archival Materials, Northern Arizona University, 2008, accessed October 12, 2022, https://www2.nau.edu/libnap-p/index.html.

28. Mahuika, *Rethinking Oral History and Tradition*, 115.

29. T. L. Cowan and Jasmine Rault, "Onlining Queer Acts: Digital Research Ethics and Caring for Risky Archives," *Women and Performance: A Journal of Feminist Theory* 28, no. 2 (2018): 124.

30. Burch, *Committed*, 6–7.

31. Gayatri Chakravorty Spivak, "Can the Subaltern Speak?," in *Can the Subaltern Speak? Reflections on the History of an Idea*, ed. Rosalind Morris (New York: Columbia University Press, 2010), 22; Cowan and Rault, "Onlining Queer Acts."

32. Fiona R. Parrott, "The Material and Visual Culture of Patients in a Contemporary Psychiatric Secure Unit," in *Exhibiting Madness in Museums: Remembering Psychiatry Through Collection and Display*, eds. Catharine Coleborne and Dolly MacKinnon (United States: Taylor and Francis, 2012).

33. Kirsten Thorpe, "Aboriginal Community Archives: A Case Study in Ethical Community Research," in *Research in the Archival Multiverse*, eds. Anne J. Gilliland, Sue McKemmish, and Andrew J. Lau (Clayton, Australia: Monash University Publishing, 2017), 903.

34. Liz Lerman, *Hiking the Horizontal: Field Notes from a Choreographer* (Middletown, CT: Wesleyan University Press, 2014), 51.

35. Pennhurst Memorial and Preservation Alliance, accessed October 12, 2022. http://www.preservepennhurst.org.

36. Pennhurst Asylum, accessed October 13, 2022, https://pennhurstasylum.com/.

37. Hartman, *Wayward Lives, Beautiful Experiments*; MarieClaire Graham, "Imagining the Archive: Speculation as a Tool of Archival Reconstruction," master's thesis (The Graduate Center, City University of New York, 2019); Taylor Thompson, "Tell Me about That World: Speculative Archives and Black Feminist Listening Practices," accessed on October 12, 2022, https://twt.sandbox.library.columbia.edu/.

38. Hartman, *Wayward Lives, Beautiful Experiments*, 17–20.

39. Spivak, "Can the Subaltern Speak?"

40. Stephanie Ban, Kenny Fries, Dustin Gibson, and Katherine Ott, "Advocating for Disability: Intersecting Movements." Online panelists, Ninth Annual Disability and Change Symposium, Disability and Justice: The Evolution and the Revolution, Temple University Institute on Disabilities, March 30, 2022; Ben-Moshe, *Decarcerating Disability*; Ben-Moshe, Chapman, and Carey, *Disability Incarcerated*; Susan Burch, *Committed.*

41. Gracen Brilmyer, "It Could Have Been Us in a Different Moment; It Still Is Us in Many Ways: Community Identification and the Violence of Archival Representation of Disability," in *Lecture Notes in Computer Science*, 12051, *Sustainable Digital Communities*, edited by A. Sundqvist et al., 485. iConference, 2020, https://doi.org/10.1007/978–3–030–43687–2_38.

42. Gracen Brilmyer, Liú Méi z.b. Chen, and Alice Wong, "Telling and Preserving Disabled Stories." Online panelists, Relating Oral History: Spring 2022 Workshop Series, Oral History Master of Arts, Interdisciplinary Center for Innovative Theory and Empirics, Columbia University, February 24, 2022, https://www.youtube.com/watch?v=wqfeOlgZBrI; Jacqueline Fox, "The Current COVID-19 Surge, Eugenics, and Health-Based Discrimination," Bill of Health (blog), Harvard Law Petrie-Flom Center, July 23, 2021, https://blog.petrieflom.law.harvard.edu/2021/07/23/covid-eugenics-health-based-discrimination/.

43. Debbie Robinson, interview by Lisa Sonneborn, *Visionary Voices*, Temple University, September 15, 2011, https://disabilities.temple.edu/voices/interviews/robinson.

44. Susan Burch, *Committed.*

45. Modified exhibits of File/Life have also been installed in two additional venues: in the Russell Rotunda of the Russell Senate Office Building in Washington, DC, in July 2023, and in the Helix Gallery at Thomas Jefferson University in Philadelphia, January–April 2024.

46. Taylor, *Acts of Conscience.*

47. Anne Carson, *Antigonick* (New Directions: New York, 2012).

Epilogue

JENIFER L. BARCLAY AND
STEFANIE HUNT-KENNEDY

The disability to come . . . will and always should belong to the time of promise.
—Robert McRuer

On June 17, 2024, just before midnight, lightning struck the Barbados Archives Department—housed in a former leper asylum—causing a fire that destroyed documents that spanned nearly four hundred years of history. To date, the materials lost include vestry records, records of the general hospital and lunatic asylum, and city council minutes. The 1661 Barbados slavery law—the first slave code of the Anglo Americas—and the 1834 Emancipation Act were also likely lost. The fire happened at a time when archivists had initiated efforts to digitize the Archive's materials and secure a fire suppression system for the building, but according to news reports neither had been fully set in motion. Unfortunately, the Archive's long-standing policy of prohibiting the use of cameras by scholars working in the collections means that few digital copies of records lost in the fire exist. This tragedy devastated Barbadians, people throughout the Caribbean, and scholars and community members worldwide who are invested in the nation's history.

On the surface of things, the fire at the Barbados Archives may seem unrelated to disability, yet upon closer consideration, it offers us important lessons about the relationships between disability, history, and power. Social, political, and economic privilege is imbricated in the acquisition, preservation, and digitization of archival materials. Digitization is an expensive process that many underfunded archives around the world struggle to accomplish, one that is exacerbated in the global South. Although digitization is often perceived exclusively as a measure of historical preservation, it is also an accessibility practice. In this case, if archivists had prioritized digitization or allowed patrons to photograph archival materials, the collections would have been more accessible—to disabled and nondisabled people alike. The sources would also have been preserved in some form, although digitization certainly would not have ameliorated the physical loss. Digitization as an accessibility measure underscores something that disabled people have long known and advocated for: that accessibility has universal benefits. Like disabled people themselves, these precarious archives possess invaluable knowledge and perspectives even as they are often unsupported, marginalized, and devalued.

The Barbados Archives, while a powerful example of archival inequalities in the global South, speaks to broader patterns of injustice and discrimination enacted on and through archives. Accountability is one factor that is key to mitigating these issues. Being responsible to the principles of "nothing about us without us" and disability justice means that archives must be accountable and attentive to the people who use them, the people whose histories are contained within them, and the power dynamics of historical production that implicitly and explicitly shape them as well as the stories we tell. The Barbados Archives embodies the connections between disability and the archive in other ways as well. As a former lazaretto, it quite literally stands as a space where disabled people were once contained, isolated, and obscured from the community, revealing a deeper archaeology of ableist violences now found in historical sources themselves and the logics of the archive writ large.

Cripping the Archive ended with one natural disaster and began with another—the COVID-19 pandemic. Although the pandemic adversely impacted individuals who were racialized, disabled, female, and poor, this global experience forced all to confront their own physicality and mortality in different ways. It gave nondisabled people some insight into the health anxiety and precarity that many disabled individuals live with daily. It also revealed that public institutions, which had long denied accessibility measures fought for by disabled people, were willing to adopt these measures when nondisabled people's lives and profits were at stake. In the face of continuing resistance to public-health practices such as remote work, social distancing, and masking, the world has reverted to a fiction of a post-pandemic life that poses great risk to vulnerable populations.

Even at the height of the pandemic, ableist anxieties shaped individual and institutional responses to COVID, from refusing vaccines based on debunked claims that they cause autism and other debilitating health conditions to the mainstreaming of eugenicist sentiments that accepted the supposedly inevitable loss of aged, chronically ill, disabled, or otherwise vulnerable people to the virus. In fact, politicians, reporters, and medical professionals of all political backgrounds invoked ableist and eugenicist rhetoric to comfort nondisabled people every time a new variant emerged. Although society engages in a widespread fantasy that we have "overcome" COVID, for many disabled people this "back to normal" mentality trivializes the ongoing threat to their lives. This revisionist narrative of the pandemic supplants the hard realities of historical truths with a triumphalist rendering that erases disabled people's lived experiences, creating documentary materials that will one day be embedded in and retrieved from archives as "the" historical record.

The COVID-19 pandemic and the Barbados Archives fire, the two catastrophes that bookended the creation of this volume, are real-time examples of how ableism and silences about disability shape the processes of historical production. According to the Haitian American anthropologist Michel-Rolph Trouillot, this silencing occurs in four key stages: fact creation, fact assembly, fact retrieval, and retrospective significance. The COVID-19 pandemic offers a unique lens through which to think about the first stage: the moment of fact creation or the making of sources. For instance, dominant narratives of the pandemic were shaped by fraught politics, yet one similarity across party lines in nations around the world was the tendency to "repeatedly evok[e] but endlessly defe[r] the presence of disability."[1] Those who had the power to create narratives, such as news reporters, medical professionals, and politicians, often curated a particular set of facts that rendered other facts invisible, such as disabled people's lives and experiences.

Select narratives—like these biased accounts of COVID—will be embedded in archives, accounting for fact assembly or the making of archives. A similar process will undoubtedly unfold at the Barbados Archives once it is reassembled without the original materials it housed or digital copies of them. Scholars will encounter an even more fragmented archive with outright erasures layered onto the previous silences produced by colonization, slavery, and global inequities. While these forces shape different archives in different ways, as the archives of COVID-19 and Barbados make clear, the process of assembling facts and creating archives is freighted with the biases and politics of the past and the present. Beyond accounting for these complex dynamics, disabled researchers must also confront ableist depictions and tropes of disability in historical materials and navigate inaccessible spaces in and beyond the walls of archives, all of which takes an often-unacknowledged toll on them.

Trouillot's fourth stage, the moment of retrospective significance or the making of history in the final instance, is the most complex because it relates the past to the present and, by extension, the future. A culmination of the various processes of historical production, this moment reflects the future acceptance of well-trodden histories as "truth." If cripping the archive allows us to recognize and trace the silencing of disabled pasts, it also affords us the opportunity to reimagine the archive and the possibilities of future historical narratives and their retrospective significance. With this approach, we can imagine future archives, and the scholarship and storytelling that will derive from them, as ones that not only make disability legible, but also acknowledge and honor disabled people's experiential knowledge. In contrast to the COVID-19 pandemic narratives that envisioned disabled people as "destined for no future," we imagine a future in which the process of historical production foregrounds disability histories, recognizes disability legacies, and commits to crip futurities.[2]

Privileging a crip practice in the archives is more than writing against ableism, because doing so still allows ableist narratives to set the agenda. Rather, cripping methodologies unearth disability from the archives and tell stories of disabled people without requiring that we speak to power. Historical narratives can recognize ableist oppression without giving it the power to erase the multifaceted realities of disabled people's everyday lives—the joys, pleasures, struggles, disappointments, desires, banalities, heartbreaks, and messiness. Such an approach demonstrates the critical importance of accessible archives created by, for, and with the input of disabled people. To crip the future, we must crip the past, which requires us, first, to crip the archive.

Notes

1. Ellen Samuels, "'A Complication of Complaints': Untangling Disability, Race, and Gender in William and Ellen Craft's Running a Thousand Miles for Freedom," *MELUS* 31, no. 3 (Fall 2006), 20.

2. Alison Kafer, *Feminist, Queer, Crip* (Bloomington: Indiana University Press, 2013), 33.

Contributors

JAIPREET VIRDI is an Associate Professor in the Department of History at the University of Delaware whose research focuses on the ways medicine and technology impact the lived experiences of disabled people. She is the author of two books, *Echoes of Care: Deafness in Modern Britain* (McGill-Queen's University Press, 2025) and *Hearing Happiness: Deafness Cures in History* (University of Chicago Press, 2020), and coeditor of *Disability and the History of Science, Osiris 39* (2025) and *Disability and the Victorians: Attitudes, Legacies, Interventions* (Manchester University Press, 2020).

JENIFER L. BARCLAY is an Associate Professor of History at the University at Buffalo, Associate Director of the UB Center for Disability Studies, and an associate editor for *Review of Disability Studies.* She is also the editor-in-chief of *Oxford Bibliographies'* Disability Studies module. Her first book, *The Mark of Slavery: Disability, Race, and Gender in Antebellum America* (University of Illinois Press, 2021), was supported by fellowships in African American studies at the University of Virginia's Carter G. Woodson Institute and Case Western Reserve University. Her work has been published in *Slavery & Abolition*, *The Oxford Handbook on Disability History*, and *Women, Gender, and Families of Color*. One article, "Mothering the Useless: Black Motherhood, Disability, and Slavery," was reprinted in the fifth edition of the classic text *Unequal Sisters: A Revolutionary Reader in U.S. Women's History* (Routledge, 2023). She is currently working on her second project, *Between Two Worlds: A Black Disability History of Southern Education from Emancipation to Integration*, supported by a Cornell University Society for the Humanities Fellowship (2024–25) and a University at Buffalo Humanities Institute Fellowship (2023–24).

STEFANIE HUNT-KENNEDY is an Associate Professor in the Department of Historical Studies at the University of New Brunswick. Her research and teaching interests focus on histories of slavery and emancipation, disability, Mad, race, gender, and poverty in the Caribbean, Atlantic World, and Early Americas. She is the author of several essays and of the book *Between Fitness and Death: Disability and Slavery in the Caribbean* (University of Illinois Press, 2020), which received the Disability History Association's 2021 Outstanding Book Award. Hunt-Kennedy is a Series Editor of the University of Illinois Press's Disability Histories series and serves on the *William and Mary Quarterly* editorial board. She is the creator of *Laws of Enslavement and Freedom in the Anglo-Atlantic World*, an open-access digital archive of slavery legislation spanning the seventeenth through the nineteenth centuries. Hunt-Kennedy is currently working on two book projects: *Slavery and the Making of Poverty in the Age of Emancipation* and *An Unusual Crowd of Strangers: Immigrants, Community, and Canada's First Psychiatric Institution.*

FRANCINE ALMASH is a doctoral candidate in Urban Education at the Graduate Center, City University of New York (CUNY), where she also holds a position as a Percy Ellis Sutton Search for Education, Elevation, and Knowledge (SEEK) Counselor. Her research on the history of disability and racial segregation in New York City's schools for so-called socially maladjusted and emotionally disturbed youth has been supported by a Schomburg Center for Research in Black Culture Archival Dissertation Fellowship, a Rockefeller Archive Center Fellowship in applied history, a CUNY Provost's Digital Innovation Grant, and a Mellon Humanities Alliance Fellowship.

GRACEN MIKUS BRILMYER (they/them/iel) is an Assistant Professor in the School of Information Studies at McGill University and the director of the Disability Archives Lab, which hosts multidisciplinary projects that center the politics of disability and archives as well as how to imagine archival futures that are centered around disabled desires (DisabilityArchivesLab.com). Their research lies at the intersection of feminist disability studies, archival studies, and the history of science, where they investigate the erasure of disabled people in archives primarily within the history of natural history museums. Their work has been published in journals such as *Archival Science*, *Archivaria*, and the *Journal of Feminist Scholarship*. Outside of academia, they are involved in disability justice, design justice, and social justice projects.

SUSAN BURCH is a Professor of American Studies at Middlebury College in Vermont (US). Her research and teaching interests focus on histories of deaf, disability, Mad, race, ethnicity, Indigeneity, and gender and sexuality. Burch is the author of *Committed: Native Families, Institutionalization, and Remembering* (2021); *Signs of Resistance: American Deaf Cultural History, 1900 to 1942* (2002); and a coauthor, with Hannah Joyner, of *Unspeakable: The Story of Junius Wilson* (2007). She has coedited anthologies including *Women and*

Deafness: Double Visions (2006), *Deaf and Disability Studies: Interdisciplinary Perspectives* (2010), and *Disability Histories* (2014), and also served as editor-in-chief of *The Encyclopedia of American Disability History* (2009).

KJ CERANKOWSKI is Associate Professor of Comparative American Studies and Gender, Sexuality, and Feminist Studies at Oberlin College. He is the coeditor of two editions of *Asexualities: Feminist and Queer Perspectives* (2014 and 2024) and author of *Suture: Trauma and Trans Becoming* (2021).

EMILY COCK is a Senior Lecturer in Early Modern History at Cardiff University, author of *Rhinoplasty and the Nose in Early Modern British Medicine and Culture* (Manchester University Press, 2019), and coeditor with Patricia Skinner of *Approaching Facial Difference: Past and Present* (Bloomsbury, 2018). Her current research explores transnational social and cultural histories of medicine and disability c. 1600–1850.

LIANA KATHLEEN COLE, PhD (formerly Glew) is a teacher, researcher, and manager of the Prison Education Program at Penn State's Restorative Justice Initiative. Her research has involved disability history, U.S. literature, and patient writing in psychiatric institutions. Her article "Documenting Insanity: Paperwork and Patient Narratives in Psychiatric History" won the 2021 *History of the Human Sciences Journal* Early Career Prize, and her work can also be found in *J19: The Journal of Nineteenth-Century Americanists* and the C19 podcast. Now she coordinates classes, workshops, and an upcoming degree program for incarcerated learners.

JESS L. WILCOX COWING (they/them) is a multiply disabled scholar and educator who teaches gender and disability studies for Goucher College's Prison Education Program and the University of Wyoming's Disability Studies Program. Their research is in the areas of nineteenth and twentieth century literary studies, feminist disability studies, and settler colonialism. Cowing served as the American Studies Association's Critical Disability Studies Caucus Co-Chair from 2017 to 2021. Their work is published in the *Journal of Feminist Scholarship*, *Disability Studies Quarterly*, and *CUSP: Late 19th/Early 20th Century Cultures*. Cowing grew up on Wabanaki homelands and lives and works on Piscataway homelands.

RADU HARALD DINU is an Assistant Professor of History at Jönköping University in Sweden. His research specializes in disability history and the modern and contemporary history of Eastern Europe. Recently, he coedited the book *Disability and Labour in the Twentieth Century* (Routledge, 2023).

WILLIAM T. ENNIS III is Associate Professor of History at Gallaudet University. His teaching and research interest is deaf history, with a special interest in the history of eugenics and the deaf community.

MARIA CRISTINA GALMARINI is Associate Professor of History and Global Studies at William & Mary. She has published extensively on Soviet history and disability history, including two monographs—*Ambassadors of Social Progress: A History of International Blind Activism in the Cold War* (Northern Illinois University Press, 2024) and *The Right to Be Helped: Deviance, Entitlement, and the Soviet Moral Order* (Northern Illinois University Press, 2016). Galmarini won the Disability History Association's award for best published article in 2018 and is currently working on several projects in the field of disability in Russia, the former Soviet Union, and Eastern Europe.

EFRAT GOLD is a Social Sciences and Humanities Research Council (Canada) postdoctoral fellow and visiting Assistant Professor at the University at Buffalo's Center for Disability Studies, engaging in mad studies. Working with records and artifacts, she explores various appearances and disappearances of mad and psychiatrized people. Critiquing psychiatric hegemony and calling attention to the naturalization of medicalized orientations to human suffering, Gold unearths a multitude of present-absences of those cast off as mad. Tracing the boundaries of normalcy, she explores practices of meaning-making that reproduce sanist and ableist cultural attitudes. Foregrounding the often-overlooked active role of mad and disabled people in pushing back against their marginalization and creating life-affirming possibilities for survival, Gold is motivated by radical politics that recognize the entwined landscape of oppression within efforts to build different futures.

SAMUEL GOLDSTONE-BRADY currently works as the Collections Engagement Officer for the National Paralympic Heritage Trust. He was an Arts and Humanities Research Council Collaborative Doctoral Partnership PhD student at the University of Glasgow and the National Paralympic Heritage Trust. His PhD research explored the social, political, and technological history of sporting wheelchairs, and his thesis was submitted in December 2023. Goldstone-Brady is also a cofounder of the UK Disability History and Heritage Hub.

BRIAN H. GREENWALD is Professor of History and Director of the Schuchman Deaf Documentary Center at Gallaudet University. He has presented and published on numerous topics in United States Deaf history. Currently, he is studying the role of eugenics in Deaf residential schools during the early twentieth century.

MARY JEAN HANDE is Assistant Professor in Sociology at Trent University. Her community-engaged research and teaching focuses on the care politics of aging, disability, and madness, and the role of care in social movements. She currently leads a community research partnership focused on building social justice coalitions for homecare transformation.

SARAH HANDLEY-COUSINS is Associate Teaching Professor of History at the University at Buffalo. Handley-Cousins is the author of *Bodies in Blue: Disability in the Civil War North* (University of Georgia, 2019), which won the Outstanding Book prize from the Disability History Association in 2020. She is also coauthor of *Spiritualism's Place: Reformers, Seekers, and Séances in Lily Dale* (Cornell, 2024) and coeditor of the forthcoming *The Nursing Clio Reader* and *Routledge History of Disability in America*. She is currently writing about race, deafness, and justice in late-nineteenth-century America. Handley-Cousins is also executive editor of the history blog *Nursing Clio* and a producer of *Dig: A History Podcast*, which translates historical scholarship into a compelling audio format.

LEALA HOLCOMB is a Research Assistant Professor at the University of Tennessee, Knoxville. Their research focuses on professional development for teachers and its impact on language and literacy outcomes in deaf students. Holcomb is an Associate Editor for the *Journal of Deaf Studies and Deaf Education* and cofounder of *Hands Land*, a nonprofit that produces sign language rhyme and rhythm educational media for young signing children.

TARA HOLCOMB is a psychologist at Gallaudet University's Counseling and Psychological Services. Her clinical and research interests include the impact of childhood trauma and community-based healing in deaf populations.

THOMAS K. HOLCOMB (PhD, University of Rochester) is a retired Professor at Ohlone College in Fremont, California. He is the author of several books and multimedia curricula on Deaf culture and interpreting, including *Introduction to American Deaf Culture* (2023) and *Deaf Eyes on Interpreting* (2018).

AUDRA JENNINGS is Professor and Department Chair of History at Western Kentucky University. She is the author of *Out of the Horrors of War: Disability Politics in World War II America* (University of Pennsylvania Press, 2016) and is currently writing *Insecurity: Disability, the Great Depression, and the New Deal State*, a project that has been funded by the National Science Foundation, American Council of Learned Societies, the Harry S. Truman Library Institute, and the Roosevelt Institute. Jennings has written articles on health and safety in the U.S. labor movement, gender and disability, and veterans' health and disabled veterans' activism in midcentury America. She is the recipient of the Disability History Association Outstanding Article Award and the James Madison Prize from the Society for History in the Federal Government.

HEMACHANDRAN KARAH is an Associate Professor in the Department of Humanities and Social Sciences, Indian Institute of Technology Madras. He has published a dozen peer-reviewed essays in academic journals and books. Karah coedits the global section of the journal *Review of Disability Studies*

(RDS). He is a founding member and a principal investigator of the Centre for Capabilities and Access Building Across Disciplines (CABAD). Under the auspices of CABAD, Karah and his fellow co-investigators gather high-quality teacher tutorials on the broader theme of disabilities and disciplines. He is also a recipient of a fellowship grant from the Indian Foundation for Arts that allowed him to pursue a collaborative research project on the theme of theological accessibility. Prior to this, Karah was one of the principal investigators of a global project on COVID-19 and mental health organized by The Ohio State University. Karah is currently finishing a coauthored companion volume on Disability studies in addition to teaching courses in the field offered on the National Programme on Technology Enhanced Learning (NPTEL) platform.

OSNAT KATZ (she/they) is an autistic historian, writer, and science studies expert. Her research interests focus on the social and cultural history of science and new ways to make scientific knowledge more reproducible, while her personal interests center around supporting other disabled and neurodivergent people in forging a more accessible and inclusive world.

SONA KAZEMI is an Assistant Professor in the Department of Race, Gender, and Sexuality Studies at the University of Wisconsin-La Crosse. Her first monograph, *Disabling Relations: Wounded Bodyminds and Active Witnessing*, is under contract with Temple University Press and scheduled to come out soon. Kazemi is currently working on her second monograph, tentatively titled "Interdependence, Feminism, and Infrastructure of Care in Prison," and two edited anthologies, one of which is under contract with Canadian Scholars Press. She is the Society for Disability Studies' 2018 recipient of the honorable mention for the prestigious Irving K. Zola Award for emerging scholars in Disability studies. She is currently the associate editor for the Global Ideas' Section at *Review of Disability Studies, an International Journal.*

ISABELLE LAWRENCE, at the time of writing, was an Arts and Humanities Research Council–funded PhD student undertaking a collaborative doctoral partnership with the University of Leicester School of Museum Studies and the British Museum. She organized and conducted the workshops and interviews discussed in her chapter as part of her doctoral research project, entitled "Hidden, Revealed: Investigating Representation and Narratives of Disability in the British Museum." With lived experience of brain injury and special educational needs, Isabelle strongly believes in the importance of representing disability histories in museums to challenge attitudes and assumptions in the present.

JAMES MCCARTHY is the current director of the Gallaudet University Archives. His focus as director is on developing a community-based approach to the collection, organization, preservation, and accessibility of Deaf history that eschews traditionally paternalistic archival practice and seeks to empower local communities to preserve and steward their own histories.

JOSEPH J. MURRAY is Professor of Deaf Studies at Gallaudet University. He has published widely in the fields of deaf history, deaf studies, applied linguistics, and language rights.

MEREDITH PERUZZI is the director of the National Deaf Life Museum at Gallaudet University. She presents internationally on the topic of making museum exhibitions and programming more accessible to deaf visitors. Her historical research focus is on Gallaudet University and the deaf community in the United States.

NICKI POMBIER is an oral historian, writer, and educator living in Brooklyn, New York. Her work in oral history is largely focused on disability history, with a particular interest in collaborations across ability and oral history beyond speech. She teaches in the Oral History Master of Arts Program at Columbia University, and won the 2021 Distinguished University Teaching Award from The New School University.

OCTAVIAN E. ROBINSON is Associate Professor of Women's, Gender, and Sexuality Studies and Director of the Center for Deaf Equity at The Ohio State University. He served as an archivist at the Gallaudet University Archives before becoming a historian. As coauthor of "Crip Linguistics Manifesto," his research areas are language attitudes toward signed languages within academia, historical attitudes about disability among deaf people, and linguistic protectionism in deaf communities during the early twentieth century.

AARON RUBINSTEIN is the head of the Robert S. Cox Special Collections and University Archives Research Center at the University of Massachusetts Amherst and the principal investigator for the Council for Library and Information Resources–funded Visibility for Disability Digitization Project, which has made over thirty thousand primary source documents related to disability available online for free. Rubinstein has been involved in the development of national and international archival description standards and has published on linked data and sharing archival metadata on the web.

SHUKO TAMAO is a curatorial fellow at the Science History Institute's Center for Oral History, conducting oral history interviews and curating oral history in museums and other public and educational settings. At the Institute, she curated the Voices of Science exhibit, to which she brought the lives and work of five scientists from diverse backgrounds, including scientists with disabilities. Tamao earned a graduate certificate in public history with an archives management concentration at the University of Massachusetts Amherst and a

PhD in history at the University at Buffalo, where she conducted oral history interviews related to the institutionalization of people with mental disabilities. Before joining the Science History Institute, Tamao was a postdoctoral fellow at the Division of Medicine and Science, Smithsonian Institution's National Museum of American History, where she participated in exhibition planning activities.

JAN VALLE is a Professor of Disability Studies and Inclusive Education at The City College of New York (CUNY) in New York City, where she teaches courses about inclusive practices in the programs of childhood education and educational theatre. She is a coauthor with David Connor of *Rethinking Disability: A Disability Studies Approach to Inclusive Practices* (Routledge, 2019), coeditor with David Connor and Chris Hale of *Practicing Disability Studies in Education: Acting toward Social Change* (Peter Lang, 2014), and author of *What Mothers Say about Special Education: From the 1960s to the Present* (Palgrave, 2009). She is currently developing a model that integrates disability studies and applied theatre to raise disability awareness in public schools and the arts community. She also consults with integrated (disabled and nondisabled) theatre and dance companies and provides professional development for various arts organizations and teaching artists.

NINA VOLLENBRÖKER is Associate Professor and Director of the Architectural Design PhD program at the Bartlett School of Architecture, University College London. Her research into intersections of disability and architecture has been disseminated internationally and is supported by the Paul Mellon Centre and the Royal Institute of British Architects.

TRACI BRYNNE VOYLES is Professor and Department Head of History at North Carolina State University. She is the author of two books: *Wastelanding: Legacies of Uranium Mining in Navajo Country* (University of Minnesota Press, 2015) and *The Settler Sea: California's Salton Sea and the Consequences of Colonialism* (*Many Wests* book series, University of Nebraska Press, 2021), winner of the 2022 Caughey Prize from the Western History Association for most distinguished work on the American West and a 2022 Choice Outstanding Academic Title.

HEATHER VRANA is a historian of disability, revolutions, student and social movements, social class, race, and the history of medicine in Central America and Associate Professor of Modern Latin America in the Department of History at the University of Florida. Vrana's current book project is *Guerrilla Medicine and Disability in Cold War Central America*; previous books include *This City Belongs to You: A History of Student Activism in Guatemala* (University of California Press, 2017), the anthology *Anti-Colonial Texts from Central*

American Student Movements 1929–1983 (Edinburgh University Press, 2017), and *Out of the Shadow: Revisiting the Revolution from Post-Peace Guatemala*, coedited with Julie Gibbings (University of Texas Press, 2020). Vrana's articles have appeared in the *American Historical Review*, the *Hispanic American Historical Review*, *Radical History Review*, the *Journal of Genocide Research*, and elsewhere.

SARAH WHITT (Choctaw Nation of Oklahoma) is an Assistant Professor in the Department of Global Studies at UC Irvine, with an affiliation in the Department of History. Her first book, *Bad Medicine* (Duke University Press, forthcoming 2025), illustrates the interconnected nature of settler institutions, and the ways in which Indigenous people mounted complex challenges to white hegemony in the Progressive Era. Whitt's work has been published in journals such as the *Western Historical Quarterly*, *American Indian Culture and Research Journal*, and *Disability Studies Quarterly*, and she has received numerous fellowships, grants, and scholarships from tribal, national, and intramural organizations such as the Choctaw Nation of Oklahoma, American Council of Learned Societies, and National Endowment for the Humanities. She is currently at work on her second book, *Prisoners of War*, which is an affective and material history of Indigenous freedom, captivity, and memory in the United States.

Index

Note: *Page locators in italics indicate figures.*

The University of Illinois Press
is a founding member of the
Association of University Presses.

Composed in 11.5/12 Adobe Garamond Pro
with Gotham display
by Lisa Connery
at the University of Illinois Press
Manufactured by Versa Press, Inc.

University of Illinois Press
1325 South Oak Street
Champaign, IL 61820-6903
www.press.uillinois.edu